CHURCH, SOCIETY AND RELIGIOUS CHANGE IN FRANCE,
1580–1730

CHURCH, SOCIETY AND RELIGIOUS CHANGE IN FRANCE,
1580–1730

JOSEPH BERGIN

YALE UNIVERSITY PRESS
NEW HAVEN AND LONDON

Copyright © 2009 Joseph Bergin

All rights reserved. This book may not be reproduced in whole or in part, in any form (beyond that copying permitted by Sections 107 and 108 of the U.S. Copyright Law and except by reviewers for the public press) without written permission from the publishers.

For information about this and other Yale University Press publications, please contact:
U.S. Office: sales.press@yale.edu   www.yalebooks.com
Europe Office: sales@yaleup.co.uk   www.yaleup.co.uk

Set in Minion by IDSUK (DataConnection) Ltd
Printed in Great Britain by TJ International, Padstow, Cornwall

Library of Congress Control Number: 009925813

ISBN: 978 0 300 150 98 8

A catalogue record for this book is available from the British Library.

10 9 8 7 6 5 4 3 2 1

To the Rektor and staff of the Wissenschaftskolleg zu Berlin

in admiration and gratitude

Contents

	List of Maps	ix
	List of Tables	x
	Preface	xi
	Prologue: the Fire and the Ashes	1

Part 1: Foundations

1	From Dioceses to Parishes: the Geography of the French Church	17
2	Wealth into Benefices	37

Part 2: Clerical Worlds in Context

3	Clerics and Clergy: the World of the Seculars	61
4	The Monastic Orders: Adjustment and Survival	84
5	From Mendicants to Congregations	105
6	A Silent Revolution: Women as Regulars	129

Part 3: A New Clergy?

7	Bishops: Adaptation and Action	155
8	Remaking the Secular Clergy	183
9	The Triumph of the Parish?	208

Part 4: Instruments of Religious Change

10	Saints and Shrines	229
11	Sacraments and Sinners	252
12	Religion Taught and Learned	277
13	The Forms and Uses of Spirituality	310

Part 5: Movers and Shakers

14	The Many Faces of the Confraternities	339
15	*Dévots*: the Pious and the Militant	366
16	Jansenists: Dissidents but also Militants	394
	Conclusion	425
	Notes	433
	Bibliography	465
	Index	485

Maps

		page
1	French dioceses, 1715	19
2	French chapters during the *ancien régime*	73
3	Growth of the regulars' presence in Burgundy-Champagne, 1598–1700	122
4	French educational institutions, *c.*1715	202
5	Expansion of the Company of the Holy Sacrament, 1629–49	380
6	Expansion of the Company of the Holy Sacrament, 1653–67	381
7	Geography and scale of clerical appeals against *Unigenitus*, 1717–28	420

Tables

		page
4.1	Old monastic orders	86
5.1	Old mendicant orders and their offshoots	107
5.2	New orders/congregations	111
5.3	New congregations	114
6.1	Female monastic and mendicant orders before *c*.1600	130
6.2	New female orders	137
6.3	New female congregations	142
16.1	Brief chronology of French Jansenism, 1640–1713	404–5

Preface

Few of Europe's churches emerged untouched by the religious upheavals of the sixteenth century. The current preference among historians for the plural 'Reformations' rather than the singular 'Reformation' reflects an increasingly clear sense of how far local or national patterns diverged from some ideal-typical 'Reformation' whose contours can no longer simply be assumed as self-evident. Religious change 'in national context' promises a more complex but also a more credible picture, even when the 'national context' in question is itself a fairly artificial construct. Furthermore, the traditional chronology and duration of the 'Reformation' have been significantly revised, and it is no longer any surprise to see the centuries from approximately 1400 to 1700 labelled as an 'age of reformation'. What used to be exclusively considered as the age of Reformation – 1517 to 1555 – now looks more like a sudden surge within a far longer spectrum of action and concern with religious matters. As a result, 'long', 'early' and 'late' (or even 'later') Reformations have become familiar notions to historians. One recent contribution to this revisionism is of particular interest here not just because it focuses entirely on France but also because its authors argue the case for '600 years of reform' (the book's title) between the late twelfth and eighteenth centuries. Within that vast timescale, Hayden and Greenshields identify two Catholic Reformations, a 'first' which runs from the 1480s to the 1580s, and a 'second' from the late 1580s to the 1680s. The two are not presented as radically distinct – indeed they run into one another more or less seamlessly – and the real intention behind the book's analysis of the two seems to have been to show that there was a genuine, if perhaps limited, precursor (the 'first' of these reformations) to the better-known Catholic Reformation (labelled the 'second' by them).[1] If a trend towards an increasingly *longue durée* standpoint threatens to overwhelm concepts traditionally applied more sparingly, it unexpectedly frees historians to reconsider the scope of religious change within shorter – but not necessarily 'short' – timescales. The pages that follow are an attempt to do just that.

Despite its apparently limited scope, doing full justice to France's religious history during the 'long' seventeenth century would be the work of a lifetime. For the historian writing on the subject, Michelet's dictum that 'tout est dans tout' (everything is connected to everything else) recurs as a constant, inexorable refrain, one that always demands a broadening of the scope of the enquiry. In this particular regard, John McManners's monumental history of church and society in eighteenth-century France stands as a model of what such a history should be, but its vast scale means it is unlikely to be imitated, let alone bettered, by any future historian of other periods of French history.[2] Despite its 'church and society' title, it devotes considerable space – nearly 600 out of over 1,400 pages – to the political ramifications of religion during an age when it might be thought that the embers of earlier conflicts had definitively cooled in the face of the Enlightenment. But the political dimensions of religious issues are inescapable for any historian of the eighteenth century, given that not even the most strenuous effort to avoid using hindsight can quite shut out the dramatic impact of the revolution on the French church and religious practices generally. The study of France's religious history in its other, non-political contexts during the eighteenth century is largely the study of a 'mature' religious system in which there are relatively few major innovations: a story whose stasis is more evident than its dynamics. By contrast, the long seventeenth century, which did so much to create what would become the 'mature' religious system of the next century, appears as a period of innovation and experiment, witnessing an ever-expanding search for the mechanisms and instruments of religious revival reform, instruction and participation. Here, by contrast, the story is one in which the dynamics are dominant and unmissable, although it is essential to account for the sources of stasis which made religious change slow, patchy and limited in important respects. On top of that, the political ramifications of religious developments were considerable: not only was there the problem of establishing peace between the rival confessions in the decades following the wars of religion, but there were challenges that arose out of changes occurring during the seventeenth century itself. The best-known instance of the latter is that of Jansenism, which in turn overlapped with unresolved problems of France's relations with the papacy. It is not indulging in misplaced special pleading to claim that a 'total' history of 'church and society' represents an even bigger task for the seventeenth century than for its successor.

However, rather than undertaking the Sisyphean labour of trying to match McManners's account of eighteenth-century France's religious history, it seemed best to redefine the scope of the challenge in a way that promised a real chance of completion. The present book is the first but, it is hoped, not the last outcome of that decision. In the pages that follow, the focus will be on the 'internal' history of French Catholicism during the period from the later wars of religion to the edge of the age of Enlightenment, which corresponds roughly to the years 1580 to around 1730. Self-evidently, this involves excluding a number of important themes which, in the interests of avoiding any misapprehension, it is only fair to indicate and explain at this point. There will be only contextually indispensable references to the political dimensions of the successive issues under discussion here, since the broader elements of the familiar 'church–state' relationship will not be treated systematically. For example, the history of France's Protestants will not feature much, even though it will be assumed that their continuing presence was a highly important reminder and stimulus to the French church of the need to put its house in order, both before and after the removal of religious toleration of Protestants by Louis XIV in 1685. The intention is that the present study will open the way for a separate treatment of these overlapping themes under the broad heading of 'politics and religion' in France during the period covered here.

Meanwhile, the present book may be regarded as a series of closely connected essays which, eschewing comprehensiveness for its own sake, seek to shed light on many of the elements that are essential for an understanding of religious change – its nature, scope and prerequisites. On the one hand, it seeks to understand the structural and cultural limits to such change, so that it becomes easier to see why particular agents or instruments of religious change were tried, abandoned or extended in ways that were sometimes unexpected. The reader perusing the table of contents may be inclined to think that the first half of the book is really more about the clergy than the French church. Although it would be pointless to deny this clerical presence, these early chapters constitute an extended effort to use the different types of clergy – male and female, secular and regular – as a way of approaching the connections between the French church and the wider society in which it functioned. The prologue stands somewhat apart as a brief snapshot of the state of the French church and Catholicism during the latter decades of the religious wars; its purpose is to provide a synchronic point of departure to which we shall return at numerous points throughout the remaining chapters. The two following chapters attempt to present some of the fundamental dimensions of the French church – its institutional geography and its 'economic' basis. The latter, entitled 'wealth into benefices', may seem to consider the church's economic status in France in terms of the clergy who held such benefices, but it is also designed to show how far the French church was 'colonised' by social and family groups at almost every conceivable level.

The same may be said of the chapters that follow on the secular and regular clergy. It is essential not to view the later sixteenth- or seventeenth-century church through the lens of the eighteenth or especially the nineteenth century, when the experience of revolution created a far more socially insulated form of clericalism than anything experienced during previous centuries. The relatively recent rediscovery of different, almost hidden categories of clergy and cleric (especially those not in priestly orders) who no longer existed in subsequent centuries is an essential element of the 'strangeness' of the French – and other European – churches of the period under study here. That strangeness is, in turn, indispensable to understanding the problems and limitations of efforts, so central to the post-Trent Catholicism, to reform the ordinary 'secular' clergy, and to understand how limited the wider impact of some of these efforts could actually be for a long time.

Likewise, devoting three chapters to the 'regular' clergy may well seem overindulgent, but they are offered here in the hope of making the role of the religious orders within the French church, and their widely varying impact on French society generally, easier to grasp. This role tends to be seriously understudied in most accounts of the period once the names, geographical diffusion and particular features of the orders have been catalogued. The historiography of the seventeenth-century French church still has a long way to go before a convincing synthesis on the orders' contribution can be written. Precisely because subsequent chapters will return to the activities of the orders in this or that sphere of action, it is crucial to grasp some of their underlying similarities and differences from the outset. With this in mind, these chapters combine a longer 'structural' perspective on the orders with an analysis of the changes they experienced during the period of the Catholic Reformation. Finally, the chapter devoted to female orders and congregations can stand as a case-study of the continuing post-Tridentine – one might also say, un-Tridentine – innovations of which the French church was capable until well into the age of Louis XIV. It is not an exaggeration to say that these innovations altered the face of the French church, at least in the sense that for the first time in history, female regulars and lay sisters outnumbered their male counterparts, while also engaging far more than in the past in charitable, instructional and pastoral works – and in ways that were often themselves new. '*Le catholicisme au féminin*' begins in the seventeenth century.

Thereafter, the bulk of the book can be seen as a set of connected essays whose common thread is the agents, techniques and instruments employed in order to alter, invent and reform a wide range of the religious practices of the period under study in ways that corresponded to contemporaries' understanding of what 'reformation' entailed. This, too, involves further attention to the role of the clergy, but this time in a more 'short-term' perspective. As the primary intended 'carriers' of such changes, the clergy, from bishops to parish priests, were themselves held to be in serious need of improvement, but the mechanisms for achieving change differed, depending on whether one was a bishop or an aspiring *curé*. Above all, in the case of the parish clergy, those instruments were much more varied than is usually imagined. After long years of trial and error, a range of educational-cum-disciplinary practices that complemented each other took shape, so we should not imagine that, at least in the minds of contemporaries, there was ever a single, magical solution called a 'seminary' for such purposes. A key theme running throughout these chapters is that of communication and autonomy. How exactly were bishops, especially those governing the huge dioceses of central and northern France, to supervise and communicate with their clergy, let alone the populations beyond them? What kind of communication channels did they have, or develop, that enabled them to make a difference within their dioceses, and what can we learn about the possibilities of change from the adequacy, or inadequacy, of such instruments?

A parallel enquiry into the role of the parish and its titular head, the *curé*, also sets some of the parameters which help us to understand the scope for engineering changes within local religious practices. The mechanisms that were developed, or at least modified, in our period in order to communicate the post-Reformation conviction that only those individuals who possessed some 'credal' knowledge of their religion deserved the title of 'Christians', form the core of several chapters which cover the rise of preaching, missions and catechisms, but also Sunday schools, confraternities, pilgrimages and processions. Here, too, the contribution of laypeople to the process of religious change should not be underestimated. It is also a field in which the activities of women became increasingly visible during the seventeenth century, even though, by comparison with the eighteenth century, it is a contribution which it is much harder to observe directly.

The book ends with a series of chapters that pursue these themes further by attempting to analyse some of the key agents and sources of action within this tableau of religious change. It is too easy to dismiss the myriad confraternities, *dévots* and Jansenists who have always figured so prominently in the religious history of seventeenth-century France as being cut off from the population at large, part of an 'elite' culture that was drawing away from 'popular' culture. There is truth somewhere in that assertion, but it can be too easily exaggerated with the benefit of hindsight. It underestimates the extent of common religious attitudes and practices among different social groups; it also understates the efforts made by individuals and groups to reach out beyond their own narrow circles to a wider public. If we take the case of the spiritual writers considered in Chapter 13, it is natural enough to imagine them as the most secluded of all, but what is most striking about large numbers of them is how far their works are distillations of actual pastoral experiences, and not academic treatises derived from putative first principles. A *dévot*, a confraternity member, a mystical-spiritual author and a Jansenist might often be one and the same individual, connected to wider movements within the French church. However impossible it may ultimately be to measure the precise impact of this or that religious idea or devotional innovation, historians should not lose sight of those on the 'receiving' end of attempts to devise and implement shifts in religious practices. In this regard, the remarkable spread of 'congregations', assemblies, sodalities, confraternities and the like testify to the capacity of ideas and new devotional practices to reach substantial audiences well beyond their original 'places' of conception; the history of confraternities, but also of pilgrimages and other collective religious activities, testify to the enduring force of lay religiosity which the 'official' church could never ignore, even when it did not quite know how best to deal with it.

Needless to say, in a field which has produced so much path-breaking research, especially in the past half-century, this book will seem to ignore some important individual topics. There is scarcely any reference to witchcraft, for example, and one could cite several others. In defence of the pages that follow, one can reply that the book's principal aim has been to plunge into – and inside – the process of religious change in seventeenth-century France, in order to examine the most prominent of its elements in some depth – and in the hope that the gain from doing so would offset the resulting loss of breadth.

That the present book exists in any shape at all is due to the initial prompting of John Nicoll, the former director of Yale University Press's London office, who embodies everything that the ideal publisher should be. That it then made the more difficult journey from proposal to completed work is due primarily to the privilege of enjoying a fellowship during 2006 to 2007 at the Wissenschaftskolleg zu Berlin, one of the scholarly world's best-kept secrets. This 'Berlin Institute for Advanced Study', which each year creates a community of around forty scholars from around the world and from all disciplines, is a place where nothing seems unachievable. The experience of writing a book in English, based overwhelmingly on French materials and scholarship, and produced in a German-speaking environment, has been a source of often unexpected exchanges, not to mention linguistic tangles, over lunch or at the bus stop, yet the support of the other Fellows and Mitarbeiter of the Wissenschaftskolleg made it seem the most natural thing in the world to be doing. It is invidious to single out anyone from such an extraordinary 'tower of Babel' (a favourite metaphor of the Wissenschaftskolleg), but conversations with, and time spent in the company of Pierre-Michel Menger,

Marta Petrusewicz, Sunil Khilnani, Alain Schapp, Beatrice Longuenesse, Georg Nolte, Wayne Maddison and Andrew Read will remain in the memory for many years to come. Last but certainly not least, the incredibly efficient Library Service of the Wissenschaftskolleg, led by Gesine Bottomley, seemed positively to relish producing the books and articles that I requested as effortlessly as rabbits popping out of a hat. The only honourable expression of gratitude for such bounty is to dedicate the end product to the institution that did so much to smooth its way to completion.

My final thanks go to individuals closer to home. Earlier versions of the text were read by Nigel Aston, Dermot Fenlon and Alison Forrestal, all of whom I thank for their forebearance and especially for their helpful comments. If I have not acted upon all of the latter, the fault is entirely my own. Finally, I hope that my wife, Sylvia, will no longer feel that she is living with the 'ghost upstairs'.

Prologue: The Fire and the Ashes

When the fog of war finally lifted on France during the last decade of the sixteenth century, it was well-nigh universally believed that the country had been reduced to a state of virtual collapse, cruelly damaged by a generation of endlessly recurring civil wars and the communal violence that accompanied them. The condition of Catholicism, its majority church and religion, was no exception. Contemporaries had long been accustomed to the denunciations of France's Calvinists as well as the lamentations of France's Catholics (especially the preachers) on the subject. The religious propaganda of the Calvinist presses painted a stark portrait of France's religious inheritance – the misguided theology and the 'abominable' and 'idolatrous' practices to which it gave rise; the inadequacies and greed of the Catholic clergy; and the inevitable morass of superstition in which the ordinary population wallowed. In due course, elements of this black legend were reproduced, albeit for entirely different purposes, by Catholic authors and preachers bemoaning the state of the French church and the culpability of its clergy and people for such a state of disrepair. It would be surprising if some of this endlessly rehearsed negative stereotype did not stick and pass into history as factual certainty. The duration of the wars of religion – rivalled only by the revolt of the Netherlands – and especially the severity of the last of them (c.1588–95), ensured that perceptions of France's condition would remain heavily pessimistic to the end. Accounts of those wars, and especially of the bloody massacres that punctuated them since the one at Vassy (1562), were widely diffused across Europe, their graphic attempts at visualising them leaving no doubt as to the kind of hostilities that they generated within families and communities.[1] Such views were also recycled and diffused by observers, travellers and diplomats. It is especially noteworthy that the Roman Curia, which had a vital interest in preserving France within the seriously diminished Catholic fold in northern and central Europe, shared much of this pessimism. With a permanent ambassador (or nuncio) at the French court who had regular contacts with leading French dignitaries, lay and ecclesiastical, it was not short of sources of information. From the 1560s onwards, the instructions issued to new nuncios, which were based on the Curia's understanding of conditions in France, habitually reiterated the established litany of lamentations and warnings.[2] It would be several decades into the next century before the tenor of these instructions started to shift into a more optimistic key.

It had not always been thus. Until the 1540s or even 1550s, France appeared as a virtual 'haven' in central-northern Europe, around which religious change swirled, often tempestuously, but to no avail. The words attributed to St Jerome, 'Gaul alone knows no monsters', were quoted to death during the decades before 1560, and their meaning was beyond all doubt: France was God's chosen land and people, which he protected from any temptation to infidelity; comparison with the rest of Europe was entirely in France's favour.[3] It had had some distinguished Christian humanists, disciples of Erasmus and Jacques Lefebvre d'Etaples, who were patronised to varying degrees by the major political and ecclesiastical figures. Despite the emergence of a crop of more openly dissident reformers from the 1520s and especially the 1530s onwards, France seemed comparatively immune to religious turmoil. Its monarchy, which at no time showed any inclination to imitate Henry VIII of England or the German-Scandinavian territorial princes by founding national churches, remained vigilant, confident of its ability to control the situation by mixing patronage and repression in its dealings with would-be religious reformers. The increasingly punitive 'heresy' laws introduced after 1534 were not a response to a massive or imminent threat, but more a matter of dissuading people from propagating 'heresy' and the 'sedition' that was increasingly its external manifestation. The French attitude towards the Council of Trent before and after its inception in 1545 reflects this stance quite faithfully: the religious problems of other parts of Europe, especially Germany, were unknown in France; therefore, France did not really need the Council to deal with its problems.[4]

With the benefit of hindsight, such complacency seems short-sighted, but within both the church and the royal government, the dominant view until the late 1550s was that serious 'reformation' had *already* been undertaken within France. Should something urgent need to be done, then the preferred option was not Trent, but a Gallican national council, which was briefly envisaged by Henri II in 1551. Provincial councils and diocesan synods had been held since the 1480s, with at least five meeting in 1528 alone at the king's request. The legislation of the Sens council of that year was regarded as a model that others, including the Council of Trent itself, could – and did – imitate. French bishops, who were often drawn from the same families or social groups as royal councillors, responded by at least legislating for religious reform, though relatively few of them felt the need to do more in order to implement change 'on the ground' (by visitations and the like); with some exceptions, it would take the experience of the wars to transform their views of their pastoral responsibilities. The Sorbonne, too, had fulfilled its historical role by its efforts at doctrinal clarification (1543) and by drafting an early index of prohibited books, both of which were to be taken up by the Council of Trent.[5] Thus, even when the Calvinist challenge grew noticeably during the 1550s, plans to have France follow the example of its neighbours in the Netherlands, Spain and Italy by introducing an inquisition were confidently, and successfully, opposed, and nothing that happened during the ensuing religious wars could induce a change of mind. In May 1588, only days after Henri III had been driven out of Paris, the triumphant duke of Guise was approached by the papal nuncio, who had not forgotten this piece of the papacy's agenda and who now urged Guise to use the opportunity to introduce the Roman Inquisition into France. The ultra-Catholic duke asked for time to think about it, but soon replied that it was out of the question, as the Inquisition – the Roman as much as Spanish – was odious in the eyes of French Catholics, even among those best disposed to the Roman Curia.[6] Decades of conflict had not changed the view that dissent and confessional conflict were not to be suppressed by mechanisms whose fearsome reputation curtailed their appeal.

Inevitably, the onset of the religious crisis in the late 1550s and the ensuing wars from 1562 onwards shattered the self-congratulatory climate that had prevailed for so long. From this point onwards, the fog of confrontation, propaganda and war, has always made it extremely difficult for the historian to 'see' French Catholicism and its condition in isolation from the politico-military events that dominate these decades. Yet it is essential to identify some key features of the Catholicism as it emerged from the civil wars, not least because so much of the energy and initiatives for religious change at work during the early part of the seventeenth century were rooted in the experiences of those earlier decades. It would make little sense to attempt to do so in the form of a narrative, however brief, of the religious wars themselves; the following pages will focus instead on a number of themes that will recur in later chapters of this book.[7] The condition of French Protestantism and the wider political context of the subject will not, for reasons explained in the Preface, be discussed directly here.

The Limits of Legislation

Once the French version of the 'colloquy' pioneered in the Empire since the late 1520s had failed to deliver religious compromise and concord at Poissy in

1560–1, the pressure was on the crown and the 'old' church to change tack and put their house in order. The decision to allow a French delegation led by the cardinal of Lorraine to attend the last sessions of the Council of Trent 'realigned' France, at least temporarily, with the rest of Catholic Europe, all the more so as Lorraine did much to rescue the Council itself from stalemate and contributed substantially to its admittedly rushed avalanche of reform decrees of 1563. What Lorraine and leading church figures could probably not have anticipated was the crown's consistent refusal thereafter to 'receive' Trent's decrees into French law, on the grounds that its reforms involved a substantial strengthening of papal control over the church, a refusal that would gradually become a litmus test for Gallican dislike of papal intentions generally. This impasse had other, more short-term political grounds: the French crown, in particular, feared a prompt Calvinist revolt if it introduced the 'provocative' Tridentine decrees into France. Until the 1620s, the papacy constantly pressed the monarchy to do as other Catholic monarchs had done, but to no avail. It had to settle for the consolation prize of the assembled French clergy declaring in 1615 that they 'adopted' the decrees as far as the governance of their dioceses was concerned. The papal nuncio exulted at the news, proclaiming that France was once again a full part of Christendom, ignoring the fact that the declaration was more a moral gesture than an effective measure, and that it included a proviso to protect the celebrated 'Gallican liberties'.[8]

But this particular issue, which provoked so much debate at the time, should not disguise the extent to which, throughout the wars of religion, the problem of how to restore and reform the Catholic church *continued* to be intensively discussed at numerous levels within France. It would be hard to find any place in Europe where it was more thoroughly debated, and in arenas quite different to the provincial councils that Trent had envisaged. These debates were nearly always conducted as part of increasingly urgent discussions about the broader Reformation – moral, political and administrative – of the realm itself. The Estates-General of 1560 and the Assembly of Notables of 1561 had already produced their *cahiers de doléances* (lists of grievances) and proposals, some of them radical, for religious and ecclesiastical reform. The conclusion of the Council of Trent in December 1563 did not put an end to such discussions for, as Alain Tallon has shown, even some of the French delegates present at Trent seem not to have paid much attention to its legislation in their own post-conciliar activities. Later, especially during the reign of Henri III, another Estates-General (1576), a landmark Assembly of Clergy (1579) and an Assembly of Notables (1583) produced further ideas, and in some instances royal commissions of investigation were despatched to the provinces in order to prepare the ground for the debates to follow. Overall, a huge range of views, complaints and proposals was recorded and summarised along the way, so it cannot be said that the different assemblies were arguing in a vacuum. This is all the more important as the French monarchy clearly continued to regard itself as enjoying the right to legislate for the church. The great reforming ordinances, from Orléans (1561) to Moulins (1566) and Blois (1579), did just that, and in many cases they silently incorporated large chunks of Trent's reform legislation into royal law.[9] During the 1580s, the crown finally allowed the provincial church councils, which should have met in the wake of Trent, to convene and engage in their own legislative activities. Several provinces did so during the early to middle years of that decade, but the deterioration of the political and military situation after that point meant that there was little scope for follow-through legislation at diocesan level. Hayden and Greenshields have shown in their study how poised the French church was at this point to move to the next phase of religious reform, but the conditions of the decade from 1585 to 1595 forced a deferral which lasted in some cases until well after the arrival of Henri IV on the French throne.[10] Years later, when Cardinal Richelieu would claim, in a bout of national self-disparagement (as he often did), that France had the best laws in Christendom, but that nobody paid any attention to them, he could well have had the reform laws of the church in mind.

In explaining the slowness of the French church, by comparison with other parts of Europe, to engage in self-reformation, it is not a case of claiming that it needed to legislate first and only then could it put precept into practice. The counter-model, as provided by the best-known post-Trent reformers such as Carlo Borromeo of Milan, involved moving back and forth between the two – and the reputation of Borromeo and others was no secret in France. It has also been argued that legislation on a grand scale, as exemplified by the French royal ordinances from 1561 to 1629, tended to be so general and moralising as to be virtually inapplicable to individual situations.[11] It is not impossible that church legislation of this period suffered from similar defects. For example, it is clear, as we shall see later, that diocesan legislation continued to retain many of its 'archaic' and 'chaotic' features until well into the seventeenth century, despite tentative moves towards a more 'methodical' format and the use of the vernacular.

Tribulations

The biggest problem facing attempts at concerted action of any kind, nationally or locally, since the early 1560s was not legislative 'archaism', however, but rather the violence, destruction and insecurity arising from the successive wars of religion themselves.[12] Physical destruction of churches and religious objects and symbols of the old church did actually precede the civil wars, since it began with the iconoclastic activities of Calvinist groups spread across France. Some of the iconoclasm was not as destructive or violent as might be imagined, and it was conducted in some places with a certain orderliness.[13] The onset of the wars ensured that the work of the iconoclasts and soldiery would overlap thereafter, and on a far greater scale. The wars did far more indiscriminate damage, but it cannot be quantified with any prospect of accuracy. Suffice it to say that such damage depended upon the duration of the individual religious wars and their geographical scale – both of which varied considerably. Some parts of France fared far worse than others, being regularly criss-crossed by rival armies; even areas that were simply along their routes rather than actual theatres of campaigning could suffer. Poitou, Touraine and the Orléanais were prime examples of such military boulevards. Provinces like Brittany escaped serious damage for most of the period, with the exception of the early 1590s. The royal commissioners and other observers of these years reported at length on the desolation of ordinary churches, but also of abbeys, convents, chapters and other religious institutions. The most common complaint of local people was that, as a result of such depredations, clergy had abandoned their posts and sought refuge in towns, so that normal religious services were no longer to be had. But pillaged churches were not always the cause of the absence of religious services, as improvised solutions were found. Instead the cessation of services was possibly more often the consequence of a related complaint, namely that much of the local church property had been seized by laypeople who tried to pass it off as their own, thus denying the clergy any kind of prospect of a proper living.[14] This was true a fortiori in those areas of France, especially in the west and the south, where the Calvinist churches were most strongly entrenched; in many such towns and villages, Catholic clergy, from bishops to simple chaplains, were highly vulnerable to physical attack, especially in the early years after 1560. But such usurpations of church property were not exclusively the action of Protestants, as Catholic nobles were not averse, for example, to confiscating the church tithe for their own benefit. And regaining possession of such properties was often far more difficult than repairing damaged churches! For all their patchiness, the early 'pastoral' visitations of the next century constitute possibly the best source for documenting the physical 'tribulations' of French Catholicism around 1600. It would take several decades to restore the damage to the basic physical fabric of many regions throughout France.[15]

As if civil war were not enough, the 'despoiling' of the church by the monarchy compounded its existing difficulties. Earlier historians of the subject deplored the fact that instead of protecting the church, as it was sworn to do, the crown engaged in a series of forced sales of church property to pay existing debts and, increasingly, to accumulate new ones. More recent research has substantially modified this picture.[16] Although we do not have a new nationwide snapshot of what really happened, local studies suggest what that might be. Church benefices in every diocese were affected by these sales, seven of which occurred between 1563 and 1587. That of 1563 was the most traumatic, since would-be purchasers were permitted to select the piece of church property that caught their eye and then had the royal commissioners grant it to them at knock-down prices. But 1563 did not set the pattern for subsequent sales, since the abuses that occurred then spurred the clergy to secure royal permission to repurchase the properties that had been alienated, and even to sell off other, less valuable ones in order to do this. Many clergy and especially, the bigger institutions (chapters, abbeys, etc.) managed to keep their most valuable assets, and often responded to the sales by using them as an opportunity, however unwelcome, to rationalise their existing holdings. During the subsequent sell-offs the clergy kept some control of the process, and above all secured the possibility of paying what was demanded of them from their disposable revenues, without touching the capital itself – a method widely practised in southern France. And in 1606, Henri IV allowed them to recover such alienated properties at the original sale prices, a concession that in due course enabled them to regain many of the properties that had changed hands since the 1560s. It would perhaps not be going too far to say that the forced sales were not without useful side benefits.

A second and more enduring financial imposition also fell on the clergy during the 1560s. Even before the forced sales began, an Assembly of Clergy at Poissy (1561) had signed a contract with the crown to pay an annual sum (the word 'tax' was strictly avoided so as to preserve the principle of the 'untaxability' of the clergy) to the crown to enable it to amortise its debts. Known as the *décimes*, the contribution was apportioned among benefice-holders within individual dioceses across France. The growing levels of non-payment in the 1570s and 1580s would suggest that benefice-holders were finding it impossible to pay, but things may not have been quite so simple. Because the assessment and apportioning of the *décimes* was conducted by the church at national (via the assembly) and local level (per diocese), there were widespread complaints that the higher clergy (bishops and cathedral chapters) were lightly assessed, because the arrangements enabled them to off-load much of the burden onto the lower, parish clergy. If there were failures or refusals to pay up, it has been argued, they may have been 'tax-strikes' or protests against abuses of power among the clergy rather than the result of any intrinsic inability to pay. Precisely because they coincided with the civil wars and the forced sales, the *décimes* were long regarded by historians as yet another 'tribulation' that the church had to endure. In fact, the alternative to them in 1561, when they were hastily negotiated for the first time, was a massive sell-off of church property of the kind that happened in 1789; that prospect had been enough to persuade the assembled clergy at Poissy to opt for a less painful outcome. At a moment of huge uncertainty about the future, the contractual relationship for the raising of the *décimes* proved to be one of those unexpected steps which brought the crown and the clergy closer together than they had been for some time. Furthermore, by giving birth to the regular assemblies of clergy, it transformed the church–crown relationship in enduring respects over the next two centuries, giving the French clergy a voice and a platform on which to discuss numerous other matters of interest to them beyond the financial one that was virtually unique in Catholic Europe. These assemblies were crucial to the gradual homogenisation of the French church's dominant groups but also to the diffusion of models of governance, reform and religious practices more generally.[17]

None of this is to deny that the wars of religion did widespread damage to the basic material fabric of French Catholicism, as they did to the wider French society. Their consequences are not hard to imagine, especially the massive fall in the numbers of new clergy, from mere tonsured clerics to priests in full orders, being ordained at the time. But a careful analysis of particular issues indicates that we should avoid adding layer after layer of black paint on the historical canvas of these decades. The institutional church and its clergy were not without resourcefulness, even when they had no option but to bend with the wind. They owed much of that capacity not just to old-fashioned 'insider' know-how, but to another unexpected contemporary development.

Mobilization

The most convincing evidence that French Catholicism was not totally overwhelmed by its tribulations is of a kind that the older historiography could not quite perceive in its own terms, because it was so heavily obscured by the more familiar military history of the wars. Yet the degree of self-defensive mobilisation generated in response to the challenge of Calvinism, and dating from the early 1560s in some areas, seems increasingly impressive. Of course, separating it from military mobilisation and activity generally still remains a tricky matter, so closely interlocking were the two for much of the time. Historians have long known, however vaguely, that the years of the second Catholic League (*c*.1589–95) were characterised as much by preaching, penitential processions, confraternities and other forms of religious mobilisation as by military activity. Recent historiography has brought this dimension of the League into sharper focus, to the point where it now seems more striking than any of the military activities of the League's commanders. But equally importantly, historians have begun to trace it backwards through the earlier decades of the religious wars, rather than assuming its sudden appearance as a *deus ex machina* during the later 1580s.[18]

There is no need to assume a simple nationwide pattern to this earlier mobilisation. A great deal depended on the degree of local danger from the new Calvinist churches and their organisations, especially in the early 1560s when their geography was more extensive than it would be a generation or so later. The initiative of local figures was often decisive here, and once again the initial format of the mobilisation tended to be military, involving associations of nobles who feared anti-seigneurial rebellion among the peasantry as much as the Calvinist churches themselves. A good example of this is provided by one of the most persistently active devisers of such 'leagues and associations', the celebrated Jean de Monluc, the royal lieutenant-governor in the huge province of Guyenne in the 1560s.[19] From Bordeaux to Toulouse via Agen and other towns across the region, uncertainty or suspicion of the crown's policies, or possibly doubts about the capacity of local aristocratic governors to afford protection against 'pratiques' and 'coups' by Calvinist groups, led to the formation of syndicates and other organisations of self-defence. Monluc engaged in such mobilisation across Guyenne from at least 1562 onwards in order to secure the major towns of the province, and once they had formed, the leagues tended to stay in being in one form or other despite formal acts of dissolution. The Bordeaux 'syndicate', dedicated to the service of God and the king, was designed to operate on four levels – the parishes, the city jurisdiction, the seneschalsy and the wider province; within each parish there was leader and a council, with subscriptions and regular Sunday meetings. In Toulouse, the major association soon diverged from its original noble stamp and evolved towards a more 'open' format that made room for urban notables to join it.[20] Needless to say, the crown itself feared such autonomous activity, especially by nobles who could call on military levies of their own. Charles IX and his mother, Catherine de Médicis declined the dubious pleasure of being greeted by over 1,000 nobles near Toulouse during the royal tour of France in 1564–5 and ordered them to return home on pain of being hanged if they failed to do so.[21] From the outset (Amboise, March 1563) the edicts of pacification that followed each religious war dissolved all such leagues and associations, but the evidence suggests that the leagues actually spread northwards to the Loire valley as early as 1564. The second war of religion (1567–8) had, if anything, constituted a bigger shock because of the number of towns captured or attacked by Huguenot forces, so there was a rash of local associations founded in their wake to prevent such surprises in the future. In the light of these early developments, it is easier to understand the fear inspired in Henri III by the creation of the first Catholic League in 1576 and his decision not to suppress it directly – as that might not have been any more successful – but to place himself at its head in order to suffocate it. The second Catholic League, organised in ultra-secrecy from 1585, proved far more immune to royal subversion than its predecessor, and it duly became Henri III's nemesis in 1588–9.

In its broad outlines, this is a variant of the familiar crown–nobility–province narrative. But as already intimated, there was far more than noble-military mobilisation involved from relatively early on during the conflicts. In the early 1560s, the governor of Burgundy, Saulx-Tavannes, drew upon the local confraternities of the Holy Ghost to counteract Protestant activities there, whence the example spread to neighbouring provinces like Berry-Limousin and Champagne. Monluc was aware of all this and tried the same approach in Guyenne. France's Protestants were already complaining by the mid-1560s that the confraternities of the Holy Ghost were actively mobilising against them.[22] In cities like Lyon, Toulouse or Rouen, which experienced Huguenot take-overs – however brief – during the 1560s, the Catholic backlash was closely associated with the re-emergence of confraternities, many of which rapidly became vigilante groups. The timescale of such developments was far from uniform, and during the early years of the religious wars it probably depended on the sense of threat felt within individual areas or towns. Philip Benedict has revealed a real lack of concern or positive activity among the higher clergy of Rouen until the mid-1580s, and it was surely not the only instance of such inertia.[23] As we shall see in a later chapter, confraternities dedicated to the holy sacrament sprang up in many places, Rouen included, during these years, and because they defended Catholic sacramental practices, they quickly became a focus for anti-Calvinist forces. Because they were not as closely connected as the older confraternities to particular social or occupational groups, they were capable of mobilising an unusually broad spectrum of the population.

At this juncture, local authorities, both secular and religious, were still suspicious of confraternities, whether old or new, but at the same time the capacity of noble leagues to protect cities as vulnerable as Agen or Mâcon from subversion was uncertain. So for all its evident dangers, some form of internal urban mobilisation seemed essential, provided it could be kept within a reliable structure. Confraternities proved to be a useful cover for militant groups within cities, especially when their associations were outlawed. As a result there was a rapid extension of confraternities such as the Penitents well beyond their circumscribed original base in Provence, Avignon and the southern Rhone valley, which saw them springing up in cities as far north as Rouen, Paris, Abbeville and Laon. Some of the latter owed their foundation to the first, short-lived Catholic League of 1576–7, but most emerged during the League's rebirth from the mid-1580s onwards. A key figure in this diffusion was the Jesuit and future confessor of Henri III, Edmond Auger, who made his reputation as a preacher in places like Bordeaux, Toulouse and Lyon, bringing the Penitents there in his wake. But perhaps the most improbable sponsor of Penitents was the Penitent-king himself, Henri III, who had first witnessed the Penitents in northern Italy and Provence on his return from Poland in 1574–5. He gave them public support as early as 1575, and by 1583 he had founded his own confraternity of Penitent flagellants at Vincennes, and was encouraging similar actions within individual cities throughout France.[24] In many towns, the alternative was to revive older and virtually moribund confraternities and to infuse them with new devotional and political objectives; sometimes cities like Lyon did both. These confraternities coincided with other forms of popular religious activity, especially mass processions, either within towns or to particularly venerated religious sites, which displayed unmistakable penitential attitudes. As has been shown for Rouen, Toulouse and elsewhere, the Penitents were well suited to channel the religious and political anxieties of the age, and they found themselves taking a leading role during the years of the Catholic League's struggle (1589–94) to prevent Henri IV from succeeding to the throne. In some southern cities during these years, membership of the Penitents was thrown open to lower social groups, which was a shift away from the previously restricted elite membership and closed meetings. That may well have enabled more radical politics to surface and to take control of the Leaguer towns. This seems particularly evident in Marseille, a city with a record twelve confraternities of Penitents by 1593 and whose Leaguer 'boss', Cazaulx, used the Penitents as a ramp to seize power within the city in the late 1580s. Marseille is not the only example of the growing impact of 'confraternal contamination' on urban politics as the wars of religion advanced.[25]

Regardless of their names and the military-political role they played, these confraternities, which we will revisit in a later chapter, were at the centre of several religious practices that are characteristic of the latter decades of the sixteenth century. The sudden shock of a serious Protestant threat, coming after years of confident assertion of France's religious purity, led them not just to military action and massacres culminating in those of August 1572, but also to adopt a combination of crusading and penitential actions that echoed the fragility of French Catholicism after 1560. As Denis Pallier has aptly put it, they were 'penitents as well as militants', so that they contributed substantially to anchoring new-style devotions among France's urban populations.[26] Calvinist attacks on particular elements of Catholic religious attachments and practices – images, the cult of the saints, shrines and so on – produced a symmetrical response in their defence, one that was collective and highly public. Among the most familiar demonstrations were the 'white' processions that were organised, especially in 1583, and which were in fact huge pilgrimages to important sites such as Chartres, Reims or Liesse across north-eastern

France. Thereafter, such exercises were mostly confined to towns, and the processions, especially of the flagellant Penitents, were depicted during the height of the Second League (post-1588) as involving a mixture of laity and clergy, some of whom carried arms under their cassocks. Penitential action of this kind in turn owed a great deal to the impact of popular preachers whose doom-laden message was, in the conditions of the time, capable of mobilising large numbers of ordinary people, especially during the Lenten and Advent stations. The message was one which called for repentance and renewal, but also, and crucially, for action against heresy and the pollution it represented.[27]

It has been argued that this readiness of the French clergy to urge people to defend their church and religion distinguishes France from other parts of Europe where similar challenges emerged. The clergy of the old church within the German lands were extremely slow to react to change from the 1520s to the 1550s and beyond, while the *Reichskirche* as a whole seems to have counted largely on help from the princes or from the outside – from the papacy, the new religious orders and so on. The Netherlanders, both lay and clerical, who experienced a similar and almost simultaneous Calvinist challenge to that of France, displayed little stomach for a fight, and only a tiny handful of their clergy did more than urge people to examine themselves and repent their sins.[28] Few apart from the Jesuits seemed ready to call for more resolute, open resistance to 'heresy'. In France, the old church did bite back – and from the early years of the religious crisis. First the Jesuits and then the Capuchins and Récollets (both offshoots of the Franciscans) appeared between the 1560s and the 1580s, and they were welcomed for the energy with which they preached *both* messages: they founded new confraternities, encouraging their religious fervour in ways that heightened their sense of being a 'Christian militia'. The orders were not, however, the only clergy to respond in this way, since much of the initial resistance to Calvinism had occurred before they appeared. A sufficient number of urban clergy had put up resistance since the 1550s and early 1560s, and they also played a vital part in pumping out an impressive quantity of printed works, both learned and polemical, which ensured that the Calvinist presses were swamped by the output of their ever more numerous Catholic rivals. This too was in contrast with what happened – or failed to happen – in other parts of Europe, and it reached a peak during the decade of the second Catholic League. These were critical contributions to the vigour with which French Catholicism defended itself during the age of the religious wars even though, as we saw above, the first instances of mobilisation in self-defence in the early 1560s were military and noble. When this initial mobilisation opened out to other social groups and drew upon the potential of the confraternities, there was considerably more room for involvement by both laypeople and clergy. The role of the clergy thereafter was scarcely to be found in any handbook, but it did not eclipse or replace that of the lay population engaged in the same combat. Some southern militants looked to Philip II of Spain for assistance, but they did not sit back and wait for him to relieve them of the burden of aggressive self-defence.[29]

Once they had come into being, there was little incentive for the militants and the confraternities to demobilise, since with virtually each edict of pacification from 1563 to 1576, the Huguenots seemed to extract ever more extensive concessions from the crown, concessions which were also increasingly described as 'perpetual and irrevocable' rather than simply as provisional pending efforts at religious reunion. Moreover, the prospect of the childless Henri III being succeeded by the Huguenot leader, Henri de Navarre, which suddenly became real after 1584, made demobilisation even less likely. The second Catholic League was soon formed and quickly spread its tentacles throughout France, taking control of numerous towns in 1588–9, during the height of the prolonged political crisis triggered by the expulsion of Henri III from Paris in May 1588, exacerbated by the murder of the Guises in December that year, and then transformed by Henri III's own assassination in August 1589 into a war of royal succession. But instead of being a standard around which to rally France's Catholic elites against the future Henri IV, the cause of the Catholic League, despite its crusading and eschatological motifs as chronicled by Denis Crouzet, proved to be a source of acute division among those elites.[30] Many were not willing – or no longer willing – to prolong civil war indefinitely, and were willing to support Henri IV's claim to be king, despite his Protestantism, hoping that he would be persuaded to convert to Catholicism, which he did in no great hurry in 1593. Families, social groups and key politico-administrative institutions like the law courts were deeply divided over this choice, and often ended up in open conflict. The exaltation and crusading militancy of the early days of the League withered gradually during the grind and chaos of civil war. The post-war recomposition of those Catholic elites, which Henri IV himself was so keen to promote under the banner of 'forgive and forget', was something in which all but a few unreconciled diehards could participate.[31] Common ground was not hard to find: the restoration and reformation of Catholicism at various levels had been a leitmotif of the mobilisation of the previous decades and could be pursued henceforth with some hope of accomplishment. Where the League had divided, these projects would reconcile. In fact, as a number of studies have shown, this initial expectation was not entirely fulfilled, and reunion could be as elusive as the 'union' that had been the mantra of the Catholic League. The erstwhile Catholic adversaries could not always forget their recent past, especially in towns where their conflicts had been violent, so they went on to sponsor and patronise the different elements of Catholic reformation that corresponded to their respective sensibilities. The classic example of this was the preference for particular religious orders – the Spanish Carmelite nuns and the Capuchins were far more to the taste of ex-Leaguers than of the former Politiques, who preferred the Jesuits (despite the reputation of the latter for peddling anti-monarchical ideas). There were, of course, exceptions to this rule, but in broad terms it still seems to fit. They may even have had, as in Limoges, their distinct preferences for certain saints' names for their children! Likewise, where ex-rivals avoided intermarriage (the classic mechanism for healing such wounds), the process of 'oubliance', as Henri IV called it, was slowed in subsequent decades.[32]

The social recomposition of Catholic elites was, therefore, not total nor perfect, but as far as supporting religious change in the generation after the wars of religion had ended, perhaps it did not have to be. As it was, it offered the prospect of a wider range of religious options than might otherwise have been the case. The record, as we shall see later, speaks for itself, amply justifying the hypothesis of André Latreille many years ago that 'during the religious wars, a long and obscure work of preparation must have been accomplished, without which it is impossible to account for the religious revival that exploded once normal conditions had returned'.[33] On paper, not much had been done to bring French Catholicism into line with the rest of post-Tridentine Europe; and the resistance to Protestantism had not advanced the indispensable but grinding work of visitation and reformation within the parishes. Yet the signs are that some contemporaries were aware that there was room for hope, and indeed some optimism. In his report to Rome on the state of his diocese in 1594, Cardinal Joyeuse, archbishop of Toulouse, wrote: 'of course, it is regrettable that our civil wars, which have been so long and brutal, have reduced or disfigured some of our good things (*avantages*). It is, nonetheless, a great consolation to see that these wars have increased piety and religion to the extent that losses among certain of our material goods have become gains by being added to the piety, zeal and ardour for religion among the population of Toulouse generally.' Two years later, and more surprisingly given its source, we find a similar 'revisionist' position taking shape. On his way to France as a papal legate with wide powers to deal with the many problems left unresolved after the wars, Cardinal Alessandro de' Medici (briefly Pope Leo XI in 1605) sensed, very soon after setting foot on French soil in the Dauphiné, that the received wisdom about the state of France and its church, which like everyone else in Rome he had accepted, was simply not reliable.[34] He proceeded to file away the instructions he had on the subject, determined to base his judgements henceforth on what he observed around him. No historian wishing to analyse the fundamental structures of the French church of the day could cavil with such sound advice.

PART 1

Foundations

CHAPTER 1

FROM DIOCESES TO PARISHES: THE GEOGRAPHY OF THE FRENCH CHURCH

By any standard of measurement, the French church of the centuries before the revolution was one of the biggest and most imposing in Europe. And as the French monarchy itself expanded again from the mid-seventeenth century onwards, so did the church that corresponded to it. There were, of course, other 'national' churches, to use an anachronistic term, which were as big or even bigger – those of Poland, the Spanish kingdoms, or the Holy Roman Empire, for example. But viewing things purely in spatial terms does not provide the full picture. For one thing, France had long been the most densely populated kingdom in Europe, with a population that, despite the persistently adverse conditions of the seventeenth century, hovered around 18 to 19 million. In addition to its geographical extension, one of the most important distinguishing marks of the French church was its compactness and institutional 'density', not to mention its highly developed sense of itself as an entity. It is the often surprising combination of these factors which, paraphrasing Marc Bloch, accounts for the 'original characteristics' of the French church, and this book will return to them more than once. At the outset, however, it is essential to become familiar with the fundamental building blocks which enabled it to cohere both locally and 'nationally', even though many of those building blocks were common coin across Christendom as a whole. Institutional geography may be largely descriptive, with limited explanatory power on its own, but it is indispensable to understanding the challenges that the French church would face during the period covered in these pages.

Dioceses

If the French church of the early modern period prided itself on anything, it was on the antiquity not merely of its traditions, but also of its key structures. Like in other parts of central and northern Europe, French dioceses were remarkably fixed and unchanging, so that however small some of them were, they exhibited none of the constant shifts in numbers that characterised the Italian peninsula, where the frequent suppression, combination and resurrection of dioceses makes counting them at any point quite problematic (see Map 1).[1] In important respects, the diocesan map of France mirrors the long process of Christianisation and the highly peculiar 'geography' which it generated. The earliest regions to be evangelised were the Mediterranean provinces of Roman Gaul, from Provence to Aquitaine. These were also the most urbanised provinces of Roman Gaul, resembling numerous other areas of the Mediterranean littoral, so it is no surprise that the contours and institutions of the new churches there would closely resemble those of elsewhere in the Roman Empire. Consequently, the 'cities', big and (mostly) small, of the future Midi quite naturally became the seats of dioceses which were themselves frequently tiny, containing by the early modern period no more than fifteen to fifty parishes in some cases. The parishes into which they were gradually subdivided for pastoral and administrative purposes were themselves based on the Roman villages (*vici*) that depended on the nearest city (*civitas*), itself the seat of civilian administration. What was important from the earliest days was the urban 'seat' of the diocese, not its territorial extension. This ancient conception of what defined a diocese continued to influence seventeenth-century thinking, thus ensuring, for example, that attempts, usually initiated by bishops, to remove their residence and cathedral church from a possibly deserted or inhospitable *bourg* to a larger, more suitable town would be fiercely resisted; and that resistance to the change of 'seat' was not infrequently led by the cathedral chapters, defending the name and honour of the diocese's founder-saint. Beyond that, local self-interest played a major part in the resistance, since for many of the 120 diocesan towns across France, the presence of a bishop, a chapter and ecclesiastical administration were vital sources of prestige and even economic viability; their loss would be more than a symbolic one. When, finally, the French Revolution and not the *ancien régime* church set about suppressing many of these old dioceses and creating a new administrative map of France, small episcopal towns like Lectoure, Lombez and Saint-Pons in Languedoc, or Sisteron or Apt in Provence protested that they were effectively facing a sentence of death.

By contrast, the evangelisation of the central and northern regions of Roman and Frankish Gaul had been much slower, but dioceses were created in several cities there from the third and fourth century AD onwards. Being

FROM DIOCESES TO PARISHES   19

1. French dioceses, 1715.

much less urbanised regions, their cities were more scattered, which in turn meant that dioceses would, with some exceptions, be far larger in overall size and also in the number of dependent parishes, than their southern counterparts. As a glance at the map shows, a large number of the dioceses north of the Bordeaux–Grenoble line fell into this category, though there were occasional exceptions to the rule. Indeed these large dioceses resemble those of the Netherlands, the Empire and England, not to mention the eastern marcher lands of medieval and early modern Europe, far more than those of the Midi. Vast dioceses like Bourges and Clermont had upwards of 700–900 parishes by 1600; dioceses like Poitiers, Chartres, Tours and Le Mans were no less extensive, but the absolute record here belonged to Rouen, with over 1,300 parishes. It is not hard to imagine how radically different the challenges occasioned by such a haphazard ecclesiastical geography might be. This applies particularly to seventeenth-century bishops and their advisers as they attempted to meet the demands of residence and active governance placed on them by the post-tridentine church. The map shows that some dioceses were not merely vast, but also misshapen, suggesting how difficult communication across them was in an age of poor travel conditions.

Despite the huge disparities in the size of dioceses, efforts to deal with them were fewer than might be imagined. A brief look at the changes which *were* made, and the reasons for them, reveals a lack of interest in redrawing the map, and the force of the opposition to it when it did happen. First of all, at no time was there any attempt made to address the question as a whole – when changes to the diocesan map did occur, it was always for particular reasons without a 'generalising' rationale to them. The only major redrawing of diocesan boundaries before the early modern period had been made as long ago as 1317–18 by Pope John XXII, mainly in order to deal with the Cathar problem around Toulouse in western Languedoc. When it came to creating new dioceses or unifying existing ones two or three centuries later, it was, significantly, the crown rather than the papacy which played the decisive role, even though in theory the right to create new dioceses still belonged exclusively to the pope. Amalgamations of small dioceses rarely received any support, especially in the areas that would be most affected by them. The tiny Provençal dioceses of Vence and Grasse, with no more than fifty parishes between them, were unified twice in our period – in the 1590s and the 1640s – but on each occasion the outcome was a failure, leading to renewed separation. Petitions for *new* dioceses were also made here and there during the wars of religion, but a weakened monarchy was unlikely to attempt what its stronger predecessors had eschewed, not least because local elements of the radical Catholic League were campaigning for change. Dijon, located on the southern end of the vast diocese of Langres, is a perfect example. A first petition for an independent diocese there was made during the 1590s, when the Catholic League dominated the city and region, but it was ignored by Henri IV and his successors. Unusually, the bishop of Langres himself took up the cause and petitioned Rome for a diocese for Dijon in the 1620s, but he was firmly opposed by his own cathedral chapter which effectively blocked any change in Rome. It was not until 1730 that sufficient support for the change materialised, especially from the crown, and Dijon was finally separated from Langres.

The ad hoc, particularist logic behind the creation of new dioceses is also evident in the few changes that did occur during the seventeenth century. Only days after the fall of the Protestant stronghold of La Rochelle in 1628, Louis XIII pledged that it would become the seat of the local diocese, but what he had in mind was the relocation of the existing diocese of Maillezais and the 'annexation' to it of a small slice of the neighbouring diocese of Saintes around La Rochelle itself. Yet it took nearly twenty years for this modest change to come about, despite the obvious challenge of dealing with Protestantism in the region. Although La Rochelle was not the only part of France with a large Huguenot population, it was not until the Revocation of the Edict of Nantes (1685) that some further thought seems to have been given to subdividing a few existing dioceses. The sprawling diocese of Chartres was the only northern one to be affected by it, and the outcome was the creation, in 1697, of a new diocese at Blois, where there were substantial concentrations of Protestants. But in the southern Huguenot heartlands, where the population densities were far greater, the only diocese to be subdivided was Nîmes, whose bishops had consistently failed to make much headway in dealing with the Huguenot communities of their elongated and upland diocese: the new diocese of Alès finally appeared in 1694, three years before that at Blois. The division of Valence and Die astride the Rhone was less problematic: they were already nominally separate dioceses, even though they had had the same bishop for centuries. But that was all: a distracted monarchy did not have the stomach for further 'rationalisation' of dioceses, despite the failure of its preferred methods of dealing with the Huguenots. On the eve of the revolution, the map of France's dioceses remained as much a patchwork as before.

The slowness with which seemingly justifiable alterations to existing dioceses were implemented offers an unusual, but valuable, first glimpse of the formidable combination of inertia and attachment to the familiar that pervaded both church and society in seventeenth-century France. It might be thought that the crown would want to subdivide the bigger dioceses and, like the Avignon papacy before it, increase its fund of episcopal patronage, but too many other factors militated against such efforts. The canon law itself favoured those arguing that change would damage them and their interests. Entrenched corporate clerical groups, like the canons of a cathedral or monks of an abbey, were formidable opponents experienced in fighting their corner. On each occasion when change did actually occur and a new diocese was created, ways had to be found to undercut such opposition and offer the kind of indemnity, material and symbolic, that would buy off opponents of change. The most difficult problem of all was finding the means of endowing a new diocese with sufficient assets to be self-financing. This could only be done by 'incorporating' existing benefices – a wealthy abbey, most commonly – into the new see, but such moves tended to multiply the number of opponents at local level. Practical and acceptable solutions were inherently slow to materialise, which explains why the creation of a new diocese usually took several years of negotiation, accompanied by much bullying and arm-twisting. In these circumstances, it is hardly surprising that the appetite for wide-ranging change or rationalisation of the French diocesan map proved so limited.

The 'interest' dimensions of such questions are relatively easy to detect, but we should not imagine they were the only considerations involved. The degree to which belonging to a particular diocese shaped contemporaries' sense of who they were, especially among laypeople, is hard to fathom. For clerics, priests or not, diocesan 'identity' was inescapable, since all official documents concerning them systematically recorded which diocese they currently belonged to, either by birth or by later attachment. Like their medieval predecessors, early modern churchmen and writers were convinced that the cathedral churches and the dioceses they 'represented' were of great antiquity, with most of them claiming their founder was a saint. Sees like Marseille, Arles or Narbonne claimed to have origins as old as the Apostles, and the widely practised embellishing of the hagiographical record served as a basis not merely for ceremonial 'precedence' in assemblies and public occasions, but also for claims to authority and jurisdiction over churches of later foundation. Lesser or more recent dioceses were just as attached to their foundation myths, the enduring power of which enabled them to defend their distinctiveness against all-comers.

Furthermore, the attack on episcopal office itself by the Protestant reformers elicited a strong defence of both dioceses and bishops within the old church. In particular, it has been suggested that the Protestant challenge triggered an almost instinctive move to revive the cult of the saintly founding bishops (and other exemplary successors along the way), something which both encouraged, and was facilitated by, the compilation (or reworking) of episcopal succession lists.[2] Major church figures like Carlo Borromeo of Milan also stimulated scholarly work on the history of their dioceses and predecessors, and the signs are that their urgings were taken seriously. In seventeenth-century France, the writing of numerous diocesan histories began, usually with the encouragement of bishops, so the outcome was often diocesan history with a decidedly 'episcopal' intention and format to it. The successive versions of the celebrated *Gallia Christiana* produced during the century are the best evidence of such a drive. In due course, more rigorous scholarship would undermine many of the earlier myths concerning France's diocesan history and its saints, but in the meantime they often created, or revived, a cult of the saintly bishop and even made the seat of the diocese a place of at least local veneration.

By then, too, the Council of Trent had firmly and quite consciously entrusted the government and reform of the church to its bishops, with the diocese as their normal sphere of operation. Henceforth, they were meant to move about their diocese and become closely acquainted with it, rather than merely govern it from their often-distant 'seat' – or even from outside the diocese itself. This same exigency is visible in the requirement, which French bishops largely ignored, that they report regularly to the pope on the state of their diocese – the visitation *ad limina apostolorum* – providing details about population, numbers of parishes, confraternities, religious houses and so on. But ignoring papal demands did not mean that such information simply went uncollected.[3] It was the financial demands of the monarchy after 1560 which first compelled bishops to acquire a more minute knowledge of their dioceses and their benefices, so that they could be assessed in order to apportion the *décimes* and *dons gratuits* payable to the crown. Ultimately, the cumulative effect of these developments was to reaffirm the centrality of the diocese within the French church.

'The diocese comes across above all as an historical reality; it was its antiquity which legitimated its existence, but it was also necessary to clearly define its territorial extension.'[4] The qualification contained in this historical judgement should not be overlooked. In France and elsewhere, the Tridentine vision of the role of the well-defined diocese sat uneasily with several aspects of inherited ecclesiastical geography. Dioceses, like parishes as we shall see later, were 'porous' in more than one respect. On even a relatively small map of seventeenth-century French dioceses, large numbers of enclaves belonging to other dioceses are visible, but the true picture is even more complicated than that. Breton dioceses seem to have experienced this phenomenon more than most: fully half of the ninety-six parishes that made up Dol diocese were enclaved within neighbouring ones, with the remaining half clustering around the town of Dol itself.[5] Possibly the most serious instance of this occurred in Alsace-Lorraine, where whole areas regarded themselves as belonging to no diocese at all, and certainly not to the vast diocese of Toul which claimed jurisdiction over them. It was partly to deal with these problems that the diocese of Saint-Dié was finally established, but that was only in

1777. The biggest 'enclave' of all was, of course, of an altogether different kind – the cluster of five dioceses around Avignon, four of which remained under papal rule until 1789. Occupied more than once by French troops during Louis XIV's quarrels with Rome or the Prince of Orange (who was still sovereign of the principality-cum-diocese of the same name), they were just as regularly returned to their masters when peace was finally made. Only Orange became a fully French diocese in the last years of Louis's reign.

The problems of Toul mentioned above can also be seen as instances of the 'frontier' diocese and its peculiarities. The problem was particularly important during the seventeenth century, since the increase in the overall number of French dioceses was due primarily to the territorial expansion of the monarchy, largely but not exclusively under Louis XIV. The small diocese of Belley, close to Switzerland, only became 'French' under Henry IV in an exchange of lands with the duchy of Savoy in 1601, while the incorporation of the crown of Navarre a few decades later (1620) officially brought the Navarre-Béarn dioceses of Lescar and Oloron into the French church. The Franco-Spanish war (1635–59) added the dioceses of Perpignan and Arras at opposite ends of the kingdom, while Louis XIV's early wars added Tournai, Saint-Omer, Ypres, Cambrai and Besançon (the latter covering the entire Franche-Comté) to that tally. But contrary to the trend of the previous century or more, Louis was forced to hand back Ypres and Tournai under the terms of the treaty of Utrecht (1713). By the later date, the French church numbered 124 dioceses, eleven more than it had under Henri IV.[6]

Incorporating and 'domesticating' newly acquired frontier dioceses was by no means straightforward, especially those like Perpignan or Besançon which, although wide apart on the map, both had long experience of the distinctive characteristics of Spanish temporal rule, religious traditions and different attitudes towards the papacy. The Flanders dioceses were regarded as being more 'French' in many respects, but they too possessed features which were deemed to make them very 'un-Gallican' – different emphases in their piety, the greater influence of the religious orders, and so on. It was no surprise that the bishops chosen to govern these dioceses were selected with great care, with the intention of introducing French practices among the populations there. Yet even dioceses like Metz, Toul and Verdun, whose cities had been under French control since 1552, were extremely slow to move into the French orbit: it was not until Louis XIV's rule that, with papal agreement, French bishops were nominated *de jure* by the crown to govern them. One reason for this is that all along France's northern and eastern borders, the papacy endeavoured to preserve for as long as it could those prerogatives to appoint to benefices which it no longer enjoyed within France itself since at least the Concordat of Bologna (1516). These and other recently acquired dioceses were thus only half-integrated into the French church. They were the church's equivalent of the crown's 'provinces held to be foreign' (*provinces réputées étrangères*). They did not belong to the 'Clergy of France', which in turn meant that they were not represented at the assemblies of clergy which debated church and religious questions and, above all, voted financial subventions to the monarchy. Here it was the ecclesiastical *pays légal* and *pays réel* that diverged, with newly acquired dioceses fitting inside France's political, but not church, boundaries.[7]

Provinces

It would be misleading to conclude from this survey that the French church was a flat, heterogeneous amalgam of dioceses which largely went their own way. They were grouped together into provinces which show similar marks of historical accident, but that did not prevent them from becoming increasingly important during the early modern period. A brief consideration of this type of ecclesiastical geography is indispensable for an understanding of questions of communication and leadership within the French church. In keeping with its large numbers of dioceses, it is not surprising that the French church should also have boasted an imposing number of ecclesiastical provinces – eighteen in all by the end of Louis XIV's reign. Some of them were as ancient and exhibited the same extremes of size as the dioceses we have just discussed. Arles was the smallest of them, with just three small dependent ('suffragan') dioceses; Bourges was by far the largest, with twelve dioceses, some of them of enormous size. Like France's dioceses, half of all the provinces were located in the southern regions stretching from Bordeaux to Vienne and Embrun.

A limited reconfiguration of the provinces occurred in the seventeenth century. By far the most important of them resulted from the belated elevation of Paris, previously a 'mere' diocese and a suffragan of Sens, to the status of an archdiocese in 1622. It now became a separate province, with Meaux, Orléans and Chartres as its suffragans. The second redrawing of the 'provincial' map occurred in 1676, when Albi, formerly part of Bourges province, became the head of a new province regrouping the southernmost dioceses of the existing province of Bourges. And, thanks to Louis XIV's conquests, the French church acquired two high-ranking existing metropolitan sees, Besançon and Cambrai, although in both cases their ecclesiastical provinces were only partly located within France's political frontiers. Thus, when Cambrai's most famous archbishop, Fénélon (1695–1715), wished to issue ordinances for his diocese, he had to prepare two versions of them, one for its new 'French' subjects, another for its Spanish or (later) Austrian ones living beyond France's borders. Here, too, we are confronted with an institutional geography that defies neat, rational explication.

In addition, at least six of these eighteen provinces went further than others, with their archbishops claiming 'primatial' status, which in each case was based largely on the administrative geography of the Roman Empire. The antiquity, nomenclature and claims to leadership of these provinces and their archbishops could easily suggest that French dioceses were firmly integrated into a hierarchical structure over which primates and archbishops presided. But for most purposes this was simply not the case. Each archbishop tried to defend and extend his jurisdictional powers within his province, but the Gallican maxims, which held that all bishops were essentially equal, did not foster a submissive attitude towards such hierarchical claims. Fewer and fewer of the provincial councils that might have reinforced primatial or metropolitan authority actually met after the sixteenth century, once those of the 1560s–90s had played their part in diffusing the reformist legislation of Trent and the great royal ordinances of Orléans and Blois. The last proper provincial council met in Bordeaux in 1624, but its legislation, inspired by a devoted follower of Carlo Borromeo, Cardinal François de Sourdis, met with a very negative response from Rome, which disliked the Gallican and 'episcopalist' accents of its decisions. The provincial councils which met in 1699, for example, to condemn Fenélon's quietism were much more limited and improvised assemblies, and not councils in the conventional sense. As elsewhere in Europe, the papacy, the crown and ordinary bishops all had their own reasons for disliking provincial councils, which met hardly anywhere apart from the generation or so after the Council of Trent.

Yet France's ecclesiastical provinces mattered considerably more by the end of the seventeenth century than a century earlier. The overriding reason was financial and political, and not internal developments of the church. Without dioceses losing any of their importance, it was provinces, not dioceses, which elected deputies to, and which were 'represented' at, the regular general assemblies of clergy during the last two centuries before the revolution. Voting in the assemblies was also by provinces; presidencies of an assembly were, until Louis XIV's reign, decided along similar lines, as was the choice of the two 'general agents of the clergy', who were normally paired along north–south lines. And to become a candidate for election as a deputy by a province, aspiring clerics needed to hold benefices within the church province in question. Thus, those most involved in French ecclesiastical politics – from royal ministers to ecclesiastical politicians and clerical hopefuls – all contributed to conferring a degree of importance on ecclesiastical provinces that they would not otherwise have enjoyed. The monarchy took the measure of this development in several ways, and for the first time under Louis XIV nobody, with a few exceptions that caused largely unflattering comment at the time, who lacked prior experience as an 'ordinary' bishop was promoted to the rank of archbishop. It was in this unexpected fashion that the crown's financial interests rather than the church's own internal dynamics were mainly responsible for the reinforcement of its particular hierarchical structures which in other circumstances might have remained without much substance.[8]

The fact that the provinces survived as functioning entities despite the decline of their historic claims to jurisdictional superiority over their suffragan dioceses also relates to the question of leadership roles within the French church. There was, it seems, no innate desire among French bishops to have a leader figure who could speak on their behalf or require them to follow his lead. If the sixteenth- and early seventeenth-century French church did have leader figures, it was usually cardinals like Tournon, Lorraine-Guise, Joyeuse, du Perron or Henri de Gondi-Retz. They were succeeded by the cardinal-ministers, Richelieu and Mazarin, whose domination of the affairs of the French church derived primarily from their roles as royal ministers, which makes it patently impossible to disentangle that leadership from their political roles. With the death of Mazarin in 1661, Louis XIV made it perfectly plain that there would be little scope for cardinals to play major political roles from then on. The most eminent cardinals of his reign – Bouillon, Estrées, Forbin-Janson and Bonzi – were kept well away from Paris and confined to diplomatic roles, essentially in Rome. One result of this was that the archbishop of Paris, despite the very recent elevation of his see, gradually emerged as the principal episcopal figure, and Paris itself the leading see of the French church. This was not immediately obvious, and for a time it depended heavily on the personality and political skills of the archbishop: François de Harlay (1671–95), for example, was infinitely more successful in this regard than his successor, Cardinal Noailles (1695–1729).

Parishes

The gap separating the pinnacle of the diocesan hierarchy just discussed from the parishes, often tiny and inaccessible, of which dioceses were made up, could hardly have been wider. Of course, there were intermediary structures: for centuries, archdeaconries, 'arch-priestships' and deaneries – the vocabulary varied considerably across the country – had been familiar, but by the seventeenth century the extent to which they still really functioned as working subdivisions of dioceses rather than as 'fiefs' held by prominent canons of the cathedral chapter is often hard to establish. To be an archdeacon within a cathedral/diocese was to be a 'dignitary' with certain prerogatives, including that of inspecting ('visiting') dependent parishes and collecting fees from them for one's pains, and such positions were keenly fought over for the prestige and revenues that they brought their holders. In large dioceses, these subdivisions could obviously serve as part of an authority-chain (*relais de pouvoir*), but in general, it seems that seventeenth-century bishops – and not just in France – were anxious to find both more flexible units of diocesan governance and more dependable subordinates, even though that did not prevent them from making extensive use of well-disposed and energetic archdeacons.

Nobody has yet successfully calculated exactly how many parishes there were in pre-revolutionary France, since all of the surviving lists contain inaccuracies and omissions, but a round figure of 32,000 seems to be the most plausible for our period.[9] Regrettable as such uncertainty may be, it does point us towards questions of direct interest to the present analysis – notably the differing status of parishes themselves, which is well reflected in the wide range of terms used in contemporary records to describe them and their incumbents. And as with the dioceses, questions of the size and shifting geography of parishes in relation to population movements and social demand are crucial for an understanding of how the French church functioned at grass-roots level.

We have already noted the Roman and village-based origins of parishes, especially in the south, where some dioceses could number as few as twenty-five parishes, in contrast to some northern and central dioceses containing up to, and even beyond, a thousand. The starkness of these disparities is somewhat mitigated by the fact that a large proportion of northern parishes were considerably smaller than their southern or western counterparts, and that the parish network of the Île-de-France and surrounding areas was an extremely dense one – and often in direct contrast to the inordinate size of their dioceses.

This suggests that the correspondence of the parish structure to social and demographic patterns in a country as varied as France was not straightforward. The parish structure evolved fairly slowly during the Middle Ages, and could not, therefore, escape being influenced by shifting patterns of habitat; in many parts of France, it was also the basic unit of government as it was of religion. Contemporary writers often assumed, carelessly, that 'communities of inhabitants' and parishes were just two sides of the same coin. But that correspondence was only partially true. It was patently not true of the bigger towns and cities, which would normally have more than one parish. Even in the countryside, where in around 1720 approximately four out of every five French people lived, it applied mainly to areas where the population inhabited villages, large or small. It was in these areas of long-standing, concentrated population settlement that the correlation of parish and community was most perfect, with the result that the parish actually served as a unit for the administration of justice and the collection of taxes, even though in theory these functions were quite distinct. Where the peasantry lived in more scattered forms of habitation, as was common in the western and central, often upland areas, a parish might cover several small communities of inhabitants, with the result that its 'secular', especially administrative and fiscal, functions were seriously diminished, and its religious ones eclipsed all others. Such differences inevitably influenced the attitudes of people to the parishes to which they belonged.[10]

Regardless of their size, parishes could be just as imprecisely defined and as porous as some of the dioceses we have already observed. The inhabitants of Quesneger in Beauvais diocese still had no fixed parochial affiliation as late as 1634, when a neighbouring parish priest described them disparagingly as 'wild Christians who acknowledge neither pastor nor flock'.[11] Sometimes places like Quesneger even alternated from year to year in attaching themselves to this or that neighbouring parish: in Tours diocese, these places were known as *tournants et virants* (hoppers and changers). Enclaves and 'immunities' were very common, especially in towns, and there was no single logic available to overcome the problems to which they gave rise. These inherited anomalies were mostly tolerated by clergy and laypeople, who had long since learned to work around them, so that it was probably the bishops of the seventeenth century, followed in due course by provincial intendants and administrative reformers, who first took a serious dislike to them. But none of these outsiders, either separately or together, seems to have had much success in rationalising them, and most of their solutions were ad hoc, short-term and more 'personal' than institutional in conception.

From the thirteenth century onwards, the medieval church had tried to insist that parishioners use their parish church in preference to others, and especially that they made their required annual confession to their parish priest, but even such a limited requirement was still not widely observed by 1600. Mostly, it gave rise to endless disputes, particularly in towns, between secular parish clergy and their direct competitors, the religious orders. By the seventeenth century, partly through the renewed insistence of the Council of Trent and then of the reformers and legislators who were inspired by it, the emphasis on the parish as the normal focus of people's religious life was finally being taken seriously. With that came greater concern about the adequacy of the existing parish network and the need to ensure that everyone 'belonged' to a parish. The jibe about the 'wild Christians' of Quesneger noted above perfectly mirrors the concern that such extra-parochial enclaves be eliminated from the map altogether.

The ad hoc development of parishes over time and the subsequent shifts in population density and settlement generated difficulties of a different kind that were not as easy to identify or resolve as that of Quesneger. Parishes could and did grow in size by taking over as 'annexes' former parishes which had ceased to function as such, either because of depopulation or failure to attract clergy willing to serve in them. It was the large multi-hamlet rural parishes that were the most likely to generate problems for their inhabitants. The most obvious physical indicator of the average parish was the titular parish church with its adjacent buildings. Furthermore, the baptismal font was a distinctive mark of the parish church itself, which could involve serious inconvenience for the parents in search of a speedy baptism for their new-born children, but living perhaps several miles from the church. Likewise, weddings and burying the dead in a 'central' parish cemetery would involve difficult travel, especially in winter and across poor or non-existent roads. The most common, ad hoc solution was for the 'central' parish church to be supplemented by 'chapels of ease', the *succursales*, usually entrusted to a curate and located in the outlying hamlets. But the inhabitants of these dependent annexes or *succursales* were still likely to feel underprivileged and neglected, since they were still required to attend the parish church – the 'mother' church – for the major feast days and could only take the major sacraments there. Plainly, serious instances of clerical absenteeism or fecklessness would aggravate this kind of situation further. It was not surprising that in such circumstances the demand for curates and, less often, for the subdivision of parishes, was particularly insistent.

The degree to which the church felt compelled to respond to these demands remains difficult to assess. It is impossible even to make an educated guess at the number of newly created parishes during our period in proportion to the existing stock. The role of local inhabitants was crucial in such creations, since they had to reckon the advantages it would bring them against the not inconsiderable costs, from the outset, of ensuring that the new parish had enough revenues to support and house a parish priest, as well as the normal round of liturgical services. These considerations may have ultimately weighed more heavily with peasant than with urban communities, which could always fall back on the services of the religious orders and their churches. When a formal demand for a new parish was pressed by the local inhabitants, an established procedure laid down by canon law had to be followed, one which began with a consultation of the principal local 'interests' (parish priest, churchwardens, for example) by the bishop's officials. The Council of Trent had stipulated that distance from the parish church should be the primary consideration, and inhabitants arguing for a new parish would commonly insist that people died without receiving the sacraments of baptism or extreme unction, or that their children were unable to attend catechism classes and so on. But if the serving clergy forcefully rebutted such claims – as they were likely to do, because they reflected negatively on their pastoral diligence – then the case for change would probably fail. In the final stages of the formal enquiry into the 'pros' and 'cons' of innovation (*de commodo et incommodo*), the views of the local royal judge were given increased weight under Louis XIV and royal letters patent were required before a new parish could be created. Clearly, with such substantial safeguards in place, change was likely to be both difficult and slow.

It is only occasionally that we can quantify the extent of the reshaping of parishes at diocesan level, or the approximate timing of such changes. The substantial diocese of Tours had only ten parishes more in 1789 than in 1330 – 298 against 288 – and the only new parish to appear in the seventeenth century, that of Richelieu 'new town', must rate as the exception that proves the rule. The diocese of Cambrai hardly witnessed any new parishes between its own creation in 1559 and the death of Louis XIV. Only *one* of the 401 parishes of the diocese of Beauvais in 1789 was added during the century between 1550 and 1650, and that was in 1648, to which we may add just two new *succursales*. It seems, therefore, that in northern dioceses with a dense existing parish network, one that was closely mapped onto village communities, the need for change was relatively limited. The already huge diocese of Besançon, which became French after 1678, grew from 660 parishes in the mid-seventeenth century to around 800 a century later, largely because of the creation of new parishes in the more thinly populated upland areas in the Jura and Vosges mountains, whereas in its more densely populated wine-producing areas new parishes were rare.[12] A few of the smaller southern dioceses with large parishes also seem to have subdivided at least some of their parishes during our period – Aix had ninety-six parishes in 1789 against eighty-four in 1668; Arles fifty-one by 1789 against thirty-eight a century or so earlier – though it is possible that the changes were made in the eighteenth century rather than in its predecessor.[13]

Almost inevitably, our knowledge of such changes is confined to the better documented urban centres. Sixteenth-century French towns and cities grew significantly in population thanks to the influx of immigrants from rural areas during a long period of demographic growth down to about 1570. But although new districts and *fauxbourgs* outside the walls developed, parish structures were slow to adapt, so there was substantial new business for the seventeenth-century church to conduct during a period of relative demographic stasis. By the late sixteenth century, Paris had thirty-two parishes, Bordeaux fourteen, Lyon twelve and Aix-en-Provence two. But the willingness to create new parishes and provide the endowments they needed varied from place to place at a time when French bishops had not yet invested much energy in reforming their dioceses. In fact, bishops who were willing to remodel the parochial map needed substantial support from urban authorities, and they could encounter formidable opposition, notably from established clerical interests. Thus, in Aix, with a population of about 15,000 people, the cathedral chapter had a tight grip on the city's *two* parishes – one of them minuscule and based on the cathedral itself, the other several times bigger and embracing most of the city's population. The chapter was unwilling to see new parishes created which might dilute its existing control of the city, so that no change at all occurred within the city during the seventeenth century, despite the tenure of Aix by a series of active archbishops.[14] At the other end of the scale there was Paris. Several of its thirty-two parishes were minuscule, located in the oldest districts of the city (the *Cité*, the university quarter, for example). But the Notre Dame chapter did not enjoy the same power as its Aix counterpart to prevent further additions. New parishes emerged in spurts during the early decades after 1600 – Saint-Leu (1617), Saint-Louis-en-l'Ile (1623), Saint-Roch (1631), Saint-Jacques-du-Haut-Pas (1633). More followed later during Louis XIV's reign – Bonne-Nouvelle (1673), Saint-Philippe-du-Roule (1699) and Saint-Marguerite (1712).[15] These parishes may have 'shadowed' the continuing growth of the city beyond the old city walls, but there were never enough of them, with the result that some parishes *intra muros* like Saint-Sulpice and Saint-Eustache still had to cope with huge numbers of parishioners. Bordeaux resembled Aix and Lyon rather than Paris, by leaving unchanged its existing tally of fourteen parishes, although the real consequences of that inertia would not be felt until the eighteenth century, when the city population grew rapidly again. Furthermore, as with Paris, eight of Bordeaux's fourteen parishes were tiny, archaic survivals located in the area around the cathedral, whereas the outer ring of six parishes which emerged subsequently and which catered for most of the population, tended to be far larger. The cathedral chapter of Saint-André was *curé primitif* to no fewer than ten of these parishes, so its grip on the parochial map resembled that of its Aix counterpart and offered little prospect for change.[16]

These examples throw their own light on the sources of institutional inertia within the French church and its underlying causes, since towns and cities were not bereft of the services of the religious orders and the un-beneficed secular clergy. La Rochelle diocese illustrates perfectly the variations in the size, population and distribution of parishes, and in both town and country. It contained 321 parishes around 1650. Its principal towns, La Rochelle and Fontenay-le-Comte, both had parochial structures that were well proportioned to their populations. But across La Rochelle diocese the picture is much more confused. Some rural areas could have extremely small parishes, with some average-sized villages divided into several parishes, each with tiny populations of 150 inhabitants or less; others again had populations varying from 3,000 to 6,000 and scattered across a wide area. The problems they gave rise to can easily be imagined: the smaller parishes were hard put to maintain their churches and religious offices while the larger ones struggled to cope with the demands of distance. Such sharp contrasts were not confined to La Rochelle, and were replicated across many areas of France.[17]

Parish and Fabrique

The 'governance' of a diocese was a monopoly restricted to the bishop and his clerical officials and advisers, but managing a parish was quite a different matter, despite its apparently more rudimentary structures and smaller scale. However numerous they might be, the clergy simply did not govern the parish as they saw fit. First of all, the parish as a distinct entity enjoyed a substantial, if indirect, say in its own religious affairs, although the manner and the extent of those rights would themselves vary enormously across the country. We shall see later how vital the historical role of confraternities was to defining parishes in many areas of France. Nearly everywhere, laypeople played an indispensable part in financing and managing the parish's material endowments in their often considerable variety, as well as in the organisation of religious services.

It seems that the administration of the local parish's goods by laymen goes back to the thirteenth century, and may have been a response to the contemporary 'confiscation' of the local tithes by outsiders to the parish, with the consequent need to ensure the upkeep of the parish church and worship from the parish's own resources.[18] That responsibility ultimately fell on the assembly of inhabitants, which gradually delegated specific responsibility for the task to regularly elected churchwardens widely known as *fabriciens* or *marguilliers*. The term *fabrique* refers both to the material endowments of parishes and the officials elected to manage them. Over time, the electing of churchwardens itself may have become a rather empty shell, dominated by the *sanior et maior pars* of the parish's households. This translated into a great deal of co-option of new wardens by their predecessors, drawn largely from the local oligarchy of the more wealthy and literate inhabitants of the parish. In big urban parishes with imposing churches to maintain, only men of real substance (magistrates, town councillors, lawyers, merchants) could expect to accede to the position of churchwarden, which carried the desirable status of 'notable' with it; in some urban parishes, like Saint-Médard in Paris, they were even expected to make an expensive gift to the church when they left office, a duty which left little hope for those of modest means.[19] But in the great mass of rural parishes, the expectation that churchwardens be solvent, of good moral character and of some education, ensured that they would be drawn from the ranks of the farm-owning *laboureurs* rather than the mostly landless *journaliers*.

Wherever parish endowments were substantial, the position of churchwarden, and in particular that of treasurer, was much prized as it entailed the handling of valuable funds. Pierre Corneille, who retired to his native Rouen by the early 1650s, took his turn, like his father before him, to serve as treasurer of his parish of origin, entering in his own hand the rents and other receipts into the parish accounts book – the longest autograph by Corneille in existence.[20] Yet Louis XIV's government miscalculated badly when, in a desperate attempt to finance his later wars, it turned the positions of church-warden into venal offices in the 1690s. The result was a serious flop: there were few takers for offices which rarely offered real prospects of profit or improved social 'consideration' at a time when taxes and money-raising expedients had exceeded all previous records.

Of course, the *fabriques* were not equally present throughout France. They were at their most powerful and entrenched in Normandy and the Paris Basin generally, where they dominated the communities of inhabitants. But in the south-east, their functions were shared by the parish priest and the community of inhabitants. In wide areas of the south and south-west, towns with well-developed councils (*consulats*) had taken over most of those functions, exercising them indiscriminately alongside their other civic obligations. The *consulats* were accustomed to regarding themselves as responsible for almost everything pertaining to the church fabric, mass foundations, processions, the materials needed for services, but also the hiring of preachers, chaplains to almshouses and schoolteachers. But even before the Catholic Reform got going, both the crown and the clergy had begun to show their dislike of such indiscriminate and extensive powers, and the confusion of the sacred and the profane that arose from it.[21]

Where they did exist, it was the *fabriques* that, regardless of their social composition, administered the glebe lands and other items of real property that provided some or even most of the parish's income. The more scattered and numerous the properties and revenues in question the more difficult it was to manage them efficiently, which in turn required vigilance towards those liable to pay the revenues in question. It was also the *fabrique*'s responsibility to provide, on behalf of the parish, a dwelling for the parish priest, which could take the form either of a sum of money with which to rent a house, or a purpose-built presbytery which also needed to be kept furnished and repaired. By the later seventeenth and the eighteenth century, newer generations of parish priest were actually more demanding than their predecessors, wanting dwellings which reflected their new-found 'dignity'. Purchasing and renewing religious objects from vestments to ciboria, crosses and the like was also the *fabrique*'s responsibility. In rural parishes at least, their annual budget would normally be small, since the parish's endowments were paltry compared to those of religious institutions generally or even the *curé*'s own 'living', with the result that they were often obliged to 'tax' the households of the parish in order to meet ordinary expenses. They could augment existing income by renting out reserved seats in the local church, for example, but any significant expense – new church bells or furniture, not to mention rebuilding of any sort – required recourse to the parish as a whole. Perhaps the most instructive illustration of these problems of power and responsibility within a parish involves the parish church itself. The patron or ecclesiastic who collected the main tithes (the *gros décimateur*) was normally responsible for maintaining the chancel, while the nave was the responsibility of the parishioners and, therefore, of the *fabrique*. Responsibility for the bell-tower was less clear cut, since it mostly depended on its precise location in relation to the rest of the building, but the tithe-owner was normally expected to maintain it. This subdivision alone suggests the kind of disputes, often leading to litigation, which might arise over who should pay for particular repairs, and how slowly decisions were likely to be taken, let alone acted upon. Repairing church bells was inordinately expensive, yet parishioners had numerous reasons for wanting them in good working order – reasons which would help to overcome their notorious reluctance to raise the necessary money. With the average *fabrique* possessing only modest financial reserves, it is not hard to see why external pressure, whether from royal officials or church authorities generally, to rebuild or decorate their church to a 'decent' standard, might not be complied with for many years.

By and large, pre-seventeenth-century parish priests and churchwardens lived and worked side by side without undue friction but, as we shall see later, this changed substantially during our period, especially in urban parishes. Churchwardens were increasingly required to render account of their stewardship to the parish priest[22] and the bishop, but the latter could not interfere directly with their management, as royal legislation had established over time. In fact, the accounts were often rendered late and haphazardly, with the disposable funds being used in the meantime by churchwardens, who might also be village tax collectors or local magistrates, for purposes other than religious ones. Despite being theoretically debarred from doing so, parish priests sometimes served as the chief churchwarden, usually in the absence of lay candidates in rural parishes. In this kind of society, keeping spiritual and temporal roles strictly separate, even at parish level, was never easy, least of all when the provision of religious services depended directly on the funds supplied by the churchwardens to the clergy. To that extent, even the smallest parish represents in a nutshell the problems which historians are more accustomed to considering at the much more exalted level of the church's relations with the crown and the papacy.

Conclusion

This brief tour of the geography of the French church has highlighted the enormous diversity of the territorial framework in which that church operated, and showed how slow historical developments spanning several centuries continued to determine its relations with French society. Just as importantly, a geographical and institutional analysis leads quickly to questions concerning church–society relations more generally. Later chapters will return to the question of how dioceses and parishes interacted when efforts at reconstruction, reform and control got under way in the seventeenth century, in a context in which the scope for institutional change, especially regarding size and location, was seriously limited, and in which the forces of continuity and inertia were well entrenched. Yet it would be equally wrong to conclude that the French church was hopelessly entangled in an institutional morass that crippled its effectiveness at every level. By comparison with the secular institutions by which the monarchy governed its subjects, there are ample grounds for regarding the church's 'territorial' institutions as comprehensive, coherent and straightforward. One need but think of the 'administrative imbroglio', as Pierre Goubert has called it, that the institutions of the monarchy constituted from the vantage point of the average village or community, whose inhabitants found themselves subject to multiple, overlapping and sometimes sharply competing jurisdictions located in several different places. Viewed in this light, the church's 'building blocks' seem positively well hewn. The population of early modern France possessed neither post-1789 experience nor modern expectations about the 'rationality' of their church's diocesan, parochial and related structures, and they were past masters in coping with what they had before them. Other legacies of earlier centuries, to which we now turn, could be no less constraining.

CHAPTER 2

WEALTH INTO BENEFICES

Across the ages the issue of the church's wealth has been the subject of a shifting mixture of curiosity, debate and hostility. Questions concerning its proper size and purpose, as well as who was entitled to benefit from it, invariably helped to define and, at times, to polarise relations between the 'church' – in its narrow sense of the clergy – and the wider lay society. It was also inevitable that a religion which exalted poverty and detachment from material goods would have problems defending the wealth accumulated by the church over the centuries. The old-style anticlericalism, inherited from the Middle Ages and still alive in our period, throve on stereotypes of an indolent, neglectful clergy enjoying incomes derived purely from the generosity of the laity, who in turn were severely short-changed by those they so generously supported. The rationale which had been worked out over the centuries to defend church property was constantly pressed into service against those critics, clerics as well as laity, who attacked not merely the allegedly excessive wealth of the church, but above all the misuse and corruption to which it led.

Most of the time, both the charges and responses read like rhetorical jousting, but occasionally there were moments of high tension when it seemed, to the horror of the clergy, that lay society was about to exact its revenge on them, depriving them of the wealth which they took for granted. The Protestant Reformation was the most momentous instance of this, quickly stripping away much, but not absolutely all, of the church's property wherever it triumphed across Europe. This was most visible and deliberate in the suppression of the monasteries, which found themselves with alarmingly few defenders in their hour of need. Leaving aside the pillages of church property by all sides during the wars of religion, the closest the French church came to such a reckoning occurred in 1560–61 when, in a context of acute political and financial crisis, the deputies of the third estate to the Estates-General of Orléans and Pontoise came up with radical proposals to sell off church property in order to bail out the monarchy. They argued that the sale of the church's property would generate sums of money which, in addition to liquidating the king's debts, would serve as a sinking fund to provide the wherewithal for the upkeep of a salaried clergy of a kind previously unknown in Europe. Had these measures been even partially adopted, the seventeenth-century French church would have been radically different, and its history would certainly have run along alternative lines.

In the event the proposals of 1560 were buried for over 200 years, only to resurface in the rather different environment of 1789, but as the solution to yet another royal bankruptcy. In the intervening years, as we have seen, the French clergy got away with some limited property sales (from the 1560s to the 1580s) and especially with paying the monarchy regular church 'tenths' and other financial subventions, timely concessions which took the sting out of the 1560 sell-off proposals. Crucially, these levies were assessed and raised by the clergy themselves, who at every turn insisted that royal officials and outsiders should play no part in their financial affairs. If the clergy of France had no precise idea during this period of the overall value of its temporalities, it was because it suited its assemblies, diocesan *bureaux* and benefice-holders *not* to know it; they had no incentive to provide such hard information to those who, especially in the eighteenth century, increasingly speculated on how much of the nation's wealth was in church hands. Had such information been gathered and, more crucially, proved to be reliable, it could never have been kept secret, and it might have been used to force the clergy into paying the equivalent of real taxes to the crown. So it was not until the complete sell-off of church property in 1790 that the full extent of the church's holdings was known for the first time in French history.[1]

This opening excursus indicates not merely how sensitive a subject church wealth could still be in our period, but also why it remains so difficult for historians to provide anything like a satisfactory account of it. There are obvious problems about using figures generated by the total sell-off of 1790 as a guide for previous generations, but those objections are less problematic when the purpose is merely to indicate the overall scale and variation of church wealth across France as a whole in, say, 1590 or 1690. Because church property was well protected by the law of mortmain, to which we will return later, it ran no major risk of depletion from the normal effects of inheritance, subdivision or market forces. Historians agree that although clerical revenues did rise markedly from the 1720s onwards, thanks to the general economic recovery, overall church wealth did not increase much in eighteenth-century France; indeed many church bodies such as convents and religious houses generally suffered rather badly from the financial measures of the latter years of Louis XIV's reign and especially from the 'law experiment' around 1720, when they saw their investments, especially in public and private annuities, virtually go up in smoke. By contrast, it was between 1590 and 1690 that additions (though some involved recovering property sold off during the wars of religion) were made to the total sum of the church's wealth, but they probably did not amount to more than 1 or 2 per cent of the 1790 total value. In its broad outlines, therefore, the 1790 snapshot is probably a fairly accurate pointer to the situation a century or so earlier. What general patterns and local variations can we extract from it? Was the view that the French church had become disproportionately wealthy before the revolution already true a century or more earlier?

The Geography of Church Wealth

Before trying to map the church's wealth, we should realise that modern conceptions of wealth as based on property ownership are only partly appropriate for our purposes. To say that church wealth was made up of two essential but quite different components is to simplify the question in the extreme, but it may be helpful to do so. The first component was *property* in its most conventional forms – land and buildings essentially, but also investments in annuities of all sorts. The second consisted in *rights to revenue* not just for the performance of services, but above all the church tithe levied on agricultural produce from lands and other 'taxable' assets that did not themselves belong to the church at all. Combinations of these categories were not uncommon, the most widespread being that much of the land owned by the church consisted of lordships which were comprised not merely of land itself, but of a multiplicity of revenue-generating rights and monopolies (milling, wine-pressing, justice for example) attached to it.[2]

The figures for 1790 show that between 6 and 10 per cent of all the land of France belonged to the church, but this national average hides significant regional disparities. It was in the northern and eastern provinces, essentially the Paris basin and its extensions into Picardy, Artois, Champagne and Lorraine that the church as landowner was most prominent, with a regional average of between 15 and 20 per cent. Within this region, there were areas, notably around Cambrai, where the figures were far higher again, approaching 40 per cent. Much of this economic power was accounted for by the large number of wealthy monasteries that had dominated these areas since the high Middle Ages. Such enormous concentrations of landed property were not to be found either in western or southern France. Here, the figure scarcely ever exceeded 5 per cent of the land surface, and that average in turn masked very considerable differences from place to place. In much of the south-west church land was notable mainly for its non-existence, often consisting, where it did exist, of insignificant glebe lands of parishes and the like.

But an accurate assessment of the church's wealth at this time cannot be derived from merely counting the acres it owned: just as important was the quality of those acres and their use. The church's landed wealth, especially that belonging to its bishoprics, abbeys and priories, both male and female, was disproportionately of high quality. Thanks to a long tradition of careful management, effective protection from the subdivision of holdings familiar to peasants and noble families alike, and economies of scale, its lands were often among the best maintained and most productive in France. Among other things, it could engage in extensive pastoral farming in the way that hard-pressed peasants could rarely afford to do in a largely subsistence economy; it also owned large tracts of highly profitable woodland, one of early modern France's scarcest resources, which brought in large returns from supplying the building trade. These same timber resources enabled some church estates to exploit, by the early eighteenth century at least, their mineral resources, and also to develop blast furnaces in the way that aristocratic landowners were doing. The benefits of institutional continuity across the generations are nowhere better seen than in the large vineyards which belonged to the church, mainly to monasteries, in Champagne, Burgundy and elsewhere, and which played their part in developing high-quality wines and other kinds of alcohol for domestic and international markets. Here and there, similar pursuits were indulged in on a much smaller scale by parish priests with an interest in the subject and the business acumen that it demanded.

The overall proportion of landed wealth belonging to the church does not of itself indicate how extensive individual 'holdings' might be. The larger the latter were, the more they involved the rights and advantages of lordship rather than landownership alone, whereas the smaller holdings were likely to be 'mere' land. The church owned lordships alongside the crown, the nobility and well-off royal officials and merchants. The biggest of these lordships were usually attached to bishoprics, monasteries, chapters and 'commanderies' of the Knights of Malta.[3] Some of them were as extensive as secular lordships, especially where 'feudal' titles (a peerage, for example) were attached to them, as was the case with many bishoprics; but most church-owned lordships seem to have been smaller than the corresponding lay lordships. From diocese to diocese, a disproportionate share of either episcopal or monastic revenues could be derived from one or more large-scale lordships, and they were usually subject to close supervision by their holders. For example, in the Velay-Vivarais-Gevaudan region of north-east Languedoc which corresponded mainly to the dioceses of Le Puy, Viviers and Mende, one-quarter to one-third of all lordships belonged to the church, with bishops and monasteries dominating their ranks. But within the region itself, there were significant variations. In the Velay, half of all lordships belonged to the church and many were substantial, whereas in the Gévaudan and especially the Vivarais, the church's share was less than one-fifth, and its lordships were small-scale and scattered.[4] Such contrasts probably existed across France. Because lordship entailed exercising rights of justice as well as a range of economic monopolies (milling, brewing and so on) over the population of the territory it covered, it clearly intensified the grip of the church on particular localities. For the majority of the population it could mean fractious relations with the church as a social and economic power; but for a minority it could mean often lucrative opportunities to operate as lessees, managers or officials enforcing church rights and jurisdiction over their fellow parishioners.

Tithes

We should not conclude from the regional disparities in landownership by the church that its presence as a socio-economic force was somehow negligible south of the Loire and in the western provinces. These areas did indeed have pockets of landed church property of the kind we have just seen, attached especially to bishoprics and monasteries. However, in these regions the wealth of the church mainly took a very different form – the tithe, a levy on agricultural produce which, unlike all other taxes or forms of property, was in principle exclusive to the church. The term 'tithe' itself suggests a one-tenth levy, but variation on an unimaginable scale was the order of the day here too. Rates varied from locality to locality, and from one kind of produce to another, sowing both confusion and endless opportunities for dissimulation as to who owed how much and on which product. It seems that it was rare enough for the theoretical 10 per cent rate of levy to be raised anywhere, though rates higher than that were not unknown in some parts of south-western France; in Provence and Dauphiné they were as low as 2 to 5 per cent. Elsewhere rates varying between 3 and 8 per cent were far more common. Yet regardless of the rate, and therefore of the economic 'burdensomeness' of the tithe, it is clear that the clergy of much of southern and central France depended very heavily on it for their livelihood. In some localities, they had virtually nothing else to fall back on. Consequently, it is not hard to imagine the determination with which they were likely to defend and even extend those rights, and how serious any threat of non-payment by the peasantry could be. By contrast, in the northern parts of France where landed or 'real' property generally in church hands was more prominent, tithe was levied at a far lower rate, and was a relatively insignificant contributor to church incomes.[5]

Strictly speaking, the term 'tithe' should always be used in the plural, since it fell into different categories – the 'great', 'little', 'green' and 'new' tithes, to cite the main ones. These were levied on grain crops, fruit, vines, animals, wool and even fish catches. They were payable in kind rather than in money, at the precise moment that crops were being harvested; their payment also took priority over all other claims on the harvest, which could not be stored until the tithe-takers had garnered their rightful share. Despite being a theoretically universal obligation from which no layperson, not even a non-taxpaying noble, was exempt, virtually nothing was straightforward about tithes. They were not in practice levied evenly on all producers of agricultural goods, and by the seventeenth century they were mainly paid by the peasantry. Originally destined for the upkeep of the parish clergy, they were now largely in the hands of other categories of ecclesiastic, and some had been appropriated centuries earlier by lay landowners. With so many kinds of tithe, some of which were defined by purely local usage 'from time immemorial', it is no surprise that they proved to be a perennial source of conflict between clergy and lay society. Tithe and trouble were synonymous, and 'trouble' could range from litigation (a common enough phenomenon, even in perfectly 'normal' times) to outright refusal to pay. For centuries, tenants of the Norman abbey of Montivilliers paid either seigneurial dues or the tithe, but by the sixteenth century the abbey decided that all should pay tithe, regardless of their other obligations, which understandably elicited strong protests, especially from wealthier tenants with access to the law courts.[6] Generally, games of cat-and-mouse between clergy and peasants occurred whenever the peasantry tried to take advantage of the different rates of tithe in order to convert land from arable to livestock, or to avoid paying it on newly cultivated lands. Peasants protested that they paid tithe on the grain they produced, and then on the animals they raised and fed with the same grain!

Nothing was more likely to sustain tension and suspicion between the clergy and laypeople, and this in turn was compounded by competition and distrust between the various types of clergy themselves regarding claims or rights to the tithes. Where the main tithe-holders were 'outsider' clergy – bishops, cathedral chapters, monasteries or other corporate clergy – with scarcely any other connection to the parishes in question, the sense of grievance could not merely be strong, but it was probably shared by clergy as much as by parishioners, all of whom felt hard done by. As always, local ire was directed most strongly at those clergy who enforced their rights to the letter of the law. A parish priest entitled to all or part of the parish's tithes was well advised not to push his demands too far if he wished to retain his parishioners' goodwill; outsider clergy were less likely to harbour such inhibitions, and if they worried about anything, it was about being fiddled out of their rights by cunning peasants while their backs were turned. For the likes of the great Benedictine abbey of La Chaise-Dieu, the main tithe-holder in over 300 parishes across the Auvergne, there would always be plenty of work and concern for its agents and leaseholders.

Towns

The discussion so far has ignored the nature and presence of the church as an economic force within towns. Yet urban landscapes were far more indelibly marked by that presence than most rural areas, since the church tended to be a proportionately more substantial and visible property-owner in towns than in the countryside. Not merely did it own large tracts of cities, but a considerable amount of the revenue that it derived from land-holding and tithes was siphoned away from the countryside and towards the towns and cities by urban-based clergy, its major beneficiaries. The most obvious examples of towns dominated by the church were those small, mostly southern, episcopal towns where the local bishop and cathedral chapter had few or no lay competitors for local pre-eminence, and without whom the towns themselves would scarcely have survived.[7] But much bigger towns and cities across the entire country could also be fundamentally shaped by the church's presence. Cities as well known and as far apart as Reims, Beauvais, Angers and Toulouse were among them, but there was a host of smaller places, with no episcopal seat or cathedral within their walls, that were exactly like them. To understand how this could happen we need to remember how severely cramped most French towns were around 1600: in an age when walls were still regarded as vital to the security of towns – and even to their identity – the population was squeezed tightly within ramparts that no longer corresponded to contemporary urban needs. However, the resulting problem would have been far less acute had the space within the walls not been so dominated by ecclesiastical establishments of various kinds – cathedral chapters, monasteries and convents for the most part, but also hospices and colleges, all of which possessed, or aspired to possess, gardens, closes, orchards and closed spaces *intra muros*. These establishments were often in the least cramped areas of towns, and they hardly changed at all during the seventeenth century, because the law of mortmain protected them quite effectively from the normal pressures or enticements to sell off land for building shops and houses. Indeed, the existing situation proved to be a bonus to these urban religious establishments, as it permitted them to build new accommodation along the façades of their own properties and then rent it out to those in search of living quarters or shops.

In such circumstances, it is not hard to imagine how problematic the arrival of new religious orders could prove to be in towns which already had their fair share of religious houses. The later sixteenth and first half of the seventeenth century was a period when such foundations reached a high point. Initial foundations were often extremely modest, and frequently made possible only by the generosity of laypeople willing to donate a house and possibly a garden for the new community. But as soon as its numbers and activities – especially if they involved teaching or nursing – began to expand, serious problems of space became inevitable, and urban authorities often found themselves seriously divided over what to do. Religious orders like the Jesuits, with high-ranking connections at court and elsewhere, could manipulate or browbeat local authorities in order to get what they wanted – usually property close to the centre of towns rather than on their peripheries. It was perhaps fortunate for these new communities that seventeenth-century municipal authorities were not yet as concerned about embellishing or modernising the urban landscape as their eighteenth-century successors would be. Thus, in a city as big and active, economically and politically, as Toulouse, about 35 per cent of all land and buildings belonged to the church around 1680; at Angers, the ratio was reckoned to be about twice that. Amiens, with a population of over 30,000 in 1698, had within its walls three chapters as well as fourteen male and nine female communities, housing or supporting a clerical establishment of approximately 1,000 individuals.[8] The presence of the church within towns was unmistakable at any time, as travellers did not fail to observe, and its visibility was not confined to feast days or processions. Urban skylines were defined by their churches in a manner which lay buildings simply could not rival.

Nor was the church's 'material' urban presence confined to property in the narrow sense. Large numbers of French cities and towns were also subject to seigneurial jurisdiction of the kind that is often wrongly associated with the countryside only. Seigneurial rights in large cities like Paris, Toulouse or Bordeaux were a lucrative source of church income, as they included the right to a sometimes hefty transfer tax when property subject to them changed hands, either by sale or by inheritance. The archbishop of Paris drew enormous revenues from areas subject to his urban seigneurial jurisdiction. And, of course, behind the revenue-generating rights lay seigneurial and political power itself. But church seigneurial power could extend much further than that. A town like Beauvais was entirely subject to the powers of justice, civil and criminal, and of police that belonged to its bishop, who was also a peer of the realm. These powers, confirmed by the king in 1596, were successfully defended by subsequent bishops of Beauvais, so that in effect their word was final in most matters of municipal government.[9] More common was the sharing of such powers between church bodies and the king, local courts or town halls. When a desperate Louis XIV decided to put up for sale key municipal offices, such as those of *lieutenant général de police*, bishops and other ecclesiastical bodies often purchased them outright in order to maintain, and even strengthen, their existing grip on the towns.

Dead Hand and Taxes

Two further characteristics of church property distinguished it from other forms of wealth in *ancien régime* France. The first of them, already alluded to, was the law of mortmain (*mainmorte* – the 'dead hand'), by virtue of which church property was untouchable once it had been designated as such by law. It also meant that the clergy themselves only enjoyed the short-term usufruct of the properties they held. Obtaining permission to dispose of an item of church property was subject to numerous safeguards, and it came with the provision that anything sold off had to be 'replaced' by something of equivalent or higher value. This did not deter some clerics or laymen from trying their luck, and even getting away with it; but such successes were on a very small scale, and usually depended on confusion about the property in question and possibly the collusion of other interested parties, clergy and magistrates included. When, as we have already seen, country-wide sell-offs of slices of church property occurred during the wars of religion, they had to be solemnly authorised by the pope who, as the *dominus beneficiorum* – the sovereign master of the church's temporalities – was the only person with the right to waive the rules of mortmain: neither the clergy in assembly nor the monarchy possessed that power, singly or jointly. But the assemblies of clergy became increasingly alarmed at each new sell-off during the 1560s and 1570s, since the monarchy went over their heads and cut a deal directly with the papacy which they could then do virtually nothing about. The last sale of this kind was authorised in 1587, after which date there was to be no repeat. Scarred by such experiences, the seventeenth-century clergy successfully scotched the very idea that they might be resumed, even in wartime.[10] That did not prevent the crown, from Richelieu to Louis XIV, from finding other ways of retrospectively imposing payments – in the form of an 'amortisation' tax – on properties which had fallen into mortmain, but on which the 'transfer of status' tax had not been paid at the moment when their status changed. Recourse to such measures produced squeals of protest from the clergy, but they should not disguise the fact that the crown had no stomach for an attack on mortmain itself.

The second distinguishing characteristic of church property – as of the clergy themselves – was exemption from the major taxes paid to the crown by its non-privileged subjects. By definition, that exemption covered the mortmain properties themselves. The subject is a surprisingly elusive one, on which the intensive research of recent decades into the French fiscal system has shed little new light, but it seems fair to assume that the parish tax assessors knew and protected church property from royal taxes. It is hardly necessary to stress the considerable advantages of not being subject to a fiscal system during a century when it really began to bite remorselessly into the incomes of ordinary taxpayers. As we have seen, the quid pro quo of such valued immunity was the obligation on benefice-holders to pay *décimes* and *dons gratuits* to the crown, but here, too, the church enjoyed two signal advantages over lay taxpayers generally – the right to negotiate and vote, in an elected assembly of clergy, the amounts to be paid and a fiscal machinery of its own to levy and collect the sums in question. We should not underestimate the part played by these institutional and legal arrangements in preserving the church's wealth intact, untroubled by the forces which tended to subdivide even the largest lay estates.[11]

Economic Trends and their Impact

By contrast, no amount of privilege could quite insulate the French church against the effects of general economic trends, both short and long term, especially given that land rentals and agricultural tithe were its main sources of revenue. The upward trend of France's demographic and economic record since the second half of the fifteenth century gradually came to a halt, with obvious regional and local variations, during the first two decades of the wars of religion after 1560.[12] The church, which had hitherto benefited from rising revenues, now found itself faced with the combined effects of economic recession, the material damage inevitable from civil wars, especially ones involving often savage religious hostility and, as we have just seen, the partial sell-off of its property. Of crucial importance here was the fate of the tithe. It appears that tithe returns reached an early peak around 1560 after decades of economic growth, but the following decades saw a drop of up to 40 per cent, for which the destruction of warfare and growing economic difficulties were only partly responsible. More novel – because wholly unexpected – was the refusal, from the early 1560s onwards, of large sections of the French peasantry to pay their tithes. The explosive emergence of the Protestant churches around 1560 emboldened peasants to go on strike over the tithe (the *grève des décimables*, as it was called) throughout France, but especially in the southwest where, as we saw, tithe was a heavy burden and where Protestantism also spread most rapidly into rural areas. But Catholic peasants also joined their Protestant counterparts in refusing to pay tithe there, and it has often been suggested that large numbers of Protestant peasants were really 'tithe Protestants' rather than convinced adherents of the new churches. It may be that the tithe-payers' revolt would have spread more widely and had more long-lasting results had the emerging Protestant churches themselves decided to countenance the revolt rather than share the old church's view that the tithe had genuine religious sanction behind it. Despite that 'failure', the collapse of royal and ecclesiastical authority in many areas of France ensured that tithe-payments would remain patchy for many years to come.[13]

The final two decades of the century, dominated by the Catholic League's virtually nationwide struggle to prevent Henri IV from becoming the acknowledged king of France, saw no improvement; nor did the return of civil peace by the mid-1590s signal an immediate return to more prosperous times. With ecclesiastical revenues at their lowest point around 1600, recovery during the following decades was slow, and it seems that by the 1630s and 1640s, at the latest, a new period of economic stagnation and recession had arrived, exacerbated by the impact of war against the Habsburgs until 1659. A mini-recovery then followed, thanks to peace and the concomitant fiscal slackening, but the last thirty years of Louis XIV's reign, from the late 1680s to the early 1710s, were among the most economically depressed of the century.

Of course, what was good for France's population as a whole – ideally, bumper harvests and modest prices – was not necessarily good for an institution like the French church, which rented out its land and sold the grain and other produce of its estates, and which would prefer high rather than low prices for its surpluses. One reason why the French church benefited from the general if limited economic recovery of the early seventeenth century was that, for reasons that are difficult to untangle, the tithe-payers proved more willing to pay the tithe.[14] They continued to rail whenever they had the opportunity, as when Estates-General met or were summoned (1576, 1614, 1649, 1651), against the absentee clergy who took the lion's share of the tithe, but they at least now paid it, possibly because the church was at last trying to put its house in order and to ensure that the parish clergy were resident and active in their parishes. Indeed, the returns from the tithe give some idea of wider trends as they affected the church: recovering in the early decades of the century, by approximately 1670–80 they surpassed the sixteenth-century records, only to drop back sharply over the next forty years or more. But property-owners like the church did not always tailor their expectations and demands to trends which would have been largely invisible to them, so that their efforts to continue raising rents could continue well past the point where they were easily affordable by their tenants. Notable for their famines and mass mortality rates, the last decades of Louis XIV's reign have been understandably labelled 'the years of misery', from which many parts of France did not begin to recover until the 1740s.[15]

What is much more difficult to see is whether the French church experienced an economic 'conjuncture' of its own which, at least in part, might have diverged from general trends. There was certainly ample scope, as we shall see, for clergy with capital or at least good 'credit' to repurchase lands, buy out indebted tenants, rationalise leases and bring abandoned lands back into cultivation. It certainly seems that the 'corporate' clergy – the chapters and monasteries, which are the best documented – set about restoring their fortunes in the decades after the end of the religious wars, even though the renewed religious–civil wars of the 1620s, especially in the west and south, and then the foreign wars, which mostly affected the northern and eastern border provinces, probably frustrated some of their efforts. Resourcefulness, attention to detail and good credit ensured that the revenues of the southern cathedral chapters such as Narbonne, Béziers and Montpellier rose notably during the first half of the century.[16] So, too, did those of most bishops from their dioceses, though for the most part less markedly than those of the chapters just cited, so the recovery may owe less to attentive management than to a simple upturn from the very low income levels of the later sixteenth century. By the early decades of Louis XIV's reign, however, these rises were beginning to taper off, and thereafter revenues seem, on the basis of the haphazard sources available, to have either remained fairly stagnant for another half century or to have continued rising in an unpredictable way which deserves closer scrutiny.

Whatever the proper explanation for these trends, they seem indicative of wider developments across the French church as a whole. We should probably not overrate the extent to which new entrepreneurial or management skills, to be discussed presently, contributed to its prosperity. The fact that the peasantry now paid regular tithes, having gradually abandoned their massive refusals to do so in the previous century, was a very significant change. And the clergy appear to have largely won the battle to impose the tithes on both new crops and lands newly brought into cultivation during the century. Likewise, the church's unchallenged fiscal privileges were a major benefit in a century which witnessed more than one harsh turn of the fiscal screw by the monarchy on its taxpaying subjects. Admittedly, the clergy did pay their own specific 'taxes' – which they refused to consider as taxes – the *décimes* and the *don gratuit*, but although the screw was turned on them too, especially under Louis XIV, the fact remains that much less of the church's wealth was siphoned into the royal coffers relative to the rest of the population. Its contribution to the overall royal budget declined by at least a half to less than 4 per cent by the second half of the century, evidence enough of the overall light royal touch on the church.

The Management of Church Wealth

It follows from what we have seen so far that, with so much property and income-bearing rights at the church's disposal, the management of its wealth represented a formidable challenge, since the manner in which it was done was just as decisive as the scale of its property-holding per se in determining its relations with French society. But given the huge differences in the scale and worth of the individual 'benefices' into which that wealth was subdivided, as well as the combinations of types of property that might make up an individual benefice, it would be absurd to imagine that there was any consistency about the management of them. Moreover, rather like the holdings of both peasants and seigneurs, the dispersal of church properties across the landscape was often the norm. And this factor was further magnified when several benefices were held by a single cleric or community, whose approach to handling their 'estate' might be significantly different to the holder of a single, local benefice. In the light of such profusion, it is only possible to offer a brief sketch of these variations in practice and the logic behind them.

Keeping in mind the parallels with lay society, it was, self-evidently, cardinals, bishops and 'commendatory' abbots who topped the pyramid of the beneficiaries of the church's endowments. The number, scale and geographical dispersal of their benefices was often considerable, while their non-residence, itself a consequence of such dispersal, prevented them from concerning themselves closely with their local management. This point is less valid for bishops than for the other two categories, especially after the disappearance of episcopal 'pluralism' by the end of the wars of religion. But although bishops were increasingly resident during our period, the size of many of their dioceses and the growing pastoral and administrative load they had to shoulder should not be forgotten, since these made it more difficult than previously to manage their temporalities directly. And, of course, many bishops were themselves holders of often-distant abbeys or priories *in commendam* which they might scarcely ever visit. The ensuing combination of dispersed benefices, cash-flow needs and other commitments ensured that these 'dignitaries', who operated on a nationwide platform, were probably the first to move towards the management of church properties through consolidated, fixed-term leases. The process whereby such practices spread throughout the French church is still poorly understood, it is not at all clear whether the church followed the lead of lay property-holders – or the reverse.

It seems likely that the leasing of church temporalities by such ecclesiastics began within the individual benefices themselves: a 'general' lease for an abbey or a priory's 'temporalities' would normally involve a relatively 'local' leaseholder (a merchant, a royal official, a lawyer or a big tenant-farmer, depending on the scale of the operation) with the capital and credit needed to guarantee regular payments to the distant benefice-holder. But the holders of several benefices, especially if they were on a grand scale such as those of Richelieu and Mazarin or other well-endowed cardinals – Guise-Lorraine, Bouillon,

La Valette, Joyeuse – would be tempted, especially as the seventeenth century advanced, to go further still and to organise a general lease of *all* their benefices – with administrative convenience and cash flow as their principal concerns. The priorities of non-resident pluralists generally were of a very different order to the mass of benefice-holders further down the ladder, but it is worth noting how closely their management resembled the techniques used by the monarchy in respect of some of its major sources of indirect taxation – and that sometimes it involved the same individuals.[17]

The next rung of the ladder below them was occupied by the chapters (cathedral and collegiate) and monasteries which had a reputation for taking the closest interest in the management of their properties. The surviving chapter deliberations for cathedrals like Béziers or Narbonne, Amiens or Chartres are replete with discussions and decisions about extending, improving and managing these properties, as well as what to do with the proceeds. The canons' own livelihoods depended – rather like modern shareholders and their dividends – on how carefully they watched over such matters, which were therefore not left to the caprice of individual members, who might prove to be uninterested or incompetent. 'Resident' by definition, chapters and monastic communities had both the time and the incentive to engage in the collective oversight of their temporalities. Monasteries were more complicated than chapters, since their abbots (mostly absentee secular clergy by the seventeenth century) would not necessarily manage their share of the temporalities in the same way as the resident community itself – assuming that their relative shares of the revenues were managed separately. Because they were such important and permanent local institutions, chapters and monasteries never wanted for lay assistance beyond their walls: a whole network of individuals and professions was involved in running their affairs in one capacity or another – as farmers, lease-takers, agents, lawyers, notaries, lenders and so on. Their properties were not always neatly gathered together, although there is evidence, especially from the period of the religious wars and their aftermath, of attempts by monasteries to consolidate them and to divest themselves of the more marginal holdings, geographically and economically: the forced sell-offs of the 1560s and later may have encouraged such thinking thereafter. Where careful management was possible, leases were likely to be confined to individual properties and revenue-bearing rights, since a general lease of, say, the temporalities of the chapter of Montpellier or the abbey of Bec in Normandy as a whole, would involve a substantial loss of immediate control by the chapter or the monastery in question. Such a surrender of control was also less likely to happen at a time when, as during the decades after the religious wars, there was much work to be done in recovering and then restoring lost or damaged properties.[18]

An unusual insight into the approaches taken to managing these church properties is provided by the career of a monk of Saint-Germain-des-Prés in Paris. Claude Coton (1588–1660) championed the reform of his abbey, but when the famous Maurists took over and reformed it in 1631, he did not join their ranks, but received instead a life-pension as a well-disposed member of the old, unreformed observance. Within a few years he was residing in, and managing, lands belonging to the abbey, in return for which he subsequently surrendered his pension. Through repairs and some innovation he engineered a two-thirds rise in income from them in only seven years. In 1637 he persuaded the abbey to sell off a small parcel of land in Paris in order to buy a substantial *seigneurie*, Cordoux, forty miles from Paris, for 67,000 *livres*, and a few years later he personally took on the lease there, his status as a monk notwithstanding! He borrowed money to make major improvements, and by the time he left Cordoux to retire in 1654, its income had risen by over half of its previous value – and this despite recession and the impact of the Fronde around the capital. Coton contributed his mite to this rise of the abbey's overall revenues, which were derived from a widely scattered property base, between the 1630s and mid-1670s, when they began to dip again in changing economic circumstances. The Maurists of Saint-Germain may have been famous by then across Europe for their scholarly pursuits, but the abbey's wealth ensured it would remain a major prize whose commendatory abbots under Louis XIII and XIV included an illegitimate son of Henri IV, a former king of Poland and a German prince-bishop![19]

As a monk, Dom Coton may have been unusual, but it is very likely that chapters and monasteries across France as a whole drew heavily on the talents of his local counterparts. Saint-Germain itself allowed three other monks to administer some of its lands in ways not dissimilar to those of Coton. Bishops, abbots and priors also had their own 'intendants' – sometimes holding innocuous titles like 'valet de chambre' or 'secretary' which disguised the important role they played in their financial affairs. There is evidence to suggest that as the seventeenth century progressed, even resident and active bishops preferred to organise their temporalities into a general lease, abandoning earlier practices of direct management via stewards and household officials. It may even be that in freeing them from the day-to-day responsibility for such management, a general lease facilitated more efficient supervision at one remove of those properties. Moreover, a general lease frequently contained exclusions, with bishops frequently 'retaining' specific properties – a favourite estate, a summer residence, vineyards and so on – for their own direct use. What is less evident is how many of them allowed their general leaseholders to negotiate and renew subleases of the numerous individual properties with its implication of relinquishing direct control over the benefice. Some newly installed bishops were keen to reclaim direct management for a time in order to restore properties that had fallen into disrepair or were in need of investment, which was always likely when lands were confided to leaseholders with little incentive to make such investments; such measures were also more likely after the death or retirement of long-standing benefice-holders generally. The seventeenth century seems to have been a long age of uncertainty and experiment with new forms of management of large-scale holdings, whereas the eighteenth century seems to have taken leaseholding for granted. And where large episcopal or monastic estates were entrusted to leaseholders of real substance, it is not hard to see how experiments with new crops, mining, metallurgy and so on could take place, since the parties involved all enjoyed access both to credit and the latest techniques.

Regardless of the form of management adopted by the great and middling benefice-holders, their impact was ultimately felt in the localities where the properties in question were situated. The leaseholders of big benefices and estates were usually urban merchants, lawyers and royal office-holders, who in turn would find themselves dealing with a host of lesser leaseholders of yet smaller properties, all the way down to parish level, where they merged and overlapped with people involved in managing parish lands and the smaller benefices. Here, too, it seems that the seventeenth century was one of transition. Numerous accounts of the sixteenth- and seventeenth-century parish (and associated) clergy show them to have been active as farmers and traders, working 'their' fields alongside their parishioner-neighbours, taking their produce to the local markets, buying and selling animals and investing their profits in land, annuities, buildings and so on. There was little in their culture, dress or demeanour to distinguish them from the farmers around them. By the eighteenth century, however, such behaviour was far less acceptable, and was under attack from all sides. Church authorities pressed the clergy to detach themselves from secular occupations and pastimes, with varying degrees of success. But just as vehemently, lay opinion was also insisting by then that the management of church property be reserved exclusively for laypeople, and the clergy be forbidden from competing with them. The sharp tone of some of these arguments suggests that there was still some way to go before that goal was achieved, but it seems by then that an increasingly outsider, urban-born and seminary-trained clergy was less and less likely to roll up their sleeves to become farmers and cattle-dealers; at best they might behave as gentleman farmers with interests in agronomy, improvement and the 'public good' (*bien public*).[20]

At parish level, where the tithe tended to be the principal source of income for the clergy, it is also likely that leases were becoming more and more common as the century progressed. This was doubly so because, as we saw, a substantial proportion of the tithe was in the hands of outsider clergy who, as absentees, would be more inclined to lease it to third parties, often wealthy local farmers, than to play cat and mouse with the local peasants over crop yields and tithe ratios. Some of the parish clergy also found that where the tithe was theirs to collect, the vigilance it required of them and the bad blood that it generated with the local population made leasing a better option than direct personal control. More surprisingly, perhaps, other parish priests during our period gave up direct title to the tithe altogether and settled for the much maligned *portion congrue*, encouraged perhaps by the crown's intervention to force up the value of the *portion congrue* itself from the 1620s onwards. But apart from the tithe, the parish cure-benefice would nearly always entail plots of land or buildings scattered about – the product of legacies or acquisitions made in previous generations – and so offering further opportunities for leasing or direct management by the parish priest. And of course, the churchwardens had 'their' property to administer, and however small its component parts were in value, especially in rural parishes, they were likely to find takers among the parishioners.

For all its brevity and omissions, this account has sought to give some idea of what a substantial economic 'enterprise' an institution like the French church actually was. The discussion could be extended in numerous ways, such as the types of employment that it provided, both directly (for example, domestic and administrative service) and indirectly (the trades, artists and so on). As a borrower, the church had possibly the best 'credit-rating' of any institution in seventeenth-century France, but it is arguable that the church's activities in *lending* money were even more widespread. The church's own property might be protected by law against forced sale for the repayment of benefice-holders' debts, but the revenues it furnished the clergy were theirs to use as they saw fit, and many of them invested them in short-term loans and annuities, public and private, as innumerable probate records from bishops right down to parish priests amply demonstrate.[21]

It is more difficult to determine how French society 'experienced' the church's wealth and responded to the ways in which it was managed, especially by comparison with other social groups such as the landed nobility. Its complexities and myriad shapes ensure that any generalisation about it will continue to be highly tentative. It does seem beyond dispute, however, that hostility remained strongest towards the absentee or outsider clergy who collected revenues, especially tithes, but who showed little readiness to acknowledge their quid pro quo obligations. Discontent also tended to arise when new benefice-holders insisted that all existing leases had automatically lapsed and attempted to raise the rental values via new contracts. Yet in many parts of France tenancies of church properties could remain in the possession of the same family over several generations, which almost certainly prevented rents from escalating unduly. The popular saying that 'life is good under the mitre' was often invoked, suggesting that the church was perceived as an accommodating landlord, lender and employer, and that it was aware of the need to retain the good will of a population who were churchgoers as well as employees, tithe-payers and tenants.

Wealth into Benefices

When contemporaries thought about the wealth and endowment of the French church they would not have thought in terms of aggregates or trends – national, provincial, diocesan or even local – which would not have made any sense to them. What they would have immediately 'seen', by instinct and habit, were the innumerable and often minuscule benefices into which that endowment was subdivided and which, therefore, formed the universal 'point of entry' to the church for contemporaries. From this perspective, the church was an immense honeycomb, one that was utterly asymmetrical in shape, given the vast differences in the status, worth and desirability of the benefices that composed it. Exceptions to this general rule did, of course, exist, the best known being the Val d'Aran, high up in the Pyrenees, where church property was retained undivided (*en indivision*), which proved decisive in sustaining a distinctive type of 'household clergy' until the eighteenth century at least.[22] Thousands of these benefices provided only a tiny income, insufficient to provide a living for an individual, which was one obvious reason for the frequent accumulation of several of them in one pair of hands. At the opposite end of the spectrum, the richest bishoprics and abbeys provided incomes that can fairly be described as princely. Such a vast range helps to explain both the ambitions of individuals and social groups to acquire them, but also the degree to which birth and social rank could be decisive in the pursuit of a benefice. No attempt at historical analysis can afford to ignore this specific feature of the church's wealth since, for all its aridity, it goes a long way towards an understanding of the interactions of church, clergy and society generally. The brief discussion that follows will focus on a few issues that were essential to the workings of the benefice system.

The law of the church – canon law – as inherited by the seventeenth century was mostly a law of benefices, while French royal law and jurisprudence were also seriously concerned with them, given how much they mattered to the monarchy and society generally. In law, a benefice could be defined as the material remuneration attached to the tenure and performance of the duties of any spiritual function or office, and the classic understanding of the connection was that the spiritual came first, the material reward second (*beneficum propter officium*, the benefice on account of the office). It was almost inevitable that, with time, the connection between them would become blurred, and that the material (financial) dimension would become detached altogether from its source (the contemporary French word for profits is *bénéfices*). Almost inevitably, the legal superstructure devised to define and conserve church benefices was always struggling to cope with the ingenuity of families and individuals, as they found ways of turning desirable, but of their nature temporary, church offices, designed with a celibate and non-hereditary clergy in mind, into more permanent gain for themselves and their families. It was thanks to the real solidity of that legal superstructure – and to the relative effectiveness of the law of mortmain – that the church's benefices did not shrivel or disappear into private hands over successive generations. Despite the tensions between them on many questions, canon and royal law together managed to preserve the specific character of church benefices, even though critics, moralists and reformers always had ample material with which to attack abuses in the system.

As might be expected, a legal system as precociously refined as canon law engaged in distinguishing between different types of benefice, and especially in establishing rules concerning their acquisition, tenure and transmission. One of the most basic distinctions was that between benefices with, and without, cure of souls attached to them, since the conditions of access and tenure, as well as the obligations attached to them, differed considerably. That particular distinction had unexpected social ramifications: it was the original legal basis for the sale of royal offices, as it was argued that church offices without cure of souls could be 'sold' without endangering the salvation of anyone involved in the transaction. Benefices with cure of souls attached to them were, not surprisingly, the subject of closer attention and regulation. By definition, such positions were incompatible with the simultaneous tenure of identical benefices elsewhere – 'pluralism' in the technical sense – but *not* with the simultaneous tenure of other benefices *without* cure of souls, which could in practice be held in unlimited numbers. There was, therefore, nothing to prevent a bishop or a parish priest from simultaneously holding several other benefices, provided none of them had cure of souls attached to it, but even such an essential distinction could often be ignored. For a relatively brief period during the sixteenth century, France experienced pluralism in the tenure of bishoprics, with leading figures like Cardinals Amboise, Bourbon, Lorraine and Joyeuse holding several major dioceses simultaneously – but the disapproval of such practices proved too strong for the practice to survive into the next century. However many abbeys they might accumulate while in favour, Richelieu and his successors never tried a similar strategy with bishoprics; quite the contrary, they now tended to divest themselves of them altogether once they gained political power. But the same standards were not applied to the monastic orders: with the spread of 'commendatory' practices, which will be discussed in a later chapter, to most of France's abbeys and priories, the offices of abbot and prior ceased, in effect, to have cure of souls attached to them, so that the door was opened to pluralism on an often breathtaking scale – Mazarin's twenty-five abbeys being an all-time record for such not-so-primitive accumulation of church-derived revenues.[23] By definition, the tenure of a parish involved cure of souls, though for a long time the tenure of parishes by clerics who were not yet priests was tolerated, provided they employed an ordained priest as their curate (*vicaire*) to perform religious services. The seventeenth-century church would gradually winkle out this practice too, and restore the observance of the law concerning benefices with cure of souls.

An important set of distinctions separated 'secular' from 'regular' benefices, in that offices within, and belonging to, religious orders were in principle reserved for members of the orders ('regulars') in question. From our perspective, this distinction applies primarily to the older monastic orders rather than the more recent mendicant orders, since it was the former that were the most seriously endowed with property. If fully respected, the distinction would have confined the regulars and the seculars to their separate spheres, but there were numerous exceptions to a rule that might otherwise have cut off some at least of the regulars from the society around them. As already noted, the spread of the *commende* to the male monastic orders – female orders were spared that intrusion – enabled members of the secular clergy to enjoy huge amounts of monastic wealth on a regular basis, a process which one might describe as 'secularisation' of a highly specific kind. The true scale of this practice remains unknown, not least because just how far it reached down into the small priories which depended on the monasteries subjected to the *commende* has still to be established. Conversely, large numbers of parishes, which we might expect to be held by secular clergy, were in the gift of monasteries, which sometimes placed their own members there as parish priests. These were far from being the only instances of such crossing of the lines between regulars and seculars.

From both an ecclesiastical and social point of view, possibly the most fundamental issue with benefices was who had the right to fill them. Here, too, canon and royal law had long been at work, even though lawsuits over such matters remained legion throughout our period. 'Patronage', in the original sense of enjoying the right to present someone to a benefice, had itself evolved over time, with such rights changing hands, so that a bewilderingly wide range of patrons were entitled to play a key part in determining which benefices went to whom, and with what consequences. Thus lay figures, often local seigneurs, had frequently acquired – or 'usurped' as critics and reformers would claim – patronage rights over numerous parishes across France, not to mention the 'simple' benefices without cure of souls. Such a development had important implications for any attempt to change the character of the clergy, as well as for the latter's relations with their hierarchical superiors. Founders of churches, hospices and chapels usually transmitted similar patronage rights to their descendants – and in many cases these 'descendants' might be monasteries or chapters rather than families by the seventeenth century. For the majority of such benefices, the patrons presented their candidate, while the actual conferral of the benefice belonged to the bishop, who could reject an unsuitable candidate, but who had no power to impose an individual of his own choice in their place. The implications of such deeply entrenched traditions were serious for any bishop aiming to extend his control over his diocese or reshape its clergy: viewed in this context, a bishop was himself only one patron among many, and not necessarily the one with the biggest portfolio of benefices at his disposal. More generally, the diffusion of patronage rights among innumerable individuals and institutions enabled particular sections of French society to control access to much of the benefice system, which was by the same token only partially controlled by the institutional church.

In reality, the rights and power of patrons within the benefice system had been seriously attenuated by the spread among benefice holders of the practice of resigning their benefices in favour of a designated successor of their own choosing.[24] It is easy to imagine the attractiveness of such a mechanism, not merely to clerics themselves, both old and young, but also to their families, which helps explain how rapidly and widely it developed during the later Middle Ages. Among a celibate clergy, such a mechanism had the potential to render large sections of the clergy quasi-hereditary, assuming that their families had young aspiring clerics in each generation, as indeed many did. Although the papacy accepted the validity of the practice, its incidence across the church as a whole varied, not least because it was suspected of promoting 'the commerce of benefices' and its concomitant trafficking, monetary exchanges and corruption. It had become widespread throughout the lower and middle echelons of the French church before the seventeenth century, and even showed signs of doing likewise within the upper reaches, as bishops and abbots tried to follow the example of those below them. But the most formidable obstacle at this level was the crown and *its* patronage rights over the higher benefices after the Concordat of Bologna. The crown was not averse to serving the interests of families within the church, and they developed their own ways of manoeuvring it into doing just that. But whenever it was politically strong enough, the crown tended to dampen down expectations of success in preserving bishoprics and abbeys (though the latter mattered much less in this respect) in family hands over several generations. Uncle-to-nephew and cousin-to-cousin successions in the French episcopate continued into the seventeenth century, but the practice of resignation to a designated successor among bishops was marginalised, and when it did occur, it was a grace that had to be negotiated in advance and in no sense the exercise of an automatic customary right.

We shall see some of the social and religious consequences of the benefice system more specifically in later chapters, but a few concluding points should be made here. Contemporaries learned almost instinctively to navigate their way through the dense thicket of law and custom concerning church benefices. Everything about benefices made people conscious of the differences between them, and so they evolved correspondingly different strategies in their attempts to get their hands on them. An entire and often sophisticated culture of what might crudely be called 'benefice hunting' existed across all social groups, with appropriate differences, depending on birth, rank, means and ambition. Because the church's wealth was indivisibly attached to the myriad of benefices, clerics and families alike were easily conditioned to think in terms of specific objectives, and to rely on their social 'capital' in seeking to snare a benefice. It is also important to grasp that bishops were benefice-holders themselves, and that they only had direct control of their own benefice and its endowments, the bishopric itself, even though they were simultaneously patrons of a certain number of benefices within their dioceses. The combined wealth of the benefices of a given diocese was simply not at the bishop's disposal, to be distributed between the clergy of the diocese as he saw fit.

One major consequence of this situation was that neither tonsured clerics nor ordained priests really looked to their bishop to support, promote and salary them as they have done in more recent times. It made far more sense to cultivate an elderly benefice-holder with a view to a resignation of the benefice in one's favour than to expect a distant, and possibly transitory, bishop to come to one's assistance. Nor would a bishop attempt to tax the wealthier clergy of his diocese to support the poorer or un-beneficed clergy, since the very idea was itself totally alien to the church and society of the day, which would never have placed such a power or right in anyone's hands. Not even the 'lord of the benefices' himself – the pope – harboured such ambitions. Consequently, the very nature of the benefice system precluded anything resembling a modern system of clerical promotion, driven by a combination of individual 'achievement' and hierarchical 'policy'.[25] This is of critical importance for an understanding of the real workings of the French church in our period, since it set genuine 'structural' limits to change. At no time did a serious reshaping of the benefice system appear on the agenda of reform, either at Trent or subsequently.

PART 2

Clerical Worlds in Context

CHAPTER 3

CLERICS AND CLERGY: THE WORLD OF THE SECULARS

General

If the previous chapter has suggested anything, it is that the French clergy were likely to be as heterogeneous, in terms of status, social origins and cultural attainments, as the benefice system that conditioned their behaviour and life-chances. Not only would the disparities between 'upper' and 'lower' clergy in general be enormous, but even among the great mass of 'lower' clergy there would also be marked differences. Yet although the benefice system may have been the matrix which ultimately 'fixed' all of these individuals within the French church, its peculiarities meant that a surprising amount of mobility was always possible for clerics with the intelligence, ambition and perseverance to make their way in a world which was less rigidly stratified than much of the society surrounding it. And this is not to mention the 'other' clergy, members of religious orders, old and new, male and female, who were especially numerous in seventeenth-century France and who merit separate examination later. This chapter will focus on the 'secular' clergy, and in particular on their major distinguishing characteristics, which cannot be satisfactorily conveyed in a purely institutional approach; it will convey some sense of their place within both the church and society of seventeenth-century France, leaving it to later chapters to examine the specific changes they experienced during the period.

Despite the impressive rise in the numbers of 'regulars' in our period, the secular clergy were by far the biggest contingent of France's clergy. The term 'secular' (meaning 'of the world') merely distinguishes them from the 'regular' clergy (meaning here 'bound by a rule' and thus belonging to the religious orders). That distinction, as we shall see, was not always watertight as far as the activities of many seculars and regulars were concerned, but it does point to important differences in the status of the respective clergies, the manner in which they lived and some of the tasks assigned to them. Elements of the secular clergy, for example, might resemble regulars in belonging to corporate institutions, such as cathedral or collegiate chapters – except, of course, that they were *not* bound by two of the three 'vows of religion' (poverty and obedience) taken by the regulars. Conversely, a tiny number of cathedral chapters in our period were still made up of either monks or canons-regular, but cathedral canons remained in principle subject to their bishops. All of which points to the biggest differences between the two groups: the secular clergy retained all the normal rights of ownership, inheritance, acquisition and disposal of their property, whereas the regulars, as individuals, surrendered all such rights and even made their will and testament prior to taking their formal vows, an act which rendered them 'civilly' dead.

Another essential precondition in approaching the seventeenth-century church is to set aside, provisionally at least, one of the major developments of French Catholicism that was yet to occur during this period – the growing emphasis on the priesthood itself. Seventeenth-century writers and reformers raised the priesthood to such heights as to place it on virtually a different plane to the other clerical 'orders' and even – a more radical step in many respects – to the religious orders themselves. One consequence of that emphasis was to single out the parish clergy in particular as those most heavily responsible for the salvation of communities, and thus to downplay the presence and value of other, less 'responsible' clergy, not to mention those clergy who were not in priestly orders at all. The subsequent development of the French clergy only added to the sharpness of this focus on the 'ideal parish priest' (*bon curé*). But for a social and cultural history of the secular clergy of our period, such a focus would constitute a real distortion, since the *curé* was just one tree in a very large wood. It would be a mistake to think of the early modern lower clergy generally, even that of the pre-revolutionary decades, as shaped exclusively by the parish system and as having a sense of 'calling' defined by parochial pastoral activity rather than by the wider benefice system of which parishes were themselves just a part.

The one obligation which all clergy, secular as well as regular, shared was that of celibacy, which ideally would be combined with a life of chastity. The consequences of this may seem too obvious to need stating. The most basic of them was that it precluded a hereditary, 'levitical' clergy at all levels of the church, since there was no provision, as in the Orthodox churches, for married and unmarried clergy, with senior positions reserved for the unmarried. The French clergy might be the first Estate of the Realm, but they were clearly not an 'Estate' like the nobles and the commons: without the capacity for reproduction from within their own ranks, they were constantly being 'colonised' from without by clerics born into the other two Estates. This meant that each generation of clergy was in some sense 'new'. The 'newness' or 'openness' of the clergy was, as already suggested, not absolute but relative, yet even that was significant at a time when the accessibility of many other corporate groups and professions seemed increasingly restricted. The venality and heredity of royal office, whether military, judicial, municipal and so on, which reached new heights during our period and which were mainly responsible for that decline in accessibility, did not formally touch the French church at all. This confirmed its relative openness, enabling it to be viewed as an avenue for advancement for individuals, families and social groups.

But it would be naïve to think that the French church could escape 'contamination' – the term is used in a morally neutral sense here – by the wider world which made it a social as well as a legal–religious entity. Clerics of every stripe were bound to bring with them some of the mentality and habits of the social groups from which they originated, notably that of wishing to perpetuate church positions within families over several generations. It is well known that some of the key techniques which enabled the venality and heredity of secular office to develop were first pioneered within the late medieval church. Those techniques continued to be extensively practised by clerics right down to the French Revolution, and some of them came so close to buying and selling benefices and offices that the offence – and sin – of 'simony' was never in danger of becoming redundant! As we have already noted, the most widely used technique was that of resigning one's benefice 'in favour' of a named successor of one's choice. Because the suspicion of underhand financial dealings was inevitable in relation to this practice, it had to be approved by ecclesiastical authority, and ultimately by the pope who alone possessed the power to lift that suspicion and give the transfer of tenure the legitimacy it so badly needed. Rigorists and reformers might vehemently disapprove of such dispensations, but the practice of resigning 'in favour' was deeply entrenched among the clergy long before the seventeenth century. This, after all, was how Vincent de Paul became *curé* of Clichy in 1611, while the *curé* who resigned it to him, François Bourgoing, would later become superior-general of the French Oratory! Of course, had it been allowed to expand indefinitely and at all levels of the French church, this practice would have produced the same kind of *blocage* that, as contemporaries remarked, occurred when secular offices effectively became private property. In this eventuality, not only would the French monarchy lose its freedom to choose bishops and abbots for major positions within the church, but so, too, would the multitude of patrons, secular and ecclesiastical, for lesser positions within the church, from that of cathedral canon right down to parish priest or chaplain. We shall see in due course how such problems were faced during the seventeenth century, but the point here is to indicate not merely that the French clergy themselves mirrored important features of the contemporary social structure, but also to show *how* particular mechanisms facilitated them and thereby made entry into the clergy feasible across the social spectrum.

Clerics and Clergy

Probably at no time in European history was the distinction between lay society and the clergy in the broad sense as blurred as in the fifteenth and sixteenth centuries. Huge numbers of pre-teenage boys were administered the tonsure, the first of the 'minor' orders, which technically made them clerics and therefore capable of holding 'simple' benefices (that is, without cure of souls). We do not need to examine here the reasons for this surge in such 'basic' ordinations, which must have made clerics as numerous in some localities as nobles in Basque or Polish villages! Evidently, families thought of such ordinations of – mainly younger – sons as an option which might lead in due course to further orders, the priesthood included, but that would be a distant prospect when those being tonsured were as young as eight or nine years. None of these 'minor' orders, as they were collectively called, obliged the clerics in question to proceed later to the 'major' orders culminating in the priesthood itself, and the majority probably did not remain clerics into adulthood. The huge discrepancy in the ordination registers of some dioceses of the later fifteenth and sixteenth centuries between the numbers taking the tonsure and the priesthood – the ratio was often as high as ten to one, if not more – gives some idea of the scale of this 'investment' in the church by families.[1]

Nothing illustrates better the distinction between status and function within the *ancien régime* church than this development. Being a 'cleric', even if only in minor orders, conferred a special status, bringing with it the 'privileges of clergy', as they were known, which included exemption from secular jurisdiction in civil and criminal matters. For centuries these highly desirable clerical privileges had been a huge bone of contention, and secular authorities throughout Europe strove hard to limit them to those who were 'real' rather than 'nominal' clergy, a difficult frontier to fix. The French monarchy was certainly moved by such concerns, and it tried, as is evident from its major ordinances between approximately 1560 and 1695, to restrict the enjoyment of such privileges to clergy who were at least subdeacons (the first of the 'major' orders effectively to debar clerics from returning to lay status) and who were exercising an office within the church. Once these measures took effect, the only 'mere' clerics (those in minor orders) who could still legitimately claim the privileges of clergy were those studying at university or holding a church benefice, both of which could still involve substantial numbers of individuals. The seventeenth-century French church would cut the inherited gap between ordinations to minor and major orders far more drastically than other parts of Catholic Europe, so that more tonsured clerics than ever would duly go on to become priests, but the process was a very slow one which ran at different speeds across the kingdom. Despite this development, to which we shall return later, what did not change much was the speed with which individuals might decide to take the successive orders: the church set a minimum age for each one of the orders, as well as the obligatory 'interstices' between them – especially for the major orders – but once these 'time-outs' were respected or papal dispensations had been obtained to sidestep them, the church did not impose a timetable by which particular orders had to be taken. It was thus not uncommon for individual clerics to take the subdiaconate or diaconate, but then to wait several years before taking the priesthood – and, of course, some never took it at all. Often it was the prospect of acquiring a new benefice or office that triggered the decision to take the remaining orders that an individual still lacked, most obviously if those orders were a formal requirement for the particular positions on offer. And, of course, many adult men continued to enter the ranks of the clergy in widowhood, and not necessarily at an advanced age. In sum, this was a world with 'an open conception of the clerical state that left room for degrees of clericalisation between the priest and the layman' and which only responded slowly to pressures to change its most basic, centuries-old habits.[2] We have, therefore, to understand the clergy and its internal differentiations in more ways than the obvious functional ones of more recent times. Changes in the numbers and types of clergy result from a range of factors, and not merely from administrative fiat or the efforts of religious reformers.

Numbers and Clerical 'Titles'

With such large numbers of clerics and priests being ordained, it would seem to follow that the lower ranks of the clergy were populated by men from all rungs of the social ladder. Contrary to what might be expected, this was not quite so, but explaining the reasons for this are not straightforward. Sons of the poor, landless labourers and cottagers – as well as of their urban counterparts – found entry into the clergy increasingly difficult, especially in the seventeenth century. This was not because of any explicit social or cultural bias against them, but more likely due to the imposition of one particular entry requirement that is not widely understood, although it was a logical result of the benefice system of the time. For centuries, clerics wanting to be ordained priests had to prove that they had the means to support themselves after ordination, so as to guarantee a minimum 'decency' threshold that would enable them to avoid activities or behaviour regarded as unworthy of their status, or which would bring the church into disrepute. Accordingly, there were various clerical 'titles', as they were called, by virtue of which one could be ordained – the most important being possession of a benefice, membership of a religious order and family patrimony. These titles had to be produced in legally certified form before ordination as a subdeacon. As we have already noted, there were always far too few benefices available compared to the number of clerics seeking them, so it was mainly the socially well connected or those from families with benefice-holding clerics who obtained them from an early age. The religious orders, both monastic and mendicant, were by definition capable of supporting their members who sought major orders, and they certainly did recruit some of those members from lower social groups. This meant that for the remainder, who constituted the majority of potential priests, a 'patrimonial' title was the only option. As its name indicates, this title entailed the setting aside of a sufficient amount of family property, usually in the form of a legal mortgage, to generate the annual income equal to the monetary value of the title required by the church authorities of the day. In the abstract, it is not hard to see how the calibration of such a mechanism could make access to the clergy more or less difficult for the not so well-off clerics and their families. Over the centuries, it seems that the actual imposition and impact of this requirement varied quite significantly from diocese to diocese: not only was the annual revenue required of those in orders itself set by individual dioceses, but it was up to their officials to police actual observance of the rules. The high numbers of priests ordained in the fifteenth and sixteenth centuries suggests a serious relaxation of those rules, thereby enabling sons of relatively modest families to enter the clergy. Regardless of the precise sums concerned, the fact remains that a large number of priests were supported primarily by their families, even though all concerned hoped that the acquisition of a benefice would in due course shift that burden of maintenance to the church itself. Where such a happy outcome did not materialise, the family's commitment remained a lifelong one. For many clerics, therefore, the search for benefices was driven not merely by personal ambition, but by family interests and pressure.[3]

There is good reason for thinking that between them the spread of Calvinism and especially the wars of religion slashed the very high numbers of ordinations of the previous generations, even though the severity and timescale of the reductions varied substantially from one region to another. Whether previous levels would have been restored once the wars had ended is a moot point, but it seems that, thanks perhaps to the continuing influence of

Catholic militancy that was itself highly critical of clerical inadequacies, there was an unwillingness to return to such permissive practices after 1600. Nevertheless, the view that the clergy were still too numerous was held in the 1660s by as influential a figure as Colbert, though his concern was mainly with the newer, less secure religious orders and congregations. Colbert's figure of 260,000 clergy of all stripes, representing approximately 1.2 per cent of France's population, was an exaggerated one, based essentially on guesswork.[4] By way of comparison, it seems that, despite the strictures of Trent and the movement of Catholic Reform thereafter, both Italy and Spain witnessed a sustained *rise* in the numbers of clergy, especially those in sub-priestly orders, well into the eighteenth century, a trend which drew similarly adverse comment from both *arbitristas* and Enlightenment authors in turn. But 'national' averages mean little here, especially in France, where no serious effort was ever made to calculate the total size of the clerical population during the *ancien régime*, so that historians have to extrapolate from often incomplete and problematic local and diocesan figures.[5]

Clerical Geography

A major feature of French history since the revolution has been a well-defined geography of religious observance and clerical recruitment which closely overlap. Early indications of both phenomena have been found by historians for the pre-revolutionary decades. There is some reason to believe that they had roots that went back even further in time, although it should be realised that the vagaries of the benefice system counted for more than religious observance per se in earlier periods.[6] It is known that even *within* certain dioceses there were regions which produced – or overproduced – clergy, and others which did not. The religious 'dimorphism' of the seventeenth-century diocese of La Rochelle was such that the hinterland of the coastal city itself depended heavily on the northern districts of the elongated, misshapen diocese to supply it with clergy; up to 70 per cent of clergy serving in southern parishes came from the northern districts. Under Louis XIV, the city and immediate hinterland of Reims were a 'desert' which depended on the influx of clergy originating in the north-eastern and south-eastern areas. A similarly high proportion of the rural parish clergy of the Paris diocese were migrant clergy, particularly from parts of Normandy; nearly one-third of the parish clergy of Beauvais diocese in 1708 were from nearby areas, especially Normandy, which also 'exported' clergy to parts of French-speaking Brittany from the sixteenth century. Similar patterns have been observed for other parts of France, such as parts of the Loire valley, the Rhone valley and the Toulouse plain by the eighteenth century. In stark contrast to such areas, the Auvergne, Dauphiné and

Provence seem consistently to have provided surplus clergy to other parts of France – mostly, but not exclusively, in contiguous regions. But as these upland areas were also ones in which communities of un-beneficed local clergy were at their most numerous throughout the early modern period, it is clear that not all of those in priestly orders were forced to emigrate to other dioceses. We know that the high numbers of clergy from the uplands being ordained in sixteenth-century Avignon declined thereafter, which may have reflected similar downward movements across French dioceses.[7]

It would be unwise to press the significance of these local contrasts too far, let alone attempt to base on them a nationwide map of clerical 'over-' and 'under-supply' during the seventeenth century. They need to be considered in relation to long-standing patterns of clerical migration rather than in terms of nineteenth-century problems of clerical 'shortages' across the board. Firstly, clergy were far more likely to prefer modestly endowed benefices in towns without cure of souls to better-endowed rural parishes with cure of souls. University graduates were more mobile than most because of the preferential treatment to which they were entitled during particular months of the year when competing for benefices. Brittany, for example, was never short of clergy during our period, and may have been one of the best-provided provinces in France, with considerable levels of inter-diocesan migration, yet it consistently attracted, as noted above, immigrant Norman clergy.[8] Once again, it was the benefice system itself, with its almost inexhaustible gradations, that was the major influence on clerical demography and mobility. In attempting to analyse the secular clergy as a whole, it makes sense to begin at the bottom of the pyramid, where the greatest number of them were to be found.

Parishes and their Clergy

Identifying the different kinds of clergy to be found in France's parishes is indispensable to any understanding of the workings of the French church, and particularly to seeing how the rigidity of both parochial geography and the benefice system could be attenuated by more informal arrangements. The idea of the parish as a pastoral charge requiring a resident holder who was in full priestly orders took a long time to take hold, and it was not really until well into the seventeenth century that it became established, as we shall see in a later chapter. Prior to then, in France as elsewhere in Europe, it was widespread for the title to be conferred on clerics who could not exercise the ministry itself, either because they were not yet ordained priests, or were still studying at university; all they had to do in the meantime was to find a substitute who would serve in their place for a fixed remuneration. In some places, this gave rise to an open auction, with the successful 'substitutes' sometimes signing an actual lease of the parish cure for a predetermined number of years. Such arrangements served all kinds of purposes, allowing university students to pay for their studies, and clerics 'on the make' to live elsewhere, invariably in towns, where they could search for better career opportunities.

This dissociation of the tenure and service of parishes facilitated the well-known practice of clerical absenteeism so decried before and during the Reformation, when both parties involved were attacked – the titular *curé* for neglecting his charge, the serving curate for his alleged mercenary behaviour. It would be tempting to imagine that these practices were confined to remote rural parishes, but that would not be true, given that in towns like Arles this kind of absenteeism was common in the fifteenth and probably the sixteenth centuries.[9] The main parish in Langres, Saint-Pierre, was in the gift of the cathedral chapter, and it was put up 'for auction' every three years until 1628.[10] Although the attractiveness of individual urban parishes could vary, it seems likely that it was in towns that the tenure and the service of parishes by the actual benefice-holder was first achieved, whence it spread thereafter, in trickle-down fashion, to rural areas. This process owed something to the growing numbers of university graduates seeking parish benefices, some of which, especially in the major towns, were progressively reserved for graduates during our period. Pressure from parishioners and bishops alike probably came later, but across the seventeenth century it gradually eliminated the older practices.

Canon law may have defined a parish as a territorial entity under the direction of a parish priest, but the term 'parish priest' (*curé*) is not as straightforward as it appears at first, and this too helps to explain the varieties of clergy to be found within early modern French parishes. Over the centuries, formal title to an impressive numbers of parish 'cures' was, like the tithe, taken over by religious orders or chapters, cathedral or collegiate – 'moral' rather than physical 'persons' which could obviously not discharge the responsibilities of the parish priest themselves. There was scarcely a monastery or a chapter across France which did not hold such rights, sometimes in considerable numbers and not always in their immediate vicinity. It was they that were ultimately responsible for the calibre of the clergy serving in innumerable parishes. Retaining the *curé*'s rights and prerogatives (such as church tithes) for themselves, via the revealing title of *curé primitif*, they would exercise their patronage right to nominate a curate (*vicaire*, 'one who takes the place of another') to serve in the parish, a priest who might either be chosen from their own ranks or, more usually, from the secular clergy. It was widely held that they discharged these obligations less than conscientiously, not least because the parishes in question could be located in distant parts of France, which made effective supervision of, or attention to, the parishes virtually impossible. On the other hand, the *curé primitif* could always nominate monks or canons from the chapters as curates, thus ensuring that the service of parishes would not be a complete monopoly of the secular/diocesan clergy.

Whatever his precise title, the *vicaire*'s tenure of such parishes was a matter of interminable disputes across the centuries: was he removable at will by the *curé primitif*, with the disruptive consequences that might be expected from such a potentially arbitrary exercise of its rights, or was he entitled to some security of tenure? Seventeenth-century bishops were keen to improve the status of these priests by having them declared 'un-removable or perpetual curates' (*vicaires inamovibles/perpetuels*). They did so partly in order to prevent excessive turnover of clergy serving in these parishes, but also to secure their own power to supervise and discipline them. Such issues were not purely intra-clerical affairs, and it was the king's council which decided, in January 1686, that these *vicaires* should be held to be 'perpetual and irremovable', to all intents and purposes enjoying the same stability of tenure as a full parish priest. Needless to say, it took more than a decree of the council to settle such long-standing problems.

Clerical Proletariat?

The average parish was home to members of the secular clergy other than *curés* and/or *vicaires*. The phenomenon of curates working under the supervision of a resident parish priest, rather than replacing him on a full-time contract, was slow to materialise, despite the growing pressure for it during the seventeenth century. It might be expected that between them the size of many parishes and the abundant supply of clergy would ensure the presence of numerous curates throughout the French church, but that would be to forget that there was no office or benefice corresponding to such a label. Being a curate was a mere 'employment', and one that offered highly uncertain prospects. A parish priest employing his own curate had to pay him out of his own pocket, so it is not hard to imagine how few there were of them.

Beyond the curates there was a far more indeterminate population of un-beneficed clergy in most parishes during our period. Some of them held minor benefices arising from legacies and foundations for the saying of masses for the dead, and in that capacity they were attached to chapels in churches, hospices, priories, and so on. In addition, we find many other un-beneficed priests, the most invisible of all to historians until relatively recently, and whose presence constitutes one of the most unfamiliar aspects of the church–society connection in the seventeenth century.[11] Unevenly spread across France, they were most prominent in mountainous regions like the Jura, Dauphiné, the Massif Central and the Pyrenees, areas which were traditionally over-providers of clergy, but they could also be found in the more lowland dioceses in Normandy and parts of central France. The names by which they were known are as diverse as their geographical presence – *prêtres-filleuls, communalistes, mépartistes, familiers, purgatoriers, obituaires, prêtres habitués* – names which sometimes suggest the type of activities in which they engaged. The *prêtres-filleuls* tag is the most widespread and also the most expressive of them, since in the majority of areas the priests in question had to be 'sons' of the parish in order to join the community or association of priests based exclusively in the parish, and if they obtained a benefice of any kind, inside or outside of the parish, they had to leave the community. Despite being communities in church law, with governing statutes that often went back to the fourteenth or fifteenth centuries, they should emphatically not be seen as variants of the communities of religious orders or of canons. They might have a meeting place, a chapel or a building of their own, and elect their own syndic each year, yet their members continued to live with their families after taking orders rather than under one communal roof. Furthermore, despite the fact that the parish priest was the titular head of their community, its members had no claim on the parish cure itself or its emoluments, but were entitled instead to the income from mass foundations, annuities and other property attached to their community. Essentially, they made a living from saying masses for the dead, attending funerals, processions and so on, as well as assisting the parish priest at particular moments of the year. The degree to which rural social life revolved around the parish church and its religious ceremonies, which constituted a densely filled liturgical year, made work for many hands such as these often-derided lower clergy. Because of their often purely local origins, they were the clergy who most resembled the lay parishioners in their lifestyle, of which the best demonstration is the fact that many of these communities became money-lending societies in several areas of France. The bishops and reformers of the seventeenth century tended to look on this un-beneficed clerical underbelly with considerable suspicion, but they were not an easy problem to dispose of, so long as requests for masses for the dead continued to be demanded in large numbers by testators who could afford them.

Not all of the un-beneficed clergy, however, belonged to 'insider' communities of this kind. Individual priests, often identified by the elusive label of *habitués*, could attach themselves to the service of cathedrals, collegiate churches, hospitals, places of pilgrimage and so on, providing similar liturgical services to those described above. Opportunities for such affiliation were not lacking in a church which generated 'holy places' in such huge numbers in both town and country. Not surprisingly, evidence abounds for their presence in major cities. In Paris, the parish of Saint-Germain-des-Prés had fifty to sixty *habitué* priests who performed such religious offices of the parish as have just been mentioned alongside its *curé*. In Angers, the parish of Saint-Michel-du-Tertre had a parish priest and eight priests or *habitué* chaplains in 1618. Big urban parishes, such as Saint-Sulpice or Saint-Nicolas-du-Chardonnet in Paris, were home to far more substantial numbers of *habitué* clergy of this kind, some of whom began to group together by the early seventeenth century into communities of a more novel type, and it was from their midst that some of the new-style seminaries for ordinands, congregations and missionary societies of the time emerged. Even where they did not form a community of any visible kind, it is clear that this type of parish-based clergy were worlds apart from the clerical communities of rural Auvergne, the Limousin or the Pyrenees.[12]

Second-Order Worthies

It is overwhelmingly in the towns and cities of provincial France that the historian encounters the kind of 'second-order' or 'intermediate' clergy which everywhere constituted the elite of the local secular clergy. Yet they remain in many ways the least studied – or least understood – cohort of the clergy. This is due partly to their contemporary reputation, which applies particularly to the chapters, as the most 'unloved' clergy of their day. It does not help that the contours of this stratum of clergy are necessarily imprecise: at their apex we find the 'dignitaries' of the great cathedral chapters – or sometimes of collegiate chapters like Saint-Martin of Tours which could enjoy more prestige than the local cathedral chapter – while their lower ranks merged more or less invisibly into that of the parish priests of the most desirable urban parishes, which were increasingly reserved for university graduates in our period. There were about 600 to 700 chapters in France, of which cathedral chapters amounted to around 125 by the early eighteenth century. The remaining four-fifths or more, consisting of collegiate chapters (*collégiales*), were scattered across towns, big and small, in addition to the cathedral towns themselves. The overall effect was to make France the 'promised land of chapters' in western Europe (Loupès), with a total population of around 15,000 by the eighteenth century.[13] Whereas half of all the cathedral chapters were situated below the Bordeaux–Grenoble line, in keeping with the geography of France's dioceses, the collegiate chapters were massively (83 per cent) located *above* that line, thanks largely to the bigger scale of the dioceses in question. Beyond that, however, the spread of chapters across the country was, as the map opposite indicates, fairly haphazard, apart from the concentrations evident in the north, parts of the Loire valley and Gascony-Languedoc, and in Auvergne-Burgundy.

2. French chapters during the *ancien régime*.

It seems that the great majority of the collegiate chapters were located in France's middling and smaller towns, but in substantial non-episcopal cities like Lille they could be the dominant type of corporate clergy. To what extent local chapters disappeared during the wars of religion or later is impossible to say, but it has been shown that some of the communities of priests described earlier in this chapter did decide to change status and become collegiate chapters during the seventeenth century. Their membership was probably small, and they were located mainly in regions which probably had not previously had such chapters.[14] Viewed as a whole, the chapters were a distinctive and extensive, and sometimes powerful, presence within the French church, from its major urban centres to its semi-rural *bourgs*.

The chapters were fewer in number – and smaller in their membership – than the religious orders, but they were often longer established than the orders, as well as being closely tied to the local social elites. Many, though not all, towns of any importance were home to several chapters whose mutual rivalries were often notorious. Of the fifteen chapters in the big diocese of Clermont, four were located in the town of Clermont itself: three of them were collegiate chapters with just thirty-four members between them, while the cathedral chapter had forty members. In the small dioceses of the Midi, the number of canons per cathedral chapter could be tiny – no more than four or five – but in northern France, they could easily be ten times as numerous. Chartres, one of France's richest, had about ninety canons, with Langres, despite being much less rich, having around eighty-four. Auxerre, Sens, Soissons and Paris each had above fifty canons. They were also far from egalitarian institutions. Within each chapter there was an oligarchy of office-holding 'dignitaries' – the dean (or provost or an equivalent title), the sacristan, the cellarer, the archdeacons and so on – who were usually entitled to a double stipend, and who also claimed to exercise authority inside, and sometimes outside, of the chapter itself; they and the remaining 'ordinary' canons made up the 'high' choir of the chapter. Below the ordinary canons, and constituting the 'low' choir, we find a frequently bigger and more heterogeneous cohort of clergy, who were either 'half-canons', prebendaries, chaplains or mere 'employees' of the chapter. Mostly ordained priests, the latter said masses for the dead and performed the numerous other services which the canons – absentee, idle, or un-ordained – might be unable or unwilling to conduct themselves. The best placed among these 'dependent' clerics might aspire one day to the rank of canon, but most of them were tied into a lord–servant relationship with the chapter they served. Thus, the forty places in the Clermont chapter just mentioned actually consisted of twenty-four 'ordinary' canonries, one 'double' canonry for each of the four dignitaries and, after 1668, twelve 'half' canonries which required their holders, referred to as 'serfs', to be in priestly orders; the remaining two full places were reserved for the bishop and for the post of chanter, so as to cover the costs of maintaining the cathedral choir.[15]

What this suggests is that the huge disparities between these chapters, and therefore the relative desirability of a position of canon there, depended in large part on their wealth, which the chapters managed as a body, thus ensuring a careful supervision of their often widely scattered properties and estates. The canons' own incomes were directly tied to the returns from the chapter's temporalities. Their relatively limited religious and pastoral obligations meant they had abundant time and energy to devote to such matters, one side effect of which was a reputation for tenacity in exacting what was owed to them and in defending what they regarded as their rights – the tithe being the most notorious example. Thus a canon-cum-dignitary's income in the richest chapters – Chartres, Paris, Narbonne or Lyon – might be half that of a bishop of a poorly endowed diocese, and it came with none of the costs and responsibilities of episcopal office; correspondingly, the poorest chapters could only offer stipends that were inferior to those of the better endowed parishes.

In the light of this it is no surprise that positions of canon were enormously attractive to clerics throughout the French church. The internal 'stratification' of chapters also meant they would appeal to clerics of different social backgrounds. The clergy of a cathedral chapter also came immediately after the bishop in the ecclesiastical hierarchy of every diocese, and they defended their status with some ferocity, especially when it came to ceremonies, processions or other public events. Canons enjoyed a comfortable, sometimes wealthy lifestyle, which enabled them to employ personal servants, acquire substantial libraries and, of course, 'set up' younger relatives for a clerical career in the next generation. Their canonries carried few unavoidable or onerous obligations, since some of the notional duties of a canon – reciting the divine office, saying mass and so on – could be performed, in part at least, by the substitute clergy mentioned above. With the growth in university graduates among them, some with doctorates in law or theology, individual canons could become important intellectual figures locally, and not just in the principal cities. Few of them, however, were of the calibre of the famous sceptical philosopher, Pierre Gassendi (1592–1665), who spent virtually all his career as a canon and later dean of the cathedral of the small hill-town of Digne in Upper Provence.

The Council of Trent insisted that canons be aged twenty-two and subdeacons (or about to be ordained as such), but many in France objected in principle to this requirement, and argued for the lower age of fourteen, corresponding to the new age for the tonsure also laid down by Trent.[16] For centuries, university graduates had been specifically entitled to seek admission to chapters, and they had absolute precedence over other candidates during the 'graduates' months' of the year. The requirements for 'dignitaries' were also made more stringent in our period, and they usually involved full priestly orders as well as a university degree. One effect of this was to ensure that non-local canons might form an important proportion of the members of the most desirable chapters. Entry into, and especially advancement within, the chapters was subject to a changing range of formal demands which it took skill and perseverance to negotiate. But, as was so often the case, legislation and reality did not always coincide. To be received as an ordinary canon in the majority of French chapters around 1600, it sufficed to be a tonsured cleric, and it was not uncommon for well-connected boys of eight years and above to join their ranks, so that their prebend probably paid for them to continue their studies elsewhere.

Yet it seems that as the seventeenth century progressed, more and more chapters raised the bar for entry, responding to wider changes within the French church and reducing, but probably never quite eliminating, teenage and non-priestly canons. Pressure to maintain their presence within the chapters meant that families would naturally seek ways around new conditions. And when elderly canons wished to retire or felt the approach of death, they were usually able to resign their benefice 'in favour' of a successor of their choice, who in most cases would be a younger family member. Such mechanisms made it possible to sustain a family's presence in a chapter over several generations, once the crucial first entry had been secured: thereafter all depended on family strategies and resources. And with persistence and good connections, it was possible to do even better still by securing one of the chapter's 'dignities'. The circulation of offices within chapters, again via the practice of 'resignations in favour', was commonplace, and it was frequently an opportunity for an established canon to move upwards, while vacating his original position for a nephew or relative whose entry into the chapter would sustain the family's presence into the next generation. The most successful families, of course, were those with several members in a chapter. This kind of success was the most obvious manifestation of the growth of a local clerical oligarchy, based on extended family ties, which was often a mirror image of the oligarchy that dominated the local royal courts and town councils during the same period.

It will be evident that chapters enjoyed considerable control over their own recruitment. The well-oiled mechanisms of co-option made for a corporate clergy that could be highly homogeneous socially and marked by strong continuity of membership; they also promoted a strong sense of corporate identity which made them formidable opponents in local conflicts. Chapters enjoyed the right to elect many of their own members in the first place; bishops also enjoyed patronage rights for a proportion of both canonries and offices in chapters, but that varied hugely from chapter to chapter. Where bishops exercised extensive patronage, the chances of a more varied corporate clergy were greater. For one thing, bishops who were themselves increasingly outsiders to the dioceses they held were more likely to bring in outsiders (some of them relatives) as canons – a convenient means of remunerating clerics who mostly served them in administering the diocese. But in some chapters it seems that resignations 'in favour' were so common as to reduce both election and episcopal appointment to relative insignificance. In Langres Cathedral, nine out of ten canons received between 1615 and 1695 owed their entry to resignations! On one occasion, in 1619, the chapter failed even to impose its preferred choice of dean, and the dignity went instead to a canon to whom the previous incumbent had 'resigned' it.[17] Everyone knew such practices came close to trafficking in 'sacred goods', but they also knew that they were too pervasive to be eradicated altogether.

The extent and effectiveness of such entry and exit mechanisms were also the key to the social profile of the chapters and their clergy. In general, France's chapters were far removed from the social exclusiveness of those of the Holy Roman Empire, with their exceptionally stringent rules about the quarters of nobility required of candidates for election. Only a small number of French chapters, mostly scattered along its eastern border-provinces, had explicit rules of that kind, but they were less demanding. The best known were Saint-Jean of Lyon, Saint-Pierre of Mâcon and Saint-Julien of Brioude (the latter a collegiate chapter), while some female chapters, such as the canonesses of Remiremont in Lorraine, had similar requirements. Canons of Saint-Jean of Lyon, the most aristocratic male chapter in France, were referred to simply as 'counts of Lyon'. The chapters of Brittany, a province dominated by its nobility, were themselves, with one or two exceptions, a faithful reflection of the nobility's power there.[18]

The social timbre of the other chapters cannot be so easily summarised, since the internal differentiations of office and rank – dignitaries, ordinary canons, semi-prebendaries and the like – obviously attracted men of correspondingly different social backgrounds. Sons of noble families were most likely to be attracted by, and gravitate towards, the dignities, especially in the more high-ranking chapters, and therefore to disdain lesser-status positions, but it does seem that the overall proportion of old nobles within chapters fell somewhat by the end of the wars of religion and did not recover fully thereafter. By that point, entry into chapters by sons of royal officials, merchants, lawyers and so on was well on its way. By the eighteenth century, the process of social change (and especially office-holding) would have transformed many of these originally commoner families into hereditary nobles, thus rendering the chapter membership increasingly noble in status; even then, nobles were less than the majority in several of the best-known chapters. It was only in the smaller semi-rural collegiate chapters that it was possible for the sons of the better-off farmers to make a timid appearance during our period. But whatever the social origins of the chapter clergy, they tended to be drawn massively from urban families, and from the towns in which the chapters themselves were located. These common features had the effect of firmly connecting the chapter clergy to the local notables.

As the epitome of the 'corporate' clergy, cathedral chapters saw themselves as the 'natural' councillors of their bishop, but over the centuries relations between the two had often been fractious, and sometimes violent. Chapters insisted that they were exempt from the bishop's jurisdiction, so that the cathedral and its immediate surroundings 'belonged' to them, and the bishop was only allowed inside them on sufferance, and certainly not as their lord and master. However, long before our period the chapters' golden age had passed, marked by the loss of their invaluable privilege of electing bishops. So long as that right had been theirs, even intervention by the papacy and the crown did not drastically diminish their influence, since the prospect of being elected a bishop by a chapter meant that canons' stalls were keenly sought after; its final disappearance may well have played a part in reducing the proportion of canons drawn from older noble families. Yet the change in their fortunes did not make competition for places any less intense, but probably made it more local in both scope and significance. A study of the five major chapters of Guyenne in the south-west found that only about eleven members became bishops during the 1600–1789 period, and that most of them did *not* owe their mitre to their career as a canon.[19] But although it might no longer open the door to the episcopate, outsider clergy still sought membership of far-flung chapters because, however nominal or temporary it might be, that membership could enable them to be elected to an assembly of clergy, which in turn might open up more exciting prospects of advancement elsewhere.

The impact of the chapters and their clergy on their surroundings was extensive, but it is easy to ignore since, as we saw above, there were few obligations on canons beyond their liturgical duties. It was they who elected, from their own ranks, the vicars-general who governed dioceses during episcopal vacancies, some of which were extremely prolonged in our period – for example, during the final confused decade of the wars of religion or during subsequent periods of tension with Rome (late 1630s, 1682–92), when the papacy refused to confirm the king's nominations as bishops. It was no less common for cathedrals, but also other chapters, to be the patrons of some or all of the urban parishes in question, and to evince a fierce determination to maintain control of them. We saw in an earlier chapter that

Aix-en-Provence had only two parishes to serve about 15,000 inhabitants, and that the cathedral chapter successfully resisted any attempt to create new parishes which might reduce its grip on the city. Such situations and tactics manifested themselves in other cities, winning the chapters a reputation for self-interested litigiousness.

Chapters also claimed jurisdiction of their own within dioceses, especially over parts of the cathedral town, while some of their members, notably the archdeacons, claimed the right to visit and inspect parts of a diocese, so that clashes with bishops unwilling to recognise such historical fiefdoms were inevitable. But conflicts of this kind, however widespread in the seventeenth century, were usually kept under local control, partly because it was realised that dioceses ran more smoothly when the two parties co-operated. In any case, such skirmishes did not prevent certain canons, especially deans or archdeacons, from belonging, as individuals, just as much to the diocesan administration as to the chapter. When bishops chose their vicars-general and other senior officials (the *théologal*, the *official*, the *promoteur* and others) from among the chapter clergy rather than from outsider clergy, it was a sure sign of common ground with the local clerical elite; the more canons who were in full orders and possessing university degrees, the bigger would be the pool of potentially capable clerics, who also had the signal advantage over outsiders of being well entrenched in the networks of local society. The bigger chapters seem to have discouraged their members from holding parishes. That of Langres had fifty-eight parishes in its gift, but only one in five was held by a canon during the seventeenth century, and that average was still falling under Louis XIV.[20] For members of the poorer chapters, however, such additional activities might not be purely a matter of choice, and the extra income from holding a parish could not be turned down; sometimes canons would abandon their chapter stall in order to take on a big parish. Beyond that, there was endless scope for action by individual canons with commitment and ability – for example, in helping to run hospices, poor-houses, the emerging seminaries and schools, as well as in preaching, missions and conducting catechism classes. It is striking how often a relatively small number of them could play a pivotal role in the religious history of France's towns and dioceses during the long seventeenth century, and how repeatedly their names surface in the surviving chronicles as agents of religious change.

The Upper Clergy

Applied to *ancien régime* France, the notion of an 'upper' clergy seems as natural and unproblematic as that of an 'upper' class or an aristocracy generally. Yet on closer inspection, the analogy is not quite as straightforward as it appears. Who belonged to this element of the secular clergy, and why? On the strictest definition, France's upper clergy would consist of its bishops, the titular governors of the 113 (around 1600) to 124 (around 1715) dioceses that made up the seventeenth-century church. To them we might add the occasional cardinal who obtained the red hat without ever being a bishop. That would make them one of the smallest elites, secular or religious, of the day, especially considering the overall clerical population and the territorial extension of the French church. But such a tightly drawn and purely functional definition of the upper clergy would be self-defeating, as it only accounts for those who successfully emerged with an episcopal mitre from a wider world of clergy whose elusive contours need exploring. Moreover, in each generation across the seventeenth century, a proportion of France's new bishops were outsiders who had *not* belonged to the higher echelons of the clergy prior to their elevation: some of them were regulars or local church figures with no obvious connections to the world of the court and the capital, with which the upper clergy are instinctively associated. But this experience of unexpected elevation to the upper clergy by royal fiat was not that of most bishops, many of whom had belonged to that charmed circle from the outset of their careers. Even though not all of them entered its ranks in the same manner, it is fair to say that it was crown patronage rather than court service alone which determined the upper clergy more than anything else.[21]

A royal court the size of that of Valois and Bourbon France was bound to attract its share of ambitious clerics, many of whom were, in any case, drawn from families of nobles, ministers and courtiers. This was not a new phenomenon, of course, and court clerics had been familiar for centuries. But by the sixteenth century, the functions of scribes, secretaries, record-keepers and so on that they had held for so long were increasingly falling into lay hands, potentially reducing the scope for a court-based clergy. There remained the individual royal households with their chapels and ecclesiastical posts. They varied widely in number and size from one generation to the next, with that of the king easily dwarfing those of other members of the royal family, though queen-regents like Marie de' Medici or Anne of Austria were not far behind. Posts of 'grand' or 'first' almoner in royal households mostly went to men who were already cardinals or bishops, and they enabled them in turn to make the careers of younger clerical clients or other hopefuls, not least when it came to filling the far more numerous positions of almoner-in-ordinary. But as these offices were venal, we should not overestimate the influence of the senior officials just mentioned in determining their distribution. As happened in other spheres of government, venality led to the proliferation of new offices, the vast majority of which were purely honorific. The effect was to draw impressive numbers of clerics to court from the reign of François I onwards.[22]

It is not clear how tough the competition was for the far smaller number of 'serving' and rotating almonerships, which brought individual almoners into close personal contact with the monarch (or other members of the royal family) and which, presumably, increased thereby one's chances of securing other desirable rewards. The early Bourbon royal households may well have broken with Valois practices, and both Louis XIII and Marie de' Medici seem to have survived with just four serving almoners each, plus thirty-four unpaid almoners for Marie in 1631 and just fifteen for Louis XIII by the year of his death, in 1643. By Louis XIV's time, the honorific almonerships no longer figure at all on the royal household lists, having probably disappeared altogether. Furthermore, in 1685 the king decided that in future none of the serving almonerships could be bought and sold, a decision allegedly prompted by the confession of an almoner to the king that he had only bought the office in order to become a bishop.

But that move did not empty the court of high-flying clergy, and whenever announcements of nominations about vacant benefices were made, large crowds of clergy were invariably in attendance. In addition to almoners, the court could also be home to stipendiary royal preachers who sometimes went on to higher positions, especially in the episcopate, but as some of them were regulars or from modest backgrounds, we should not assume that the power of the word alone was capable of making them truly part of the upper clergy before episcopal office beckoned. The same might be said of another category of court clergy. Preceptors, tutors and 'readers' to royal children were often clerics, a few of whom, like Bossuet and Fénelon, went on to enjoy illustrious careers, while lesser-known figures were most commonly rewarded with church benefices including the bishop's mitre.[23]

It would, however, be misleading to conclude that the growth of a court-centred upper clergy was driven by the opportunity and the desire to serve at court, where most of the daily services were actually conducted by the more menial 'chaplains' and *clercs d'office* (as they were in the cathedrals and *collégiales*). What mattered far more, especially to those holding honorific positions, was the expansion of royal church patronage to embrace not just bishoprics, but also the far larger constituency of abbeys and priories belonging to the old male monastic orders. We shall examine the effects of this on the orders themselves later, but suffice it to say from the present vantage point that the expansion of the *commende*, as it was called, did more than anything else to give the terms 'court clergy' and 'upper clergy' real substance. Court offices were attractive primarily because they held out the real prospect for members of the secular clergy of obtaining abbeys or priories tenable *in commendam* and which were increasingly in the king's gift after the Concordat of Bologna.[24] Tenure, actual or prospective, of such benefices was the major common denominator among the upper clergy, one result of which was the increasing use of the title 'abbé' by clerics who might never have seen the inside of a monastery! Success in gaining such benefices bred the expectation among those concerned that further largesse might follow – a better abbey, or more abbeys – and perhaps also a bishopric, if the circumstances were favourable. And of course the substantial revenues they derived from accumulating such benefices enabled their holders to lead the life of a courtier-abbé, but also of a scholar or man of letters without needing to seek official positions in the church or elsewhere. We find many of these figures frequenting the law and theology faculties of seventeenth-century universities. Under Louis XIV nominations to these benefices and to bishoprics were made and announced simultaneously.

Not all of this upper clergy saw an episcopal career as a necessary culmination of their ambitions, as many had no desire at all to take on the increasingly onerous responsibilities that it entailed. An unknowable number of these figures actually declined bishoprics when they were offered them; some did so provisionally, because they wanted a better diocese, but this did not always materialise later. Beyond that there was the fact that many dioceses throughout France, and particularly in the south, were undesirable in the eyes of clergy comfortably ensconced at court or in Paris, with the result that a varying proportion of bishops in every generation were 'outsiders' chosen, as suggested earlier, from beyond the court-based upper clergy. Nor did bishops cease to belong to this 'generic' upper clergy on taking up office, 'exiling' themselves to sometimes distant dioceses; on the contrary, two-way movement was constant and considerable. Some bishops continued to engage in court activities – as more 'senior' almoners, preceptors, preachers, advisers, councillors of state and so on. In France, abbeys held *in commendam* did not have to be surrendered on receipt of a diocese, and bishops continued to solicit further royal largesse throughout their subsequent careers; as the seventeenth century wore on, they were probably the major beneficiaries of this fund of royal church patronage. Bishops seeking to retire often secured an abbey *in commendam* as a pension in return for giving up their see.

This upper clergy differed from the remainder of the First Estate in significant ways, apart from the obvious ones of birth and family connections. Unlike the parish clergy, especially rural, and the canons of chapters, most of whom were natives of the places in which they served, they were the least local and the most 'mobile' element of the clergy. The loss of episcopal election rights by cathedral chapters and the gradual emergence of the *commende* meant that their ambitions could no longer be fulfilled within local contexts or by local patronage: these might still play a part in their careers, but only as part of a wider world of connection and influence. These clerics were also by far the most likely to have been educated in the bigger university cities like Toulouse, Aix, Bourges and, of course, Paris. The best-connected and most successful of them remained 'free-floating' for most of their careers, willing to accept benefices or positions as cathedral canons and 'dignitaries' (often regarded by them as sinecures not requiring residence) or as abbots *in commendam* in parts of France to which they had no prior attachments.

Furthermore, as the seventeenth century progressed, bishops increased the size of their own personal and administrative entourages, in which members of this high-flying non-episcopal clergy could find a place. That the latter were willing to do so may well have been a response to the decline in the number of court offices available to them and a realisation, notably in the latter years of Louis XIV's reign, that a number of years of activity, especially as a vicar-general in the service of a reigning bishop, was increasingly desirable as a qualification for entry to the episcopate itself.[25] Where previously *abbés de cour* would have waited for their turn at court, many now joined the curias of bishops, especially those known to have good connections to the court and the ministry. Powerful, influential bishops could 'talk up', especially in correspondence with the royal confessors and ministers, the qualities of particular clerics in their service, and in some cases could engineer their election either as deputies to assemblies of clergy or, more decisively, as 'general agents of the clergy', which by the later seventeenth century virtually guaranteed episcopal preferment at the end of the five-year term of office. Thus, despite the differing ambitions of many of these clerics, by the early eighteenth century the evidence is of an increasingly integrated and 'fluid' upper clergy of possibly no more than 1,000 individuals who together constituted the apex of the secular clergy.

CHAPTER 4

THE MONASTIC ORDERS: ADJUSTMENT AND SURVIVAL

Introduction

It would not be exaggerating to employ the expression coined around the year 1000, 'the white mantle of the churches', to describe the presence of the religious orders within France, so heavily dotted was the landscape with old and new, male and female religious orders. It was in France, after all, that many of the greatest of them had been founded and where they developed with remarkable vigour over the centuries. And with the Catholic Reformation, the latest and perhaps the most intensive round of foundations ever began, adding new 'religions' – as religious orders were commonly described since the Middle Ages – to the existing ones, which by way of response often found themselves regrouping, reforming and sometimes expanding in new formations.

If the sheer scale of the presence of the regulars in France, in both town and country, is difficult to convey as a whole, it is largely because of the considerable plasticity of the successive forms which that presence possessed, which can lead historians of the *ancien régime* church to underestimate them. Precisely because of the kind of communities they formed, the regular clergy were infinitely more visible, even in towns, than their far more numerous secular counterparts. Not the least of the many differences between the secular and regular clergy was the presence among the regulars of women in large numbers, in whose history the seventeenth century occupies a highly distinctive place. It was not the old monastic orders but rather the mendicant and newer orders, especially female, which accounted for the spectacular surge in the number of regulars throughout France, which amounted by around 1750 to approximately 30,000 male and 55,000 female members. Such figures, however approximate they may be, underline the scale of the regulars' presence in France.[1] An historical analysis of the orders in our period has to focus mainly on innovation and movement rather than describe a 'mature' structure represented by the orders of pre-revolutionary France. Yet innovation needs to be understood with a longer history and traditions, of which the orders themselves were always acutely conscious. While touching on the specific characteristics of individual orders, this chapter will also suggest some comparative perspectives on their development over time.

The monastic orders, which constituted the historical bedrock of the religious orders, had as their common source the Rule of St Benedict and the tradition that it inspired during the early medieval centuries. A parallel movement produced the Augustinian canons-regular who observed the much less fully developed 'Rule' of St Augustine. The Benedictine tradition emphasised separation from the world outside the monastery walls, silence, contemplation and communal living (dormitory, refectory, study), as well as manual labour. Its monks took the three vows of religion (personal poverty, chastity and obedience to their superiors) and expected to remain attached for life to the monastery in which they had taken their profession (the key notion of monastic 'stability', which the mendicant orders would largely abandon later). Yet the size of these monastic communities made it inherently difficult for them to shut themselves away like hermits, especially because, over time, they came to possess substantial endowments – lands, lordships, buildings and so on – which made them major economic, social and even political forces in their localities.

The Benedictine tradition shared another feature with the Augustinian canons-regular, namely that of being more concerned with 'observance' than with governance. It readily allowed individual monastic houses to be governed independently by their own abbot or prior, without having to belong to a bigger, organised structure: it was the rule that communities lived by which determined their monastic affiliation. In due course, internal 'revivalist' movements appeared in their ranks, often intent on reforming the existing observance which they judged to have 'lapsed' from its primitive purity. To achieve their objectives, they invariably banded individual monasteries together into 'orders' or 'congregations' characterised by a hierarchical governing structure, with an abbot- or superior-general, central office-holders, a regular general chapter and so on – structures which could also be at least partly replicated within the constituent 'provinces' of the congregations in question. Over time, these new formations developed their own 'constitutions' and interpretations of the Benedictine or Augustinian rule, which gradually set them off from other groupings elsewhere, or of later foundation. The most classic instance of this was Cluny, in Burgundy, which was strictly speaking a Benedictine congregation rather than a separate order, but Cluny may also serve as a crude approximation of similar developments within other religious orders, monastic and non-monastic alike, over the following centuries. The Cistercians, 'white' monks in contrast to the Benedictine 'black' monks, themselves broke away from Cluny, because they found it had lapsed from its initial austerity, which they tried to recover by founding new monasteries remote from existing centres of population. In due course, subgroups with similar reformist intentions formed within the Cistercian 'family', all of them striving for, or even obtaining, a substantial measure of autonomous self-rule from the original order in the pursuit of their objectives. This concomitant process of reform and internal fragmentation across several orders, both monastic and mendicant, giving rise to successive 'strict' or 'reformed' observances and the congregations that brought them together, had not finished by the seventeenth century.[2] On the contrary, it was to be expected that the church in a century as fixated as the seventeenth on a bygone golden age of Christianity should wish to recreate earlier monastic austerity and purity of observance, but equally that views might differ sharply on what constituted the essential core of true observance – perpetual silence, complete abstinence from eating meat, strict enclosure, avoidance of book learning, to mention just a few among the monastic orders. Thus clashes between different types of observance – 'primitive', 'strict', 'mitigated' and 'common', to use the vocabulary of the day – became part and parcel of their history. Differences of emphasis and disputes over such questions could be all the more vehement and protracted because those involved in them could agree on so much else, as in the long-running dispute under Louis XIV between Abbot Rancé of La Trappe and the reformed Benedictine Jean Mabillon over whether monks could devote themselves to scholarship or should avoid learning altogether. There was scarcely a religious order, monastic or otherwise, which did not experience some or all of these phenomena.

Table 4.1 – Old monastic orders

Benedictines	**Cistercians**	**Augustinian canons-regular**
Cluny (910)	Feuillants (1577)	Saint-Ruf (1039)
Celestines (1240)	Strict Observance (1618)	Val des Ecoliers (1200)
Chezal-Benoit (1479)	La Trappe (1664)	Prémontré (1121)
The Exempts (1580)		Saint-Victor (1503)
Société de Bretagne (1603)		Congrégation de France (1624)
Saint-Denis (1607)		Notre Sauveur (1622)
Saint-Vanne (1604)		Chancelade (1622)
Saint-Maur (1618)		

One result of these complex long-term developments is often a rather confused picture of the place of the monastic orders within the seventeenth-century French church. Table 4.1 provides a limited snapshot of the principal monastic orders (as well as the Augustinian canons-regular) and their subdivisions, especially the new ones appearing during our period. As already noted, the Benedictines and the Augustinian canons were 'generic' orders based on an original rule rather than structured organisations, so it is no surprise that they spawned more congregations than the Cistercian order, which from its inception had a centralised – or at least federal – structure. Some of the congregations listed here were purely regional or provincial in their extension – as will be obvious with the Benedictine 'Société de Bretagne', but it was also true of the Exempts (mainly southern France), Saint-Denis (the Paris area), Saint-Vanne (Lorraine) or the canons-regular of Saint-Ruf (Dauphiné), Notre Sauveur (Lorraine) or Chancelade (south-west). Some of them were relatively ephemeral and small in scale (Exempts, Saint-Denis, Société de Bretagne), so that when they had run out of steam or lost control over their individual member houses, they found themselves being absorbed by more recent reform movements, though in some cases a fierce battle to protect their autonomy and privileges proved successful (the Augustinian Exempts, Saint-Victor). Among the Cistercians, the relatively small reformed 'Strict Observance' failed in its initial ambition of taking control of, and reforming, the entire order; but it enjoyed a generation of precarious autonomy from the 1620s onwards until it was reabsorbed into the main body of the order during the 1660s; even then, however, its particular features were recognised and accepted by the much bigger 'Common Observance'. Among the Augustinian canons-regular, most of whose houses remained self-governing into our period, a series of relatively small congregations had already appeared, while seventeenth-century efforts at reforming them inevitably produced new ones, since a congregational structure was by now regarded as indispensable, not merely to build and extend reform but, above all, to preserve it into later generations.

Of the smaller, more marginal monastic 'families' not listed above, the best known were the Carthusians, whose motto *numquam reformata quia nunquam deformata* ('never reformed because never deformed') echoes their reputation for consistent observance across the centuries. The order's continuing vitality derived largely from the unique way in which it combined the eremitical and the conventual traditions of monasticism. Another reason was that because it did not have abbots like the other monastic orders, it escaped the manifold effects of the *commende* (see below). It added seven new foundations during the seventeenth century to the sixty or so that it already possessed a century previously. Such a numerical increase was tiny compared to the expansion of the newer orders, but it contrasts with the stasis or even decline in the numbers of truly active communities among other monastic orders. It is easy to think of the Carthusians as living in remote rural sites like the Grande Chartreuse near Grenoble, but even in the mid-eighteenth century, their most populous communities were located in France's larger cities. Some of these houses, like Vauvert in Paris or that of Avignon, enjoyed exceptional local influence, acting as magnets for those in search of retreat, contemplation and a deeper spiritual teaching.

The *Commende* and its Impact

One major development within the monastic orders, occurring mainly in the century after the Concordat of Bologna (1516) and deeply affecting their relations with the society and church around them, was what contemporaries referred to simply as the *commende*. It was confined to the male monastic orders (apart from the Carthusians, as noted above) and did not spread to either the mendicants or female monasteries, old or new. Its growth, relatively rapid and extensive in scale, also set off France from much of the rest of Catholic Europe, where the practice either did not exist or was much more limited. For these reasons alone it merits attention here.[3] Essentially, it was a mechanism that allowed clerics who were not members of the religious orders in question to become titular abbots or priors of monastic houses, thereby circumventing one of the basic rules of classic church law, namely that 'regular' benefices should be reserved for 'regulars'. Separating title and function at the head of monastic houses, it also meant there was nothing to prevent the accumulation of several such benefices in one pair of hands; being an abbot or prior *in commendam*, to use the technical term, did not require residence, let alone the exercise of the normal powers of the superior of a monastic community. The latter were henceforth confided to a prior who was a member of the monastery in question. But the *commendataires*, as they were usually called, continued to enjoy important patronage rights over subordinate houses, where they existed, and crucially, the right to a substantial share of the monastic revenues. In theory, the abbot's share (his *mense*) should have been limited to one-third of the revenues, with a second third going to the monastic community itself, and the final one reserved for upkeep and repair of the material fabric, alms and so on. But in practice this tripartite division was not always observed, and other subdivisions were possible. It took a very long time for the French monastic system to adjust to the expansion of the *commende*, which was still in train in the early seventeenth century, and to define its exact scope.

The *commende*, originally devised by the papacy to enable cardinals to meet their expenses, has been heavily criticised for allowing a class of absentee and parasitic 'abbots' and 'priors' of court-aristocratic origin to plunder a whole sector of the French church by taking advantage of the monarchy's insatiable patronage needs, especially during the wars of religion. Certainly, the best-known beneficiaries of the practice were the great aristocratic families, royal favourites, ministers and major courtiers – categories which often overlapped significantly. The Guises, Joyeuses and Epernon-La Valettes were followed in due course by cardinals like Richelieu, Mazarin and Dubois. Viewed in broad social terms, the crown's use of the *commende* made the nobility, and especially 'outsider' rather than local nobility, masters of the monastic orders in which they had not previously figured at all prominently; and their mastery was facilitated by the toleration, by both the crown and the papacy, of the practice of 'resigning' these benefices to designated successors – usually family members of the younger generation.

The *commende* also had a broader impact on the status of the monastic orders within the wider French church. In the narrow sense of imposing outsider 'secular' clergy as abbots and priors, it secularised the monastic orders subjected to it. The *commendataires*' powers of intervention in strictly monastic affairs may have been limited, but their very existence tended to diminish the place of the old orders within the wider French church. Outside the monasteries exempt from the *commende* or belonging to the reformed congregations – about one-eighth of all French monasteries – there were henceforth relatively few opportunities for monks to emerge as important church figures, as they had in the past in France, and as they continued to do in Spain, Italy and the Holy Roman Empire during the early modern period. The roles they might have played, for example, in sessions of provincial estates were now taken by secular clerics intent on making their own way in the French church. The monastic orders were not even represented in the regular assemblies of France's clergy, which provided a platform for many an able cleric. By the same token, it is hardly surprising that the numbers of monks entering the episcopate shrank dramatically during the seventeenth century and had virtually dried up by Louis XV's reign, while it was only exceptional figures like Rancé or Mabillon – both, significantly, members of a reformed congregation – who exercised wide-ranging personal influence without holding high church office. The *commende*, where it held sway, largely confined monks and monasteries within a secondary, local role.

The expansion of the *commende* had a further unintended consequence whose importance only emerged gradually during our period. With a substantial proportion of monastic revenues being siphoned off into the pockets of secular clergy, the idea that institutions rather than merely individual clerics might benefit from it also began to take shape. Some of its earliest manifestations were connected to projects sponsored by the monarchy itself as, for example, when Henri IV endowed the new royal college of La Flèche, to be run by the Jesuits, with the revenues of monastic benefices in 1608. Louis XIII and Louis XIV imitated his example for similar royal projects – the famous nobles-only convent of Saint-Cyr, to which Louis XIV granted the huge revenues attached to the title of abbot of Saint-Denis, the richest benefice in France, being the best-known instance. Such 'incorporations' of monastic benefices could encounter stiff opposition, but once it had been demonstrated that they could be reassigned in this way, there was nothing to stop petitions for causes unconnected with royal policy to be supported by such means. For all the church's endowment with property, it was widely accepted that many bishoprics, but also the colleges, seminaries and general hospitals, to name but a few, which appeared under the early Bourbons, were seriously under-resourced and therefore unable to function properly, while the chances of increasing their resources from clerical taxation, royal largesse or private benefactions were decidedly limited. Initially, the simplest solution appeared to be to assign pensions payable out of monastic revenues to individual clerics associated with the 'good works' in question. But the drawback of that arrangement was that as it was purely ad hominem; it would automatically lapse when the individual died. The real innovation would be to assign in perpetuity all or part of an abbey or priory's revenues, especially where it no longer housed a monastic community, to a bishopric, college or hospital – an institutional rather than a personal arrangement. The new dioceses created under Louis XIV – Blois and Alès – were endowed exclusively by such means, for which there were precedents from earlier centuries.[4] A single example may suffice to illustrate the shift occurring in the seventeenth century. The abbey of Saint-Cyran, famous for having as abbots *in commendam* between 1620 and 1678 the Jansenists Jean Duvergier de Hauranne and his nephew Martin de Barcos, ceased to be an independent institution altogether in 1712, when the abbot's *mense* was incorporated into the under-endowed bishopric of Nevers, while the monks' *mense* (there were no monks at Saint-Cyran by then!) was assigned to the Jesuit college of Nevers, a far from unique example of new orders benefiting from the problems of their predecessors. Interestingly, as heir to the prerogatives of the abbot of Saint-Cyran, the bishop of Nevers acquired the presentation rights to ten parishes within the diocese of Bourges – a revealing instance of how patronage rights over parishes within the French church could become fragmented.[5] The Saint-Cyran-Nevers transfer was preceded by many others of its kind under Louis XIV, and in 1712 it seems to have elicited few objections. It seems that for many colleges, seminaries and general hospitals the permanent acquisition of monastic revenues became a standing aspiration. The proportion of France's monastic wealth redeployed for such purposes during the seventeenth century was probably quite modest, because it was done on an ad hoc basis, and bore no comparison to the redistribution attempted by the more ambitious Commission of the Regulars in the 1760s.

The *commende* had several other effects, one of which is of particular relevance to what follows. In ways that differed from one monastery to another, it regulated the size of monastic communities. Regardless of how it was arrived at, the division of monastic revenues between secular abbots and monastic communities nearly always entailed specifying the number of monks to be catered for, especially where the abbot agreed to pay them individual pensions from the abbey's revenues; even agreements made to turn over an abbey to one of the new reformed congregations usually contained a similar clause establishing a *numerus clausus*. Only those monasteries which escaped from the *commende* altogether, such as La Trappe, had the freedom to increase the number of monks they were prepared to accept within their walls. A major consequence of the *commende* was to reduce – or at least set a ceiling on – the number of monks across France's old orders, so that a substantial increase in its monastic population was highly unlikely without the foundation of new houses.

With only a minority – possibly one in eight – of monastic abbeys exempt from the *commende*, it has been relatively easy to blame it for the limited contribution of the old orders to religious renewal in the seventeenth century. The accusation assumes that abbots and priors *in commendam* would respond to reform in a purely self-interested, 'bottom-line' manner. No doubt many did so, but it is equally clear that many of them supported the reform of 'their' monasteries, some in a limited 'permissive' way, others in a frankly enthusiastic manner, even to the extent of taking the initiative at key junctures. As the seventeenth century wore on, *commendataires* were increasingly more than mere *fils de famille*: a sizeable proportion of them were bishops, vicars-general, royal almoners and the like, who participated in the affairs of the French church in other capacities, and who were thus in a position to push for reform within their monasteries. The fact that they were 'outsiders' with wider connections across the French church was actually an advantage, since it enabled them to attract the interest of the reforming congregations in a way in which 'regular' abbots – and especially very local abbots – might have been unable to do, and then to maintain the pressure for reform until a 'concordat' paving the way for change was agreed.[6]

The *commende* and its beneficiaries were not the sole obstacle to the reform of the monastic orders after the religious wars. Existing monastic communities across France were just as likely to reject it without any lead from above; they were also capable of doing so *despite* a favourable response to reform from the *commendataire* himself. When questioned if they would accept a reformed observance, individual monks were inclined to reply in the negative, arguing they could not be required to embrace an observance which did not exist at the time they took their original vows! At best, this stance might lead them to consent to an external reformed group of monks entering their monastery and enjoying a monopoly of recruiting future members. In that event, the unreformed 'old' monks, the *anciens*, would usually agree to withdraw from the main cloister buildings and accept individual life-pensions payable by the new community, enabling them to live out the rest of their days within the general monastic precincts; for some, reform was an opportunity to seek refuge in parishes in the gift of their monastery. This approach, which was used mainly for self-governing monasteries, ultimately led to reform 'by contract'; but the negotiations could be protracted and uncertain, given the number of parties involved (the abbot *in commendam*, the local bishop as well as the 'old' and 'new' monks themselves), all of whose consent was needed for the formal agreement to be signed and ratified by a *parlement* or the royal *grand conseil*, since legal appeals against the proposed changes were always a serious prospect. A major consequence of this approach was that 'double' communities were the order of the day in many monasteries for a generation until the *anciens* died out and the successor community gained full control of the house and its affairs. Friction between two communities living in close proximity to each other was hard to avoid, but seems to have been reasonably contained.[7]

Reform by contract hardly seems a heroic 'way of proceeding'. Yet despite its piecemeal character, it was ultimately more successful than the more familiar alternative, namely the imposition from above of a reformed observance and the dispersal to other houses of those unwilling to adopt it, so as to enable new communities to take control of individual houses from the outset. This solution tended to be tried within those orders, such as Cluny or Cîteaux, which possessed the hierarchical authority structures that autonomous houses lacked. But such an authoritarian approach could create more problems than it solved: the dispersed often became troublemakers in their new places of residence, where they were either unwelcome or unwilling to settle; they were also inclined to bide their time and hope that changed circumstances would eventually allow them to return to their house of origin. Their strongest complaint was usually that reformers arbitrarily flouted the key tradition of monastic 'stability', which guaranteed monks a permanent place in the monastery in which they took their vows. Given the mainly local nature of so much monastic recruitment, such accusations were likely to win sympathy within localities, and especially from families whose offspring belonged to the monastic communities in question. Even reform by negotiation and contract could be disliked on these grounds, since the reforming congregations usually insisted on new recruits being sent to 'central' novitiates elsewhere and, once they had taken their vows, that they accept being moved about from house to house as their superiors judged best.[8] This policy, which the reformed congregations borrowed from the mendicant orders, represented a limited 'modernisation' of monastic practices that were not always welcome among the old orders.

Recovery and Reform

The havoc wreaked by the wars of religion on the monasteries of the old orders, especially those located in vulnerable rural areas, meant that large numbers of them were either completely empty or had tiny populations by the early seventeenth century. It was precisely for these reasons that it became possible, as we have just seen, to consider assigning their revenues to other, more deserving church institutions. The physical restoration of damaged monasteries after the religious wars was hampered not so much by the *commende* but by the fact that so many of them were really under the control of laymen who used straw men to disguise the situation. This would only begin to change during the ministry of Richelieu who made serious efforts to appoint *commendataires* with an interest in reform. In some regions that were heavily exposed to military conflicts from Richelieu to Louis XIV, especially in eastern France, monastic houses remained vulnerable to depredation for far longer.

It would be naïve to suppose that the standards of monastic observance were not seriously affected by all this. Where communities of monks survived at all, individual monks often lived in private quarters of their own, drawing a personal pension from the monastery's revenues, while some even returned to their families when the damage to the monastic fabric was extreme. Clearly, such consequences made normal communal observance impossible, so that restoring it to even minimum levels was no mean achievement. That in turn presupposed, among other things, the renovation of the material fabric of the monastery, the recovery of alienated or usurped lands and a modicum of internal reorganisation. One reason why the precise scale of the recovery of French monasticism in the long seventeenth century is so hard to measure is that we have no idea of the monastic population around 1560 or 1600. But, as noted already, with the pervasiveness of the *commende* among male monastic orders working to restrict the numbers of monks, a substantial increase in numbers following 1560 and before the religious wars began seems highly unlikely. The recovery of church revenues during the seventeenth century would have been enough to sustain a rise in their numbers, and it may well explain why it was temporarily possible to envisage having two communities – one reformed, the other not – living off the same monastic revenues as a result of introducing reform from outside. Contemporary travellers, especially from the latter years of Louis XIV's reign, contrasted the fine, often restored monastic buildings with the small number of monks living in them.

Yet the old orders did experience some stirring of reformist activity while the religious wars were still in progress, although achieving and sustaining momentum for reorganisation and reform proved increasingly difficult by the end of the wars.[9] The Council of Trent demanded that independent monastic houses band together in congregations, but in France progress was extremely slow. By contrast, such congregations did emerge along the peripheries of the kingdom, especially among the Benedictines and Augustinian canons-regular in Flanders, Alsace and Lorraine, which were to have a major impact on the growth of French Benedictine reform after 1600 – and long before these areas became French. Moreover, French royal legislation *did* incorporate Trent's injunction on congregations, with the result that from 1580 onwards congregations such as the Benedictine Exempts, based on the abbey of Marmoutier, began to take shape, followed in the 1600s, during Henri IV's reign, by the congregations of Saint-Denis and Brittany.

But as already noted, putting together a congregation did not necessarily entail reforming its member houses, as it could just as well serve to protect monastic privileges in the face of bishops or commendatory abbots. Among the early seventeenth-century Benedictines, it was the new Lorraine-based congregation of Saint-Vanne which was the real flagship of reform, and it soon spread into Spanish Franche-Comté as well as French Champagne and the Metz-Toul-Verdun region controlled by the French crown; individual monasteries elsewhere in France were reformed with its assistance between 1604 and 1616. But since any expansion into Gallican France by a foreign congregation like Saint-Vanne was fraught with political and jurisdictional problems, Saint-Vanne itself called for the establishment of a *separate* French congregation which would take up the challenge. This was the origin of the most famous of all the reformed congregations, that of Saint-Maur, launched in 1618 and given papal approval in 1621, and which subsequently adopted the great Parisian abbey of Saint-Germain-des-Prés as its head house (1631). Its expansion was rapid among the previously independent monasteries, while it quickly absorbed existing congregations like Saint-Denis, Brittany and Chezal-Benoît. In consequence, it rose from having about 40 member houses in 1630 to 100 by 1650, 180 by 1680 and 193 by the end of Louis XIV's reign. The number of monks rose from a correspondingly modest 80 around 1620 to over 2,200 by 1700, with most of that increase occurring between 1620 and 1670. These figures, it may be noted in passing, also give us some idea of the average size of reformed monastic communities.[10] No other congregation from any of the old orders could match such a record. Above all, institutional growth was accompanied by an unrivalled reputation in other spheres – the monastic, spiritual, and literary – which was at its height from the 1680s to the early eighteenth century, when the hostility of many of its members to the anti-Jansenist papal bull *Unigenitus* got them into trouble with church and state authorities, especially in the early years of Louis XV's reign.

Reform from Above and its Limitations

It would be wildly misleading to interpret the origin and success of the Maurists, who ended up by bringing together under one roof the majority of France's Benedictine monasteries outside of Cluny, as typical of the extent of, or approach to, reform within the monastic orders. The growth of Saint-Maur was anything but tranquil and inevitable, since for almost all of its first thirty years it was caught up, sometimes willingly but mostly reluctantly, in much grander schemes devised by senior churchmen and royal ministers for reforming and reorganising the entire Benedictine order, Cluny included, into a single entity. The creation of Saint-Maur in 1618 did nothing to diminish the belief, that had been growing steadily during the 1610s among some contemporaries, that progress towards reform was so slow that some kind of concerted action to force the pace of change was imperative. Indeed, within a year of Saint-Maur's foundation, the idea of a special commission to promote and direct the reform of the old orders, monastic and mendicant, won the support of senior church and political figures at the court of Louis XIII, and in 1622 the energetic but short-lived Pope Gregory XV accepted a strategy that the more cautious Paul V had firmly rejected. In March 1622 a papal commission, timed to run for six years, to reform the monastic orders only – essentially the Benedictines (Cluny included), Cistercians and the Augustinian canons-regular – was issued to Cardinal François de la Rochefoucauld, then nominal president of the king's council and grand almoner of France, a man with limited political ambitions and skills, but with long experience as a reforming bishop. The crown strongly backed his commission, providing him with the legal and institutional support that would enable him to proceed with what was a staggeringly ambitious task. In undertaking his commission, he drew on the advice of senior church figures, influential members of the religious orders (including the Jesuits, to whom he was personally close), as well as a group of committed lay councillors of state and masters of requests. But it was also made clear from the outset by both crown and papacy that there was no chance that reform would involve rolling back the *commende* and returning to elected abbots. La Rochefoucauld was heir to a long royal tradition, of which we shall see more, of patronising and supporting the reform of the religious orders.[11]

It is unnecessary to follow here the story of the complex and often conflict-laden commission, which did not have the same consequences from one order to the next. Yet because the cardinal's objectives and methods were subsequently adopted in differing degrees by both Richelieu and Mazarin, even though neither of them was ever a papal-cum-royal commissioner like him, a few general points can be made in order to see how far they determined the fate of the monastic orders for over a generation. Having invested so much effort in establishing a full-blown commission for reform, it was unlikely that La Rochefoucauld and his supporters would be satisfied with merely nurturing or waiting for internal movements of reform to emerge within the orders. From the outset, they saw his task in a much more active light: that of structuring – or restructuring, in the case of Cluny and Cîteaux – the institutions of the orders in order to perpetuate as well as promote reformed observance. Although the proper observance might differ from order to order, there were some key common objectives. One was to restore full community life, beginning with the suppression of personal pensions and other privileges, which would enable the practice of the vow of poverty to be fully restored. It seemed no less vital to ensure that the recruitment and formation of new monks would no longer happen in individual monasteries, but in dedicated novitiates, after which the professed monks would be sent by their superiors to reside for variable periods of time in designated houses. Monasteries should no longer recruit whoever they pleased, while 'central' novitiates would ensure that a uniform observance would be the norm in the future. This was contentious enough, given how much it undermined the autonomy of individual houses and the 'stability' to which they were so attached. But plans for recasting the governance of the orders, notably that of superiors would be elected for only limited terms of office, produced the biggest shock, and therefore the biggest reaction. Orders like Cluny and Cîteaux had long experience of defending their autonomy and customs, and when changes were decided and imposed by outsiders their natural instinct was to become defensive and fight back in every way they could.

Within Cluny and Cîteaux, La Rochefoucauld's firmest supporters were the existing groups of reformers who saw his commission as a means of gaining control of the orders and reshaping them from above. As far as Cluny and the Benedictines were concerned, La Rochefoucauld could also call on the Maurists, while the Cistercian Strict Observance's members were champing at the bit to impose their version of reform. But in both cases, the reformist groups were both too small and isolated, and La Rochefoucauld's tactics only stiffened internal opposition to them. In both orders, his efforts ultimately played into the hands of Richelieu, who in 1629 and 1635 had himself elected abbot-general of Cluny and Cîteaux respectively. He played a more subtle game, as one might expect of him, but his objectives were ultimately not much different from La Rochefoucauld's. Not even Richelieu could work the miracles needed to reform these two giant orders by decree in such a short time. He proved even more ambitious than La Rochefoucauld by attempting to unite *all* of France's Benedictines, Cluny included, into a single body, with the Maurists as its engine. But when he died, his plans were almost immediately swept away, and Mazarin's half-hearted efforts to revive and modify them in the 1650s fared no better.[12]

Richelieu's ambition to see these great orders reformed cannot be doubted. Like La Rochefoucauld before him, he was not content to wait for and nurture reform, but tried to engineer it from above. In his case, papal commissions were dispensed with, and he preferred to use his considerable powers as both abbot-general and chief minister. While he lived, opponents were cowed, reduced to biding their time. After his death in late 1642, the mirage of a grand union of all France's Benedictines evaporated. It is, therefore, all the more remarkable that the Maurists emerged largely unscathed from the attempts to use them as the spearhead of reform and restructuring the entire Benedictine order. Their own caution about the project played a part in this, while La Rochefoucauld and Richelieu's support of reform may have, indirectly at least, helped them to continue their ad hoc absorption of both smaller congregations and autonomous houses into their ranks. By mid-century, their own congregational structures were working remarkably effectively, and they had the advantage of being led by some inspiring yet eminently practical superiors-general. There were, after all, more than enough independent Benedictine monasteries needing or seeking their assistance, so that not gaining – or not keeping – control of Cluny did not prove disastrous to the Maurists' fortunes after Richelieu. By the end of the century, their 190 houses actually outnumbered those of Cluny itself (which had eighty-five in all) by a factor of over two to one! It also seems that in terms of the average number of monks the Maurist communities outnumbered those of Cluny, and possibly by the same proportion.

In their efforts to reform the Cistercians, both La Rochefoucauld and Richelieu relied primarily on the nascent Strict Observance – or Abstinents – whose members were allowed to take over the abbey of Cîteaux itself after 1636.[13] The cardinal-minister's support enabled them to double the number of their houses from fifteen to thirty in six years. But they could not retain control of the order thereafter. Richelieu's death ushered in a generation of internecine warfare, replete with legal appeals, counter-appeals and successive royal council decrees concerning the validity of La Rochefoucauld's plans – which the Strict Observance still considered essential to successful reform. Finally, in

1666, the papacy worked out a modus vivendi for the rival parties, based on a common observance (with the exception of abstinence from meat for the Abstinents). It brought the Abstinents back inside the Cistercian institutional fold, while allowing them a large measure of self-government. The Strict Observance ended up with approximately one-third of all the populated Cistercian houses in France, totalling about 800 monks, by the next century.

It was among the Augustinian canons-regular that La Rochefoucauld had his biggest success, and that was largely because his approach here was radically different.[14] Their lack of an institutional structure with entrenched authority positions made his task easier in one respect, but it did mean that reform would be infinitely slower, since he had to proceed on a purely house-by-house basis. His initial intention was to create several reformed congregations across France, beginning with one based in Paris and its environs. But by the time that first congregation actually came into being in 1635, he had changed his mind, and it was therefore entitled the Congregation of France, whose seat was his own Parisian abbey of Sainte-Geneviève (hence the name Genovéfains by which its members were known). The congregation's title proved a misnomer in the longer term, as its geographical extension remained highly uneven. The early hope of building the new reform around the existing Paris-centred Congregation of Saint-Victor was quickly shattered by its flat refusal, both in 1623 and later, to be drafted into other's people's schemes. A mere five houses had been reformed by the time La Rochefoucauld's first commission ended in 1628, but the papacy and the crown continued to renew his powers until 1641, thereby sustaining the momentum of growth and, crucially, forming a new generation of reformed canons-regular capable of taking up the challenge of expanding the congregation of France from the 1640s onwards. By 1645, when La Rochefoucauld died, membership had risen to forty-five houses. That rate of growth was largely sustained until the early 1670s, by which time the membership had more than doubled again, and it reached a total of 106 houses by early the next century. The fact that only forty-six independent houses of canons-regular still existed in the 1760s gives some idea of the scale of this achievement. Sainte-Geneviève did not, however, carry all before it. It reformed only a scattering of houses in southern France, where the tiny congregation of Chancelade (six houses only), created by the famous bishop of Cahors, Alain de Solminihac (1593–1659), successfully defended its independence and made it difficult for the Paris-based congregation to interlope in the south-west. Older congregations in south-eastern France, like Saint-Ruf and Saint-Antoine-de-Viennois, were also beyond its reach, and survived until the mid-eighteenth century with scarcely any effort at renewal.[15]

By comparison with these enterprises, other monastic stirrings inevitably seem puny. From the late sixteenth century, the reformed Feuillants had broken away from the Cistercians and, with strong support from the monarchy, ploughed their own furrow, but even they were only comprised of twenty-eight monasteries by the middle of the seventeenth century.[16] A serious challenge to the Cistercians might have emerged in the age of Louis XIV had not the creator of the Trappist Reform, Abbot Rancé (1626–1700), flatly rejected gathering a reformed congregation around his Norman abbey of La Trappe. His career appositely illustrates many of the contradictions of the French church of his day. Scion of a ministerial family and a godson of Richelieu, he was an abbot *in commendam* at the age of eleven. But after an extended conversion experience in the early 1660s, he decided to become a professed monk of La Trappe in 1664, of which he was henceforth the 'regular' abbot. At this point, the Strict Observance appeared to be the only practical vehicle for his own ideals of monastic austerity and self-discipline, but after the 1666 compromise he decided to go it alone at La Trappe. The community there went from six monks in 1662 to ninety by 1700 – a hugely untypical achievement for its time. Cistercian monks from other monasteries came to La Trappe to experience its observance and take it back with them to their own houses, but Rancé refused all appeals to launch his own reformed congregation. His personal influence was immense, not just because of the impact of his published works and polemics, but also because through his extensive correspondence he acted as mentor and guide to an astonishing range of individuals, from kings and princes, cardinals and bishops downwards.[17]

Reforming the old monastic orders of France in a way that encompassed even the majority, not to mention the totality of their houses, was thus an extremely complex undertaking. It was so in part because these orders belonged to the benefice system in which the crown and the papacy had a major stake; so, too, did France's social elites and, therefore, to a large degree its ecclesiastical elites, given the ways in which royal patronage within these orders worked. For centuries, moreover, some of them, especially Cluny, Cîteaux and Prémontré, had also been of major political importance, since they were the head houses of great orders scattered throughout Europe. Both the crown and the orders in question strove to preserve their authority over foreign houses, although the growth of congregations among foreign houses had already weakened that authority by the early seventeenth century, while the attempts of a Richelieu or a Mazarin to take control of them inside France risked further alienating foreign houses on political grounds. At crucial junctures, these factors could determine both royal and papal support for one or other of the parties to reforms within France itself. Needless to say, the orders were also heavily embedded in the French legal system of appeal and counter-appeal which could effectively be used to neutralise those seeking to change them from inside. All of this made it hard to resist the temptation to engineer change from above – whether by a special commission like that of La Rochefoucauld, or by the intervention of a Richelieu figure combining political power and the role of abbot *in commendam* – when there seemed to be little evidence of internal renewal. But the danger was that by reorganising the orders in such a way as to give reformist minorities control of their institutions and future recruitment, they would alienate a majority that was not without allies, locally and 'nationally', and that was prepared to bide its time until the political situation changed. Only within the canons-regular, who for the most part had no such authority structures to begin with, was this danger largely avoided. The efforts at reform of the 1620s and 1630s were pushed hard by a generation who believed strongly in the necessity of a *general* reform of the orders rather than leaving it to grow organically at its own pace. Thereafter, such an approach only lived on as an aspiration within reformist groups like the Cistercian Strict Observance. The outcome was a partial but still substantial reform within all of the major orders in question, embodied in the new congregations that emerged during that crucial period.

In chronicling the successes and failures of the reformed congregations, it should not be forgotten that many monasteries preserved the Benedictine and Augustinian canons-regular tradition of individual self-government which they were loath to give up. Some had never known anything else, while others had joined a congregation at some point but later slipped out of its embrace as it lost control over the member houses. Bishops, whose office made them the natural higher authority over these self-governing houses, were often highly reluctant to see their powers as visitors and reformers taken away by outsider-reformed congregations. There is also some evidence of isolated reforms, which are by definition hard to detect, in some of these independent houses. Only local diocesan studies could establish whether the reform of the abbey of Fontgombault in Bourges diocese, conducted by its prior, was an exceptional event or not.[18] But such studies would probably not alter the fact that it was the reformed congregations which, once they had acquired a minimum of critical mass, became the most attractive options for many independent houses which could see their future secured by joining their ranks. It was this prospect which enabled the congregations to continue expanding until well into the reign of Louis XIV.

Scholars, Educators and Pastors

The age-old tension between monasteries' withdrawal from 'the world' in order to expiate sins by prayer and penance, and the many other roles that they accumulated over time, was revived by the post-Tridentine church's efforts to impose rigorous enclosure on them. In theory, that should have reduced their visibility and activities within the communities that lived around them. Of course, as in the past, the more holy and austere, even remote, individual monastic communities became – like La Trappe, Port Royal des Champs or the Carthusians – the more they were likely to be sought out by the world beyond their walls. But only a tiny number of French monasteries were ready to embrace absolute withdrawal, while the austerity and separation adopted by even reputable reformed groupings like Saint-Maur was 'reasonable' and moderate. So although enclosure might make interaction with local populations more regulated and indirect, people still came to worship in monastic churches, took retreats in them, sought spiritual instruction and guidance from their members and so on. Even where the orders did not directly take part in the running of parishes, their members would participate in parish life in other ways, such as by preaching Advent and Lent sermons. To some extent, the capacity of the old monastic orders to meet expectations, whether strictly monastic or more broadly social and pastoral, depended on their finances, which in turn determined the material fabric of individual monasteries. For any kind of reformed observance to function, it needed full conventual facilities and buildings, and that meant that the reformed communities were the most likely to build, or rebuild, the essential elements of a monastic compound. Given the post-Tridentine emphasis on enclosure, this could mean extensive remodelling of individual sites, even where they had not been extensively damaged by war. It would be misleading to judge this process from the telescoped evidence of surviving buildings and their (mostly) eighteenth-century date and style. During the preceding century, it is likely that physical restoration and rebuilding was erratic enough, given the limited revenues of the individual communities due to the *commende*, and to the need during the early decades of reform to pay life-pensions to the unreformed *anciens*. Strapped for cash, most reformed communities were correspondingly slow to embark on projects extending beyond their immediate needs. In the case of the Maurists, it was only late into Louis XIV's reign and beyond that they had both the means and the experience to redesign and rebuild what were in some respects new monasteries. Reformed congregations such as the Maurists were also far more likely to scrutinise carefully the needs of their individual member houses and to supervise building work itself; in so doing, they may even have encouraged the spread of particular architectural styles to places which would not otherwise have adopted them.[19]

The revival of monastic learning was something which the majority of reform movements felt the need to promote. The founder of Saint-Vanne, Didier de la Cour, famously declared that 'an unlearned Benedictine is a thing that cannot be defined'. The Maurists whom he inspired seem to have taken his point almost literally, and from very early in their history they made provision for scholarly work, mainly in patristics, liturgy and history, as part of the monastic regime, thereby laying foundations for the achievements of Mabillon, Montfaucon and others under Louis XIV. Saint-Germain-des-Prés, with its great library, became one of Europe's most active centres of learning.[20] The canons-regular of the Congregation of France and Prémontré also engaged in scholarly activities, albeit with less spectacular results. It is not hard to see why these congregations were capable of such efforts: the Genovéfains, stipulated seven years of study for their members after completing their rhetoric course, thereby ensuring a solid grounding in philosophy (two years) and theology (three years). Unlike the Maurists, it seems that the activities of Sainte-Geneviève were limited to Paris and never really became congregation-wide. The only authoritative dissenting voice here was Rancé, who famously challenged the Maurist philosophy of the learned monk and whose own far more austere reform at La Trappe in Normandy denied any place to monastic learning, on the grounds that it dissipated observance and opened the door to un-monastic worldliness and pride.[21] The heat generated by these controversies makes it easy to miss the extent to which the scholarship engaged in by congregations like Saint-Maur contributed directly to the key religious debates of their time. For example, the Maurists' great edition of St Augustine (1681–1700) was particularly contentious in an age when the Jansenist dispute was so divisive, and it was no accident that so many Maurists were – as, for obvious reasons, were the Augustinian canons-regular – highly sympathetic to the Augustinian–Jansenist camp then and later.[22] One of the major objectives of the Cistercian Strict Observance during the 1630s was to gain control of the college of Saint-Bernard, their order's house of study in Paris, in order to use it as a seminary, in the broad sense of a place of 'formation', which would produce new generations of monks with higher university degrees to their name. The Cistercians never rivalled the Maurists' scholarly achievements, but their members regularly took theology degrees in Paris and elsewhere. Some of their houses developed a reputation for scholarly pursuits, based on having good libraries, and one of them, Perseigne near Alençon, became Malebranche's favourite place of refuge and study.[23]

It is often forgotten that the reformed monastic orders did not just produce a handful of great scholars, but they sometimes opened and ran their own schools. The pressure for enclosure and the renewed emphasis on proper monastic observance did not exactly encourage such activity, of course, and the intense competition from the likes of the Jesuits, Oratorians and Doctrinaires further restricted it. Saint-Vanne was hostile to opening schools, but the Maurists took a less negative view from the 1630s onwards, supporting the foundation of 'seminaries' for young nobles, possibly in the hope of recruiting future monks from their ranks. Such seminaries were duly opened at Thiron and Pontlevoy in the 1640s, while the Genovéfains did the same in Senlis and Nanterre in the 1630s. Later still, the Maurists opened similar establishments at Sorèze and Saint-Germer, near Beauvais, in the 1680s. By the eighteenth century the Maurists had fifteen such institutions, which over time evolved into academies providing an education designed for young nobles destined for the court and the army rather than the church.[24] The Genovéfains remained closer to their original intentions. They organised *conférences ecclésiastiques* for the theological and pastoral instruction of clergy, including their own members, serving in parishes. They also responded to invitations from French bishops to run diocesan seminaries, especially during the key decades of the mid-century when seminaries were appearing across France. Such invitations sometimes grew out of their previous activities within the dioceses in question – preaching missions or retreats for ordinands being the most common. If, in the end, the Genovéfains only managed to direct a few seminaries, led by those of Reims and Meaux, it was partly because French bishops and clergy alike were not always comfortable in dealing with independent congregations of regulars, and because Sainte-Geneviève was not well served by its association with the theology of St Augustine, which to some meant being just too close to Jansenism.[25]

Scholarly and educational activities like these only reached a relatively small fraction of the social elite and clergy. The contemporary vision of what constituted a reformed observance was inherently unlikely to encourage monks or canons-regular to serve in the world beyond the cloister either in large numbers or on a regular basis. But, as we have already seen, France's abbeys controlled huge numbers of parishes which were in their patronage. One such example was the unremarkable Benedictine abbey of Déols, located in Bourges diocese, which in 1603 was *curé primitif* of 182 parishes, of which 103 were within Bourges itself, with the remainder scattered across those of Poitiers, Limoges, Tours, Nantes, Orléans and within Brittany.[26] Regardless of whether it experienced reform or not, Déols would not have been able to appoint monks to more than a handful of these parishes, so the appointment of secular priests as *vicaires perpetuels* was the only available solution. However, the Augustinian canons-regular, including those of Prémontré, traditionally had a strong attachment to pastoral activity, one that La Rochefoucauld's Congregation of France did not wish to abandon. One of the best-known *curés* of the entire seventeenth century, Christophe Sauvageon, was *curé* of Sennely-en-Sologne for thirty-four years from 1676 onwards. Yet the congregation's leaders fully shared the wariness of many reformers towards the tenure of parishes, because it guaranteed incumbents the kind of independence, financial and legal, that could be destructive of community observance. In order to square the circle, the congregation imposed a special vow on its members: they were required to promise that they would not seek a benefice without their superiors' explicit permission, and would undertake to surrender it when asked by them. Evidently, it was hoped that this vow, along with the emphasis on obedience generally within their observance, would eliminate the danger represented by service in parishes. To ensure compliance, the parochial patronage of individual monasteries joining the congregation was transferred to the superior-general at Sainte-Geneviève itself. At the height of its influence, the superior had in his gift some 800 parishes, some of them important urban parishes, and half of all the Genovéfains served in parishes as a matter of course by the eighteenth century.[27] Such an accumulation of patronage would have been well beyond the dreams of any French bishop, but also suggests how inadequately the stereotypes in the standard accounts convey the engagement of the old orders with the world of their time.

CHAPTER 5

FROM MENDICANTS TO CONGREGATIONS

With the overall membership of the monastic orders not rising markedly during the seventeenth century, the sharp rise in the numbers of male regulars must be credited to their 'mendicant' counterparts. This, too, is not surprising, given the scale and variety of the mendicants' historical presence in France, but it results above all from the continuing resourcefulness of the French church, especially in the period we are dealing with, in 'inventing' new types of religious communities which stretched the continuum of mendicant religious life well beyond what previous centuries had managed to do. At the 'new' end of the spectrum we find congregations, male and especially female, which, by eschewing nearly all of the rules and structures of the classic orders, were determined to remain 'seculars'. The paradox is that despite their rejection of 'regularity', they often kept elements of the orders' way of life which could make them behave in ways remarkably similar to the older orders in their relations with the wider church and society.

The contrasts between the monastic and the mendicant orders have always been more immediately visible than their common features. The very first of the mendicants, the Dominicans, did not appear until the early thirteenth century, a full century after the last of the great monastic orders, the Cistercians, had been founded. The mendicants foreswore the large establishments and material endowments characteristic of the monastics, and the most radical disciples of Francis of Assisi, *il poverello*, even preached absolute poverty, not merely on the part of individual Franciscans but by entire communities, whose members should, if necessary, beg – hence the epithet 'mendicant' attached to them – for their upkeep. The monastics were mainly but not exclusively anchored in rural society, while the invention of the mendicants coincided with the revival and growth of towns and cities, so much so that historians have seen their emergence as a direct response to the challenges of new, unfamiliar social formations. The mendicants also abandoned many features of traditional monastic observance in order to engage in an active apostolate in the towns, where they were soon busy preaching, teaching, administering the sacraments, and performing the other pastoral tasks which the secular clergy were mostly incapable of doing until well into the seventeenth century. From the outset, the mendicant orders were endowed with centralised governing structures; they preferred elected and temporary office-holders to life-tenure superiors; and they moved their members from house to house depending on needs and circumstances – all of which, as we have just seen, represented a significant departure from monastic practice.

This brief inventory of differences could be extended much further, but that would be to ignore the borrowings and cross-fertilisation between the monastics and mendicants over time. As noted in the previous chapter, seventeenth-century efforts at internal reform among the monastic orders seemed to demand the adoption of particular structures (such as congregations, elected superiors, central novitiates) and practices (for instance mobility of individuals rather than 'stability' within orders) that were largely inspired by the mendicants. Cardinal La Rochefoucauld's most influential advisers in his efforts to reform France's monasteries were themselves mendicants, especially from the newer orders. This at a time when yet newer orders were themselves pushing the existing conceptions of the regular life in unfamiliar directions! And the one-dimensional identification of the monastic orders with rural society and an agrarian economy also ignores the massive presence of monastic houses, especially female, within towns, something to which the sustained violence of the wars of religion gave further impetus. In view of the weight that historians have always attached to the reform of the French secular clergy in our period, it is all too easy to underestimate the extent to which the religious orders continued to develop and contributed hugely to the needs – pastoral, educational, charitable and many others – of French lay society. It is perhaps because the orders were so numerous and could differ so much that they have not been given their historiographical due. The present chapter aims, therefore, to identify who they were, and how or why they mattered. A diagrammatic presentation of the orders and their offshoots will serve as a (minimalist) point of departure, but beyond that some degree of selection is unavoidable, if only to avoid serving up an indigestible guidebook. For presentational purposes, the orders have been arranged under three headings here – old, new and secular congregations – but it will quickly become apparent that these are by no means watertight categories, which in itself is testimony to the creativity of the orders in question.

Medieval Heritages

Table 5.1 provides the simplest possible outline of the 'old' mendicant orders, even though some of their offshoots (such as the Capuchins and the Récollets) were new creations of the Catholic Reformation across Europe. Like their monastic counterparts, most of the mendicant orders belonged to a few major 'families', and had also been subject to the same internal pressures – revivalist, reformist, separatist – as Cluny or Cîteaux were across the centuries. The principal 'families' of old mendicant orders were the Dominicans, Franciscans, Augustinian hermits and the Carmelites. The first two merit fuller consideration later. What the table cannot effectively indicate is just how much the scale (numbers of houses and members) and internal development of the different orders varied. At the low end, there was the order of Grandmont, which consisted of just one abbey and fewer than fifty full members even after its reform in 1643! France's Servites, who were of Italian origin and whose most illustrious early modern member was Paolo Sarpi, were settled almost exclusively in Provence since the later fifteenth century, where they had seven houses and fewer than 100 members in 1692. The Augustinian hermits were typical of the evolution of many other orders. The original medieval creation, which still had about 110 houses scattered across France around 1690, had spawned a post-Trent offshoot, the Discalced Augustinians (nicknamed the 'little fathers') who, from their Italian beginnings, spread into France after 1596, mostly in Dauphiné and Provence, and finished with forty houses but possibly no more than 400–500 members by around 1700. As for the male Carmelites, their older medieval root engaged in a relatively successful internal reform in early seventeenth-century France, and by the century's end they had around 130 French houses, with nearly 2,000 members. Like their Augustinian

Table 5.1 – Old mendicant orders and their offshoots

Grandmont – Old and Strict Observance
Dominicans
Franciscans – Conventuals, Observants
Récollets
Capuchins
Third Order of St Francis
Augustinian Hermits (Grands Augustins)
Discalced Augustinians
Carmelites
Discalced Carmelites
Servites
Minims

counterparts, the Discalced Carmelites emerged in France from 1600 onwards, where their reputation as a reformed order of high spiritual attainment made them welcome, so that by the end of the century they had approximately sixty-two houses and around 1,200 members. But both branches were eclipsed by the reputation that attached to the *female* French Carmelites in our period.[1]

The Dominicans

Up to the Protestant Reformation, however, the big battalions of the French mendicants belonged essentially to two orders – the Dominicans and the Franciscans. Like many others, both of them had female branches, but their numbers were modest compared to the male houses and membership. Of the two, the Dominicans were the first to appear in France, having been created in Toulouse in 1215 in the aftermath of the Albigensian crusade. Nicknamed the Jacobins (because their Paris house was on the rue Saint-Jacques), their real title, the Order of Preachers, conveys their major activity, though academic teaching and study also became a distinguishing mark of Dominican activities. Organised into 'provinces' either side of the Loire, they had experienced several movements of internal reform before the Reformation when, partly because of their intellectual activities, many individual members joined the new religious movements. Reform efforts continued thereafter, with most of the initiative coming from the Midi, where Sebastien Michaelis (d.1618) played a key role in banding together a reformed observance which went on to win adherents in northern France, especially in Paris, by the early seventeenth century. The internal politics and the shifting affiliations of the order's individual houses before and after Michaelis's time are particularly difficult to follow, but they do not seem to have radically altered either the roles or the reputation of the order generally.[2] The Dominicans were not racked, as were the Franciscans, by acute differences over matters of observance, and appear to have been capable of agreeing on internal reforms that were not divisive. This 'reasonableness' may explain why, despite the number and geographical spread of their houses, the Dominicans enjoyed the kind of stability – 175 houses with approximately 1,500 members in the mid-eighteenth century – which makes them the most discreet and elusive of the mendicant orders of early modern France.

By the later sixteenth century the Dominicans lost much of the influence which had previously come from having one of their members as the royal confessor and, in the longer run and more intangibly, from the shift away from Augustinian-Thomist thinking in theology and ethics generally with which they were associated. It seems that it was their preaching, spiritual guidance and confessing, as well as the devotional confraternities they ran, that enabled them to retain or attract laypeople in towns, especially in southern France, where their tenacious defence of older theological positions during the Jansenist conflict endeared them to adversaries of the Jesuits. To some extent, the Dominicans were eclipsed, intellectually at least, not just by the Jesuits but by another mendicant order of much later provenance: the Minims. The Minims enjoyed considerable success in France, not least because they attracted royal patronage since their appearance there in 1483. With just thirty-eight houses in 1600, they experienced rapid expansion under Henri IV and his successors, claiming to have 112 houses in 1623 and 150 by 1673, a pattern which makes them as much a 'new' as an 'old' order. Although Minim houses were fewer and probably smaller in membership than the Dominicans, several of them were distinguished for their spiritual and intellectual activities. That of the Place Royale in Paris was associated with the *savant* Mersenne (1588–1648), and became a virtual academy where he received learned visitors and corresponded with scholars across Europe. Combining intellectualism, some of which was directed towards combating Protestantism, and real austerity, the Minims appealed to several 'constituencies' at once. The leading lights of the Catholic Reform in France, but also figures like Anne of Austria and Mazarin, held them in the highest esteem, which probably also explains why a number of their members became bishops in our period.[3]

Franciscans

Few orders in any age resembled the Franciscans, and few were so successful in terms of numbers and geographical extension, despite remaining highly susceptible to the subterranean workings of a unique radicalism deriving from their origins. The Dominicans endured no such turbulence as to their underlying *raison d'être* and fidelity to their founder's intentions. Less intellectual than the Preachers, the popular demotic ways of the Franciscans, the rough clothes (their French nickname of *Cordeliers* derived from the rough cord worn around the waist), the simple lifestyle and austerity, all won them widespread support and saw them spread rapidly. But from its early days the order was more beset than any other by internal dissensions, especially on the question of poverty, institutional as well as personal, so that reformist or breakaway groups – the mainstream of which became known as the 'Observants' – constantly called for a return to the founder's intentions and rejected the 'mitigated' conditions of subsequent generations. By the time they were divided by the papacy in 1517 into two separate orders all across Europe – the unreformed Conventuals and the reformed Observants – newer offshoots were on the verge of appearing and would soon establish themselves, sometimes as independent orders in their own right. Meanwhile, the great majority of the existing Franciscan houses in France opted to join the Observants, but without always embracing a genuinely reformed observance! By the middle of Louis XIV's reign, the Observants and Conventuals still had around 300 houses and 4,500 members.[4]

The least known of the 'new' Franciscans, the Récollets, originated among the observant movements in Spain and Italy, but were slow enough to settle within France, where they began as a congregation of the Strict Observance within the Franciscan Order, but in practice they enjoyed almost complete autonomy. By the time the Récollets' first French houses opened in 1583, a combination of the religious wars, opposition from the established Observants whom they aimed to reform, and intense competition from the equally new Capuchins restricted the scope for expansion and confined them mainly to the smaller towns. Nevertheless, despite the slow start and their failure to absorb or replace the Observants, the Récollets did make serious headway, especially in the first half of the seventeenth century; by the later seventeenth century they were second only to the Capuchins among France's mendicants, with a total of over 220 houses and 2,500 members scattered across eight 'provinces'. As well as absolute poverty and the familiar pastoral activities of the Franciscans, they added an intense spiritual life of retreat and withdrawal – the 'recollection' to which their nickname alludes. This record would have been hugely impressive by any standards, were it not eclipsed by their greatest rivals, the Capuchins.[5]

The emergence of the Capuchins as an emblematic Catholic Reformation order was not radically different to that of their Récollet confrères. For nearly a century, they too were an observant *ad fontes* movement within the wider Franciscan 'family', and it was only in 1619 that they finally became a fully independent order. They had already founded their first French houses in Paris and Lyon in 1578, and recruits and houses would increase rapidly for the next seventy or more years, not least in the larger towns and cities which competed to welcome them inside their walls.[6] From a mere 400 members in 1596, they had risen to 5,000 by 1643, divided into seven French 'provinces' and possibly 300 houses. That total would rise further to around 6,500 members by 1711 with some 411 houses by 1726, at which point the Capuchins accounted for half of all France's 'Franciscans'.[7] These figures also put them far ahead of any other order, old or new.

Along with, but even more than the Récollets, the Capuchins rediscovered the authentic strains of Franciscanism. The Capuchins were also the most 'popular' of the new religious orders, as evidenced by their clothes and their hood, the *capuchon*, yet the order was not initially as plebeian in its recruitment as is sometimes imagined. Paradoxically, as it might seem, it recruited strongly from among the old nobility, the 'robe' and the professions, and much less from the lower classes of town or country; it seems to have been only from the 1720s onwards, at least in their Lyon 'province', that more plebeian and rural recruitment became prominent. From its earliest years in France, it attracted individuals with famous names like Ange de Joyeuse, Brûlart de Sillery, Joseph Leclerc du Tremblay (Père Joseph) and Bochart de Champigny (Père Honoré de Paris), whose dramatic changes of career heightened the aura of heroic abnegation that surrounded the Capuchins. Their 'popularity' derived not from their social origins, but from their activities and lifestyle. They practised the Franciscan ideal of poverty more fully than any of the order's other offshoots, even though the austerity of the Récollets was not far behind. Both orders displayed genuine responsiveness to popular expectation. Their behaviour during plagues and other disasters, when they risked their lives and often died in considerable numbers, contrasted with the behaviour of most of the social and clerical elites of their time. Their preaching and 'pastoral' methods were designed to reassure and comfort rather than terrorise people, though 'fire and brimstone' sermons were undoubtedly preached, especially during times of missions, as devices to lead communities towards the sacraments.[8]

The effect of the success of the Récollets and Capuchins was to hugely reinforce the presence of the Franciscans throughout France, which is evidence of the willingness of urban and especially small town elites to find the means to support them, in return for their pastoral, liturgical and other services. By adding the Observants to the list, the total Franciscan population in France around 1700 would have been somewhere in the region of 12,000 – which in turn accounted for about one-third of all French male regulars, old and new. It should also be realised that the neither the Récollets nor the Capuchins, any more than the Dominicans, owed their success to having expanded the scope of traditional Franciscan activities: they did not become involved in opening colleges or schools, nor in running hospices, seminaries or charitable organisations. They were not, therefore, competing directly with the newer orders and congregations which we shall now turn to discuss.

The number of entirely new male religious orders taking shape during the reformation era and afterwards can easily be exaggerated. As we saw, the Récollets, Capuchins and Minims were hybrids, at least as 'old' as 'new', and so

Table 5.2 – New orders/congregations

Barnabites
Doctrinaires
Jesuits
St John of God

were the reformed branches of the Carmelites and the Augustinian Hermits. Of those orders that were genuinely new, some had a relatively confined impact within France. The Italian Barnabites, after their redefinition by Borromeo in Milan, were introduced into France by François de Sales, but although they attracted royal patronage, from Henri IV to Anne of Austria, they remained relatively discreet, working initially on crown-sponsored missions in Calvinist Béarn, but above all running schools, mainly in the south-west. The Brothers of St John of God, whom Marie de' Médici was instrumental in bringing to France in 1602, were of Spanish origin; their members were primarily lay brothers and they took a fourth vow to devote themselves to caring for the sick. Their numbers remained relatively small, and the world they worked in, that of hospitals, was, as we shall see later, increasingly dominated by female congregations.[9]

In many respects, only two of the new orders can be regarded as having a significant impact, although the differences between them remain enormous. The Doctrinaires (*recte* Fathers of the Christian Doctrine) were the only order to begin life on 'French' soil, albeit in the papal Comtat Venaissin near Avignon, in 1592. Their real inspiration was Italian (Borromeo, the Roman Oratory), and they spread across southern France, with Avignon and Toulouse as their key focal points, but they hardly made any advances above the Bordeaux–Gap line. The name 'Doctrinaires' suggests a pedagogical mission, and it refers not to study or teaching of academic theology but, more characteristically for the age, to the instruction and catechism of laypeople. But as happened with other orders or congregations, such activities almost inevitably led them into formal teaching, in the guise of secondary schools, as well as into clerical reform, in the guise of the running of seminaries. In both capacities, they were often the most serious competitors of the Jesuits across southern France. Finally, the Doctrinaires oscillated almost from the outset between being regulars with full vows to being a secular congregation with simple vows of the kind that we shall see presently.[10]

Jesuits

No such uncertainty beset their – and many others' – greatest rivals, the Jesuits.[11] Their history in France can hardly be summarised without serious risk of misrepresentation, and it does not help that, despite some recent scholarship, they remain little studied beyond the polemical frameworks inherited from their chequered history.[12] For all their origins in Montmartre, controversy clung to them in France from the beginning, and no good Gallican, Catholic or Protestant, could stomach what seemed to be their political allegiance (to Rome) or values (for instance the defence of regicide) – sentiments that would be shared by many of the secular clergy and the universities. As we shall see, they elicited further kinds of opposition in the seventeenth century.

Unusually for a new order, serious high-level opposition to their establishment in France emerged in the early 1560s, and their activities during the wars of religion created further division of opinion about them. When one of their former students attempted to murder Henri IV in 1594, the Paris *parlement* swooped immediately and ordered their banishment from its area of jurisdiction, which was subsequently extended to Burgundy and Normandy. But neither the southern *parlements* nor the newly converted Henri IV himself followed the *parlement*'s lead, so that the northern Jesuits could take refuge elsewhere in the country. Other orders, such as the Dominicans and the Feuillants, had been compromised by their conduct during the wars, but the readmission of the Jesuits to northern France was so hot a potato that it was not resolved for nearly a decade. Finally in 1603 and after many a diplomatic faux pas, the terms for their return were finally agreed. It would be excessive to say that the Jesuits jumped from pariahs to favourites as a result of this, but Henri IV (and by inheritance, his successors) played a very good hand in seizing the chance to bind the Jesuits to the crown as never before, and in making it clear to them how far their presence in France depended henceforth on absolute loyalty; for those who did not register that message immediately, the crisis following Henri IV's assassination, the Estates-General of 1614 and the Santarelli affair of 1626 made things crystal clear. As we saw, other orders such as the Récollets, Minims or Capuchins enjoyed royal favour in varying degrees, but the Jesuits took it all a step further, building upon the even more unexpected choice by successive monarchs to employ exclusively Jesuit confessors, whose role was a guarantee of the company's good behaviour.[13]

Once these terms had been set and tested, the Jesuits could return and recruit in force across the country. And France's elites, with some exceptions, were not slow to call upon their services, especially as educators in colleges and certain universities. The speed with which their colleges, old and new, opened after 1603 is remarkable enough, but even more so when account is taken of the competition from the Oratory, the Barnabites, the Doctrinaires and others. It is also evidence that the Jesuits' own recruitment levels were consistently adequate for the challenges they faced.[14] But the 'internal' history of the Jesuits, especially its social dimensions, remains largely unstudied. Subdivided into five provinces after 1616, France's Jesuits grew in numbers from approximately 1,400 to about twice that figure by the end of Louis XIV's reign; above all, their houses rose from 45 to 115 in the same period, though the bulk of that growth seems to have occurred up to 1650. If these figures place the Jesuits far behind the Franciscans, Capuchins and Récollets on both counts, their success was built on other foundations. Ninety-one of their 115 houses were colleges, and most of the rest were residences, novitiates or houses of study for Jesuits exclusively. But, as with the other 'teaching' orders of the day, it would be misleading to see these colleges as exclusively teaching institutions; each college fitted within a wider strategy, determined by the Jesuits' own hierarchy, which dictated its wider 'mission'. Both financial resources and the deployment of individual Jesuits could subtly modify the *raison d'être* of this or that house, so that preaching, parish missions, 'controversies' with Protestants, and so on could be expanded or contracted according to need or the talents of their members. Even if the Jesuits still had their critics, there were far more potential patrons and partners – bishops, the crown, towns – in search of their co-operation. By the mid-seventeenth century at the latest, they had left behind them the early years during which their patrons could largely determine what commitments they would undertake. Nowhere perhaps is this more evident than in what may seem like their surprising refusal for many decades to become involved in running seminaries, which they judged inferior to their own colleges. But once they had accepted the new showcase seminary in Strasbourg in 1683, under pressure from the one patron who could not be rebuffed, Louis XIV, the floodgates opened, enabling numerous French bishops worried about the orthodoxy of the Oratory, Sainte-Geneviève and the Doctrinaires to approach them with seminary direction in mind. It was, in fact, seminaries that accounted for most of the expansion of Jesuit houses in the decades either side of 1700, although the numbers involved in them were limited.[15]

Breaking the Mould

The emergence of new religious orders – or of observant, reformed branches of existing orders – during the Catholic Reformation was predictable enough. It is not to underestimate the distinctiveness of orders like the Jesuits to argue that the strongest claim to originality in our period belongs to the new 'secular' congregations which began appearing shortly after 1600, and some of

Table 5.3 – New congregations

Oratorians
Congregation of the Mission
Saint-Sulpice
Priests of Holy Sacrament
Eudists
Missions Étrangères de Paris
Community of St Joseph
Brothers of the Christian Schools

which were still starting up a century or so later. We have already seen that the Doctrinaires were as much a 'secular' as a 'regular' congregation. The brief survey of the main congregations that follows will also reveal some of the 'constitutional' problems that novelty produced and how they were resolved.

What is particularly interesting is the pattern that was set from early on by the founder of the first of these congregations, Pierre de Bérulle (1575–1628). After the experience of the Parisian Catholic League and its religious reverberations, Bérulle initially decided to enter the Jesuits as they seemed to offer the most satisfactory balance of action in, and withdrawal from, the world, but he left them after a brief spell, convinced that they did not have the answers that he was seeking. For all their activism, they remained essentially a religious order with their own internal priorities and activities. A decade later, in 1611, Bérulle founded the French Oratory, based on Filippo Neri's Roman Oratory, but with its own characteristics and organisation. Above all, it was intended as a congregation of secular priests, who were emphatically not intended to be members of a religious order. This key distinction reflected the evolution of Bérulle's thinking on the priesthood as a special state which not even the most observant could aspire to as a regular. Suffused with mystical influences, Bérulle's thought may not have been typical of the early decades of the century, but in his theological concern with the priesthood itself he provided a highly original and distinctive blueprint for the reform of the secular clergy, one which went far beyond anything that the Council of Trent or its interpreters had managed to articulate before him. With hindsight, all of this seems unexceptional, but Bérulle's idea of a secular congregation was far from unproblematic in Gallican France. The normal superior of secular priests was the bishop of the diocese they were attached to, so that creating a country-wide congregation with its own superiors could easily be interpreted as trespassing directly on episcopal authority. This difficulty was ultimately resolved by reserving the superior's authority over members to internal Oratorian affairs, thereby ensuring respect for episcopal direction in other (especially pastoral) spheres of action. At a time when the age-old seculars–regulars controversy reignited with a vengeance in France, such solutions were indispensable, and in this case, they opened the door to a large number of secular congregations to follow the Oratory's lead.[16]

The Oratory itself was intended, unlike its Italian predecessors, to be a structured congregation, with the familiar provisions for a general chapter, an elected superior-general and a set of constitutions. But its members would not take the classic vows of religion, so that exit from the congregation itself, whether voluntary or imposed, would not entail any real change of status for them: they remained what they always had been – priests. As the first 'general' of the Oratory, Bérulle himself guided its early development, but the impact of what he created was magnified by the fact that he simultaneously emerged, less by his writings than by his personal aura, as an extremely influential figure within higher church circles. Respected by senior church figures, he also became the mentor for a younger generation of reformers, both within and without the episcopate, whose names would become synonymous with the 'generation of saints' of the mid-seventeenth century – Saint-Cyran, Vincent de Paul, Jean-Jacques Olier, Jean Eudes and others. Some of them, like Bérulle before them, had been either educated or influenced by the Jesuits, and went on to create their own congregations. As early as 1613, Richelieu, then bishop of Luçon, offered the Oratorians the direction of his new seminary, and other bishops would duly follow his lead. Yet like the Jesuits, the Oratory soon found itself involved in related educational activities which could be justified as helping to prepare a new generation of secular clergy, but which, in the form of its colleges attended mainly by the social elites, quickly went far beyond such a commitment. The future rivalry between the Jesuits and the Oratory would therefore have multiple sources – institutional, theological and even ecclesiological – and would endure until well into the next century. By 1630, the Oratorians had seventy-three houses in all, but some were no more than parishes or retreats, while seventeen were colleges and a further eight were either seminaries or houses of study. Under Louis XIV, they would close many of their original smaller houses but add a further fifteen seminaries and eleven colleges to their tally. Yet by 1700, their Jansenist-Augustinian leanings had lost them much of the favour which they had previously enjoyed within both church and state. This flexibility of Bérulle's creation is evident in the variety of tasks and houses just mentioned, yet by 1714 there were no more than approximately 650 Oratorians in France. It was not always the biggest battalions which contributed most to religious change in seventeenth-century France.[17]

If the Oratory was the intellectual 'aristocracy' of the new congregations, others like the Lazarists, the Sulpicians and the Eudists had no such ambitions. Conceived by disciples of Bérulle, they were all equally focused on the Berullian objective of forming a new type of secular clergy. Founded in 1625, Vincent de Paul's Lazarists (*recte* Congregation of the Mission) aimed, in keeping with their official name, to reach out into towns and rural areas which desperately needed evangelisation, but de Paul was adamant that they would not follow the Oratorians in taking on colleges as a way to further their preaching and related activities. Even when they began running seminaries in due course, it was on the understanding that they would form clergy in a robustly practical manner, eschewing intellectual ambitions beyond the minimum required for their pastoral duties. Their early history is a good example of the highly experimental way in which new-style congregations were still taking shape up to mid-century. Approved by the papacy in 1633, the Lazarists remained without clearly defined structures until 1651 when, after nine years of preparatory work, a set of general rules was finally agreed. De Paul insisted that members take the three vows of poverty, chastity and obedience, but that they should not become regulars! This distinction, which the archbishop of Paris strongly approved of, was only possible because the vows in question were private, not public and 'solemn' as in conventional religious orders.[18] Like Bérulle before him, de Paul was an influential and highly respected figure in the French church, so by the time he died in 1660, his congregation totalled twenty-one houses in France, of which six were designated seminaries and five as mission houses only. Their unfailing theological orthodoxy, which they shared with Saint-Sulpice, helped to make the reign of Louis XIV the period of greatest expansion for the Lazarists. By 1700 or so, they were running twenty-seven seminaries, and more would be added thereafter, while the proportion of purely mission houses dropped further from what it had been around 1660: the congregation's mission had taken a direction that de Paul would probably not have approved of.[19]

The origins of the most enduring and perhaps the most famous of these new congregations, Saint-Sulpice, are of interest here because they highlight another characteristic feature of religious change in our period. The original community of three, led by Jean-Jacques Olier, was initially based at Vaugirard, then a village outside the walls of Paris, and they only moved into Saint-Sulpice parish in 1642 when Olier – another Berullian who knew Bérulle only via his successor, Condren – became its *curé*. Similar parish-based clerical communities had already been put together elsewhere in Paris and other cities where, as we saw earlier, some parishes had large numbers of resident, non-beneficed clergy. Few of these ever survived or grew into anything remotely similar to Saint-Sulpice, although the Paris community of priests of Saint-Nicolas-du-Chardonnet parish gradually moved to establishing a seminary in the early 1630s. Olier and his companions thus had models to follow and, although they had considerable experience of preaching missions, from the outset they saw a seminary as the primary vehicle for their mission to improve the parish clergy. Even when it did become a seminary in subsequent decades, the Saint-Sulpice parish and its large clerical population remained an important source of support – men like Fénelon belonged to it without ever formally being a seminarian at Saint-Sulpice.

Jean Eudes (1601–80) differed from both de Paul and Olier in having himself been a member of the Oratory under Bérulle. After serving ten years as a preacher and missionary, he left the Oratory in 1643 to found his own congregation, with missions and running seminaries as its specific objectives. Thanks to Eudes's long career, the congregation also became an effective vehicle for the devotions to the heart of Mary and Jesus of which Eudes was an indefatigable proponent. At his death in 1680, the Eudist congregation ran six seminaries, all located in Normandy and Brittany, where Eudes himself had been most active. Yet the congregation's membership was probably still well short of one hundred![20]

This exploration of the new congregations ends with the Congregation of Christian Brothers schools, which were founded by Jean-Baptiste de La Salle in 1680 and grew steadily over the next century, initially around the congregation's birthplace Reims and north-eastern France generally. La Salle's creation was more radical than anything we have seen so far, since he refused to allow any of its members to be a priest! This was why he himself, a priest and former cathedral canon, declined to take the title of superior-general. Its members would remain lay brothers, despite the fact that they would renew the vows of religion every three years, and would observe a strict rule and community life. What lay behind this reworking of existing models was a determination to educate young boys from poorer social groups. Unlike the Jesuits or Oratorians, the Christian Brothers took on schools provided by local municipal authorities rather than founding their own, and they insisted on using French as the language of instruction in subjects chosen essentially for their practical value to their pupils. Such a drastic departure from the educational practices of the earlier orders and congregations evidently called for an equally startling break with some of their key constitutive features.[21]

However selective it has to be, no account of growth among seventeenth-century France's regulars and congregations should lead us to overlook the fact that a plethora of smaller groups appeared across the country, but they either remained within a small area, such as a diocese or region, or else failed to preserve their independence. In some instances they were absorbed by larger and more dynamic groups: what the Maurists did by absorbing older Benedictine congregations could occur here, too. One example will suffice here, that of the congregation founded by Raymond Bonal in 1638 in the Rouergue, which was devoted, like so many others of the period, to reforming and educating the secular clergy. But Bonal's initially promising congregation remained unstructured, without any central novitiate or leadership. Over time and with each house gradually going its own way, there was a failure to expand and especially to cohere beyond the first generation, leading the congregation to seek rescue in the form of absorption by the Lazarists in the early decades of the eighteenth century. Indeed, the Lazarists' success in expanding into parts of western and southern France came about precisely because they had the institutions and leadership to absorb congregations such as Bonal's. A similar congregation, that of the priests of the Holy Sacrament, operated in parts of south-east France from the early 1630s but, unlike Bonal's, its efforts to merge with the Oratory and the Lazarists came to nothing, and from the 1670s onwards it seems to have gradually dissolved into its component houses.[22] One possible reason for such 'failures' may be that French bishops often encouraged the development of groups which remained purely diocesan in scope, though that preference usually affected female orders rather more than male ones. As we have already seen, episcopal concern that the church could exert little control over members of orders or congregations whose superiors were based outside their dioceses was a constant, and even growing feature of the period. By contrast, local congregations subject to episcopal authority could be usefully recruited into serving episcopal policies, whether they involved teaching, missions or running seminaries.

Local Densities

No account of the successive waves of orders and congregations to sweep across France can provide a satisfactory idea of their density on the ground and, as a consequence, of their potential impact on the localities they settled in. Constructing an overall map of these phenomena across France would in theory be possible, but the outcome would not be a particularly legible one. It could be expected to show that, as already suggested in this chapter, some religious orders were over-represented in some parts of France and almost entirely absent elsewhere. A more limited but nevertheless more illuminating alternative to a nationwide map is to focus on a number of cities, beginning with Paris, and on a region embracing a fairly representative spread of smaller cities and towns.

The experience of Paris, even more so than France as a whole, during the decades following the religious wars, has often been described as an 'invasion' by religious orders, new and reformed, male and female – an 'invasion' that has also been labelled 'mystical' because of the heavily contemplative bias of the most prominent orders concerned. Despite the defeat of the Catholic League, the religious militancy which years of defying the king and his predecessor, Henri III, had generated went hand in hand with more pacific efforts to generate religious revival. Between the mid-1590s and 1650, something like sixty-five new religious houses, forty-five of them for women, opened in the city, but these figures convey relatively little of what was really happening. We shall return in the next chapter to the significance of the rise in the number of female religious houses. It is not a question of estimating how typical Paris was at this point, since so many of the orders, including those with a mainly remote provincial base, wished to possess a house there that would give them greater 'visibility' and, above all, protection and patronage. For example, the southern Dominican reformer Sebastien Michaelis founded his own house in

Paris, at Saint-Honoré, as a rival to the unreformed house close to the university, while the equally southern-based Doctrinaires and Barnabites managed, after considerable time and effort, to find a place in Paris, albeit not always in the most favourable locations. Even within the older monastic orders, reforms originating elsewhere often sought to establish their head house in Paris – the Maurists with Saint-Germain-des-Prés being the best known example, the canons-regular at Sainte-Geneviève another. Such moves illustrate the city's emergence as a kind of religious capital of France. Many of the new foundations there led a perilous existence, chronically short of funds and buildings, and relying heavily on the goodwill of lay sponsors and the families of their members. With more new houses failing and disappearing than is usually realised, it was a geography which took a long time to stabilise. In 1666 the English expatriate cleric, Thomas Carre, published his admiring *Pietats Parisiensis*, which was in large part a guidebook to the capital's many religious houses.[23]

Lyon has as good a claim as any French city of the period to the title of a monastery-city. The city had long been the 'gateway' to Italy, as much for religious groups as for merchants, and its substantial printing trade enhanced its attractiveness to those engaged in religious and intellectual activity. The diocese of Lyon saw seventy-five new religious houses appear in the years down to 1653, of which thirty-nine were male, even though within the city itself new female houses were more numerous than male ones. Year after year, almost from 1602 onwards, the municipal authorities received petitions from orders, old and new, for a locale within the city walls – petitions which often enjoyed high-profile support from the provincial governor, the archbishop or the lay elites. The city council estimated the number of religious houses in 1628 at twenty-nine, and in 1656 at forty, with a comparable growth in the number of churches and chapels. It is hardly surprising that by the mid-1620s the Lyon printing presses were turning out twice as much religious as secular literature, compared to a mere decade or so earlier, nor that a large number of devotional movements took strong root there in connection with its resident religious orders. By way of comparison, it may be noted that Toulouse saw approximately twenty-one new orders or congregations settle in its midst between 1590 and 1709 – twelve of them before 1650. Although the *parlement* had banned all further religious building *intra muros* as early as 1624, the royal intendant, Basville, estimated in 1698 that the orders occupied half of the city! Yet not all of the urban regular communities were of the same size, influence or connections. In early eighteenth-century Bordeaux, the male regulars may have numbered just over 500 in all, with the Jesuits as the largest group with ninety members, but the Capuchins, Récollets, Dominicans, Carmelites and others averaged around forty to fifty members each. Here too, urban space was a severe problem, and most of the new foundations had to seek locations outside the historic urban centre.[24] Such experiences were common across towns and cities elsewhere, and the prominence of the regulars across urban France down to the French Revolution was the direct consequence of these 'invasions'.

The problem with these snapshots of the larger and well-documented cities is, needless to say, that they give little idea of the situation beyond their walls. Indeed, they can easily create the impression that the high urban concentrations of regulars had a 'desert effect' elsewhere across a country as large and non-urban as France. A brief regional comparison will provide a useful corrective, not least because it can be represented cartographically (see Map 3). Across the two large dioceses of Auxerre and Langres, situated in southern Champagne and northern Burgundy and with only two middling-sized towns between them, Auxerre and Dijon, the overall growth in the regulars' presence between 1598 and 1700 is no less remarkable. Not only did Dijon and Auxerre, already well provided, experience a major influx of regulars, but secondary towns such as Gien, Tonnerre, Noyers, Châtillon, Clamecy, Bar-sur-Aube, Chaumont and Saint-Jean-de-Losne did likewise. It is hard to know how sizeable the smallest communities inherited from the later medieval period were around 1600, and some of them, especially in the smaller towns and villages, may have been just hospices or *beguinages*, but the map does show that even at this virtually rural level, religious houses not merely survived but expanded in number after 1600. After allowance is made for the relatively few houses that disappeared from the map altogether, the impression remains unmistakably one of a *monde plein*.[25]

Success and Social Insertion

For the regulars and congregations to have fared so well in urban centres or across entire regions, it is obvious that an appealing combination of leadership, way of life, religious practices and so on was at work within each of them. But the responsiveness of the wider church and especially lay society counted for just as much, since little could be achieved without their sustained goodwill and energy. Municipal authorities held a decisive say in whether a new community could settle in their town, but as we saw in the case of Lyon above, strong support, especially if it was backed by financial commitment, from nobles, bishops or other groups, could sway the council's decision. It is easy to think that by the seventeenth century, hard-headed councils were seeking to admit religious communities with something unfamiliar or 'useful' to offer, such as education, charitable work, the management of hospices and the like. But the greatest influx of mendicants and congregations, up to around

122 CLERICAL WORLDS IN CONTEXT

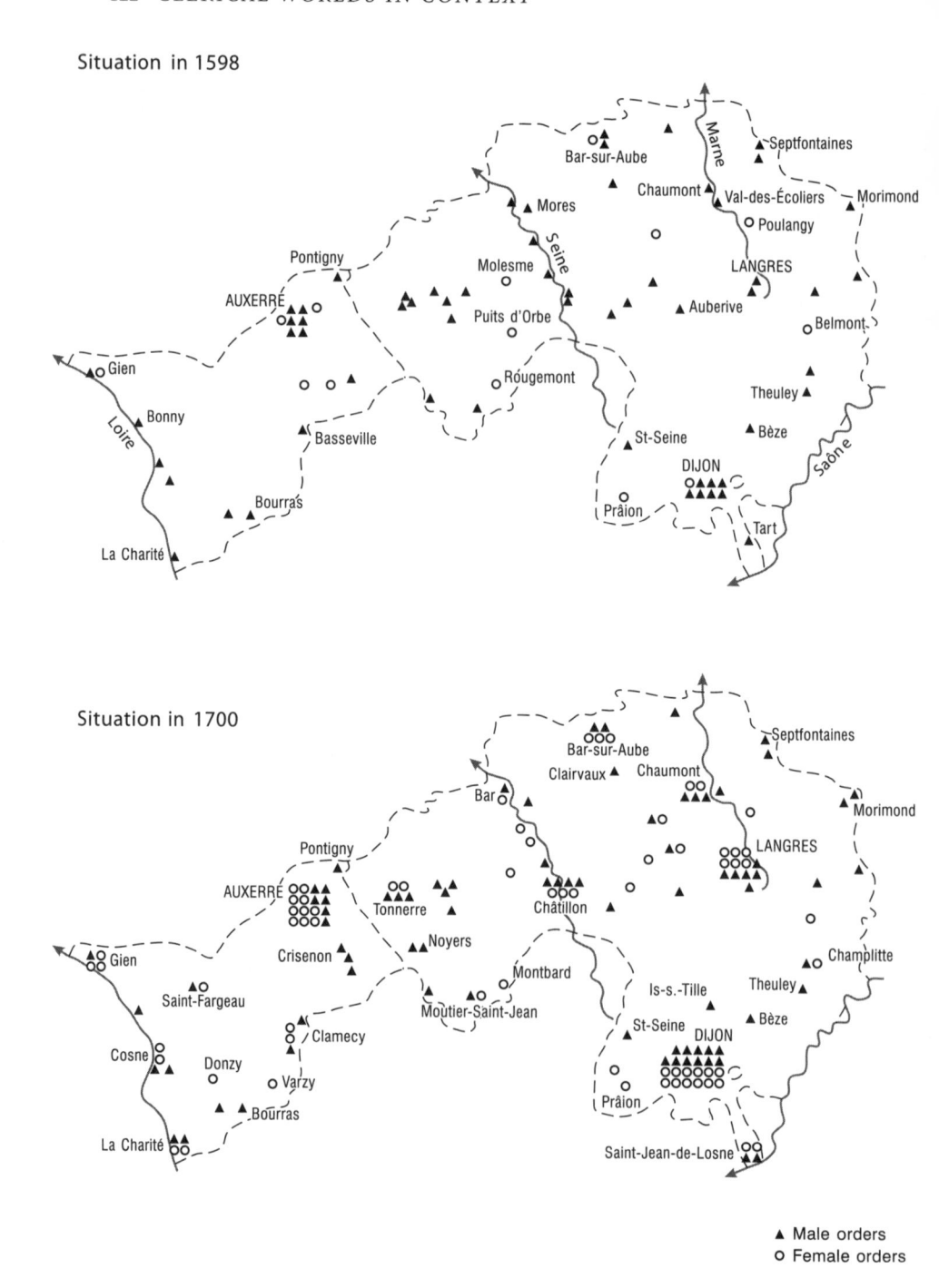

Situation in 1598

Situation in 1700

▲ Male orders
○ Female orders

3. Growth of the regulars' presence in Burgundy-Champagne, 1598–1700.

1650–60, was not characterised by either such supply or such demand. The success of the 'new' Franciscans, Récollets and Capuchins, did not depend on their offering anything radically different from earlier Franciscan recipes, which had always gone well beyond merely preaching or administering the sacraments. And none of these considerations would have any point had not local families been willing to offer their offspring to orders and their individual houses even before they had acquired a firm footing in a particular area, and to maintain that willingness subsequently. Family fidelity to particular orders or religious houses was not new, and the seventeenth century may have encouraged them to vary or extend such attachments. Mutual bonds between French society and the orders, especially but not exclusively the mendicants, were also strengthened by the fact that several of them also had female branches, whose houses were often in close proximity to their own, especially at a time when female regulars were growing exponentially in numbers. This constituted an additional reason why large numbers of families were attached to the religious services provided by the regulars.

The bonds with local society were also strengthened immeasurably by means of confraternities and 'third orders' which were guided and directed overwhelmingly by the mendicants, where they so often had their own private chapels, and where they confessed and conducted their religious observances.[26] We shall return to the subject of confraternities later, but it should be noted here that some were based on the crafts, some were purely devotional and that confraternities also experienced renewal and innovation in the same way that religious orders themselves did. What seems particularly pertinent here is that, as a result of the shocks of the Reformation and wars of religion, many of the older confraternities which had previously kept the clergy at a distance now found themselves moving back towards co-operation with them. By the early 1600s at the latest, they were ready to accept a substantial role for the clergy in directing their members and activities, and there is evidence that the Récollets and Capuchins were particularly sought after for such a role. The newer confraternities of Penitents, whose entrance and initiation rites for new members uncannily resembled those of new entrants to religious orders, had no such problems with the presence of regulars. The proliferation of new confraternities in our period expanded the role of the regulars, especially the mendicants and new congregations, across France, especially in the smaller cities and towns.[27]

Confraternities and third orders may be considered as two degrees of integration between lay society and the mendicant orders. The third orders were exclusively linked to religious orders to a degree that was not true of confraternities, but it seems that we should not regard the differences between them as rigid, and that degrees of flexibility were common. 'Third' orders, so called because they came after the first (male) and second (female) orders, existed mostly among the Dominicans, Franciscans, Minims and the Augustinian canons of Prémontré, and were designed to allow lay people of both sexes to adopt a demanding devotional life and a form of 'belonging' to the orders in question, taking vows and observing celibacy while remaining active in the world as laypeople. These highly elusive associations in their successive guises were also valuable instruments for the diffusion of new forms of devotion – to the Holy Sacrament, the Rosary, the Sacred Heart and many others during our period.[28] In seventeenth-century France, 'tertiaries', as their members were called, included Louis XIII, Anne of Austria, Marie-Thérèse and major court and ministerial figures, so despite the difficulties in charting their growth and activities, they were anything but obscure in their membership and social cachet; and the fact that their membership was mostly female and that they were largely self-regulating meant that the third orders gave devout women considerable opportunities. By also encouraging spiritual reading, meditation and direction of conscience, third orders offered some part of the ascetic, renunciatory ideal of the orders to people unable to leave the 'world' and their families, but they also strongly urged involvement in charitable and other good works. Not surprisingly, given the combination of individual religious discipline and social responsibility, France's *dévots* belonged massively to these bodies. It is within this wider context that the Jesuits' well-known sodalities and associations of devotion to the Virgin Mary and the Holy Sacrament, which were not third orders, could achieve so much success; they may not be the main reason why the Jesuits were in such demand across France, but the Jesuits knew well that forming, guiding and attaching such groups to their houses immeasurably strengthened their own roots within French society.[29]

Moreover, at a time when new congregations like the Oratory were demanding only 'simple' rather than traditional 'solemn' vows from their members, the gap between the orders and certain lay devotional organisations was becoming ever narrower. It was only to be expected that the third orders could themselves sometimes be the starting point for new orders and congregations, especially of women, and that some third orders were – or went on to become – full 'regulars'. Taking vows as a tertiary was an act whose logical conclusion might be full religious vows, as occurred with the 'penitent priests' of Picpus, who were founded in 1594 and had around sixty houses across France a century later.[30] The Récollets went a step further and, in addition to the 'priestly' and 'lay' members of the order, they established an *internal* third order which grew in numbers by the early eighteenth century; these full-membership tertiaries took simple vows, but were expected to observe the order's rules like its other members.[31] With such numerous options available to urban lay society, it is not hard to see how difficult it would be for the parish clergy, even a reformed one, to persuade the most religiously committed of their parishioners to regard the parish church and priest as their 'natural' spiritual homes. Had the mendicants' pastoral activities not gone well beyond merely preaching or administering the sacraments to lay populations, it might not have been difficult for a competent and well-trained secular parish clergy to lever them out of such a role by the latter part of the seventeenth century. But their appeal and activities were far wider than that, and in the confraternities and the 'third orders' that they organised and directed, they had found a social base that was infinitely more rooted and enduring. One historian has aptly suggested that 'in the age of Catholic renewal, the third orders represented the religious orders' contribution to promoting new models of Christian life that were detached from the template of the regular life'.[32]

The pastoral activities of the regulars have remained comparatively unstudied in their proper context. This owes something to the earlier prejudices of both clerics and lay elites as to the kind of religion that the orders purveyed; in more recent times the neglect owes more to historical methodology than to religious sensibility, given the emphasis placed by historians of religious practice on the records of pastoral visitations of parishes by bishops and their officials, which dealt essentially with the parish and its secular clergy, and which had little to say about the regulars and their activities. For a very long time, it was the regulars who manned the missions and preaching campaigns throughout France; to the extent that the secular clergy became involved in them, it was mainly the elite, organised 'seculars' belonging to the new congregations such as the Lazarists who did so. Before they appeared, the Jesuits, Capuchins, Récollets and others had carried out such campaigns, and they continued doing so into the eighteenth century; the extent of such engagement by regulars becomes clearer still when it is realised that even the Maurists undertook such missions in the late 1660s and 1680s, and based their approach on those of the Oratory and the Eudists.[33] Jesuit colleges often had members whose main task was mission work rather than teaching. As in previous centuries, the orders continued to supply urban churches with most of their Advent and Lenten preachers, which often represented major religious occasions when new devotions were first introduced or when individual preachers sparked controversy. In Paris under Louis XIV – admittedly not a typical example – Mme de Sévigné and her friends earnestly debated the relative merits of this or that Lenten or Advent preacher, many of them regulars. The Capuchins and Récollets were probably the most 'popular' preachers of their time, and beyond their fidelity to Franciscan traditions and saints, they were welcome because they preached a religious message of reassurance, salvation and divine mercy. As already noted, the regulars' churches had acted as the base of operations for the confraternities from the earliest Penitents onwards, and it was their continuing ability to attract social elites which accounts for the fact that the regulars' churches were usually more attractive physically than their potential rivals, the parish churches. If the regulars were often preservers of religious traditions (such as confraternities dedicated to particular saints), there is abundant evidence to show that they were also the first to diffuse newer devotions such as the Rosary, Holy Sacrament, the Forty Hours' and many others.

Conclusion

Despite the prevailing historiographical emphasis on the secular clergy and their steady improvement – an emphasis which itself reflects the agenda of the seventeenth-century French church – it is clear that a combination of internal renewal and the arrival of new groups ensured that the regulars, who brought with them new trends in spirituality and pastoral philosophy (for want of a better term), had a very big impact on both church and society across our period. Competition among the orders themselves for recruits and the wider support of lay society ensured that they would be responsive to the aspirations of towns, families and individuals. The chronology of this 'invasion' – the term enshrined in French historiography, despite its limitations – is also relevant to any judgement of its wider importance. In fact, it was an explosion as much as an invasion, given how many of the new institutions were French. It is well established that the bulk of the influx took place in the decades between 1600 and 1660, with an initial tapering-off setting in by around 1640. This chronology fits the old and new mendicant orders best, but it is far less applicable to the new congregations, mostly of seculars, which emerged in the wake of Bérulle's Oratory, some of which had either not appeared or were only in the early stages of elaboration by 1640 or 1660. The new secular congregations were also significantly smaller, especially in their membership, than the likes of the Jesuits or the Récollets, but because of the nature of their activities, such as running colleges or seminaries, their impact on the French church could be disproportionate to their numbers; this also meant they were still expanding their activities into the early eighteenth century at least. Because of the relative tailing off after 1660, it has been easy to argue that France was saturated by that point, and the concerns of Louis XIV's minister, Colbert, about the size of the orders and the need to prevent new foundations with insufficient means to support themselves, seems to be the evidence that confirms such an argument. But this point creates some misleading perspectives on what had been happening.[34] The wars of religion had deterred many orders from trying to expand within France, so there was a massive effort to catch up in the decades that followed, especially among female regulars, as we shall see. These were decades during which there was unparalleled enthusiasm for groups and institutions that seemed to embody the old church's robust response to the challenge of French Calvinism, and such a trend was probably unrepeatable as well as unsustainable in the longer term. That some of the new creations should have been fragile and experienced difficulties is not really surprising, and if account is taken of the timescale of the expansion of the different orders and congregations, it is evident that after a 'heroic' founding age there was a correspondingly 'normal' age of consolidation when few new houses were opened, but when in all likelihood the membership of the existing houses continued to rise towards their maxima under Louis XIV. The 'saturation' argument tends to ignore this key point by focusing almost entirely on the numbers of new houses *founded*, regardless of their subsequent history. Colbert's intention was to set rules for new foundations, not to terminate existing ones.[35] He would have been aware that in the 1650s, Innocent X had ordered the closure of no fewer than 1,500 religious houses throughout Italy alone, but it was not until the eighteenth century that the French crown was willing to imitate papal precedent.

There is probably no single explanation for the differing chronologies of the creation and expansion of new orders and congregations. Particular reasons can be adduced to explain why some failed to expand more than they did, and some of them are political and 'ideological'. For example, the increasingly assertive Gallican bishops often disliked the privileges and self-governance of the religious orders, which flew in the face of their claim to govern their dioceses with full powers. Individual bishops became embroiled in sometimes acrimonious conflicts with particular orders – Cardinal Le Camus of Grenoble (1671–1706) with the Jesuits, Percin de Montgaillard of Saint-Pons in Languedoc with the Récollets, to mention only two.[36] Cardinal Noailles of Paris actually banned the king's confessor and other Jesuits from preaching in the capital for several years in the early 1710s! For the same reasons, many bishops preferred the new congregations of secular priests, given that they explicitly recognised the bishops in whose dioceses they operated as their superiors. This could also work in favour of smaller orders or congregations with purely local roots. But there were times when other factors might override these. Some of the most distinguished congregations were compromised by their theological and pastoral principles, so that institutions as different as the Feuillants and the Oratorians lost favour with the crown and many bishops for their Augustinian views which made them suspect of holding views close to Jansenism. Being compromised in this way could seriously restrict their development. So in the final decades of Louis XIV's reign the Oratorians, for example, found themselves being subjected to unwelcome intervention in their affairs and being removed from many of the seminaries they ran, which were then turned over to their more orthodox rivals, the Jesuits or the Lazarists. And when eighteenth-century bishops refused to ordain as priests Oratorians who would not accept the papal condemnation of Jansenism of 1713, the congregation faced the prospect of gradually becoming a lay society rather than the priestly body so keenly desired by Bérulle and his successors.[37] By contrast, both the Capuchins and the Récollets benefited from the anti-Jansenism of the Franciscans generally.

Historians of the regulars in this period have often charted the foundation, early expansion and consolidation of the orders, with an eye to the crisis they experienced in the eighteenth century. They have usually seen the problem from the perspective of an individual order rather than providing a wider picture of the orders as a whole. But individual orders were in competition with others for new members and for lay support, and given how numerous they were, it is not surprising that a recipe for success in the early seventeenth century might no longer work a century or so later. The later phase of consolidation was sometimes accompanied by active accommodation to social convention and expectation, as for example in the mitigation of the 'heroic' ideal of poverty among the Capuchins and Récollets, or the use of lay brothers to conduct the begging 'campaigns' in the places where the authorities gave them permission to beg. It is also possible that the spirituality diffused by individual orders did not adapt to changing times and tastes.[38] Some lay associations, such as the Company of the Holy Sacrament, took over traditional regular activities in relation to poor relief and so on. Newer orders or congregations specialising, like the Brothers of the Christian Schools after 1680, in educating people further down the social scale than those attending Jesuit, Oratorian or other schools, responded to needs as yet untapped by their predecessors. Beyond the successes and failures of particular groups of mendicants and secular congregations, there remains the 'total' fact of a massively reinforced and deeply entrenched regular presence across the length and breadth of France.

CHAPTER 6

A SILENT REVOLUTION: WOMEN AS REGULARS

Historians have long been aware of the upsurge in female orders and congregations during the seventeenth century, whose record is bettered only by the nineteenth, when more female religious orders were created than during any other period in the history of Christianity. But the scale as well as the significance of the seventeenth-century additions has often been difficult to grasp, for several reasons. One is a limited sense of the context and prehistory of the developments that occurred then: only when these are well understood – for they exhibit many of the characteristics we have seen among the male religious in the previous chapter – can the real importance of the new female regulars and congregations be properly measured. Likewise, the fact that for centuries male and female orders were often 'paired' together, with the male orders usually exercising extensive control over their female 'branches', is easily forgotten, yet it remained a powerful model well into the early modern period. Female orders or congregations wishing to break free of it could find themselves facing stiff resistance, both from church circles and even from the ambient lay society; even those which were highly conscious of their separateness continued to rely heavily on particular male orders. One result of all this is that the houses and population of the female orders are usually more elusive than their male counterparts, both in general and for individual orders and houses. Rather like the analysis of the church's wealth, which as we saw depends heavily on 'retrospective' data from 1790, the history of France's orders tends to work backwards from the figures derived from the mid-eighteenth century *Commission des réguliers*, which collected statistics on religious houses with a view to deciding whether to close them down or not. But the commission's relevance to France's female orders is nil, since its remit did not include them at all.[1] That was because forty years earlier, in

1727, the female regulars had already attracted their own *Commission des secours*, which closed nearly 250 fragile or unviable houses over the following sixty years. The best estimate to date of an overall figure for male regulars around 1760 is about 30,000, yet the total for female regulars for the same date is almost double that figure at around 55,000, a remarkable statistic.[2] Unfortunately, no such estimates are possible for earlier periods, but when it is realised that female regulars were far fewer than their male counterparts around 1600, it is clear that our period experienced a transformation that dwarfs anything observed in the previous chapters. It is also likely that the rise in the female religious population was more sustained into the mid-eighteenth century than among the male regulars. The pages that follow will, inevitably, take for granted some of the generalisations about the religious orders made in previous chapters, though it is impossible to avoid recapitulating some points of detail or argument made earlier, in order to understand both particular developments among the female orders and, above all, the reasons for the scale of the changes they experienced.

The Monastics

The mere enumeration, in tabular form, of the older female orders immediately reveals the 'complementary' nature of those orders to their male counterparts, monastic and mendicant. Indeed, there were scarcely any medieval female orders that were *not* emanations of male prototypes, each genre of which – black monks, white monks, Augustinian canons, and Hospitallers – had at least some female houses. The one exception which stands out here is the great abbey (and order) of Fontevraud, a highly aristocratic and wealthy abbey which was sometimes governed by female members of the French royal family, and which subordinated its male houses and members to female rule. But the

Table 6.1 – Female monastic and mendicant orders before c.1600

Benedictines
Cistercians
Fontevraud
Augustinians of various types
Hospitallers of St Augustine
Carmelites
Dominicans
Franciscans – various *Clarisses*
Annonciades
Récollettes

Fontevraud 'model' found no imitators, and it remained a distinguished, if also tiny, anomaly, since the order numbered only five member houses in all. Yet the older female monastic houses did resemble Fontevraud in certain other respects – the rural site, the often extensive 'temporal' endowments and a tendency to more socially exclusive recruitment than was current among the male monastic orders. This particular pattern is more visible along the eastern borders of France, where some initially Benedictine houses abandoned the Rule of St Benedict altogether, and their nuns gradually mutated into canonesses resembling their aristocratic counterparts in the Holy Roman Empire. Similar trends, albeit limited in scale, occurred within France – in Normandy, the Paris region, the Loire valley and elsewhere. It is impossible to calculate accurately the overall number of female monastic houses across France as a whole by approximately 1600, but a crude order of magnitude, based on the figures available for the crown's patronage rights over the religious orders, might be a 1:3 ratio against male houses, with around 250 female ones being so 'listed' during the eighteenth century. The new female monastic foundations occurring during our period only marginally increased earlier totals.

By the sixteenth century, there was increasing concern about the vulnerability of female religious houses located in rural areas, and both the rise of Calvinism and the ensuing civil wars amply confirmed those fears. In its final reform ordinances of December 1563, the Council of Trent explicitly encouraged the houses in question to move inside the safety of walled towns. The wars of religion wreaked havoc on many of them, even in areas of France not usually thought of as having a large Huguenot presence, such as Champagne and Burgundy. But the Huguenots were not the sole nemesis of the orders – German *reiters* and Catholic League troops seem to have behaved no better towards them at times. As with their male counterparts, the big, wealthy female monasteries were an attractive target, while the smaller ones were a soft target. While there may have been individual abbeys untroubled by the wars, it is more likely that extensive damage and loss of lands and revenues, leading in time to the abandonment of community observance and a serious drop in membership, affected France's female monastic orders by the 1590s.[3]

By then, also, these old orders had been brought within the reach of the crown's patronage. But this, as already noted, did not entail a female version of the *commende*. Even though the crown quietly extended its right to nominate abbesses who should in principle have been elected, there was no female equivalent of an 'outsider' secular clergy, court-based or otherwise, from which to select its favoured candidates: to become an abbess, one had already to be a professed nun, although not necessarily in the same order. Given that monastic vows could be taken at the age of sixteen, there was no great obstacle to precocious nominations and, as the celebrated case of Jacqueline (in religion, Angélique) Arnauld showed, even those rules could be broken: she was effectively nominated to Port-Royal as its future abbess when aged just ten. As with the male abbots *in commendam*, the crown's choice of abbesses usually favoured daughters of well-born families, all of which strengthened the nobility's grip on big established abbeys like Longchamp, Chelles, Maubuisson, La Trinité of Caen and numerous others, which found themselves governed by abbesses with illustrious names like Orléans, Montmorency, Guise, Béthune and so on. Moreover, the ease with which the crown accepted prearranged successions of abbesses (via co-adjutorships) ensured that quasi-dynastic rule would apply in many of these abbeys, although underaged successions like that of Port-Royal in 1602 were gradually phased out thereafter.[4]

Mendicants

Much less is known of the female branches of the older mendicant orders. Their elusiveness derives in no small part from the fact that many individual communities were not part of any wider, structured order, but remained local and mostly self-governing, nominally subject to overall episcopal supervision; others again might have moved at a particular moment under the mantle of a well-known order, mostly as a result of adopting the religious observance of that order. Because of this high level of fragmentation, it is simply impossible to obtain reliable figures about the numbers, location, or observance of many communities. This applies even to the Dominican and Franciscan nuns, the dominant female mendicant orders. They were, like their male counterparts, town-based and, in principle at least, they were also cloistered contemplatives. As with male mendicants, neither the social cachet nor the endowed wealth of the female Dominicans and Franciscans was such as to attract the patronage-scanning antennae of the crown. Interestingly, the only exception to this involved a branch of the Franciscans known as the 'rich Clares' (the *Urbanistes*), on whom Louis XIV tried to impose crown-appointed abbesses in the 1680s, only to give up in the face of stiff resistance.[5] This did not, of itself, mean that the crown was indifferent to the mendicant orders since, as was noted in the previous chapter, many of them did indeed attract royal favour and support at crucial moments in their development, something which played its own part in their reception by French towns. In the past, members of the royal family had sometimes taken the veil and founded either a house or even a branch of a religious order. One of the most prominent offshoots of the female Franciscan family in early modern France, the *Annonciades*, were founded in Bourges in 1501 by Jeanne de Valois, daughter of Louis XI and repudiated wife of Louis XII. In Bourbon France, it was the more recently introduced Spanish Carmelites who attracted some of the highest-profile nuns, from Louis XIV's mistress, Louise de la Vallière, to Louise de France, youngest daughter of Louis XV.[6]

The female Dominicans and Franciscans resembled their male counterparts in another important manner. True to form, the female Dominicans retained their original observance without evident difficulty, while successive reforms in Avignon (1512) and Toulouse (1605) enabled them to found new houses elsewhere in France thereafter. To them we should add those previously lay 'third order' groups which, after the Council of Trent, were gradually compelled to adopt enclosure and a full 'regular' way of life. Dominican unity was tested by increasing episcopal supervision of individual convents in our period, but even that was not enough to produce schism or lasting division among them.[7]

By contrast, the female Franciscans, known generically as the *Clarisses* after their founder St Clare, had already developed several branches by the sixteenth century, the consequence of successive attempts to return to their original observance, especially of the vow of poverty. Each male Franciscan Observant province had female communities of *Clarisses*, 'grey' sisters, or *Annonciades* attached to it, and each continued to attract previously independent communities under its wing during the period we are dealing with, so that by around 1680, it has been estimated that French Franciscan nuns numbered around 4,000, spread across eight provinces. The 'new' male Franciscans, such as the Capuchins and Récollets, did develop their own female offshoots, but surprisingly few female Capuchin houses materialised in France, while the name 'Récollettes' seems to be a very loose term that covers a range of reformed Franciscan convents rather than merely the male Récollets' own dependent female nuns. That the Franciscans were not solely dependent for expansion on newly created offshoots is illustrated by the 'rich Clares' who, having been reformed by the male Franciscan Observants or by post-Tridentine bishops, opened a string of new houses by offering education to girls and by engaging in charitable activities.[8]

Perhaps the main reason why so many of these 'mendicant' nuns are more 'hidden from history' than either the monastics or the newcomers of our period is that, in addition to being cloistered contemplatives, they retained the medieval tradition of being a 'second' order, constitutionally dependent on the male ('first') order when it came to determining their observance, way of life and activities. Individual communities could enjoy a measure of autonomy through having their own female superiors and office-holders; others, however, had exclusively male superiors. But all, needless to say, depended, on a virtually daily basis, on priests, whether from the 'first' order or outsiders, to say masses, preach, hear confessions, administer the sacraments and so on, and this easily translated into effective male control of communities, especially in a period when recourse to the sacraments loomed far larger than previously in their religious practices.

Invasions

As already observed, the French Catholic Reformation was characterised by an unprecedented 'investment' in female orders and congregations of almost every imaginable type which, by the eighteenth century, saw the female regulars outnumber their male counterparts by a ratio of nearly two to one. It was not a movement consisting exclusively of new creations, but was much wider than that. Several of the existing orders were borne along by it, and to a degree reinvented themselves, either by attaching themselves to a new reforming movement – as happened within the male orders – or by taking on activities not hitherto associated with them, especially teaching and charitable work. It remains difficult to judge just how far the older female orders were affected by the previous efforts at reforming the orders during the period from about 1460 to 1520, but one of the main effects of the wars of religion was the widespread abandonment of cloister and community life within convents, and a greater reliance on the families of nuns to replace the lost wealth and revenues, leading almost inevitably to increased family intervention in the convents' affairs. Even where this did not lead to scandalous behaviour by ex-claustrated nuns – which was never more than marginal – most efforts at reform began by trying to reverse these trends. The *journée du guichet* of 1609, when Angélique Arnauld finally refused her family entry inside Port-Royal, is only the most celebrated instance of the conflicts that a reformist reshaping of the ties between convents, families and local society could raise. Yet the original suggestion that she become abbess at a young age had come from no less a figure than the abbot-general of the Cistercians, in the hope that her family's money and connections would benefit the then dilapidated Port-Royal![9]

Not all reforms produced dramatic 'moments' like this, but resistance to and incomprehension of reforms that entailed major changes in lifestyle – enclosure, silence, fasting and so on – were never far below the surface, and many communities instinctively regarded them as an attempt to rewrite the 'contract' which they had accepted when taking their vows. Rejections of change were therefore numerous, as they were among male orders, but it would be mistaken to regard them as firm evidence of a lack of observance, let alone of scandalous behaviour, in the houses concerned: all too often that was propaganda designed to discredit houses that reformers had in their sights. As within the male orders, aversion towards reform could be linked to fears that local recruitment of new members might be threatened, and that particular fear was one which their families and local social groups instinctively shared. Within established female orders, it was the intervention of authority figures like bishops that was most likely to trigger conflicts involving local interests, conflicts in which the monasteries were usually trying to defend their immunities and exemptions from episcopal jurisdiction and inspection. Barricaded doors, violence, anathemas and lawsuits were not uncommon outcomes of such clashes in an age when bishops took their responsibility as 'natural' superiors of female monasteries with increasing seriousness. The number of such clashes can easily be exaggerated, and they were more likely to involve the older and more independent monastic houses, especially if they had aristocratic abbesses, than their less well-connected mendicant counterparts.[10]

It seems likely that the sheer difficulty of reforming existing houses was an important reason why the new orders founded in such numbers after the wars of religion were so widely welcomed across France. Despite that, it would be a mistake to ignore the extent to which the successful reform of abbeys such as Port-Royal, Montmartre and many others provided encouragement to similar attempts in lesser-known houses. A handful of small reformed congregations, of a type already familiar from the old male orders, also took shape among female Benedictines and Cistercians. Port-Royal may be the most celebrated of the reformed Cistercian convents, but its highly individual style of observance prevented it – rather like Rancé's La Trappe – from becoming the head of a Cistercian reform movement. It seems that the majority of Benedictine and Cistercian convents that did experience reform tended to do so within a diocesan framework that entailed episcopal supervision, which obviously limited the congregational drive. On the other hand, it was difficulties in reforming the aristocratic Fontevraud in the 1610s that led to the creation in neighbouring Poitiers of a Benedictine congregation, Notre Dame du Calvaire, whose expansion throughout western France owed a great deal to the energy of the famous Capuchin, Père Joseph du Tremblay, Richelieu's so-called 'eminence grise'.[11]

But it was the enormous religious energy, especially its ascetic and intensely meditative spirituality, released by the Catholic League that was essential for the success of the 'new' orders and congregations that seemed to flood France in the half-century or so after the ending of the wars of religion.[12] Nothing exemplified this altered climate more than the arrival in Paris in 1604 of a group of Spanish Carmelite nuns belonging to the reformed observance of the great mystic, Teresa of Avila. France already had Carmelites of its own, though they were confined to Brittany and the west, and were otherwise largely unremarkable. The Spanish newcomers were strikingly different, and they exemplified the most rigorous form of enclosed, ascetic and contemplative existence then available to pious women. Their arrival in France was the culmination of the efforts of a group of *dévot* men and women grouped about Barbe Acarie, who had been an ardent supporter of the League – though other members of her circle had not been *ligueurs*. Acarie and some of her supporters themselves became Carmelites during the early years after 1604. Despite initial linguistic, cultural and even political difficulties (arising from scepticism in some circles about welcoming Spanish influences so soon after war with Spain), the Carmelites began to attract recruits in the capital and beyond. By 1630, no fewer than forty-six of these Carmels had been founded, usually in substantial towns and cities, after which new foundations tapered off; by the end of the century, there were approximately sixty-three of them. Individual houses often acted as spiritual magnets for individuals, men as well as women, seeking religious guidance as to how to live their lives in the unenclosed world outside, as is abundantly clear from the correspondence between Chancellor Séguier and his sister (a nun at Pontoise) or the *dévot* Gaston de Renty and several nuns of Beaune and Dijon.

Despite their expansion, the Carmelites' way of life was clearly designed for a tiny minority of spiritual athletes. Yet nothing better indicates the enthusiasm and eclecticism of the early seventeenth century than the fact that it was Barbe Acarie and her friends who were instrumental in introducing the Ursulines to Paris in 1608, only four years after the Carmelites, and that the first Ursuline nuns there had failed to obtain entry into the Carmelites.[13] Even before arriving in France, the Ursulines had already experienced the kind of problems that would regularly cause so much soul-searching and debate during the seventeenth century. The early Italian Ursulines were unenclosed women who lived in their own homes without the usual religious vows, while engaging in an active apostolate among the poor and sick, but by the 1580s, thanks to the efforts of both Carlo Borromeo and the papacy, they had been compelled to accept both a form of community and full religious vows, as Trent had required. With the active support of the male congregation of the Doctrinaires, a small group of women came together in papal Avignon in 1592 and, after a few years of uncertainty, they adopted the Borromean-papal format of a congregation with vows. Without a chapel and related buildings of their own and because they were active in catechising children – thanks to the Doctrinaires' overt encouragement – these Ursulines were not initially cloistered, but by the early 1600s they, too, had moved towards a partial form of enclosure. The way was already open, therefore, for the Paris Ursulines, located symbolically in close proximity to the Carmelites, to adopt full cloister from the outset. A papal bull of 1612 would confirm that requirement, while also allowing them to take a fourth vow to dedicate themselves to the teaching of girls. Within a few years, enclosed Ursuline convents would be springing up in cities and towns across France, combining an evidently attractive mix of the

Table 6.2 – New female orders

Ursulines (Fr. 1592)
Company of Our Lady (Lorraine, 1597)
Carmelites (Fr. 1604)
Capucines (Fr. 1606)
Company of Our Lady Mary (1606)
Visitation (1610)
Annonciades Celestes (Fr. 1612)
Our Lady of the Refuge (1624)

NB Fr. *indicates date of first French foundation by a foreign order.*

contemplative and active life, teaching girls in their schools, while living withdrawn from the outside world behind the walls and grills of their cloister, a combination which tested the ability of builders as much as the ingenuity of writers of rules and constitutions! The speed with which they were actually transformed, by a combination of episcopal pressure and social expectation, from loose groupings of unenclosed women into fully fledged nuns inhabiting conventional convents, varied enormously from area to area, since not all church authorities regarded full cloister as appropriate for them. Some of their own leading figures were against it and one of their congregations, based in the Spanish Franche-Comté, resolutely rejected it. Full enclosure was not achieved in the papal Comtat Venaissin and Provence region until the late 1650s, where one of its most convinced early opponents was the sister of Louis XIII's great favourite, the duke of Luynes.[14]

However, these vicissitudes did nothing to halt the Ursulines' staggering rate of expansion during the same period. Nearly 320 Ursuline convents opened in seventeenth-century France, most of them located in the provinces on each side of the Rhone, Saône and Seine valleys from Provence to Picardy, but with significant densities in Brittany and the Garonne valley. The overall population of these convents may have been somewhere between 10,000 and 12,000 nuns, whose main function was to teach girls who sometimes included boarders from better-off families. Not all Ursuline nuns were continually involved in teaching, and some houses operated rotas for the purpose, allowing individual nuns to return to full contemplative life after a spell of teaching. From what we can tell, it seems that the great majority accepted enclosure with little or no difficulty, while viewing teaching as an intrinsic part of their own road to salvation and sanctification, rather than a socially 'useful' activity. The move towards cloister also reassured families who were suspicious of the idea of women coming and going independently, and who instinctively preferred the prospect of a firmly controlled community with safeguards against the outside world. By the same token, the new regime enabled the Ursulines to recruit members from well-placed families of office-holders, lawyers, merchants and so on, while the teaching of boarders from the same social groups ensured, along with the nuns' own dowries, the financial underpinning of the communities themselves.[15]

During the early decades of the seventeenth century the Ursulines were shadowed by another congregation which resembled them to a remarkable degree, the Congregation of Notre Dame, founded by a niece of Montaigne, Jeanne de Lestonnac, who had been unable to endure the austere regime of the female Cistercian Feuillants of Toulouse. Drawing her inspiration from the Jesuits, she sought to found a congregation of nuns who would teach girls, especially in Protestant areas, in order to assist in the recovery of Catholicism. Her congregation was approved in 1607, before the French Ursulines were, and it involved roughly the same mixture of the active and contemplative life, of teaching and cloister, which the Ursulines would adopt in the coming years. Intriguingly, the foundress's desire to create a centralised congregation caused problems with her original sponsor, the archbishop of Bordeaux, who insisted that each house remain autonomous so that it could be subject to episcopal authority. This obstacle, which female orders and congregations faced far more than male orders, seems to have prevented the congregation from expanding on anything like the scale of the Ursulines whom it resembled so much in its objectives. When the ninety-four-year-old Lestonnac died in 1640, there were about thirty houses spread across the major towns of the south-west.[16]

The closest rival to the Ursulines in terms of numbers and extension was the Visitation Order, and it too was confronted from early on by the question of cloister. Its co-founders, Jeanne de Chantal and François de Sales, bishop of Geneva/Annecy, envisaged a form of female religious life which would attract women who either could not, or would not, accept the rigours of conventional reformed observance; they also proposed a community that would practise a Christocentric spirituality based on the 'devout humanism' which was de Sales's hallmark and which made considerable room for the religious needs and sensibilities of women. The first such community was formally founded in 1610 at Annecy, in Savoyard territory. It reflected sixteenth-century Italian experiences of 'open' and flexible female communities, whose members visited the sick, and which also accepted women wishing to retire or to 'retreat' there for a time. It is therefore highly paradoxical that the first French house, that of Lyon, was opened at the instigation of its archbishop who had spent much of his career in Rome, yet who now insisted on a tightening of the original Salesian format to suit French expectations over vows and cloister, not to mention episcopal control over the houses to be founded. De Sales yielded to Archbishop Marquemont's arguments, so the French Visitation promptly embraced cloister, solemn vows and the Rule of St Augustine, but retained the possibility of laywomen entering its houses for periods of retreat. These amendments were duly sealed by a formal papal bull issued in 1618.[17]

By that point, the flood of requests from towns across France already noted in relation to other orders, male and female, was already in motion, and a steady stream of new foundations followed thereafter.[18] Having satisfied the archbishop of Lyon, the Visitandines were soon widely sought after by other bishops throughout France, partly because of their readiness to act as educators like the Ursulines. The fact that they also attracted members who came from well-born noble and robe families meant there was no shortage of lay patrons and sponsors. Thus a varying combination of powerful families, the Jesuits and local bishops frequently overrode the opposition of local towns when it came to installing a new convent within their walls, but that phenomenon was not confined to the Visitation. This explains, for example, why there was a Visitation convent in Bayonne, the only one for many years in the entire region. It was founded there in 1640 because the then bishop of Bayonne, the well-connected François Fouquet, eldest brother of the future *surintendant des finances*, had three sisters and an aunt who already belonged to the Paris convent. The total number of Visitation houses reached eighty-seven by the death, in 1641, of Jeanne de Chantal, who over the years had constantly issued hard-nosed warnings to her *consoeurs* over the dangers of accepting invitations not based on adequate financial resources. She warned equally forcefully against rapid expansion because of the danger it represented for the consolidation of the 'spirit' of the order itself.

Some of these early foundations were indeed ephemeral, but that, too, was hardly confined to the Visitation, given that by the 1620s at the latest, the competition between religious orders of both sexes for houses in individual towns had reached cut-throat dimensions, in which resort to underhand tactics was not unknown. Mme de Chantal's other key requirement, it should be noted, was that foundations should, as far as possible, be located in the bigger towns which already had a Jesuit house, so that the nuns would receive spiritual direction from an order that she and de Sales trusted completely.[19] Despite her fears, there was no let-up in the pace of expansion, especially throughout the 1630s and 1640s, so that by the end of the Fronde there were some 124 Visitation houses in all, all but 17 of which were within France's contemporary borders. The pace dropped thereafter, and there were hardly any new houses established post-1670, a chronology which the Visitation shares with several other orders, male and female, and to which we shall return later. As to the Visitation's geography, it strongly resembled that of the Ursulines in its north-east to south-east profile, one in which the 'broader' Rhone valley, dominated by its 'founding' houses in Annecy and Lyon, and its neighbouring provinces, were especially prominent.

The New Congregations

It is clear from the early histories of the orders just examined that the question of what the standard way of life for female regulars should be was increasingly unavoidable. The Jesuits had caused a stir at their inception when they abandoned many of the conventional practices of the male mendicant orders, so it is not hard to see why moves to jettison cloister and its attendant life-routines among women would evince such reticence. But the conflicts over the active versus contemplative life which ensued should not be interpreted as a collision between repressive misogyny and a kind of proto-feminism, since the battle-lines were not drawn up in such a conveniently clear manner. For both practical and religious reasons, leading female reformers could be just as much in favour of enclosure and contemplative lifestyles as the male church establishment, some of whose members were capable of seeing that there was no good reason why all female houses should adopt strict enclosure. It is possible that the strong penitential piety that was one of the legacies of the later wars of religion favoured the installation of female religious orders which practised austerity, fasting and contemplation rather than action in the world around them; such a legacy would certainly explain the unexpected attractiveness of orders like the reformed Carmelites. It is also possible that the French church emerging from the wars was on the defensive, unsure of how to respond to the challenges of the day, and thus all the more likely to fall back on the traditional format for female orders – not least because enclosure and contemplation also had the firm sanction of the Council of Trent.[20] But there is clear evidence of an increasing willingness to contemplate less enclosed and more active formats, even if there was a visible hesitancy in accepting their full implications. Likewise, it would be artificial to pit a 'first' and 'second' generation of reformers and founders against each other, with the first preferring the traditional and the enclosed, and the second the simplified structure of the 'secular' congregations. There were simply too many overlaps based on personal ties and mutual influences at work during the early decades of the seventeenth century for such a distinction to carry conviction. After all, Vincent de Paul, who is associated with one of the most successful of the secular congregations, the Daughters of Charity, was a superior of the Visitation in Paris for many years. It is also the case that the leading religious figures of the period, both female and male, were themselves well aware of the many groups of pious women who, unbidden, came together of their own accord to pray, visit the sick and engage in other charitable activities, but who were reluctant – and also at times too poor – to exchange the informality that made them resemble conventional 'third' orders or confraternities for a formally regulated religious life behind convent walls.

The readiness of the church's authorities to approve a more simple style of female religious life was first successfully tested on a substantial scale by the celebrated Daughters of Charity.[21] As with so many female foundations, there was a male–female partnership, in this instance Louise de Marillac and Vincent de Paul, both deeply anchored in the leading *dévot* milieux of their time. Their connections to some of France's most powerful politicians and families, experience and reputations acted as indispensable reassurance that what they proposed was acceptable to the French church. Even so, the route was a tortuous one. It began with the parish-based confraternity of charity for devout laywomen, the Ladies of Charity, which de Paul started in his rural parish of Châtillon-les-Dombes in 1617. It might well have ended in failure, since the well-off Ladies were reluctant to engage in the messy and unpleasant work of assisting the sick and poor, but that obstacle incited Marillac and de Paul to invent a two-tier solution in which lower-class Daughters of Charity would assist the Ladies of Charity, drawn from the higher social groups that included many of de Paul's patrons, in their good works. It was only in 1633, after several years of experiment and uncertainty, that a rule was drafted for twelve women living in Marillac's house. It was clearly stipulated that the Daughters of Charity were not – any more than the Ladies of Charity themselves – to be cloister nuns, but rather secular women living in a community who were free to come and go in the service of the poor, prisoners, abandoned children and the sick. With the Ladies drifting further away into a fund-raising role, the Daughters began taking 'simple' vows in 1640 which, because they were renewable annually (with the option of quitting altogether that this entailed), did not make them a religious order nor require them to adopt cloister. As de Paul himself famously put it, 'the houses of the sick will be their sole monastery, a rented room their convent cell, the parish church their chapel, the streets their cloister, obedience their enclosure . . . the fear of God their convent grille, holy modesty their veil, unceasing confidence in divine providence their vows of profession'.[22] By the time Marillac and de Paul died in 1660, they had nurtured into maturity a form of female religious life that proved highly attractive, consisting at that point of about sixty houses within France. In 1668, when Clement IX granted the congregation papal approval, he designated them as a confraternity rather than as a religious order, as this seemed to be the only label that the post-Tridentine papacy could find that fitted the Daughters of Charity. In the no less difficult aim of gaining episcopal approval in France for unenclosed women, the decision formally to subject the Daughters to the Congregation of the Mission was probably crucial: here, too, an older model could serve new purposes.

The Daughters of Charity were only one, albeit the most successful, of the new secular congregations of women founded in seventeenth-century France.

142 CLERICAL WORLDS IN CONTEXT

Table 6.3. – New female congregations[23]

The Daughters of the Cross of St Quentin (1626)
Hospitallers of Dieppe (1629)
Daughters of Charity (1633)
Daughters of Ste Geneviève (Miramionnes) (1636/1658)
Hospitallers of St Joseph, La Flèche (1643)
Our Lady of Charity, Caen (1643)
Sisters of Charity of St Charles, Nancy (1651)
Sisters of St Joseph, Le Puy (1651)
Congregation of St Thomas of Villanova (1661)
Christian and Charitable Schools of the Infant Jesus, Rouen (1662/1669)
Sisters of the Holy Sacrament and Charity of Bourges (1671)
Daughters of Instruction of the Infant Jesus, Le Puy (1667/1676)
Daughters of the Trinity, Valence (1676)
Sisters of Charity and Christian Instruction of Nevers (1680)
Sisters of St Charles of Lyon (1680)
Christian Union of Fontenay (1680)
Sister of Charity of Our Lady of Evron (1682)
Hospitallers of Our Lady of Charity, Dijon (1683)
Congregation of the Daughters of the Holy Virgin ('the Retreat') of Vannes (1674–8)
Sisters of St Anne of Providence, Saumur (1693/1709)
Sisters of St Paul of Chartres (1696)
Sisters of Charity of Sainville (1697)
Daughters of Wisdom (1703)
Sisters of the Sacred Heart of Ernemont (1711)
Daughters of the Good Saviour of Caen (1712)
Mathurines of Paris (1713)
Sisters of Holy Sacrament of Autun (1732)

Table 6.3 lists only the most prominent of the other congregations founded by the early eighteenth century, and it does not include a small number of congregations which subsequently adopted full cloister and became recognised orders. The table also indicates how sustained across the seventeenth century the foundation of new congregations was, though it cannot of itself convey the fact that many of them remained local and relatively small in their membership. Of the approximately thirty congregations to appear between 1600 and the revolution, the majority were founded under Louis XIV; on the other hand, a few of them, such as the Daughters of the Cross, were actually a few years older than the Daughters of Charity. The table shows that several of these congregations also made a point of calling themselves 'daughters' (*filles*) in order to demonstrate that they were seculars, and not classic 'choir' nuns (*religieuses*).

The misery and social distress that mid-seventeenth century France experienced through war, harvest failure and growing poverty provided limitless scope for the Daughters of Charity and their imitators, as is clearly suggested by both the chronology and the geography of their emergence, to which we will return later. From the outset a high proportion of their members were attached to the hospices and hospitals, old and new, of the day, but were also involved in providing assistance to people in their homes.[24] Women were indeed edged out of the medical profession, but the world of nursing was almost entirely 'feminised' during the seventeenth century: the Brothers of St John of God were the only male group to remain active in it, but in France they ran only around thirty institutions before 1750.[25] The claustration of the female Augustinian hospitallers which followed Trent and the wars of religion tested their ability – and especially their willingness – to continue to work full-time in hospitals. Despite claustration, they did retain many of their nursing activities, especially in northern France, where they were historically most numerous. Yet combining cloister and such activities created real difficulties both for the nuns and for the local authorities, problems that became far less acute when the new congregations developed.

But it was not just a matter of replacing one set of nursing personnel with another: seventeenth-century France also witnessed a major expansion in the kinds – and therefore the numbers – of 'medical' institutions compared to earlier centuries. Some older institutions like leper-houses were by now redundant, and a raft of new ones such as hospitals for orphans, abandoned children, the mentally deranged, 'fallen' women, the incurable – not to mention the military hospitals and the grand 'general hospitals' of the reign of Louis XIV – transformed the hospital and nursing landscape.[26] Consequently, the demand for nursing sisters, however limited their professional skills might be, was insatiable, and it continued well into the eighteenth century, gradually bringing new, if often small, groups of nursing sisters into large numbers of middling and small towns which probably never had such communities hitherto.

The congregations listed in table 6.3 reflect this demand and suggest how it was met. Instead of a few major congregations fanning out in almost every direction, we see essentially local initiatives across many provinces, mainly in northern and central France; southern France retained its municipal institutions run by lay personnel for much longer. The new congregations typically began with a number of *dévot* women gathering together informally to assist the poor of their town or neighbourhood; in due course, under the leadership of an individual woman and with the assistance of a local clerical mentor, they would form a community, which also meant adopting a rule of life. Gaining episcopal approval was a key step, since bishops could add additional features to their observance, such as the taking of vows, annual or triennial.[27] Obtaining royal approval in the shape of letters patent could be infinitely more difficult, and the discrepancies from one congregation to the next over how long that took – anywhere from twenty to a hundred years – are striking. These successive milestones along the road to full recognition as a congregation makes assigning precise founding dates to them somewhat arbitrary; we are looking at processes rather than events.

Another important reason for the proliferation across France of the new congregations has already been alluded to – episcopal authority. France's bishops were even more wary of female orders with centralised structures than of their male counterparts, and increasingly insisted on their authority to control them. Louise de Marillac actually feared that her congregation would face possible fragmentation and enclosure if it became subjected in this way; that fear, as we saw, led her to resort to the medieval male–female 'twinning' format with the Lazarists. Some bishops were content simply to grant recognition to locally based groups, but others invited members of existing congregations from elsewhere in France to settle in their dioceses. New congregations, such as the Daughters of Charity, Hospitallers of Le Havre and La Flèche, or the Sisters of Saint Joseph of Le Puy owed some of their expansion to such invitations. But as often as not the outcome was less expansion than the creation of a purely diocesan congregation, one based on adapting the model provided by the outside congregation in question and making it fully subject to episcopal control. Episcopal initiatives like these seem to have grown during Louis XIV's reign, as bishops sought to ensure that the 'general hospitals' (of which they were sometimes the real founders) in their dioceses were well staffed.[28]

It would, however, be a mistake to see these congregations as highly focused 'nursing' organisations like their successors of more recent times. Precisely because of the religious impulse that brought them together in the first place, their nursing activities were part of a broader charitable 'mission'. Their involvement with hospitals and nursing arose, as we saw, from two sets of circumstances – the claustration of the older medieval female hospitallers and the growth of a far greater range of hospital-style institutions during the seventeenth century. But from the congregations' point of view, the distress of France's poorer classes was more than medical in nature; the religious instruction of people in the various 'hospitals' was just as important as treating their illnesses.[29] Visits to people in their homes had the same objectives, and were no less widely practised. The progressive 'discovery' of popular religious ignorance also lay at the origin of several of these congregations – as will be evident from the names of some of them – while others owed their existence to the drive to catechise and educate the daughters of Protestant families in the decades either side of the Revocation of the Edict of Nantes (1685).

The schoolmistresses or nursing sisters belonging to these often small groups were worlds removed from the enclosed environments of the boarding schools for the social elites of the Ursuline or Visitation orders: they were frequently dispersed throughout small-town schools or hospitals, in some cases living totally outside the religious community for much of the time, and relying on regular reunions – retreats, in fact – in order to maintain their sense of belonging to a religious congregation.[30] In some ways, they resembled the male congregations of lay brothers founded by Jean-Baptiste de la Salle and his imitators. Between them, however, the orders and congregations which engaged in teaching girls and staffing hospitals transformed the internal balance of France's female orders, as well as their relation with French society generally. Considering the widespread reservations about such un-cloistered *dévotes* in the early seventeenth century, it is intriguing to find the bishop of Cahors in 1673 forbidding the members of a new congregation that he had approved from conceiving, as he put it, 'any desire to form a religious order or found convents, as has sometimes happened. We order that these widows and women who have come together in their houses to run schools shall be, and shall remain, seculars, wearing secular clothes with the appropriate modesty, without being compelled to take any vows or to observe cloister'.[31] That Bishop Le Jay could speak in such terms at all shows how significantly attitudes had shifted since Archbishop Marquemont's stance towards the Visitation in the 1610s.

With the spectrum of acceptable forms of female 'regular' life expanding to such an extent, especially during the middle decades of the century, the scope for new foundations and new recruits itself grew, even if none of those created after mid-century came remotely near to matching the Ursulines, Visitation or Daughters of Charity. The emergence of numerous local, diocesan groupings brought the phenomenon to towns and areas often untouched by the bigger orders, old and new. Just as crucially, these developments considerably enlarged the *social* scope of recruitment, since many of the later congregations of seculars did not require dowries of new entrants. That alone enabled women from lower social groups to join these communities at little or no expense to themselves or their families. Taken together, these changes help to explain why the numbers of female regulars in France continued to rise beyond those of their male counterparts well into the second half of the seventeenth century and beyond.

Local Impact

The local impact of all the changes discussed so far could be dramatic, transforming the social and religious profile of towns and cities, even when allowance is made for their smaller scale and fewer resources compared to the existing orders. We should not forget that new female houses were being founded at the same time as new male ones, and that all of them were competing for support, resources and space in more or less the same places. Wherever we turn, the pattern observed seems broadly the same. The 'explosion' in Paris is well documented, where forty-five new female houses were founded in the years 1600–50, compared to twenty for men. Bordeaux and Angers had only one female house each in 1600, but that rose to eight by 1650 for Bordeaux and to thirteen for Angers by 1692. By the time it became French under Louis XIV, Lille had moved from ten religious houses for men and women in 1588 to twenty-seven by 1667, when female regulars outnumbered men by nearly two to one (610 compared to 350). Douai, also in northern France and with a population of 15,000 people, had thirteen female houses (one fewer than for men) by 1687, compared to just two in 1568.[32] The same pattern is apparent in towns as diverse as Troyes, Blois and Saint-Denis. The scale of the phenomenon can be measured via dioceses rather than merely towns, and the figures for the three contiguous and highly rural central dioceses of Clermont, Limoges and Tulle show how from one decade to another the pace of new foundations could vary, with female houses outstripping the numbers of male foundations (by fifty-one to thirty-four) despite a slower start before 1600.[33]

Throughout France, in towns where there had been for centuries no more than one female religious house, there were now up to three or four, and such proportions were replicated in the larger cities. The religious lives of these towns were subtly altered by the presence within their midst of female communities that were quite distinct in their status, reputation and activities, not to mention the social background of their respective members. The enclosed orders attracted the daughters of the better-off who could afford dowries and other gifts, but even among their members there was a clear hierarchy between choir nuns (*religieuses*) and lay sisters (*converses*), who did not bring a dowry and who performed many of the menial tasks that the choir nuns could not be asked to do. The sisters joining the secular congregations were usually a further step down the social ladder, since many did not require dowries or accoutrements such as the habit worn by full choir nuns; they wore ordinary clothes instead, and usually dressed in a manner that made them resemble widows.

Despite the rising numbers, female orders and congregations did experience many of the problems faced by the male orders from the mid-seventeenth century onwards. Without attempting to pinpoint a 'saturation point' occurring around 1650 or 1670 or later, it is nevertheless evident that a slow-down, rather than an end, to foundations occurred from around mid-century; at least seven new congregations were founded between 1703 and 1762.[34] But that is only part of the picture. The process of 'catching up' with the male regulars had its own dynamic, and it is likely that the actual numbers of women within individual houses continued to rise under Louis XIV and later. In a town like Angers, it is clear that the new female houses from the Ursulines onwards tended to have consistently higher numbers of members than the older male orders.[35] The real worry for most parties – church authorities, town officials, families and the nuns themselves – was how financially secure these new communities really were at a time when recruitment was still buoyant. More generalised fears were expressed that the influx of both men and women into religious orders was an unhealthy sign, and that the orders, especially the female ones, were siphoning off too much of the wealth of families in uneconomic directions.[36] It was this which led to a royal edict of December 1666 regulating, for the first time on such a scale, the establishment of new orders and religious houses, even though its prime mover, Colbert, wished to go much further and close down the most insecure of the existing establishments, male as well as female. In particular, he wished to raise the minimum legal age for joining orders among women from the canonical sixteen to twenty (and to twenty-five for men), but he had to settle for a set of rules mainly governing *future* foundations. Henceforth, new foundations would need to be approved by the grant of royal letters patent which required a prior enquiry on the ground and consultation with the local authorities concerned.[37] It would be wrong to think that royal legislation of itself significantly prevented new foundations – the list given above demonstrates that they continued – but when and where it echoed local sentiments, it could slow them down considerably. It was the secular congregations involved in nursing, charity and teaching that were most likely to cope best with such restrictions.

Dowries and Finances

As already noted, the finances of the orders loomed increasingly large in both society's and the crown's attitudes towards them by, at the latest, Louis XIV's personal rule. Individual communities, old and new, had to look after their own finances as best they could, since they could not usually count on much support, even when in distress, from the other houses belonging to the same order or congregation as themselves; the predicament of entirely 'independent' houses was even more dramatic in such circumstances. Older, established orders and convents could rely on their endowments, but like their male counterparts, they still needed to manage their assets carefully, and it took only one incompetent or corrupt 'treasurer' to jeopardise severely a house's entire future. The newer orders were more reliant on initial benefactions if they were to get off the ground, and they usually needed to provide evidence of such endowments in order to obtain the permission of church and municipal officials in order to settle in a given place. It was only when revenues were sufficiently secure that they could borrow money to build or extend their premises as their numbers, needs and activities dictated. But it was not unknown for funds promised by early patrons either not to materialise at all, or to do so tardily or in instalments, making the juggling of community finances even more fraught, and leading in some cases to the closure of individual communities by the law courts at the request of creditors.

One of the most familiar and long-standing 'institutions' of female religious orders, the dowry, mirrors many of the changes occurring in seventeenth-century France.[38] In some ways, the dowry can be compared to the 'clerical title' required of male clerics wishing to take priestly orders. But there were differences between them: if a male cleric already possessed a benefice, the title cost his family nothing; no such option was available to future nuns and their families. Moreover, whereas the monetary value of the clerical title was identical within a given diocese and, increasingly, across several dioceses in our period, that of convent dowries varied markedly from one convent to another within the same town. In this respect at least, placing daughters in the church was more expensive for families than placing sons, because virtually all convent dowries were of much higher value than clerical titles. But that consideration has to be set alongside another contemporary yardstick: convent dowries fell far short of marriage dowries, which could be several times greater in value.

Dowries were a vital source of funds for convents, especially those belonging to enclosed orders, since outright cash gifts were probably fewer and smaller than usually imagined. Setting the value of a dowry was itself critical for individual houses, and nothing better reflected their relative place within the hierarchy of female orders than the dowry 'tariff' they operated.[39] The figure was determined in part by the expectations of families placing daughters, particularly in towns with two or more convents, but also by the nature of the houses in question (contemplatives, teachers and so on), since some social groups, for example, found manual work for their daughters wholly unacceptable. Teaching orders, for instance, could not command the same dowries as those which did not teach. The value of the dowry would in turn 'stratify' a town's convents along different social lines, drawing particular social groups and families towards one, sometimes two, convents over several generations, since generational overlap within convents was highly prized by families which could rely on older-generation members to look after their younger relatives. Dowries could also be used as levers by families seeking special privileges or dispensations for their offspring, and convents in financial difficulties did not always find such offers easy to refuse, even if they threatened to undermine the rules of common observance within the convent walls. Large numbers of convents, old and new, replaced the payment of dowries in annuities with cash down-payments from the early seventeenth century onwards, a step that elicited protests until well into the next century, protests which seem to have involved older noble families with limited revenues and, therefore, little chance of raising the capital required for dowries.

While convents might be driven to set the bar for dowries on the high side, families, local authorities and churchmen were apt to take different – and differing – views. For the bishops, high dowry requirements could deny entry to women with real talents and a real wish to become nuns but who did not have the means to do so. For local authorities, dowries could mean too much wealth being 'drained away' by religious orders into mortmain. As for families, self-interest drove them to negotiate the convents' demands downwards, and the period between a daughter entering a convent as a 'postulant' and taking her vows was dominated by negotiations between the two parties over the size of the dowry and the modalities for payment. *Ceteris paribus*, successful negotiations led to a religious profession, unsuccessful ones either to outright rejection of the postulant or to her becoming a lay sister, whose status was well below that of the professed 'choir' nuns. Even if negotiations were successful, families might still find themselves juggling their own financial commitments, just as they did with the dowries of married daughters – borrowing, paying by instalments, defaulting and renegotiating. The fact that many of the secular congregations did not demand dowries put them in a very different position to the full-scale orders, which partly explains the different impact on them of the financial crises of the later years of Louis XIV and the regency that followed it.

It is not surprising, therefore, that the question of female dowries loomed large when the crown felt moved under Louis XIV to regulate the religious orders. Worries over dowries had already been expressed in several quarters, with law courts like the *parlements* of Dijon and Paris attempting to limit them to a percentage of what the future nun would have inherited had she remained in the world. A royal declaration of 1693 insisted that dowry contracts be drawn up and signed before a notary, and fixed a maximum figure of 8,000 *livres* in Paris and 6,000 *livres* for other towns; it also allowed families to pay a life-annuity of 500 *livres* for Paris and 350 for elsewhere.[40] If the crown set such figures, it was almost certainly because actual dowries at the time were already higher than those figures themselves, but it is equally likely that dowry values varied considerably from place to place across France, depending on local levels of wealth.

The crown's interventions in the orders' affairs could also take a financial rather than a regulatory turn. Early attempts, under Richelieu, to extract a one-off tax from the orders had largely failed, as did Colbert's later plans to that effect, but in 1689, the crown's financial position was so bad that such self-denial was no longer possible. The tactic it now used was not entirely new – to impose an 'amortisation' tax on all property acquired by the religious orders since 1641 and which had consequently passed into mortmain. One contemporary called the 1689 tax 'the Saint Barthélemy [i.e. the massacre] of the clergy'. However, its impact was not uniform, since it was bound to hit the more recent and more vulnerable religious orders and congregations most heavily; the older an individual house was, the less likely that its property had been acquired since 1641; the new orders had frequently used the dowries of their nuns to acquire house property, a safe investment of the kind that nuns' families themselves would have approved of. Previously knife-edged budgets were now thrown into disarray by the crown's sudden demands, and communities were forced to borrow well beyond their means in order to meet their immediate obligations. And all this occurred during the darkest decades of Louis XIV's reign – 'the years of misery' – which in fact extended into the early 1720s. If the 1689 taxes were bad enough, the financial experiments known as the 'Law System' (1718–20) were far worse in their impact, although they did not only affect the religious orders. The financial crash of 1720 meant that religious houses whose main source of revenue came from investments in government bonds (*rentes*) now found them being redeemed by their creditors for virtually nominal sums with increasingly worthless banknotes, while their worsening situation enabled families, who had probably themselves suffered financially, to beat down the value of new dowries or not pay existing ones.[41] The Ursulines of Bordeaux, who had to accept the redemption of 56,000 *livres* of capital in banknotes, were virtually bankrupted as a result, and they were not alone.[42] A few years later, in 1727, the crown responded to the pleas of the female orders by establishing the *Commission des secours* which, as its name suggests, was meant to assist them in weathering the crisis, and which included closing down houses that were no longer financially viable.[43]

Conclusion

It would be abusing the benefit of hindsight to regard 1727 as a turning point in the history of France's female orders. All the signs are that they continued to recruit in large numbers, and more successfully than the male orders, for several decades more. The variety of forms invented by seventeenth-century

France to get round the precepts of the church after the Council of Trent's strictures on full enclosure was impressive by any standard, and they broadened significantly the social constituency of those who could envisage joining an order or congregation. The religious lives of these women cannot be easily summarised, since the lifestyles of choir nuns and those of nursing or teaching sisters could hardly have been more different. Enclosed convents become primarily liturgical communities, where religious services and the recitation in common of the divine office – the *opus Dei* – took up much of the day, with private devotions varying in importance from order to order; such routines were more onerous than we might imagine, and in convents where teaching also occurred it was not unknown to find nuns complaining that teaching obligations disrupted their spiritual lives.[44] Mastering the tensions between the religious and professional activities was far from easy, even among the new non-cloistered congregations brought up on Vincent de Paul's 'work is prayer' philosophy, as is evident when the lay administrators of hospitals complained that the sisters spent too much time praying and not enough tending the sick. We should not take such accusations as factual truth: the administrators wanted as much as they could get from the sisters, whose working days were probably as onerous and labour-intensive as any other occupation of their time.[45] Indeed, what is surprising is that more of them did not opt out of an 'active' apostolate altogether and retreat into a contemplative environment.

Despite their success in engineering a degree of self-government for themselves, the female orders retained numerous ties, some more voluntary than others, with their male counterparts. Many elements of the spiritual culture of individual houses derived from the male clergy, themselves mostly members of religious orders, who acted as their confessors, preachers and directors of conscience. Where it continued to exist, the traditional 'pairing' of male and female orders obviously removed the element of choice here; where no such pairing existed, houses and orders made their own spiritual choices. Mme de Chantal, as we saw, preferred the Jesuits above all others as preachers and confessors for the convents of the Visitation. Some male orders, such as the Maurists and the Oratory, refused to take on such activities at all, but alternative sources of guidance, especially among the new Capuchins and Récollets, were not in short supply. Long-term connections between orders were built upon such intimate connections, but it was not unknown for individual convents to change their affiliations.

As for the secular congregations, some were founded by influential spiritual directors like Jean Eudes (Congregation of Our Lady of Charity, Caen), Charles Démia (St Charles of Lyon) or the Minim, Nicolas Barré (Christian and Charitable Schools of Rouen, Ladies of St Maur). These individuals also founded parallel male congregations, and acted in close liaison with local female *dévotes* when founding female congregations. It seems that some members of the smaller secular congregations were barely literate, and the onerous tasks they shouldered, especially as nurses, probably left them with little time or energy for intense religious experiences.[46] Indeed, their religious lives were probably not hugely different from those of the 'ordinary' *dévote* women who belonged to the third orders or confraternities of the average parish, and from whose ranks they were themselves so often drawn. At this particular point of contact between French society and its religious orders, the differences between the two would not have been easily visible to the uninitiated eye. And since a majority of convents and communities were engaged in some form of teaching, they contributed to the religious education of substantial sections of French society of the day.[47] It is unfortunate that such activity has left so few documentary traces but, as we shall see later, this early chapter of 'le catholicisme au féminin' played a significant part in the diffusion of religious change across France during our period.

PART 3

A New Clergy?

CHAPTER 7

The Bishops: Adaptation and Action

The reform of the church that was so universally demanded across sixteenth-century Europe depended crucially on the clergy, regardless of the conflicting views that emerged during the Reformation about the exact nature of their orders or ministry. As befitted the most distinctively 'clerical' of church councils to date, Trent went to great lengths to underline the centrality of clerical action at every level of the church, and its repeated emphasis on dioceses and parishes as the central units in church life was accompanied by corresponding demands on the clergy in charge of them. The council's well-known but belated enthusiasm for episcopal authority collided sharply with the competing claims of papal power, a clash that nearly paralysed Trent. The crisis was resolved by simply burying the subject altogether, and the Gallican traditions of France, which themselves exalted episcopal power to an extent unrivalled elsewhere in Europe, were in no way diminished by this contretemps. Indeed, the heat generated by the 1563 debate on the source and nature of episcopal power has too often obscured the fact that the actual decrees of Trent showed a real awareness of the different circumstances of individual churches and, therefore, of the need to leave the conduct of reform to the judgement and initiative of local bishops rather than placing it under the direction of the growing papal bureaucracy.

Crown and Episcopate

France was not the only country in Europe in which the principal generators and agents of religious reform were themselves regarded as being seriously in need of reform. But 'reforming' the episcopate was quite a different matter to reforming the rest of the clergy, and certainly one that could not be accomplished by a period of preparation in a seminary or college. Bishops might be entrusted with reforming those under their jurisdiction, but who would reform *them*? Trent itself used forthright language to express its disapproval of the worldliness of many contemporary bishops, but while it prescribed the kinds of attitude and behaviour that were desirable in a bishop, it said virtually nothing about how its ideal of the *bonus pastor* was to be realised. It is worth noting that it merely recapitulated the clauses of the Concordat of Bologna as to the minimum age, university degrees and clerical orders required of incoming bishops, and extended them beyond France to the wider church.[1] In doing so, Trent tacitly accepted that episcopal reform was intimately dependent on the practice of church patronage at the highest levels throughout Europe. The evolution of the French episcopate in our period cannot be understood without reference to it.[2]

At the outset, it may seem surprising that until well into the seventeenth century the Concordat of Bologna, despite its role in setting explicit standards for entry into the episcopate, was widely held to have led to a decline in the calibre of France's bishops. It upset what was regarded as the proper balance of the relationship of church and crown by giving the crown too much power within the church. As a result, the crown was perceived as being too prone to misuse its church-patronage rights by pursuing short-term objectives – making 'political' appointments, favouring particular families or court clerics, buying the support of possible malcontents and so on. The spread of 'pluralism' within the episcopate, whereby powerful church figures might hold several dioceses simultaneously, the granting of dioceses 'in administration' to cardinals or bishops, not to mention the nomination of underage bishops – all of this, and other forms of patronage-driven horse-trading, were held responsible for the condition of a church whose natural leaders were inadequate precisely at the moment when competent bishops were most necessary. As a result, until 1615 the assemblies of clergy pleaded in vain for a return to episcopal elections. Alongside many observers, French and non-French, successive papal nuncios commented negatively on the post-Bologna episcopate, and their judgements found their way into the instructions which Rome issued to each new papal nuncio, accompanied by an injunction to act vigilantly over dubious episcopal nominations. It was not until the ministry of Richelieu that this pattern ceased, and the reputation of the French episcopate finally entered a new and, viewed from Rome at least, more positive phase.

Such a transformation in the fortunes of France's episcopate had not occurred overnight, during the 1620s. For much of the wars of religion, parts of the south and west, whose dioceses had large Protestant populations, were wholly or partly inaccessible to their bishops, some of whom found themselves having to reside elsewhere. Likewise, there seems little doubt that as the wars dragged on, the crown partially lost effective control of its fund of church patronage, and it often found itself rubber-stamping practices such as the exchanges of dioceses, prearranged successions, grants of massive pensions off episcopal revenues and so on, which were initiated by third parties rather than by the king and his advisers. It is likely that the predicament of many of France's numerous abbeys was far worse than that of its bishoprics at this point. Such practices were sufficiently evident by 1579 for the Assembly of Clergy to draw up an impressive, albeit by its own admission incomplete, list of the dioceses – mostly in the south – that had been granted in this way to clerics who were acting as dependents and 'seat-warmers' for more powerful parties, most of whom were noble families whose local powers or connections the crown desperately needed to satisfy. It took more than a new king and dynasty after 1589 for things to change; by 1595, approximately one-third of all French dioceses had no bishop at all. For many years, Henri IV had far more urgent problems than episcopal patronage to deal with, problems which also led him to sanction many dubious nominations. When the assembly of 1605 congratulated him on his choice of bishops, it was more of an exhortation to improve his choices than an accurate historical record of his decisions so far. Indeed, the king's murder in 1610 and the long decade of political uncertainty that followed it saw the crown again using episcopal patronage to satisfy large numbers of noble families wishing to place their sons in the episcopate; its willingness during the 1610s to accept an unprecedented number of prearranged successions (co-adjutorships) for dioceses led Paul V to complain that the king of France was effectively depriving himself of patronage in years to come.

It was not until the ministry of Richelieu that the crown (re)gained something approaching real mastery of episcopal patronage, and that a template of the French episcopate for the next century or so took shape. It was from this point onwards that papal nuncios no longer received specific instructions to keep a close eye on episcopal nominations, which are rarely commented upon in nuncios' despatches thereafter. Richelieu's own career is a classic warning against systematically assuming that because bishops were appointed for reasons that contemporaries deplored, they could never shake off the 'original sin' enshrined in the circumstances of their elevation. Originally nominated a bishop by Henri IV when no more than sixteen years old and as a recognition of his late father's services to the crown, Richelieu was approved by the pope at twenty-one, even though the minimum age for a French bishop was twenty-six, itself by far the lowest in Europe. Long before he became Louis XIII's chief minister, he had emerged as one of an energetic younger generation of bishops who threw themselves into repairing the damage done by the wars of religion. Moreover, his generation owed a great deal to an even older cohort of bishops, some of whom had belonged to the Catholic League, and who were still in office under Henri IV and the young Louis XIII. As a minister, Richelieu was, of course, not averse to using church patronage for his own many purposes, but as an experienced church figure with a large and ever-growing clerical clientele, he was better placed than any lay royal minister would have been to improve the calibre of episcopal nominations. He took several years to tighten his grip on the system, and was aided in no small measure by the fact that Louis XIII seems increasingly to have trusted him in this particular sphere of activity; the results are evident in the kind of episcopal nominations occurring during these years.

Richelieu's successor, Mazarin, was prevented for almost a decade (1643–53) by his political vulnerability from matching his predecessor's mastery of church patronage. Interestingly, one reason for Mazarin's limited grip was the emergence in 1643, the same year that he became chief minister, of a body usually known as the *conseil de conscience*, whose purpose was to advise the king – or rather the Queen Regent, Anne of Austria, since Louis XIV was a minor until 1651 – on questions of church patronage and religious affairs generally for 'the discharge of his conscience', as the contemporary phrase put it. The idea of such an advisory role had originally been adumbrated by the assemblies of clergy under Henri IV, but it was for a long time a quite tentative notion – it was not clear, for example, whether it could be exercised by one person, or by several individuals meeting as a council of some kind. Characteristically, Richelieu seems to have taken the view that he would himself be a one-man *conseil de conscience* to Louis XIII, but in 1643 Mazarin, the ministerial debutant, was unable to monopolise that role for himself. Ten years later, after the end of the Fronde, he was finally strong enough to elbow aside the remaining members of the *conseil* established in 1643, and engage in his own inimitable *combinazioni* involving France's dioceses. Crucially, however, neither Mazarin nor Louis XIV after him were able – or perhaps anxious – to turn the clock backwards: the *conseil de conscience* had become entrenched as, at least, an idea and an aspiration; its precise shape and composition were another matter, and were subject to variation, as the early years of Louis XIV's reign would again demonstrate. What is decisive, however, is that the king now felt compelled to take regular advice on church matters, patronage included, from members of the clergy, usually his confessor or the archbishop of Paris, but from others too, if he so wished.

The crown's recovery of control over episcopal patronage had been accompanied by a powerful demand that church patronage, especially concerning bishoprics, be treated as a distinctive element of royal patronage, with implications for the royal conscience. The fact that the handling of nominations to abbeys, male and female, was far less subject to such considerations, may be regarded as proof, *a contrario*, of this assertion. Under Louis XIV, the process of choosing bishops became gradually more organised and ritualised (decisions were finalised and announced on major feast days from the early 1680s onwards) than was previously the case. What France did not do, however, was imitate Spain by establishing an elaborate bureaucracy charged with administering its church patronage. Under Louis XIV, the king regularly met his confessor, who kept most of the relevant paperwork in his personal possession, or the archbishop of Paris (or other clerics) in a routine manner, even when there were no major decisions to be made; the names of individual clerics deemed worthy of promotion were added to the confessor's list, which was regularly updated so that a pool of potential bishops, abbots, court almoners and the like was available when nominations had to be made. It was the confessor's responsibility to seek out individual names and to obtain information from his wide network of sources within the French clergy that those being considered for preferment were worthy and reliable. For all its limitations, this mechanism, which retained a good deal of informality, enabled the crown to prepare major decisions well in advance and to abandon the 'first-come, first-served' habits of previous generations. Equally importantly, it also enabled the crown to send out strong signals as to the kind of cleric who would henceforth be favoured for episcopal office – signals which tended to be quickly picked up by the clerical milieux at which they were directed.

Origins

The kind of episcopate that emerged in the course of the century reflected both the fluctuations in royal power and the shifts in attitudes towards the exercise of its patronage rights. The diversity of backgrounds – geographical, social, intellectual and otherwise – of the 600 or so individuals seated as bishops from Henri IV to Louis XIV also means that simple, lapidary characterisations of them would be both trite and misleading. Perhaps the first point that should be made is that the episcopate of the long seventeenth century was not nearly as socially exclusive as its eighteenth-century successor, whose aristocratic image has generally tended to be surreptitiously backdated to earlier periods. The episcopate of the wars of religion and the Henri IV years (*c.*1560–1610) included some of the lowest proportions of nobles – one-third to one-half of the bishops were from bourgeois, commoner or otherwise undetermined social backgrounds – of the entire early modern period. Such an unexpected profile had far less to do with a monarchy preferring a socially diverse episcopate – a preference which it would have been far too weak to impose anyway – than with its political difficulties and the exigencies of the nobility during this turbulent period. The presence of 'seat-warmer' bishops, mostly of commoner origins, was one manifestation of these developments, and it did not endure beyond the circumstances of the period in question. By contrast, the renewed weakness of the crown after Henri IV's death in the 1610s had the opposite effect of heralding a return to the ranks of the episcopate of sons of established noble families. It was, as we saw, only from the late 1620s to the early 1640s that Richelieu was able to impose his personal choices of bishop. They, too, happened to be more socially diverse than Richelieu's *Political Testament* would lead us to expect: he may indeed have instinctively believed that sons of the nobility like himself 'naturally' made the best bishops, since they were born to govern, but his own practice belies that assumption. It was not really until the 1640s and 1650s, with the shock of the Fronde acting as a catalyst, that the nobility began to regain a dominant position within the episcopate. Non-noble bishops declined from a record high point of 38 per cent of newcomers under Richelieu to an average of around 22 per cent across the personal government of Louis XIV, a proportion that would again shrink dramatically in the next century.

It is also clear that the noble bishops of the seventeenth century were not quite as 'aristocratic' as those of the sixteenth or eighteenth centuries. Great names did, as always, figure among them – Guise, La Rochefoucauld, Estrées – but most of them were drawn either from the ranks of the older, middling-rank 'sword' nobility or from families that had been ennobled, sometimes very recently, by the tenure of royal office, itself an increasingly significant source of noble status. There were more episcopal sons of peers under Louis XIV than previously, but there were also far more peers *tout* court in France by then. There were more Colbert bishops (six plus two Desmarest cousins!) under Louis XIV than from any other family, a pointed reminder that ministerial and court connections were as valuable as ever for entry into the episcopate. Because intermarriage between 'old' and 'new' families was easier and more widespread in France than in the Empire, continuity of family presence within the episcopate over several generations was considerable, despite the fact that the virtually automatic mechanisms for keeping benefices in family hands (resignations in favour of a designated successor, exchanges of benefices and so on) were formally inoperative among the higher clergy. That prearranged episcopal successions did occur, as we have just seen, either side of 1600 was due to the crown consenting to them for reasons of its own. Louis XIV made it quite clear – and the message was effectively diffused by his confessors – that he disliked 'arranged' successions to bishops who were still in office, especially if they involved an uncle to nephew or some other family-centred succession, and they virtually disappeared as a result. But it was the mechanism itself, which smacked of 'proprietary' attitudes to particular dioceses, that was unacceptable, and emphatically not the idea that individual families might continue to provide bishops to the French church. In fact, what is striking on a closer examination of the French episcopate is how many of its members were related to predecessors and contemporaries in the episcopate, and this trait was not exclusive to bishops of the highest social status. The relative importance of kinship ties obviously enabled bishops to 'make' the careers of their younger relatives, but without the crown's increased attention to the demands of episcopal office itself such grooming might only have secured them second-rank positions in the French church rather than membership of the episcopate. What were those demands? Were they formal or informal?

Education

In requiring future bishops to have taken a degree in law or theology from a 'famous university', or to have attended an equivalent academy, the parties to the Concordat of Bologna might appear not to make heavy demands on future bishops. The terms in which they were expressed suggest a desire to avoid a single inflexible standard, and that a good education was what they had in mind. Trent, as we saw, reiterated rather than elaborated on Bologna, being more concerned with other aspects of episcopal activity. Some of the most distinguished bishops of the sixteenth and early seventeenth centuries had not attended university at all, let alone taken a degree; the Renaissance dislike of university learning, and especially of scholastic theology, drove many to study elsewhere and to steer clear of law and, especially, of theology, which seemed to many to be a quasi-monopoly of the religious orders and to be neither well suited nor necessary for the higher ranks of the secular clergy. For sons of the nobility who did attend university, taking a degree was even less of an obligation, and some regarded it as beneath their dignity. But as the religious and educational landscape began to change, so too did the educational cursus of the clergy from which future bishops would be drawn. The new Jesuit, Oratorian and other colleges increasingly provided a full and more 'modern' educational menu, which often included philosophy and theology courses leading, in some instances, to degrees. If French bishops during the early decades of our period took degrees at all, it was overwhelmingly in law rather than theology, on the grounds, no doubt, that law would be more useful in a 'governing' role; the fact that many law degrees were short and undemanding was another attraction. Yet, under the pressure for a more pastorally active episcopate, this pattern, too, was to alter by the middle decades of the seventeenth century, when both Richelieu and then the *dévots*, who were the driving force behind the *conseil de conscience* after 1643, showed a growing preference for bishops with a theological training.

Crucial to this shift was the willingness of prominent noble families with high ambitions for their sons to send them to universities and take theology degrees: had that not been so, the French episcopate might have resembled its German counterpart whose members disdained such intellectual attainments. By the 1650s, the number of bishops with theology degrees equalled the number of those with law degrees for the first time, before drawing ahead substantially in the next half-century, so that by Louis XIV's death, there were only a handful of law graduates still left among the French episcopate. What is more, a very significant majority of the theology graduates had studied, though not necessarily taken their degrees, in the Paris theology faculty. Hailed as early as the 1670s as the 'seminary' (in the original sense of 'seed-bed' rather than of the seminary as an institution) of France's bishops, the Paris faculty steadily became a more self-consciously elite institution, with close ties to the episcopate. Its golden days as the oracle of the church were long over, but the faculty, which had expanded continuously in numbers since the 1630s, increasingly attracted the elite of the French clergy. For that reason, perhaps, the Tridentine seminaries that had developed in mid-seventeenth-century France played only a limited role in the 'formation' of France's bishops; even the celebrated seminary of Saint-Sulpice (and other Paris institutions like Saint-Magloire or Saint-Lazare) attracted relatively few of them during Louis XIV's reign, and not all of those who frequented them should be considered as 'seminarians' in the conventional sense.

What is more difficult to deduce from these developments is the real intellectual attainments of the French episcopate. It seems clear that the Paris theology course was more demanding than that of other faculties across France, and that theology continued to be both longer and more demanding than the study of law. Yet, from Cardinal du Perron to Fénelon via Antoine Godeau and many others, it might be said that the finest *esprits* of the episcopate were not really products of a university environment at all. Fénelon's theology degree was taken at the university of Cahors, whose 'coma', as its historian labelled it, probably began well before the eighteenth century. In fact, we should not regard seventeenth-century universities as closed hothouse environments, and other sources of intellectual engagement were available beyond their confines, whether it was in Paris or Toulouse. On the other hand, bishops who had studied abroad, especially in Italy, had entirely disappeared by the age of Louis XIV.

The gradually increasing dominance of Paris theology graduates suggests an episcopate that was growing more intellectually homogeneous and more sensitive to differences within theological and moral debates, broadly defined. Without such an educational and intellectual cursus, it would be hard to explain not just bishops' personal engagement with contentious questions, whether it be on church–state–papacy or secular–regular clergy relations, or on the increasingly tricky questions of grace which were central to the prolonged Jansenist affair, but also the energy and arguments with which they defended their positions. The fact that growing numbers of bishops went beyond the traditional publication of statutes prepared in synods to issuing often lengthy and detailed pastoral instructions of a more discursive, didactic kind can be traced to similar roots. Doubtless much of the preparatory work for such pronouncements was done by their officials, and some bishops were regarded as being in thrall to them, yet such developments represent the bishops' increasing self-image as doctors and protectors of the faith of their diocesans. Such a self-image was most visible among Jansenist bishops and those close to them, but it would be a mistake to think of it as the preserve of a tiny minority.

Careers Before Mitre

When the Concordat of Bologna stipulated that incoming bishops should be of a certain age, possess major orders and hold a university degree, it was concerned with the *status* of given individuals rather than with any putatively 'qualifying' activities that they might have undertaken and that would in some way justify their elevation. For many sixteenth- and seventeenth-century bishops, it would indeed be difficult to find any distinctive activity to record in their pre-episcopal curriculum vitae. This is particularly true of those descended from high-ranking noble, court or ministerial families, for whom the receipt of other benefices (abbeys, court almonerships, canonicates in particular chapters) in the crown's gift indicated that a bishopric might follow in due course, since such grants signalled the favour that individuals (and/or their families) already enjoyed in the royal entourage. The changing social make-up of the episcopate from the 1560s to the 1630s was bound to alter that picture somewhat, as bishops with less exalted social origins had usually filled a variety of roles – administrative or pastoral – within the church which did not depend on royal bounty. It is significant that, despite the return of noble dominance from the 1640s onwards, the earlier pattern of birth and connections being sufficient for preferment did not return with it – or that it now applied only to a steadily diminishing number of bishops.

It took much longer for something like a 'royal road' to the episcopate to evolve and to be widely acknowledged as such. For much of the seventeenth century, it would have been hard to predict any such outcome, as the picture remained one of huge diversity in pre-episcopal careers. Where some future bishops manifestly relied on family connections, especially at court, others engaged in a wide range of activities, and often simultaneously, so that the modern notion of career 'progression' bears very little relation to what they did. By far the largest single cohort of bishops – almost one in two across the entire century – had been members of cathedral or collegiate chapters, while a proportion of them had been 'dignitaries' – dean, archdeacon, canon-theologian, sacristan and so on – in these same bodies. Although the latter positions themselves were benefices often obtained from an early age as a direct result of family connections, they would have at least helped to familiarise their incumbents, unless they were out-and-out absentees, with some of the business of governing a diocese. Cathedral chapters might no longer enjoy the right to elect bishops, but a canon's stall, with very few obligations attached to it, continued to attract future bishops more than any other type of benefice, which made them part of the higher echelons of the 'second-rank' secular clergy discussed in an earlier chapter. Many of these canons were simultaneously royal almoners, court preachers or tutors to the royal family, so the real source of their preferment lay elsewhere. By contrast, only a tiny proportion of France's future bishops had direct experience of 'cure of souls' as it was then understood, namely tenure of a parish. In fact, it was something of a miracle that a dozen of Louis XIV's 250 bishops were parish priests; some of them still held the post at the moment of their nomination, but they were mostly based in prominent parishes in Paris and, in any case, were known to the court for other reasons. Increasingly as the century wore on, incoming bishops had preached, conducted missions, acted as directors of hospitals and so on.

It was not until the latter decades of Louis XIV's rule, from the 1690s onwards, that the career pattern which triumphed in the following century began to establish itself – namely, that of vicar-general to a reigning bishop. It was a signal that was quickly picked up by the dominant clerical circles, and soon both well-connected royal almoners and recent Paris doctors of theology were seeking out bishops who would employ them in such positions. It was probably the increasing sophistication and bureaucratisation of episcopal government that enabled bishops to respond to so many requests, the result of which was that bishops were increasingly surrounded by often large teams of vicars-general anxious to prove their abilities. It did not mean that henceforth all vicars-general had, in principle, an equal chance of ending up as a bishop – *au contraire*. In an age when, owing to the Jansenist and related controversies, church and crown increasingly wanted bishops of impeccable orthodoxy, a stint as a vicar-general placed potential bishops under the spotlight and provided the opportunity for them to impress the decision-makers.

Things in Common

One major consequence of these social, educational and career patterns was that the French episcopate became increasingly detached from its earlier local origins. Foreign, especially Italian, clerics who had figured so prominently in the sixteenth-century episcopate, declined sharply after Henri IV's reign, despite a brief and unsurprising revival under Mazarin. Thereafter, every French bishop was a natural subject of the king, with only natives of Lorraine or the papal enclave around Avignon representing a minor exception. Across the century as a whole, by far the largest single contingent of bishops was of Parisian origin, though some of them, especially from noble families, also retained their provincial roots. Fewer and fewer sees were held by bishops who were natives of the diocese concerned, or even of the province to which it belonged. There were some exceptions – in lower Brittany and Navarre-Béarn, where linguistic differences long ensured that local clerics would become bishops – but they, too, were falling away by the later seventeenth century. Provence represents something of an exception here, in that some of its smallest dioceses were sufficiently unattractive to outsiders for natives of Provence to fill them with considerable regularity.

But the crown was just as likely to award such dioceses – in Provence and elsewhere in France – to members of religious orders as to native candidates. The regulars, especially mendicants like the Franciscans and their offshoots, were not seen as bishops *comme les autres*. It was as if the mitre could never quite efface their original identities as 'mere' friars who had renounced wealth, honours and power. The fact that a steadily declining number of regulars made it into the ranks of the episcopate, especially under Louis XIV, is another indication of an episcopate moving towards greater internal homogeneity. At the highest level of all, the triumph of the secular clergy over their regular counterparts was indisputable, and that, too, sharply set off France from contemporary Spain, Flanders and Italy.

The French episcopate may no longer have been local in origin, but this should not be misconstrued. After the pluralism and related 'abuses' of the sixteenth century had been eliminated, the episcopate settled down into a relatively high degree of stability. Complaints about too many transfers of bishops from one diocese to another never disappeared, but like many other such complaints they do not reflect the overall pattern of episcopal tenure. The fact is that the great majority of France's bishops could expect to govern only one diocese during their career. No more than one in five of them experienced transfer or promotion, and a far smaller number governed more than two dioceses. Doubtless many more of them dreamed and schemed to engineer their translation from dioceses that were isolated, under-endowed or troublesome, but their chances of success were slim enough. Surprisingly, perhaps, it was not until Louis XIV that the crown began to make it clear that only reigning bishops could become archbishops; previous to that no such rule or custom had existed, and it was not uncommon to become archbishop of Paris or Lyon without any prior episcopal experience. In an age when the assemblies of clergy played a larger role than ever in church–state relations, having archbishops of proven reliability at the head of church 'provinces' mattered more than ever. And when Louis XIV broke his own rule about such appointments, he was roundly criticised for it – and even promised not to repeat it. The more the new dispensation was observed, the more it became the principal source of episcopal mobility.

This picture of stability is evident in other respects, too. One of the most tenacious misconceptions about the early modern French church is that of clerics impatiently seeking, and obtaining, episcopal office at an early age. The very fact that the Concordat of Bologna demanded that French nominees for episcopal office be aged only twenty-six, when it was twenty-nine elsewhere in Europe, might even suggest that this view was true. Underaged nominations were not uncommon through the sixteenth century, and Richelieu was not the last of them when nominated to Luçon around 1602. The last Guise archbishop of Reims was only fourteen when nominated in 1628, by which time Richelieu himself was principal minister and a determined foe of such practices! There were no more nominations like this one, and on the rare occasions thereafter when the French crown nominated individuals who were short of their twenty-sixth birthday, the papacy was prepared to dig in and refuse, or at least delay, their confirmation more openly than in previous generations. As might be expected, these exceptional cases nearly always involved well-connected sons of great nobles or ministers – the last of them was a son of Colbert in 1679! – but because they attract disproportionate attention, they tend to hide the far more significant fact that the average age of France's incoming bishops during the seventeenth century crept up from around thirty-seven under Henri IV to around forty-two a century later. Neither of these figures may seem especially high, nor the rise in the average age remarkable, but they show that incoming French bishops were over ten years younger than their Spanish or Anglican counterparts. Crucially, they also mean that, on average, French bishops were taking up office while in the prime of life, and therefore enjoyed the prospect of relatively long tenure of office – typically around twenty-four years across the century. Needless to say, arithmetical averages conceal a wide range of real-life ages, and France did have its share of long-serving octogenarian, and even nonagenarian bishops, whose reigns virtually always tailed off into prolonged inaction and drift.

The evolution of the French episcopate, especially towards long periods of stable tenure of individual dioceses, provided a firm basis for the kind of reform that between them Trent and French legislation envisaged. But would these preconditions suffice to transform episcopal behaviour on the ground? At Trent itself, the French bishops had argued strongly in defence of the idea, which nearly wrecked the Council, that episcopal residence was a duty under divine law, from which they could not be dispensed, even by the pope. Such a stance was far more 'ideological' than practical in nature, in the sense that the real issue at Trent was the papal claim to wield superior dispensing powers across the entire church, something that Gallican clerics were not disposed to accept.[3] They readily agreed with Trent's perception of bishops as the lynchpin of church governance and religious reform at every level, something that was deeply rooted in their own Gallican traditions. However, that did not prevent France's bishops from being as widely and frequently accused as their counterparts elsewhere of not residing in their dioceses, accusations that continued until the end of the *ancien régime*. The charge usually made against them was that they spent too much time at court – or in Paris, which came a close second when the court left for Versailles in 1682 – and that such non-residence amounted to neglect.

In principle, at least, French bishops had far fewer excuses for non-residence than, say, their Spanish counterparts, since very few of them held political office at court or outside their dioceses. Archbishop Villeroy of Lyon under Louis XIV was highly unusual in serving as lieutenant-general of the province of Lyon, Forez and Beaujolais for its absentee governor, who happened to be his brother. In fact, the post provided him with an additional reason for residing there, which he did assiduously for nearly forty years (1653–93). Other bishops, such as Cardinal Bonzi, archbishop of Narbonne, became power-brokers and major political figures, especially in provinces with their own estates and financial machinery, to such an extent that the Bishop of Lavaur, an 'ordinary' figure among Languedoc's bishops, could complain in the mid-1670s that the political business of the province simply overwhelmed him. Yet it seems that long-term, non-resident bishops were few enough at any time, but equally that they never wholly disappeared. Those who were 'alienated' from their dioceses for whatever reason were, as we saw, unlikely to be offered another one more to their taste, unless they had compelling arguments or, more likely, powerful patrons. The much bigger cohort of temporarily non-resident bishops is by definition far more elusive, but contemporary criticism of these absentees was not constant. After all, resident bishops could be indolent, withdrawn and neglectful of the needs of their dioceses, while those spending periods at court or in Paris could just as easily be more combative and effective defenders of the best interests of their dioceses, given the number of issues and lawsuits that could only be resolved there. The problem was to strike an acceptable balance between the two. By the later seventeenth century, French bishops were increasingly supported by well-oiled diocesan governing structures which could function effectively in their absence and which could, for a time at least, be directed from a distance by their well-informed master. It was that which enabled Bishop Laval of La Rochelle to spend nine months every two to three years in Paris, and his more austere neighbour, Bishop Barillon of Luçon, nine months every three to four years under Louis XIV.[4] It never occurred to anyone at the time to accuse either of them of absenteeism.

It is no paradox to suggest that the cohesiveness of the French episcopate owed much to the 'official' opportunities they had for periods of absence from their dioceses, even though those opportunities did not fall to all of them equally. The sessions of provincial estates only concerned certain provinces, and they tended to decline rather than remain constant across the century with the demise of certain estates. Never frequent at the best of times, church councils ceased altogether after that of Bordeaux in 1624, effectively 'replaced' by the provincial assemblies that met to elect deputies to general assemblies of the clergy. Attendance at the general assemblies themselves provided unrivalled opportunities to network with fellow bishops, present and future, and with ministers and major royal officials. As Pierre Blet has shown, it was in the assemblies that the respective 'frontiers' of church and state were negotiated and defined for practical, working purposes.[5] One need but follow the debates of an average 'major' assembly of clergy to realise how many of the issues discussed were, not surprisingly, precisely those which were of greatest interest to the bishops themselves – especially the defence of ecclesiastical jurisdiction against secular courts, the authority of bishops over the religious orders and the ordinary secular clergy, but also questions of pastoral practice. It is easy to forget that the 1615 assembly's adoption of the decrees of Trent, a highly symbolic gesture bereft of real legal force, was followed up by 'spiritual regulation' of its own, intended to serve as a programme for action throughout the French church. This was not the last 'declaration' of its kind.

Yet an underlying, if normally invisible tension endured within this part of the Gallican edifice – between the general voice of the 'Clergy of France', as expressed through the assemblies, and that of individual bishops insisting on their sovereign right to govern their dioceses as they saw fit. It surfaced only on occasion, as when some bishops opposed the official line over the anti-Jansenist Formulary in the 1660s, the *régale* in the 1670s and 1680s and the anti-Jansenist bull *Unigenitus* after 1713. In normal circumstances, the assemblies did speak for the 'Clergy of France' in a real sense, channelling the grievances and protests of individual bishops upwards, and then diffusing their attempts to find a common stance on the issues downwards to all bishops. The extent to which the assemblies remained in touch with the bishops across France shows how closely their deliberations were followed, with substantial numbers of bishops who were not deputies often coming to court or to Paris during their sessions. Through speeches, resolutions, sermons and addresses to the throne, the assemblies consistently exalted the role of the episcopate within the church, sometimes to the point of making Rome worry whether they saw themselves as the national council of the French church.

It might seem from this discussion that 'political' activities in this broad sense were the prime source of the self-image of France's episcopate in our period. But that is only partly true. Models of what a good bishop should be and do were strongly embedded in Gallican tradition, and they were further influenced by the content and language of Trent's decrees.[6] Thereafter, the emergence of 'iconic' bishops such as Carlo Borromeo or François de Sales went a long way towards translating Trent's demands into something like attainable, lived experience. The rapid canonisation and the proliferation of edifying 'Lives' of these figures had an equally significant impact, and French bishops who consciously identified themselves as their disciples were not in short supply. Like the emerging literature on the *bon curé*, that on the 'good pastor' could develop the more recent ideas of Bérulle and his disciples on the nature of the priesthood, by insisting that bishops possessed a higher form of priesthood and were more than merely 'external' and hierarchical superiors of the rest of the clergy precisely because they enjoyed a 'plenitude' of the priesthood. Here too, hagiography, 'mirrors of bishops' treatises, diocesan histories and other occasional works disseminated an image of bishops as being more than efficient governors of dioceses; they insisted that bishops develop a personal spirituality that, along with its accompanying daily routines, corresponded to their high office. Even the biting Jansenist critique of the courtier-bishop served to reinforce that message. Needless to say, the degree to which individual bishops imbibed such influences and developed a distinctive personal 'style' varied considerably. It would be pointless to characterise more than a small fraction of them as being obviously or exclusively Borromean, Salesian or, later on, Sulpician, Lazarist or Oratorian in spirit. De Sales clearly thought of himself as a Borromean even as he was seriously modifying the austere, disciplinary image provided by his model. In fact, what this suggests is that ideas about the episcopate did not remain static or derivative, but that those earlier Borromean or Salesian models were subsumed into more recent ideas of home-grown provenance on the subject.

This movement of ideas itself mirrors the expansion of episcopal activities across France's dioceses during the same period, not least because many of its subsequent contributors, from Jean-Pierre Camus to Antoine Godeau, were heavily involved in religious reform. It may also owe some of its dynamism to the need they felt to defend episcopal authority against the regulars and the spokesmen for the rights of *curés*. Two instances may illustrate these concerns. The first was the attempt, made on behalf of the 1625 Assembly of Clergy, to disseminate among the episcopate an 'advice' comprising 156 articles, and which was mainly an attempt to paint a detailed portrait of what a true bishop should be like. But it was never officially published: it was its author's ultra-Gallican views on papal authority, not his ideas of the *bonus pastor*, which were the problem. Over two decades later, in 1649 and 1656, the famous 'Borromean' bishop of Cahors, Alain de Solminihac, gathered his episcopal neighbours together for a retreat of several days designed not just to examine their occupations and obligations as bishops, but also to develop their spiritual lives.[7] The well-documented correspondence between several Jansenist or philo-Jansenist bishops during the reign of Louis XIV shows how intimately they connected their episcopal duties and their inner spiritual life.

Communication and Action

The gradually changing profile of the episcopate outlined above did not of itself alter the fact that much of what bishops did continued to be traditional in nature. The 'good pastor' was not a pastor *comme les autres*, with the possible exception of preaching, in which many French bishops engaged with remarkable success from Cardinal du Perron to Bossuet and beyond. Otherwise, his pastorate had to fit in with the business of governing a diocese which remained a heavily 'political' and administrative activity. Indeed, seventeenth-century developments actually increased rather than diminished that dimension. Bishops still belonged inside the old feudal hierarchy, possessing secular titles and rights attached to their sees. Developing and maintaining good relations with powerful families could be crucial for a successful bishop, and as late as the 1680s a bishop of Dax who fell foul of them found himself quitting his post altogether. Given that these families were frequently patrons of benefices, cultivating them could be more than a merely 'social' exercise. The famous Bishop Vialart of Châlons-sur-Marne (1640–80) was so effective at it that he seems to have gained de facto control of most of the benefices of his diocese.[8] Clearly, in the surviving *pays d'états* the bishop's political role was far more explicit and time-consuming than elsewhere. Everywhere, the duties of hospitality and 'representation' were equally inescapable obligations. Quite how much time bishops might spend on such matters could depend in part on their financial means, but the damage done during the civil wars frequently meant that regaining control of properties involved disputes and lawsuits – a further reason for periods of non-residence. For much of the century, bishops did not yet have the mastery of their temporalities or the administrative support that would allow them to rely on subordinates in such matters. Yet despite the broadly unfavourable economic trends, there was a fairly sustained rise in episcopal revenues, which in due course enabled bishops to expand their activities within their dioceses.

A combination of earlier criticisms and changing objectives ensured that episcopal governance did witness significant shifts during the seventeenth century. Given the considerable differences in size between dioceses, any generalisation may prove risky here. For relatively small dioceses, 'governing' arrangements could remain fairly simple, although the desire to emulate larger ones could complicate the picture. The existing diocesan curias, with their limited number of officials – such as the vicar-general, the *official*, the *promoteur*, the syndic, the *procureur fiscal* – found themselves expanding in size. The Council of Trent had demanded that each diocese also have a canon-theologian (*théologal*) and a canon-penitentiary (*pénitencier*) and, with some exceptions, these duly appeared throughout France during the following century or so. Although both were clearly meant to be members of the cathedral chapter, it seems that they really belonged to the episcopal curia and depended mainly on the bishop for opportunities to carry out their functions. Outsider bishops naturally wanted the freedom to bring in their own trusted counsellors alongside experienced local figures, but they were usually averse to wholesale purges of their predecessors' officials; it was often these latter who guaranteed continuity from one bishop to another.

Mention has already been made of 'teams' of grand vicars appearing by the latter decades of Louis XIV's reign, but the timescale of that development remains obscure. The main reason for their growth was episcopal determination to exercise full control of their dioceses and a corresponding unwillingness to accept the claims of the archdeacons, who were members of the powerful cathedral chapters, to exercise an autonomous jurisdiction within 'their' territorial subdivision of the diocese. In the bigger central and northern sees, more administratively convenient subdivisions of diocesan space were regarded as essential, and they were usually confided to individual vicars-general; although some of the latter might also be archdeacons, the significant difference now was that they would act as the bishop's delegates rather than as independent agents.

As the business of governing dioceses became more complex and more bureaucratic, involving for example the managing of a seminary or organising preaching missions, the numbers of vicars-general and other lesser officials grew accordingly; and these men were increasingly experienced and well educated graduates, and often doctors of theology. Several seventeenth-century bishops are known to have established an advisory council of vicars-general and other major officials (*théologal, promoteur* and others) formally to assist them in diocesan government. That of Rouen, one of France's biggest dioceses, dated from 1641, but scarcely anything is known about its activities beyond a few years in the late 1690s, when it is known to have met twice a week and dealt with all of the routine business of governance. Cahors had its episcopal council from at least 1654 onwards under Alain de Solminihac. In the early 1700s the new bishop of Poitiers (a vast diocese with over 750 parishes) drew on his experience as a former vicar-general of Lyon and applied its practice to Poitiers: he delegated most of the ordinary matters of government to six vicars-general, each of whom had his own territorial area of responsibility; they brought matters arising from it before the weekly council meeting where they were discussed by the entire team of vicars-general under the bishop's overall control.[9]

It should also be remembered that some French bishops followed the model of Milan under Borromeo, who had divided up his diocese into districts (*vicariats forains*) supervised by one of the resident clergy known in French as a *vicaire forain*. As early as 1600, the well-known 'Borromean', Cardinal Sourdis, archbishop of Bordeaux (1599–1629) placed the government of his diocese in the hands of several 'congregations' which were entrusted with different *types* of diocesan business rather than with distinct territorial areas. One of them, the 'congregation of examination' (dealing mostly with the ordination and appointment of the clergy to benefices) seems to have come closest to being the key governing council, especially during Sourdis's many absences.[10] These few examples suffice to show how varied the practice of individual dioceses could be, and that it would probably be misguided to expect a high degree of uniformity from one to another, especially early in the century. What we can expect, however, is a high degree of borrowing and imitation thereafter, facilitated by the high levels of contact and communication within the French episcopate.

Synods and Assemblies

Perhaps the weightiest challenge facing most bishops, especially in the big dioceses of northern and central France, was to develop regular and effective means of communication with the lower clergy.[11] No doubt the 'territorial' officials and other intermediaries discussed above were a part of the response, though the survival of independently minded archdeacons continued to cause friction for many years. These problems are well illustrated by synods, which rarely detain historians of the period unduly. The conduct of synods was a conventional feature of episcopal rule since the central Middle Ages which seventeenth-century bishops were usually keen to revive. It is too easy to imagine them as legislative exercises, of interest to historians only when they produced statutes that reveal something about the priorities of the bishops who compiled them. But synods which formally legislated were always a distinct minority. Historically, synods were a notional attempt to recreate the actual community of bishop and clergy which had existed in cathedral towns before the dispersal of the clergy across the parishes and churches of the dioceses. By our period, synods were mostly intended to be annual or twice-yearly gatherings of clergy holding benefices with cure of souls, for whom attendance was in principle obligatory – with fines and even excommunication threatened for failure to do so. If many clergy were reluctant to attend, or even claimed they were exempt from doing so, it was precisely because synods were a recognised instrument of episcopal government, enabling bishops to exercise a form of supervision over their clergy. The latter might be obliged to report on the state of their parishes at synods, where they might also face criticism for their stewardship, and they would certainly be recipients of episcopal directives and reminders concerning the administration of the sacraments, preaching, record-keeping and other issues relating to the duties of their office. The changes in sacramental and liturgical practices characteristic of the Catholic Reform were often introduced, channelled and harmonised in individual dioceses by means of synods whose regularity made them the most useful vehicle for such purposes.

It was also possible to go much further, especially in our period, and to use regular synods in order to sustain an *esprit de corps* among the clergy present and, through the sermons and exhortations given during them, to play a role, especially during the pre-seminary age, in nudging the parish clergy towards a better understanding and practice of their pastoral obligations. Although little direct evidence has survived about these 'normal' twice-yearly synods, it would be unwise to minimise their value both as sounding boards for clerical grievances and, especially, as vehicles for diffusing episcopal priorities among the clergy during an age of limited communication within the average diocese. Equally, we should not minimise the obstacles to success. In a diocese as accustomed to twice-yearly synods as Saint-Malo, the attendance rates, though rising from the 1590s to the 1650s, still fluctuated between one-third and one-half of the parish clergy, despite efforts to hold synods in different places in order to facilitate greater attendance.[12] Saint-Malo was far from being France's largest or most impassable diocese (162 parishes), so its record may suggest the scale of the difficulties elsewhere. The experience of the diocese of Coutances suggests that by the eighteenth century the usefulness of synods had seriously diminished, overtaken by other mechanisms of episcopal rule such as the publication of instructions, the use of clerical conferences and so on. Interestingly, the synod which still mattered by the eighteenth century in Coutances was the so-called 'small' synod composed of the bishop, his principal officials and the twenty-three 'rural' deans, and not the much larger and unwieldy 'general' synod of all the beneficed clergy.[13]

With the parish clergy so often trying to avoid attending synods, especially in the early to middle decades of the century, French bishops found themselves seeking ways of complementing them in order to reach down into and influence the lower clergy. 'Calends' – assemblies of clergy held within a deanery with a view to preparing for synods – existed in some dioceses of France, though the precise difference between them and non-legislating synods is hard to find, since their purpose was also to regulate the 'disciplinary' problems of the clergy. In Coutances, they met in the interval between the Easter and autumn synods, and dealt with the business of an individual rural deanery, generating reports on the parishes and on the deanery as a whole which were then transmitted 'upwards' for use at the diocesan synod to follow.[14] The 'ecclesiastical conferences' were another such initiative. In principle they had the advantage of meeting more often – up to once a month for nine months per annum – and involved only the clergy of a small part of a given diocese, closely supervised by the local *vicaire forain*. Their objective was also more explicitly pedagogical than disciplinary, in that the conferences were intended to educate the clergy about their pastoral duties and the moral–theological premises on which they were based. For this reason, more detailed analysis of them will be left for the following chapter.

The evidence of the published synodal legislation of the seventeenth century shows a curious persistence of medieval approaches, with many dioceses sticking for a long time with Latin rather than French texts, and also publishing statutes that were in no obvious order whatever. Likewise, some bishops who are known to have held regular synods of their clergy were content merely to reprint statutes going back to the sixteenth century or even earlier. Yet statutes following a *plan méthodique* and grouped under coherent sets of headings or subject matter did gradually become more common, aided no doubt by the pattern set by Trent and the French provincial councils that followed it. Such publications occurred mainly in the early decades up to the 1630s and again from the 1650s to the 1680s, when some of the most comprehensive legislation of the entire early modern period appeared. The statutes of Angers of 1680 ran to 937 pages, and those of Bordeaux of 1686 to 512 pages, but both were outdone by the Saint-Malo statutes of 1620 which ran to 1,200 pages, complete with index.[15]

That comparison suggests that the drive towards comprehensiveness was not always a slow cumulative one, but that encyclopaedic legislation could occur at any time; so, too, could a mere recapitulation of later medieval legislation, whose exact purpose often escapes historical comprehension. But in general, seventeenth-century synodal statutes witnessed a noticeable shift in emphasis from the inevitable commands and prohibitions so dominant in earlier centuries to a pastoral stance that was more supportive of the clergy with cure of souls. The uneven pattern of synodal legislation may owe something to the development, especially in the age of Louis XIV, of a relatively new form of episcopal action – the pastoral letter or instruction. These were more 'single-issue' exercises for which synodal statutes were unsuited, and they fitted better than did statutes the purposes of bishops who were by then more theologically literate and more imbued with the belief that they were the 'doctors of the faith' of their dioceses. These instructions mostly concerned pastoral questions – or theological matters with direct pastoral consequences, notably for the practice of the sacraments. The most contentious of them related to questions raised by the Jansenist controversies, and were sometimes widely diffused beyond their dioceses of origin, provoking further polemic and criticism.

Visitations

What could bishops do beyond these mostly traditional and 'top-down' acts of authority, all of which could be performed in the comfort of their residence? The injunction to 'know your flock' was not a seventeenth-century invention, but it was probably taken much further then than previously. Here, too, it was largely a matter of rediscovering established practices and to some extent using them with a new sense of purpose. Visitations of dioceses – inspections would be a more accurate term – were themselves an ancient practice, but in previous centuries episcopal inactivity often meant that archdeacons, cathedral chapters, monasteries or other 'dignitaries' had laid claim to the right to conduct them and charge a fee (the *droit de visite*) from the parishes subject to them. When they insisted on the right to collect the fee even without taking the trouble to visit them, it was obvious that it had become yet another fiscal device; when they did visit, their main purpose could simply be to remind those subject to them of their authority.[16]

In the past half-century or more, historians have made such extensive use of the material contained in seventeenth-century visitation reports to study religious practices that the visitations themselves – their context, purpose and development – have often been somewhat lost from sight. There is no denying the value of the contents of visitation records, but historians should not confuse the evidence which they provide about religious practices with a judgement of their effectiveness. A contextualised discussion of the practice can illuminate both its limits and possibilities for an understanding of France's episcopate in action.[17]

To begin with, the 'rediscovery' by bishops of visitations as a mechanism not just for expanding control of their diocese, but for their attempts to reshape the clergy and popular religious practice, was a relatively slow one, despite calls from the sixteenth-century monarchy, Trent itself and the example of leading post-Trent reformers. Compliance was not facilitated by conditions during France's wars of religion, but the Tridentine requirement of a full visitation yearly or biennially was, especially in the larger dioceses, quite unrealistic – and it remained so for the rest of the *ancien régime*.[18] It has been calculated that it would have taken 200 days to visit La Rochelle diocese, whose 325 parishes did not even put it in the league of truly big dioceses.[19] For the generation of bishops in office around 1600, visiting their dioceses must have seemed as daunting as it was necessary. It was an unfamiliar task for virtually all of them, and in middling to large dioceses it took on aspects of an expedition. Bishops on visitation would travel with at least a minimum entourage of officials and householders, so the logistics of travel and lodgings could be vexatious, especially as few of them were accustomed to spartan living conditions, let alone ready to endure them for months on end. Large numbers of dioceses, and most obviously those with mountainous terrain and poor roads, were hard to move through at any pace. The months from Easter to All Saints (1 November) were regarded as the only possible time for visitations.

Only a tiny, heroic minority from each generation of bishops was ready to impose such a regime on itself, year in, year out. For the others, especially in middling to large dioceses, the only option was to establish a crude rota for visitation, one deanery or archdeaconry after another, in a cycle that might be spun out haphazardly over several years. For the bishop of a large diocese to visit all of it just once in his career may seem a poor record indeed, but that is to ignore both contemporary conditions as well as the purposes of visitation. It took the young Archbishop Colbert of Rouen seven years to visit his huge diocese (1680–87), but he would never try to repeat that exploit. As the surviving records indicate, it was common practice to delegate the task to officials such as vicars-general or reliable archdeacons. What bishops were unwilling to countenance was the *right* of archdeacons or other dignitaries to visit parishes over which they claimed autonomous jurisdiction, and it does seem they were largely, but not completely, successful in eliminating such claims by the later seventeenth century. Where they were successful, visitations could be conducted more frequently and perhaps also more meticulously than if the bishops themselves conducted them.

The objective of visitations was rarely, it needs to be said, to achieve familiarity with one's diocese for its own sake: the knowledge derived from them was meant to assist in governing the diocese. Thus a first visitation might be delayed until the new bishop felt capable of using it to full effect; or it might be timed to coincide with the bishop's administering the sacrament of confirmation for the first time in several years across his diocese.[20] Visitation was first and foremost an act of jurisdiction, and the rituals surrounding it were designed with that in mind. For precisely that reason, too, they could easily provoke not merely disputes, but on occasion actual physical confrontations. Moreover, visitations invariably brought to light the different enclaves of exemption generated during previous centuries. The chapter of Angers, for example, enjoyed 'episcopal authority' over at least six parishes, and had the right to hold its own annual synod – and successfully preserved it into the eighteenth century.[21] Efforts by bishops to suppress these privileges commonly led to appeals to the royal courts against an alleged abuse of church power (the *appel comme d'abus*). Visitations were one way for bishops to stake out their power within the more remote areas of their dioceses, especially if they were home to powerful abbeys with claims to independent jurisdiction; visitations then became an instrument for making diocesan boundaries 'real', but once that was achieved, the job could be delegated to officials and proved relatively unproblematic.

But the most formidable obstacles to visitations usually lay right under the bishop's nose, in the form of his own cathedral chapter and the religious orders of the episcopal city itself whose local roots gave them additional force. Episcopal efforts to wring acceptance of the right to 'visit and correct' them punctuated the entire century and beyond, and were increasingly supported by the monarchy.[22] Bishops could not normally insist on visiting the houses of regulars unless it was on the grounds of an evident failure of religious observance, but proving that was itself contentious and likely to mobilise opposition from the wider order in question. Visitation of female regulars was usually much less of a problem, since episcopal 'superiority' of their houses was more readily acknowledged, with the exception of the older monastic houses which treasured their independence and had both the will and the connections to defend it. The 'pastoral' element in many of these visitations may well have been the least important one, even if it became more prominent and far more explicit during the seventeenth century.

Because visitations were regarded as onerous, all but the most ad hoc exercises needed serious planning. However brief individual parish visitations might be – a few hours at best – clergy and parishioners needed to be informed in advance of the event, especially if the bishop conducted them in person, in which case the ceremonial dimension would be considerable and designed to impress the parish. Episcopal visitations might involve some preaching and administration of the sacraments, especially of confirmation which only bishops could perform. Those conducted by vicars-general or others would doubtless have been more mundane, businesslike affairs, given their limited powers to act. In virtually all cases, they began with an examination of the physical state of the church and any adjoining buildings, with a view to ensuring they were 'fit for purpose'. Likewise, all visitors would seek to question both clergy and laity, especially the churchwardens, about the state of the parish generally, focusing mainly on religious behaviour and its extensions. Where they had suspicions of clerical misdeeds or conflicts between clergy and parishioners, they might interrogate them separately in the hope of ascertaining the true state of affairs.[23] But it should not be imagined that this was undertaken lightly, despite some well-documented instances of mutually protective silence by laity and clergy in the face of questioning by outsiders whom they might never see again. Nor should we inflate the desire of visitors to know every unpleasant truth about individual parishes, as they might have little possibility of dealing with them or might be wary of action that would stir up further trouble there. Most if not all visitations, especially when conducted by a bishop, ended with an ordinance requiring the parish to make certain changes which could range from improving the church fabric and its furnishings, purchasing new liturgical books or vestments, insisting that the clergy catechise their parishioners to enclosing the cemetery or, later in the century, to building a house for the parish priest.[24]

This purely formalist account cannot show how visitations evolved from a relatively simple to a far more elaborate format during the seventeenth century. From as early as 1620, individual dioceses began to impose a single format for all visitors to follow, so that the idiosyncracies of particular visitors would not render their reports impossible to use effectively. That process was still incomplete in a diocese like Limoges before the 1710s, by which time printed visitation forms had already become widespread elsewhere. To a large extent, especially in places were visitation was reasonably frequent, the early 'voyages of discovery', especially of popular religious ignorance, gave way to more measured and co-ordinated efforts, which themselves reflect the growth of episcopal administration across France's dioceses. It is well known that by the second half of the seventeenth century, often quite detailed questionnaires were prepared for advanced circulation and answers to them were required before the visitation started. The questionnaires might be identical, but it was the individual responses that would enable the visitors to identify the potential issues from one parish to the next, and plan how to deal with them, rather than assuming that all had identical problems. Such a development had its own logic, so that by the eighteenth century, the despatch and return of the written questionnaire often replaced the physical act of visitation altogether in many dioceses: the questionnaires themselves could be used by the diocesan bureaucrats in other ways, now that they had developed other mechanisms for keeping checks upon their clergy and parishes.[25]

Above all, the use and development of questionnaires points to the expansion, not so much of the visitations themselves, as of the nature of episcopal concerns. During the opening decades of the century, the major concern of visitors was the rebuilding and restoration of churches after the damage of the religious wars, damage that was perpetuated by the wars, civil as well as foreign, that occurred thereafter, especially up to the 1650s.[26] Neglectful bishops and foot-dragging churchwardens often left much for their successors to do in this respect until well into the second half of the century, so it should not be assumed that these concerns were somehow dealt with definitively during the early decades after 1600. It was not, for example, until the reign of Archbishop Le Tellier (1668–1710) that the diocese of Reims fully recovered from a long combination of neglect and war damage. Furthermore, expectations themselves changed significantly from one generation to another, and what might have been acceptable around 1620 might no longer be regarded as such around 1680 or 1720. Greater concern for the 'decency' and holiness of churches – especially the altar, the pulpit, the sacristy, the baptismal font – lay behind the steadily widening injunctions issued by visitors to improve and embellish them.

All this suggests that the agenda of bishops and their administrations had been gradually expanding beyond questions of the 'material' foundations of religious practice.[27] The 1687 questionnaire for Toul diocese ran to no fewer than eighty-eight questions. Questions like 'Does the church have a pulpit?', 'Are men and women placed separately in church?' or 'Are hymns sung in French?' all clearly reflect an agenda of religious change which had expanded in previous decades; other questions about sorcery, superstition, schoolmasters and so on, did so just as explicitly.[28] Around the same time, having visited all of his vast diocese, Archbishop Colbert of Rouen devised a questionnaire for future use and covering 130 points of interest. If the questionnaires tell us anything, it is as much about the 'knowledge-is-power' priorities of the church authorities as their curiosity about popular religion per se.

The official 'memory' of visitations was consigned in a written record, the *procès-verbal*, drafted by whomever acted as secretary to the visitor. The tone is usually formulaic, the content often cursory, especially when the pace of a visitation was itself rapid. Sometimes, the original on-the-spot accounts, which also include the ordinances issued at the end of a visitation, were edited and tidied up at some date after the event, which led them to lose even more of their 'original' flavour. Thereafter, the *procès-verbal* could serve as a reference for diocesan administrators and future bishops, who would use it for several purposes, not least of which was deciding whether or not to conduct further visitations in particular places. They knew perfectly well that visitation ordinances, especially where they required parishes to spend money, were unlikely to be acted upon unless placed under sustained pressure – but a new visitation was not necessarily the best way of doing that. Furthermore, what was *not* recorded in a *procès-verbal* may have been just as important a part of a visitation as what was. For bishops and their officials it was, as already mentioned, an occasion to preach, administer the sacraments and encourage or interrogate the clergy, but also to resolve disputes and patch up relations between feuding families or religious orders. Some of this was conducted 'off the record', or during interruptions to the visitation process itself which, by comparison, may have been regarded as more routine in nature. Thus, information gleaned about clerical misdeeds might be kept out of the official account altogether, and recorded only on separate sheets of paper for use in due course. Above all, the contents of visitation records convey the views and agenda of the visitors rather than the 'reality' of local religious communities.[29]

Yet the more that was learned from visitations, the more other kinds of action and response beyond the obvious recourse to further inspections were required. The most common instance would be synods, which did not necessarily produce published legislation; and even where they did, the exact connection between visitations and the ensuing synodal legislation is frequently far from self-evident. At any rate, synods constituted the most frequent 'supervisory' forum where information on particular parishes and *curés* could be used to repeated effect, especially by requiring 'problem' *curés* to account for changes demanded of them during a visitation. By the later decades of the century, there were even seminaries where the most recalcitrant clergy could be confined for an obligatory retreat. In some dioceses (Rouen, Coutances), calends were also used for similar purposes, with *curés* being required to bring accounts of the state of their parish under specified headings.[30] It was the interaction between these different practices which led to those lengthening questionnaires, and which enabled them to become perhaps the most telling evidence of the scale of religious change. Visitations played their part alongside other mechanisms in the growing ambition to produce a better clergy, which would be equipped to improve local religious practices. Paradoxically, the more such activity consolidated the episcopate's administrative grip on individual dioceses, the less indispensable visitations themselves came to seem in the eyes of the church's leading figures.

One Bishop's Agenda

This account of France's bishops and their normal modus operandi has been unavoidably 'general' in tone, eliding exceptions and differences in practice across a vast diocesan network and a long time frame. However arbitrary it may sound, a brief evocation of the early years of a newly installed bishop from the 1690s should restore a sense of the specific to the picture; it also has the advantage of allowing us to penetrate some of the bishops' own thinking about the problems they still encountered at the end of the century. In early 1696, the bishop of Angers wrote to an unnamed colleague, doubtless at the latter's request, to relate what he had attempted since their last encounter just before he left Paris for Angers in January 1693. Michel Le Peletier, son of a former finance minister of Louis XIV and a product of the rising seminary of Saint-Sulpice, was a mere thirty-two years old when he succeeded the famous nonagenarian Jansenist, Henri Arnauld (1597–1692), who had been infirm in his latter years. Energetic, well organised and well counselled, as his background enabled him to be, Le Peletier was manifestly a 'hands-on' bishop whose drive, much of it anti-Jansenist, upset some local figures.

By his own account, he spent his first year, 1693, familiarising himself with his diocese (*c.*460 parishes), not by conducting formal visitations, but rather by touring it to administer the sacrament of confirmation. This, he claimed, enabled him to introduce 'several measures for the good order of the parishes and the repair of churches' where he officiated. He also held synods that year in each of the Angers deaneries for the purpose of 'devising rules for parish priests on how to live'. He spent 1694, the year of the great famine, travelling around the diocese raising funds, especially from the clergy, to assist the poor. The next year, after careful preparation, he visited those parishes whose *curés* were not 'fully disciplined', launching lawsuits against the most ill-disposed and recalcitrant of them; one such case alone cost him, he confessed, 1,000 *livres*. Although he already knew a great deal about his diocese, there was, clearly, still much for him to do, since the visitation 'season' in 1695 lasted – though not necessarily without interruptions – from Easter until mid-November. The most 'infected' *curés* (possibly a codeword for Jansenists) he obliged to follow a special retreat in the seminary, which Le Peletier himself attended, and which was, he concluded, so effective that he planned to reproduce it, in less punitive mode perhaps, twice a year for the rest of his clergy in future. He had also used the 1695 visitation to ease out some of the unsuitable or overaged clergy from individual parishes, another difficult task given the nature of the benefice system, and which he could only accomplish by finding pensions or alternative benefices (without cure of souls) for them elsewhere.

By the time he was writing, in early 1696, Le Peletier had evidently worked out a routine, which entailed using the winter months to prepare for his next 'campaigning season', one which would not be a repeat of the previous one, but an attempt to implement the lessons he had learned from it. Having concluded that the lesson of 1695 was that the ignorance of ordinary people was a consequence of clerical ignorance, he prepared an ordinance the following winter designed to impose the duty on 'all parish priests and curates to teach catechism and preach the homily, to prepare from week to week the text of their sermons, and to examine carefully their moral principles and the sacraments'. To make this obligation both feasible and inescapable, he prepared no fewer than three catechisms – one each for the clergy, adults and children – a particularly complex task, he admitted, and which he undertook only after 'having consulted all the catechisms that had been prepared by France's greatest bishops'. It was duly published in 1697. His 1696 'season', from Easter to All Saints, would, he added, consist of visitations conducted, as always, at his own expense, but this time only in the principal towns to which the *curés* would be required to travel. The visitation he had in mind was to be the most thorough so far, and a genuine ordeal for the clergy subject to it. 'During my next visitation, I shall confer every day with eight parish priests – four during the morning, four in the evenings – on moral questions and the sacraments. I shall require them, in my presence, to teach the catechism to the children whom I may encounter in the places I am visiting. I shall read through their written homilies, which they will submit to me. I shall then send to the seminary for as long as I deem it necessary those I find to be ignorant in these matters . . . I shall have plenty of work to do until All Saints, and there will be no way of escaping from such a worthy undertaking, having informed the parish priests of it. This is the only way that I have discovered to banish ignorance and negligence from their ranks, and I hope it will succeed.'

Le Pelletier's own account of his early years ends there, with the promise of further exchanges with his correspondent, who may well have been a recently appointed bishop himself.[31] No doubt, the early years of numerous episcopal careers were characterised by similar optimism and energy, with routine, discouragement or inactivity following in later years. In Le Peletier's case, independent sources show that his dynamism did not diminish after 1696 – his age certainly helped here.[32] It was probably no great surprise, therefore, that he was chosen ten years later, in 1706, to be the new bishop of Orléans, but he died suddenly in transition between the two dioceses, still in his prime and aged only forty-five. Because Orléans was regarded at court as tainted by Jansenist influences, the succession there was deemed too vital to be entrusted to an untried novice-bishop. Le Peletier's sudden death was clearly a setback, but in a church the size of France there was no lack of relatively young but already proven bishops. So a few months later, Le Peletier's cousin and fellow 'graduate' of Saint-Sulpice, Louis Fleuriau d'Armenonville, bishop of Aire in Gascony since 1698 but still only forty-four years old, was summoned northwards to restore good order in Orléans. He set about his task in a manner which demonstrated how strongly 'episcopal', compared with the rest of Europe, the French church had become.[33]

CHAPTER 8

REMAKING THE SECULAR CLERGY

The intricate layering of France's secular clergy, which resulted partly from their differing social backgrounds and partly from the complex and essentially unchanged benefice system in which they were anchored, was bound to pose major problems for any attempt to transform them. Yet the generations of bishops portrayed in the previous chapter increasingly viewed their objective of a well-regulated diocese in terms of a disciplined, resident and conscientious lower clergy, of whom the parish priests were to be the lynchpin. But such a specific objective could not be pursued on its own, as if the parish clergy were merely the servants and appointees of the bishops. Nor could it be divorced from the problem of what to do with lower ranks of the populous secular clergy as a whole. Consequently, there was no miraculous 'one-size-fits-all' remedy that could single-handedly transform the lower clergy, actual or future, so that a combination of measures, both old and new, had to be tried. Transformation, when it came, would be a slow, uneven and composite result of the overlapping of these efforts. Conventional as most of these methods were, as we saw in the case of visitations and synods, they nevertheless echoed the prescriptions of the Council of Trent and its major interpreters, for all of whom improvements in the religious behaviour of the population generally could only be the result of prior improvements in the calibre of the clergy. In the longer term, this 'curate's eye' view of the world could easily generate a fixation on the creation of a 'perfect' parish clergy almost as an end in itself, virtually guaranteeing that everything else within a parish was satisfactory. It was, as we have seen, one reason why actual visitations gradually ceased in many dioceses by the eighteenth century, to be replaced by written reports and extensive questionnaires. There was little immediate prospect of that happening during the century being examined here.

It may seem unnecessary to begin by recalling that each generation inherited the clergy provided by its predecessor. For that reason, the question of how to improve them was never as simple as designing a blueprint for the next generation. Even when seminaries began to produce new cohorts of clergy, the problem was not necessarily solved, since even clergy who had been to seminaries, universities or colleges continued to be largely independent figures, whose access to advancement or benefices was not necessarily tightly controlled by their bishops. Thus improvement via visitations, synods and similar interventions had to be maintained and strengthened, and no single mechanism was ever likely to deliver definitive results; as we shall see, the relations between these mechanisms would also change over time.

To contemporaries, the basic requirement for an improved parish clergy was that they be resident. Most parishes, as we saw, did not lack for clergy of different types, so the real issue was the residence of the *curé* or, if he had a legitimate reason for absence, of his stand-in. Such replacements were very widespread during the sixteenth century and continued until well into its successor. Visitations regularly recorded such arrangements and, especially during the early decades after the religious wars, tried to verify their conditions and validity. Thereafter, visitors were increasingly determined to regulate and police them. Slowly, this pressure, which was backed up by other, less visible measures, brought about a far higher level of residence by *curés*, especially in rural parishes, by the second half of the century.

Far more difficult to deal with by such methods was the behaviour of the resident clergy within their parishes. Sexual misdemeanours, alcoholism, violence and other forms of clerical delinquency were traditionally dealt with by diocesan lawcourts, but finding evidence and witnesses against those involved was not always easy. Parishioners were, for reasons of fear or self-interest, not always willing to denounce their clergy to outsiders, episcopal or otherwise. Some of the clergy of Chartres diocese in the 1650s were being effectively protected by the silence of their parishioners when questioned by visitors, at a time when individual priests were facing trial for various misdemeanours in the diocesan courts; it is not hard to imagine that such silence, if widespread, would protect many clerics against initial detection.[1] Nor did laypeople always share the official church's hostility to concubinary clergy: across many areas of France, they were willing to accept a priest cohabiting with a woman, provided that relationship was stable and 'respectable', whereas priests who attempted to get their hands on the virtuous women of the parish, married and unmarried, were often the object of considerable resentment. But the pressure from above did gradually tell, and the practice of celibacy by the clergy became more widespread as the century progressed – at least as judged by the fall in the numbers of those accused of, or tried for sexual offences. This trajectory was in turn helped by a gradual shift in attitudes among laypeople themselves, which is much harder to account for. In 1614, it seems that some electors of Third Estate deputies were prepared to accept that their clergy live in stable relationships with one woman, but that a generation later, in 1651, they firmly disapproved of all such practices. It seems reasonable to imagine that other parts of France evolved in the same way.[2]

Beyond such specific issues, there was the traditional general involvement of the clergy with the everyday life of their parishes, the extent of which the seventeenth-century church increasingly judged undesirable. Here, too, pressure was gradually exerted on them to withdraw as far as possible from some of the most obvious forms of such involvement – farming, jobbing, buying and selling goods and so on. Over time, laypeople supported clerical withdrawal from economic activities, if only out of self-interest: it provided them with opportunities to lease and work church property hitherto conducted by the clergy themselves. Accompanying these kinds of withdrawal was a growing insistence that clergy wear the tonsure and the clerical garb that would distinguish them from their lay neighbours. Symbolic though it was, this demand probably took the longest to achieve and, as in so many other spheres, it was achieved less by inspection, reprimand or penalty than by the changing formation of the younger generations of clergy, increasingly 'socialised' into such forms of behaviour.

Clerical Titles and *Prêtres Habitués*

Efforts to change the lower clergy must be placed in the perspective that contemporaries would have understood, and attempts at explanation must incorporate social factors as well as institutional pressures from above. The clerical 'title', briefly discussed in Chapter 3, was one of those traditional mechanisms that proved unexpectedly useful during the seventeenth century.[3] The need to ensure that clergy about to take orders be able to support themselves, either without or while waiting for a benefice, was strongly reaffirmed by the Council of Trent and in post-conciliar legislation, and in due course both the French crown and the bishops moved towards a more systematic imposition of the rules, while also raising the monetary value of the annuity itself. Whereas 50–60 *livres* a year was a common enough requirement in the late sixteenth century, the norm a hundred years later was more likely to be around 80–100 *livres*, a rise that was only marginally offset by the effects of inflation in the interval. Some dioceses, such as Coutances and Lisieux in Normandy, set the bar higher again – at 100 and 150 *livres* respectively; Reims and Lyon both required 100 *livres* by the later seventeenth century. Above all, the signs are that these tariffs were gradually enforced, to the extent that clergy seeking major orders had to furnish an authentic notarial contract as evidence of the financial settlement itself. The bishop of Tarbes was probably not the only bishop to insist on treating the titles like marriage banns to be read out publicly in church on three successive Sundays, so that their legal validity could be challenged if necessary; he may even have suspected that some of the titles were fraudulent.[4]

The effect of these measures was to quarantine for an indefinite period family property to the capital value of somewhere between 1,600 and 2,000 *livres*, since an unforeseeable proportion of the clergy concerned might never hold a benefice throughout their careers. Whether calculated in terms of annual income or notional capital value, the effect of such demands, where they were actually enforced, was to thin the ranks of the clergy in general and to exclude sons of the poorer social groups in particular. Such investments were well beyond the means of labourers, peasants and many artisans, whose sons may well have been attracted instead by the religious orders, especially the newer ones, which made no such demands of their recruits. Some dioceses also established 'special' titles for poorer and/or bright young clerics, as did Reims under Archbishop Le Tellier (1671–1709), which were attached to attendance at the seminary rather than at some distant university college. This particular reinvention of a long medieval tradition of bursaries for poor clerics was probably not enough to make a significant difference in regulating access to the clergy, while Le Tellier seems to have seen it as a way of creating a small pool of priests that he could deploy tactically in parishes needing capable clergy.[5] At any rate, the reduction in clerical numbers that occurred across the seventeenth century was more 'successful' than anticipated in different parts of France (Vannes in Brittany is a good example), with the result that some early to mid-eighteenth-century bishops found themselves reducing the value of the title to make it easier for these middling to lower social groups, in country as well as in towns, to re-enter the ranks of the clergy.

It seems likely that these measures had the greatest impact on the lowest rungs of the secular clergy, especially among those *prêtres-filleuls* or *prêtres habitués*, whose financial situation was the most fragile. There were exceptions of course, and these communities survived quite effectively in many areas of France – the Auvergne, parts of the Pyrenees and various other upland areas where the clergy remained distinctly more 'familial' than elsewhere in France – until well into the next century. Some of these communities turned themselves into collegiate chapters in order to protect themselves from episcopal assault. There is no doubt that seventeenth-century bishops and allied reformers took a strong dislike to this category of parish-based clergy, who seemed to them to enjoy too much autonomy and were not readily amenable to control from above or outside the parish. Moreover, they also represented that segment of the clergy which was least distinguishable from the ordinary inhabitants of parishes, at a time when the 'separation' of clergy and laity was becoming increasingly important to church authorities. Revising and tightening the statutes governing the *habitué* clergy was one response; another was to strengthen the role of the parish priest as the head of their 'communities'. These and other restrictive measures gradually brought about a shrinking in the size and the geographical location of the communities of priests in question.[6]

The *Concours* and its Alternatives

One major reason for the way these efforts developed was that the workings of the benefice system severely limited the capacity of bishops and their officials to discipline, shape or promote 'deserving' clergy. In many dioceses, the bishop's own right to appoint directly to parishes was as low as 5 per cent (Cambrai), with scores of 14 per cent and 22 per cent being recorded by its neighbours, Arras and Boulogne respectively. The archbishop of Reims may have been 'the first peer of France', but he only filled thirty-two out of his 517 parishes. These differences were reiterated across the whole of France, although episcopal patronage was considerably higher in many other dioceses. As we have seen elsewhere, presentation rights to the remaining parishes were shared by a bewilderingly large number of 'patrons', especially formidable institutions like chapters or abbeys: there were over 200 such patrons in the huge diocese of Clermont alone (840 parishes). Challenging *their* habits – which were often openly 'clientelist' in nature – where parishes in their gift were concerned, could be fraught, as they did not flinch from high-level litigation to protect their privileges, and the ensuing conflicts could blight the parishes concerned for years on end. Few bishops relished the prospect of repeated conflict with powerful bodies whose good will might be indispensable to them in other respects, so for a long time they did not enquire too zealously into the qualifications of those they presented for their approval to hold vacant parishes.

Unable to abolish and unwilling fundamentally to transform the benefice system, Trent had attempted to propose ways of mitigating the impact of such practices. It urged bishops to organise competitions (*concours*) to fill vacant parishes, even where they were themselves the patrons, so that the 'most deserving' candidates obtained them.[7] Trent actually gave more thought to this question than it did to the creation of seminaries, so its fate in post-Trent France may offer some useful clues about 'success and failure' in reforming its clergy. The *concours* was one of those disciplinary decrees of Trent adopted by the post-Trent provincial councils across France, as well as in successive royal ordinances from 1580 to 1629. Indeed, the 1629 ordinance explicitly stipulated the need for a real competition, a *concours*, in which the 'most worthy' candidate was granted the benefice and that in the case of a dead heat between candidates, the one with the better morals be preferred to the one with greater learning!

Yet the evidence indicates that late sixteenth-and early seventeenth-century bishops found the *concours* extremely difficult to operate, even in the then non-French peripheral regions (Flanders, Lorraine, Franche-Comté, Avignon) where Trent had been officially 'received'.[8] Brittany represents a curious exception here, as the papacy organised its own *concours* for parishes in its gift that became vacant during the 'pope's months' of the year, with the bizarre result that, until 1740, Breton priests found themselves journeying all the way to Rome to take an examination.[9] Across France generally, synods were regarded as a useful moment for appointing examiners of future *curés* and, in some instances, for examining those seeking benefices, but these examinations were not part of an actual competition to fill specific parishes that were vacant, but were rather a test of fitness to hold benefices with cure of souls generally. For most of the seventeenth century and beyond, French bishops settled for such 'aptitude' tests rather than the full *concours*, which remained beyond their grasp, mainly owing to the hostility of the patrons of the parishes, who also enjoyed some support from the law courts. So long as the latter remained opposed to the principle of the *concours*, its legality was fragile in Gallican France, royal ordinances notwithstanding.

It may be the persistence of such opposition that compelled many of France's bishops to look for ways around these obstacles and to insert themselves into the relationship between patrons of, and clergy seeking after, benefices. Giving up on the *concours* in the strict sense, many went ahead with the examinations of clergy just mentioned. Examiners would be appointed during the annual synod, candidates for vacant parishes would be examined at published times on a range of topics (usually theology and the administration of the sacraments), after which the bishop would either rank them or declare a given number of them fit to serve. This approach may also have helped to avoid some of the undesirable and unintended consequences of the *concours*. One bishop found that 'outsider' university graduates would obtain the best parishes via a *concours* and would then refuse to reside in the parishes concerned, frustrating the ambitions of the better local clergy while leaving replacement curates of inferior value to serve there instead. Likewise, excessive severity in examining and approving priests, especially in Jansenist-leaning dioceses, could scare off contenders, leaving only the mediocre from whom to select future *curés*.

Much less is known about the means employed by bishops to convince patrons to accept that they should have a voice in the filling of vacant parishes, yet it was of decisive importance. The secret was not to attack patrons' rights per se, but to impress on them the need to accept their duty in conscience to fill parishes with worthy clergy, who had, by definition, been formally examined and approved. It is not hard to imagine how unpredictable such a process could be, since being confined to selecting candidates from among clerics already approved by the bishops was a serious erosion of the patrons' liberty. Yet that liberty was already being eroded by the existing clergy who were accustomed to resigning their cure to successors of their own choosing, often younger members of their own families. Since this practice also enjoyed recognition by both Rome and the French law courts, there was no prospect of eliminating it outright. Across seventeenth-century dioceses, the proportion of *curés* entering and exiting parishes through resignations could be as high as two-thirds or three-quarters. The more this became – or remained – common practice, the more it effectively hollowed out the rights of patrons from the inside, even though those rights were nominally invoked and respected throughout the process of changing benefices. Yet, paradoxically, it may have suited bishops in the long term, insofar as it sidelined potentially troublesome players (chapters, abbeys, nobles and so on) and left them to deal with individual clerics in search of parishes and other positions in the church.

Very gradually, the principle that the designated successor must be examined and accepted by the bishops as suitable for the parish was imposed. But caution was advisable, as litigious *curés* might find willing allies in the courts, and any hint of episcopal arbitrariness in rejecting or accepting proposed successors could torpedo the policy. Here too, it is difficult to plot the growth of such episcopal intervention across France, but by the later decades of the seventeenth century, it seems clear that many bishops had effectively inserted themselves into the process which determined the renewal and placement of parish clergy. It was all the easier to do so by then, since they were accustomed to intervening in earlier stages of individuals' progression towards priestly orders: at the moment of tonsure and the subdiaconate, bishops and their officials were examining and, in some cases, denying individuals judged unfit the right to take the orders in question; approving or rejecting future parish priests was in some respects an extension of such exercises. And the clergy themselves were accustomed by then to supervision and intervention of this kind. It has been suggested that some bishops learned to use the surplus of clergy to their advantage here: by imposing curates on many parishes and then observing their track record, the best organised bishops could, like Le Tellier of Reims, keep files on potential candidates and then pressure retiring parish priests to resign their benefice to a successor from among their number.[10] Once the momentum towards such solutions gathered, it became easier for bishops to ensure that the existing clergy knew in advance whether their succession plans stood any chance of success and what the conditions would be if they pursued them.

It is all the more paradoxical, therefore, that the *concours* staged a belated arrival in eighteenth-century France.[11] By then, the French church's 'investment' in improving the clergy's intellectual and pastoral attainments had the gradual effect of *increasing* competition for parishes generally, so that recourse to the *concours* seemed an obvious means of coping with the problem from the 1740s onwards. By that point, patrons of benefices and the wider French society had come to accept the validity of the *concours* in one form or another, and France's bishops had gained an indirect, yet reasonably firm grip on a benefice system that on the surface at least was no different to what it had been a century or so earlier.

Conferences for Clergy

One of the earliest expectations of a *concours* after the Council of Trent was that it would encourage future clergy to attend college and university in order to acquire the educational baggage that would enable them to compete more successfully for posts. There were some such incentives within the French church already, such as the rights of graduates to obtain benefices during certain months of the year, or the increasing tendency, backed by royal legislation, to reserve parishes in the bigger towns and cities for doctors of theology. But university graduates did not always have the reputation that this might suggest: as noted above, they were frequently accused of grabbing the most lucrative benefices available and then farming them out to substitute clergy with highly precarious tenure and dubious motivation. Something of that mistrust surfaced in the 1629 ordinance's article on the *concours*, which explicitly placed priests with good morals ahead of those with learning. By then, however, the French church had largely decided *not* to persist with the *concours*, preferring instead to concentrate on improving the calibre of the clergy, mainly but not exclusively through college and seminary education.

But here, too, there could be no question of relying on the next generation to resolve problems which were only partly intellectual, since it was the ability of clergy to conduct religious services, administer the sacraments and catechise their parishioners which was of greatest concern. Visitations endlessly recorded these deficiencies and synods repeatedly legislated on how to deal with them, but neither offered practical solutions to the problems identified. The subdivision of dioceses, especially the bigger ones, into *vicariats forains* was a significant step in that direction. These rural deaneries tended to be smaller than the historical subdivisions of dioceses (archdeaconries, or their other names), and had none of their unwelcome aspirations to autonomy. The best-known model of these vicariates was that of Carlo Borromeo in Milan, and it was as a self-conscious 'Borromean' that Cardinal Sourdis introduced them to both France and his diocese (Bordeaux) in 1609. In Bordeaux, there were to be twenty-seven of them in all, each covering ten to twenty parishes, and each led by a *vicaire forain* drawn from among the clergy of the district. Other 'Borromean' bishops followed and adapted Sourdis's lead in subsequent decades; in Limoges, Tulle, Clermont and Meaux, the *vicariats* did not materialise until the 1650s, and they were probably not the last. In 1652, Dominique Séguier of Meaux divided his diocese of 239 parishes into ten unequally sized 'conferences' meeting in principle twelve times yearly from April to October.[12]

It is possible that other vicariates/rural deaneries and their conferences emerged more informally elsewhere, especially in northern France, out of older, local associations or 'confraternities' of priests, especially in towns, and that at some date during our period they were reshaped and made more uniform by episcopal intervention. They are well attested for the town of Beauvais for which, unusually, the record of their deliberations has survived.[13] They also seem to have existed in parts of Rouen diocese (France's biggest in terms of parishes) from the 1660s, if not earlier, but Archbishop Colbert decided to restructure them in the 1680s as an extension of his synods and calends. He was probably only formalising a pattern established by then when he laid out a timetable for the assemblies, a range of issues for discussion and the keeping of an official record of the discussions themselves which would be submitted to the archbishop's council.[14]

These ecclesiastical conferences, as they were called by then, were also intended in part as a means of supervising and 'educating' the clergy in smaller, more effective units. The *vicaire forain* was expected to organise and lead the conferences, and develop them as a forum for mutual education among the parish clergy. Ideally, they met monthly – or even fortnightly – during the April to November period, moving around from one parish to another. But they did not always escape the problems of absenteeism that plagued synods and calends – and for similar reasons arising from the passage from the voluntary-associational to the obligatory. Conferences were also liturgical occasions which could involve preaching, which was especially useful during their early history. But their main purpose was to discuss set topics, theological, ethical and especially pastoral, with the better-educated clergy expected to help the less educated. In the Norman diocese of Coutances, clerics who were not yet priests attended these conferences during Louis XIV's reign as part of their preparation for orders, and proof of attendance at them was required for ordination.[15] Apart from Beauvais, not many records survive of the actual discussions – as distinct from the published 'proceedings' of the later seventeenth and eighteenth centuries – but we know that the Rouen discussions of the 1690s ranged widely from the clergy's own vocation and its demands on them in their relations with laypeople to cases of conscience involving ethical-religious problems like usury. At Rouen, too, detailed attention, stretching over several years, was given to the Ten Commandments, some of which received far more attention than others. The Coutances clergy of the late seventeenth century regularly discussed the duty of catechising their parishioners and the best ways of doing so.[16]

In the most ambitious assemblies, the clergy brought their own written submissions which were then examined by the deans who, in some cases, would refer them onwards to the bishop's officials, to whom the formal record of the discussions and their decisions was also submitted. The most successful 'conferences' developed elaborate programmes of moral and pastoral divinity; some of their proceedings were edited and published in several volumes, and became a staple part of the educational cursus and libraries of future generations of clergy. For example, the conferences of Le Puy of 1672 and 1673 were published in the same year as they occurred: there were seven conferences per year, all devoted to the question of superstition, and each published volume consisted of seven four-page *cahiers* based on the discussions of individual topics relating to superstition.[17]

By the mid-eighteenth century, when seminaries were offering a basic theological education, the conferences could afford to move on to more complex issues of moral theology and 'cases of conscience'. Not every diocese persevered with the conferences, however: in some they were suspended because of fears of theological 'contamination' owing to the circulation of Jansenist ideas, which could have a significant bearing on the key sacraments of penance and the Eucharist; in others such as Meaux, where complaints about their cessation arose in both the 1710s and the 1730s, the problem was a more familiar one – absenteeism rather than perceived intellectual dangers.

However difficult they may be to isolate and evaluate, the ecclesiastical conferences can legitimately be seen as both cause and consequence of the rising standards of the parish clergy of the time. One historian has rightly seen in them 'an essential element of clerical formation', not least because the teaching they provided was put to concrete use, being recycled in sermons, for example.[18] Whereas synods brought together only holders of benefices, including *curés*, the conferences were usually open to the wider population of curates, *habitués*, chaplains and clerics in sub-priestly orders. This alone made them a major form of clerical sociability, especially in large dioceses where isolation in rural parishes was a serious problem. Their success may have hinged on the degree of compulsion or liberty governing participation by the local clergy, and the signs are that by the later seventeenth century they were increasingly part of a chain of command (*relais de transmission*) controlled by bishops and their officials. Their educative and disciplinary functions overlapped, with *vicaires forains* sometimes reprimanding individual clergy for their misbehaviour and threatening them with further action; and it is not hard to imagine this kind of problem finding its way into the agenda of subsequent visitations of the parishes concerned.

The conferences' educational mission, 'to banish ignorance from the sanctuary', related closely to another specific concern of visitors to parishes throughout the century, that of ensuring that the clergy possessed the books deemed necessary for their pastoral duties.[19] Obviously, the requirements would vary across dioceses, and especially over a century and a half. In the early seventeenth century, bishops and visitors generally were keen to ensure that the most basic books, essentially liturgical in scope, were available in churches; priests' own libraries were still a rather secondary consideration. Much of the time, this involved replacing older versions of the missal, the ritual, the breviary, the diocesan synodal statutes and other key books with new ones resulting from the post-Trent revisions. But by mid-century, visitors had begun to insist on more than that. The demand that priests have a copy of the Roman Catechism, alias the Catechism of the Council of Trent, was virtually universal, given that it was far more a manual for pastors than a catechism in the strict sense of the term.[20] Where, in 1623, the bishop of Maillezais required his clergy to have their copy of the Roman Catechism, the decrees of the Bordeaux provincial council and one or two manuals of casuistry, in 1669 his successor added the entire Bible and the works of Gregory the Great and St Bernard, as well as Thomas Aquinas's treatise on ethics. The scale of such demands varied across France, and their chronology did likewise. As early as 1638, Alain de Solminihac, newly installed as bishop of Cahors, required his *curés* to have a Bible, the decrees and the Catechism of Trent, the Cahors synodal statutes of 1638, Cardinal Toledo's summa of cases of conscience, the Roman ritual, missal and breviary, as well as the Spanish Carthusian Molina's *Instruction for Priests*. He also exhorted them to acquire commentaries on the Ten Commandments and the full edition of the *Guide for Sinners* of the Dominican Luis de Granada.[21] This particular selection of titles amply shows, among other things, the continuing influence of Spanish writers even among the most advanced French reformers at this juncture.

As these basic, indispensable demands were met over a number of decades, rising standards among the clergy opened the way for a corresponding rise in what was expected of them: the possession of books that were less purely liturgical and more indicative of the pastoral and spiritual calibre of the clergy. Of course, books whose purchase was prescribed by visitors or during synods might not always materialise in parochial 'libraries', but the independent evidence of visitation records and, especially, of probate inventories shows that the efforts made in this domain during the seventeenth century did bear fruit by the early decades of the next one, when *curés'* libraries, especially in the bigger towns, could be considerable. Borromeo's *Instructions for Confessors*, Luis de Granada's *Guide for Sinners* and de Sales's *Introduction to the Devout Life*, were commonly to be found alongside the Bible, lives of the saints, the Roman Catechism and so on. For the most part, the clergy's books point to a greater concern with pastoral and moral matters than with the more problematic questions of doctrine or scripture. Such shifts were incremental, generational and probably also regional, since the *curés* of La Rochelle diocese and parts of Brittany still possessed very few of the items considered essential as late as 1720–30. To that extent, they are yet another barometer of the pace of change within France's lower clergy.[22]

Seminaries and Colleges

The growth of clerical seminaries in seventeenth-century France makes a great deal more sense when viewed in the context of these attempts to invent 'in-service' training for serving priests. The converse is also true. After all, the most common accusation made against the clergy before, during and after the Protestant Reformations was that not only were they ignorant, but that their ignorance was a prime source of their inadequacy as pastors. The new Lutheran and Calvinist churches looked to universities and academies to make good that educational deficit among their clergy; the wave of new academy and university foundations that accompanied the Reformations is evidence enough of their prime concern, namely to create a clergy capable of preaching the word of God. The old church could hardly avoid the issue, yet it was only in the very last sessions of the Council of Trent that, like so many related issues of church reform, the question of what to do about clerical education – understood in the broader sense of 'formation' or preparation – was finally addressed. Interestingly from a French perspective, the first draft of the Council's decree on seminaries was made by the bishop of Verdun, Nicolas Psaume, a confidant of the Cardinal of Lorraine who later did so much to propagate Tridentine reforms inside and outside of Lorraine.[23]

Unlike Protestant Europe, the old church was not proposing radically to reduce the huge numbers of adolescent tonsured clerics in Europe at the time, so it proposed the creation in each diocese of a seminary for clerics aged twelve and over, who already had basic writing and literacy skills, and in which they would be both educated in the conventional school syllabus of the day and 'formed' in the habits and virtues expected of future clergy. This hardly sounds revolutionary, and much of the decree reads like an attempt to revive the choir schools of the cathedral chapters. Trent was also thinking mainly of supporting poor clerics: the future seminaries could take candidates from well-off families, but they would have to pay to live there. Most paradoxical of all is the fact that while Trent required bishops to found seminaries, it did not explicitly oblige future clergy to attend them. Consequently, the question of what a bishop who founded a seminary might do in the face of clerical boycott or indifference – not an unlikely prospect, as we have seen in other contexts – remained unanswered. Trent also insisted that the seminary should be diocesan and not simply episcopal, which meant that members of the diocesan clergy (usually drawn from the cathedral chapter) were expected to be involved in founding and governing it. Given the often tense, even hostile, relations between bishops and their chapters, this was not likely to be an easy partnership. And, of course, the question of how to finance seminaries (by a tax on benefice-holders, the 'incorporation' of benefices into the seminaries themselves, or some other mechanism) was left entirely open. That, too, proved to be an enduring source of headaches for founders and administrators in subsequent generations.

Such were the unpromising beginnings of an institution, the 'Tridentine' seminary, that has long been seen as a defining element of early modern Catholicism. France's experiences are of particular interest, and it is no exaggeration to say that the seminary system that subsequently developed there was *un*-Tridentine in important respects.[24] Initially the French church did what it could to follow the Council's precepts, encouraged no doubt by the great royal ordinances of Blois (1579) and the edict of Melun (1580) which incorporated many of Trent's decisions into French law.[25] About sixteen seminaries were established between the 1560s and the end of the 1610s, but only one or two of the earlier ones survived into the seventeenth century. Some of the reasons for this relatively inauspicious start are already familiar: the disorders of the religious wars, the weakness of episcopal control of the clergy and the inability to put the seminaries on a proper financial footing. But there were, arguably, other, perhaps more illuminating, reasons for this state of affairs. The new seminaries *did* resemble the old cathedral choir schools too closely, so not surprisingly the cathedral chapters often refused to co-operate in creating what looked like direct competition to their own educational activities. Some French bishops reacted no differently, failing to see quite how yet another breed of colleges for adolescents would or could solve the problem of clerical recruitment and training.[26]

It was precisely during this period – from 1560 to around 1620 – that the largest contingent of the newly developing *collèges* spread throughout France. These schools owed much to the humanist educators of the Renaissance, and proved hugely attractive to those seeking careers in the church, the professions or the service of the monarchy. Most of them taught the 'humanities' but a growing number, especially in the larger towns, added the 'higher' subjects of rhetoric and philosophy. In many ways, they offered virtually the same educational facilities as the seminaries outlined by Trent, even though the *collèges* were, of course, not confined to future clergy. Indeed, in the decades after Trent some of the towns petitioning to have seminaries appear to have imagined that seminaries really were *collèges*. Such a confusion seems all the more understandable when, in the early decades of the seventeenth century, the running of more and more of these initially lay and municipal *collèges* was confided to religious orders like the Jesuits, the Oratory and the Doctrinaires.[27] The Jesuits, in particular, were long *un*interested in running seminaries in France, convinced that their own *collèges de plein exercice* (those teaching humanities, rhetoric, philosophy and even theology), whose foundation owed much to episcopal patronage and support, were far more useful than those rather fragile, marginal institutions with a mere handful of students, such as the seminaries of Toulouse or Rouen, the only survivals from the first crop of post-Tridentine foundations. Moreover, the fact that most of these new seminary foundations quickly became boarding houses whose adolescent 'boursiers' actually followed the courses of instruction in the neighbouring *collège*, whether Jesuit or not, only seemed to prove the point. Indeed, as Marc Venard has pointed out, several French bishops contemplating the creation of a Tridentine seminary saw it as operating alongside one of the new *collèges*, especially those of the Jesuits; between them, they would raise the level of the diocesan clergy.[28]

This wider educational shift, unplanned by any church council, and the collapse of most of the early seminaries, helps to explain the long hiatus before the next round of seminary foundations during the middle decades of the seventeenth century. In fact, those most active in the drive to reform the French clergy found themselves having to rethink the entire strategy, and did not have ready answers to the problems they faced. A few seminaries of the 'Tridentine' type were founded as late as the 1610s and 1620s. A good example is that established by Richelieu in his western diocese of Luçon in 1612. He persuaded Bérulle's new Oratory to take charge of it. But it is doubtful if it contributed much to the improvement of the Luçon clergy. It was virtually defunct by the time Richelieu resigned his see in 1623 and, once he had left, the Oratorians, too, were anxious to disengage from the enterprise.[29] Similar foundations, in Paris for example, also seemed to produce little effect. This uncertainty was famously summed up by Vincent de Paul in 1644: 'the decree of the council of Trent must be respected because it is of the Holy Spirit. Yet experience shows that the manner in which it is implemented in respect of the age of the seminarians means that it does not work, neither in Italy nor in

France. Some of them leave before finishing, while others have no attraction to the ecclesiastical state; some join religious orders, and others again flee the places where they have obligations arising from their education, preferring to try their luck elsewhere. There are four in France – at Bordeaux, Reims, Rouen and one previously at Agen. None of these dioceses has benefited from them and I fear that, apart from Milan and Rome, things are no different in Italy.'[30]

By 1644, de Paul was as well placed as anyone to make such a devastating judgement. The Rouen seminary which he mentioned is a case in point. Founded by Cardinal Joyeuse in 1613, it was initially located not in Rouen itself but in Paris, where large numbers of young clerics from Rouen, France's largest diocese, went to college and university. Joyeuse was only following the logic of the Council of Trent's decree in acting as he did, and he was not alone: the bishop of Mirepoix reported to Rome in 1594 that a college in the university of Toulouse served as his diocesan seminary. A study of the Joyeuse seminary has shown that it only produced about 2 per cent of the Rouen diocesan clergy during its first fifty years, while by the 1640s *half* of its 'graduates' did indeed pursue non-ecclesiastical careers once their education was completed.

In other words, the evidence shows that de Paul was not too wide of the mark in his 1644 observations. As the founder of what would become one of the most successful congregations of seminary directors in French history, de Paul had himself been wrestling with these problems since the 1610s. He was in good company, since other influential figures within the emerging reform movement, such as Pierre de Bérulle, were similarly challenged. Through his personal influence and his numerous disciples, inside and outside of the French Oratory, which he dedicated deliberately to reforming the secular clergy, Bérulle exercised a profound and subtle influence on several generations of church reformers. Less celebrated figures such as Adrien Bourdoise, *curé* of Saint-Nicolas-du-Chardonnet in Paris, used his own parish as a laboratory to experiment with the idea of a clerical community of present and future clergy coming together in order to learn and practise the necessary pastoral skills. Bourdoise's immediate influence may have been limited by his intransigence and abruptness, but the idea of using parish-based communities of clergy as agencies for clerical education in the broad sense was attempted in several French cities. De Paul himself regarded this type of seminary as the best because there learning was born directly out of experience. The most famous of them began in Saint-Sulpice parish in the early 1640s and only slowly evolved into an institution that would be recognisable as a seminary; and even when it did so, Saint-Sulpice retained its other concomitant features of a parish, a retreat and a community of priests.

The full extent of such experiment across France remains elusive, but it suggests that a new generation of religious figures tacitly agreed that the

'Tridentine' model of a seminary was no solution – or, at best, only a very partial solution – to the problem of clerical formation, and that they would doubtless have accepted the reasons de Paul gave in 1644. Above all, the solutions that slowly emerged from the different experiments of the early decades of the century derived more from direct personal experience of the state of the parish clergy in both town and country by those involved – especially in rural missions or preaching campaigns – than from conciliar decrees or subsequent treatises. But such experience did not necessarily entail a uniformity of approach to the problem. When, for example, *curé* Olier of Saint-Sulpice, who had seen the realities of rural France as a missionary during the 1630s, wrote his *Project for the Establishment of a Diocesan Seminary* (*Projet de l'établissement d'un séminaire dans un diocese*) in 1651, the celebrated bishop of Cahors, Alain de Solminihac, responded pointedly that Olier's proposal was 'not merely very difficult, but impossible, for practice and speculation are quite distinct things'.[31]

By the mid-seventeenth century, the wider context had changed enough for a new wave of seminaries to appear. Some perennial obstacles did remain: finding the funds to establish and then finance seminaries was as problematic as ever, since the French clergy were as reluctant as their counterparts elsewhere in Europe to be 'taxed' for their upkeep. Only the odd seminary managed to get hold, via incorporation, of a slice of the monastic revenues discussed in Chapter 4. Yet the recovery and rise in the revenues of ecclesiastical properties made the financial problem less intractable than it had been a generation or so earlier.

More vital still was the fact that there was no shortage throughout France of energetic individuals who were prepared to find the funds, acquire or donate the lands or properties needed for a seminary, and even deal with the inevitable litigation arising from such transactions in the law courts. Many of these figures were *dévots*, lay as much as clerical, among whom the members of the Company of the Holy Sacrament were probably crucial to the entire process, especially in the early uncertain stages.[32] Likewise, the 'corporate' opposition or indifference of cathedral chapters did not prevent individual canons from playing decisive roles in developing seminaries. Finally, given the Jesuits' continuing preference for schoolteaching, it was invaluable that the new congregations of secular clergy, with their specific commitment to reforming the lower, especially parish clergy, were taking shape in these same decades. In addition to the Doctrinaires, who were scattered through towns south of the Bordeaux–Gap line, they included Bérulle's Oratorians, de Paul's Lazarists plus the Eudists and, later still, the 'Company' of Saint-Sulpice, to mention only the most prominent. All had their own particular views on clerical education and reform, with differences of emphasis which would define the ethos of the seminaries which they would later direct. The Oratorians were drawn into running *collèges* like their rivals, the Jesuits, and their seminaries thus tended to become elite institutions. But the Eudists, the Lazarists and the Sulpicians were determined at all costs to avoid those broader teaching commitments, however much their own work depended upon the existence of such schools in the first place. The growth and evolution of French seminaries has to be seen in close proximity to that of these specialist congregations, their objectives and their place within the wider French church.[33]

Put simply, one can say that Vincent de Paul and his contemporaries concluded that Trent had focused its attention on the wrong category of cleric. Educating adolescents could safely be left to the many *collèges* now operating, especially as they were increasingly run by religious orders anyway. If necessary, poor scholars could be taken into what would later be called *petits séminaires* and board there while they attended classes at the local college; indeed, the *petit séminaire* often became an almost indistinguishable 'annexe' to the college in question, and was governed by the same religious order as ran the *collège*. What de Paul and his contemporaries proposed was to redirect the focus of attention to those clerics who, having wholly or partly completed their education in the humanities, were intending to take the 'major' orders. Neither the colleges nor the Trent-style seminaries made any provision for them, yet it seemed increasingly essential to test and prepare those about to cross the major threshold that full priestly orders represented. Dioceses might not have *concours* or bishops much control of the benefice system, but access to the 'major' orders was in principle their preserve. Orders could legitimately be denied to the undeserving or the unfit, after an examination of the candidates. There might be little hope during the seventeenth century that bishops could really require universal clerical attendance at a seminary but, as we saw in connection with clerical 'titles', they were increasingly willing to use other means available in order to get round such problems. And here, too, church law offered them a possible way forward, since it stipulated a gap of virtually two years between the subdiaconate (the first of the three major orders) and the priesthood. Surely, such an obligatory and extended timescale could become the focus of efforts at improving the incoming generation of clergy?

This is the background to the gradual transformation of the parish-based communities created by the likes of Bourdoise and Olier into seminaries, but also to the initially informal retreats or conferences for ordinands that de Paul and others organised from the 1620s onwards. Initially lasting no longer than a week or more, the latter were of a purely practical nature, designed to provide the prospective clergy with a 'crash course' in liturgical, sacramental and related matters, and with no room for intellectual ambitions. Yet their fame came from the fact that they also attracted high-flying theology students from the Sorbonne such as the future Cardinal de Retz. Such activities, often ad hoc and experimental, developed without a blueprint over many years before they grew into anything remotely resembling an institution. From the late 1620s, at least, de Paul at the Bons-Enfants college and the Oratorians at Saint-Magloire Abbey in Paris were both 'receiving' clerics who were referred to them by the archbishop of Paris before being allowed to take the major orders. The 1625 Assembly of Clergy debated these questions and urged that the pre-ordination retreat or conferences should be made obligatory, so clearly these initiatives were attracting wider interest.[34] Twenty years later, by the mid-1640s, Paris alone could be said to have three seminaries – the Oratory at Saint-Magloire, de Paul's Lazarists at Bons Enfants and the emerging seminary in the Saint-Sulpice parish – yet none of them was yet quite like what would conventionally be thought of as a full seminary. In 1640, de Paul stated that his 'seminary' was attended only by those referred to him by the archbishop and his officials before taking orders, that they usually stayed about eleven days in all, and that their time was devoted to basic moral theology, the sacraments and the liturgy generally.[35]

Tentative and unpromising as they may seem, these efforts were the real starting point of the huge rash of seminary foundations that followed – thirty-six between 1642 and 1660, fifty-six between 1660 and 1682 and a further twenty-five between 1683 and 1720. Only seven more were added between 1720 and 1789, and only six of the smallest southern dioceses never had a seminary of their own. This evidence is impressive, though we should not overestimate the speed with which some at least of these seminaries became fully operational. It was one thing to 'found' an institution, and another to bring it to a state of normal working, and in some places that could take several decades. It is often claimed that crown intervention in 1695 and especially 1698 provided a stimulus to a new generation of seminary foundations, but this probably refers to the crucial post-foundation task of financing them and making them fully operational.

Likewise, as early as the 1650s, a number of bishops and seminary directors agreed that a total stay of two years in the emerging seminaries was the target they should aim for.[36] But reality lagged a good way behind for decades, and in many dioceses for up to a century. While clerics seeking the major orders were increasingly being routinely required to attend the available seminaries for ordinands, the fact is that they tended to spend discrete periods of weeks or months there preceding the taking of the *individual* orders. The inconsistent pattern of such attendance in seminaries, which was determined more by the taking of specific orders than by an educational cursus, should be borne in mind when attempting to estimate their possible impact on each new generation of priests. And of course, seminaries were also used to discipline already ordained clergy, especially those seeking benefices or whose behaviour was found to be unsatisfactory during pastoral visitations.[37]

The management of these new seminaries was confided mainly to religious orders or congregations with differing views of what they should be doing, which sort of candidates they were dealing with and which type of cleric they wanted to produce, all of which ensured that the seminary map of France would not evolve in a uniform manner. The term 'seminary' still had a variety of meanings, and contemporaries of Louis XIV sometimes pointed out that although their diocese might not yet have a seminary, it did have a proper *collège* and, therefore, it should not be regarded as totally lacking in the proper educational provision for future clergy. It was not until 1683 that the Jesuits finally agreed to drop their opposition to running seminaries and took on the new seminary in the recently conquered city of Strasbourg, a move which opened the floodgates for them as seminary directors elsewhere in France.[38]

An equally decisive development by the later seventeenth and early eighteenth century was the imposition of educational prerequisites on those entering these seminaries for ordinands. Depending on the type of seminary in question, the prerequisite might involve having completed the humanities or philosophy; others again might demand some familiarity with theology, based on a year or more's study of the subject in a *collège* or a university, depending on the educational cursus offered in the *collèges* in question. The assumption was that the core of their formal education could be left to the network of *collèges* and universities, with which the small-scale seminaries, with their severely limited financial and other resources, simply could not compete (see Map 4). Individuals entering the seminaries for ordinands now had to produce the required evidence of their scholastic attainments. Seminaries in large rural dioceses or run by de Paul's Lazarists usually had modest educational ambitions for their candidates, compared with those of the Jesuits, the Oratorians or Saint-Sulpice. Early on, many local *collèges* did not have the classes in philosophy, let alone in theology, to meet more than limited demands, but the growing provision for the teaching of philosophy and theology in the *collèges* during the second half of the century may well have been an improvised response to a rising demand stimulated by a growing seminary movement.

Thus, French seminaries, far from being uniform, actually played their own part in stratifying the clergy, even if they did not initially create such stratification. By the second half of the century, as we have seen, French dioceses required their ordinands to produce solid evidence that they could support themselves decently once ordained. By the same token, those who could aspire to clerical careers increasingly came from families who could afford to give them an education in a *collège*. The social profile of the clergy which this

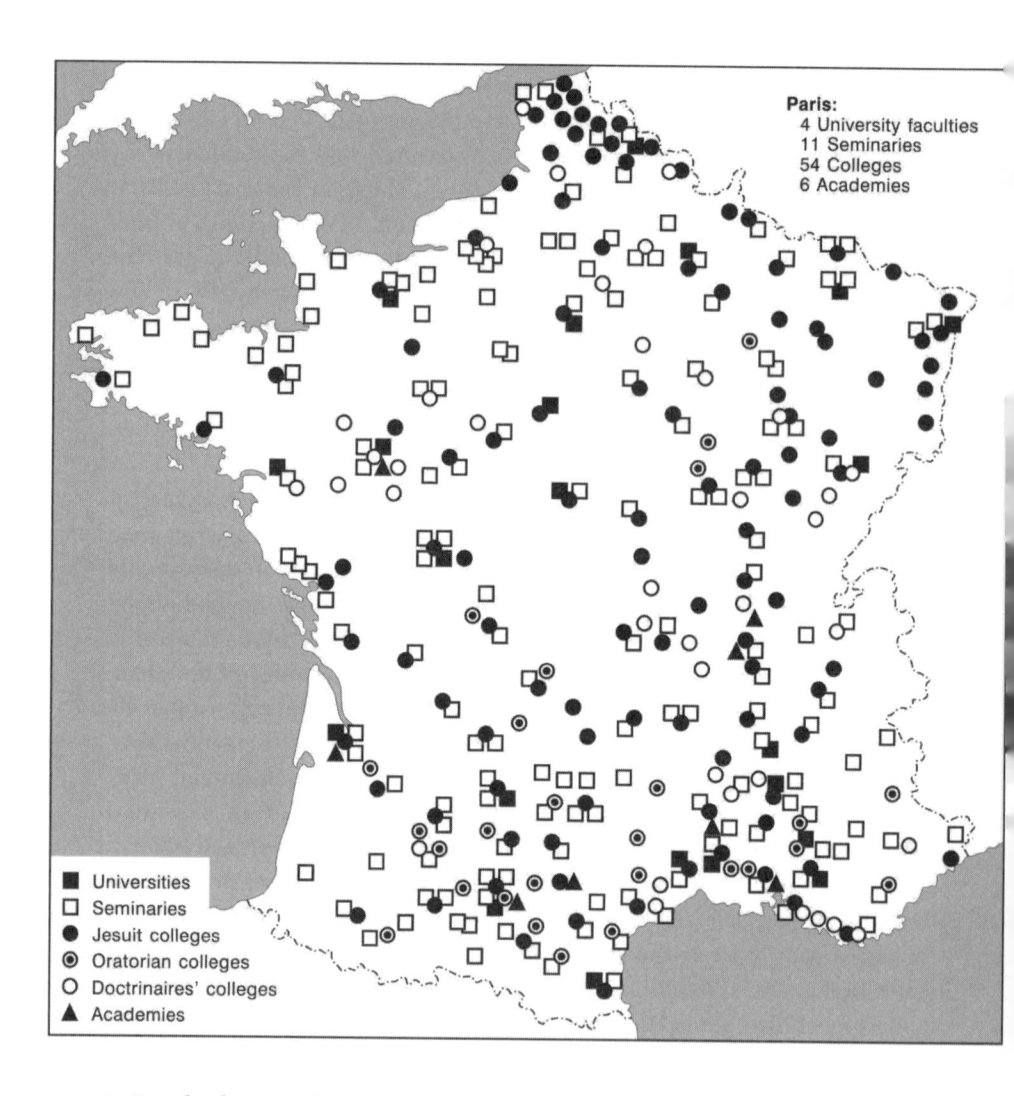

4. French educational institutions, c.1715.

brought about ensured that intending priests were likely to be attracted by different types of seminary. Saint-Sulpice in Paris gradually became the most influential of all, the one which produced future bishops, vicars-general and the like, many of whom were graduates of the Paris theology faculty. The Oratorian and Jesuit-run seminaries produced the cultivated middle-ranking clergy, especially cathedral canons, diocesan officials and the holders of urban parishes, while the Lazarists, the Eudistes and the Doctrinaires catered mainly for the lower tier of the secular parish clergy. Some big metropolitan dioceses – Lyon, Rouen, Toulouse – developed two or more seminaries, which differed in their clientele and ambitions. The Joyeuse seminary in Rouen eventually became known as the 'seminary of the rich', which led Colbert's son when he became archbishop of Rouen to found his own seminary, which became known as the 'seminary of the poor'.[39] Thus, a certain differentiation emerged within seminary provision, one result of which was that by the eighteenth century, the clergy themselves and commentators generally were keenly aware of the variations in career prospects that were realistically open to the 'alumni' of particular seminaries.[40]

Given their 'experimental' beginnings, it is hardly surprising that the mid-seventeenth century's seminaries for ordinands continued to evolve in subsequent generations. Much depended on the relations between individual bishops and the religious order running a particular seminary. Episcopal control of seminaries tightened progressively, with little room left for other members of the diocesan clergy to play an independent role in their affairs. Bishops' Gallican sensitivities could also mean that they were not simply content to allow a religious order to direct their seminary. On the contrary, many of them held out for a very long time against such a prospect, preferring to employ members of their own diocesan secular clergy, on the grounds that they could exercise direct authority over them at all times; as late as the 1780s, three out of every ten French seminaries were still run in this way.[41] The fact that the remaining seven were run by orders or congregations owed much to the fact that the congregations themselves were composed of secular clergy. French bishops often clashed with seminary directors and the orders that they represented, so that contracts with particular orders to run a particular seminary might be torn up or renegotiated with a different order. A change of bishop in a diocese could of itself signal such a change of direction.[42] Even de Paul, as respectful as anyone of episcopal authority, found this particular burden irksome, lamenting the fact that his congregation had to render regular accounts to the local bishops on how individual seminaries were run.

Towards the end of the century, a new factor appeared that would further complicate such arrangements, the fear of Jansenist ideas penetrating seminaries and thus contaminating the next generation of clergy. Consequently, several bishops rescinded agreements with the Oratory, which was suspected of Augustinian and therefore Jansenist sympathies. The Jesuits were welcome in many dioceses for precisely that reason after 1683, despite the considerable reservations in many episcopal hearts about their theology and politics. Jansenist bishops, needless to say, had equally clear ideas of the kind of seminary and clergy they wanted and even more so of what they did *not* want – namely, anything that smacked of Jesuit–Molinist theology. Above all, the Jansenist scare was an important reason why from around 1700 onwards, seminaries slowly began developing their own formal teaching programmes, starting obviously with theology itself and imperceptibly expanding to embrace philosophy and canon law. Over a period of time, the net effect of such efforts was to lengthen the duration of the average cleric's sojourn in the seminaries. By taking on more and more of the intellectual tasks previously left to other institutions, seminaries gradually became less and less places of immediate preparation for orders, and more the mature institutions of the pre-revolutionary decades. This shift is neatly exemplified by the success of several such seminaries in obtaining affiliation to universities which ensured that their 'in-house' courses would lead to university degrees and their students would gain the proper academic recognition for their studies.[43] Thus, the privileges that graduates still enjoyed when pursuing benefices within the French church became a further incentive to attend a seminary.

The seminaries which took shape during our period did not single-handedly transform the French secular clergy: they were far too small and limited in what they could do for that. The Lazarists were not alone in developing, as early as the 1630s, the idea of a seminary where individual seminarians' vocations would be closely tested and observed, but it would be several generations before such a programme could be put into practice.[44] Meanwhile, seminaries took their initially very modest place in a whole range of measures which were gradually reshaping the clergy. It would be misleading, for example, to attribute responsibility for clerical residence to them, when it is evident that other measures had almost achieved that objective by the time the seminaries were getting off the ground. By 'piggy-backing' on the *collèges*, they freed themselves from the constraints of having to educate adolescent clerics, many of whom might not wish to pursue clerical careers once they had acquired an education. For a long time, the seminaries were often heartily disliked by the clergy, especially wherever they were used as clerical 'houses of correction'. Bishops and reformers all regarded them as necessary, but in practice even the best-run among them never 'produced' more than a modest proportion of the newly ordained clergy.

Ideals of the Priest

If the ultimate outcome of the efforts chronicled so far was a 'Tridentine' clergy, it raises the question of whether there was a model of such a clergy at work in seventeenth-century France. There is good reason to think that the frequently invoked Tridentine model was far from fixed. The Council's own thinking about the priesthood was limited, defined as it was by the need to resist the Protestant reformers' assaults on the concept of a priesthood set apart from the rest of the Christian community by its own special sacrament. So Trent defended the sacrament of orders and reiterated the 'separateness' of the priest, whose essential mission was to consecrate (the mass) and pardon (penance) rather than, say, to preach God's word, which would have been too much of a concession to the reformers. This emphasis was in line with the general conservatism of its doctrinal decrees, although Trent's 'disciplinary' decrees took a more positive, pastoral view of what priests should do. Within less than a generation after Trent, a significant layer of interpretation had been added, some of it 'official' (for instance the Roman Catechism, papal decrees), some 'unofficial' but no less authoritative for all that. The most decisive exemplar of this type was, inevitably, Carlo Borromeo's *Acts of the Church of Milan*.

In few parts of Europe was the process of interpretation and adaptation of Trent's work more intense and more sustained than in France, where Trent was more likely to be seen as a point of departure than as an obligatory model. A critical figure here was Pierre de Bérulle, whose understanding of the priesthood as participation in Christ's sacrifice of himself for humanity was to be so influential among successive generations of writers and reformers. In Bérulle's thinking, which crystallised many ideas that had previously circulated in disconnected fashion, the 'merest' priest was in a different category to everyone else, including the most 'perfect' members of religious orders who were not priests, since priests alone could mediate in a unique way between God and men. This rarified vision, with its historical roots in Platonism and later medieval mysticism, was set out most fully in his *Discours de l'état et des grandeurs de Jésus* (1623). For the rest of the century, it was combined with other currents of thought by Bérulle's most influential disciples – Condren, Saint-Cyran, de Paul, Olier, Eudes, Tronson – and it led them to insist on the theological and spiritual gap between priests and the 'world' in which they lived. Some of these figures belonged to the generation most heavily involved in the seculars-versus-regulars controversies, especially during the 1620s and 1630s, which led them to accentuate their exalted claims for the priestly vocation.

The Berullian vision was also capable of being complemented by other understandings of the priesthood, such as that of the *bon curé*, whose profile was essentially pastoral, or the *saint prêtre*, who was seen as a model Christian that other people could imitate. Saint-Cyran, perhaps Bérulle's closest disciple, declared that 'having as his model Christ, who was crushed to nothingness, the pastoral life of the priest lies in the exercise of charity, and one could not become a suitable instrument for the transmission of grace unless one possesses it to the full oneself'.[45] The different approaches to shaping the next generation of clergy all placed growing emphasis on the virtues of self-discipline, humility, detachment from worldly values – and, in a more generic sense, on clerical 'civility'.

Nor were these elucubrations confined to the literary sphere, since so many of those promoting them were themselves actively involved in the process of religious reform and, in many cases, in the running of seminaries. The seminary 'movement' and its successive phases reflect the scope of these intellectual developments, so that the two went together rather than either one being the consequence of the other. One major outcome was that by the early decades of the eighteenth century, France's seminaries were becoming an increasingly closed environment governed by professional directors and by ever more minute regulations that defined the daily lives of those living in them. This was to ensure that when they emerged as ordained clergy, they would have internalised the virtues that would make 'perfect ecclesiastics' of them, enabling them both to live a life apart and behave as models of Christian virtue. Nor were such ideas applied only in seminaries at the outset of clerical careers. As we have seen, identical themes were adapted and recycled for use during the synods, ecclesiastical conferences and calends, where the priestly vocation and what it entailed was a constant topic for discussion.[46]

Needless to say, reality often fell dismally short of such vaulting aspirations, and only a small percentage of the clergy approximated to them before the eighteenth century. But accepting this should not lead us to underestimate the interlocking efforts made during our period to develop a distinctive clerical 'mentality', and to 'form' future clergy accordingly. They lay behind the countless practical efforts made 'on the ground' to disengage the clergy from the secular pursuits of their parishioners, such pursuits being increasingly deemed unworthy of their priestly status. In 1674, the bishop of Séez in Normandy even forbade priests from attending confraternity banquets on pain of suspension, because 'it is wholly indecent for priests to be in a position of inferiority to laypeople in the church'. Equally, the same mindset lay behind attempts to prevent laypeople from performing actions that were now 'reserved' for the clergy. Finally, these ideas, endlessly recycled and discussed, were capable of generating a strong sense of self-worth among the secular clergy which had not previously existed, though in practice their influence during the seventeenth century would have been limited to the better educated clergy of the cities and larger towns. They had the potential to embolden the lower clergy to think of themselves as being as indispensable to the church as their hierarchical superiors, the bishops, who were equally intent on imposing their authority on the lower clergy. One of the paradoxes of the next century was a clergy who could be no less recalcitrant than their predecessors in the face of authority, but who had gradually acquired novel reasons to justify it.

CHAPTER 9

THE TRIUMPH OF THE PARISH?

The growing emphasis on the *bon prêtre* has often been coupled with a development frequently designated as 'the triumph of the parish'. In each case, the results are more visible during the eighteenth century, but their foundations are held to have been laid during the previous one. As with so many such endeavours, the drive to make the parish central and indispensable to the lives of ordinary Christians was portrayed at the time as a return to a putative status quo ante, but there was a large degree of innovation at work behind this rhetoric of returning to the proper order of things. Many of the prescriptions of the later medieval church about parishes had remained a dead letter because of a want of resources, or an inability to enforce the prescriptions themselves or simply because of the more attractive alternatives close at hand, such as the offerings of the religious orders. The Council of Trent seized on this agenda and went on to 'canonise' the parish, a message that was amplified by subsequent generations of reformers and administrators, both secular and clerical, some of whose attitudes gradually outstripped their Tridentine origins. This chapter will examine the efforts made in France to put the parish at the centre of normal religious life, and to evaluate the successes and failures it encountered.

Rebuilding Churches

The prospects of a 'triumph of the parish' must have seemed extremely remote in France during the years either side of 1600, especially as the material fabric of parochial churches was in a very poor state in much of the country. The process of rebuilding and 'modernising' churches, which had been so prominent from about 1470 to the 1560s, came to a halt under the impact of the expanding religious wars, which damaged huge numbers of churches, old and new, finished and unfinished, until well into the 1590s. Thereafter, the Huguenot wars of the 1620s and then the foreign wars from the 1630s to the 1710s caused much further destruction, in the western and south-western provinces in the first case, and along France's northern and eastern frontiers in the second. Furthermore, the economic recovery of the decades after the 1590s was shorter and less significant in its effects than that of the period 1470–1560, so the process of reconstruction was correspondingly more haphazard, especially as parishes could not always muster the same resources as the regulars or the chapters for this purpose. Rural churches were more vulnerable here than urban ones, and the prospects of rapid rebuilding were less good the more remote they were from the financial resources concentrated in urban areas. In some parts of France, the proportion of churches awaiting rebuilding around 1600 was the same as that of the aftermath of the Hundred Years War.[1]

If there was one major difference by the decades after 1600, however, it was the pressure exerted on communities to rebuild and repair their churches by church and, somewhat later, secular authorities. This is not to argue that they should be credited with the reconstruction that did take place, merely that they played a key role in coaxing local communities into action when circumstances were not especially favourable. Clearly, the timescale of such pressure and, more importantly, of the responses to it varied enormously across dioceses and localities. The image we have of damaged early seventeenth-century churches derives largely from the visitations conducted by bishops, archdeacons and other officials, when they inspected and recorded the poor physical state of churches and their furnishings. Churches without roofs, windows, doors or bell-towers were widespread, and the first priority had to be to ensure they were sufficiently well refurbished to meet the minimum demands of worship.[2] It was not the clergy who were most affected by this problem: it was the parish itself, through its representatives, the churchwardens, which had to find the money to repair and improve its church, something which poor economic conditions and increasingly heavy royal taxes could seriously limit.

More difficult still was the task of persuading seigneurs and clergy, particularly where they were the 'owners' of the major tithes, to provide funds; the major tithe-owners (the *gros décimateurs*) were usually the most neglectful and reluctant of all. Studies of particular areas have revealed the resulting variations in the pace of reconstruction. A visitation of Reims diocese in the 1650s chronicled widespread damage, some of it due to continuous war in the region since the early 1630s. In the less exposed and perhaps more 'typical' diocese of Rodez, two out of three churches still needed repairs according to a visitation of 1665. The damage experienced by Franche-Comté churches during the 1670s took about twenty-five years to repair. By contrast, the damaged churches of the Paris region seem to have been repaired relatively quickly after both the religious wars and after the Fronde, no doubt in part because, unlike some other regions, it had ready access to financial resources, thanks to its many wealthy landowners and village notables.[3] Finally, many other churches escaped damage in wartime, but accumulated so many structural defects over the years that partial or even total reconstruction was unavoidable.

Parish visitations always involved questions about the condition of local churches, but these questions gradually became qualitatively different in the seventeenth century.[4] Church authorities generally may well have become more demanding, not because the buildings they wanted to see rebuilt were necessarily in an objectively worse state than previously, but because their ideal of a church that was suitable for proper worship had itself been evolving in the meantime. Indeed, as the century progressed, something resembling a programme for the embellishment of churches as 'sacred' places took shape, a programme that was not fully articulated from the outset, but one whose scope expanded as it gathered pace. The more sacred the church ought to be, the more its existing condition and accoutrements were examined and found wanting. Synodal statutes and visitation ordinances are a prime indication of the shift in question, but are much less useful when it comes to judging how effective such pressure for change was. An early manifestation of this concern, which was not particularly novel in itself, was the insistence on having a baptismal font, ideally situated near the church entrance, so as to convey the symbolism of the sacrament of baptism as entry into the community of believers. In addition, the baptismal font belonged exclusively in the parish church, hence the attempts made to rail it off and decorate it, so that parishioners would not treat it too casually – for example, by using it as a place to store goods and objects. The railing-off of church altars was prescribed with a similar emphasis on those parts of the church deserving of the greatest reverence.

More subtle, but also more revealing of seventeenth-century religious thinking, were the changes effected to the interior layout of churches, even where there were no damaged parts to rebuild. The prominence of the main altar, and the desire to ensure it was the visible focus of churches, reflected an increased emphasis on Christ's sacrifice and the Eucharist. Where possible, this altar was embellished in order to capture the attention of congregations during the mass and, especially, to ensure that the elevation of the host by the priest during the mass was clearly visible to all. One of the most spectacular methods of doing this was to commission large-scale altarpieces (*retables*), which were also designed to communicate some of the new forms of devotion emanating from the Catholic Reformation.[5] The churches of the new religious orders, especially of the Jesuits, were just as influential in diffusing the new architectural styles as the devotions to which they were connected. It has been argued, too, that seventeenth-century France, virtually alone in Catholic Europe, witnessed the early phases of a similar 'modernisation' of (mainly) cathedral and collegial churches as far apart as Bayonne, Carcassonne, Tours and Meaux, with a move to replace the roodscreens and closed choirs of previous centuries with an unobstructed view of the main altar which, in the wealthier churches, tended to 'expand' upwards and outwards via its new-style embellishments. This change, which grew in pace during the eighteenth century, was hardly ever a matter of rebuilding damaged structures, but was part of an agenda to open up churches and the liturgy to lay congregations. There is evidence of similarly inspired attempts to simplify and unify the interior spaces of smaller urban churches, for example, by removing secondary altars located close to roodscreens to another part of the building, and either to make transparent or to remove other obstacles preventing a clear sight of the main altar.[6]

The vast majority of parish churches across village and rural France did not have to make such choices, since their layout was far simpler. But they did experience the effects of the post-Tridentine church's efforts to establish the primacy of the 'main' altar, since the latter had to compete with saints that were venerated locally, the confraternities that supported them, the sidechapels devoted to them and the priests who said masses there. Generalising about these changes is problematic, as only local studies can really track them with any accuracy. The fate and popularity of local devotions can be viewed in part through the demotion and promotion of the 'secondary' altars in relation to the main altar within churches. Visitations often paid what might seem like disproportionate attention to these chapels, demanding information on the legacies that funded their masses, and so on.[7] The records can also indicate altars that had been deserted and left unmaintained, because popular devotions had shifted, or a new confraternity had taken them over. In some cases, abandoned altars were ordered to be removed and replaced by a confession box! Other chapels moved out of the main church altogether to sites elsewhere within the parish, but it is not always easy to grasp the significance of this: was it escape, as is sometimes alleged in the case of certain confraternities wishing to keep their independence, or was it banishment?[8]

At least two other additions to the average church layout deserve special attention here, because of their direct connection to religious changes that will be examined later – the pulpit and the confessional. Pulpits were no invention of the Catholic Reformation, and had existed, especially in urban churches, both parochial and regular, for generations. But the emphasis on preaching and the widespread conduct of missions in the seventeenth century saw pulpits gradually spread into smaller, even rural churches. And it seems that some care was given to the siting of the pulpits in relation to both the main altar and the instructional possibilities arising from closer proximity to the congregations gathered in the nave of a church. The confessional, on the other hand, was an invention ascribed to Carlo Borromeo of Milan, and his many disciples throughout France pushed to have confessionals erected in churches as part of a drive to impose and facilitate the practice of individual confession. The earliest confessionals were in all likelihood flimsy affairs and, especially in smaller, more cramped churches, little more than a pair of chairs with a screen to hide the faces of confessor and penitents from each other; many churches would not have an obvious space to locate larger confessionals, and we know that some confessionals initially located in the choirs of churches were later moved to more 'private' areas. Only gradually did more robust confession 'boxes' appear, but the changes and recycling over the centuries of these constructions makes it hard to trace their successive shapes. It does seem, though, that by the early eighteenth century the vast majority of parish churches had some kind of confessional.[9] By contrast, church organs were probably too expensive for most parishes, especially in rural areas – unless, of course, a benefactor appeared who was willing to pay for one.

Decorating Churches

The growing emphasis on the Eucharist, to which we will return later, probably sharpened concern for the holiness of worship itself and, consequently, the 'fitness' of the materials used in parish churches. The records, especially of visitations, are full of demands for new chalices, patens, ciboria and other objects used in celebrating the mass. Particular care was devoted to making the tabernacle visible by placing it either on the altar itself or suspended just above it; altar cloths attracted similar attention; and dirty or threadbare materials were ordered to be replaced. Bishops like Guillaume Le Gouverneur of Saint-Malo (1611–30) ordained that each parish church possess a wide range of liturgical vestments for individual services (such as for masses of different types), and the local clergy themselves increasingly pressured churchwardens into purchasing them. Older receptacles, especially those of enamel or pewter, used to keep communion hosts, were to be replaced by more 'noble' metals, especially silver- or gold-plated ones. A 'holy horror' surfaces in comments upon the state of many churches and the slovenly attitude of the local clergy, for example towards the conservation of consecrated communion wafers. The demand that a separate sacristy be built had similar origins, reflecting a desire that religious objects, vestments and records be properly housed, while also freeing the spaces around the altar from unsightly clutter. Such a demand suggests that the traditional use of churches to store parishioners' goods and chattels was no longer acceptable, except perhaps in extraordinary circumstances. As in so many other respects, the injunctions to make religious services more decent and reverent had a better chance of success when and where the mechanisms for (re-)educating the clergy already discussed began to take effect: at that point the pressure came as much from inside the parish as from the outside.[10]

A similar pattern of pressure and response is evident in relation to liturgical books. Sixteenth-century parishes already had their printed collections of the 'handbooks' needed for a wide range of religious services – missals, breviaries, antiphonaries, graduals and rituals – but from one region to another the number of such volumes per parish could vary by a factor of one to three. From the beginning of our period, their renewal was increasingly regarded as necessary, because new editions of virtually all of these key books had appeared in the decades after the Council of Trent; and new texts, such as the Catechism of the Council of Trent, were duly added to the list. From as early as the provincial councils of the 1580s, church authorities insisted upon the acquisition of the revised versions.[11] Although they were cheaper than the manuscript copies of earlier centuries, actual replacements were often delayed, and the churchwardens had to be chivvied along to do their duty.

Nor was the programme of 'sanctification' limited to buildings, books or liturgical instruments: it is also visible in the efforts made to introduce a new regime of Tridentine religious representation that defined a whole range of objects as sacred/profane or decent/indecent. This campaign shows that at least some of the Protestant critiques of images as forms of superstition had left their mark.[12] Thus, many a piece of sculpture or painting fell foul of visiting bishops or officials for whom the representation in question was either profane, and therefore had no place in a church, or it was an indecent, inappropriate representation of a figure or a theme which did have a place in a church. Examples would be representations of saints, such as Martin of Tours, on horseback rather than kneeling or rapt in prayer, as now seemed appropriate for France's patron saint; other instances might involve saints traditionally associated with particular trades or animals but represented too realistically as artisans rather than as saints. Images involving nudity or 'folkloric' themes were also marked down for removal. Most known instances of the banishment of these objects derive from visitation records, but it is not hard to imagine others occurring on separate occasions.[13]

It would be misleading to describe this process as one of official iconoclasm, since the injunction was usually to replace the pictures or statues with more acceptable substitutes. As the century progressed, however, the official disapproval of what were regarded as grosser forms of religious images from earlier periods is unmistakable, especially when they were associated with popular superstition. Some of these efforts were not specifically part of an effort to 're-clothe' parish churches, many of which, especially in rural areas, would have had relatively little decoration to begin with. Yet it does seem that seventeenth-century churchwardens everywhere spent more money on church vestments and religious objects for regular use than in the past, and that the resident clergy, rather than occasional outsider inspectors, were increasingly concerned to ensure the 'decency' of religious services by the age of Louis XIV. But the degree to which new paintings or statues, not to mention the more expensive altarpieces, materialised in parish churches depended considerably on the generosity of individual parishioners who might also be churchwardens, a factor which helps to explain the varying speeds of change from one parish to the next.[14]

Cemeteries

The aim to put an end to burials within churches surfaced strongly for the first time during our period, when the practice came to be regarded as disruptive and damaging to the church fabric itself.[15] The paving of church floors, which began as an urban phenomenon, slowly spread outside town walls, although it was relatively contained until the eighteenth century. The seventeenth-century clergy were the strongest advocates of such a change; some of them even argued that the 'sacredness' of the church building was such that only God's own anointed, the clergy themselves, could be buried there! But for the better-off families of a parish, the long-standing practice of burial in church was not easy to forego, especially if their ancestors were already buried there; being buried alongside ordinary folk in the cemetery cannot have had much appeal for them. In towns, of course, there was always the option of burial in the chapels of the religious orders. Throughout the seventeenth century, it seems that in towns like Marseille, Tarbes and Paris the majority of individuals making a will chose to be buried inside a church, which was increasingly that of the parish; such requests were harder to resist when the testators were also leaving legacies of one kind or another to the churches of their choice. The pressure was no less intense in rural parishes, with seigneurs, churchwardens and other notables pressing for burial in the holiest place of the parish, near the altar of the parish church.[16] It need hardly be said that the majority of the population, who were too poor to make a will, had little chance of making such demands at all. A major exception was the western area of Brittany, where there was an intense cult of the dead, which witnessed extremely high ratios of burials in churches throughout the seventeenth century, and often violent resistance to attempts, from the 1680s onwards, to force the use of the cemetery instead.[17]

One possible way of dealing with such pressure for church burial was to try to 'sanctify' the cemetery surrounding the church by fencing it off to a greater degree than previously, and by preventing parishioners from meeting, holding fairs and grazing their animals there! Making the cemetery an integral part of the church 'compound' could partially compensate for the loss of burial rights inside the church. It also made the parish church itself more distinctive and 'withdrawn' from the world around it. But despite extensive synodal and secular legislation to that effect from the later sixteenth century, there was considerable resistance throughout the following century to making a 'sacred' space of the cemetery, one that was off-limits to the social and business events which were so frequent there; even the *curés*, who lived in dwellings attached or very close to the parish church, came and went as they pleased through the cemetery with their horses and other animals. Until that anomaly had been resolved and the clergy themselves, under persistent pressure from their bishops in many cases, had adopted a different approach, laypeople were hardly likely to respect demands for strict enclosure.[18] It is ironic that by the time – the mid-eighteenth century – attitudes really changed and the 'sacredness' of the cemetery as an extension of the parish church was widely accepted, the French monarchy was about to envisage, essentially in towns, the removal of cemeteries from churches altogether, on health grounds.[19]

Perhaps the major exception to the pattern discussed above was in areas of mixed confessional population, where the Calvinist denial of the whole notion of 'sacred' spaces, such as cemeteries, did not quite extinguish the desire of French Huguenots to be buried beside their kin in the existing cemeteries. This proved a highly divisive issue, one that often led to armed violence in localities from the 1560s onwards, but the Catholic rejection of Huguenot demands gradually ensured the separation of burial sites.[20] It is likely that rejecting Huguenot burials as a profanation of the local cemetery sharpened Catholic perceptions of it as a distinctive, sacred space.

One consequence of measures and improvements like these was slowly to accentuate the superiority of the parish church and its immediate surroundings over the other churches and chapels within the average parish. As we shall see presently, there were some crucial exceptions to this generalisation, mostly but not exclusively in towns. Parish churches already possessed enforceable monopolies – including burial in the 'central' cemetery, the performance of key sacraments like baptism or marriage, and so on – that they were determined not to share with chapels-of-ease elsewhere in the parish. By making them more attractive to parishioners, the embellishment of parish churches provided a stronger 'affective' grounding for their primacy. Thus, the 'great' mass (*grande messe*) was celebrated on Sundays and feast days at the main altar of the parish church. It was intended for the adult population, and especially heads of households, as it was during it that the *prône*, with its public announcements as varied as the banns of marriage and the *vendanges*, was delivered by the *curé*. Other masses were available, particularly in large parishes, especially as the need to mind children and animals made it impossible for everyone to attend the same service; but these other masses were 'relegated' to a subordinate status. The private masses said on side altars in the main church were no longer supposed to coincide with the 'great' mass, and these altars were, as we saw, often moved to positions where they would not distract from the main altar. And when small outlying chapels got into difficulties, mainly because of the devaluation of their assets over time, *curés* increasingly insisted on closing down the chapels in question and 'repatriating' the service to the main altar of the parish church.

Changes like these derived essentially from clerical pressure and corresponded to the clergy's view of what constituted the best conditions for public worship. But it is also clear that seventeenth-century parishioners were willing to go along with, and pay for, what was being demanded of them. A revealing instance of this was the pressure exerted on parishes, especially by the second half of the century, to provide purpose-built dwellings for their parish priest. Inevitably there was much foot-dragging and disputing over the cost involved, especially when repairs to the local church were also outstanding.[21] A visitation of the Forez district of the Lyon diocese in 1662 concluded that the uninhabitable condition of some presbyteries was the main reason for non-residence by *curés*. Large numbers of presbyteries were duly built, especially during the eighteenth century, but half of the parishes of the Périgord already had a presbytery by 1688.[22] Most of them were probably ordinary enough constructions, yet their existence did 'distinguish' the parish priest in a visible way, bringing him considerably closer to the 'notables' of the parish.[23] The gradual but never quite total withdrawal of *curés* from economic activities, which both parishioners and the authorities demanded, had a similar effect on their local social standing, one that did not exclude a passage from money making to money lending.[24] Finally, the building of presbyteries may also be seen as evidence of seventeenth-century parishioners' growing satisfaction with their *curés*, as well as of the *curés*' own expectation of living conditions that corresponded to their increased sense of their own worth and separateness. In its own way, the built landscape could mirror the forces that were slowly altering France's parishes and their clergy.

Triumph of *Curé*?

The most obvious precondition for such developments was that parish priests be resident. Until that point had been reached, the idea of the *bon curé* directing his parish could be little more than a pipe-dream. The combined pressure from diocesan authorities and parishioners was strong enough to ensure extensive compliance from the middle decades of the century onwards (before seminaries began to have an effect on the clergy), but this development needs to be viewed in a wider context. As we saw in the previous chapter, with more and more priests either holding benefices or possessing 'clerical titles' worth between 50 and 100 *livres* per annum at ordination, the likelihood is that their families had also provided them with a correspondingly good education, and for many that meant attendance at the new Jesuit, Oratorian and other colleges which embodied the values of post-Tridentine Catholicism. If it also suggests a growing tendency to restrict access to the clergy to those with connections and disposable wealth, there is reason to believe that they were still being drawn from a wider range of social groups than their better-known eighteenth-century successors. Much depended on the tariff set in individual dioceses for the clerical title, and then on the speed and the strictness with which it was enforced.

Of course, the social profile of clerics taking orders and those obtaining parishes should not be confused, since the latter were usually drawn from the better connected social groups. For example, the proportion of nobles among the parish clergy remains highly obscure, but it seems to have remained fairly constant in some areas like south-west France and Brittany throughout the seventeenth century, when one-quarter of all parishes in Tréguier diocese were held by nobles; in many cases, the parishes and other benefices that they obtained were in their own families' patronage. Overall, however, the indications are that noble clergy were less and less attracted by the cure of souls as the century wore on, preferring canonries or other benefices without pastoral obligations. The vast majority of parish-based clergy were drawn from the professions in the broad sense, sons of middling to minor royal officials, merchants, lawyers, notaries, artisans and some prosperous farmers, with a small and probably declining proportion from poorer social groups. Such a pattern in turn suggests that as the century wore on, more and more *curés* were of urban rather than rural origin, as has been demonstrated for dioceses with relatively limited urban densities such as Reims, Châlons-sur-Marne, Autun and the Forez region of Lyon, and that they brought with them to their parishes the assumptions and prejudices of their background and education.[25]

Unfortunately, we know relatively little about the career patterns of the French secular clergy of our period, but we should not be surprised to find considerable variation from one area to the next. For example, out of 397 priests ordained between 1693 and 1710 in the small northern Breton diocese of Tréguier, only 35 managed to obtain a benefice of any sort in later life, with only 19 (4.8 per cent) of them becoming parish priests. By contrast,

70 per cent of the Reims clergy ordained between 1683 and 1709 became parish priests, 13 per cent curates, while the remainder found other posts.[26] These percentages suggest either that the 'fit' between parishes available and priests ordained was extraordinarily good, or that the Reims clergy were more closely vetted before ordination than their Breton counterparts. It seems, too, that the archbishop of Reims had a far better grip on the benefice system than M. de Tréguier, in whose diocese nobles monopolised a large proportion of the parish cures.

What is much harder to determine is the extent to which *curés*, once they had obtained a parish, remained in it for the rest of their career or found a better one elsewhere. It seems that those who succeeded in moving did so relatively soon after obtaining their first parish. At any rate, they would have only rarely, at least before the eighteenth century, been able to count on anything resembling 'promotion' if they did wish to move, so the best chance of moving was to negotiate one's way into another parish, usually via a resignation 'in favour' with an outgoing or retiring *curé*. But it is likely that only a minority of *curés* would have had the connections that such mobility necessitated: changing a parish in this way has been described as 'risky and expensive' even for the eighteenth century.[27] If this hypothesis stands, then France's *curés* would have resembled their bishops in the limited prospects of mobility open to them.

When combined with consistent residence, such stability strengthened the *curé*'s position within his parish; it certainly helped to integrate those who were outsiders. Like many others, Jean Lardière, *curé* of Saint-Aubin de Branne, in Bazas diocese, may have acquired his parish thanks to the outgoing *curé*'s resignation in his favour in 1660, when Lardière was only twenty-two years old and still three years short of the priesthood, but he duly stepped into his new office in 1663 and remained in it until 1706. Likewise, Christophe Sauvageon, a canon-regular of Sainte-Geneviève, served as *curé* of Sennely-en-Sologne from 1676 to 1710.[28] Paradoxically, the fact that clergy did not have to wait long years before obtaining a parish meant that extended, stable careers were always possible.[29] Between 1680 and 1706, three of out every five parishes in Reims diocese still changed hands through resignation, but by this point it seems clear that the resignation mechanism itself had lost much of its earlier autonomy. Twelve per cent of the resignations were forced by the archbishop upon the *curés* concerned for unacceptable behaviour, and many others were only accepted because the incoming *curés* were either proposed by, or known to be acceptable to, the archbishop. Many of these resignations also involved clergy changing parishes rather than simply retiring, which suggests that the archbishop was using the practice to engage in promotion of some kind rather than simply tolerating high levels of mobility.[30] This example need not be taken as typical for the end of the seventeenth century, but it offers a glimpse of what was possible by then – and in a diocese in which the bishop technically only nominated up to around 5 per cent of all parishes.

Residence alone, even when prolonged, does not explain everything, and *curés* could still face problems on several fronts within their parishes. For a long time, they resisted pressure to employ curates to assist them in running the parish. Because they had to be paid by the parish priest out of his own resources, the proportion of curates in parishes was slow to rise during the seventeenth century. It is not hard, for example, to imagine that a *vicaire* installed by a monastery or chapter in a parish would not wish to diminish his already limited stipend further by hiring a curate. The combined efforts of bishops and the crown to make a curacy more attractive for those in search of one, by raising the stipend attached to it from the 1630s onwards, cannot have made parish priests more eager to fill these posts, and it is unlikely that the crown's decision, in 1695, to reserve the choice of a curate for the local bishop made curates popular with the parish priests either. We should not underestimate the novelty – and therefore the difficulty – of accepting curates working *with* parish priests rather than, as previously, serving in their place. Resident *curés* took some time to adjust to this redeployment, and not just for monetary reasons. That curates did actually increase in numbers, however, was due mainly to the pressure on parish priests to take them on, exerted by both parishioners and church authorities. Such pressure often came in the wake of visitations which enabled bishops and officials to gauge the real pastoral needs of parishes. Yet the curates' status remained precarious, since they could be dismissed by the parish priest. Nor did serving as a curate necessarily constitute a strong claim on a parish in due course. It should be clear by now that the inherited clerical *cursus honorum* took little account of questions of service or merit, so that a curate might find himself obliged to remain a curate for his entire career. For this to change and for better career prospects to appear, as happened in Reims diocese by around 1700–1720, bishops needed to gain a somewhat better grip on the benefice system than was the norm in earlier generations. And there is some evidence that this did happen.[31] In 1682, Archbishop Villeroy of Lyon declared that he would not confirm anyone in the position of *curé* unless he had served for at least a year as a curate, a limited and tentative measure.[32] But there was no guarantee that episcopal control, where it became a reality rather than an aspiration, would always benefit deserving but untenured curates who remained a major anomaly in a church where most functions had long since been transformed into benefices.

Most French parishes were also home to a cluster of clerics, some ordained and some not, who tended to be less easily accessible to disciplinary pressures from outside the parish. The parish priest was increasingly expected – at least by his superiors – to control and discipline these clerics. By tradition, these men, even if not yet ordained priests, were considered to be 'serving' the parish. The *curé*'s 'seat' in the parish's main church, at a time when its importance was growing, gave him a major advantage over the chaplains and other benefice-holders of the parish. And he was not hampered by the situation that obtained in many Italian parishes, where the 'title' to the parish was held collectively by a group of clergy, no individual member of which enjoyed higher status than the others; co-*curés* like this were rare in France, though some have been found in the Franche-Comté, Normandy and Anjou.[33] It also helped that the parish priest had always been the nominal head of the different 'communities of priests' that were scattered across urban and rural areas of France. During the seventeenth century, this previously rather 'virtual' title was put to new uses, of which discipline and control was only one. *Curés* also had a strong interest in co-opting some of these clergy into the widening range of pastoral activities within parishes.[34] Curates, *habitués* and chaplains alike could be employed in catechising the children of the parish, a task that *curés* themselves often balked at, and in teaching in the *petites écoles*, where they existed. Their participation had always been needed in the main parish church – for high masses, sung Vespers, assistance at funeral masses and so on – and this remained as true as ever during a period when the desire to add greater solemnity to religious services was growing. Missionaries, too, could appreciate the usefulness of this kind of clergy during their 'campaigns', although it is not clear if that extended beyond a limited range of skills. Despite that, they continued to attract negative attention from the church authorities in several regions. The act of banning some of them from administering the sacraments was not just a response to their perceived incompetence, but also a measure to preserve the *curé*'s control of the parish's religious services.

Curés' Responsibilities

Many of the parish priest's responsibilities were legal and administrative rather than strictly religious, and their effective discharge did not necessarily require a *curé* with unusual pastoral skills. And those non-pastoral roles were growing steadily during the seventeenth and eighteenth centuries. The list would be tedious to rehearse, but some idea of their variety is essential if we are to grasp their significance for the present discussion.[35] The parish priest had a more or less absolute veto over the hiring and firing of schoolteachers, catechists and midwives, for whose orthodoxy rather than strict competence he was responsible. After the revocation of the Edict of Nantes, his 'say-so' could condemn 'new' Catholics to incarceration or punishment if he judged them obdurate and recalcitrant. The requirement that parish priests keep registers of births, marriages and deaths was inaugurated by the crown as early as 1539, but it was only over a century later that it, like many other legislative acts, was finally being respected by many of them. The church, for its part, tried to oblige parish priests to keep other records, such as lists of parishioners who did (or did not) take communion at Easter, and registers of the 'condition of Christians' (*états des âmes*) generally. 'Dimissorial' letters from one's parish priest were required if someone wished to marry in another parish or take orders in another diocese. Outsider clergy could not normally preach or confess in a parish without his explicit permission. Other 'certificates' from one's parish priest were required for a variety of purposes, especially when individuals, lay and clerical, were moving to other places. By the early eighteenth century, *curés* were being asked to vouch for younger clerics seeking orders, and specifically to confirm whether they had performed as catechists and attended ecclesiastical conferences during the periods between orders when they were not required to reside in seminaries.

Throughout much of rural France, the parish priest was for long one of the few fully literate inhabitants, hence his right to receive and transcribe people's wills and testaments; towns may well have had larger concentrations of literate and professional laypeople, but since the more urban parishes were 'reserved' for university graduates, their *curés* were capable of holding their own. Under Louis XIV the days when 'enlightened' provincial intendants like Turgot would routinely use the *curés* as sources of information, collaborators and conveyors of their demands, were still well into the future, but it is not hard to see why such a thinly staffed form of regional administration would look to the clergy for assistance.[36] With so many different tasks and responsibilities flowing in his direction, it is hardly surprising that the profile of the *curé* should have become so pronounced, but also that only a better-prepared clergy could discharge the role in question.

Nor is it surprising that, by the end of the seventeenth century, more and more *curés* were viewed by both the ecclesiastical and secular authorities of the day as allies and collaborators rather than as subordinates in need of vigilant surveillance and discipline. Such co-operation was all the more likely when the *curés* in question were themselves outsiders, far less securely integrated into their parishes than previous generations of native clergy. But by the same token, it is likely that such an outsider clergy was better able to stand above the rivalries and disputes among parishioners that could so easily descend into violence, and to emerge as arbiters and reconcilers. Taken as a whole, these obligations, old as much as new, could only be discharged by *curés* enjoying both respect and authority.

Inside Parishes

On other fronts, a *curé*'s outsider origins made clashes with other groups or individuals within the average parish more likely. Confraternities will be discussed in more detail in a later chapter, but it is well known that seventeenth-century church authorities were keen to control them. Behind this move lay the conviction that not only were some of them too 'profane' and 'carnival-prone', but also too independently spirited, even in the manner in which they conducted their religious affairs. Regaining control of them was the first part of an agenda designed to make them more religious in orientation, and this, too, was a task for which the parish *curé* was judged best fit. Church authorities insisted on their right to inspect and approve the confraternities' statutes. Above all, they were anxious to stamp out any inclination among the confraternities to use their chapels to compete with the parish church and its religious offerings – hence the ban on them distributing the *pain bénit* (blessed, but not consecrated bread) which was reserved for the parish church masses, and on their conducting their services at the same time as those of the parish church. The practical problem of how to deal with confraternities whose members belonged to several parishes was one of those factors that obliged church authorities to focus their attention on the need for a parochial religious framework that would be the norm for the 'average Christian' (*le chrétien moyen*).

When it came to dealing with the churchwardens who constituted the *fabrique*, the *curé* was often dealing with the same parishioners who might belong to these confraternities and, beyond them, to the most prominent families of the parish. The clerical urge to domesticate them, too, which was so marked from the sixteenth century, was tempered here by the clergy's expanding need, as we saw earlier in this chapter, of the *fabrique*'s co-operation in myriad ways. Never, it could be said, were the funds of the *fabrique* more solicited than in our period, given how much more expensive religious services could be.[37] The pressure to spend more came from external authorities and it was relayed through *curés* who were themselves increasingly outsiders, and that represented a major shift from earlier centuries when clergy were mainly of local origin. There are well-documented cases of *curés* becoming so exasperated with the *fabrique*'s slowness to provide funds for new vestments or liturgical books and so on, that they went and purchased them themselves, and then presented the bill to the *fabrique* – all of which might easily lead to lawsuits between them. But for the most part, disputes like these between *curés* and *fabriques* were limited in both scope and threat to their continuing co-operation. 'Ideological' disputes such as those which divided *curés* and the parish churchwardens because one of the parties was Jansenist or not, were probably confined to the major cities. That which wracked the parish of Saint-Médard in Paris – and to a lesser extent, neighbouring parishes – during the 1730s showed how effectively a well-supported group of churchwardens could make life truly miserable for a new *curé* who had been 'parachuted' into the parish by the archbishop of Paris to replace a well-loved Jansenist predecessor.[38]

Curés and Urban Parishes

However slow and incomplete the rise of the *curé* may have been across rural France, and whatever complaints the peasantry may still have had about their *curés* or their parishes, the sense of identity of those populations was essentially parochial, especially where communities of inhabitants and parishes overlapped. By contrast, the situation in towns and villages big enough to house more than one parish and/or houses of religious orders was always likely to be different. Despite the fact that religious practices came far closer to meeting the standards of the post-Tridentine church, urban identities were not really parochial. Urban parishes, as we saw in an earlier chapter, often ranged from the too big to the too small, but from the present perspective, all were too 'porous' to serve as the only focus for their residents' religious activities. There was little to stop people attending services in other parishes, confessing to other priests and communing elsewhere. The sermons, processions and other festivals or feast days that they attended were similarly chosen – unless of course their own parish clergy, backed by the *fabrique* and its financial resources, competed successfully with what was available a few streets away. But this was to join the market in religious services rather than to invoke the parish's right to impose its own offerings on the parishioners. Offsetting this atomisation was the presence in many towns of a sense of 'neighborhood', which could be closely connected to a given parish and its churches. Once again, it would be unwise to generalise from the experience of Parisian parishes, but it does seem that their *curés*, through a combination of education, combativeness and a sense of their rightful place within the church, managed to establish a degree of parochial 'belonging'.[39]

This 'pick and mix' approach of urban populations might not have attracted much attention at the time had it involved only other parishes and their churches. That it gave rise to so many disputes was because most of the other religious services and churches belonged to the religious orders. The ancient 'secular versus regulars' dispute, as it is known, reignited in seventeenth-century France, acquiring a new dimension that is of particular interest to us here. Ever since the Fourth Lateran Council (1214) had required people to confess their sins to 'their own priest' (*proprius parrochus*) as part of their annual Easter obligation, there had been disputes over the exact meaning of the term 'one's own priest', and specifically whether the

Council had intended all Christians to confess exclusively to their *parish* priest. This question pitted spokesmen of the secular and regular clergy against each other over their respective fields of pastoral responsibility, although for centuries the debate was more academic than practical, given the inadequacies of the parish clergy when faced with the pastoral superiority of the regulars.

However, with the emergence of a secular clergy that was more capable, but also more conscious of its responsibilities, the conflict moved to another level in seventeenth-century France, with the seculars disputing the regulars' claim that, based on long-standing papal privileges and their exempt status, they were entitled to conduct pastoral activities, such as preaching, confession, the administration of the sacraments and so on, largely free from restriction. The seculars did not wish to prevent them from engaging in such work, but insisted that they could only do so if, and when, they were authorised by local bishops; they also pressed the regulars to accept that Catholics were primarily parishioners committed to the care of their parish clergy, whose role the regulars should respect at all times. Thus did a classic intra-clerical dogfight become much sharper in post-Berullian France now that the cause of the secular clergy was championed by the new secular congregations which made a point of allying themselves with the bishops and the parish clergy.[40]

Because they were reinforced by the arrival of highly active new orders like the Jesuits, the Capuchins and many others, the pastoral activities of the regulars were not about to wither away after the religious wars – on the contrary. It would take a long time before the parish clergy of the major towns were in any position to compete with them. So the social elites of individual parishes continued to patronise the orders, send their children to their schools and novitiates, join their sodalities and confraternities, attend their sermons and services, and finance them in numerous ways. Even the chapels of the regulars were physically more attractive than all but a few parish churches, thanks to the bequests flowing in their direction. And as far as 'advanced' pastoral services such as preaching, confession and spiritual direction were concerned, few parish priests could rival the 'professionals' that the regulars turned out – and when they could, it was a case of the one against the many. In urban areas, arresting the 'flight' of the lay elites towards the regulars – not a new phenomenon – was a Canute-like challenge, and the best that the parish clergy could hope for were those symbolic recognitions of their position, such as, precisely, their exclusive right to confess and 'communicate' their parishioners at Easter. Other demands included agreement by the regulars not to conduct services during the main mass (*grande messe*) in the parish church. The existing tensions were rendered much sharper when, by the second half of the century, sections of the secular clergy began objecting to the content of what regulars like the Jesuits taught and preached, rather than just their right to do so. The confessional and moral practices of the Jesuits, in particular, were regarded by some seculars, mainly but not exclusively those with Jansenist leanings, as too laxist and too much of a compromise with contemporary social values.[41] It was these clergy who were also most likely to have developed the strongest sense of the *curé* being the master of his parish – like the bishop of his diocese – and to have the least desire to see their flocks being fed by other hands.

Conclusion

The verdict emerging from this chapter is that the 'triumph of the parish' as a nationwide phenomenon needs to be nuanced. It certainly did not occur in towns and cities, where parochial forms of religious life struggled to cope with many problems in addition to the competition from the regulars. The often lopsided parish geography of the cities did not help, but there was more to the problem than that. For centuries the religious orders had been entrenched as the real specialists in providing religious services to the urban populations, especially the better-off and better-educated social groups. The new religious orders ensured that this tradition would not only continue, but that it would be carried into the middling and smaller towns which prior to the seventeenth century had relatively little exposure to them. And, of course, some of these orders, especially the Capuchins and the Récollets, went beyond the towns in search of people to preach and minister to. Yet it is certainly true to say that in urban parishes, religious services and pastoral care improved substantially across the century, and that their *curés* were increasingly competent and conscientious. It has been shown that the Jansenist-leaning parishes of Paris were the best administered of the city under Louis XIV, because their *curés* brought to the task a sense of responsibility which they extended beyond the strictly religious sphere, and into the administrative and financial aspects of their charge. This example cannot be easily applied to other parts of France, but there is no reason to think that only Jansenist *curés* were capable of comparable efforts.[42] What both types of *curé* seem to have done quite successfully was to involve the un-beneficed, parish-resident clergy in the catechetical, devotional and charitable tasks devolved to them.

Rural parishes did not face the same problems of laypeople deserting the parish church or the fallout from intra-clerical rivalries. As the century progressed a certain normalisation of relations between *curés*, curates and other resident clergy took place, largely to the benefit of the *curés*. Much of that process was due to pressures exercised on the parishes from outside and from above – by church and secular authorities – but we have also seen that parishioners themselves learned to use it as a lever in order to obtain changes or improvements, such as the hiring of a curate. Regardless of how different the fortunes of parishes and their *curés* may have been from town to country, they were all to be marked significantly by the changes to the religious practices of the period.

PART 4

Instruments of Religious Change

CHAPTER 10

SAINTS AND SHRINES

The historiographical commonplace, that pre-modern Europeans were surrounded, from the cradle to the grave, by the supernatural, loses none of its validity for being repeated one further time. Any historian attempting to inventory and analyse early modern religious practices can appreciate the appositeness of Michelet's phrase, 'tout est dans tout', but can also see that it hints at an intractable problem. It still remains far easier to make general statements about the pervasiveness of things religious than either to apprehend them at close quarters or to grasp their meaning for those who experienced them in one form or another. 'Everything' was connected to 'everything' precisely because social and cultural life in the widest sense was suffused with religious imagery, language, sounds and gestures, which made it impossible for all but a handful of people to view the world as other than governed by supernatural forces. But rather than attempting an impossible inventory-cum-analysis of all of these phenomena, the most useful thing that a historian can do is to focus on a selection of examples which best illustrate the range of contemporary practices as well as the efforts made to distinguish between what was religious and what was not. Seventeenth-century Catholicism could not escape the consequences of the often quite radical rejection by Protestant churches, of which the French Calvinist church was among the most militant, of so many of the practices and rituals of the old church. Their rejection of the saints and their inextricably confused roles of models, intercessors and miracle-workers is only one instance of this impact.

Religious Calendar

The most obvious indicator of the degree to which religion infused people's lives is the calendar, which had long been evolving very slowly towards its modern shape.[1] It was not until 1564 that 1 January was declared the beginning of the new year in France; until then it fell, significantly, on 25 March, the feast of the Annunciation to the Virgin Mary. Yet the real beginning of the liturgical calendar itself was Advent in early December. The average year was packed not just with Sundays, which were holy days by definition, but also with a parallel cycle of religious feast days which could vary greatly in number, as we shall see presently, and which were regarded as 'feasts of obligation', when people were forbidden to work and had to attend religious services. The two types of holiday sometimes overlapped (as when Christmas or another feast fell on a Sunday), but otherwise they represented two interlocking cycles within a single liturgical calendar. The first cycle, known as the Temporal, consisted of Sundays and other feasts relating to the life of Christ; the second, called the Sanctoral, contained, as its name indicates, the fixed-date feast days of the saints (angels and the Virgin Mary included). Many individual saints' days might be a major holiday of 'obligation' in one diocese, but not in another. As is well known, several of the feast days, from Christmas itself to St John's Eve (24 June) and All Saints'/All Souls' Days (1–2 November) were 'baptised' versions of pre-Christian festivals of one provenance or another, and many of them had their origins in the agricultural seasons. At any rate, between them, they constituted what has been called an 'agro-liturgical cycle' whose 'religious' basis was, for that very reason, open to doubt and criticism. The cycle as a whole was unevenly 'charged' religiously: its high points were the penitential seasons of Advent and, especially, Lent, but that was counterbalanced by large numbers of overtly 'festive' moments (Pentecost, Corpus Christi, All Saints/All Souls) which attracted popular favour. The feast of a parochial patron saint was a major highlight because of the preparation it required and the combination of festivities it generated.[2]

It would be a mistake to think this calendar was ancient and untouchable, especially the feast days of 'obligation'. There could be substantial differences from one diocese to the next, and 'new' saints brought new saints' days with them. The diocese of Rennes and the changes made to its calendar may serve as an illustration of this point.[3] It had sixty feast days of 'obligation' per year, on top of the fifty-two Sundays, in the early sixteenth century, having had a few added, subtracted or even restored to that list by its bishops since as recently as the 1460s. Only one feast day was removed during the century before 1609, when the bishop decided to excise a further ten. This did not prevent two significant further additions later, that of St Louis in 1620 and St Joseph in 1665, both championed by the monarchy. Things then remained unchanged until the year after the terrible winter of 1709–10, when the bishop of Rennes decided to remove, at one stroke, no fewer than twenty-seven feast days, nearly all of them saints' days. The end result was, well before the better-known reforms of the later eighteenth century, a reduction of around 30 per cent of holidays across the seventeenth century, which left Rennes with a relatively modest twenty-four feasts of obligation which, when Sunday overlaps are taken into account, meant about seventy holidays per year. Such a total probably meant that by 1710 it probably had fewer holidays of obligation than elsewhere.

The fate of Rennes's holidays of obligation, even if it is not wholly typical of French experiences of calendar reform during our period, is nevertheless instructive in several respects. Reducing the number of non-working feast days clearly pre-dates the Enlightenment. Individual bishops were the ultimate arbiters of which saints' days should or should not remain obligatory in their dioceses, and neither king nor pope seriously attempted to take away that power. Urban VIII's attempt, in 1642, to gazette thirty-four 'universal' Catholic holidays was widely ignored in France, on the good Gallican grounds that it was none of his business to dictate to local churches, but his list would probably not have worked anyway. More surprisingly, perhaps, Louis XIV's efforts, in 1661, to generalise the feast of St Joseph were also ignored: if some dioceses, among them Rennes, complied with his wishes, others did not respond at all. Colbert's well-known attempt (1666) to reduce non-working days was taken up by a few dioceses, but some of them later restored the suppressed holidays. The mix between local and general holidays was one that could not easily be resolved by pope, king or assembly of clergy, but there is some evidence that France's bishops ended up copying each others' decisions, enabling a reasonably coherent 'reformation' of the religious calendar to take shape by the mid-eighteenth century. A diocese like Angers still had sixty-three holidays of obligation until 1693 when its new bishop, Le Peletier, reduced them to thirty-nine, a figure that remained unchanged until 1781.[4]

Given the crown had little to do with the suppressions, the motives for doing so were unlikely to have much to do with political or Colbertian economic arguments. It is, of course, possible that the massive suppression in Rennes in 1710 – and those since the 1690s across France generally – reflected the economic conditions of these 'years of misery' and, consequently, a desire to alleviate popular distress. But it was just as likely that natural disasters would have the opposite effect, and it is remarkable that a philo-Jansenist bishop like Le Camus of Grenoble found himself restoring, during the terrible year 1693, no fewer than seven saints' days 'of obligation' that he had previously suppressed, declaring that he hoped that they would 'reheat and nourish people's piety and devotion'.[5] Significantly, the most frequent argument deployed for reducing holidays of obligation was that because there were so many of them, they were not being properly respected; instead of being occasions for religious activity, it was argued, they were excuses for scandalous behaviour – frequentation of taverns, drinking and many other abuses. A reduced level of obligation would, therefore, be more bearable and would facilitate the proper observance of religious injunctions.[6] In that respect, it should be realised that for many of these holidays, abstinence from meat on the previous day was enjoined, and people were not merely expected to attend mass on the day, but also to return for vespers in the afternoon.

If Rennes is at all typical of seventeenth-century France's approach to the religious calendar, it is in the choice of those holidays that were 'demoted' to non-obligatory status. In 'culling' a disproportionately large number of 'ordinary' saints' days from the list, the French church was attempting to privilege the more Christocentric holidays and their accompanying devotions, so that the Virgin Mary, St Joseph and the apostles were the most likely to survive. And such a cull of the saints made it easier to lighten the burden of obligation at the busiest times of the agricultural year, when holidays were the least observed. The most difficult choices lay with those holidays associated with long-venerated local saints: there was a limit to the extent to which they could be dethroned, since they were likely to be the most popular. A holiday like St John's Eve, a thinly baptised version of the summer solstice, was the biggest bête noire of seventeenth-century reforming clergy, given their loathing of the profanity that it generated. But because it was associated with a 'universal' saint, John the Baptist, the church was never likely to 'demote' it, which left clergy fulminating against the rites (especially the lighting of fires) and 'debaucheries' (in other words festivities) associated with it.[7]

Saints

It should already be clear from this purely 'external' analysis that the status of particular saints was not as secure as might be imagined within seventeenth-century French Catholicism. It is much easier to establish what the hierarchical church thought and did than to grasp how the mass of the population related to saints, old and new. In a top-down fashion that did not emerge overnight, the French clergy increasingly took its cue from the Council of Trent's defence of the medieval cult of the saints against Protestant and other critiques of 'idolatry'. Trent's judgements had, as we shall see, further implications for a very wide range of religious practices – ranging from the weekly liturgy to the practice of procession and pilgrimage. Against Luther, Calvin and many others, it defended the legitimacy of a cult of the saints as models of Christian virtue, as intercessors with God and as guides for individuals.[8] The terms of the defence were simultaneously an attempt to reject older and widespread views of the saints as miracle-workers in their own right, to whom one addressed directly one's prayers and vows for protection, healing and other benefits. Putting such a new dispensation into practice was a whole lot more complicated.

The French church's initial response was dictated far more by local circumstances, and particularly by the shock of the Calvinist assault not just on the theology of the saints, but above all against its destruction of the material, iconographic manifestations of the cult. Throughout the religious wars, talk of purging the cult of the saints took a back seat, all the more so as the confraternities and other associations which mobilised to defend Catholicism were characterised by their devotion to individual saints, whose images they paraded and feast days they celebrated with revived enthusiasm.[9] Such a mobilisation of the saints could hardly be forgotten in a hurry, however much the next generations of clergy wished to tackle what they believed were the excesses and supersitions surrounding the saints. That particular agenda could draw upon earlier Erasmian-humanist critiques of idolatry, some of which would be expanded upon by the seventeenth-century 'learned libertines' in their attacks on credulity and superstition. The continuing presence of Protestantism within France after 1600, and the hefty doctrinal controversies which ensued, also precluded any premature closure of the debate on the place of the saints within Catholic religious practice. Indeed, famous works like Jean-Baptiste Thiers's *Treatise on Superstitions* (1679) or Pierre Lebrun's *Critical History of Superstitious Practices* (1702) would be unthinkable without these controversies. No less noteworthy is the fact that these and other works were drawn upon by later seventeenth- and eighteenth-century reformers seeking to demote or eliminate 'saints' or religious practices that now seemed without any credible warrant.[10]

One of the major difficulties facing a Catholic Reformation church programme that attempted to present the saints as models of individual virtue was that existing devotion to the saints was massively collective in nature and was, precisely for that reason, embedded in local structures and institutions which could not be removed or changed with a wave of the hand. Many saints' devotions were borne by confraternities within parishes, notably that of the patron saint; innumerable older confraternities existed almost exclusively to sustain that cult and to organise the annual feast of the patron saint. The most popular saints always had their own chapels, either inside or outside of the parish church, which meant that they enjoyed financial resources of their own, derived from legacies or mass foundations. Altars or chapels without such 'foundations' could nevertheless survive through ad hoc gifts from parishioners. But whatever their circumstances, they had their own 'chapel' priests, whose function was to say the masses that were specified by contract or by testament. And when new chapels were erected in the seventeenth century, it was mostly by well-off families, the nobility included, whose preferences and support could hardly be ignored by the local clergy. The overlapping interests involved here are easy to detect, so that any major change in the cult of the saints could only succeed by some persuasion and adaptation. Episcopal ordinances arising from synods or pastoral visitations could not create *ex nihilo* the collective enthusiasm that this required. After all, the cult of particular saints was no more obligatory than was membership of the confraternities that were so often associated with them. It was always possible to boycott or simply ignore new saints deriving from the more elite/clerical milieux of the Catholic Reformation church.[11]

A complete catalogue of the saints in 'use' across an area the size of France around 1600 does not exist, and it is not clear how useful it actually would be. Shifts in saints' popularity, and the factors which might explain them, can really only be apprehended in localities, which in turn makes any generalisation about them highly provisional. The core group of universal church saints that the post-Trent church wished to promote, and to whom we shall return later, was relatively small compared to the remainder of the pantheon in question. The most obvious feature of the latter was the association of individual saints with particular human needs, dangers and fears. In a massively agrarian society, that involved the cult of saints who could not merely protect people from natural disasters (floods, avalanches, storms), but who could also protect their crops, livelihood and chances of survival against those same natural disasters (drought, excess rainfall, pests and so on). In an age frequently visited by epidemics and related enemies of humankind, the protection of the saints was invoked by virtually the entire population; the combination of medical impotence and the mysterious incidence of disease and sickness ensured that recourse to the saints was frequent and sustained.[12]

There is no reason to think that, all other things being equal, a society as plagued by wars, civil and foreign, epidemics and severe mortality crises related to food shortages as seventeenth-century France, would not generate even more healing and protecting saints – or at least would not cleave strongly to those it already had. It is easier to categorise the kinds of danger against which protection was sought than to list the saints who were 'assigned' to each one, as the attributions varied hugely from place to place for no obvious reason other than that many of the cults in question were the result of local bricolage spread across time. Some of these long-standing popular saints were more 'universal' than others in the sense of being recognised as having similar powers in provinces as widely separated as Brittany and Dauphiné. Some were more thaumaturgic, others more therapeutic in nature, but all were protectors. St Sebastian and St Roch were very widely seen as protecting people against the plague, and many later medieval confraternities had adopted them as their patron saints. Despite their being 'old' saints, it is remarkable how widespread their appeal became throughout the early modern period in a province like Brittany, where they had been scarcely known or venerated previously; and the more popular they became, the more they were associated with other religious practices (and their confraternities), such as the souls in purgatory or preparation for a good death. St Anne was, as befitted the mother of the Virgin, another 'universal' saint, but from one place to the next, her other, more local attributes could change. In the Alpine areas, she was held to offer protection against avalanches; elsewhere, in lowland provinces, her powers were, needless to say, viewed quite differently. St Anthony is a good example of the many 'all-purpose' saints: he was widely venerated as a protector of animals and crops – but endless specific local additions to his 'portfolio' were always possible – and he was regularly depicted accompanied by his pig.[13]

It is not hard to see why such a religious culture – universal in its recourse to the saints but bewilderingly diverse in its local adaptations – was bound to create problems in the age of Europe's reformations. Despite retaining the cult of the saints, the Catholic church, in France at least, increasingly found the gap between official teaching and actual practice hard to reconcile. A huge number of the saints venerated across Europe had become saints by local popular acclamation, and the basis of their status as saints was impossible to establish using criteria imposed in later times. Those who had been through some process of verification in previous centuries were relatively few, so it was not surprising that the post-Tridentine church, and specifically the papacy, attempted to define and control sainthood in a much more thorough fashion than hitherto. It culminated in Urban VIII's decree of 1634, which forbade the attribution of the term 'saint' to anyone who had not been officially acknowledged as a saint by the church, and reserved the right to canonise saints exclusively to the papacy.[14]

The new rules requiring miracles and evidence of holiness of life were far stricter than they had been previously, and the result was a serious decline in the numbers of those acknowledged to belong to what may be called 'canonised sainthood'. The latter was now effectively reserved for those corresponding to the Catholic Reformation's ideals of saints as heroic exponents of Christian virtues, so it is no surprise that nearly all of its official saints were clergy, both male and female, and especially members of religious orders; the secular clergy did far less well, and laypeople hardly figured at all.[15] Among them, new French saints were few and far between from 1665 (François de Sales) to 1737 (Vincent de Paul). De Sales, like Carlo Borromeo before him, was a model of what a bishop should be, but regulars or founders of orders like Ignatius Loyola, Teresa of Avila and Francisco Xavier were more common. But establishing them as models for the average Catholic or translating their sanctity into an idiom that might attract 99 per cent of the population was a very tall order indeed. Despite being projected as a 'universal' saint, actual veneration of de Sales was mostly confined to his native Savoy, though it did spill over in a limited way into neighbouring Dauphiné, thereby making him an unusual kind of 'local' saint! Interestingly, Carlo Borromeo (canonised in 1610) was portrayed in several ways in seventeenth-century French paintings and other representations, and not merely as a model bishop. He was often depicted as assisting people suffering during plague outbreaks, which made him appear as a possible protector against the plague. Yet this particular version of Borromeo's sanctity did not 'take' in France – as if, somehow, it remained inhibited by his episcopal reputation which effectively confined him to the veneration of the clergy.[16]

The historical genuineness and provenance of the saints was not necessarily the most pressing problem for the church at this juncture – after all, it was in no rush to scrap the great majority of the inherited plethora of saints. More problematic, arguably, was the attitude of people from virtually every walk of life, and not merely from the popular classes generally, towards the saints. The representations mentioned above of Carlo Borromeo during the plague were intended to convey his heroic sanctity (he died during the 1584 plague in Milan), but it was virtually impossible to prevent people from seeing such a figure as capable of acting as a protector against danger. And if that was possible with a 'new-style' saint like Borromeo, how much more often had it already happened with the others.

The seventeenth-century reformers saw their task as one of weaning people away from the habit of seeing saints as wonder-workers or protectors in their own right. This might seem a relatively straightforward question of re-education through the instructional mechanisms that we will examine later. But inherited practices reached deeply into local cultures. By analogy with the 'familiarity' with which people treated their local church as a place to use for all kinds of needs, it was the 'familiarity' with the saints that seemed to disturb reformers most: it eliminated the distance between saint and living individuals necessary for the saints to be seen as models of virtue and behaviour. A wonder-working saint was not perceived as totally 'different' or treated with due awe by parishioners. Such familiarity enabled individuals to make vows of a 'if you help cure my illness, I will do the following' variety to the saint whose help they were invoking. This kind of vow was highly contractual, and it summoned the saint to prove his or her value first; only then would the individuals in question have to fulfil their part of the bargain. It is well known that images, especially the statues, of saints who failed to behave as requested, were assaulted and beaten![17]

In the case of major threats like plague or crop failure, it was often the parish as a whole that would make a collective vow to a particular saint, for which it might promise to restore an abandoned chapel, embellish or rebuild parts of the parish church, or go on pilgrimage to a particular site.[18] In any event, the protector or wonder-working saint had to justify the faith put in him or her, and repeated failure might see people switch to other saints who seemed more effective to them. Devotion to the saints could be fickle, and the fact that they were 'popular' was not evidence that they were also ancient in particular localities. Either way, this kind of familiarity was increasingly regarded by reforming French clergy as unacceptable: it treated the saints as 'friends of man' rather than as 'friends and servants of God', which was the official church view of them.[19]

Unwilling to canonise any but a handful of new saints, the post-Tridentine church found itself having to work with the existing population of more or less approved saints; though it did strike a few of the most dubious among them off the calendar entirely. Its objective could be described as one of re-orienting the cult of the saints towards more Christocentric and Marian devotional practices, which would be individual as much as collective in nature. This was entirely in keeping with the changes within contemporary Catholic, and particularly French spirituality, the impact of which we will see in later chapters, especially that on confraternities. These attempts to reorient the cult of the saints meant that some were more suited than others for the purpose, since the miracle or wonder-work at the centre of this entire project was the incarnation, Christ's sacrifice and the ensuing promise of human salvation. In this perspective, saints were not expected to compete, as more or less 'independent' miracle-workers, with these key mysteries of the Christian faith; the most appropriate and valuable saints here were those who were witnesses to, or models of that faith, who would be content with the role of intercessors with God on behalf of backsliding, sinning Christians.

It is obvious that the best candidates for such a role were the members of God's own family – Christ, the Virgin, St Joseph, the Virgin's mother St Anne, followed by the Apostles. The challenge was nevertheless a major one, as they had to straddle the gap that tended to separate popular religious practices and the higher spheres of theological-spiritual reflection. Christ himself was the most problematic figure here, despite the emphasis during previous centuries on his humanity and suffering which gave rise to the penitential confraternities devoted to the passion of Christ. The Catholic Reformation made huge efforts of its own to promote Christ-centred devotional practices, especially Eucharistic ones. It is noteworthy that a figure like Pierre de Bérulle managed, despite the mystical slant of his thinking and the difficulty of understanding his writings, deeply to influence the French church from the 1620s onwards by developing a new view of Christ's humanity that could yield significant devotional benefits. His apprehension of the successive 'states' of Christ's life – of the Infant Jesus, the Word Incarnate – offered possibilities which were subsequently diffused as devotions that spread well beyond elite circles.[20] Devotion to the Sacred Heart or the Forty Hours' emanated from such thinking, but they were uneven in the speed with which they caught on throughout the seventeenth century. Yet it seems that such Christocentric devotion, for all its focus on phases or elements of Christ's human life, did not quite make him a saint *comme les autres*, and was not perhaps even intended to do so. For example, devotion to the Sacred Heart was criticised in some circles by the early eighteenth century as theologically unsound. Bérulle's 'Word Incarnate' or 'Infant Jesus' were *not* meant to be treated 'familiarly'.

By contrast, Marian devotions were considerably easier to diffuse, given how popular her unique combination of roles as virgin, wife and mother had always made her. Her humanity was in no doubt, despite the doctrine of her assumption into heaven; and the French church remained resolutely traditional in refusing to support the Spanish push to have the idea of her immaculate conception declared the official teaching of the church. The evidence provided by chapels, altars and confraternities clearly shows that Marian cults recovered and expanded during the seventeenth century. Around 1500 in Grenoble diocese, Marian chapels and altars were mainly dedicated to Our Lady of Pity or of Consolation; by the 1660s, Our Lady of the Rosary had already appeared, and over the next half-century or so the Rosary would become by far the most common type of the Marian cult, and indeed the most widespread cult of *any* saint there.[21] That pattern of reorientation within an overall envelope of continuity was probably repeated across most of France in this period.

The emergence of St Joseph as a model saint was, when seen in the longer historical framework, probably the most unexpected development of the century. Despite the medieval emphasis on the saints as friends of man, Joseph's status as a husband who was not a father made him an ambiguous and elusive kind of saint whose miracle-working capacities were hardly blindingly obvious. Within the 'official' post-Trent dispensation, Joseph's place as a friend and servant of God was far less problematic: he was a witness to the life of Christ who accepted his non-paternal status by practising the virtues of poverty, chastity and obedience, all of which made him a model of what a saint should be. This alone would probably not have done much for his popularity, and it was rather his association with dying and preparing for a good, Christian death during the seventeenth century which really brought his cult to life. The many chapels, altars and confraternities of *Agonisants* and especially *Agonisants* 'of St Joseph' bear clear witness to this, though his other persona as the patron saint of carpenters still existed in the minds of many artisans.[22]

The last member of the holy family was St Anne, the mother of the Virgin, whose cult we have already noted briefly. But her marginality within the

Catholic Reformation increased after her husband, St Joachim, was officially dumped from the breviary in 1572. Again, the evidence from Grenoble diocese suggests that the number of chapels dedicated to her had reached a high point by the 1660s and remained stable thereafter, but also that they were sited in increasingly marginal parts of churches, or even in chapels outside of the parish church, which would indicate that the cult of St Anne remained largely local and had limited, even declining clerical approval.[23]

Because so much of what we know about the cult of the saints is derived from information recorded in pastoral visitations of parishes, it has little or nothing to say about the cult of the saints proposed by the religious orders in their churches – through preaching, confraternities, images, devotions and so on. But ignoring the regulars and their contributions makes it extremely difficult to grasp the process of religious change, given that they were usually among the first to formalise the cult of many individual saints. Unfortunately, far less is known in detail about their activities. The most 'popular' of the religious orders, namely the Franciscans and their later offshoots, the Capuchins and the Récollets, were also among the most successful in adopting and adapting local saints' cults for wider use. And of course they all shared the cult of Francis of Assisi, perhaps the most popular of all saint-founders of a religious order, something which none of his early modern counterparts could ever match. St Anthony of Padua was another immensely popular Franciscan saint. The 'capital' which these orders possessed made them more effective vehicles for diffusing perhaps more user-friendly variants of Catholic Reformation saints and their cult – the Rosary, the Passion of Christ, the 'good death', St Joseph and so on – than the often inconsequential proclamations of bishops and their officials. Their churches had the important advantage of possessing far more relics and images of the saints than their parochial counterparts. The reputation of some barefoot Capuchin missionary-preachers was such that they themselves sometimes became the objects of popular devotion, so that when they died there was a stampede to snatch items of clothing or other potentially 'sacred' things belonging to them. Needless to say, such behaviour drew rebukes from sceptics and rigorists alike, for whom such association with popular attitudes to the saints was increasingly distasteful by the later seventeenth century.

In chronicling the fortune of the saints, it appears that it was the local parish clergy, especially in rural areas, who were probably the most exposed to contradictory pressures. Even the most indulgent bishops and their officials tended to push for action against saints' cults that they judged idolatrous or magical, but for much of the century, local clergy, especially the *curés*, were far less inclined to take the axe to the root. A great proportion of them were themselves natives of the areas in which they served, and thus firmly anchored in local religious culture. As outsider *curés* became more frequent, a different approach became possible, but they too had to measure the impact of interdicting particular cults of the saints on their own standing within the parish, particularly its effects on their subsequent ability to communicate with their parishioners. The *curé* of Sennely-en-Sologne is a good example of this: 'I could not carry out the [bishop's] order, and granted a respite to its seditious opponents, hiding *their* St Anthony under the altar of St Fiacre.'[24] In such circumstances, it probably took regular pressure from bishops and their officials (vicars-general, archdeacons, *vicaires forains*) to achieve results, but for various reasons, the size of many dioceses being only one, that pressure could not always be effectively applied from above. Such intervention usually took a negative form – injunctions during synods or visitations to remove unacceptable images or suppress particular 'idolatrous' cults. These were more easy to police thereafter in areas where hierarchical supervision was relatively well established. Since it was not the cult of the saints per se that was the problem, such intervention also sought to promote the acceptable form of the cults under scrutiny. But this was far more difficult to achieve unless there was local support for the reformed or new format. Where support was lacking, *curés* were unable to do very much on their own, so that a good deal of foot-dragging – duly noted in subsequent visitations! – took place.

Preachers and missionaries were the most common introducers of new religious devotions, but they were themselves well aware, as we shall see later, that they would only take root through confraternities sustained by local people; where that readiness did not exist, the missionaries' confraternities often rapidly disappeared. But confraternities needed their own spaces, and people were more likely to join them if they enjoyed some distinctive form of identity. One of these was a chapel, located inside or outside the parish church, with its altar, statues and images, where members could meet to venerate their favourite saints and engage in the approved devotions. For this to happen, however, parishioners themselves had to put the hands in their pockets and find the funds for the buildings and commissions involved, and these sums were really only affordable by the wealthier inhabitants – nobles, officials, churchwardens and the like. No amount of external pressure was likely to produce such results if these 'best sort' of parishioners were unwilling to embrace the religious changes in question.[25]

Yet when allowance is made for all the different 'drag' factors, it does indeed seem that there was a genuine acceleration of change within the cult of the saints during, broadly speaking, the reign of Louis XIV. As we saw, judging by the prominence of chapels and confraternities of the Rosary, Marian devotion became the single most common cult, even in upland areas like the Grenoble diocese, where it was run a close second by that of the Holy Sacrament, which gradually gained ground on the cult of older saints. Their success, and notably that of the Rosary, owes a great deal to their appeal to women, while the fact that their chapels and altars were resolutely inside the parish church alleviated possible anxieties about female – or even about lay – autonomy generally in religious matters.[26] Judging by these results, it seems that there was enough local support for Catholic Reformation devotions to the saints – if not to Catholic Reformation saints per se – for them to take root, with newer generations of *curés* capable of mobilising the parish *dévots*.

The impact of such gradual change can also be seen in the realm of images of the saints whose influence, even subconsciously, on those venerating them must have been considerable. Once again, generalisations are extremely difficult to make, as they are liable to overlook the innumerable local hesitations and compromises over images which bring such changes into true focus. As we saw, iconographic revisionism accompanied architectural restructuring within many seventeenth-century churches: if the main altar was now meant to dominate the church, a single altarpiece of substantial dimensions was, wherever possible, intended to complete that recomposition, and to dominate the congregation's line of vision. The patron saints of parishes and religious orders were now depicted in poses which emphasised their virtues and their role as intermediaries and intercessors. Such revisionism was not confined to the main altars, as it was soon extended to the chapels, usually maintained by the confraternities for the saints they venerated. The records of visitations show an often close interest in these questions – the physical state of the altars, the objects kept in the chapels, the representations of the saints in statues and paintings. A major target for visitors' strictures was anything that smacked of 'indecent' or too 'familiar' representation of the saints, especially the more popular ones, who were often depicted with animals or other inappropriate 'signatures'.[27]

But there was more at stake than merely sanitising existing images of the saints. A study of eastern Provence has traced a gradual shift away from the hieratic, 'frozen' saints' images of later medieval art, in which individual saints do not relate to a wider universe. By contrast, seventeenth-century altarpieces place the saints in a landscape in which they are no longer the primary forces, but one in which their relation to God, Christ and the Virgin is emphasised; the hieratic saint gives way here to the saint who is apprehended through his or her virtues, and is portrayed as an intermediary who leads the ordinary worshipper to seek the divine and the heavenly. 'The seventeenth century', it has been said, 'thus appears as the period in which there was a move away from a form of sainthood which was a manifestation of supernatural power towards one in which it is defined as intercession in a quest for a more intense spiritual life ... from a religion of recourse to a more personal one in which the believer seeks intimacy with God.' But, perhaps as a sign that such a one-sided and heavily didactic message was hard to swallow, it seems that the iconographic shift was not quite total, in Provence at least.[28] Chapels, confraternities and individual patrons continued to commission and pay for altarpieces in which the protecting saint still appears dominant, even when it concerned an archetypical 'new' devotion like the Rosary.

Processions

Regardless of their place within 'the economy of salvation' and of the kinds of power that were attributed to them, saints were inseparable from miracles and relics. As is well known, the vast majority of saints' cults had begun with marginal individuals, such as hermits, or in out-of-the-way places, where apparitions occurred or unknown statues were found by shepherds, peasants or young women. As they became objects of popular interest, miracles of various kinds, especially cures for illnesses, were reported, generating heightened interest and drawing crowds of expectant visitors. The death of a wonder-working individual, whose 'sainthood' was already asserted by local inhabitants, was often a crucial moment, since it was usually then that objects associated with him or her were avidly sought after, and were dispersed as relics for their potentially miraculous powers. It is not hard to see why such a culture of saint-making was not to the liking of the post-Tridentine church, as we have already noted, but that dislike was of itself powerless to arrest this kind of encounter with as yet uninstitutionalised manifestations of the 'holy'. However, the tensions that resulted in the seventeenth century were widespread, since the earliest reactions of the official church to new sites of miracles or saints tended to be sceptical, even dissuasive. But if the initial bubble did not burst and a cult grew, the authorities' usual response was to seek to guide it into approved channels, circumspectly removing along the way those elements they judged no longer tolerable in the developing cult. The clergy, often members of religious orders, who were entrusted with the maintenance of such sites and their cults, were under instructions to compile detailed accounts of miracles occurring there – and they complied, realising that this was also perhaps the best way to secure official support of the cult involved.[29] The most important of these sites were, as we shall see, the 'great' centres of pilgrimage, 'national' and international, but they were not radically different from the more recent and more modest shrines and the processions that they attracted.

Thus the geographical density of holy places, with their chapels and shrines, continued to grow in the period under study here. It had already started to do so during the wars of religion, as part of a response to Huguenot attacks on such places and their relic collections; similar 'revivals' occurred in or close to Huguenot areas, no doubt serving as a focus for local Catholic identity, until well into the seventeenth century. A related phenomenon also surfaced during the religious wars. The 1580s and 1590s in northern France witnessed penitential processions to big sanctuaries like Liesse and Chartres that were on a scale unseen anywhere else in Europe. These 'white' processions came at a time of heightened confessional anxiety, and were paralleled by many more local ones, especially within towns where the Catholic League was entrenched during the final decade of the wars. But large numbers of peasant communities also appear to have downed tools in order to participate in these mass outpourings of religious guilt and anxiety.[30]

This was not quite the normal format of processions, since they came far closer to the pilgrimages that we will discuss later. New-found sites or destinations were not absolutely necessary, since the opportunities for procession in an average seventeenth-century parish were frequent enough. Bagnères (in Tarbes diocese) appears to have had a procession every Sunday between mid-May and mid-September, and one every Friday morning throughout the year to commemorate Christ's Passion.[31] In many communities, participation in processions was obligatory under pain of a fine, but that threat was probably unnecessary, since the willingness of people to process seems nearly inexhaustible. After often long services in church, the opportunity to process outside must have been welcome, even in an age when there were no seats or pews to constrain people's movements within churches. One procession may seem the same as the next, but they differed in important respects, depending on the occasions, the purposes and the destinations involved. The routine, common-or-garden procession was on one end of a wide spectrum, which embraced many other varieties, some of which may seem at times indistinguishable from pilgrimages.

The celebration of the major feasts of the calendar usually gave rise to a procession, but some were far more elaborate than others. Those of Rogations (three days before Pentecost), Corpus Christi (May–June), the Assumption of the Virgin (15 August), not to mention the feast of the parish's patron saint, were moments of huge collective festivity and solidarity, which were not really undermined by the all too common disputes concerning precedence and status while actually processing, especially in the more socio-professionally segmented urban areas. The 'great' processions, particularly that of Corpus Christi, usually featured a musical band of some sort, the banners of the local community and its saints, and the various professions (in towns) dressed in their finery. The sacrament was taken out on display from the parish church to the other chapels of the parish. Such events took time to organise, especially as some feast days lasted more than a single day, and involved mystery plays and the like. It was usually the main purpose of the older confraternities to prepare the patron saint's celebration, while others feasts were traditionally organised by youth groups, the *royaumes* or *reinages*, as they were often called, whose own rowdiness and pranks increasingly set them at odds with the parish clergy. The most common period for processions was, understandably, from mid-April to mid-October, especially in rural areas, where processions to bless the crops, pray for rain or sunshine when either was sorely needed, and seek divine benevolence for a good harvest, were a routine part of the calendar.

In often sharp contrast to the institutionalised procession, we find those triggered by extraordinary circumstances occasionally welcome but mostly threatening. Processions to new shrines belong to the first group. Far more common, however, and especially during the seventeenth century, were those moments of acute crisis, of which 'plague' was by far the most enduring and most common. If nothing else explains the continuing recourse to 'protector' saints and rituals, it was helplessness in the face of the prospect of sudden death on a large scale. Stalwart saints like St Roch or St Sebastien, but also the Virgin as mother, were invoked not just by individuals, but by entire communities, urban and rural.[32] It was in such circumstances that devotions to particular saints were the most strenuously tested, or perhaps hitherto less familiar saints enrolled. Vows of numerous kinds – to go on pilgrimage being just one – were also made at these moments. And these vows were not merely individual, since the response to such threats was also communal. The usually lugubrious procession around the parish which ensued was thus only the first gesture of atonement for the sins which were held to be the ultimate cause of the plague or other disaster which personified God's wrath against them. From Amiens to Tarbes, collective vows were also made then – to go on procession/pilgrimage to a site well beyond the parish; to build a chapel to a saint, to rebuild part of the parish church that needed repair, to fund the saying of special masses and so on. The fact that plague was averted or that a community was protected against, for example, earthquakes (as in 1660 in the south-west) also led to expressions of thanksgiving, which themselves could generate further processions to particular sites.

The act of processing itself, its routes and its destinations, also varied considerably, depending on the occasion in question. The choice of routes and destinations was infinitely greater than we can now imagine, given how dense the average parish's long-vanished collection of chapels, oratories, crosses and other *monjoies* could be. Not all could, or needed to be visited en route each time, so those which had some link to the motif of the procession of the day would be singled out as a 'station' along the route. The normal annual processions frequently reaffirmed the boundaries of the parish in a gesture which was not as gratuitous as we might imagine, since parishes, especially rural ones, were an important part of a local people's identity. Pauses at chapels on the way were stations where particular prayers might be said, while songs or chants were sung at other intervals.

But increasingly processions beyond the parish boundaries were undertaken, especially if there were well-known sanctuaries in the area. In keeping with their origins, numerous sanctuaries were located on the boundaries of parishes, and if they had any reputation at all, they would attract processions from several parishes on particular feast days. Normally, the different groups involved would be led by their own clergy, who actually tended to fear that abstaining from such a procession could lead to unspeakable disorders! Processions through several parishes towards a bigger sanctuary were widespread in our period, and were frequently the result, as we have just seen, of vows taken in moments of crisis. Precisely because there were more such sanctuaries within a radius of approximately 15 to 20 miles, such 'long' processions – or 'short' pilgrimages, depending on one's perspective – were feasible. When perennial, such pilgrimages were usually organised by a parish confraternity or by the churchwardens. As one historian put it, 'seventeenth-century believers travelled more than ever, but also increasingly in groups, and for that reason did not travel too far'.[33] This is particularly true of the rural populations, who could rarely afford long absences: the agro-liturgical calendar was not quite so perfectly dovetailed as to allow them to decamp en masse at regular intervals.

The fact that processions can be seen through different lenses raises the question of what kinds of religious practices they constituted. If those held in times of grave threats were of their nature sombre, recollected affairs, the great majority were infinitely more festive. The bigger a procession and the longer it lasted, the more likely it was to develop other dimensions too – hence the fairs, markets and rent-settling activities associated with some of them. Others generated what were in effect 'sporting' competitions between the different villages present, especially when the procession's end-point was located at a parish boundary; but serious fracas and physical violence were just as likely between natives of parishes known to dislike each other! Other processions again featured masques, farces and carnival-like swipes at the established order, in which youth groups were heavily involved. For centuries, large numbers of the clergy had participated directly in ceremonies whose dubious religious content attracted increased criticism in our period – firstly, for their profanity and, secondly, for the inappropriateness of clerical involvement in them. The cathedral canons of Amiens sponsored a service for the patron saint, St Firmin, including a representation of an incident at his death that was enacted each year by a 'green man' clad in ivy. The ceremony was only abolished as late as 1737.[34] It is an example that makes it easier to imagine how much greater clerical participation at lower levels of town and country could be.

Processions themselves could be very rumbustious affairs, as attempts at social mixing might be countered by people wishing to keep their social distance from others. For all that it was common enough, such indiscriminate intermingling of men and women, especially of adolescents and the unmarried, worried the authorities, clerical but also secular. A procession held during a mission at Aubarède in Tarbes diocese in 1683 was policed by the missionaries themselves, the Capuchins, whose efforts were successful on that occasion because, as the *curé* noted, they 'kept people in line as captains do with their soldiers during a pitched battle'. The *curé* confessed he had never seen the like before, but may well have doubted how long its effects would last, since the very next procession during the same mission was reserved exclusively for the 'best' women and girls of the parish.[35] That option, which excluded the majority of the parishioners from the procession, was not tenable for normal processions throughout the year. The clergy would have to work harder if they were to obtain the kind of devout processions that they wished for, even though many of them knew well how little real control they had over them once they were under way.

Pilgrimages

This account of widely shared religious practices may conclude with what might seem the most marginal and insubstantial among them for our period – that of pilgrimage. Few kinds of religious behaviour have experienced such a change of historiographical fortune in recent times as pilgrimage, the practice of travelling, sometimes over long distances, to a holy place, such as Jerusalem, in order to seek a variety of spiritual or even physical benefits. Pilgrimage has long been regarded as a medieval tradition which declined into picturesque insignificance by the sixteenth century when, in reality, it expanded considerably and took on some important new features. The medieval tradition was, almost inevitably, savaged by the Protestant reformers, who denied the very possibility of 'holy' places of any sort, Jerusalem included. Before that a sharp humanist critique, deriving from the *Devotio moderna* and Erasmus, had already appeared, arguing that true pilgrimage was an 'internal' voyage to be taken by the individual Christian, and not a misguided search for miracles and indulgences in faraway places. Views like these resurfaced within seventeenth-century French Catholicism, especially among Jansensists and Catholic rigorists like Bossuet, who regarded pilgrimage with disdain as the epitome of 'external' religion.

The historiography of early modern Catholicism could find no real place for it until recently, when French historians, inspired by Alphonse Dupront's work on crusades and other 'extra-ordinary' forms of religious behaviour, began to map its incidence across not just France, but Europe generally, for the entire early modern period. For Dupront and his disciples in the historical anthropology of religion, pilgrimage deserved attention precisely because it signified the abandonment of normal life – normal religious life included. It was, therefore, an extraordinary gesture for any individual to make, because it represented a leap into the unknown, mentally as well as geographically, and a readiness to accept the possible consequences of a close encounter with the sacred in a completely unknown environment. Furthermore, since pilgrims travelled and lived in wholly random groups, they escaped the institutions and hierarchies – especially the tutelage of the clergy – that prevailed in normal life. So, if not exactly 'Carnival', pilgrimage was a still version of the world turned upside down. Seen in this way, pilgrimage was at the opposite end of the spectrum to the humble procession, which involved a temporary and orderly group of worshippers and neighbours (usually) walking around their own parish, and which ended with them quickly returning to 'normality' within their local church itself.[36]

Pilgrimages could only exist when and where 'sacred' places were to be found, whose sacrality derived from a local incursion of the holy, usually in the form of miracles produced there by saints, the subsequent cult of whom spawned a plethora of relics, images, tombs and so on at the place in question.[37] For many people, the decision to go on pilgrimage derived from vows made to do so in situations of immediate personal danger – sickness, injury, anxiety and so on – and once taken, such vows were binding under pain of sin, unless one could obtain release from it from the church, usually one's bishop. The latter did happen, though to what extent is not known. Whether more vows of this kind were made in the seventeenth century than previously is also unknown – and unknowable – but there was, it seems, a noticeable rise in the number of vows that were written out and then despatched to the sanctuary of the person's choice, so that no actual pilgrimage ensued. Proxies were also used by individuals incapable of travelling themselves to a sanctuary.[38] But one very important incentive to the performance of a pilgrimage remained firmly in place – that of the special indulgences which they brought. Another incentive, which particularly concerned long-distance pilgrimages to Rome, was the multiplication, from 1575 onwards, of jubilee years, which henceforth occurred every twenty-five rather than every hundred years. When successive popes declared ad hoc jubilees in 1730 and 1740, they were simply ignored in Gallican France, which seems to have preferred to support the more demanding 'regular' jubilees.

The golden age of Catholic Reformation pilgrimage probably ran from the 1580s to the 1730s approximately, though it was still growing in Germany and Austria after 1730. The practice recovered from the damage done by Reformation attacks, and the Council of Trent came to its defence in its very last session, when it defended the legitimacy of venerating the saints viewed as models of holiness to be imitated rather than as 'mere' miracle-workers. It flourished on a wide scale until eighteenth-century secular authorities began acting on the view (which already existed in places such as France since the mid-seventeenth century) that pilgrims were vagabonds, and pilgrimage had no place any more in an age which increasingly rejected the very idea of miracles.[39] During the intervening generations, pilgrimage not merely survived, but its centres multiplied across Europe, trickling downwards into regions and localities. With the ending of pilgrimage to Jerusalem in the fifteenth century, it was Rome and Compostella which became the major centres, with intermediary 'stations' like Loretto, Milan, Einsiedeln and others emerging from almost nowhere, while the proliferation of relics from the Holy Land via Rome enabled smaller and more local sites to develop thanks to the possession of relics or copies of venerated relics held at the major sites.

France may not have possessed a truly major place of international pilgrimage to rival the sites just mentioned, and Louis XIV may have tried to prevent his subjects from going abroad on pilgrimage (without success, as it happened), but it developed its own 'sacred' geography nevertheless. The small Burgundian village of Alise-Sainte-Reine may have welcomed up to 60,000 pilgrims a year during the seventeenth century, though it is impossible to know how many of them were engaged in a longer-distance pilgrimage to another site. The older French sites included Rocamadour, Le Puy, Chartres, Reims, Liesse, Saint-Denis near Paris and Mont-Saint-Michel. The more recent ones (at least in the sense of the scale of the pilgrimages they attracted) included Saint-Maximin, Auray and Ardilliers. All were scattered unevenly across the kingdom, but not all enjoyed equal favour during the long seventeenth century, when Chartres was, compared to later centuries, of little importance. Surprisingly, it was Liesse, near Laon in north-eastern France, that drew the biggest annual crowds by far during our period. Below this category we find regional or local sanctuaries which had a more restricted clientele and which were sometimes sites restored after being desecrated during the wars of religion and which became attractive because of the miracles alleged to have occurred there subsequently. Judging by the miracles recorded at Auray near Vannes between 1625 (when pilgrimage began there) and 1684, it seems that it was essentially a site of pan-Breton pilgrimage, with a few neighbouring dioceses also participating.

A complex, interlocking geography of national, provincial and local sites of devotion and pilgrimage thus evolved during the Catholic Reformation, so that a long-range pilgrimage could include visits to smaller sites along the way, and those disinclined to travel long distances could engage in pilgrimage nevertheless. Cities like Paris and Marseille not only had an abundance of sanctuaries and their related *intra muros* processions, but they had pilgrimage sites that were conveniently close at hand – Mont-Valérien and Saint-Maximin respectively.[40] To that extent, the most 'local' of pilrimages may not have been entirely different for their participants than the extended procession which we have just studied – so that the radical 'difference' ascribed to pilgrimage may need some qualification.

A highly important factor in the success of many of the major sites was their connection, reaching back into previous centuries, with successive royal dynasties, whose patronage of them (especially Reims, Saint-Denis and Chartres) was deliberate and sustained, and was especially intended to contribute to the monarchy's own sacrality.[41] Louis XIII and Anne of Austria were inveterate pilgrimage-goers whose health, long-standing lack of a male heir (from 1615 to 1638) and other political problems provided them with ample opportunities to make, and fulfil, vows of pilgrimage. Though it did not of itself involve a pilgrimage, Louis XIII's consecration of his realm to the Virgin Mary in 1638 was the culmination of such dynastic identification, while his choice of dedicatee was typical of Catholic Reformation religious developments generally, and not just an isolated gesture.[42] Pilgrimage to Marian sites generally was greatly boosted as a result. The adult Louis XIV turned his back on such practices, in sharp contrast to his fellow Catholic rulers in the German and Hasburg lands. Pilgrimage sanctuaries that were patronised by princes and elite social groups often received large sums of money and expensive gifts (many designed for religious services), which then went into embellishing the sites and conferred on them an even greater éclat. The miracles recorded at Auray in Brittany in the years 1625 to 1684 show an over-representation of nobles, clergy and bourgeois among their beneficiaries – 42 per cent compared to 58 per cent for the rest of the population. The pilgrims who went to Saint-Méen near Rennes or to Saint-Marcoul of Corbeny between Reims and Laon were, it seems, mostly peasants, but at Corbeny they attracted only 8 per cent of the recorded miracles. If these figures are representative – and the profile of Liesse's miracles suggests they probably are – they show that here, as elsewhere, the higher social groups benefited disproportionately from their efforts.[43]

Beyond that, however, it is difficult to offer a general account of who went on pilgrimage and why they did so.[44] Insofar as the often very scrappy records allow us to judge at all, it seems that the majority of those participating in long-distance ones were young, unmarried males, sometimes artisans whose trade may have induced such mobility anyway. Gilles Caillotin (1697–1746) was one of these, a textile artisan from Reims, who began going on pilgrimages virtually every year from the age of fifteen, sometimes with his entire family, to places like Liesse and Corbeny in his native Champagne. His Roman pilgrimage of 1724 was the highlight of a career which continued thereafter, to at least 1732, when he visited Alise-Sainte-Reine in Burgundy. This 'walker for God' (*marcheur de Dieu*) even went to Fontainebleau and Versailles in 1724 and 1729 respectively in order to be touched by Louis XV, doubtless because he suffered from scrofula.[45] Like Caillotin himself, whose piety was impeccably orthodox, many of these pilgrims were members of devotional confraternities, which actively encouraged such practices among their members. The more local a pilgrimage was, the more likely it was that pilgrims would travel in sometimes large groups drawn from the same parishes, which in turn could mean that an established tradition or a 'one-off' vow lay behind their actions. Nor, as already indicated, was pilgrimage the preserve of the lower social groups or embedded in a putatively 'popular' religious culture, since higher social groups readily engaged in it, following the example of the Bourbon dynasty itself. The prince of Condé famously extricated himself from French politics in 1622 on the grounds of a vow to make a pilgrimage to Loretto, from which he did not return until 1625. That in turn suggests how mixed *individual* motives – and not just those of large groups – could be, so that religious fervour might well have had to make room for various combinations of wanderlust and pure curiosity.

By the eighteenth century, when official attitudes were turning far more negative in France, pilgrims were often depicted by secular and (some) religious authorities as running away from their family and other responsibilities; arrest by the constabulary for vagabondage was a constant threat by the early eighteenth century. But while there were always some 'professional' pilgrims, the accusation seems highly egregious. Long-haul pilgrims heading for Rome or Compostella would confess and take communion, usually during the principal mass on a Sunday, before commencing their journey with a blessing and a festive send-off from their parish. For many people, it was a rite of passage or the consequence of a vow, and on their return they fully expected to re-enter the society they had temporarily left behind, enjoying perhaps increased prestige from having completed a pilgrimage.[46] It also seems that confraternities devoted to the cult of the saint of a major pilgrimage site were founded by returning pilgrims, especially those who had obtained what they had been seeking. Needless to say, such confraternities would in turn promote further pilgrimages.

As for the impact of pilgrimages on individuals, especially to the major sites, we can only judge, in the absence of contemporary accounts, from what we know of how pilgrimage centres were organised. Contrary to what a 'world-upside-down' view of pilgrimages might imply, it is clear that the

Catholic Reformation church attempted, as it did in other spheres, to turn the places in question into 'pedagogical' opportunities. Genuine success was far from guaranteed, partly because the smaller pilgrimage sites which attracted proportionately the largest crowds were perhaps not the best organised, and pilgrims did not stay very long there. But since the main reason for pilgrimage was the undiminished fascination that miracle-working saints exercised over pilgrims, it was not always amenable to domestication or readily commutable into approved kinds of devotion. Sanctuaries could not retain the favour of pilgrims if miracles dried up, but the fact that three out of every four miracles recorded at Auray, for example, were therapeutic in nature must have encouraged the belief among those seeking miracles that saints actually possessed the power to cure rather than merely being intercessors with God.[47]

The seventeenth-century church's initial scepticism, followed by its reluctant acceptance of such miracles at new sites of pilgrimage, shows how tenuous its purchase on the phenomenon really was. Its principal response, however, was to put religious orders such as the Jesuits, the Capuchins or even the Oratorians, in charge of the sites, and to instruct pilgrims during their stay via preaching, catechism, confession and other 'exercises'.[48] Chosen for this task partly because of their ability to counter the Protestant presence in the regions where many of the sanctuaries were located, and also because they could counteract popular superstitions about saints and miracles, these orders contributed to the diffusion of particular devotions, especially those of the Marian type so favoured by the Jesuits. Even in these places of ecstasy, the opportunity to shape and instruct individuals who would soon return to a normal religious life was not overlooked. Put differently, a profound religious experience there was judged not to be enough in itself, and pilgrims were held to need more than thaumaturgy and therapy. The instructional effort was deemed all the more worthwhile if the individuals concerned were members of confraternities, since the latter could then be used as local vehicles for devotional change. For a seemingly marginal activity as pilgrimage to be conceived as offering opportunities for religious education testifies to the extent to which the seventeenth-century church, drawing on the pastoral abilities of the newer orders, attempted to bring it within the bounds of 'normal' religious practice.

CHAPTER 11

Sacraments and Sinners

It should be evident from the previous chapter that the religious aspirations and activities of the average Catholic (*catholique moyen*) of our period were not easily contained within the narrow confines of the local church or of an official canon. The very fragility of life itself in a century punctuated by war, famine and epidemic ensured that people would continue to seek 'salvation', in the widest sense of the term, wherever or in whatever form – the saints, relics, holy places, processions, pilgrimages – they could find it. As we saw, their instinct was to do so in groups rather than merely as individuals, but that also applied to the more 'normal' religious activities associated with saints' days and other major holidays. Other occasions of the liturgical year, from the most festive to the most penitential, were equally characterised by a strong element of sociability. But the very fact that the church authorities were attempting, however unevenly, to discipline and regulate such activities shows that even the most 'mobile' and elusive religious practices of the period were not entirely beyond the reach of the post-Tridentine church. Indeed, it has been suggested that the decline in the numbers of French pilgrims and the relatively limited proportion of peasants among them should be seen as evidence that attempts to improve the quality of 'normal' parochial religion were beginning to make their mark by the early to middle decades of Louis XIV's reign. Some of the elements of that effort we have already seen, notably in the concern to improve the calibre of the clergy, ensure the primacy of the parish church, embellish churches and develop the liturgy itself; more evidence of which will emerge in later chapters. Indications that such measures were bearing fruit would include, inter alia, the increasing volume of testamentary legacies made in favour of the local parish church and its religious services. Only if and when people were reasonably satisfied by what was on offer within their own parish communities, it is argued, would they make gestures of this kind; and such a shift in behaviour signalled an end of the 'time of miracles'.[1] Before any judgement can be made, we must examine some of the key elements of 'ordinary' religion, the changes to them initiated by the Catholic Reformation church and, when possible, the responses that they elicited.

There is no disguising the sustained efforts to put the sacraments that the Council of Trent had so stoutly defended at the centre of normal religious practice. But preserving all seven of them against their Protestant critics, who reduced them to two, was only the beginning.[2] The work of definition and clarification faced its own problems, but that was perhaps a more tractable challenge than that of translating them into practice in such a way that their significance was grasped by those receiving them; the gap between theological rationales and everyday practice could be a mighty one. In the Thomistic definition, a sacrament was an external sign of God's grace that was more than a 'mere' sign, since it possessed agency by actually 'causing' the grace to be communicated to individuals. But in a world swamped by religious gestures, symbols and signs, it was asking a great deal of people to acknowledge the distinctiveness of the sacraments, given that they, too, involved gestures and representations not easily differentiated from non-sacraments. There was a long road to walk before the difference between the sacraments and the plethora of 'sacramentals' (ritual actions like blessings, the sign of the cross) could be understood. On the other hand, in a world suffused with religious symbolism, it was at least possible to imagine ways of bringing people to accept that certain signs might be more important than others.

It is convenient to refer to a 'sacramental system', but important to realise that this term should only be very loosely defined. Firstly, there was the simple fact, which could be turned to advantage at times, that the seven sacraments were far from being a homogeneous series. Four of them – baptism, confirmation, marriage and extreme unction – coincided with rites of passage, but only the first two of them were, like a normal rite of passage, absolutely unrepeatable. Marriage, which was also by far the most complicated sacrament, was in principle unrepeatable, but at a time when the lifespan of marital unions was often extremely short, remarriage was far too widespread for clerical reservations about it to carry much weight. The sacrament of the dying, extreme unction, was administered only when death seemed really imminent, partly because the church authorities were deeply ambivalent about allowing it to be repeated. The sacrament of holy orders was wholly *sui generis*, even though it was the 'completion' of lesser orders already taken over a period of several years, because it was reserved to a tiny fraction of the (male) population. All of which left only two, penance and the Eucharist, which were fully repeatable, but which were in no way restricted (like holy orders) to a particular group or connected to any rite of passage. Finally, the sacraments differed in terms of those who could administer them: two (confirmation and holy orders) were reserved exclusively for bishops, and two others (confession and communion) were reserved for priests; another (marriage) was self-administered by the couple getting married, while baptism and extreme unction, though also normally reserved for priests, could be administered by laypeople in cases of emergency. It follows from this heterogeneity that the inherited culture of the sacraments would be one of genuine internal variety, and that any substantial change in it would require much time and effort. The analysis that follows here will concern itself as much with the wider cultural and historical 'envelope' as with the 'ideal-typical' theological sacrament hidden inside it.

Baptism

Birth and baptism must have seemed virtually indistinguishable to seventeenth-century contemporaries, all the more so as the parish registers that the clergy were required to keep recorded the dates of baptism rather than of birth. Between them, rampant infant mortality and the view that unbaptised infants were, at worst, damned for all eternity or, at best, confined to an indeterminate space called limbo, had long ensured that there was little need to encourage people to have children baptised soon after birth.[3] There were some exceptions to this, but they were more socially than statistically significant. Aristocratic and other prominent families often had newborn children simply *ondoyés* (a kind of 'provisional' baptism), and then waited for a suitable opportunity, sometimes a few years later, for the equivalent of a 'society' baptism in full pomp. The only other newborns to be *ondoyés* were those who were in real danger of imminent death, and they were normally formally baptised later in church. For everyone else, the sacrament was conferred by a priest within a day or so of birth. Priests who were unavailable to perform the ceremony, either because of negligence or unwillingness to travel long distances to do so, were subject to harsh criticism from their parishioners; such distances were, as we saw, one reason for demanding either a curate or the subdivision of a parish. The fact than anyone could perform the *ondoiement* of a child in emergencies by saying a simple formula was only a partial insurance against clerical fecklessness. The normal place for baptism was, of course, the parish church itself, not some other chapel elsewhere, and parish priests usually insisted strongly on their church's prerogative.

Needless to say, over the centuries the move towards universal infant baptism had the effect of 'collapsing' the successive elements of earlier church practice into one highly condensed rite. The firm insistence, evident from hundreds of seventeenth-century visitation ordinances, on parish churches having a proper baptismal font, ideally near the church entrance and properly decorated, was integral to the attempt to convey the religious meaning of the sacrament; the repetition of such demands suggests that local churchwardens and clergy were not always immediately responsive to them. The act of admitting a new member of Christ's church was preceded by the (partial) washing away of sin, especially the 'original' sin of Adam and Eve, and by an exorcism of the devil and his minions from the person being baptised; then followed the anointing, the words of the baptismal rite itself, and the profession of faith. Parents, if present, could only be observers of, rather than participants in the sacrament, a key element of which was the presence of godparents who undertook, in the name of the child, to observe the baptismal vows until the infant reached the age when he or she could do so for themselves.

The rise of godparenthood over the previous centuries gave the sacrament of baptism its real social-historical substance, especially when the numbers of godparents involved, both male and female, multiplied. Like marriage contracts, they displayed the social spread of the newborn's family, adding new kin to existing blood relations and possibly strengthening the latter, too. The Council of Trent had attempted to reduce godparents to three at most, but in many parts of Europe this remained a dead letter. It seems to have caused fewer difficulties in France, even though the strictures of both church and state to perform baptisms quickly, culminating in the royal declaration of 1698 that they be performed within twenty-four hours of birth on pain of a fine, seem to have been designed essentially to prevent numerous godparents from assembling in time for the baptism, and also perhaps to limit the scale of the 'profane' baptismal festivities that followed. The church also attempted to 'baptise' the much older rites of 'purifying' mothers allegedly defiled by giving birth through a version of its own, that of 'churching', known in French as the *relevailles*. Occurring some weeks after the baptism, 'churching' mimicked to some degree – by commencing at the door of the church, for example – the baptismal ceremony at which the mother had not been present, in order to emphasise her reintegration into the religious community after giving birth. But it is hard to know how many contemporaries would have understood the difference between this sort of thanksgiving and the older purification rituals.[4]

The most disturbing problem, for contemporaries at least, with the church's view of baptism concerned stillbirths, which were extremely common until the mid-eighteenth century. All kinds of anxieties arose from the impossibility for the unbaptised to be saved: did that mean they were really no different from adults who had knowingly sinned and were, through their own fault, damned in hell? More immediate and unavoidable was the fact that not only did they not have a name, but they could not be buried in Christian ground or alongside other family members. This denial seemed particularly harsh to parishioners who had their own strongly held if theologically unsophisticated understanding of the community of the living and the dead. It is evident in the widespread resistence to the compromise often proposed by church authorities during our period, namely that the stillborn be buried in an unblessed area of the parish cemetery, because the compromise still entailed separation and exclusion. If such a prospect was itself yet another incentive to rapid baptism after birth, stillbirths were almost bound to introduce other gestures which could not be easily policed. Desperate efforts, sometimes involving magical recipes, would be made to bring the stillborn to life and to revive those who had died before they could be baptised.

The practice of taking children to holy places so that a miracle that would enable baptism to take place could happen shows just how far people were willing to go. And some such places inevitably claimed miracles had occurred, thus attracting interest from further afield. They were known as 'sanctuaries of respite', where it sufficed for a 'sign of life' from a stillborn child to enable him or her to be baptised. French 'respites' seem to have been most common in the eastern provinces, from Flanders-Picardy to Provence, and places such as Moutiers-Sainte-Marie in Provence attracted desperate miracle-seekers from considerable distances. Such practices generated considerable unease in higher church circles by the later seventeenth century, but the local clergy appear to have been more understanding and even complicit in them.[5]

Equally revealing of the seventeenth-century church's approach to the birth-baptism association was the manner in which it dealt with midwives. Their numbers spread gradually as the century progressed, especially in the period from 1670 to 1730, and their subjection to the parish priest was simultaneously affirmed, with the consent of the civil authorities. However technically competent they might be – and most of those in rural areas had no real training at all – it was their religious knowledge which was meant to be decisive as they presented themselves before the parish priest; only if he was satisfied with it, and specifically their ability to administer the *ondoiement*, the provisional form of baptism, could they take the oath and serve as midwives. He could subsequently dismiss them if there were negative reports – possibly of sorcery or infanticide, each a source of much rumour and fear of midwives at the time. Their primary responsibility during a birth was the interests of the newborn, which included the *ondoiement* if there was an obvious danger of death, and the duty to urge families to baptise their children quickly; by comparison, the life of the mother was a secondary consideration.[6]

Finally, it is worth noting how considerably baptism was reworked in a different register during this period. Rather than ignore it as a once and for all ritual which nobody could recall, religious writers, preachers and missionaries magnified it as crucial 'moment' of grace that Christians could try to recapture at different points in their lives. The most obvious and most public instance of this was at the end of missions, when the preachers called upon the assembled congregation to repeat their baptismal vows, rededicating themselves to Christ and renouncing the devil and his works.[7] Public cursing of the devil might also occur at this point, and one participant related that he had cursed so hard 'that he did not think the devil would dare to bother him any more'.[8] Such practices only seem to have spread in the decades after 1700.

Confirmation

Of all the sacraments, confirmation was perhaps the most anonymous and uncertain, a position which the Council of Trent did little to rectify when deciding to retain it.[9] It was intended as the sacrament which, literally, confirmed the engagements of baptism, now that the Christians receiving it had reached the point of entry to adulthood. This, of course, made it a rite of passage. Apart from holy orders, it was the only sacrament whose administration was reserved exclusively to bishops. And that, in turn, was the nub of the problem: bishops who were either absent elsewhere or disinclined to visit their dioceses, especially if they were large, were unlikely to administer the sacrament all that often, short of compelling their diocesans to travel to the episcopal seat, something that would only work in the smallest dioceses. Relatively few seventeenth-century French dioceses had resident 'auxiliary' bishops who could have performed such a duty more frequently. Consequently, visitations, because of their pastoral concerns, became the most common occasions for confirmation, and many contemporary accounts show vast numbers of people waiting patiently – even heroically, hagiography *oblige* – during long hours for their turn to take a sacrament that was theoretically viewed as the rite of passage into religious adulthood. In fact, not infrequently, middle-aged people who had perhaps not seen a bishop for decades, joined the queue alongside their children and grandchildren to be confirmed! However much one might dispute the figures given by eyewitnesses for the numbers of those confirmed in our period, there can be no doubt about the 'popularity' of the sacrament itself. One reason why bishops on visitations took increasingly large retinues with them was to prepare parishes for the sacrament, through preaching, catechetical instruction and examination. The seventeenth-century French church relied on the sacrament's popularity to introduce a brief test of religious knowledge, to be conducted by the bishop's officials, before admitting individuals to take it. How searching the tests were at any time is hard to say, but on the occasion of 'monster' confirmations, they must have been fairly perfunctory.[10] Ideally, seventeenth-century catechetical efforts would have culminated in this sacramental occasion, whereby adolescents became

Christian adults, but its infrequency meant that this ideal coincidence only happened rarely.

The sheer unpredictability of confirmation, when viewed in terms of its status as a rite of passage, meant that a gap was left in the life cycle of parishioners that could be filled by some other rite, and in France that proved to be the long-lasting and no less popular 'first', or solemn, communion. It was targeted at roughly the same age group, those between twelve and fourteen years of age. It originated in late sixteenth-century France, in the 1590s, but it really took off during the following century or so, proving to be one of those clerical initiatives that corresponded closely to popular aspirations.[11] It also enabled the seventeenth-century church to do two things – firstly and as already suggested, to provide a culminating point for catechetical activity, after which people could, at least in principle, be confirmed without the question of their religious instruction or ignorance raising major problems; and, secondly, to push the gospel of Eucharistic devotion generally. Its success as a rite of passage was such that catechists complained that it was no longer possible to persuade young people, especially male adolescents, to continue with catechetical instruction once they had taken their first communion.[12]

Confession and Penance

The growth in the popularity of the first communion should not lead to the conclusion that regular communion became common throughout French parishes during the seventeenth century, however much the intention behind promoting the first communion was to encourage it. The first communion could very easily stand alone, since the subsequent taking of communion during a 'normal' year had no such 'rite of passage' appeal. Secondly, whatever rite of passage potential it may conceivably have had was offset by having as its Siamese twin the sacrament of penance in its post-Trent format of private confession, the most daunting of all the sacraments for the mass of the population. It was, in theory, possible to separate these two sacraments, but this seems rarely to have happened in practice, and it was not recommended except to the most devout. Confession, the normal shorthand for the sacrament of penance, might not have to be followed by communion, but the insistence on confessing before communing became so strong that it became inconceivable, at least psychologically, to break the connection that this entailed. And since communion was itself sheet-anchored to the celebration of the Mass, without which there could be no consecrated communion hosts at all, those wishing to take communion were confronted by a three-part sequence in which individually taxing religious rites were bolted together. Put in such stark terms, we might expect the outcome to be high levels of abstention, even among those with strong religious commitment. But the historical record is far more complex than that, since abstention from communion, for example, could just as easily be based on a sense of reverence and personal unworthiness as on fear or indifference.

Given the pivotal position of penance/confession within this sacramental cluster, it deserves careful scrutiny. It is also a potentially inexhaustible subject, since so much of the post-Tridentine church's moral-theological system became bound up with it. Yet because confession was the most 'secret' of sacraments, even when taking place in public spaces, and because no direct evidence of any individual confession has survived, historians can only approach it indirectly. A flood of works of guidance for both confessors and confessants accompanied the post-Tridentine drive to encourage people to take the sacrament not only more frequently, but more 'knowledgeably'. Yet the value of these texts as evidence of actual shifts or emphases within contemporary practices is problematic, given how many of them bear the imprint of particular schools of thought, disputes peculiar to a particular period or place, or the conventions of theological argument. Thus, despite their range and detail, even the larger tomes of 'cases of conscience' only provide highly indirect echoes of actual behaviour. However, for all their drawbacks, historians have little choice but to use these 'external' sources to eavesdrop on contemporary attitudes and behaviour. At the very least, these publications suggest the scale of the reorientation of confession after the upheavals of the Reformation and the need to elaborate its practical implications.

The evolution of the practice of confession cannot be understood without at least some reference to its theological underpinnings, which themselves underwent shifts in emphasis.[13] Briefly, the requirement laid down by the Fourth Lateran Council (1215) that all Christians confess to their 'own priest' and communicate at least once a year, preferably during the Easter season, provided an important stimulus, but the relation between, and the relative importance of the different elements of the sacrament itself – the sorrow for having sinned, the act of confessing those sins and the absolution granted by the confessor which closed the sacrament – were far from settled by the age of Luther. It is no small irony that the major target of Luther's attack on the sacrament, namely the power of the confessor to absolve sins, was originally based on a pessimistic view of the capacity of any Christian to evince the perfect sorrow needed to merit divine mercy. The emphasis on 'the power of the keys' held by the confessor that resulted from it was widely interpreted before and after Luther as evidence of 'laxism', since it seemed to downplay the attitudes of the penitent; and it was even more widely viewed as the epitome of clerical power hunger.

The sixteenth century would bring further theological clarification which in turn would be put to the test during the post-Tridentine centuries, gradually pulling the practice of both penance and communion along in its wake. It now seems that the thesis of populations being terrorised into spiritual anxiety by confessors in pre-Reformation Europe is quite unfounded, based as it was on Luther's own explosive personal angst and, perhaps, a too-literal reading of official texts and confession manuals.[14] On the contrary, the practice of confessing and communing yearly around Easter seems to have become virtually universal precisely because it was seasonal and communal, with the individual element seriously underdeveloped compared to later generations. The preaching and fasting of Lent generated the right kind of environment for engaging in an act of self-accusation that was often perfunctory and limited in scope when it did come. There was no popular demand for, or little pressure from above to, promote more frequent recourse to either confession or communion. Nor will it come as any surprise that the vast majority of the clergy were quite incapable of 'spiritual terrorism' of any kind, and that when people did complain it was mostly about clergy trying to charge them fees for confessing them! So it was not 'hardened' sinners fleeing condign punishment who avoided the sacrament, but mainly those who were excommunicated or in various states of enmity with other parishioners or, just as frequently, with the parish clergy themselves. Fear of the clergy divulging personal secrets also existed, but it was probably a lesser irritant. Many of these elements of popular behaviour remained largely unchanged until well into the period that concerns us here – and, in some areas of France, well beyond it.

Despite some misgivings at the time, mainly arising from debates about justification by good works and/or by faith, Trent reaffirmed the three core elements of later medieval Catholic teaching concerning confession – sorrow for sin, confession and absolution.[15] Thereafter, it was the first of these which generated the most controversy, especially in France, where Trent's acceptance of a weaker form of sorrow for sin – 'attrition' rather than 'contrition' – was at the heart of the Jansenist dispute.[16] Apart from that, most of the efforts henceforth were directed towards streamlining the conduct of the sacrament itself, but above all towards making it more integral to the religious life of even ordinary people than ever envisaged in previous centuries. The scale of this particular shift was perhaps not immediately obvious, so that it took several decades for the format of the 'Tridentine' confession fully to emerge. The process began with the gradual elimination of anything resembling a general confession of sin by the congregation during the Sunday mass and the concomitant absolution pronounced by the priest which existed in many areas, especially in northern France, until the sixteenth century and possibly later.[17] Secondly, as with baptism, the exact words of the formula of absolution pronounced by the priest took on greater importance in an age of enclosed confessionals which precluded the earlier physical gestures of absolution. With the exception of the seriously sick, confessions were to be held exclusively within churches, and ideally in easily visible places there.

The invention of the enclosed confession box during the reign of Carlo Borromeo at Milan (1564–84) has, in retrospect, come to symbolise the disciplinary ambitions of the Counter-Reformation church generally. In its own time, it was an answer to the long-standing conundrum of how to make confessions both secret and private – only the first of which they had been hitherto – while still being conducted in a public space within the church.[18] The reputation and canonisation of Borromeo ensured that he would be widely copied across Europe, albeit at greatly differing local speeds. Confession boxes appeared as early as the 1620s in Brittany and probably earlier elsewhere in France, but it is not clear how 'full dress' they were at that point. Contemporary paintings present a rudimentary structure with a chair or stool on each side of a grille through which confessor and penitent could speak but not make physical contact, not even for the traditional laying of hands that had hitherto symbolised the act of absolution. The most fully developed confessionals of the later seventeenth century were impressive structures, with their own iconography, and their presence was a constant reminder to parishioners of the sins they would have to confess. In these confessionals, the confessor sat in the middle, with a partly or fully enclosed box on either side of him, mainly so that women and men could confess separately.[19] No doubt, these physical arrangements also evolved gradually towards greater anonymity and individuality to make them more tolerable to parishioners who might otherwise have been intimidated by them. But the length of time it took to persuade churchwardens and parish priests to install them suggests that the demand for them was not insistent. When the confession box arrived in Sennely-en-Sologne under Louis XIV, the locals refused to go into it, because doing so seemed tantamount to admitting that they had serious sins to confess, which was the last thing they wanted their neighbours, fellow penitents and parish gossips to imagine. The upshot was that the parish priest had to abandon using the new confessional altogether, reverting instead to sitting on a chair in an open space and avoiding eye contact while confessing his parishioners, whose secrets were once again within earshot of the curious! We can assume that Sennely was not the only French parish to cold-shoulder this particular element of the Borromean legacy.[20]

But there was much more to the post-Tridentine developments than re-arranging the furniture of parish churches. The council's decisions emboldened newer forces within Catholicism to make confession and communion more central to normal religious practice. The emphasis on taking communion more frequently had obvious implications for confession itself, so that it is nearly impossible to treat the two sacraments entirely separately. New orders like the Jesuits were particularly keen to promote such Christocentric devotions, while their own techniques of regular self-examination could be adapted for wider, lay use, for which their Marian congregations would become the chosen agents of transmission. By the early to mid-seventeenth century, the Jesuits were pushing the more devout elements of French society towards monthly and even weekly communion. Needless to say, at that rarefied level, the function of an equally frequent confession was significantly different to the annual Eastertide shriving. Confession was now intended to be a regular discipline which operated all year round and, in certain respects, was a means towards an end – that of developing a sustained spiritual life – rather than an end in itself. In other words, Lent would ideally expand across the entire year rather than remain a conventional 'season'; regular confession itself would be based upon the practice of examing one's conscience at the end of each day. Individuals who embraced this kind of sacrament-focused religious practice were also advised to have a personal spiritual director or confessor, whose role it was to guide them along the route they had chosen to take.[21] Such 'familiarity' with the sacraments, even though it was confined to a small elite, was not always welcomed with open arms, and perhaps the most famous religious treatise published in seventeenth-century France, Antoine Arnauld's *Frequent Communion* (1643), was a vehement rejection of the Jesuit approach. Its title may refer to frequent communion, but the real issue at stake, both in 1643 and for the rest of the century, was frequent penance and *its* preconditions.

Arnauld's polemic was a response to changes in sacramental practices that generated considerable unease by his time.[22] Behind his stance there may well have lurked an assumption that frequent confession and communion might just be appropriate for clergy, especially regulars, whose lives could be geared accordingly, but not for laypeople surrounded by the cares and snares of a sinful world. The enormous outpouring of 'practical' works of various kinds – catechisms, manuals for confessors and confessants, cases of conscience and so on – testify to the extent of the efforts needed – and duly made – to cope with both the demands and the consequences of changing approaches. Approximately 600 manuals for confessors appeared across Europe in the century after Trent! Because they were practical in scope, they were attempts to adjust first principles – most commonly, the Ten Commandments – to contemporary conditions, so that both penitents and confessors could navigate their way towards solutions that would 'salve' individual consciences. The manuals, but also other works of spiritual advice, often extended their analyses beyond disembodied sins and their potential mitigation, and into the realm of professional occupations and, for want of a better term, social class. For that reason, they usually spent infinitely more time and space considering what might be called 'economic' sins – theft, usury, fraud, questions of restitution and so on – rather than, as is usually imagined, sexual sins. Discussions specific to social groups included, for example, questions of 'honour' and its ramifications (for example, duelling and its legitimacy) for the nobility. Inevitably, the forensic skills that went into reconciling Christian precepts with early modern social practices sometimes produced resolutions which seemed to undermine those precepts altogether, especially when they involved resorting to arguing that such and such a resolution was 'probable' because some previous 'authority' had supported it. It was this growing culture of casuistry and accommodation that elicited such a backlash by the 1640s in France, one which led in subsequent decades, as we shall see later, to a rigorist 'turn' within the French church's official attitudes.[23]

The problem with these discussions, as already noted, is that their connection to penitential practices 'on the ground' was highly oblique, and that they cannot simply be quarried as evidence in matters of detail. That the gap separating canonists and casuists from the vast majority of the population, clerical as much as lay, was wide will be self-evident. That conceded, changes over time were indeed possible, especially if we avoid regarding the 'clergy' and 'laity' as two ice-floes, divided rather than united by a sacrament like penance, owing to their respective positions being so different. As we shall see, varying types of intermediary already existed or would evolve over time, and on both sides. The French church did not have the option of a Spanish-style inquisition, whose interrogations of individuals were the equivalent of confessions, and which was capable of bringing pressure towards uniformity of belief and practice to bear on even rural populations.[24] For a very long time, the French church relied mainly on the religious orders, especially the new ones, to diffuse the post-Trent approach to confession and communion. The Jesuits were not the only champions of more frequent participation, as the Capuchins, Récollets and many others were not far behind them. The regulars also had far better practical experience than the seculars, with the exception perhaps of the urban *curés*. In 1619, Bishop d'Estaing of Clermont probably spoke for many across France when giving his reasons for supporting the foundation of a Récollet house in a small town in Auvergne: 'seeing that the people has a greater need of being instructed and consoled by confessions than by preaching and other good examples, both of which seem sterile without the practice of such confessions ... I desire that they [Récollets] be preferred to others, particularly because they confess, and because of confession's greater utility for the service of God'.[25] The spread of the regulars into the small and middling towns that we saw in earlier chapters broadened the scope of such efforts at diffusing more frequent confession and communion. Only much later would the local secular clergy be able to imitate, let alone compete with the regulars.

As for the 'laity', we must recognise internal differentiations among them, too. The most 'receptive' elements were urban and accustomed to having ties to the regulars, as we have just seen. It was among them that we find the earliest groups of sacramental 'activists', such as the members of Jesuits' various Marian congregations, as well as the third orders and, as the seventeenth century progressed, the growing numbers of confraternities, especially of the Holy Sacrament or the Rosary. Some confraternities were more overtly sacramental than others, and that of the Rosary was less so than the Holy Sacrament.[26] But this religious culture found much less of a welcome in the parishes of village and rural France, where neither the local clergy nor the parishioners were much predisposed to move beyond the traditional rituals of the annual Easter confession and communion. The clergy, who in most places only made provision for hearing confessions around Easter itself, were frequently reported as being too ignorant to do much more than that, but they were also in no rush to facilitate large-scale confessions at other times of the year. In this context, preaching tours or longer-lasting parish missions conducted by regulars could play a major role in encouraging parishioners to confess and communicate outside of the Easter cycle. Moreover, it was much easier to confess to strangers than to one's neighbour-cum-*curé*, and if a mission coincided with a jubilee or a special indulgence, one could confess even one's more shame-inducing 'reserved' sins – sins which, the prior of Sennely claimed, his parishioners would not otherwise confess until they were at death's door.[27] For all the exaggeration involved in accounts of missions and their effects, the numbers of people queuing to confess during them can hardly be ignored. Such confessions can be compared with those of Easter as a 'stand-alone' event, in which it was easy to engage alongside virtually everyone else from the parish. But missions were highly irregular events, so their capacity to transform confessional practice was distinctly limited.[28] Other possible occasions for confession, apart from the parish's patron saint's day, were the great 'universal' festivals of the church such as Pentecost, All Saints' and Christmas, but the results here seem decidedly patchier for the seventeenth century.

Parish missions and confessors' manuals are a useful vantage point from which to examine another important question regarding post-Trent France – namely, the extent to which the church's pastoral strategy failed because it was based on instilling fear into individuals. Because missions were often occasions for 'fire-and-brimstone' preaching, it has often been assumed that the confessions that followed them were equally frightening. But, as far as we can judge, this kind of preaching was consciously tactical, and once it had achieved the desired effect of 'stirring' people, the confessors encouraged and 'consoled' rather than terrorised those confessing their sins. This was certainly the maxim of Jean Eudes, one of the most indefatigable missionaries of the mid-century, who probably reflected widespread practice.[29] The relation between the confessors' manuals and what was actually practised in the confession box was similarly conditioned. In principle, the post-Trent confessor was both judge and doctor vis-à-vis his penitents, who were expected to confess in detail their sins and the circumstances in which they occurred. But the widely used metaphor of the confessor as doctor was double-edged in an age when medicines could harm as much as help a patient!

Although the newer generations of secular clergy gradually became more competent as confessors, there are fewer indications than might be imagined of a pervasive pastoral rigorism resulting either in an emptying of the confessionals or sustained conflicts between *curés* and their parishioners. It is likely that, faced with perhaps at times sullen resistance, the parish clergy took a broader view of their parishioners' religion and chose not to make regular acts of confession its litmus test. By the same token, a generation of parishioners who by the very end of the seventeenth century had been catechised and perhaps schooled, even in a limited way, had been prepared from an early age for the confessional, their modest 'competence' in the subject mirroring that of their *curés*; confraternity membership would have had similar consequences. The 'coaching' of children by parents or catechists on how to confess their sins was denounced by numerous authors, so we can assume that some form of it was practised. Whether or not the approved alternative to such coaching, namely the guiding of individuals in the confessional itself by confessors, reached beyond the religious elites or parish *dévots* may also be doubted.

We know far less about the degree of recalcitrance, or perhaps better, the specific reasons for refusing confession and communion in seventeenth-century France. In Italy and doubtless elsewhere, there were feuds and hostilities that were not susceptible to resolution via the confessional, because confessing one's sin and forgiving the other party involved unilateral disarmament without a quid pro quo, something that did not fit into the moral universe the protagonists lived in. The best option in such circumstances was to take the problem out of the confessional and, as in the case of duelling in France, to mobilise confraternities or similar groups to take over the task of reconciliation, after which a confession might have some chance of success.[30]

Mass and Communion

Because confession was not itself a liturgical event and was not encased within one, hiding its harder, especially post-Tridentine edges was never easy. By comparison, communion was always, with the exception of its administration to the sick, taken during the mass, attendance at which seems to have been virtually universal throughout the seventeenth century. But this in itself did not drive people to communicate in droves, even though it was at least conducive to promoting the new Christocentric devotions, of which the Eucharist was the core. Not even the fact that the post-Trent mass was probably more inaccessible than previously to laypeople, because of the stricter rules about the use of Latin throughout the service, which culminated in the wholly inaudible consecration of the bread and wine, made people any less willing to attend it. The Council of Trent had strongly reaffirmed, against Protestant criticism, the doctrine of the re-enactment of Christ's sacrifice in the mass and Christ's 'real presence' in the Eucharist. The efforts made to embellish churches and liturgical vestments, the increasing prominence of the main altar and its tabernacle, and the ban on saying other masses simultaneously in side chapels that we noted earlier – all of these were designed to enhance the solemnity and spectacle of the parish mass. Beyond that, however, there was no real encouragement towards any kind of 'union of intention', as it was called, with the priest's actions on the altar until well into the eighteenth century. Despite the enhanced primacy of the priest's mass over the laity's mass, the church did demand that laypeople attempt to grasp the theological core of the sacrifice of the mass, something that had not previously been required of them.[31]

As part of this effort, some of the catechisms diffused during the seventeenth century included questions not just about the mass generally, but also on *how* people should hear the mass, in the sense of which mental dispositions they should bring to it, as well as the prayers, such as the rosary, that they should say while the priest conducted the service. But it seems unlikely that more than a limited proportion of any congregation was capable of such an understanding, especially when they were unable to participate in those parts of the mass (the priest's mass) which were central to the whole event. As in previous generations, they were content to focus their attention on the key elements of the so-called laity's mass – the offerings of candles, bread and alms; the sermon (*prône*); the elevation of the host; the kiss of peace; and the distribution of the *pain bénit* which had been part of the offerings just mentioned.[32] The gap between post-Tridentine expectation and established custom was thus a hard one to close. Clergy frequently complained that parishioners were constantly gossiping and moving around the church during services, which was all the easier given the absence of pews for all but a handful of those in attendance. The parish church may have been a 'sacred' place, but that did not prevent it being treated 'familiarly' – or 'profanely' as contemporary reformers would have claimed – by the parishioners.[33]

It would be easy to imagine, in strict logic, that the average churchgoer had fewer problems with taking communion than with confession and, moreover, that the desire to take communion would itself make it easier to confess one's sins either at Easter or throughout the year. But there are at least two reasons for thinking that this was not so. The first was the inherited attitudes of reverence and worship of the sacrament, attitudes reinforced over the centuries by the growth of the idea of the Eucharist as Christ in person rather than the spiritual 'nourishment' of souls. The evidence for this is widespread, yet easily overlooked. Even later medieval mystics hesitated to take communion, regarding 'spiritual' rather than 'physical' communion at the altar as entirely appropriate. The early confraternities of the Holy Sacrament honoured and venerated the 'real presence' of Christ in the Eucharist, but it took many of them until perhaps the later sixteenth or seventeenth century before they would practise frequent communion of any kind. Devout women often took a similar view, though there are well-attested exceptions of some communicating virtually daily, like Mme Acarie in early seventeenth-century Paris. Secondly, the Catholic Reformation church's methods of emphasising the centrality of the Eucharist did not necessarily bring it closer to ordinary people. The gradual disappearance before 1700 of the *pax vobiscum* ('peace be with you') rite from the mass in France helped shift the emphasis away from any residual participation in, or collective 'ownership' of, the event by the laity. Moreover, the often extremely elaborate arrangements made for conserving, displaying and venerating the sacrament, whether in churches or during processions and the like, served to make it even more 'numinous' than before. The elevation of the bread and wine after the moment of consecration during the mass was calculated to have a similar effect on congregations, who increasingly demanded that the elevation be clearly visible. Many of the new devotions of the Catholic Reformation, such as the Forty Hours', involved saying prayers in the presence of the sacrament in churches. The well-documented obsession with acts of stealing, misusing or defiling the communion wafers that accompanied this development would not have encouraged familiarity with the sacrament for the great majority.

In such a context, the sheer difficulty of successfully preaching the gospel of what Bossy described as the 'asocial mysticism of frequent communion' – or perhaps of combining reverent worship with the intimacy of actually taking communion – should not be underestimated. The great majority of people were content to receive the *pain bénit* that was distributed after the Sunday mass. They would have understood that it was not the Eucharist, but would not necessarily have regarded the *pain bénit* as an inadequate symbol of communion.[34] They were nearly all willing to communicate as required at Easter because that communion was a communal rite rather than an individual act. As we saw with confession, the new religious orders and confraternities embraced head-on the challenge of promoting frequent communion. It should be realised that the inherited notion of 'frequent' communion around 1600 meant communicating somewhere between two and four times per year, usually on a major feast day. Through their schools and sodalities, the Jesuits in particular emerged as the champions of a more intensive version of the practice, building on the growing practice of the first communion among their college students. They recommended communion at least monthly for many people, and weekly for a smaller elite. The more such people frequented the two sacraments, the more likely they were to be taking active spiritual direction from the regular clergy.

As already noted concerning confession, the drive towards frequent communion generated unease among those who took a less instrumental view of the sacraments. Objecters to the approach most associated with the Jesuits claimed that frequent communion and confession were devaluing the sacraments qua sacraments. To Antoine Arnauld, the Jansenists and many others, this approach was tainted with laxism, since frequent confession in particular seemed necessarily to make light of human sinfulness by offering absolution for confessions that could only be perfunctory in their view. This was to ignore completely the discipline – and indeed self-discipline – that the regular practice of the sacraments entailed, in favour of another form of discipline that came from abstaining from the sacraments and preparing oneself for their proper reception when one did take them. This conflict between two opposed views on the same question would seriously divide the French church from the 1640s onwards, sowing uncertainty among the religious groups to which both the Jesuits (and those of their persuasion on the sacraments) and their adversaries were most closely connected. Many bishops and writers of the first half of the next century would claim that the Jansenists had put people off taking communion, by which they meant 'frequent' communion, in contrast with earlier generations. Such historical nostalgia for an age of more frequent communion seems misleading, while the impact of Jansenist-rigorist thinking was probably limited to people from higher social groups. Where it may have had wider effects was when secular parish clergy adopted such thinking and attempted to implement infrequent confession and communion, the deferring of absolution so as to test individuals' commitment, and sometimes the imposition of public penance on sinners. There is also some evidence from parishes where *curés* insisted that adolescents know their catechism by heart that their first communion could be postponed for several years.[35]

Marriage

Of all the sacraments, marriage was by far the most heavily freighted with social, economic and political considerations which threatened to drown out the religious primacy which the post-Trent church was so anxious to develop for it. Until Trent's famous – or notorious – decree *Tametsi*, the sacramental character of marriage was disputed on numerous counts, not the least of which was that its sexual core undermined its religious status; and there were numerous other thorny problems about the freedom of individuals to marry spouses of their choice, as well as about divorce, separation, remarriage and the 'impediments' to marriage arising from degrees of affinity, being in religious orders and so on. It is hardly surprising, therefore, that marriage was on the Council's agenda longer than any other sacrament, and that it defied consensus or resolution until its penultimate session in 1563.[36] Potentially, it was the most treacherous terrain of all should the church's position diverge from those of the civil law and society generally. Such a divergence had already appeared by the 1550s when the French monarchy legislated drastically to limit individuals' freedom to choose their spouses by insisting on the absolute necessity for parental consent up to the age of thirty for male and twenty-five for female children, on pain of nullity. Numerous other back-up restrictions – especially the convenient legal fiction of 'abduction' (*rapt de séduction*) designed to annul and punish unions lacking parental consent – would be added up to the early eighteenth century, ensuring the triumph of the secular law of marriage over the ecclesiastical. As Chancellor Pontchartrain put it in 1712, if there was not a valid marriage contract, there could be no sacrament.[37]

The church's refusal to condemn marriages lacking parental consent, which it regarded as sinful and 'detestable' but nevertheless valid, placed it on a collision course with the monarchy and families, who were more united on this issue in France than anywhere else in Europe at the time.[38] Yet the French clergy, as keepers of marriage registers, were also legally required to uphold royal policy. In the event, the French church found itself with little choice thereafter but to accept royal legislation, which incorporated piecemeal rather than *in extenso* those elements of Trent's legislation that dovetailed with French customs. Paradoxically, this approach, despite gradually undermining the canon law of marriage, ultimately helped to enlarge the religious elements of marriage.[39] It is only possible to consider here a few aspects of this vast topic.

Rather than clashing head-on with the crown and families over the parental control of marriage, the French church concentrated on tackling clandestine marriages by other means, insisting on the publication of marriage banns and the conduct of the wedding in church before the parish priest and in the presence of other witnesses. Strictly speaking, the priest's role was that of a witness, since it was the marrying couple themselves who administered the sacrament, but it suited both the church and the secular authorities that the clergy's role should extend beyond that of a largely passive witness. By the end of the seventeenth century, at least as far as royal legislation was concerned, it would have been hard for the average person *not* to think on seeing and hearing the priest pronounce the words 'I hereby join you together in marriage' that he actually administered this sacrament as he did most of the others. By then, the parish priest kept the registers of marriage, which were the only acceptable legal proof of a valid marriage, while marriages contracted in his absence or before a notary were liable to be declared null and void. By insisting that, as far as possible, marriages occurred in the parish in which one of the future spouses was fully domiciled, both church and monarchy tried to ensure that parishes and their *curés* would be the lynchpins of the system by the final years of Louis XIV.[40]

The post-Trent church tried equally hard to break the widespread habit of cohabitation and sexual relations among engaged couples who traditionally considered the promise to marry as tantamount to marrying. In southern France, it proved possible to eliminate engagement altogether, as it had little popular support. Elsewhere, through the relatively rapid publication of the successive marriage banns and the foreshortening of the period between engagement and marriage, it seems that the church persuaded more and more couples to return to church a few days later for the religious ceremony of marriage itself.[41] The evidence that illegitimacy levels were at a record low for the *ancien régime* during the seventeenth century, despite the increasingly late age of marriage for both men and women, would seem to show that the population largely respected the new dispensation, even to the extent of abstaining, once married, from sexual relations during the penitential seasons of Lent and Advent.[42]

It was no small success to persuade an adult population to marry in a religious 'format', with the local church and priest replacing the tavern and the notary for the occasion. Not that either of the latter really disappeared. The negotiation and signing of marriage contracts before a notary remained widely practised and were decisive for the future household. The tavern or its equivalent also survived clerical efforts to reduce marriage to a 'mere' sacrament and their denunciations of the 'disorderly' counter-culture of post-church wedding celebrations. More than the other sacraments, marriage was chronically susceptible to 'rite-of-passage' customs such as charivari, performed by the young males and designed to ridicule outsiders or older men, especially widowers, who married younger women, and so on. An infinity of practices and beliefs – increasingly denounced by the educated clergy and laity as 'superstition' – flourished, and the folklore surrounding marriage would fill volumes. Not surprisingly, rituals and gestures relating to fertility figured prominently at this key moment of the life cycle, and the biggest fear was that some of them would be hostile towards the couple marrying. The most feared of all were those words or gestures designed to render a marriage childless.[43]

Overcoming and undermining the 'superstitions' surrounding marriage was, as in other spheres, held to depend on success in 'educating' people to consider the sacrament in a new light. This was an extremely tricky task for the post-Tridentine church because of its concomitant and increased emphasis on the superiority of clerical celibacy. Even without this complication, there were other obstacles, such as the traditionally negative clerical view of marriage and the family depicted by Briggs. Because marriage was a condition as well as a specific event, it figured in the wider search for a spirituality for laypeople, which will be considered alongside other forms of spirituality in Chapter 13.

Holy Orders

In principle, marriage and holy orders were mutually exclusive sacraments, except that an unknowable number of widowers drawn from a wide range of social or professional groups continued to take orders during our period. Discussions of the clergy in previous chapters means that it is unnecessary to expatiate further about the sacrament of orders, beyond perhaps underlining how 'peculiar' it was in relation to the others. Apart from its obvious characteristic of being available only to males, it was the sole adults-only sacrament, one for which even a minimum age was specified, so that an individual could easily have received all of the other sacraments before reaching the age stipulated for the priesthood. Moreover, with the exception of those taking it later in life, it was probably the sacrament for which the period of preparation was, in principle, the longest. Trent's stipulation that the tonsure, the first of the orders, should not be taken until the age of fourteen, was only gradually implemented throughout France. A ten-year gap then separated it from full priestly orders, during which the intermediary minor and major orders would be taken; the final ordination thus capped a long, if very unevenly intensive cursus.

It is unnecessary to recall here the efforts made by the seventeenth-century church to form a better-qualified clergy, and we can assume that it took some time for the Berullian ideas about the dignity of the priesthood to reach down into the ranks of the lower clergy. Yet it is worth noting how early such efforts did begin. Alongside the familiar catechisms for different age groups produced throughout French dioceses in our period, we frequently find specially prepared catechisms for those seeking to take the tonsure. No doubt, their main purpose was to ensure the candidates passed the oral examination before the conferring of the order itself, which might coincide with, or follow shortly after, their first communion. The composition and distribution of such catechisms itself testifies to a change of approach to what was increasingly viewed as the first step in the direction of a sacrament whose uniqueness was so regularly exalted in this period. That such cathechisms existed at all reminds us of just how large the number of young tonsured clerics remained in the seventeenth century.

Extreme Unction

It might be expected that, by analogy with the universality of baptism for the newborn, the 'last' sacrament, extreme unction or the sacrament of the dying, would be equally in demand in a society which so strongly highlighted the moment of death. But it has to be said that extreme unction, the final anointing of the dying person, enjoyed a thin and ambiguous role among the last moments of early modern Catholics. The whole 'culture' of dying was too multifaceted to be absorbed into one sacramental rite that would be the equivalent to baptism for birth. The problem was partly that extreme unction was normally accompanied by two other sacraments, penance and communion; they could already be regarded as more than sufficient preparation for a good death, thus leaving extreme unction as possibly little more than an optional reinforcement of the other two.

Theologians, manuals of advice and local practices differed over the sequence in which communion and extreme unction should be administered: some felt that communion should be reserved until last because it was the true culmination of the effort to 'die well', while others took literally the idea that extreme unction was the last of the sacraments. It is possible that these differences of approach, which are well documented across seventeenth-century France, were themselves influenced by contemporary attitudes towards the purpose and implications of the sacrament. Belief in the therapeutic capacity of the sacramental rite, which included anointing parts of the body, to heal the sick had declined over the centuries, and such a belief was not encouraged by the church authorities. More problematic still was the widely held view that summoning a priest to administer the last rites was tantamount to summoning death itself, so that instead of being a beneficent 'extra' sacrament after confession and communion, it was perceived – and therefore feared – as final and life-ending. Beyond that lay the perhaps even greater fear that once these final rites had been administered, the dying person would be abandoned by those who had supported them up to then with their presence and prayers.[44]

Relatively little is known about the actual practice of the sacrament. It appears to have been largely ignored in sixteenth- and early seventeenth-century France, and the church authorities were its main promoters thereafter.[45] How far they succeeded in the face of inherited lay attitudes is much more difficult to say. The taking of the Eucharist from parish churches to the sick in their homes was obviously common enough for members of certain confraternities, and even of the famous Company of the Holy Sacrament, to accompany the priest to and from the church. But to what extent the sick or the dying merely confessed and took communion but declined the last rites is impossible to gauge; it seems likely that only those whose condition was judged utterly hopeless did so.

However, the fact that the sacrament of the dying did not quite fulfil the role assigned to it should not lead us to forget the scope of the religious culture surrounding death. The forms that it took, both approved and 'superstitious', were numerous, but only a small number of directly relevant points can be discussed here. The act of making one's last will and testament – 'a magnificent thermometer of religious fervour' (Chaunu) – was not always left to the last minute, although very frequently those making them were described as sick and bed-bound, so that their first clause invariably refers to the uncertainty of the hour of death. French historians have ingeniously mined this almost inexhaustible source for evidence of attitudes to death and the shifts that they underwent.[46] First of all, the making of a will remained a religious act of major significance throughout our period, one which always began with a familiar – one might even say 'ritual' – invocation of God and the saints to help the testator to secure his or her salvation. However formulaic these expressions may sound, the choice of formula was the testator's and not that of the priest or, increasingly, the notary who drafted the text of the will. But this preamble was not the only religious dimension of wills: until well into the eighteenth century, testators invariably assigned legacies for the saying of masses for their salvation, establishing 'foundations' for good works, leaving money to the poor, the religious orders or the local parish church, to mention only the most common ones. It is no exaggeration to say that without the last testaments of millions of people, the huge superstructure of religious services, notably masses for the dead, and the large population of clergy, male and female, would have been deprived of the financial oxygen indispensable to their survival.[47]

Since the later Middle Ages, Catholicism had developed the idea of a 'good death' that could and had to be prepared for, so that one died in a state of grace, shriven of one's sins.[48] This happy ending was open to hardened sinners who experienced a death-bed 'conversion' and repented sincerely of their sins, yet might elude those who normally lived as 'good' Christians but were unfortunate enough to be in a state of sin at the moment of death. Dying was, therefore, widely viewed as the 'moment' when one's eternal destiny was decided, as one's previous behaviour was no guarantee of the outcome; for that reason, too, it was the moment when the devil and his agents were held to besiege and beguile people into making the wrong decisions. The bed or the room of a dying person was thus a battlefield in which the forces of good would normally triumph, but it was also one where, in keeping with the Catholic theology of free will and good works, the dying individual's own contribution was crucial to the very end. An extensive literature on 'dying well' already existed, to which significant additions, in both quality and quantity, were made during the seventeenth century.[49] Classics of the genre such as Crasset's *Sweet and Holy Death* and his *Guiding Angel* ran through dozens of editions, and between roughly 1600 and 1725 approximately 200 new titles on the subject were published. The iconography, both old and new, of churches, chapels, confraternities and books of devotion ensured that a similar message was diffused by as many media as possible.

Given the high stakes involved, it was essential that the dying should not be left to face the wiles of Satan alone. It was also essential that a good death be witnessed by the living, especially one's family and acquaintances: it would not only 'fortify and console' them, but it would also perpetuate the religious message that a good death represented. Hence, too, the continuing circulation of exemplary narratives of the last moments of figures as elevated as Louis XIII or even Louis XIV, forgiving their enemies, giving advice to their successors, blessing individual family members and so on. This kind of death scene, regardless of one's rank or reputation, was one in which the dying were fully conscious of the approach of death which would have to wait until they finished their leave-taking and final prayers. *Et tibi, Domine.* It seems that it was not until the eighteenth century that the practice of leaving the dying person entirely alone during their last minutes of life came into vogue.

After and, ideally, during one's last moments, the presence of members of local confraternities, to which the dying person might belong, was also greatly desired. For some confraternities like the Norman 'charities' and those of the Holy Ghost, such assistance, followed by participation in the funeral services, were their principal activities. Not surprisingly, the Catholic Reformation church witnessed a new wave of such activity, increasing the number of groups focused on the 'last things'. Members of the new confraternity of the *Agonisants* were expected to inform the *curé* and go to their local church on learning that one of their number was dying and to offer their prayers before the Eucharist exposed on the main altar; those who could not do so were asked to pray in their houses or places of work. Alongside them there developed a later confraternity with a confusingly similar title, that of the Good Death or the Agony of Jesus, which was launched in mid-seventeenth-century Rome by the Jesuits and which gradually spread to France over the following century. Although, strictly speaking, it was more a loose 'association' of individual devotion than a confraternity with collective obligations like the *Agonisants*, its members were chiefly expected to prepare, on a daily basis, for their own good death! Here, collective solidarity in the face of death gave way to the challenge of death as it affected individuals, but such a highly spiritualised and self-conscious approach to dying was reserved for a minority, so that the confraternity's appeal only grew rather gradually before the early decades of the eighteenth century. Not altogether surprisingly, the patron saint of these confraternities was St Joseph, the model intercessor-saint rather than the wonder-working saint.[50]

Needless to say, for a rite of passage as important as dying, there were innumerable customs and practices that even the most 'creative' church could not quite control or 'baptise'. This was partly because most of the arrangements for burial were made by individuals themselves before death, especially in their testaments. In the age of ostentatious 'baroque piety', which lasted until well into the eighteenth century, this could mean specifying in great detail the kind of church furnishings one desired, the number and weight of candles to be used, how many priests or poor of the parish should accompany one's coffin to the grave, how they should be dressed and paid for their pains and so on. Families and descendants could go beyond the strict letter of a will in organising burials, and there is evidence to suggest that testamentary requests for modest, unspectacular funerals could be simply ignored. Death, like birth and marriage, was also an occasion to display family status. What occurred in churches and graveyards could be controlled to some extent by the clergy, but many other customs regarding death escaped them entirely. Among the most visible were the 'wakes' and post-funeral banquets: they were so widespread that uprooting them seemed both impossible and inadvisable. Popular views of the continuing presence of the dead among the living – as *revenants*, ghosts and so on – remained so powerfully entrenched, especially in rural societies, that myriad 'folkloric' practices flourished on, or beyond, the margins of ordinary religious life, increasingly denounced as the century progressed for their paganism and superstition.[51]

Finally, there were also regions of France where the cult of the dead was far more deeply embedded in social life than elsewhere, particularly in Lower Brittany and certain upland areas of the centre and the south-west. In the latter regions, the cult of the dead was clan and family-based, and was probably an ancestor cult as well. Because it had its own parish-born *habitué* clergy to say the masses for the dead, which were financed by foundations, testamentary or otherwise, provided by the families, this kind of cult could survive intact for as long as the social demand for it was there.[52] In Lower Brittany, the cult of the dead was such that virtually everyone demanded to be buried in church and, as a result, it was necessary periodically to remove the bones to an ossuary inside, and sometimes outside, of the church. This familiarity with the dead, with heaven and hell, was used effectively by the seventeenth-century missionaries themselves.[53]

Conclusion

The extensive attempts made in post-Tridentine France to promote the sacraments to a central place within religious practices was to achieve highly uneven results. Thinking of the sacraments as a streamlined 'system' can all too easily obscure how much they differed from each other and, consequently, how rates of success and failure were always likely to vary. The effort to distinguish them as clearly as possible from other signs, gestures and symbols risked placing them beyond the comprehension of ordinary mortals, as the taking of the *pain bénit* rather than communion suggests. Historically, the liturgical calendar with its Sundays and saints' days was not impregnated by the sacraments, the most common of which (baptism, marriage, extreme unction in particular) were not tied to particular times or holidays of the year at all. This, in turn, suggests how difficult it might be to impose a 'sacramental' revolution which, if successful, would have effectively downgraded the saints and their works. A great deal depended upon the ability of the clergy to rise to the challenge of inculcating a new sacramental culture that demanded a minimum of knowledge and understanding, but it also entailed a high level of lay willingness and involvement. Like Europe's post-Reformation churches everywhere, that of seventeenth-century France was increasingly conscious of the need to combine old and new methods, from preaching in its several formats and missions to catechetical practice and schooling, in order to turn church-goers into believers with some grasp of the key teachings of Catholicism.

CHAPTER 12

RELIGION TAUGHT AND LEARNED

Introduction

One of the most enduring challenges posed by the religious upheavals of the sixteenth century to all of Europe's churches was to ensure that their members acquired an understanding of the essentials of their religious beliefs and practices. Some elements of the challenge itself and the French church's response to it have already surfaced, albeit obliquely, in previous chapters. This chapter will consider some of the major ways in which the French church met the challenge of educating its members. Although the discussion will fall under headings such as preaching, missions, catechism and schooling, it should be realised that these terms disguise a good deal of overlap and mutual interaction. For example, preaching was itself reshaped in part by developments such as missions and catechism, while missions themselves increasingly involved both preaching and catechism. And schooling may be regarded as the ultimate extension of all of these endeavours, even if the history of schooling in our period has other dimensions not necessarily connected to religious priorities. It is also worth adding that some older methods of communicating religious knowledge were squeezed out by developments of our period. A good example was the religious plays that had flourished during the later Middle Ages. Increasingly regarded as an unacceptable mixture of the sacred and the profane, they were either suppressed or, especially during missions, replaced by more recent and edifying models. Not everything from the medieval past was so sacred that it had to be preserved against innovation and critique.

The conviction that to be a true Christian required individuals to have knowledge of their religion, and not merely to 'live' it through ritual and routine action, was fundamental to all of the post-Reformation churches. It had already been gaining ground through the works and writings of later medieval and humanist writers, from Gerson to Erasmus, but Luther, Calvin and their contemporaries 'canonised' it by insisting that some explicit knowledge of revealed truths rather than an implicit faith (believing in what the church believes and asks one to believe) was required of all Christians. The concomitant 'discovery' of popular ignorance goes back at least to the age of Erasmus and the 'pre-Reformers', and it is significant that it was specifically religious ignorance which appalled them. A century later, French Catholic reformers were making the same discovery all over again, with Vincent de Paul declaring in 1625 that 'there are 10,000 priests in Paris but the poor of the countryside are lost in the most frightful ignorance'. The Protestant reformers had already been tackling the problem, using methods that would be partially copied later by the old church, but all too often they found that their attempts to create a 'godly' people were stymied by popular indifference and ignorance. Of course, the new churches were attempting to go further than the medieval church had ever envisaged: they wanted congregations to be literate and learned enough to read, understand and meditate on the Bible; they measured success and failure by new rather than by older standards.[1] But it was not a matter of simply replacing a *tabula rasa* of 'pure' ignorance with sound knowledge, since reformers of every stripe constantly railed against a more elusive and subtle enemy, namely 'superstition'.

In responding to the challenge, the old church found itself constrained, here as elsewhere, by the options already taken by the emerging Protestant churches. In particular, it was not willing to jettison the liturgical and sacramental core of traditional religious worship, and to replace it with the proclamation of the word of God through readings from the Scriptures and preaching. As in other spheres, the difficulty was to respond positively to the Protestant challenge without seeming to concede the correctness of the opposing position. This dilemma was well reflected in the debates and decisions of the Council of Trent, which as early as 1546 reiterated the duty of bishops to preach themselves, and to have preached, the 'holy gospel of Jesus Christ', while clergy with cure of souls were obliged to 'feed the people committed to them with wholesome words in proportion to their own and their people's mental capacity, by teaching them those things that are necessary for all to know in order to be saved, and by impressing upon them with briefness and plainness of speech the vices that they must avoid and the virtues that they must cultivate' for their salvation.[2] These were cautious, carefully chosen words, and they did not envisage major shifts of emphasis within Catholicism. Nor did the *Catechism of the Council of Trent for the Use of Parish Priests* (translated into French in 1567 as the *Catéchisme aux curés*) when it was finally completed in 1566. As its full title hints, it was neither a guide for preachers nor a catechism in the conventional sense, but rather a pastoral manual for priests in the conduct of the cure of souls generally. Not surprisingly, this was the reason why church authorities would insist, in France and elsewhere, that every parish priest should have a copy of it, but it was only a modest step towards the broader tasks that awaited them. As we shall see presently, it would take some time and no small amount of experiment before the catechism could be defined in simple terms as 'a little book which contains, in the form of questions and answers, a summary of the Christian religion'.

Preaching

Meanwhile the time-honoured method of proclaiming the gospel and its practical consequences was preaching. It took many forms, depending on who was preaching and in what circumstances. Although bishops were formally responsible for its provision, there is little indication that up to the sixteenth century France's bishops discharged this particular duty any better than their counterparts elsewhere in Europe, especially if we are to believe the quip that bishops who preached were as rare as flying donkeys. Yet by the 1620s papal nuncios to France were reporting on their 'considerable ability' as preachers. This particular reputation was probably based on sermons preached by bishops at court or in Parisian churches, especially during assemblies of clergy, when the opportunities for them to preach were frequent. It is possible that the challenges of the wars of religion and the Catholic League drove more bishops to preach in person, and that this was sustained into the post-war decades. Quite how widely they preached in their own cathedral churches or dioceses is another matter, and the ability to preach did not necessarily lead them to do so at every obvious opportunity. There are innumerable instances of episcopal preaching during pastoral visitations but, equally, many bishops preferred to leave that task to members of their entourage. That some of the most admired of seventeenth-century bishops, such as François de Sales or Jean-Pierre Camus, were eminent preachers, and that each generation of bishops, from Cardinal du Perron and Nicolas Coëffeteau in the early seventeenth century to Bossuet and Massillon nearly a century later, included some of France's best-known preachers *tout court*, was certainly instrumental in keeping the French church aware of the ministry of the word, and it no doubt encouraged younger clergy to develop oratorical skills that might one day raise them to the higher ranks of the church. In his memoirs, the abbé Le Gendre recounts his own brief efforts to compete with the best preachers after his arrival in Paris in the 1670s, only for the sheer strength of the competition to persuade him to abandon his efforts at making a career by that route.[3]

However, in its most common forms and for the population generally, preaching was for centuries a virtual monopoly of the religious orders, especially the Dominicans and Franciscans, whose many sixteenth- and seventeenth-century successors among the mendicants and secular congregations perpetuated and expanded that tradition. Significantly, the preaching talents of individual mendicants were often decisive in persuading individual towns to allow them to found a house within their walls. They preached primarily in their own (mainly urban) churches, where they attracted many of the local elite in search of something more than what their parish churches could offer. But historically, preachers from the orders were also the most itinerant, often attracting large crowds as they moved across entire regions. The preparation, intellectual and practical, that they received in their own houses of study made them superior to all but a small section of the secular clergy in key areas of pastoral action – confession, the sacraments and preaching. The most active order houses had individual members whose prime task was to preach. This enabled them to dominate the 'best' preaching stations in late seventeenth-century Paris, a constant which competition from individual members of the secular clergy should not obscure; and the imbalance was probably greater still in provincial cities and middling-sized towns. But throughout French towns generally, it was the regulars who dominated the pulpits during the penitential seasons – unless there was a local university that produced 'secular' theology graduates capable of competing with them.[4]

Their dominance became more visible when it came to the two 'high' penitential seasons of the year, Lent and Advent, when many urban churches employed – and paid for – special preachers who would mount the pulpit several times per week and draw large daily attendances. However much the seventeenth-century church might attempt to diffuse preaching throughout the year, there was no question of scaling back Lent and Advent, both of which were deeply embedded in the religious calendar and popular psychology.[5] There was undoubtedly much mutual rivalry and competition between urban churches and the religious orders themselves when choosing Lenten or Advent preachers, and as the seventeenth century wore on, churches may also have selected preachers who reflected their own preferences for either Jesuit or the more rigorist, sometimes philo-Jansenist, pastoral theology. Churchwardens, parish priests and even local bishops all took a close interest in the choice of preachers and jockeyed to have the decisive voice in selecting them. Both the ecclesiastical and political authorities were keen to control preaching, given the experiences of the sixteenth century, when preachers could either propagate heterodox religious teaching or launch into politically dangerous onslaughts against the crown, especially during the Catholic League.[6] If Paris – where the number of churches there offering a full Advent and Lent preaching 'programme' *doubled* from the early 1630s to the early 1650s – is any guide, then those towns which had experienced the 'invasion of the convents', male and, to a lesser degree, female, since 1600, saw a corresponding rise in such 'seasonal' preaching.[7] How far these practices penetrated beyond the towns in question is by no means easy to say, and it is risky to generalise from just a few instances where it did happen. The towns, villages and some rural parishes of Auxerre diocese regularly experienced such Advent and Lenten preaching throughout the seventeenth century, when the Dominicans and the Franciscans were the most prominent preachers.[8] Almost inevitably, the rural areas scored less well than the urban ones, with such preaching occurring perhaps every second or third year rather than annually, depending essentially on the funds available to them from pious bequests.

As this suggests, perhaps the biggest challenge of all was how to ensure that the parish clergy of small-town and rural France would 'preach' in one form or another. It was here that objective need was greatest, and the capacity to meet it at its lowest. Given the local clergy's own often minimal educational and pastoral abilities, improvement would only come very slowly; it was, after all, a genuine shock for the ecclesiastical system to discover that preaching was an obligation for all those with cure of souls, and not just the business of outsider 'professionals' like the mendicants. By custom, priests celebrating the main mass on Sundays and some feast days were expected to 'interrupt' the mass proper to conduct the *prône*, which one bishop defined in 1706 as 'an explanation in simple language of the gospel text of the day or of some point of Christian morality, for the instruction and edification of the people'. This definition, while increasingly true for the early eighteenth century, was an inaccurate account of historical practice: while the *prône* could include a sermon of some kind, it had long served primarily as a 'hold-all' that enabled the political, seigneurial and ecclesiastical authorities of the day to communicate their demands to the assembled parishioners; there was no other forum of any kind that was remotely as convenient for such purposes. So during the average *prône* priests might issue announcements and denunciations of a truly bewildering variety, from the record of village assembly meetings, marriage banns, excommunications for debt or non-payment of tithe to threats of excommunication for failure to reveal information about offenders or crimes; they also notified parishioners of royal decrees, seigneurial ordinances and other village events. The religious events announced might include visitations, the conferment of the sacrament of confirmation, the start of a mission and many other items. It was during the *prône* that the clergy were also instructed to read chapters from the synodal statutes, as well as to recite the Credo, the Pater, the Ave Maria, various 'bidding' prayers and so on, all of which were accepted until the seventeenth century as the normal form of religious instruction. Synods had long exhorted priests not just to read the key credal statements or prayers, but also to comment upon and explain them to their parishioners. However, actual expectations were so limited in this regard that synods went on to recommend priests simply to read out sections from 'canonical' pastoral works like Gerson's famous *Opus tripartitum*, so called because it was a commentary on the Ten Commandments, how to confess one's sins and how to die as a good Christian. And for a long time, this was all that many seventeenth-century *curés* were capable of doing.

The untidy clutter that was the *prône* was thus hardly a promising format for the development of parochial preaching. With this in mind, the seventeenth-century church tried to purge it of the non-religious elements that had invaded it over the centuries, but progress was slow and it was not until the royal edict of 1695 that secular matters were, in principle at least, excluded from it altogether.[9] By then a younger generation of parish priests capable of basic preaching was settling into rural parishes, but there were probably many areas which would have to wait longer still to hear their *curé* actually preach. The fact that some bishops were still issuing directives for the conduct of the *prône* in the latter decades of Louis XIV's reign is a clear sign that many parish priests were still unable to do any better. Even a *curé* as conscientious as the prior of Sennely-en-Sologne, Christophe Sauvageon, confessed that he alternated between reading the *prône* and delivering his own sermons on successive Sundays, but he said nothing of other holidays.[10]

In the meantime, huge efforts were made to provide Sauvageon and other clergy with the raw materials for even a basic *prône*-cum-commentary on the gospel text of the day, the credo and other prayers. As a result of visiting parishes in the vast diocese of Rouen, the ever-prolific episcopal author, Jean-Pierre Camus, composed five volumes of *Prosnes* in 1649–50, each with a different set of scriptural texts. The first volume consisted of 'parish *prônes* for every Sunday of the year', plus one general *prône*. He recommended them to Rouen *curés* as containing more solid doctrinal nourishment than most of the heavily rhetorical sermons of his time, adding that *prônes* should be in 'a popular style, clear and understandable to the less intelligent'.[11] Camus and his contemporaries composed equivalent texts for use in more 'advanced' forms of preaching, with model sermons, sometimes 'themed' in particular ways, being published in huge numbers throughout the century. It was certainly not because of the absence of such carefully pre-packaged materials that *curés* failed to preach to their flocks. We saw in an earlier chapter how, by the mid-1690s, Bishop Le Peletier of Angers was planning to compel his *curés* to present the drafts of their sermons to him for scrutiny during visitations. As seminaries slowly began to develop beyond immediate preparation for orders, they attempted to educate future clergy in the basics of preaching, even organising practice sessions where seminarians preached to each other. But all of this was slow to bear fruit, and it seems certain that many of the pulpits installed in seventeenth-century churches did not suffer from overuse. Rural parishioners' experience of preaching in many areas would have been largely limited to the occasional itinerant preacher, and to sermons delivered either during pastoral visitations or, in more heavily concentrated doses, during a new-style mission. None of these would have been frequent or prolonged.

Of the various reasons for the reluctance of *curés* to preach to their parishioners one deserves brief notice, as it may come as something of a surprise. It concerns the language of communication itself. Whereas bishops and church legislation generally insisted on the need to communicate in the local dialect, there is some evidence that parish priests could take this amiss. Ordinary daily communication in patois, even for something like the catechism, might be acceptable to them, but preaching was a different matter: in some areas of France, to preach in patois was to endure cultural *déclassement*, and that was a prospect at which many *curés*, who identified themselves with the French-speaking social elites, blenched. The 'syndicate' of opposition priests in Cahors diocese in the 1640s and 1650s demanded the right to preach in French as part of their campaign against Bishop Solminihac, who was insisting that they use patois.[12] By contrast, in places like Brittany and Béarn, where the local vernacular was regarded as something more than mere patois, that reluctance seems to have been largely absent.

Missions

Missions, in the sense of intensive preaching in a particular place, lasting from several days to several weeks, were not an invention of the Catholic Reformation; it refashioned and considerably expanded something that already existed in a more limited form. Late medieval France had witnessed celebrated 'missioners', some of whom were not French or French-speaking at all, operating across wide areas, but they had worked largely on their own, delivering rousing sermons to huge audiences attracted by their often theatrical modus operandi. During the wars of religion, many localities were 'worked over' by inflammatory preachers emphasising confrontation with heresy rather than religious renewal, an experience which rendered uncontrolled preaching so unpalatable to the Catholic Reformation church. Yet the contrast between seventeenth-century developments and earlier periods should not be exaggerated, not least because Advent and especially Lenten preaching remained as much in demand as ever. Moreover, Lenten preaching, for example, already contained some elements of what would later become commonplace during missions, notably catechetical instruction.[13] At the risk of simplification, one might characterise the change as a gradual transition from instruction to conversion, even though such a lapidary formula cannot convey a full sense of the developments in the practice of missions.[14]

By the later sixteenth and early seventeenth century, the Jesuits and other new orders had begun to commit themselves to introducing into France the kinds of missionary strategies that they had been developing elsewhere in Europe, notably in Italy, and which involved whole groups of preachers undertaking lengthy campaigns not just of preaching, but of catechising and confessing in particular areas for a predetermined period of time.[15] This approach was, as we shall see, still evolving throughout the seventeenth century, the end result of which was a substantial distinction between 'ordinary' preaching and missionary work by around mid-century. The heroic, itinerant missionary of a previous age did not disappear overnight, however, and he could still attract large crowds. Some famous 'transitional' figures like the Jesuit, Jean-François Régis (d.1640), were both old-fashioned itinerant preachers and new-style missionaries. Significantly, by the 1630s the Jesuits themselves were distinguishing 'missionaries' from 'preachers' among their own members. A major practitioner of new-style missions, Jean Eudes (1601–80), was at pains to separate his Lenten preaching from the missions that he conducted *during* the Lenten season.[16]

Like preaching, missionary work was initially the preserve of the religious orders and congregations, especially the new ones. It was they who first developed and refined the methods and the objectives of their missions. This was due in part to the fact that missions were regarded as integral to the religious lives of their members who devoted themselves to such activity, so that mission work became part of their order's spirituality. The Jesuit superior-general, Claudio Aquaviva (1581–1615), went out of his way to make missionary activity central to the order's self-understanding, constantly recalling the 'pilgrim' motif associated with Ignatius Loyola. This internal, top-down pressure coincided with the early stages of the Jesuits' settlement in France and, even more crucially, with their return, in 1603, to central and northern France after nearly a decade of exile (1594–1603). More to the point, it ensured that the French Jesuits would not abandon missionary work for colleges and other activities. It soon led them to found special 'mission' houses in certain towns, especially in the 1610s and 1620s, and to take measures so that most members of their other houses would participate in missionary work at some time during the average year.[17] The Jesuits' greatest and earliest 'rivals' in this field were the Capuchins who arrived in France in the mid-1570s and grew rapidly in numbers and activities thereafter. Their approach to missionary activity was, like their overall image, more demotic than that of the Jesuits, who were more reserved about popular religious practices, and who therefore placed more emphasis on religious instruction during missions. The Capuchins did not ignore such considerations, but tried to build upon existing forms of popular piety, and organised new manifestations of it, such as special processions, devotions like the Forty Hours' and so on. Needless to say, other orders would evolve a missionary style of their own, with a considerable amount of imitation and cross-fertilisation.[18]

One of the most noteworthy developments in these new-style missions was that from the early 1610s onwards they attracted groups rather than isolated members of the secular clergy, many of which would later go on to form congregations dedicated in part to missionary work. The mission preached at Brou in Chartres diocese in 1615 by Adrien Bourdoise and the priests of Saint-Nicolas-du-Chardonnet in Paris is often regarded as a turning point, not simply for the community of Saint-Nicolas itself, but for the conduct of missions of this type. Bourdoise mobilised for the 'campaign' between thirty and ninety clerics – depending on which account one is to believe – among whom were several doctors of the Paris theology faculty. Like so many other missionaries of the age, they saw themselves as going into battle as God's militia fighting the legions of Satan.[19] Not for the last time, the mission revealed the severe pastoral needs of the rural populations and, equally, the urgency of improving the calibre of their parish clergy themselves. For this reason, too, missions developed into more than purely preaching exercises, as they attempted to combat clerical inadequacy and the popular ignorance that was its logical consequence.

Such a context makes it is easier to understand how a group of secular clergy could emerge, only a decade after the 1615 mission, calling itself the Congregation of the *Mission*. Founded by Vincent de Paul, it was destined to expand, numerically and geographically, at an impressive pace over the next half-century.[20] Above all, their foundation charter stipulated that they should avoid preaching in towns, except in cases of real necessity, and focus on rural districts.[21] The Lazarists, as they were called, were also dedicated to creating a new kind of pastorally capable priesthood, particularly in the severely neglected countryside. Indeed, this last was one of the key objectives of the new French secular congregations involved in missionary work of this kind, and is a major distinguishing factor between the new missions and the conventional Advent and Lenten preaching. As might be expected, there were numerous differences of approach and expectation. The experience of Bérulle's Oratory here is symptomatic, given its underlying objective of reforming the secular clergy. Many of its members engaged in missions, and one of them, Jean Lejeune, was among the most famous of all French 'interior' missionaries of the entire seventeenth century.[22] For a time, during the 1640s and 1650s, its superior-general, François Bourgoing, laid great stress on the importance of missions. But in subsequent decades missions were again considered to be just one of several activities that Oratorians engaged in, one that did not deserve to take precedence over the formation of a new clergy. This shifting attitude was possibly one reason why figures as diverse as de Paul, Jean Eudes and Jean-Jacques Olier, all of whom were heavily influenced by the Oratory (or, in the case of Eudes, were former members of it), decided to branch out and found their own congregations.[23] By the 1650s, the secular congregations, many of them highly local in origin and range, were as widely active in missions as the regulars, and their concern with improving the local clergy gradually added a distinctive pastoral dimension to the missions.[24]

For the new-style missions and those conducting them, preaching itself became a means to an end, which was to convince people of the urgent need to change their ways and, specifically, to confess their sins individually and take communion; but for that to happen, some prior instruction in the form of catechism was considered essential. This approach, which depended on a combination of activities shared out among different members of a missionary 'team', ultimately sought to get to grips with individual consciences via the confessional. In that sense they contrasted with the preaching campaigns of a previous age, which were directed at the congregation as a whole, whose members would collectively repent of their sins. Limited in time and extension, the new missions constituted dramatic interruptions within the normal religious calendar, when a parish and its clergy found themselves briefly taken over by outsiders and subjected to unprecedented pressure, of which preaching was only one element. Although no longer an end in itself, preaching remained no less vital for all that, since its objective was to trigger repentance and conversion of a personal kind. The more missions were conducted in rural areas, the more the preachers realised that they had to adjust their style and content for a very different audience to that of the larger towns and cities. Vincent de Paul, in particular, insisted on sermons that were 'simple and plain', like those of the apostles, shunning the elaborate rhetoric employed by preachers in other circumstances.[25] It is less clear how many missionaries followed the example of the famous Julien Maunoir who learned Breton in order to preach to the parishes of Lower Brittany.

During the average mission, sermons were usually preached twice daily, early morning and evening, so as to enable as many people as possible to attend, and they focused largely on 'the four last things', in order virtually to shock listeners into realising the urgency of responding to God's grace, which the mission was instrumental in bringing to them. 'Fire and brimstone' preaching may not have been invented for missions, but it certainly flourished during them, particularly in rural areas, where missionaries clearly felt the need to challenge people via their senses, and to implant in them a fear of divine retribution. Preachers used their imagination, sometimes to excess, to conjure up for their listeners the terrible prospect of eternal damnation and punishment, and the urgency of preventitive action. Not surprisingly, many missionaries developed shock techniques in order to move their listeners, and they used whatever aids – a skull, representations of hellfire, evocations of the physical presence and evil powers of Satan and so on – that would achieve their goal. But the prowess of the mission preacher was henceforth judged less by his congregation's weeping and lamentation than by the number of people confessing their sins and taking communion by the end of the mission. It is this spectacle of people waiting in their dozens or hundreds to be shriven which dominates the accounts that contemporaries – beginning with the missionaries themselves – wrote of missions, in which the real 'heroes' were the often exhausted confessors rather than the preachers.[26]

But there was an important intermediate station between preaching and confession, and that was instruction, usually in the form of catechism of one kind or another – a subject that will be explored further later in this chapter. The ignorance of sin that the missionaries deplored among the mass of the population was regarded as an emanation of an equally deplorable ignorance of the key doctrines of the church. By definition, ignorance of sin was an invincible obstacle to a true confession, and it could only be overcome by intensive indoctrination. Consequently, different types of catechism 'classes' were organised during each day of a mission to provide adults and children who had already taken, or who were about to take, their first communion, with the kind of knowledge that would enable them to conduct an examination of their consciences, itemise and confess their sins, and reply to the questions asked of them by the confessors. So memory techniques, songs and the like were devised to facilitate the indoctrination process. Canticles, often sung to familiar 'profane' airs, were widely used to facilitate the memorisation of basic doctrinal and moral principles. Obviously, a great deal depended on the length of individual missions, and it is not hard to imagine how superficial their catechetical achievements could be.

The psychological pressure on those attending missions must have been considerable, since they were also strongly encouraged to engage in a 'general' confession of their sins, on the grounds that previous confessions, made in a state of ignorance of what really constituted sin, were of dubious value. Despite such a fearsome prospect, it seems that large numbers of people accepted the demands of the confessional and proved more willing to avow their worst faults to confessors who were migratory outsiders than to their own resident clergy. Social conformity undoubtedly exercised its own pressure on individuals, but it also helped that the missionaries, especially those belonging to the religious orders, were able to offer indulgences to those who followed the mission to its logical penitential as well as sacramental conclusion. The reconciliation of enemies and the ending of feuds, often within families, was another task that missionaries set themselves. Reporting on the missions conducted around Maubeuge in 1664 which had led to 4,800 general confessions, the Jesuits claimed that 800 families had been reconciled and peace was restored within 250 marriages.[27] Whatever the accuracy of the figures themselves, they are evidence that missions like this were not so focused on terrifying individuals into compliance that they were blind to the social fabric of religious life, but were capable of developing a pastoral style that could combine social pacification with individual repentance born out of fear of damnation. A successful mission would end with a day of general communion, a procession, the planting of a cross or, in some places, the renewal of baptismal vows to cleave to God and to avoid Satan, the great enemy of all Christians. Such events brought a kind of collective 'closure' to an experience that was both highly unusual and potentially unsettling for large numbers of communities across France.

No account of the format of an 'average' mission can presume to cover the enormous variations in actual missions across France or the changes that occurred in their format across the century. A great deal depended on the duration of a mission: from four days to four weeks, the efforts and the results were clearly not the same. The Jesuits and the Oratorians, for example, placed more emphasis on instruction than on conversion and confession, although these were by no means neglected, while the Capuchins organised collective expressions of popular piety such as processions to achieve their aims. Beyond these particular emphases, however, there was at least one major point on which all missionaries were in agreement. They were realistic enough to accept that the 'afterglow' of a mission would not last indefinitely – after all, nobody could say when a particular parish might have its next mission – so they gave some thought to establishing practices or institutions that would help to perpetuate its effects and, indeed, the memory of the mission itself as a time of grace. In this way, the internal dynamic that was already present during the average mission – towards conversion and confession, the reconciliation of enemies and so on – could be extended beyond the end of the mission itself.

The most obvious success would be to persuade an individual or a family to endow a mission for future years, but this was more a wish than a practical objective for departing missionaries; and it might also seem much less urgent in parishes which already had a Lenten or Advent preaching endowment. The establishment of catechism classes, especially for children, the proper respect for Sundays and feast days and so on, were more realistic aims. Perhaps the most important legacy of a mission was the foundation of a new parish confraternity, sometimes regardless of whether other confraternities already existed there.[28] These confraternities were designed to perpetuate the devotions with which the clergy, especially the regulars, who conducted the mission in question, were themselves most closely associated. Where the Capuchins introduced the so-called Forty Hours' devotion to the Holy Sacrament, a confraternity of the Holy Sacrament was the most likely outcome. Other groups founded confraternities of charity, the Rosary, the Sacred Heart and so on. These confraternities were also meant to bring together the *dévots* of the parish, female as well as male, in the expectation that they would prolong the religious revival inaugurated by the mission. Lazarist missionaries had standing instructions to found a confraternity of charity, consisting exclusively of women willing to offer spiritual and material assistance to fellow parishioners. For them and the other secular congregations, as we have seen, missions were also consciously devoted to improving the local clergy *in situ*, so yet another objective was the perpetuation of the ecclesiastical conferences that were often improvised during the mission for the further reform and education of the parish clergy.

From their early days, French missions entailed confrontation and controversy with the Huguenots, and this legacy continued into the seventeenth century. Even before the Roman *Propaganda Fide* (1622) set about organising such missions across Europe, the French Capuchins, led by the famous Père Joseph, conducted a large-scale mission in Poitou, a major area of Protestant settlement (1617). Despite that, French missions to Protestant areas tended overwhelmingly to avoid direct engagement with the Protestants themselves with a view to converting them, and focused instead on fortifying the local Catholic populations. However admired he might be in other ways, François de Sales's celebrated endeavours to convert the Protestants of the Chablais region were not a model that French bishops or missionaries particularly wished to follow. Vincent de Paul took this position to its logical conclusion by actually forbidding his Lazarists from engaging in 'controversial' missions (those which involved disputations with Huguenot pastors) and many of the new congregations followed the same line. The very low levels of success in converting Protestants when the latter were not simultaneously under heavy pressure, military or political, doubtless facilitated the decision to leave that problem to be dealt with by other means, yet the Protestant presence meant that the Catholic populations of these internal 'frontiers of Catholicity' probably experienced more missions than the other regions of France.[29]

For obvious reasons, however, missions to the Protestants could not be completely abandoned, especially with the recovery of control by the crown of places like La Rochelle, Montauban, Montpellier and Nîmes from the 1620s onwards. The crown itself was willing to aid in restoring Catholicism to these areas, funding missions in confessionally mixed areas, as it did in the Cévennes in the later 1620s. Richelieu himself financed similar enterprises – the 'Richelieu missions' – by the Jesuits in several Protestant-dominated areas of southern France, but they may not have always targeted Protestant populations.[30] The mid-century decades saw a reduction in such activity, only for it to return in force by the 1680s as part of the moves leading to the revocation of the Edict of Nantes in 1685. Indeed, the biggest single mission of the entire century was sponsored by the crown – that of 1685–7 to the 'new' Catholics. Orchestrated and overseen by the king's Jesuit confessor, La Chaize, it mobilised nearly all of the religious orders and large numbers of secular clergy, some of whom, like Fénelon, were not members of any particular congregation. The approaches, experiences and conclusions of the various missionary groups involved were correspondingly diverse. From Poitou to Montpellier and the uplands of the Dauphiné, teams of missioners set to work on the nominally Catholic inhabitants. Some missionaries were accompanied by the dragoons who had already been terrorising the Protestant populations; others tried to do without them but hinted that they might be the ultimate solution if the ex-Huguenots proved too obdurate; while in western France Fénelon pioneered a more eirenic approach that was not to everyone's liking because it seemed to undermine the mission's immediate objectives of turning purely nominal Catholics into confirmed ones.[31] The Oratorians also took part in the 1685–7 campaigns, but they seem to have lost their taste for missions almost entirely thereafter.[32] The use or the threat of force merely produced minimum conformity among the new Catholics, not least because the avoidance of missions to the Protestants (with the exception of those financed by the crown) in previous decades meant that the classic format of a 'normal' mission was unsuitable for the task in hand.

Despite the huge 'investment' involved, these missions ended in failure and left a bitter taste. Their failure did not discredit missions in general, precisely because the average mission was rarely directed specifically towards the Protestant population. It is, therefore, paradoxical that – these Protestant missions apart – the geography and chronology of France's 'internal' missions throughout the seventeenth century are difficult to pin down. They have left surprisingly uneven and fleeting traces in the surviving records, and the often hagiographic accounts composed by missionaries and contemporaries are only of limited value to the historian.[33] Yet it is essential to complement the analysis thus far with a provisional summary at this point. Until the 1620s, at least, the field was dominated by the Jesuits and the Capuchins, with the Barnabites, the Franciscans, the Récollets and the Dominicans playing smaller and more localised roles. Until then, the orders seem to have conducted missions virtually when and where they saw fit, but from the mid-1620s onwards the situation began to change, and not just because the seculars became involved. The

Roman congregation *de Propaganda Fide* took it upon itself to assign responsibility for conducting missions in regions where 'heresy' was entrenched to particular groups of clergy, and in France it was the Capuchins who were entrusted with most of those in the areas of high Huguenot population density (Cévennes, Languedoc, Poitou). But beyond that, the French church felt little need to co-operate with the plans of *Propaganda Fide*, whose intervention had, if anything, the negative effect of pricking Gallican sensitivities. By 1625, France's bishops were already beginning to assert their rights over the authorisation and control of missions within their dioceses in a way that they had not previously done. But this flexing of episcopal muscles in 1625 was not a prelude to any concerted missionary push from above: here as in other areas, the actual means at the bishops' disposal simply did not match their rhetorical claims. Nor did it lead to more than fairly limited conflicts with regulars who still tended to regard themselves as free agents and exempt from episcopal control.[34]

In the decades that followed, the list of orders and congregations undertaking missions lengthened, ensuring a growing volume of activity, but also of experiment and reflection. The latter was stimulated less by the activities of the Roman *Propaganda Fide* congregation, whose interventions in French affairs were actually quite discreet, but by the fact that by then missions were taking shape in French Canada, the Caribbean and elsewhere, and that questions about their methods and objectives were fed back into thinking about missions within France itself. This applied in particular to missions in rural areas which approximated most closely, as it seemed to contemporaries, to the new-found societies abroad. Perhaps the most significant outcome of such interaction was the formation, in 1663, of the very first group of foreign missionaries from the secular clergy anywhere in Europe, the *Missions Étrangères de Paris*. Domestic and foreign missions were not yet separate domains, which ensured that the famous sixteenth-century motto which equated the mass of the population with non-European pagans – 'Your Indies are here' – was guaranteed a busy afterlife until well into the age of Louis XIV.[35]

To claim that there was relatively little that was new in French missions from mid-century onwards would be to set up artificial timescales. Yet the predominant impression is one of the honing and improvement of existing approaches rather than of invention of new ones.[36] By this point, the secular clergy were actually overtaking the regulars in numbers and in geographical spread as missionaries, which had the gradual effect of bringing the style and content of missions more into line with the developing pastoral practices of the French church than was previously the case. Obstacles to the generalisation of missions across the country as a whole remained numerous and familiar – insufficient resources and too few missionaries, the variable size of dioceses, the topography which made many areas hard to access, to mention only a few. Bishops and their officials were increasingly involved in determining how widely or how often missions could occur, but they could not conjure them out of thin air. They often had their own clear preferences when it came to selecting those who would conduct missions, avoiding or even banning those orders or congregations of whom they disapproved. For example, Cardinal Le Camus of Grenoble (1672–1706) barred the Jesuits, with whom he had serious conflicts, and entrusted his diocesan missions to the Josephist congregation of Lyon which, like Le Camus himself, was known for its rigorist pastoral positions; the Jesuits were also banned at various times in dioceses like Sens and Auxerre. Not surprisingly, Le Camus's successors changed tack completely with a view to undoing the damage allegedly done in Grenoble by the Josephists.[37] Le Camus's more 'political' confrère, Archbishop Harlay of Paris (1671–95) organised a large-scale mission in his diocese *extra muros* soon after his arrival there, in April–May 1672, and paid for them out of his admittedly deep pockets. Dividing his diocese into eighteen districts for the purpose, he called upon large numbers (approximately 160 in total) of clergy, regular and secular, to conduct the mission. The teams, some of which were at least fifteen strong, were based in the bigger *bourgs* and were expected to fan out from there into the rural areas.[38] But it proved to be the only mission of its kind during Harlay's twenty-five years in Paris, which makes it hard to read his real intentions at the time. Similar examples could be cited for other dioceses.

The rural parishes of Paris had not been neglected before 1672, and since the 1610s missions had been conducted there by some of the most highly regarded clergy of the century, in particular the Oratorians and the Lazarists. A useful idea of the distance travelled by 1672 may be derived from the fate of the first foundation of a new-style mission dating from 1613. It was established by an Oratorian, Etienne Brice, and it stipulated that four times a year an Oratorian would spend two weeks preaching in a different parish of the Paris diocese. Within a decade of the 1672 mission, the Oratorians decided to change the terms of the 1613 foundation: henceforth, five priests would work together, but the mission itself would occur only once every five years.[39] The growing conviction, which the 1672 Paris mission already embodied, that longer missions (of three or more weeks' duration) conducted by larger groups of missionaries (most of them working as confessors rather than as preachers) were more likely to be effective, did not of itself lead to the demise of the individual missionary 'athlete'. A whole raft of individuals with distinctive and evidently charismatic styles remained at work until at least the 1680s. Exceptional figures like the Jesuit Julien Maunoir, Jean Eudes, the Oratorian Jean Lejeune and the Capuchin Honoré de Cannes each conducted literally hundreds of missions, sometimes in particular regions of France, like Brittany, Normandy and the Limousin. They remained in constant demand, and usually worked with only one or two assistants.[40] The history of France's missions across the century is not just a history of 'bigger means better'.

An enduring obstacle to an increase in missionary activity was, quite simply, lack of disposable funds. From the outset, it was universally accepted that, unlike Lenten or Advent preaching, missions should not be a charge on the parishes in which they were conducted. In any case, there was little prospect that even well-off parishes would be willing to pay for the shorter missions of the early seventeenth century. Thereafter, few bishops were ready to imitate Harlay and personally finance missions on a large or sustained scale, and their most common response was to invite smaller groups of missionaries, usually from the religious orders, who would operate, sometimes with limited financial subsidy, on a smaller scale over a period of several years. Many of the missions that were conducted must, therefore, have owed their existence to a familiar source – legacies and foundations left by benefactors, who might also stipulate the frequency or the format of the mission they founded. By definition, such foundations were haphazard across time and place.[41]

A good instance of how these factors could come together is provided by the diocese of Saint-Malo, which experienced yearly missions by the Lazarists from 1645 onwards, thanks to a perpetual annuity of 500 *livres* from the bishop, who simultaneously confided his seminary to them, on condition that two of the five Lazarists resident there would act primarily as missioners. Over the next fifty-five years for which records survive, they conducted 162 missions in over half the parishes – and in some of them twice or, very rarely, three times – of Saint-Malo. The other parishes were not entirely neglected, as it seems that the parishes were chosen partly for their favourable location, so that people from neighbouring ones could – and in the event, did – attend the missions. That calculation, in turn, was the principal reason for the disproportionately large numbers of penitents and communicants recorded at the time and which, for once, seem not to be the product of the fertile imaginations of hagiographers. It is unusual to find a mission foundation that is, in relative terms, so well documented, but it is not difficult to imagine that similar missions were replicated throughout other areas of France until well into the eighteenth century. The fact that the only missions conducted by the Saint-Malo Lazarists in neighbouring dioceses were due to special invitations and financial bequests that they received for that purpose, underlines the continuing haphazardness of missions 'by contract'.[42]

Despite these constraints, it is clear that by the end of Louis XIV's reign, at least, the organisation and format of missions were well rehearsed. A mission held by a Jesuit in Brissac (Anjou) in 1707 shows that further refinements were still possible, in this instance by identifying the needs and capacities of particular groups of local people. Thus the four weeks that this mission lasted were subdivided so that children, girls, women, and men and boys were each the target of one week of specific attention (sermons and 'exercises'); at the end of 'their' particular week of intensive preparation, rather than at the end of the mission itself, they confessed and communicated. With catechism classes now reserved for the younger children who had not yet, or had only recently, taken their first communion, preaching took on greater importance than previously as the principal means of instruction and exhortation to live Christian lives. This kind of reorganisation of missions is evidence of a pastoral technique that had reached a certain maturity. Also revealingly symptomatic of such change is the fact that in Brissac, Brittany and elsewhere, missionaries could by now draw upon the assistance of various categories of *local* clergy, especially for confessions and catechism, all of which required considerable man-hours. Catechetical work, for example, could be entrusted to clerics in sub-priestly major orders or even to seminarians, both of whom might need to provide evidence of such activity as part of their preparation for taking orders.[43]

The involvement of a very wide spectrum of clergy, especially that of pastorally aware seculars, in France's missions, as well as the extended timescale in which this involvement took place, served to test the techniques and aims of those missions. This in turn helped to limit the grounds for overt criticism of missions as an evangelising strategy. After all, virtually all of the best-known reformers of the period, from Bourdoise to Olier and beyond, had themselves tried their hands at missionary work, and incorporated it into their later thinking and the congregations they founded.[44] One major consequence seems to have been the limited tolerance of the more exotic or 'baroque' penitential missions associated with the Capuchins or the Jesuits in Italy and elsewhere. Criticism did appear all the same, if only because it was well known that some preachers swayed their congregations too much, leading to scenes of barely controllable weeping, lamentation and general disarray. As early as the 1650s, Antoine Arnauld expressed reservations about the mass confessions and absolutions to which they gave rise, questioning the genuineness and durability of such 'conversion' experiences.[45] Increasingly, this kind of doubt was shared by rigorist and Jansenist-leaning clerics, mainly seculars who, because they were inclined to defer absolution to penitents who could not prove the sincerity of their confessions, were not impressed by sudden, mass conversions. Crucially, however, it did not lead them to spurn missions themselves, but rather to apply their own more rigorous demands to those participating in them – assuming that there were bishops like Le Camus of Grenoble to authorise them to do so.[46] The Jansenist critique of popular missions seems to have become more systematic only in the wake of the quarrels over *Unigenitus* after 1713, when the missions of the anti-Jansenist orders were pilloried as theatrical deviations from what true Christianity should be.

Clearly, seventeenth-century France was very unevenly 'missionised', at both the macro and the micro levels. Big efforts were made for areas like Languedoc, Dauphiné, Poitou and related western provinces, where there were large Protestant communities, yet these missions were mostly directed towards fortifying the Catholic populations of these areas. Elsewhere, within smaller spaces, such as dioceses, efforts were correspondingly patchy, and missions often became 'permanent' fixtures more as a result of individual, and thus somewhat haphazard, benefactions to fund them than of anything resembling official 'policy'. The frequency with which they occurred depended on the size of the endowment, while the increased emphasis on longer missions tended to make them rarer still. Contrary to what is sometimes imagined, missions may also have been more often based in middling- to small-sized towns, where the religious orders conducting them were already based, rather than in remote rural parishes. This is not to deny that rural missions took place, or that congregations like the Lazarists and the Capuchins did not move into rural districts. But it is hard to avoid the sense of a relative over-investment in towns, which already had better religious provision, intensive Advent and Lenten preaching included. In this respect, much depended on the density of settlement, especially in the smaller towns, of the orders and congregations willing to devote men and energy to missionary activity.[47]

Modern research has substantially revised traditional views of the success of missions, often based on fairly uncritical acceptance of the enthusiastic accounts by contemporaries, themselves narratives which described the cathartic effect of shaking parishes out of their torpor – and sin – and of achieving dramatic results in a few short weeks of intense activity. Historians' instinctive suspicion of such grandiloquent declarations of victory over the devil – which was often how the missionary enterprise was still seen by many in the early eighteenth century – led them to downplay the long-term effects of missions, especially given that the parish clergy was still too inadequately equipped to follow up the potentially beneficial effects of such ventures. Yet by the early to mid-eighteenth century, this problem had become far less acute, with a better-equipped parish clergy able to tap into the 'fruits' of a mission. It is significant that as early as the 1610s, Vincent de Paul and others not only realised that for missions to take full effect, good *curés* were essential, but also that this discovery was *itself* the result of their missionary efforts. Thereafter, close connections between missionary activity and the preparation of new generations of clergy were a distinctive mark of the post-Berullian congregations. It was this kind of mutual enrichment which enabled the missions to become attuned to the pastoral needs of the population, as understood at the time.

Missions did not take place in a vacuum. After nearly a century, the wider religious and cultural context had also changed considerably. The shocked discovery of popular ignorance and the conviction that Satan held the mass of the population in his grip gradually gave way to a situation in which popular ignorance was perceived as a condition that could be tackled by human means, while superstition gradually dissolved into particular superstitions which an appropriate 'education' could also gradually erase. French peasants could be perceived again as Christians rather than as the local equivalents of the 'savages' of America or elsewhere.[48] It was this shift that enabled one of the most controversial missionaries of the early to mid-eighteenth century, Grignion de Montfort, to declare the purpose of missions to be 'to *renew* the spirit of Christianity among *Christians*'. It was no doubt this same sentiment which enabled the Capuchins, 'the Demosthenes of the people' who were still active missionaries and whose membership seems to have become increasingly 'popular' in its social origins, to envisage the restoration of religious practices of an earlier age, on the grounds that these were no longer suspect.

Catechism

A key element of the 'search for effectiveness' that has been seen as a distinguishing mark of seventeenth-century missions was a growing emphasis on instruction as a crucial intermediate step between preaching and its desired outcome, 'conversion'. As the author of one catechism, Claude Fleury, put it, 'one can only do good by accident when one does not know what it actually is'.[49] But as we have just seen, the catechism conducted during missions was only a short-term, emergency solution to the problem of popular religious ignorance, and missionaries themselves were acutely aware of the need for more normal and constant provision of instruction.

The medieval church held that godparents and parents were the natural educators of each new generation of Christians.[50] Although this principle was never formally renounced, it was clear well before the sixteenth century that it was not enough – in a world of mass illiteracy, who was to educate the educators in the first place? At best, parents would 'teach' their children to say their prayers, but few could go any further and explain their meaning. As successors of the Apostles, the 'mission' of the bishops made them specifically responsible for spreading the word of God and, by extension, for instructing those who were already baptised as Christians. This meant that the obligation fell, in practice, on the parish clergy. But their ignorance caused increasing problems, so that for several generations before our period, real, if also limited, efforts were made to provide them with the wherewithal to discharge this particular responsibility. It is too easy to assume that before the age of fully developed catechisms, there was little or nothing for them to work with. On the contrary, what there already was continued to influence religious education in the broadest sense until well into the seventeenth century.

Synodal statutes and rituals provided the earliest basis of catechetical action, in the form of the explanatory material they contained for the parish clergy about the ceremonies, sacraments and other religious acts of the religious calendar; many of them went further still, not least during the sixteenth century, by adding explanatory sections on the articles of faith, the commandments, sin, penitence, the virtues and vices, and so on. But these materials were often scattered pell-mell alongside disciplinary articles and instructions to the clergy in the volumes of statutes, and many continued to be published in Latin rather than the vernacular. They also tended to be far more disciplinary than pedagogical in tone and format. So however close they might be in some respects to the catechisms of a later date, they remained limited in value, especially as they were addressed almost exclusively to the clergy who, particularly in rural areas, had only the rudiments of an education, and who might also have had little more than a 'see and imitate' training for the priesthood itself. These texts were also limited in the way their use was intended. They were meant to be read out by priests during the *prône* at Sunday services, but it is not clear quite how the clergy were expected to gloss them, despite the fact that many of them would have been completely unintelligible without some commentary. In recognition of this problem, some synodal statutes and rituals also appended, as we have seen, 'extraneous' pedagogical texts, notably Gerson's *Opus tripartitum*, which was still being widely used and reprinted in the early seventeenth century. By then other approaches had begun to appear which would change the entire process of popular instruction in religion.

Catechism, therefore, was an activity and an objective well before it became a specific method of religious education. The raw materials for it already existed in one form or another, as we have just seen. What was new in the sixteenth century, on both the Protestant and the Catholic sides, was the realisation that a new format was needed, one that was geared towards inculcating individual knowledge and personal assent to specific religious tenets.[51] Luther's 'small' and 'great' catechisms of the late 1520s started a major shift, and within less than a generation they were followed by a series of others – with those of Calvin, the Jesuit Peter Canisius and the Council of Trent being the most prominent – though it should be remembered that Trent's was really a pastoral manual for the clergy rather than a catechism in the stricter sense. The preface to the Trent catechism even acknowledged that the Protestants had gained an advantage over the Catholic church through their catechetical innovations. The first French-language catechism to have a major impact was published by another Jesuit, Edmond Auger, in 1563, but it was hobbled thereafter by its explicitly 'controversial' origins and format, since it was a question by question rebuttal of Calvin's catechism. The French Jesuits themselves soon preferred that of the less controversy-focused Canisius, not least because, like Luther's, his 'catechism' actually consisted of three complementary works – one for adults, one for schoolgoers, one for younger children. This differentiation was to be a major feature in the later development of the genre, but already Canisius's catechism for children had another major advantage: it avoided the danger of unnecessarily familiarising them with heretical ideas. His catechism, as well as that of an equally famous Jesuit of the next generation, Robert Bellarmine, was frequently reprinted in French until well into the 1680s, thanks largely to the engagement of the Jesuits themselves in catechetical activities, especially in towns where they founded colleges.[52]

All the uncertainties and changes of format should not hide the relative consistency of the content of catechisms. From the outset, they possessed a triple focus – what people should believe, what they should do and what they should refrain from doing, in order to be saved. The Apostles' Creed provided the core around which questions of belief were organised. But what differentiated Catholic catechisms most from their Protestant counterparts was their strong emphasis on doing or not doing certain things – an obvious consequence of the continuing belief in the efficacy of good works and the role of individuals in attaining their salvation. 'Doing' focused primarily upon the seven sacraments, the Ten Commandments and the commandments of the church as well as the seven works of mercy and the 'cardinal virtues'. 'Not doing' also related mainly to the Ten Commandments as well as on the 'seven deadly sins'. The importance of the sacraments, especially of confession and communion, in catechisms may well have encouraged the church to concentrate its catechetical efforts upon children rather than adults, as we shall see presently.

The emergence of distinctive 'question and answer' catechisms did not of itself lead to an immediate jettisoning of existing practices and attitudes. The reasons were manifold. Adults were perennially reluctant to attend specially organised catechism sessions, whether during Sunday services or afterwards, not wishing to see themselves, or to be treated by catechists, as schoolchildren. And many of the clergy were no less reluctant to play the (inferior) role of a mere teacher. Thus, for their own different reasons, both clergy and adults were happier with the familiar *prône*. It is hardly surprising, therefore, that it took several generations of uncertainty and experiment for significant change to occur. Trent and the post-Tridentine reformers put increasing pressure on the parochial clergy to catechise their parishioners, but without a prior transformation of the clergy through better education and preparation, the prospects of improvement remained poor enough. Until well into the seventeenth century, therefore, the best that could be hoped for was that *curés* would read out short texts explaining key elements of the Christian faith and practice and perhaps occasionally add their own commentary during the *prône*. This may well be the reason why it took longer in France than in neighbouring countries to move towards a catechism that proposed short and memorisable answers to specific questions; catechisms with a more substantial dialogue form still had wide appeal.[53] Richelieu's widely used *Instruction du Chrétien* (1618), often known as the Catechism of Luçon, was one of many early seventeenth-century works which proposed often lengthy responses to short, specific questions, which made it a halfway house between a *prône* and a new-style catechism. Clearly, there was still some uncertainty about the most useful method of catechising 'the simple people', and some, like Richelieu, still felt that the priest conducting a *prône* in church on Sundays or feast days was the most inclusive and workable medium of instruction. The widespread use and reprinting of the Richelieu 'Catechism' shows how attractive his particular approach was, despite the fact that long, discursive answers to questions tended to be beyond the capacity of ordinary people.[54]

By the 1650s and 1660s, however, it is evident that a number of major changes were in train. More and more catechisms devised by French authors were appearing, the fruit of an osmosis between the earlier non-French texts and French experiences of catechising 'on the ground' over the previous decades. Another important change was the drive towards official diocesan catechisms, after nearly a century of laissez-faire and unco-ordinated experiment.[55] French bishops became increasingly keen to impose some kind of uniformity on a rather chaotic landscape, in which a plethora of catechisms flourished and were used indiscriminately by catechists from one parish to the next; the suspicion that some of them might be conveying unorthodox, mainly Jansenist ideas (especially about the sacraments) was also a concern for some bishops after mid-century. This response did not involve the sudden appearance of a distinctive catechism for each diocese, but rather a number of those already in circulation being officially adopted as diocesan catechisms. It took at least another generation for the transition from catechisms authorised 'for use in diocese X' to catechisms 'to be taught exclusively in diocese X' to occur.[56] In the meanwhile, some idea of the influences criss-crossing France can be derived from the pattern of adoption. The catechism of Saint-Nicolas-du-Chardonnet in Paris, which was the fruit of the Bourdoise community's experiments over a generation, effectively became the Paris diocesan catechism in 1646, even though it was not regarded as the only one that could be used there. And because of its reputation, it was subsequently adopted, and occasionally emended, by several other dioceses as far apart as Gap, Poitiers, Coutances and Laon.[57] But Paris was by no means a model other dioceses felt compelled to adopt. The Bourges catechism of 1688, composed by the *curé* of Saint-Sulpice in Paris, was far more successful than anything published in Paris.[58]

By the 1660s and 1670s, a new generation of bishops was preparing to go further still by compiling and publishing their own diocesan catechisms, and on a scale that had no precedent anywhere in Europe. With approximately twenty catechisms in existence around 1650, no fewer than forty new ones were produced between then and 1685; by the end of the century, sixty-six dioceses in all had their own catechisms, and the rest would acquire one during the following century.[59] That development is also reflected in the interest in catechism teaching evinced by the records of parish visitations. While few visitors before the 1610s enquired about catechesis, thereafter and down to 1730 the interest rose steadily to encompass 80 per cent of all recorded visitations.[60]

Where episcopal efforts went beyond merely adopting what was already available, they could provoke unease of their own, both locally and nationally. The famous catechism of 'the three Henries', issued by bishops Arnauld of Angers, Laval of La Rochelle and Barillon of Luçon in 1676, was a tri-diocesan catechism, yet its distinguished authorship did not prevent it from being seen by many as being too influenced by Jansenist ideas. It is hardly surprising, therefore, that Arnauld's highly orthodox successor at Angers, Le Peletier, wanted to produce a catechism for his diocese of Angers alone, and by his own admission he did so after reviewing the catechisms issued before the 1690s by other French bishops. Yet bishops who increasingly thought of themselves as 'doctors of the faith' of their diocesans were not always infallible judges when it came to practical applications of their own principles! Le Peletier's Catechism, which duly appeared in 1697, actually proved to be too difficult for ordinary use, and it was replaced by a more accessible one produced by *his* successor. Archbishop Harlay's Catechism of 1687, which was intended to replace the classic Saint-Nicolas-du-Chardonnet one of a generation earlier, was prepared not by experienced catechists but by theologians with their minds focused on the more recent Jansenist and (post-1685) Protestant problems, thus making their catechism's somewhat relentless logic a pretty bloodless and dry pedagogical experience. A number of catechisms published shortly after 1685 were different again, being explicitly designed for use by 'new' as well as by 'old' Catholics.[61] Later still, the famous and widely used Catechism of Sens (1732) was marked by anti-Jansenist origins, its author, Archbishop Languet, having already published an identical work for his previous diocese of Soissons in 1718. But Languet's orthodoxy could not prevent the accolade for the most successful French catechism of the *ancien régime* from going to the Montpellier Catechism issued by Bishop Colbert de Croissy, a hardline Jansenist. Composed by an Oratorian and first published in 1702, it was repeatedly reprinted and widely used as a source for other catechisms, albeit shorn of its more extreme views, down to the revolution.[62]

Within a half-century or so, the emergence of diocesan catechisms was the major source of the 'normalisation' of catechetical practice across France. However, as with other forms of executive action, changing the manuals may only have had limited immediate impact on the actual practice of catechism in the localities. Regardless of the catechisms' content, it was essential to print large numbers of copies and distribute them, ideally free of charge, to the parish clergy and the catechists themselves, otherwise they would drag their feet for years about purchasing them. Thereafter, it was a matter of bringing as much pressure as possible, via synods, ecclesiastical conferences, visitations, seminaries, clerical retreats and so on, to insist on the exclusive use of the official catechism. It is not hard to imagine that, where frequent changes of catechism took place, a certain scepticism about the current version might take root.[63]

For many years, however, the major difficulty was not so much which catechism to use, but how to ensure that it was conducted at all. The post-Trent provincial councils of the 1580s, as well as countless diocesan synods and ordinances thereafter, tried to hammer home the message of how indispensable religious instruction was, but the response of France's clergy and parishioners was slow and haphazard. As already noted, the tenured parish priests tended to regard such an obligation as beneath them, preferring the more familiar *prône*. At best, they wished to see catechetical duties farmed out to curates, chaplains or even laypeople, but this was doubly problematic during the generations when the only readily available catechetical material was designed primarily for parish priests! The speed with which the situation changed cannot really be measured with any precision, but it is clear that rural areas lagged well behind cities and towns, which during our period also had the benefit of seeing a substantial growth in schools of various kinds. When the teaching of the catechism in rural areas of the Paris diocese was regarded as unsatisfactory during the 1672 visitation, it is not hard to imagine how much further behind other parts of France must have been.[64] Continuing inertia and resistance by *curés* seems to have been a major cause of this. But change was gradually engineered by a combination of pressures. As we saw, the spread of missions, for all their unevenness, brought catechetical activity into the regions exposed to them, and the foundation by missionaries of confraternities of Christian doctrine was designed to ensure it would continue thereafter. Ecclesiastical conferences, visitations and the gradually emerging seminaries delivered the same message but, arguably more importantly, a modicum of catechetical training for the future clergy themselves.

As with missions, it was often the establishment of foundations specifically designed for catechetical instruction which kick-started things within individual parishes. Many of these foundations were set up by laypeople, but a surprising number of priests did likewise, either as legacies to their parishes when retiring from service or to their native parishes. Because these arrangements involved contracts signed before a notary, their founders could, and often did – especially in the early decades of the seventeenth century – specify the kind of activity they had in mind, as well as by whom it should be conducted. An illuminating example of this is provided by Nicolas Quintaine, a parish priest based just outside Paris, who in 1650 established a catechetical foundation for his native parish in the diocese of Coutances. He evidently felt he needed to spell out in great detail what the catechist's task should be: 'The said founder wishes and requires that the catechist teaches children and the uneducated the principles of the faith, the commandments of God and of the church, and the manner of praying to God and of invoking the saints. He shall also teach them how one should love and practice virtue; avoid sin and the occasions of sin; attend and devoutly follow the mass; know, love, serve and adore God; what one must know and do in order to be saved, confess one's sins in a holy manner and take communion piously; frequent the sacraments with profit; and finally to live well and die as a Christian in the Catholic, Apostolic and Roman church.' And, as if to make sure his intentions were absolutely clear, Quintaine insisted that 'at the end, the catechist shall deliver a moral homily for the support and edification of those present, as it is not my intention that he deliver grandiloquent sermons which remain without fruit, *there being a great difference between a catechist and a preacher*'.[65]

Similar but probably less prolix foundations took place before and after 1650 in Coutances diocese, where Jean Eudes's many missions must have acted as a spur in this instance. Even so, it took several decades more at least for them to have a wider impact on the mainly rural parishes. The situation was not markedly different in the rural parishes of Paris *extra muros* in 1672, despite the fact that the presence there of rich Paris-based landowners ensured that such foundations were numerous and occurred earlier than in lower Normandy and elsewhere. Furthermore, a high proportion of these foundations specified that the catechism be taught by clerics, sometimes members of particular religious orders or congregations, rather than by laypeople. Indeed, it was often the annuity attached to the foundation that finally persuaded many parish priests to hire curates, something they were notoriously reluctant to do from their own resources. With the spread of such practices, parishioners themselves could use their parish priest's failure to catechise as a weapon against him in pressing their bishop to oblige him to hire a curate. Clerical catechists, whether they were curates or chaplains, were also doubly welcome, since they could perform other religious services that laypeople could not, an advantage that was not lost on the inhabitants of extended rural parishes.[66]

The great ambitions of the early reformers, Protestant and Catholic, were gradually, if reluctantly, scaled back until the focus of religious instruction was essentially on children and young adolescents. Adults remained consistently resistant, and only during missions was it possible to persuade them to participate in catechism. Within Catholicism, the fact that much of the material in catechisms was about religious practices generally, and about key sacraments like confession and communion in particular, probably facilitated, *faute de mieux*, the resultant emphasis on catechising the young. Preparing children for the sacraments became a major consideration in the way in which catechism developed, since admission to those sacraments could be made conditional on catechetical instruction which would be verified by an oral test. The 'invention' of the 'first' or 'solemn' communion, which dates from the late sixteenth century onwards in France, further increased that emphasis, creating the conditions needed for a workable 'carrot and stick' approach. This investment may seem obvious in retrospect, but we should remember that the refusal of most adults to attend catechism did not of itself make them keen to send their children in their place, especially in rural areas. They argued that they needed them for all kinds of farm work, especially from late spring to harvest time; many parishes suspended catechism altogether during that season, but the remaining winter months were no more favourable towards attendance in the parish church for instruction. Persuading parents to send their children was thus a constant struggle for most of the century, and it was only by the early eighteenth century that a generation which had itself been catechised as children appeared more willing to accept the obligation to send their own children to catechism classes. Meanwhile, instructions and ordinances constantly reiterated how crucial it was to instil sound doctrine in young minds and to shape them for life, while some expressed the hope that their good example would rub off on their parents and families. If the rise of the 'solemn' communion, taken by those usually aged between twelve and fourteen, proved an effective instrument for catechising children, it also became a cut-off point beyond which it became increasingly difficult to persuade people to take further instruction. From then onwards, their instruction came from the *prônes* and the sermons they listened to during normal church services.

The need to provide children with memorisable statements of Christian-Catholic beliefs and religious obligations pointed the catechisms that were being produced in seventeenth-century France towards the familiar question and answer format. A good deal of experimentation went into this over the years, and one outcome was a highly 'tiered' system of catechisms, adjusted towards the different age groups and their intellectual capacities. Each catechism contained the same chapter headings and questions, but from one level to the next they provided fuller answers for the older learners. As one contemporary practitioner optimistically put it, children have only memory to start with, and an understanding of things comes later when they are capable of questioning what they have learned by heart. In its own perhaps limited way, catechetical pedagogy participated in the 'discovery of childhood' during this period, since it forced authors and catechists alike to think about the appropriateness of materials and ideas for individual age groups in ways that they had not done hitherto. As we saw earlier, catechisms were not immune to the fallout from the doctrinal disputes of the day, so France's bishops tried to ensure that they were wholly orthodox, and that in turn might mean that on thorny subjects like God's grace and its availability to individual Christians, for example, authors of catechisms were likely to say as little as possible, for fear of opening up unnecessary debates or criticism. Tightening up the texts in this domain, especially those destined for adolescents, adults and catechists, coincided with another trend, that of excising from catechisms most of the stories – whether biblical, profane or folk-wisdom in provenance – that had previously been used in attempts to explain particular questions, especially religious or moral commands. Of course, the slimmer catechetical texts that were the outcome of these pressures could also be produced more cheaply and more abundantly for distribution in those parts of France where literacy rates were high enough for instruction to be conducted with a written catechism.

If the overall pattern of development was towards a more standardised format, it is evident from a scrutiny of the catechisms themselves that this did not prevent the insertion of many other, shorter texts, which dealt with specific religious practices. The sheer variety of such insertions, which might vary from one edition or one diocese to the next, defies easy summary, but their very heterogeneity indicates their perceived utility at the time. Many of them were instructions (mini-catechisms, in effect) for the saints' days of the year, preparations for confession, communion and confirmation, 'exercises' to be performed during the day, the examination of one's conscience, the duties of Christian families and many others. Bossuet composed a separate catechism for the feast days and other ceremonies of the church as part of his Meaux Catechism of 1687.[67] The text of morning and evening prayers was nearly universally present in these catechisms, many of which added prayers to be said while assisting at the mass.

A general sense of the overall scale of catechetical activity is, not surprisingly, hard to convey. An inquiry of 1672 in the Paris diocese concluded that fewer than one in five of the 135 parishes inspected had regular catechism classes, and that one in four had irregular ones.[68] Extrapolated across a country with few cities capable of having an impact comparable to that of Paris on its hinterland, this would suggest a highly patchy degree of penetration. On the other hand, the record of the diocese of La Rochelle since the 1650s indicates that its clergy had already massively accepted the obligation to catechise their parishioners.[69] Geography was not the only factor at work. The Paris visitation occurred at a point where a number of factors were beginning to coalesce into more sustained pressure for action, the results of which would only become visible a generation later. Those bishops who prided themselves on the catechisms that they produced not only wanted to see them used, but were increasingly able to enforce their wishes, often with the de facto consent of parishioners who had gradually come to expect the church to provide some religious instruction. The various mechanisms for improving the clergy's pastoral competence that we saw in an earlier chapter were readily serviceable for pressing the clergy to educate their parishioners religiously. It was not for lack of clergy that this had not happened heretofore, but now, through foundations and the pastoral requirements for taking the major orders, more of them were either given the opportunity, or faced the obligation, of engaging in catechetical work. Later in the seventeenth century, with a view to forcing the pace further, parish confraternities of Christian doctrine were brought under episcopal direction and parochial supervision. Catechetical instruction went on to become well-nigh universal in eighteenth-century rural France generally, thus finding, according to one historian, its place in 'the measured routines of village life'.[70] The Bordeaux Catechism of 1704 asked the question, 'What should one do to learn the mysteries of the faith?' and promptly gave as the answer – 'Attend the sermons and catechism classes'.

Schools and Schooling

The practice of catechism was also influenced by the differences in literacy rates between northern and southern France. In the regions above the Saint-Malo–Geneva line levels of literacy were high enough for printed catechisms to be distributed and used (mainly) by schoolchildren, whereas south of the line, lower literacy levels ensured that catechism long remained an oral memorisation exercise. For this reason, any discussion of the pattern of religious instruction needs a brief consideration of schooling. Of course, there were many reasons, not all of them religious, why different kinds of schools were sought after in our period, so only those issues that have a direct bearing on the themes of this chapter can be discussed here.

It will be immediately obvious that, as far as the availability and accessibility of schooling was concerned, cities and towns, especially those housing the colleges for boys, old and new, which increasingly dotted the urban landscape after the religious wars, had serious advantages over the *bourgs*, villages and rural areas. Furthermore, with increasing numbers of the colleges being run by the Jesuits or congregations like the Oratory and the *Doctrine Chrétienne*, their students received as advanced a religious education as was available anywhere at the time. This education was not confined to the classes devoted specifically to religious matters, since the entire syllabus and the daily routines of pupils were enveloped in a religious framework. In the Jesuits' La Madeleine school in Bordeaux, students even learned their catechism during mealtimes! And, as is well known, the Jesuits gathered together selected students into sodalities that resembled devotional confraternities in order to inculcate a spirituality that assumed, but went far beyond, mere catechetical instruction. Other orders may have been less single-minded, but together they aimed fundamentally to reshape the religious behaviour of France's social and political elites well beyond our period. This minority, lay and clerical, within an (urban) minority of the population should not be underestimated, as they provided much of the energy and money which drove forward many of the religious changes occurring during the seventeenth century.

The connections between religious instruction and schooling are more visible further down the social ladder, because it was by no means obvious to contemporaries that lower social groups should be educated at all.[71] In addition, the French church began the century with extremely strong suspicions of schoolmasters, blaming them in part for transmitting heresy during the sixteenth century; that experience made it reluctant to push hard for the spread of primary schools, the *petites écoles*. This reluctance was accompanied by a relative absence of social demand for primary schools throughout the country, especially in rural areas where the value of an education was only rarely felt. On the other hand, the old church could not ignore the challenge from the Protestant churches and *their* educational advances. Above all, it wanted to exercise tight supervision of the *petites écoles* that did exist, and particularly to vet, hire and, where necessary, dismiss schoolteachers. It was in urban areas that the most interesting experiments in this kind of schooling occurred during the decades after 1600. Early reformers like *curé* Bourdoise of Saint-Nicolas-du-Chardonnet in Paris clamoured for parish schools whose *raison d'être* would be essentially religious, and the next generation continued to push for schools that would encompass poorer social groups. Several of the later congregations of seculars were keen to engage in religious education beyond the merely catechetical. Bourdoise could not have been clearer when he wrote in 1649 to Olier of Saint-Sulpice: 'the well run and well conducted

Christian *petites écoles* are the seminaries of the seminaries'. Olier himself, as it happened, founded over thirty such schools, while Charles Démia established sixteen in Lyon after 1666.[72] And, as we saw, catechetical practice itself gradually moved in the direction of increased use of printed materials by this point, especially in northern and eastern France.

The pressure to open schools for those social groups which would otherwise not have had them came about gradually and cumulatively, as the realisation spread that the drive to catechise the population and tackle popular ignorance, still viewed mainly as a religious issue, would work better via schools. It is no accident, therefore, that synods and other pronouncements by the French church increasingly insisted upon the need for schools in the second half of the century. The earlier problem with schoolteachers' reliability in religious matters had largely disappeared by then, and indeed their assistance as catechists was increasingly valued at a time when the parish clergy were still unwilling to instruct their parishioners. The need to educate France's 'new' Catholics after the revocation of the Edict of Nantes in 1685 brought the crown increasingly into the picture, but its role was largely indirect: it legislated in 1698, and again in 1724, for compulsory schooling until the age of fourteen, but in practice it pushed the responsibility for action, and especially for funding it, onto local communities, many of which were heavily burdened by taxes and debts incurred by Louis XIV's wars.[73]

Consequently, it was mostly local and private initiative which led to the founding of *petites écoles* during our period. Ferté's study of the rural areas of the Paris diocese found very little evidence of the institutional church – from the archbishop to the wealthy abbeys – providing funds for this purpose, and it is likely that the picture applied across the country generally.[74] On top of the thin film of such schools that existed around 1600, there slowly appeared a new layer which, rather like provision for missions and catechism, owed its existence mainly to individual benefactions (some testamentary) throughout the seventeenth century and beyond. Only some urban *fabriques* had the funds to remunerate a schoolteacher without having to impose a possibly unpopular new tax upon their parish; the new foundations were thus indispensable, and owed much to the activities of the *dévots*, broadly speaking, and the confraternities and other 'ginger' groups that translated their aims into social reality. So long as such firm financial support was lacking, schoolmasters were always likely to charge more for tuition than families could, or would, pay. Where the schoolmasters were clerics – parish priests or, more usually, chaplains or curates – the financial problem became less acute, and the orthodoxy of the schoolteachers was easily verified. Substantial numbers of un-beneficed clergy appear to have acted as schoolteachers until well into the eighteenth century, especially in regions with high clerical densities, and they did so with the encouragement of church authorities.

This is perhaps why only one congregation, Jean-Baptise de la Salle's Brothers of the Christian Schools (1683), emerged during our period with a deliberate vocation to run *petites écoles* for boys, a vocation which was exclusive and unusual enough to rule out its members becoming priests. La Salle's congregation was also unique in accepting that unless the *petites écoles* offered something more than religious education, parents would not send their children to school – hence its strongly vocational focus. In the great majority of schools, 'reading' literacy rather than 'writing' literacy was the priority, and regardless of whether the teachers were clerics or laymen, religious instruction was a major component of the curriculum.[75] The ability to sing and to teach children plain chant was much sought after in schoolteachers, a revealing indication of what both the church and large sections of French society expected of such schools. And, needless to say, within the envelope of formal instruction lay the daily saying of prayers, attendance at church services and the endless repetition of many other religious gestures, which contributed just as much to the religious formation of those engaging in them.

There was one well-known downside to the church's quest, taken on its own terms, for a religiously educated population, and that was its attitude towards the education of women.[76] It increasingly accepted the need for them to be fully catechised, both as future mothers who could act as the first religious educators of their children and, more generally, as mistresses of households containing servants and others. But whether they needed any further education was a different proposition, and doubts about that were not confined to the male clerical establishment. That more general debate need not be addressed here, but particular elements of the French church's approach to it are of key interest. Firstly, it was adamantly opposed to mixed-sex schools, a stance which left the door slightly ajar for girls-only schools, but that was certainly no guarantee that they would materialise. Secondly, if there were doubts enough about whether laymen, even schoolteachers, could be employed as catechists, those doubts were far stronger in relation to women.[77] Opposition was so potent, especially in the early part of our period, and seemed to have such unassailable biblical foundations, that those pressing the case for women catechists were sometimes reduced to arguing that women would not be catechising per se, but merely repeating the words and message of the actual catechists – in other words that their role was purely mechanical and limited. It was the magistrates of Dôle, in Franche-Comté, who thundered, in 1606, that 'there is nothing more dangerous than to allow women to explain the sacred texts and for them to claim to teach girls the *grande doctrine* . . . we wish that it be stated more clearly that they will simply teach the girls to repeat the catechism by heart, without attempting to add any interpretation of their own'. The catechist, especially the female one, stood on a fault-line, and the precise nature of their activity was capable of fuelling such an outburst, one which, coincidentally, rejected the more welcoming attitude of the local church authorities towards female catechists.[78]

In addition to this, the prospects of female education being boosted by religious objectives seemed to be drastically reduced by the post-Tridentine enclosure of the existing and new religious orders that we examined earlier. Admittedly, orders like the Ursulines and the Visitation fought successfully to maintain their teaching function, but their schools did not reach out beyond a socially limited 'external' clientele. For this reason, the emergence of the new 'non-standard' congregations of *filles séculières* with simple vows represented an unexpected bonus.[79] Although the earliest of them were more concerned with pastoral and charitable work than with education, the former gradually opened the way for the latter, despite the fact that teaching and catechising, unlike charitable action, were still regarded as domains reserved in principle for the clergy. Many of the female congregations which grew rapidly from the 1630s and 1640s onwards were keen to tackle popular religious ignorance via education; some of them originated in tiny groups of women, widows or unmarried, who had previously banded together to teach local girls, but who at a certain point wished to move beyond purely informal arrangements. Given that it was far more difficult to find female teachers with any training beyond catechesis itself, congregations such as the *Demoiselles de l'Instruction* of Le Puy found themselves first training their own members to teach, and then sending them to the towns and villages nearby; in Le Puy diocese, the principal focus of their work was the women, often immigrants of the poorest kind, employed in the local lace-making industry.[80] The congregations also took on the training of lay schoolmistresses, thus expanding the possible scope for female educational action. It was in order to support this drive that the bishop of Cahors declared in 1673 that these *filles seculières* should not become full convent nuns.[81] The 'schools' they opened were often the most 'basic' imaginable, thinly dispersed across the landscape and, in stark contrast to the convent-schools of the Ursulines or the Visitation, they often had just one or two teaching sisters.[82] It is no surprise to learn that they were unable to make an impact equivalent to their male counterparts, clerical and lay, during the seventeenth century, perhaps because most of them were limited to individual dioceses and perhaps also because the efforts to spread female education were slow to gain momentum. It was not until the eighteenth century that more substantial progress would be possible.

CHAPTER 13

THE FORMS AND USES OF SPIRITUALITY

Introduction

Any understanding of religious change during the period under consideration must include the major currents of religious thought, primarily of the 'applied' rather than speculative and academic kind. The instruments and techniques of religious change, as well as the religious practices examined in previous chapters, were all, to one degree or another, vehicles for conveying religious ideas that were themselves subject to recycling and further development by thinkers and writers of varying originality and appeal. In the case of seventeenth-century France, the claims of spirituality to be regarded as an agent in the process of religious change is enhanced by the fact that so many of its authors and propagators were themselves highly active within the French church.

Like the history of ideas generally, spirituality has usually been studied by historians through a corpus of published works, with a tendency to focus on individual works designated as 'classics' or on long-term motifs. But this approach tends to remove the subject from its proper context – that of actual religious uses and practices; to paraphrase a leading historian of the subject, it can easily lose sight of 'those who pray and who suffer'.[1] In this chapter, the term 'spirituality' is employed in a deliberately elastic fashion, which enables it to range from 'high' spirituality, as exemplified by mystical and related thought, to devotional advice and direction on the other. The latter dimension is particularly important, since it helps to connect spirituality to religious practices observed in previous chapters.

French spirituality took on the forms and importance that it did in our period because the thrust of all of the sixteenth-century reformations was to persuade as many people as possible to 'interiorise' the religious principles of the church to which they belonged. They should pray, read and meditate, according to their capacities and status, in order to 'sanctify' their actual religious practices, and to breathe a living 'spirit' into the 'letter' of familiar ceremonies and collective observances that made up most people's religious lives. The idealised Christian would thus develop his or her own interior religious life, which existed beyond and outside of collective religious events, perpetuating and 'expanding' the latter into private devotions and thoughts. As far as France is concerned, this was not mere wishful thinking. Lucien Febvre argued many years ago that the period from 1590 to 1620 witnessed a silent revolution, during which large numbers of people began to 'pray' methodically – by which he meant *oraison*, a personal prayer that was distinct from the public prayers of routine liturgical occasions.[2] Such a step may seem inevitable and unproblematic in retrospect, but at the time it required a great deal of *encadrement* – guidance and assistance, both personal and in the form of books of devotion and reflection – if it was to be sustained and become a *habitus*. Febvre's timescale – 1590 to 1620 – was doubtless too short and too dramatic, and should be regarded as kick-starting a much longer-term development.

Because France boasts some of the greatest spiritual writers of post-Reformation Catholicism *tout court*, from François de Sales to Fénelon, there is a strong temptation to assume that their impact is somehow self-evident. But leaving aside the perennial question of the 'representativeness' of major writers, the historian of spirituality – as is the case with the history of ideas generally – needs to look for a middle ground, so that ideas emerging at the time can somehow be connected to contemporary religious practices and aspirations. This means, among other things, taking account of the different genres of spiritual writing, as well as the different 'constituencies' to which they were directed, rather than assuming a 'one-size-fits-all' development of a few 'grand' ideas. The term 'spirituality' itself constitutes a wide continuum into which fit the mysticism of a tiny elite at one end, and the prayers and meditations of ordinary people wishing to develop their religious life beyond mere physical participation in church services, at the other. The first category brings to mind the practices of contemplatives following in the footsteps of, say, Teresa of Avila, while the second based their devotions, inside but also outside of church, on more basic fare, the devotional books pumped out in industrial quantities by the presses of Catholic Reformation Europe. Consequently, the history of spirituality has to consider the media as well as the genres that were employed to diffuse ideas. The best-known attempt at a comprehensive account of this subject for seventeenth-century France is Henri Bremond's celebrated and partially translated, though now little read, monument in eleven volumes, the *Histoire littéraire du sentiment religieux en France* (1916–36). Its scale suggests how vast the topic really is, all the more so as Bremond's was explicitly a 'literary' history largely detached from the actual pastoral concerns of the authors that he studied. For all his tiptoeing around certain controversial issues, his presentation of the idea of a distinctive 'French school' of spirituality argued for a strong underlying coherence to a set of ideas deriving initially from the ubiquitous Pierre de Bérulle and then developed by disciples of his like Condren, Jean Eudes, Jean-Jacques Olier and beyond. What follows here is necessarily far more limited, with a choice of issues for discussion that is biased towards making connections with questions of religious change considered elsewhere in this book.

Historical Background

In discussing the roots of seventeenth-century spirituality, there is no obvious 'zero' moment or starting point.[3] A complex compound of themes, methods and genres of greater or lesser antiquity was already in circulation, sometimes reworked by later authors, and 'translated' for wider use by preachers, confessors and directors of conscience. It should be realised that much of this output was initially designed by, and intended for use among, religious orders, male and female, and that the idea of a 'spirituality' for laypeople beyond the cloister was a relative latecomer. The proposition that a truly 'spiritual' life was possible among the occupations, cares and temptations of a sinful world did not come naturally, especially to regulars, and it was not facilitated by the belief, still quite powerful among laypeople themselves in our period, that 'withdrawal' and 'retreat' from the 'world' were still the safest option for those seeking such a life. But in the generations preceding the Protestant Reformations, the attractiveness of books of hours, the *Imitation of Christ* and Erasmus of Rotterdam's campaigns to promote the idea of a 'Christian militia' living in the world at large ('to be a monk does not equate to piety'), showed that things were changing. Simultaneously, the printing presses diffused more widely than was ever conceivable in the age of manuscripts 'literary' genres like saints' lives, books of hours (essentially texts of prayers) and above all expressly didactic works of various kinds about dying, confession and praying. Jean Gerson's moral and pastoral works now reached much bigger audiences than he did in his own lifetime, and they remained in vogue until well into the seventeenth century.

The advent of printing was the one totally unpredicted factor in facilitating such changes, and the predominance of religious books in the early output of the printing presses is no accident. How things might have evolved without the explosion of the Protestant Reformations can only be surmised, but the combination of printing and unprecedented religious upheaval across sixteenth-century Europe, especially when we bear in mind the reformers' emphasis on lay religiosity and vernacular religion, meant that even the old church could not ignore the challenge they represented. For all its instinct to control publishing in order to eradicate heresy, it was forced by events to compete with the latter, in France as elsewhere. Its consistent attempts, reinforced by the decisions of the Council of Trent, to restrict access to the Bible and liturgical books in the vernacular did distinguish it, however, from its Protestant counterparts, because for the vast majority of the literate Catholic lay population it closed off the prospect of a spiritual life that revolved primarily around bible-reading and meditation.[4] In practice, France was the Catholic country least affected by such restrictions, since the continuing presence of Protestantism there created a space, however uncertain, for continuing familiarity with the Bible, which was available in French translations.

The decades dominated by the wars of religion not only saw an unprecedented outpouring of books, pamphlets and ephemera dealing with religious matters and from almost every conceivable angle, but the wars also lasted long enough to disrupt many inherited patterns.[5] Not surprisingly, the great majority of these published items were confrontational contributions to waging religious war 'by other means', especially during the periods of the greatest anxiety (1560s, 1580s and 1590s). An acute sense of 'immediate and present danger' tends not to generate the kind of serenity required to compose enduring works of spirituality, even though such works may sometimes have their origins in periods of acute anxiety. By contrast, it seems that the post-1598 context of inter-confessional controversy was sufficiently 'domesticated' by the terms of the Edict of Nantes for spiritual, theological and historical works of more than passing use to appear. However, it is clear from perusing the works of key sixteenth-century figures like René Benoist, Edmond Auger, Claude de Sainctes and others that they were fully aware that engaging in controversy with the Protestants was not enough: the Catholic population needed spiritual resources divorced from controversy. Most of the time, however, their own efforts were limited enough. Benoist translated the Bible and a book of hours, and wrote his own devotional treatises, while Auger, Henri III's confessor, revised and extended the 'Formulary of Catholic Prayers' in 1576.

In fact, this generation and its immediate successor relied to a degree not seen in French religious history, before or after this period (c.1550–1610), on translations of works from neighbouring parts of Europe. Some of this had already happened with the works of the Flemish and German mystical writers of the later Middle Ages, and that pattern continued. An established 'favourite' like the *Imitation of Christ* broke all the rules, since it was successively translated in the first half of the seventeenth century by figures as famous as Michel de Marillac, Le Maitre de Sacy and Pierre Corneille! But what was really novel during the period from roughly 1550 to 1610 was the degree of concentration on translating works of Italian and Spanish origin. Scarcely a year passed until the 1610s without several such publications, and some titles were translated more than once.[6] In retrospect, the translations of the great mystics, Teresa of Avila and John of the Cross, may appear to be the most significant, but both authors were relatively slow to be translated, given that suspicions of 'illuminism' had long been attached to mystical writing generally in Spain itself.

By contrast, more 'accessible' writers like Luis de Granada (1504–88) and Luis de la Puente (alias Du Pont in French translations), caused fewer problems and, in the case of the prolific Granada, his connections to figures like Carlo Borromeo were a positive guarantee of his worth. Indeed, he was sometimes translated from the Italian rather than the Spanish original. Individual works rather than the entire opus of an author like Granada were especially cherished, in particular his famous *Guide for Sinners* of 1556. The Italian Theatine Lorenzo Scupoli's *Spiritual Combat* was arguably even more successful, running through fifty editions between 1589 and 1610 alone. It is scarcely necessary to note that the titles of such widely read works already indicate their approach: the life of the Christian was a combat in which every possible assistance was needed. While the translations of foreign works of spirituality made during this period show a desire for comprehensiveness, it is hard to escape the impression that the growing predominance among them of 'guides' was not accidental. It reflected a corresponding wish on the part of the French translators themselves – who were drawn from an impressive range of clergy and laity – to address practical problems of religious instruction and individual conduct.

Scupoli, Granada, La Puente – these and most of the authors writing in, or translated into French were members of religious orders, whose spiritual traditions were naturally reflected in their works. The history of confraternities, third orders and the *dévots* generally shows that the orders dominated the 'supply' of personal spiritual guidance and advice; until the seventeenth century, the same is largely true of spiritual writing generally. Their members not merely inherited their traditions, but their experience as confessors and spiritual directors enabled them to apply and adapt their orders' traditions to new circumstances and to a new public, as was increasingly the case from the sixteenth century onwards. As lay literacy and religious exigencies grew, their skills were increasingly linked to the development of a 'method' of regulating the spiritual lives of individuals: it was not enough for people to pray, read or meditate; they should do so in a consciously planned fashion in order to achieve the greatest benefit from them. The orders' own regulated lifestyle gave them a distinct advantage here, a kind of template from which to map out the circumstances or times of the day when laypeople should read or meditate. Obviously, such a translation of the 'ordinary' day of a cloistered community to the world outside was accessible only to a lay elite, among whom it may well have heightened the tension between the secular and contemplative life.

This was one of the many reasons why the need for clergy capable of acting as guides for individuals became so extensive during and especially after the wars of religion. It also explains why the new orders of the Catholic Reformation found such a demand for their skills, and why they were widely welcomed, as we saw earlier, in so many small to middling towns across France. The Jesuits quickly became the best-known practitioners of spiritual direction in the broad sense, and for good reason, but other orders, particularly the Capuchins, were scarcely less active. Their demotic image should not disguise the extent to which the Capuchins' pens contributed to their apostolate, especially in the first half of the century. From Benoît de Canfeld to Père Joseph and Yves de Paris, they produced influential spiritual writers whose works ranged from high-level mystical explorations (Canfeld) to treatises on how to relate one's devotional life to one's social or professional standing (Yves de Paris).[7] The Jesuits' reputation was founded on the most methodical of all approaches to the spiritual life of the individual, Ignatius of Loyola's *Spiritual Exercises*, which were explicitly designed to be read and, especially, *practised* under the guidance of an experienced director. The *Exercises* had the enormous advantage of being readily adaptable for laypeople, and following them was intended to lead to a 'lifestyle' choice to follow God rather than Satan in the 'estate' in which one lived. But this moment of 'conversion' was only the trigger-point, and from then onwards, the individual was invited to engage in continual self-examination and daily religious actions which were no less methodical, and which left little to personal fantasy.

This 'methodical' development of an interior religious life entailed the kind of introspection and self-discipline that is more usually associated with the most challenging forms of Protestantism. Historically, the *Spiritual Exercises* preceded the involvement of the Jesuits in schools, but once the connection between the two was made, it became a major source of the order's success as a purveyor of spirituality and spiritual discipline to the elites of Catholic Europe. The Jesuits quickly realised that there was a better chance of success if they began by directing their efforts towards selected members of the senior classes in their colleges, who were gathered together in the Marian sodalities or congregations, and were placed under the wing of an experienced spiritual director capable of following an individual's progress; and the same basic format applied to the alumni and other congregations of adults that the Jesuits organised throughout the towns where they were installed.[8] The originator of the *Spiritual Exercises* may not have imagined such a development – which one Jesuit described around 1580 as a 'seminary for a truly holy life' – but it was certainly in line with with the kind of spirituality that Loyola proposed for the Jesuits themselves, one of an active apostolate in the world, in which activity was no longer a mere distraction but a form of true asceticism. This maxim would become common coin among many of the new congregations of seventeenth-century France, which in turn spread the message into their lay surroundings.

Mystical Invasion?

Nothing may seem more antithetical to the approach of the Jesuits than mysticism, yet the fact that many late sixteenth-century Jesuits were tempted to adopt and diffuse it is clear evidence of its continuing power of attraction. Strange as it may seem in retrospect, the Jesuits lacked an authoritative spiritual tradition, since Loyola did not attempt to provide one, and that partly accounts for the internal tensions between the active and the contemplative impulses that arose in their ranks during later generations. In the 1580s and 1590s, it took resolute action from the society's leadership in Rome to reaffirm the active, non-contemplative character of their mission yet, as we shall see, seventeenth-century France was home to some eminent and influential Jesuit mystics.[9] There is no short definition or description of the term 'mysticism' that could adequately convey the complexity of the search for a 'union' with the divine that it involves, one that goes well beyond conventional religious practices, even among the highly devout. This 'total' union was to be achieved through intense prayer and meditation. The dominant metaphor in most accounts of the search for such mystical union was that of a journey of several stages, during which the individual was tested and purified by successive experiences of privation, abandonment and the 'dark night of the soul'. Its final, highest stages were characterised by differing degrees of recollection, abnegation, stillness or indifference, leading to the surrender of self – or rather of one's 'interior', the favourite metaphor of seventeenth-century writers – to God, who takes possession of the soul and the will of the individual, thus bringing about the desired union. We shall return later to the implications of this vocabulary, since attempts to turn the experiences of individuals into a general 'method' for adoption by others were often met with suspicion and criticism.

In his *History*, Bremond went as far as to claim that seventeenth-century France experienced a 'mystical invasion', followed by a 'mystical conquest', both of which were essentially confined to the first half of the century. Historians have subsequently qualified the extent of both of these phenomena, along with the inference that mysticism did not previously exist in France. However, in rescuing them, as he did, from the almost total ignorance that had surrounded mysticism generally after the papal condemnation of Fénelon in 1699, Bremond opened the way towards a fuller understanding of the overall range and vitality of the spirituality of the age. It would be a mistake to imagine 'mysticism' as a rarefied plant of extremely limited interest: during the century we are concerned with, it frequently carried a 'charge' which invigorated the wider realms of spirituality, practical and theoretical.[10]

Among the deluge of translations of spiritual works of the early seventeenth century, the mystics were especially prominent; for the first time, these translations made a large body of spiritual writing accessible to a wide audience, lay and clerical. The work of some Rheno-Flemish mystics – Tauler, Ruysbroeck, Harphius – was already known in some circles, but the leading Spaniards and Italians were translated for the first time from the 1600s to the 1620s. As early as 1597, the young Pierre de Bérulle translated one such text, the 'Brief compendium of Christian perfection', composed by an Italian Jesuit, Gagliardi, at a time when the Italian original was still circulating in manuscript form because it was too dangerous to publish it in Italy. Bérulle's work was followed not merely by other translations, but in due course by something far newer – namely original works of a mystical bent composed in French by leading figures of the nascent *dévot* movement. In fact, both translations and new works were consubstantial with the *dévots*, especially the Acarie circle in Paris, since they were the prime consumers of such works, several of which were based directly upon *their* spiritual experiences.[11] This pattern would continue to be a fundamental feature of mystical writing and spirituality for the rest of the century. The religious experiences of the likes of Mme Acarie, Marie Guyart or Jeanne de Chantal were the subject of observation and correspondence prior to serving as the basis of general treatises written by acquaintances or directors of conscience. Hagiographical works, as we shall see later, could serve a similar objective and in a more accessible format. Such 'treatises' were not based on scholastic or theological premises, but built up from experience and observation, a development which led the Jesuit mystic, Surin, famously to describe mysticism as an 'experimental science', whose purpose was, as always, to find the secret of a perfect union with God. The place of women in this trend, especially as the actual practitioners of mystical-spiritual themes, is simply too massive to overlook, a fact which cuts right across conventional notions of spiritual direction and authorship. This frequently compounded the difficulties encountered by mystical authors with political and ecclesiastical authorities. And when women themselves took up the pen and proposed their own approaches to the secrets of union with God, the problems could be far worse, as Mme Guyon discovered after writing her 'Short and Easy Method of Prayer' in the 1680s.

As it does in so many other contexts, Bérulle's career offers an excellent illustration of the development of French religious thought and practice at a decisive moment in its history, but its impact on wider spiritual trends was far greater than we might imagine.[12] His earliest works show he was under the influence of the so-called 'abstract' school of northern European mysticism, which was God-centred (theocentric) in the sense that it conceived the mystical union of the individual with God as direct and without a 'facilitating' intermediary. But Bérulle, who had also been influenced by his education under the Jesuits, was sufficiently open-minded to seek a different, more Christ-centred form of spirituality. This happened progressively, and he was perfectly placed, due to his involvement in the Acarie circle (with its collection of mystics like Canfeld and Beaucousin), in the introduction of the Spanish Carmelites to France, and in the founding and direction of the Oratory, to soak up and reorient the major currents of thought of the time.

The outcome, which only became evident by the 1620s, was a Christocentric spirituality, at the heart of which stood not an abstract and infinite godhead, but Christ as the Word incarnate. Christ as both a human and divine figure was the natural and indeed the obligatory mediator between God and man, the spiritual equivalent, as Bérulle himself put it, of Copernicus's sun within the universe. It is Christ the priest and redeemer who brings mankind to God as a result of his incarnation; for Bérulle, there is simply no shortcut to union with God which excludes Christ. This was a startling claim to make at the time, and one that had considerable implications for a raft of religious attitudes. Bérulle also emphasised Christ's humanity, especially the different stages of his life (his childhood, in particular) and the attitudes that were appropriate to each of them (*états*, in Bérulle's language). They served as means whereby individuals 'adhered' (another key term of Bérulle's) to Christ and were infused with divine grace. Such 'adherence' was imagined by Bérulle as ultimately leading to a sort of 'servitude' or 'slavery', and it led him as far as to impose a vow of servitude to Christ and the Virgin on members of the Oratory and the Carmelites – a move which sparked internal resistance as well as external attacks upon Bérulle, mainly by the Jesuits, in the late 1610s and early 1620s.

Bérulle and his disciples also insisted on the role of Mary, Christ's mother, in their understanding of the 'economy of salvation', thus making 'adherence' to her a natural prelude to adherence to Christ. For all its difficulties, intellectual and practical, Berullian spirituality was much less metaphysical than its 'abstract' predecessor, and it had solid theological foundations. Nor was it intended for a tiny elite, least of all for a cloistered one, since one of Bérulle's most abiding goals was to find a spirituality suitable for the needs of the secular clergy. His and his disciples' relative success in this means that it is easy to forget how novel and unexpected it was at a time when most people doubted if the secular clergy, any more than laypeople generally, could have a genuine spiritual life at all! Bérulle laid the foundations for it by associating the ordained priest with Christ, the only true priest, whose priesthood was an essential feature of his mission to redeem humanity for God. The sacrament of orders was, therefore, a participation in Christ's priesthood, giving the priest the immense privilege of making Christ present in the Eucharist and communicating him to others. Such an interpretation elevated even the most mediocre of priests into a special category of Christian, placing him above everyone else, members of religious orders included. A distinctively 'sacerdotal' spirituality was the outcome, and Bérulle's many disciples – institutional as well as individual, such as Saint-Cyran, Condren, Vincent de Paul, Olier, Jean Eudes, Tronson, the Oratory, Saint-Lazare, Saint-Sulpice – all reworked his ideas over the next century or so, sometimes with scarcely any reference to their original begetter. Because so many of them were also involved in attempts to reform France's secular clergy, their applications of Berullian thinking were practice-based rather than just book-lore, thus ensuring that there was more to the process of clerical reform than behavioural amelioration.

The 'French school' of spirituality, with which Bérulle is so closely identified, is often reduced to a spirituality for the clergy, but it will be evident from the account above that Bérulle's thought and its subsequent modifications cannot be so easily pigeonholed. He had himself absorbed numerous influences, so it is hardly surprising that his ideas continued to ramify after his death. As for the manner in which they did so, some of the reasons go back to Bérulle's own modus operandi. He was not a clear or attractive writer in an age which increasingly boasted many fine stylists. Constantly engaged in political, diplomatic and religious affairs, he tended to write in a highly ad hoc way, often in response to criticisms or immediate preoccupations; and several important texts remained unpublished for a very long time. Most of his influence on contemporaries – and his circle was a remarkably wide one – was exercised through personal connections and liberally dispensed advice, some of which can be seen in his impressive surviving correspondence. The resulting absence of a complete or closed corpus of thought provided his closest associates and disciples with the incentive and the freedom to develop his ideas further, which has led one historian to claim, paradoxically, that the more widely Bérulle's influence spread, thanks to his followers, the less he was himself known or read after his death in 1629. Important examples of the continuing expansion of Bérulle's thought were those of the 'sacred heart' of

Jesus and of devotion to the Virgin Mary, which disciples like Jean Eudes and Olier did much to promote; both devotions grew during the seventeenth century, and were widely adopted by *dévots* and confraternities. Equally, Bérulle's emphasis on the Word incarnate offered a new basis for the development of the Eucharistic devotions also discussed in previous chapters, as well as to revitalise others. But they and other continuators of Bérulle did not simply write broad, general treatises for others to interpret and apply; their spiritual works were often – or even mainly – manuals for practising the devotions that they preached, explaining how to engage in them, which prayers to say, how to progress from one stage of devotion to another, and so on. If their efforts were not as successful as they would have wished, it was certainly not for lack of didactic intent on their part.[13]

Salesian Themes

One older contemporary of Bérulle who had no difficulty in writing for a wide audience and in a style that captivated generations was François de Sales (1567–1622), who from 1602 onwards was bishop of Geneva (in practice, however, of Annecy).[14] A former pupil of the Jesuits like Bérulle, he had studied in Paris during the Catholic League, was entirely French in culture and encountered the Acarie circle in Paris in 1602. His return visits there were triumphs, thanks to the impact of his personality, but also of his preaching, spiritual direction, correspondence and writings. A better example of the extent to which a spirituality grew and spread by a combination of media would be hard to find in any period. Behind the *douceur*, however, there was a religious message that was startlingly simple: prayer and union with God was for everyone; the holy grail of 'perfection' was available for each person, according to their 'state' in life, and it should no longer to be a monopoly of the cloister. As he himself put it, it was heresy to banish the devout life from among the barracks of soldiers, the family of married people, the courts of princes and the workshop of artisans. An irate Capuchin reacted by describing him as a 'true successor of Calvin in that chair of plague, Geneva'! De Sales is often regarded as the first to develop a spirituality for laypeople, but this does not seem quite the way he saw it – he appears to have envisaged a spirituality that extended across all social and professional conditions, rather than one specially reserved for the laity. Like so many other spiritual writers, what he wrote was a distillation of his experience of spiritual direction and reflection on actual experience. His two great works, the *Introduction to the Devout Life* (1608) and the *Treatise on the Love of God* (1616) both derived from directing women, the first a laywoman (Mme de Charmoisy), the second a nun-cum-widow (Jeanne de Chantal) with whom he founded the Order of the Visitation.

In his tireless reiteration of God's desire to save all men and, therefore, to ensure that the means of salvation were readily available to them, de Sales was unlikely to cause a theological stir. As a former student of the Jesuits, his underlying thinking was close to theirs, particularly in his emphasis on the centrality of the will in human life. Sin only weakens our capacity to love God, and God's compassion is so immense and active that it bridges the gap between the human and the divine. On this basis, de Sales invites individual Christians to take advantage of what is available to them and systematically to seek a union with God, which can, after several stages, reach a state of repose and contemplation which does not entail the 'annihilation of self' or the total surrender of the will of earlier writers. There was a genuinely mystical end-point which gradually emerged in de Sales's thought, but it is easy to underestimate it because of the everyday language in which he formulated his approach and his efforts to simplify what it entailed. He made the stages towards 'perfection' appear sufficiently easy and logical as to sound wholly feasible and normal. The individual's relation with God was one which should be devoted to pleasing God and to doing His will, and that brought an important 'psychological' element into Salesian spirituality. No fewer than thirteen chapters of his *Introduction* dealt with 'the elevation of the soul to God through prayer'. The persuasiveness of de Sales's message was reinforced by the format of his works, which took the shape of letters and which could, consequently, speak directly to readers as if they were being personally guided along the path to the love of God by de Sales himself. It may be added here that de Sales did more than any other major figure of his time to underline the importance of having recourse to a competent spiritual director, and not to undertake unusual devotions without proper guidance.

The Bishop of Geneva's beguiling prose was entirely *sui generis*, and it added incalculably to the attractiveness of his message. That, and the fact that he was made a saint as early as 1665, meant that those – such as the augustinian-Jansenists – who disagreed with the theological or anthropological bases of his approach, were invariably reluctant directly to attack or disown him. Indeed, it is not often realised that the very Berullian and Augustinian abbé de Saint-Cyran was influenced in several important respects by de Sales – especially on the importance of charity as the key virtue – and transmitted that influence to his principal disciple, Antoine Arnauld, who paid eloquent homage to de Sales in his *Frequent Communion* (1643). Unlike Bérulle, however, de Sales's spirituality was diffused rather than further developed after his death in 1622. His own huge correspondence had already ensured its diffusion among the religious elites of France and Savoy, but its inimitably 'personal' expression and characteristics made it difficult to rework it much further. There was at least one indefatigable preacher of Salesian spirituality, Jean-Pierre Camus

(1584–1652), who from 1609 to 1629 governed the diocese of Belley adjoining de Sales's Annecy. In literally dozens of works, which enjoyed an enormously wide readership, the prolific Camus reiterated the main themes of de Sales's work, suggesting methods for meditation and supplying the text of prayers for use in different circumstances. He even managed to do so in the format of the 'devout' novel, which he seems to have invented. It may well have been this kind of 'vulgarisation' that led the 'general' of the Benedictine Maurists, Grégoire Tarisse, to discourage his monks from reading de Sales's works on the grounds that 'they did not sufficiently inspire men to the love of tribulations and austerities'.[15]

What emerges from comparing these two apparently highly contrasted approaches to the spiritual life, as exemplified by Bérulle and de Sales, is that there were indeed possible 'crossovers' between them. These were perhaps less evident during the lifetimes of the two protagonists but, as we saw, the Berullian tradition was continually broadened during subsequent generations. De Sales had always been more explicitly 'mainstream', and part of what Bremond called the movement of 'devout humanism'. This ambiguous notion has had many critics, partly on the grounds that it glides too rapidly over the different emphases among many of the spiritual writers that were claimed to belong to it, and because it extended too far into the seventeenth century the Renaissance search to accommodate Christian and classic pre-Christian values. But scarcely any seventeenth-centry French spiritual writer would have cared to follow Erasmus in 'canonising' Socrates and declaring his virtues to be Christian: this approach, which could easily lead to a preference for pagan virtues (such as those of the Stoics), was increasingly left to the secular moralists and 'learned libertines'. The shock and challenge of the Protestant Reformations had sufficed to weaken such approaches, and the reassertion of Augustinian themes of human sinfulness that followed within Catholicism – a kind of 'rigorist turn' – was bound to affect not merely professional theologians but, as we shall see again with Jansenism, spiritual writers and directors more broadly. Borrowings and combinations of different strands of thought were common, suggesting that terms like 'devout humanism' or 'the French school' are no longer ideally suited to identifying the more subtle and nuanced works of spirituality.

A good example here is the Jesuits, who throughout the seventeenth century regularly produced authors of hugely successful works of devotion. Partly because of the criticism to which they were subjected by Antoine Arnauld, Pascal and the Augustinian-Jansenists, they are often credited with a fairly undemanding 'devout humanist' approach, one that was almost predetermined by their upbeat views of human nature and man's capacity to effect his own salvation. It seems undeniable that a certain number of highly prolific and widely read Jesuit authors such as Louis Richeome, Étienne Binet or Paul de Barry corresponded *grosso modo* to such an evaluation, overplaying the 'Salesian card' by reducing the search for salvation to unchallenging duties or observances. But no less eminent Jesuits of the first half of the century took a different line with their readers and *dirigés*. Pierre Coton, the first Jesuit confessor to the French Bourbon monarchy, argued strongly in 1606 that the French Jesuits were too absorbed in their activities and insufficiently contemplative. Two years later, in 1608, he published his 'Interior occupation of a devout soul' in 1608, a title which immediately evokes de Sales's 'Introduction to the devout life' of the same year. For the most part, this and other works by Coton share common ground with de Sales, especially his optimistic take on man's prospects of salvation, but simultaneously there are also traces of a pessimistic vision of human nature which inclined Coton towards a certain mysticism. Later Jesuit royal confessors such as Jean Suffren and Nicolas Caussin were tougher still, especially Caussin, who practised what he preached during his brief and tumultuous few months as Louis XIII's confessor in 1637. Both men exhibited a rather sombre view of human nature and were critical of many contemporary mores, especially among the social elites, but unlike the Augustinians they still firmly believed, as de Sales did, that God's design was to save rather than damn humanity.[16]

Spirituality and *Devoirs d'État*

One feature uniting many of the authors discussed above was a conscious pursuit of the idea that is most associated with de Sales – that 'ordinary' Christians can live a full religious-spiritual life in the world, and can sanctify themselves through their daily activities.[17] To a great extent, this effort was a response to the spread of new devotions, especially the greater frequentation of the sacraments, and the correspondingly increasing recourse to spiritual direction, rather than a sudden burst of initiative by spiritual writers themselves. De Sales's early proclamation of this message was significant, and it had a wider impact than if it had been the work of, say, a Jesuit or an Oratorian. But since de Sales did not himself go into detail about individual conditions or status, there was ample scope for others to do so. Richelieu was quite explicit in his belief that religious values had to be adapted to social situations, and that the world could not simply be turned into a monastery or retreat. It has to be said that relatively few of the authors or directors who pioneered this kind of 'applied' spirituality are known to more than a handful of specialists, yet quite a few of them were endlessly reprinted and widely read during our period.

The Jesuits were among the first to respond to the challenge, with their published works doubtless reflecting prior experience of directing individuals, but also of organising particular socio-professional groups in their own Marian congregations. Adjusting religious maxims to individuals' conditions and status in society was a far from straightforward question of judgement, especially during the early decades of the seventeenth century. Some of the most successful spiritual guides for laypeople of the era, such as Père Le Moyne's *Devotion Made Easy*, were later subjected to a full-on assault from Pascal and others for what they regarded as their wilful 'dilution' of Christian precepts that, in their view, should apply equally to everyone. Part of the problem here was the format in which this application was presented. Writers like Le Moyne (also a widely read poet) adopted a literary style what was often flowery, precious and highly ornamented – 'baroque' – and their advice was often larded with classical analogies, moral tales and historical examples of all kinds, whose immediate relevance was not always apparent. The justification for such 'decoration', which entangled pagan classical and Christian models, was that the intended audience was already accustomed to, and expected such didactic methods, and that it was better to use the latter rather than one that was wholly unfamiliar to them.

This kind of approach was judged most likely to work in relation to a category of lay Christians that was of particular interest, courtiers and the nobility generally.[18] The concern with their behaviour and culture – notably that of failure to control their passions – was not exclusively 'religious' in seventeenth-century France, since moralists and educationalists generally produced their own recipes for a nobility that would emulate ancient models of gravity, restraint, wisdom and other virtues. Not everyone in seventeenth-century France thought that elite religion and the religion of the elite were synomymous. Both François de Sales and the abbé de Saint-Cyran thought that 'sanctification' at this level of society required a certain reserve or 'withdrawal' towards the world in which one lived, but Saint-Cyran was more pessimistic about the chances that the rich and powerful generally would be saved.

The Jesuits, who were increasingly the principal educators of nobles in their ever-expanding network of colleges, were themselves heavily committed to shaping the Christian version of the 'honnête homme'. But with so many noble students finishing their studies in early adolescence, formal education alone was not enough. Hence the resort to Marian congregations and other methods that we have already seen, but also the readiness to act as spiritual directors to former students, whether court-based nobles or not. In this connection, it was hardly an accident that one of the first seventeenth-century attempts at spiritual guidance for laypeople was that of Henri IV's confessor, Pierre Coton, and he had courtiers especially in mind. Père Le Moyne's much more widely read *Dévotion aisée* set out to persuade laypeople that devotion was for them, and that it was as normal and rational to pursue devotion in their religious life as it was to pursue social and career goals in life generally. He conceded that most social customs – even gallantry – were compatible with devotion, and that with the proper 'interior' intention many otherwise questionable practices were acceptable. Why should the devout be a social, and why should they not be happier than their more indifferent contemporaries![19]

It is not hard to see why the apostles of a more severe moral standard would find Le Moyne's best-seller so lamentable. They found far less to fault with his fellow Jesuit, Nicolas Caussin, who between 1624 and 1631 produced a massive three-volume best-seller, the *Cour Sainte*, which went through fifteen editions before his death in 1651. Caussin was only briefly royal confessor in 1637, so his work was not based on the kind of court experience that Pierre Coton had. His approach also differed from Le Moyne's, since he postulated the replacement of a profane, pleasure-oriented court with a Christian one based on regular devotion, clear moral standards and constant self-discipline and surveillance. Courtiers were not meant to be monks, he conceded, but the 'way of perfection' was as available to them as to everyone else; it was a question of 'sanctifying' oneself by religious practices on a regular daily basis within the life of the court. There was no ground for arguing that this was asking the impossible of them, and Caussin was blunt enough to give them the option of quitting the court altogether if they thought it prevented them from pursuing their salvation! In fact, in pitting the Christian court against its profane counterpart, Caussin was developing an analysis which was adaptable to wider, non-courtly situations, and the enormous success of the *Cour Sainte* shows that it attracted a wider readership than courtiers, actual or potential.[20]

Further works to guide the 'spiritualised' courtier or noble continued to be published in the second half of the century. Others, such as Antoine Godeau's *Instructions chrétiennes*, provided prayers to be said by different categories of people – merchants, artisans, judges and so on. But it appears that from around mid-century onwards, this genre merged into a broader current of advice and guidance for laypeople generally, in which social distinctions now mattered less and less, and the inner spiritual development of the individual became central.[21] This would explain why some of these works were virtual encyclopaedias, replete with advice, texts and prayers for almost every individual, occasion and circumstance. In 1637, Caussin himself published the *Treatise on Spiritual Behaviour in the Spirit of François de Sales*. In the early 1640s, one of Caussin's predecessors as royal confessor, Jean Suffren, added his *Christian Year*, whose four volumes ran to over 4,000 pages in all, with two dedicated solely to the liturgical year! Suffren, for all his prolixity, was closer to Caussin than to Le Moyne in the moral standards that he set for the average Christian living in the world.[22] And it would be a mistake to overlook, merely because the genre itself was no longer novel, the continuing high output of works devoted to preparation for a good death, for example, during Louis XIV's reign.[23] A particularly successful example, *The Happiness of a Christian Death*, first appeared in 1688, and was reprinted numerous times in the next twenty or so years. Its author, the Oratorian Pasquier Quesnel, would become far better known for his Jansenist affiliations.[24]

A useful key to the success or failure of attempts to spiritualise the life of laypeople is how the question of marriage was handled. As an institution in which secular and 'customary' practices had, without major objections from the church, long been so dominant, marriage needed a broad theological-spiritual reappraisal that would correspond to the post-Trent church's expectations for it.[25] An initial basis for such revision was provided by Trent's own revision of the classic 'ends' of marriage, which was more optimistic than the traditional teaching, based on St Augustine, for whom these ends were, in descending order of importance, procreation, avoidance of occasions of sexual sin and mutual support between spouses. Building upon Thomist and more recent humanist ideas, Trent placed the desire to live together first, followed by the bringing of children into the world, with the avoidance of sin coming last. But there were several reasons why any rethinking of marriage might be more limited than Trent's decisions would lead us to expect. In a world where married women were regarded as subject to their husbands' authority, it was not easy to find an idiom capable of expressing mutual affection and, thus, some kind of 'equality' among spouses. Also working against a full rehabilitation of marriage was the equal but opposite emphasis on the superiority of the clerical condition (which included regulars and, therefore, women) over all others; the celibacy of the latter was the ultimate form of love of God, with which human love could simply not compete. As we saw, the prime movers in any revised presentation of the 'dignity' of marriage, the French clergy, were the clergy most heavily committed to exalting the importance of the priesthood.

If we take our cue from what the early to mid-eighteenth century church was preaching in books, catechisms and other media, it would seem as if the older message of marriage as a refuge from concupiscence and its function as essentially procreative had not changed at all. But this semblance of unbroken continuity of views on marriage is somewhat misleading, although it is necessary to be clear about our terms. During the intervening generations real efforts were made to broadcast a more appealing message. The first major figure to take full advantage of the shift signalled by Trent and to translate it into a language accessible to a wide audience was de Sales, whose *Introduction to the Devout Life* was written for a cousin who was married and the mother of two children. He rehabilitated not just the religious life of laypeople generally, but paid specific attention to married people, to whom he clearly offered the possibility of mutual sanctification within a normal married life, going as far as to reassure readers that normal sexual relations and sanctifaction were not mutually exclusive. This assertion was far bolder at the time than it seems. De Sales drew to some extent upon the approach of the Jesuits to combining a religious life with a career and obligations outside of the cloister, but it seems that it was not until the 1640s that his lead was really followed, if we are to judge by a series of works published by a younger generation of writers thereafter. During the 1620s and 1630s the Salesian flame had been kept alive by his most prominent disciple, Jean-Pierre Camus, whose numerous religious novels of a highly didactic kind presented an upbeat portrait of companionate Christian marriage. Some of the most influential and longest-lasting treatises and guide books on the subject were written from the early 1640s onwards; edifying lives of selected 'exemplary' couples were also used to convey a similar message, notably on the tricky subject of the role of the wife as partner rather than as a subordinate figure.

Obviously, works like these were destined for a literate, mainly urban audience, but it was typical of seventeenth-century developments in religious pedagogy that manuals and even catechisms for married people should begin to emerge at this juncture. From Jean Cordier's *La Sainte Famille* and Claude Maillard's *Le Bon Marriage* (both 1643) to Père Féline's *Catechisme des gens mariés* and Pierre Sandret's *Règlement des familles* (1719), there was, judging at least by the number of editions they went through, a steady demand for such advice. Women were portrayed primarily as mothers and spouses, and not merely legal minors under their husbands' authority. For their part, husbands were pressed to see the necessity and benefits of reciprocity if couples were to form a spiritual union in which they could sanctify themselves and their children, so as to become, as Agnès Walch recently put it, 'the infantry of the Catholic Reformation'. There was a considerable variety of biblical texts from both Testaments, and particularly the letters of St Paul, on which to construct a spirituality of marriage. Above all, the model of Christ's own 'mystical' marriage to his church was endlessly recycled. Human couples were poor copies of this higher one, yet were called upon to imitate Christ's virtues. For most of the seventeenth century, the emphasis of this spirituality seems to have been less on the family created by married couples than on their own mutual love for each other, a love which, it was hoped, would in turn engender the virtue of charity.

It does seem, however, that by the latter decades of the seventeenth century, a reaction against the Salesian-Jesuit approach to marriage began to take effect. It is likely that some of the recent casuistry surrounding marriage gave offence because it made too many concessions to human sexuality. The

Augustinian-Jansenist-rigorist approach, which we shall see more of in other contexts, exploited this to the full since it took a dismal view of human nature as intrinsically sinful, with sexual passion and sin as a characteristic weakness of fallen humans. The 'eagle of Meaux' himself, Bossuet, forthrightly rehabilitated the Augustinian view of the ends of marriage in his catechism of 1687, and he had numerous imitators then and later. Ultimately, as Briggs has shown, inherited negative views of the family generally remained too widespread among the French clergy for a new spirituality of marriage to flourish; it would be left to the secular and pre-romantic writers of the next century to celebrate it in a very different idiom.

Twilight of the Mystics?

Around 1650, according to Louis Cognet, 'French mysticism was like a beautiful tree covered with flowers, but whose roots were infected'.[26] Its health was not purely a question of its own intrinsic content or attractiveness: there was also a strong anti-mystical current at work within France, and it became stronger with time. The more seventeenth-century mysticism acquired its own vocabulary, methods and systematic treatises, the more it became independent of theological method generally. Suspicion and rejection grew accordingly, mirroring perhaps the experience of Spanish mysticism during the previous century. Because France had no Inquisition to track down its 'illuministi', there were periodic 'scares' or 'incidents' arising in connection with this or that alleged mystical deviation. The period of Richelieu's ministry, roughly speaking, was so peppered by them that, despite consistent failures to find convincing evidence of such deviations, they appear to have become one of his obsessions. Bérulle was attacked in the 1620s, the 'illuminés' of Picardy were persecuted from 1627 onwards and Richelieu came close to charging Saint-Cyran in the late 1630s with 'illuminism'. *Cas célèbres* of alleged diabolical possession, such as those of Loudun (1635) and Louviers (1643), did even greater damage, as it was not difficult to pin the blame for them on the supposed deviant spirituality of the spiritual directors of the convents involved. Jesuits like Surin and Saint-Jure, who acted as directors to Loudun's Ursuline nuns, in 1635 and later, came under heavy attack, and their attempts at defending themselves only exposed their cause even further. Surin, however, managed to stage something of a comeback: having endured a twenty-year mental breakdown after the Loudun affair, he re-emerged in the 1650s as a highly reputed spiritual director whose major works, published between 1657 and 1667, continued to be widely read for the remainder of the century.[27]

On the other hand, the Jesuit mystic of this period who would exercise the greatest influence in later centuries, Louis Lallemant (1588–1635), published nothing in his lifetime. His untimely death and the fact that his disciples kept their notes of his teaching out of sight until the 1690s meant he remained largely unknown before the next century. This fate seems perplexing, given that he was attempting to develop a mystical spirituality that would be at the service of an active apostolate.[28] At the very least, it suggests that the majority of France's Jesuits were unwelcoming to this kind of approach, to the point of effacing the mystical dimensions of Ignatius Loyola himself at this point.[29] Above all, from mid-century onwards, the neo-Augustinian Jansenists entered the fray, and in Pierre Nicole (1625–95) they had probably the most single-minded and destructive critic of any spirituality promising the prospect of direct union with God. Like many others of his generation, Nicole, a man of formidable learning, was wholly tone-deaf to such thinking. Christian spirituality was a matter of focusing one's attention on the humanity of Christ and engaging in methodical, discursive prayer, and not on the expectation of illusory contemplative experiences. On this one issue, at least, Jesuits and Jansenists were largely in agreement.

It would be wrong to imagine that only the religious orders or the clergy generally were interested in the higher realms of spirituality. The strong lay element of the Acarie circle, beginning with Mme Acarie herself, is clear evidence to the contrary. The most indefatigable translator of the Spanish mystics, René Gaultier, was a member of the circle and a magistrate in the Paris *parlement*. Further evidence of such lay involvement lies in the fact that lay mystics continued to emerge in the following generations. Even if it did not see itself as a school of spirituality, let alone of mysticism, the Company of the Holy Sacrament was a magnet for several mystics, lay and clerical. As early as 1632, some of its Parisian members decided to meet privately each week in order to conduct 'a kind of course in mystical theology in order to advance souls in meditation and in interior perfection'.[30] Two of the company's most prominent members were the Normans, Jean de Bernières and Gabriel de Renty. Renty, who died in 1649, had been the driving force of the Paris chapter of the company during the previous decade, but he also found the time to act, via correspondence, as a spiritual director to, among others, a Carmelite nun in Dijon! His own spiritual director and fellow mystic, the Jesuit Saint-Jure, published a biography of Renty (1651), significantly entitled *The Idea of a Perfect Christian*, in an attempt to diffuse his spirituality among laypeople. Renty's fellow *compagnon*, René de Voyer d'Argenson, is, thanks to Michel de Certeau's study of him, a particularly interesting instance of a lay mystic whose political career exposed him to the increasingly conflicting logics of the service of God and of the prince. His *Treatise of Christian Wisdom, or the Rich Science of Uniformity with the Will of God* (1651) underlines, as its title suggests, the need to cultivate renunciation and 'indifference' so as to purify and prepare oneself for 'abandonment' to God's will.[31] Other works offering a mystical spirituality were based on the experiences of female mystics like Marie des Vallées (directed by Jean Eudes) or Jeanne des Anges (directed by Surin).

The last stand of seventeenth-century French mysticism came much later in the century, and revolved initially around another female lay mystic, but by the time it had played out, it involved leading figures of the court and the church.[32] The mystical spirituality was different again to what we witnessed earlier in discussing Bérulle and his disciples, in that it placed the emphasis on contemplation and complete abandonment of oneself to God in prayer. The word 'quietism' was coined to describe, and discredit, it as an open invitation to moral laxity. It reached France from Spain via Italy, where its principal protagonist, the Spaniard, Miguel de Molinos, was imprisoned and his *Spiritual Guide* (1675) was condemned by Rome in 1687. Equally significant was the fact that a large number of major works of mystical spirituality, some of them French, had been condemned and placed on the Index by that point. On that list, alongside Canfeld, Surin and Bernières, was Jeanne Bouvier de la Motte (1648–1717), better known as Mme Guyon. After years of experiment and reading of earlier writers like Canfeld, Teresa of Avila and John of the Cross, as well as Molinos under the guidance of a spiritual director, Guyon published her *Short and Easy Method to Pray* in 1685 and, like Molinos's *Spiritual Guide*, it had considerable immediate success. She proposed a spirituality in which 'normal' discursive prayer would be superseded as the individual, through successive stages, gradually reached the level of pure non-intellectual contemplation, a state in which one becomes indifferent to everything, including one's interests and even one's own salvation. Her message was that action mattered less than docility and passivity – hence the 'quietist' label it acquired – in achieving union with God, and it, too, seemed to dispense with the need for intermediaries. Mme Guyon was treading on dangerous ground here, despite the fact that much of what she said was anything but new. On such a slippery terrain, her understandable lack of a precise theological training or vocabulary did not help either. As with Molinos, however, it was only when it transpired that she had acquired a serious following that the alarm really began to sound. In this case, the scare was much greater than usual, since it appeared that her influence reached as far as the foot of the throne, via Mme de Maintenon's school at Saint-Cyr and via the brilliant Abbé Fénelon, who was then preceptor to Louis XIV's grandson and spiritual mentor to several high-ranking aristocratic court families.

We need not enter into the complex political details of what followed and which ended in 1699 with the papal condemnation of Fénelon's attempts to defend Mme Guyon's work. For many historians this decision, taken extremely reluctanctly by Rome, represents a – or rather *the* – 'twilight of the mystics' (Cognet), and the ultimate victory of a more rationalist and intellectualist approach to spirituality, as personified by the ageing Bossuet who, for all his other abilities, was quite incapable of understanding mystical thinking of any sort. For the likes of Fénelon, mystical experiences were a possible, even 'normal' development of the process of individual sanctification, whereas for Bossuet they were wholly exceptional, almost miraculous events and, therefore, reserved for a tiny few, so that attempts to extend them to a wider population were both misguided and dangerous.[33] The heavy blows traded during the Bossuet–Fénelon combat, especially by the unscrupulous Bossuet, during their 'books war' of 1697–8, briefly captured the interest of public opinion for a subject of which it knew virtually nothing, but the outcome was to send any spirituality with mystical accents further into the wilderness. Fénelon, who possessed the culture and the sensibility to inflect the French church's growing moralist and rationalist approach to religious questions, found his influence and career prospects shattered by the 1699 dénouement. Mme Guyon herself was dealt a much sterner hand of cards: with her *Short and Easy Method* already on the Index, she spent several spells in prison from 1688 to 1703, and her ideas survived mainly through being taken up by Protestant writers outside France.

The latter decades of Louis XIV's reign cannot be regarded as obsessed only with the orthodoxy of mysticism. This question concerned relatively few people, even though the fate of mysticism had 'knock-on' effects for spirituality generally. It is well known that no enduringly influential works, mystical or otherwise, were composed after about 1680. But that did not halt the output of more mainstream works of spirituality and devotion. One example may serve here to introduce an important and relatively new ingredient of such writing in these decades. Pasquier Quesnel's *Moral Reflections*, to which we will return later, enjoyed sustained success from its first appearance. For all its later notoriety, it is primarily interesting as evidence of the effects, on spiritual writing destined for normal readers, of the campaign for the production of the Bible in the vernacular, an objective that the Augustinian-Jansenists – but others, too – fought so hard for.

Until the 1660s there was no satisfactory version of the New Testament in French, but one was provided in 1666 by the so-called 'Mons' Bible, translated by Isaac Le Maitre de Sacy of Port-Royal. By then, an established pattern among spiritual writers was to paraphrase the Bible or choose short extracts and then briefly gloss them, adding their own suggestions as to the thoughts and prayers that were appropriate as one read them. Quesnel was following this method when his first version of the *Moral Reflections* appeared in 1668, only two years after the Mons Bible. The later fate of his book – condemnation by

Rome in 1713 for its Jansenism – has overshadowed both its origins and the common features it shared with so many other works of spiritual guidance. Quesnel's later insistence that all Christians *must* read the Bible was, unsurprisingly, not widely shared, but an increasing use of biblical texts in devotional and liturgical works in the latter part of the seventeenth century did have an impact on French spirituality, even to the extent of curbing certain features of Marian and other devotions that were regarded as too sentimental or adventitious.[34]

Diffusing Spirituality

It will be obvious by now that the seventeenth-century French church witnessed successive and sustained efforts to expand the spiritual traditions which the religious crisis of the sixteenth century had challenged so directly. Of the demand for works of spirituality and devotion there can be no doubt: it was, indeed, so strong that, until the second and third decades of the century, it could only be satisfied by translating an impressive quantity of foreign works, both old and new, into French. The ensuing appropriation of these works laid the foundations for the more 'original' productions of younger generations of home-grown spiritual writers, though we should not imagine a simple cause and effect relation between them. It is worth noting that historians of this subject have sometimes appropriated the language of 'generalist' historians, writing of a shift from a Spanish 'golden century' to one of 'French preponderance'.[35]

The major problem, however, is how to measure the broader impact of such efforts. Ultimately, the question is unanswerable, except perhaps at a microhistorical level. It would entail making distinctions between the later sixteenth and the early eighteenth century, but also between town and country and, above, between social groups with widely contrasting literacy rates. Partial answers may be derived from looking at the mechanisms that were available and the methods that were employed to ensure the diffusion of spiritual and devotional ideas throughout the population. Some of these issues have already been examined, at least indirectly, since confraternities, catechism, preaching, schooling, ecclesiastical conferences and missions were all used for the purpose.

The continuing mobilisation of the printing press, long after the wars of religion had ended, for the diffusion of religious works as visibly different as the handsome editions of the Bible and the cheap, small-format books of devotion, is beyond doubt. The religious wars themselves increased the scale and geography of France's printing trade more than might otherwise have happened, since rival 'Catholic' and 'Protestant' towns across France (for instance in Anjou, Protestant Saumur versus Catholic La Flèche) generated business for the presses; they also habituated people to the massive use of the vernacular in the religious sphere. The return of peace in the 1590s witnessed not so much a decline of publishing as a displacement of its focus, especially within Catholicism, whose geographical spread was greater than that of French Protestantism. The installation in towns across France of religious orders like the Jesuits, the Capuchins and the more recent congregations, especially those with schools, increased – or even created – the demand for printers in many provincial centres. At a more modest level, episcopal towns, of which there were over 120 across France, often provided enough 'copy' for local printers to make a living at this juncture. Between them, teaching, preaching, missions, the conduct of 'congregations' and confraternities contributed to creating a local need for different kinds of works of devotion and meditation. But we can only guess, in the absence of exhaustive studies for our period, at the extent to which local presses satisfied local needs. Publishing as a business itself evolved considerably during the seventeenth century, and became increasingly concentrated in big centres like Paris, Lyon, Rouen, Reims, Avignon or Toulouse, which supplied a disproportionate quantity of religious works – from the high theological and scholarly treatises to the best-selling devotional works – and often used local printers as intermediaries to 'shift' their stock. Of course, some of these centres were players in international markets, so part of their output was destined for sale elsewhere.[36]

Henri-Jean Martin's study of publishing in seventeenth-century Paris is the only substantial one of its kind that we have, and although generalising from Paris's history is always problematic, it does suggest some interesting orders of magnitude.[37] One-third of all books produced in Paris under Henri IV and Louis XIII (1598–1643) dealt with religious subjects of one sort or another. It was not merely the overall percentage that was notable: the number of religious titles published per year rocketed from about fifteen for the decade 1600–1609 to around 600 for the year 1644 alone! Up to half of the stock of printers–booksellers consisted of religious works. Martin also detected a watershed in the decade between 1635 and 1645. Prior to that there had been a massive effort to produce and diffuse what he called 'the arsenal of the Catholic Reformation'. The post-Trent revisions of standard liturgical works were a substantial part of this effort, but so too were works of 'controversy', history, exegesis, theology and casuistry, not to mention older 'standard' works of spirituality and devotion. The demand for them was unprecedented and sustained, but the supply seems to have been no less so, as a result of which a point of saturation was finally attained by the end of Louis XIII's reign.

There was henceforth a greater demand for more accessible vernacular works for use by ordinary people. Books of hours in cheap, accessible editions remained in high demand. Classics like the *Imitation of Christ* competed with newer works like those of de Sales, Camus, Godeau, Yves de Paris and the numerous best-selling Jesuit authors of the day (Binet, de Barry, Le Moyne). Some individual works of these authors went through edition after edition over several decades – with editions ranging between 5,000 and 10,000 copies. It should be realised that the 'great' devotional classics had numerous imitators, as we saw in the case of Caussin's treatise on spiritual behaviour 'in the spirit of François de Sales'. But for every Caussin openly admitting his sources of inspiration, there were many others who simply plundered and recycled for perhaps less 'advanced' readers the themes and arguments of influential authors, old and new. Many other devotional best-sellers had yet to be written, of which Jean-Jacques Coret's *Guiding Angel* (1673) was probably the single most successful devotional book of the century before the French Revolution. Martin claimed that around 1700–20 France had become the biggest single producer of theological works in Europe, with Italy and Germany well behind it, but it seems equally likely that its production of devotional-spiritual works was just as substantial.[38]

The most difficult question to answer is how far all of this penetrated French society beyond an educated *dévot* elite, broadly defined. Historical research into book-holdings, based on probate inventories, is rarely as useful in tracking the spread of devotional ideas as it is for other ideas, because devotional works are nearly always the most poorly identified in the inventories. The survival rates of such works were very low in any case. Moreover, the financial value of 'ordinary' devotional works was so insignificant within an individual's estate that notaries usually lumped them together indiscriminately and rarely bothered to record their titles. However, the fact that they figure so frequently in surviving inventories and, more tellingly, were commonly described in them as 'worn' or 'bashed about', indicates high use-levels compared to the more expensive books bought for show and perhaps seldom ever opened. Such a process of diffusing spiritual-devotional works occurred gradually and required intermediaries, especially the clergy. It was not until the later decades of the century that clerical libraries began to resemble what Catholic reformers regarded as adequate, and the probate inventories of each generation of clergy show an improvement on its predecessors in this respect. Such a clergy was indispensable in small towns and *bourgs* for making known and propagating spiritual works, often through the membership of the local confraternities, whose own slim *livrets* were probably the most widely diffused devotional works for much of the century.

Missions, too, were often important moments for the further diffusion of spiritual works, and by 1700 at the latest, we see booksellers actually 'shadowing' missions, offering the kinds of devotional works that corresponded to the mission preached, and sometimes even producing books summarising the mission in order to perpetuate its effects; the same can be said of sermons, whose publication was not always initiated by the preachers themselves, but sometimes by listeners who had taken notes while in church.[39] The 'bibliothèque bleue', invented by the booksellers of Troyes in the early seventeenth century, is perhaps the best-known attempt anywhere in Europe to diffuse seriously cheap devotional works – canticles, books of instruction, lives of saints, pilgrimage accounts and so on – in a 'popular' format, which included images and texts set in verse. One of its surviving catalogues, from 1709, shows that two-thirds of its titles were religious works, which suggests that the proportion may have been higher still in previous decades. The presence of images and texts in verse form shows an evident concern to reach the illiterate or the barely literate among the population.[40]

Hagiography and its Uses

The attempts made by the Catholic Reformation to communicate spiritual values, old and new, to the wider lay society are well illustrated by the abundant biographical, autobiographical and other hagiographic works turned out in our period. Diffusing such works was not wholly new, but it is hard not to be struck by the quantitative leap occurring during the seventeenth century. Even the writings of mystics were elucidated by 'life' writings of various types, most famously by Teresa of Avila's own autobiography. But this is not the only difference. Older, even very famous works of spirituality, such as the *Imitation of Christ* or the *Cloud of Unknowing*, were usually the work of unknown authors, and so were entirely devoid of an authorial-biographical context. By contrast, virtually all the major spiritual writers of the seventeenth century published under their own names, were the subject of more than one edifying 'Life' after their death, and had nearly always engaged in written exchanges with individuals under their direction. Selections of letters of direction were regularly published, sometimes in their 'Lives', as part of a response to the increased demand for this new form of religious dialogue.

Hagiographic literature was a well-tried subgenre of spiritual writing, with a potentially far wider public. But for most of the sixteenth century, French writers contributed little of interest to it, which also had the result of pushing publishers and readers in the direction of Italian and other sources. 'Lives' of key figures like Carlo Borromeo, Filipp Neri, Ignatius of Loyola and others filled the gap for a time as exemplars of *dévot* lives – a situation rather similar, as we saw above, to that of spiritual works generally. But from the 1610s onwards, hagiographies of home-grown French models began to appear, and the demand for them remained steady for at least the next half-century. In this way, the heroic virtures of 'saints' like Mme Acarie, Vincent de Paul, Pierre Fourier and many others appeared, often relatively soon after their death. All were dynamic figures in the Catholic Reformation, the values of which their life-story was designed to diffuse and perpetuate; while the repetition of clichés from earlier hagiography was defended against sceptics as proof that they rightly belonged to that tradition.[41] The publication of later editions of such 'Lives' in small, cheaper formats enabled them to reach a wider public among whom the hagiographic medium remained highly popular. For the same reason, new or revised lives of patron saints of towns, parishes, places of pilgrimage and so on continued to sell well.

By contrast, it seems significant that a work like the *Histoire Catholique* (1625) of the highly popular Capuchin preacher Hilarion de Coste enjoyed little success, even though it was a celebration of Catholic 'martyrs' of the sixteenth century. Coste was writing in a 'controversial' rather than a hagiographical vein, and about a specific group, which may explain the lack of response.[42] Indeed, as already suggested, the relative decline in spiritual works directed towards distinctive social groups after mid-century may have made the spiritual life stories of individuals a more attractive source of 'timeless' models for people to follow. It was less doctrine than *exempla* that the readers of these works were looking for. As Claude Martin (1619–96), an eminent Maurist and son of the famous Marie de l'Incarnation, one of the first French Ursuline nuns to settle in French Canada, put it, 'Since my purpose is to write a history and not to engage in questions of spiritual controversy, I shall confine myself to relating the opinions and the words of our mother in all their simplicity.'[43] The life stories of eminent figures had many advantages, not the least of which was that they could avoid the traps awaiting systematic attempts at treatises on spiritual method, which were vulnerable to counterattack from the guardians of theological orthodoxy who seem to have become more vigilant than ever in the age of Louis XIV.

PART 5

Movers and Shakers

CHAPTER 14

THE MANY FACES OF THE CONFRATERNITIES

Introduction

It may come as a surprise, in the light of the earlier discussion of preaching missions and catechism, and in particular of the efforts made to found confraternities that would perpetuate their effects, to learn that seventeenth-century France already had a dense network of confraternities. Its geography ensured that it would house both the northern and southern European variants of that elusive, malleable and endlessly changing phenomenon. Indeed, the discovery during the past century of the scale and historical significance of confraternities was due largely to the work of French historians, whose most influential figure, Gabriel Le Bras, regarded the thirteenth and seventeenth centuries as the two great ages of confraternities. Since Le Bras himself and most of his disciples were medievalists, their attention naturally focused on the first of those 'great ages', which they gradually expanded to encompass the fourteenth and fifteenth centuries, when the the first confraternities had to respond to the conditions that followed the Black Death. These historians viewed the confraternities – especially where they were based on the professions within towns – as the social, associative, political and even religious 'cement' which structured the (mainly) urban populations, giving a sense of identity and coherence to a wide range of occupational groups. Furthermore, the frequently close ties between confraternities and the religious orders, particularly the mendicant Dominicans and Franciscans, enabled religious history to connect to urban history in ways that broadened the understanding of the scale of religious ritual and sentiment in the pre-Reformation age. At the other end of Le Bras's chronological spectrum, Maurice Agulhon diagnosed, in a justly famous study, the demise of confraternities in a region of France which was saturated by them – Provence – and showed how the eighteenth-century social elites which had previously dominated the confraternities began withdrawing from them, only to replicate much of their confraternal rituals and behaviour in the new Freemasons' lodges that they now patronised.[1]

By comparison, Le Bras's second great age of confraternities has attracted much less attention, perhaps because it prompted no grand hypothesis capable of explaining their recovery and expansion after a time of acute crisis. For this reason, their place in the religious history of our period remains tenuous, even though – as with the religious orders – no historian would dispute the massive scale of their presence across France. Yet the changes occurring in the generations after, roughly speaking, the Council of Trent were not merely quantitative (in other words, more confraternities), they were also qualitative, witnessing the emergence of new forms and activities that justifies Le Bras's characterisation of the long seventeenth century. If there is one major reason why this shift is difficult to grasp, it is that the term 'confraternity' itself covers a bewildering and constantly evolving kaleidoscope of groups with names and activities that changed over the generations, which often makes it virtually impossible to ascertain their real history, geographical distribution or specific activities. Many seventeenth- and eighteenth-century confraternities viewed themselves as having a long, proud history stretching back to the later middle ages – rather like the genealogies with which ennobled families adorned themselves – but this memory frequently ignored long periods of inactivity and even refoundations during the intervening generations, all of which could entail a significant refocusing of their socio-religious practices and objectives along the way. This flexibility and capacity to mutate across time is itself a major reason why confraternities survived for so long, outliving crises that seemed, especially during the sixteenth century, capable of burying them for ever. This chapter begins by considering some key characteristics of the legacy of Le Bras's first great age of confraternities before focusing on their sixteenth-century crisis.[2] This longer perspective is essential for an understanding of later developments. Old confraternities vastly outnumbered new ones in the seventeenth-century church, which found itself seeking ways to bring them into line with more recent religious aspirations and practices.

Nothing might appear easier than to define the 'average' confraternity – 'an association of Christians under a patron (God, the Virgin Mary, an individual saint) of supernatural status' – but even this minimalist approach raises difficulties. The absence from it of terms that seem so obviously to belong there – such as 'lay', 'urban', 'voluntary' or 'devotional' and 'good works' – offers a first hint of the sheer elusiveness and range of the confraternal impulse throughout its history.[3] The universal objective of the early confraternities was, simply, 'mutual love and assistance': fraternity was an end in itself, as the statutes of innumerable confraternities show in great detail, and fraternity did *not* require elaborate religious activities or personal devotions. Their understanding of the communion of the living and the dead was most clearly revealed at the high point of their year, their feast day (often that of *Corpus Christi* after Pentecost), which was celebrated with masses for members living and dead, a banquet of fraternity, the distribution of alms, the reading of their statutes and the election of new officers for the next year. Good 'works' such as the reconciliation of enemies, helping the sick and dying and, most frequently of all, attending the funerals of, and saying prayers and masses for, dead members during the year, might also attract them. Many of these early confraternities acquired their own chapels or altars, either within the parish church or that of the religious order with which they were often associated. Others again, as we will see later, built their own separate chapels where members met, kept their papers and property, and conducted religious services using a chaplain they hired for the purpose. How far they went beyond that to perform specific 'good works' is another question.

It is conventional to contrast the 'voluntary' character of a confraternity with the 'obligatory' character of membership of a parish, but in practice this distinction, too, is often inoperable. Firstly, there were the well-known 'professional' confraternities, *confréries de métier*, comprised exclusively of the masters and artisans of the individual trades or professions.[4] Members of the groups concerned joined en masse, and their families with them, because such membership was obligatory and written into the statutes of the occupation in question. In those places where there was no form of 'civil' incorporation available to them, essentially in the northern provinces of France (and neighbouring Flanders), the confraternities were, historically, the corporation of the profession or trade in question; in southern France, where 'civil' incorporation, in the guise of established guilds, did exist, the confraternity attached to them was less important, yet visibly present. Because the northern confraternities were far more than religious associations, their religious dimensions might easily seem inconsequential when compared to their often considerable political and social clout. Recruiting members among the artisans and professions, they were able to accumulate the kind of funds that other, more voluntary confraternities could not, so they could afford forms of conspicuous display and consumption that would attract heavy criticism long before the age of reformation. Alongside them, other non-occupational confraternities (such as the Norman 'charities', the Holy Ghost) existed in which the whole population of a parish enrolled, as households rather than as individuals.[5] Clearly, this type of confraternity was in no sense a rival of the parish with which it was, in fact, coterminous, nor was it 'voluntary' in any obvious sense of the term.

In addition, confraternities are easily assumed to have been purely 'lay' associations and, for that reason, enduringly caught up in tense, at times hostile, relationships with the clergy, local and hierarchical. This view of them, as a potential vehicle of anti-clericalism within the church, should not be conflated with the question of their membership. Eighteenth-century lawyers defined confraternities as 'societies consisting of lay people', but this is historically misleading. It is clear that medieval confraternities were highly mixed in membership, with male and female, lay and clerical members. Given what we have seen of the clergy's own internal diversity, it is hardly surprising that large numbers of them joined confraternities, and indeed often took the initiative in founding them. In some towns, especially in northern France, there were longstanding clerical associations exhibiting the key characteristics of confraternities, especially that of mutual assistance. When clergy joined confraternities in parts of Brittany, they usually chose those catering for the local noble and bourgeois elites. There are numerous indications, especially for Normandy, that some of the earliest confraternities 'of devotion' were founded by groups of clerics or had a large clerical membership. In towns like Beauvais, these clerical confraternities were at the forefront of efforts to improve the clergy, precociously absorbing and defending Berullian ideas of the priesthood during the seventeenth century. Finally, the most secretive of all seventeenth-century confraternities, the Aa, was an exclusively clerical one.[6]

It would also be mistaken to imagine that, for all their apparent urban characteristics, later medieval and early modern confraternities were confined to urban areas. In regions as far apart as Normandy-Picardy, Franche-Comté and the Lyonnais-Dauphiné, their equivalents existed in rural areas, often in parishes that were simply too big to be regarded as a single community. In such cases, it was the local confraternity, often labelled that of the Holy Ghost, which embraced the entire population of the villages where they were located. Here, the confraternity was the parish to all intents and purposes, closely integrated with the *fabrique* and frequently run by officers who were simultaneously churchwardens; parish meetings and business were routinely conducted in the confraternity house, as there was usually no other available.[7] In areas where confraternity and community were virtually synonymous, pastoral visitations rarely paid any attention to them, since their specifically religious dimension was practically inseparable from that of the parish generally. In Normandy, the situation was different again: the mainly rural 'charities', as they were called, were extremely numerous and widely scattered, with some parishes having more than one. Their essential function was mutual assistance among members, especially burials and masses for the dead. The Catholic Reformation would attempt to bring new confraternities into rural areas, regardless of whether they previously had them or not, and would try to remodel those that did exist there in its own image and likeness.

Finally, perhaps the most surprising feature of the pre-seventeenth-century confraternities was the limited nature of their 'devotional' activities by comparison with the aspirations of the Catholic Reformation and later. This point is wide open to misinterpretation.[8] As already noted, a great many of the confraternities inherited by the sixteenth century were concerned with mutual assistance, especially for the dying and the dead, and with charity towards their members living in a state of necessity, and it made no great difference whether their patrons or titles were of the Holy Ghost, Corpus Domini or the Holy Sacrament. It was common practice for their formal activities to be confided to officers and 'serving brothers' – often twelve in number, with obvious reference to the Apostles – who were required during their term of office to perform the good works prescribed by the confraternity's statutes. By contrast, the 'ordinary' members simply paid an entry fee and annual subscription to fund their confraternity's activities, but otherwise they had little involvement with its 'works'. This was one reason why confraternities in towns like Caen or Cherbourg could have in excess of 1,000 members by the sixteenth century.[9] There was, therefore, nothing to prevent individuals from belonging to several such bodies, or parishes from having more than one confraternity. Indeed, dual or multiple membership increased the prospect of better treatment in and after death (at funeral and post-mortem masses), but without making spiritual athletes of the confrères, since the devotions of the confraternities in question were minimal and, in many places, scarcely distinguishable from those of the parish.

It was for that reason, too, that individual confraternities could add several patron saints to their initial title: this was because the patrons in question were not 'exclusive', let alone objects of intense devotion, even though many of them were long-standing and highly popular 'healing' saints like St Roch or St Sebastien. Occupational confraternities all had their protector-saints, whom they were extremely reluctant to give up, even in the face of Catholic Reformation pressure for more religious activities. Adding new saints' names was simply a way of obtaining greater protection, but did not necessarily alter their devotions fundamentally. These confraternities of intercession rather than of devotion, as they have been designated, had a principal patron saint whose feast day they celebrated with varying degrees of expense and display. The annual fraternal banquet – 'no confraternity without a banquet' – with its distribution of alms either to all of the members or simply to the poor, was perhaps the most evident and, to them, essential sign of their inextricably mixed socio-religious *raison d'être*, one that the Catholic Reformation, with its dislike of such promiscuous mixing of registers, would do all it could to bury. Yet for all the changes to confraternities that characterised the post-Tridentine church, we should not forget that the majority of them long remained relatively untouched by its devotional agenda.

Penitents and Crisis

The existence of so many significant exceptions to common assumptions about the term 'confraternity' is perhaps the best indication of their potential as vehicles of practices – old and new, parochial and particular, religious and social – and of their capacity to survive and mutate. One of the most original and exotic types of confraternity to be found in seventeenth-century France deserves attention at this pont because its early history encapsulates so many of the key questions about confraternities during the age of the Reformations.[10] The so-called Penitents appeared during the last phase of confraternal expansion before the Protestant Reformations. A small number of confraternities of that name had existed since the thirteenth century, but a new wave of foundations began, mainly in northern Italian cities, in the later fifteenth and early sixteenth centuries. They deliberately set themselves at odds with the existing and by now largely domesticated confraternities. They drew heavily on the penitential, 'disciplinary' spirituality of the age of Savonarola, adopting an austere religion of atonement and self-discipline, including flagellation, which was characterised by an intense devotion to the passion of Christ. Regular confession and communion, attendance at mass during the week, private prayer, attendance at various 'offices' and so on, were prescribed as early as the 1490s by the statutes of the Cannes confraternity, a programme that sounds positively 'Borromean' in its breadth and aspirations.[11] Their best-known 'signature' was the long robe (of different colours, hence their nicknames of 'black', 'grey', 'white', 'blue' Penitents) and the tall, peaked hoods (with slits for the eyes) that they wore in church and during their often spectacular processions. The first of the new-style Penitent confraternities on French soil was founded in Marseille in 1499; over sixty more were added across Provence over the following century or so, ensuring that the Penitents would become a familiar presence in the main towns there.[12] And they would spread further afield, northwards and westwards, from the later sixteenth century onwards. It was not just their exoticism and austerity that made them so attractive across southern France in this period. Their devotion to the passion of Christ was anything but passive in a sixteenth-century context: it made them born enemies of the Protestant reformers who threatened the very basis of their devotion. By the late 1540s, they were confraternities *de combat* as much as *de dévotion*.

Perhaps because the new-style Penitents were still numerically and geographically marginal, the religious-cum-devotional activities of confraternities generally were not what impressed most sixteenth-century churchmen and reformers.[13] Long-standing criticism of their independence within the church itself, their (mis-)use of funds for banquets and socialising, and their excesses generally reached a crescendo during the sixteenth century when it was widely shared by leading clerics and royal officials. How and why the confraternities emerged from this crisis that literally threatened their very existence is indispensable to understanding their later evolution. Up to the 1560s and beyond, French provincial councils and diocesan synods, especially in the northern provinces, regularly catalogued the 'abuses' of the confraternities and prescribed remedies of varying severity to purge them of their distempers; criticism was far more limited in southern provinces.[14] Of course, they were brutally outflanked by Luther, Calvin and other Protestant refomers, all of whom denounced confraternities as embodiments of a religion of 'works', calling for their immediate dissolution and the transfer of their assets to schools and hospices. That did not deter continuing 'official' criticism from within the old church. Indeed, a defining moment seemed to arrive in 1539, when François I abolished all the occupational confraternities, owing to a strike by Lyon print workers the previous year, on the grounds that such confraternities were engaged in 'closed shops', price-fixing and other dangerous practices. Even-handedly, the king also abolished the Penitents of Provence in the same year. But this blanket abolition was too blunt an instrument to work, and within a year exemptions were being widely granted, with the result that the decree had no lasting effect, in Provence or elsewhere, though it did interrupt the further spread of Penitents in the south-east from 1540 to 1560. This climb-down did not mean that the crown had discarded its dislike of confraternities, since it renewed the ban on them twice up to 1561 – partially to defuse Protestant criticisms of them – while in 1562, on the eve of the religious wars, it actually requested the Council of Trent to abolish them. Trent, for its part, did not give the problem much attention, possibly because it was not under severe pressure to do so, and it limited itself to stipulating, not altogether surprisingly, that confraternities be brought under episcopal control.

So much criticism from within the social and ecclesiastical elites could not but have an impact on the confraternities. Many experienced serious disaffection, with declining membership and for some at least, extinction, permanent or temporary, as the outcome. Many of those who would embrace evangelism and, later, Calvinism, belonged to these same elites, and they would abolish confraternities altogether wherever Calvinism seized power in the 1560s and later. The royal suppression of 1539 most likely affected those confraternities that were already in serious decline.[15] Yet, just when their prospects seemed at their most dire and when church and crown were openly critical of them, the emergence of Protestantism gave many confraternities a new lease of life from the 1540s onwards. As already noted, the Penitents were virtually predestined for a defensive role, given the nature of their spirituality and the threat that Protestantism represented to it. But their geographical sphere of action was still largely confined to the south-east. Elsewhere there is evidence of confraternities of the Holy

Sacrament, which had not hitherto been associated with any specific devotional activity, adopting new statutes, especially from the 1540s onwards, which included provision for specific acts of veneration of the sacrament – usually the first sign of a combative local response to Protestant assaults on the Catholic Eucharistic practices. It is worth noting that these new devotional elements were initially adopted by confraternities with a significant clerical presence and, in many cases, leadership. As we have already seen, in areas facing a growing Protestant threat, such as Normandy, the south-west and the Midi, the confraternities were a key part of the process of political and religious counter-mobilisation.[16] A major example of this was the Rouen 'association' of the Holy Sacrament of 1561, which set out quite explicitly to atone for the outrages committed against the sacrament of the altar and which, no less unusually, aimed to recruit its members from across the entire city rather than within a single parish. No longer a confraternity of the familiar parochial kind, it would be a prototype for an approach that became common during the following century.[17]

As we saw in the opening chapter, the Catholic backlash in cities like Lyon, Toulouse or Rouen which had experienced Huguenot takeovers – however brief – was closely associated with the re-emergence of the confraternities; it would later spread to middling and smaller towns like Cahors and Angers, depending on the sense of threat felt within individual areas or towns.[18] But local authorities, secular and religious, remained highly suspicious of any new associations that might provoke disorder or unwanted confessional strife, while their dislike of the older confraternities did *not* simply evaporate. In this context, the process of borrowing from and imitating existing confraternities could be haphazard and uncertain, especially in the southern dioceses with their numerous Protestant strongholds.[19] These strongholds were the main stimuli to the extension of the Penitents beyond their circumscribed original base in Provence and the southern Rhone valley. Penitent confraternities sprang up in places as far north as Rouen, Paris, Abbeville and Laon – initially during the first, short-lived Catholic League of 1576–7, but mostly during the League's rebirth in the 1580s or early 1590s. And, as we have also seen, Henri III and his Jesuit confessor, Edmond Auger, were among the key promoters of the penitential piety that they represented.

Towns were not reduced to deciding whether to 'import' confraternities of Penitents, since in many places older and virtually moribund confraternities (such as the Holy Ghost, Holy Sacrament, Name of Jesus) were revived and infused with new confessional and, to a lesser extent, devotional objectives during the religious wars.[20] These confraternities coincided with other forms of popular religious activity typical of this period, especially mass processions, either within towns or to particularly venerated religious sites, and they displayed unmistakable penitential attitudes. In southern cities like Marseille,

Toulouse and elsewhere, the Penitents were well suited to channelling religious and political anxieties, and they found themselves taking a leading role during the Catholic League's struggle (1589–94) to prevent the succession of Henri IV. In Lyon and especially Marseille, membership of the Penitents was thrown open to lower social groups during these years, and that shift away from the previously 'selective' elite format may well have enabled more radical politics to emerge and to take control of the Leaguer towns during these same years. It was no wonder, therefore, that François I's abolition of the Penitents of 1539 was repeated by several *parlements* in 1595, but also that, outside of northern areas, the effect was equally limited.[21]

In major respects, the defence of French Catholicism from the 1560s onwards owed far more to lay initiative and activity than to the established clerical-institutional church. Of course, there was clerical involvement at many levels, not least in the confraternities themselves, and that often proved crucial to the mobilisation process, but that should not hide the weaknesses of the 'official' church and its institutions. The defeat of the Catholic League and, therefore, of the militant confraternities most clearly associated with it, threatened to reverse all that, all the more so as the 'Tridentine' church councils of the 1580s remained sharply critical of confraternities.[22] But a purely 'political' perspective on the issue would misread their standing in the aftermath of the religious wars. Both the surviving statutes and what we know of the practices of the new or reformed confraternities clearly indicate efforts were being made to develop individual and collective devotional practices among their members.[23] If the confrères could no longer be warriors, they could at least be ascetic and devout in ways which bore the imprint of the combat against heresy. By 1600, therefore, talk of suppressing confraternities outright had virtually ceased, giving way to a long-term process of gradual and highly uneven transformation, much of it 'under the radar', as we shall see later. That and the emergence of newer forms of devotional confraternity made it possible to describe them as 'the true school of *individual* piety', something which would have been unthinkable a half-century earlier. This is not to claim that confraternities emerged triumphantly from the religious wars: their recent history of militancy and confrontation made the authorities, ecclesiastical as much as secular, nervous of them and keen to bring them under control. How to ensure that this did not undermine the goal of encouraging lay devotional practices was a major challenge.

A Changing Environment

In the visitations, legislation and other actions of the French church authorities for decades after the religious wars, there is a steady emphasis on the need for confraternities to have approved statutes – themselves a symbol of submission to episcopal power, as Trent had demanded – and equally on the absolute primacy of the parish in normal religious life. There was nothing especially novel about the content of the legislation itself, but there was increasingly a will to enforce it, with all the potential ramifications for clergy-laity relations within localities that that suggests.[24] Intriguingly, the surviving visitation records suggest that the authorities' interest in confraternities' activities was virtually non-existent outside of the southern provinces until around 1600–1610. It then picked up across all areas of the country during the decades from 1610 to 1670, while the following period from 1670 to 1730 witnessed a surprising reversal of the earlier north–south difference: by now, it was the northern authorities who showed the greater interest in them. That century-long evolution of interest can be seen as a prolonged learning process, which gradually enabled the authorities to deal with the multitude of confraternities.[25] From what we have already seen of the pace of reconstruction and religious reform in earlier chapters, we should not be surprised that early efforts to regulate the confraternities were authority claims rather than actions or statements of fact. They did at least have firm support from the papacy, thanks to Clement VIII's bull of 1604, *Quaecumque*, which reiterated the absolute need for confraternities to have written episcopal approval.[26]

In practice, however, France's bishops mostly left *existing* confraternities undisturbed, tacitly approving their customary activities and subjecting them to very limited, occasional oversight. By contrast, it was easier and more effective to insist that all new confraternities seek explicit approval by submitting their draft statutes for examination and approval; the same applied to confraternities seeking to alter their existing statutes. Otherwise, most seventeenth-century confraternities were relatively safe from the authorities' gaze, unless their reputation or behaviour drew attention to them; it was during the next century that far more systematic attempts at detailed information-gathering, statute-writing and codification were made.[27] Pastoral visitations in our period were often preceded by demands for details about local confraternities, but few of them have survived.[28] Thus, we are unlikely ever to know just how many confraternities there were without any written statutes, or which did *not* attempt to draft new ones despite changes in their activities, simply because they had no wish to become trapped by external bureaucratic oversight. Yet by the second half of the century, the growing numbers of signed petitions to change statutes or establish new confraternities are evidence that the authorities had managed to insert themselves into the process of confraternal change. We should not expect the timescale of this shift to be the same across France. What could happen in one diocese as early as the 1630s or 1640s might have to wait until around 1700 in others. For example, the old confraternity of the Holy Ghost at Sainte-Foy-les-Lyon only acquired statutes in 1726, having relied on immemorial custom up to then. Crucially, it was the parish priest who drafted the new statutes, since he was keen to divert the confraternity's funds away from traditional socialising and towards charitable and religious purposes more in line with post-Tridentine Catholicism.[29] And along with such change came clerical control of its principal activities under episcopal-diocesan surveillance.

This kind of success was, as suggested above, also driven by the desire to affirm the primacy of the parish, an ambition which was closely connected with dislike of several features of confraternities which became more pronounced by the seventeenth century – their socialising and autonomy, the lay leadership that came close to usurping clerical functions, and the inferior position of clerics within some confraternities.[30] The rewriting and approval of statutes, old or new, provided ideal opportunities to correct such 'abuses', at least on paper. The Penitents took lay autonomy further than most, their elected lay 'priors' enjoying extensive powers of direction and discipline over their members.[31] This particular development was mainly a product of the wars of religion, when church authorities were at their weakest, and it was probably not confined to the Penitents. Reversing such relationships would take much longer, and could be highly fractious, because of the number of symbolic acts or situations which signified the opposite of what the 'normal' post-Tridentine order of things should be. A revealing example of such 'disorder', in which laypeople 'usurped' clerical functions, emerges from a declaration by the bishop of Séez as late as 1674: 'It is completely unfitting to see priests occupying an inferior place in church to laypeople, so we forbid the latter, when they are "brothers" [officers] of the charity [confraternity], to occupy any seat in the church choir other than one behind the clergy.' Parish priests were now expected to act exclusively as directors of local confraternities, so that they would not find themselves subject to its lay officers or obliged, as in the past, to engage in actions such as visiting and escorting the newly elected lay 'prior' to the annual banquet. Other members of the clergy could join confraternities, but only provided that their separate status was fully respected. As the dean of Lisieux put it in 1675, 'it is forbidden for a priest to be elected to office in any charity or confraternity, or to assemble together with their members, because such a function is too inferior and unworthy of the sanctity of the priesthood' – a formulation which has the incidental value of showing how far Berullian ideas on the priesthood could permeate 'official' thinking.[32]

Redefining clerical involvement with confraternities along these lines led almost inevitably to altering other aspects of their organisation and behaviour. One of the most important objectives was to ensure that the services or processions of the confraternities did not compete directly with those of the parish, so that their members could not regard themselves as having a 'portable' parish and clergy of their own choosing. The early Penitent statutes had specified their own devotions, while also insisting on attendance at parish services on Sundays. But in practice that injunction was widely ignored thereafter by their members, who affirmed their independence by increasingly conducting separate services in their own chapels. The problem of enforcing the primacy of parish religion was probably less intractable in places where the chapels or altars of the confraternities were located within the parish church itself. In this regard, the ultimate goal of the church authorities was confraternities that were located, as contemporaries put it, 'in the nave of the church' – that is, with no altar of their own other than that of the parish itself. Where confraternities were based in the chapels of religious orders or had their own buildings, physical separation could easily lead to defiance and conflict. This is doubtless the main reason why seventeenth-century synods and other ordinances insisted so strongly on eliminating competition from confraternities for the Easter ceremonies, the high mass, Sunday vespers and other 'offices' in the parish church.[33] We have already seen that this problem of competition existed in relation to services in the chapels of the religious orders generally, but it was complicated further when confraternities were based there.

It would be misleading, however, to dwell unduly on the points of conflict between confraternities and church authorities, since a variable degree of conflict had always figured in their relationship; total clerical control over them was a fantasy that risked turning confraternities into empty *caisses de resonance*. It is important to realise that a distinguishing feature of the French church of the Catholic Reformation was its increasing insistence that confraternities be open and accessible, unlike many of their medieval forebears.[34] Occupational confraternities apart, membership should be available to women as well as men, and entrance fees or annual subscriptions should not act as a bar to restrict accession. Thus, seventeenth-century statutes increasingly avoided setting a fixed payment for entrance, suggesting instead that members pay what they could afford, *à leur dévotion* – a particularly apt formulation in this context! These trends could be, and were, resisted, however, so that Penitents and several Jesuit-led confraternities, for example, continued to recruit male members only and levied dissuasively high entry fees.

Nor was the new-style confraternity of devotion dear to the Catholic Reformation church simply the product of official efforts at change from above. By the time the efforts at disciplining the confraternities just described were beginning, some of the existing confraternities were already moving the way that reformers had been calling for. The earliest evidence of such a shift is often 'negative', in the form of statutes which insisted on members avoiding certain kinds of behaviour – swearing, blasphemy, drunkenness and so on. More and more new foundations were to one degree or another confraternities of devotion which, although a small minority for many years, constituted a promising foundation for the seventeenth-century church to build upon. As we saw, the 'new' Penitents and the revived confraternities of the Holy Sacrament were quite explicit about the devotions they required their members to perform. Militancy and devotion belonged together, and the latter could survive militancy's demise. Not only were members required to attend mass on Sundays and feast days, but they were strongly exhorted, inter alia, to confess and take communion once a month. The new Penitents are a particularly cogent example of this: they were to flagellate themselves not just four times a year, as previously required, but every Friday, in memory of Christ's Passion. In addition to the familiar communal religious activities of all confraternities, a perceptible emphasis on individual, private performance was also developing. Prayer became an occasion for meditation, as in the case of the rosary, on the mysteries of the life of Christ. Confrères who could not attend services were exhorted to recite private prayers at various times during the day, and everyone was asked, before retiring at night, to engage in a personal examination of conscience regarding their actions during the day.

Another trend emerging within some of these confraternities before and especially after 1600 was the greater synchronisation of disciplinary and religious practices than previously. For example, the reformed Penitents of Marseille, the Bourras, founded in 1592, began exhorting their members to confess their sins *before* engaging in acts of flagellation and to take communion afterwards – the objective being to derive greater spiritual benefit from the combination of such acts, whose sequence was defined to facilitate that effect. Of importance for the growth of devotional confraternities generally was the gradual extending of the intensive religious practices traditionally associated with Advent and Lent across the entire liturgical year, making the latter a continuous devotional-penitential cycle rather than a relatively flat landscape dominated by a few isolated, seasonal peaks.[35] From another perspective, members were to embrace an extended year-long 'Lent' and shun 'Carnival', whose 'debaucheries and excesses' they were to atone for by prayer and self-discipline. The struggle against 'heresy' may have gradually abated, only to be replaced by the need to atone for the misdeeds of Christians generally. Ideally, the confraternities would become champions of a sustained and 'regulated devotion', long before the term was invented in the eighteenth century. However fraught relations with the Penitents and other confraternities close to them might become in our period and later, there is little doubt that their precocious efforts to develop devotion and asceticism showed the way forward for later confraternities, including those that shunned flagellation and related austerities.

Finally, it is evident that such devotional shifts reveal the long-term influence of the regulars, regardless of whether they hosted or directed the new-style confraternities, since it was their spiritual practices that were being 'recycled', however discreetly, for use in the world outside the cloister. A telling example of this is the requirement, increasingly present in the new devotional confraternities, that before admission new members not only recite the Tridentine profession of faith, but confess and take communion immediately afterwards, and even that they don a habit on doing so – a ritual clearly adapted from that of reception or profession among the religious orders, and which was previously unknown for lay confraternities.[36] The spread of confraternities across seventeenth-century France also bears some resemblance to that of the new religious orders, with their successive 'waves' of foundation and expansion, unexpected innovations and striking rates of female participation. The comparison is not fanciful since to a considerable extent, the religious orders, old as well as new, took a direct hand in their diffusion, building upon their extensive prior experience of confraternities. And because for at least the first half of the seventeenth century the parish clergy were largely unable to adapt these devotions themselves, they had to rely upon the regulars to diffuse them, especially outside of urban areas. The impact of such activity meant that the orders remained heavily involved with lay religious practices until the following century.[37]

By contrast, the older confraternities were less likely to have – and some never had – connections with the orders; by our period, they were either self-standing or, more frequently, purely 'parochial' in character. It is only natural to expect a wider range of confraternities within urban areas, with the more explicitly devotional among them appealing to the educated and *dévot* social groups, but the seventeenth-century church was attempting to transcend these limitations. Missions, as we saw in an earlier chapter, were widely used for such purposes, but as they were not especially frequent and the challenge was to introduce unfamiliar types of confraternity to rural France, the pace and nature of change was bound to vary considerably from place to place. It was not until Louis XIV's rule that the secular clergy assumed a greater role in the life of local confraternities.[38]

'The True School of Individual Piety'?

It was an order of newcomers, the Jesuits, who spread one of the most novel and high-powered of devotional associations. Placed under the protection of the Virgin Mary, and developed first in their Italian colleges, their Marian sodalities or 'congregations' already existed in France by the 1570s.[39] This approach set the Jesuits apart from their 'competitors', since their initial focus was schools and students, not hitherto a common target for confraternities. As we noted in the previous chapter, their efforts began with the senior (rhetoric and philosophy) classes, and involved the deliberate selection of those judged best fit to belong to a devotional congregation while still at school. But the Jesuits' strategy did not stop there, and gradually their aim became one of devising analogous congregations for people from different walks of life: each congregation would be relatively homogeneous in background, which would enable its members to focus on religious matters rather than bringing their conflicting social and professional preoccupations into their chapels with them. In some colleges, there were separate congregations for boarders and day students! A key ambition was to ensure that their best alumni would continue to frequent the Jesuit chapels in later life, hence the most important of all these Marian congregations was that of the *messieurs*, designed to embrace magistrates, lawyers and nobles generally; the congregations of the artisans (subdivided into 'great', 'small', 'young') followed in due course. By the eighteenth century, cities like Lyon could have half a dozen Jesuit confraternities differentiated primarily by socio-professional standing, but engaged in broadly similar religious practices.

The social and political significance of the Jesuit congregations has attracted more attention than their spiritual activities. They may have been 'Marian' in inscription, but their devotions were more novel and wide-ranging than this label suggests. The Jesuits proposed a very wide range of activities ranging from regular confession and communion, daily examination of conscience, individual spiritual direction, weekly meetings, monthly retreats, and so on. Eucharistic rather than Marian devotion was the real fulcrum around which the members' religious lives turned.[40] According to the 1683 *Abrégé des pratiques et règlements* of the Dijon Students' Congregation, candidates for entry there had to engage in a ceremony that closely resembled that of entering a religious order, yet the Jesuit congregations encouraged a full life of action in the world, with their members seeking ways of translating their religious fervour into practical good works.[41]

The Jesuit congregations acted as social and religious magnets across the ever-increasing number of cities and towns that housed their colleges. Some congregations of *messieurs* and artisans were enormous in size. The Rouen *Messieurs* numbered around 1,500 by around 1650, higher than the total number of students at the city's college. The various Jesuit sodalities in Lille had twice that number, for a much smaller population, by 1630.[42] In the modest episcopal town of Langres, the artisans had 300 members and the students (*écoliers*) 200 in 1720. Yet, the Jesuits, as already mentioned, vetted those seeking membership of the sodalities, and were prepared to levy high entrance and membership fees in order to keep control of them. Their sphere of action was deliberately confined to the different strata of the urban elites, but that restriction was compensated by a city-wide, non-parochial recruitment. Furthermore, they made no effort to develop comparable congregations for women. It was left to the Ursulines, who were close to the Jesuits, to attempt this via their congregations of the Penitents of the Virgin, but that was primarily with a view to forming female catechists.[43] It is no paradox that those Jesuits who conducted missions and preaching campaigns in our period were primarily interested in founding parochial confraternities of the Holy Sacrament, since they corresponded better than the conventional Marian devotions (the Rosary, for example) to the Jesuits' own pastoral and devotional goals.

It was the Confraternity of the Rosary that stood at the other end of the Marian devotional spectrum that characterised the seventeenth century.[44] Older, than the Jesuits, it was founded in Cologne in 1475 by the Dominicans, who acted as its principal promoters thereafter, but it gained a huge new lease of life, with papal support, after the victory of Lepanto (1571), the anniversary of which was celebrated as Our Lady of Victories on the first Sunday of October. The Dominicans retained their monopoly, granted by the papacy, over the indulgences to be gained by members of the confraternity, but other orders such as the Franciscans, Capuchins and Récollets, were heavily involved in its diffusion over the next two centuries. The early Jesuits regarded their Marian sodalities as belonging to the Rosary. Its diffusion also benefited from the fact that veneration of the Virgin was not confined to the orders in seventeenth-century France, but was fully shared by Bérulle and his spiritual heirs.[45] When Louis XIII dedicated his kingdom to the Virgin in 1638, 'Marian' devotion seemed to know no bounds, but France remained largely unreceptive to the Spanish cult of the Immaculate Conception and the devotions and confraternities that it spawned.

Although nestling under the same Marian umbrella, the Rosary confraternities of this period scarcely resembled those of the Jesuits. As they spread, they became overwhelmingly parochial in nature; they were in no sense confined to cities or the socio-religious elites of the age; they were, like others we shall see presently, open to women and men alike, and there was no monetary obstacle to joining, let alone a process of selection for entrants. The confraternities' formal religious practices were not extensive or highly demanding, and were essentially 'Marian' in focus. Members were expected to attend a confraternity mass in the parish church once a month, followed by a procession around the parish and its cemetery; to recite the rosary in common three times weekly; and to participate in the five major Marian feast days per year. Public and collective devotion like this did not exclude private ones; regular confession and communion was not a condition of membership, however many confrères might privately do so. This type of confraternity was fundamentally inclusive in character, unlikely to scare off ordinary people. For that reason, they were often able to step into the shoes of the older, numerous 'Notre-Dame' confraternities, and to carry on some of their activities, despite the change of label. Missions were frequently the moment of foundation, since the Rosary seemed well suited to the task of sustaining a parish's collective religious enthusiasm thereafter. It also had the blessing of the clergy, hierarchical and local, since it fitted well into their vision of parish Catholicism – it did away, for example, with the confraternities' annual banquet. And the Rosary retained enough features of the earlier confraternities for lay initiative to play its part – which was considerable – in its diffusion into small villages and rural areas.

The scale of the growth of Rosary confraternities across France is not easy to convey, but in certain central regions, from Auxerre to La Rochelle, for example, the period of greatest diffusion was relatively early, from 1620 to 1640.[46] There was no sharp falling-off after the latter date, however, and new foundations were being added until into the eighteenth century. Wherever we look – from northern Brittany to Lyon-Grenoble – the pattern seems to be one of high-density expansion. It was not uncommon for Rosary confraternities to exist in one out of every two parishes in central France, and in some places the ratio was higher again – as high as 80 per cent in parts of the south-east. The Rosary's combination of new and old ingredients appealed to a wide spectrum of the population, lettered and unlettered, for whom the Virgin was the most attractive protecting saint, regarded as more effective than many conventional saints because of her closeness to divine power itself. In regions where one parish in every two had a Rosary confraternity, it was not uncommon for one out of every two adults to be a member. Equally significant, regardless of these local ratios, was the fact that, over time, the Rosary recruited more and more female members. Across central France the picture by around 1700–20 is one of male withdrawal and a massive female presence.[47] The rude good health of Rosary confraternities until well into the eighteenth century was probably due to this phenomenon, which in many places disguised the disaffection of former male members.

If there was a rival to the Rosary for the most 'popular' confraternity of a Catholic Reformation type, particularly in northern and central France during this period, it was that of the Holy Sacrament.[48] As we saw, it too had late medieval roots and was widely spread across France, but during the sixteenth century, under the impact of Protestant assaults on Catholic sacramental belief and practice, it began to experience important internal shifts. By the seventeenth century, a series of such confraternities with different names existed, all devoted to the Eucharist in one form or another. As we saw, the 'original' Penitents were among them, but now there were others such as the confraternity of the Passion of Christ, the Five Wounds of Christ, the Cross, the Penitents of the Holy Sacrament and so on. It seems that these confraternities were relatively slow to spread, almost certainly because they required more of their members than the Rosary – in particular, regular confession and communion. By comparison with the Rosary, demand for these particular devotions was more likely to emanate from laypeople in towns than those in small villages and rural areas, although it appears that they were also welcomed by Catholics in areas with strong Protestant populations.

The new devotion of the 'Forty Hours', which involved a round-the-clock adoration of the Holy Sacrament by confraternity members when it was exposed on the main altar in churches, boosted the Holy Sacrament confraternities from mid-century onwards.[49] A further factor in their expansion seems to have been the support of newer generations of clergy by the later seventeenth century, but it probably needed the prior or continuing impact of preaching, missions, catechism and schooling for their prompting to elicit a positive response from their parishioners. Louis Pérouas has suggested that the tapering off of the Rosary by the later seventeenth century was due to concerted pressure from the clergy for these Eucharistic confraternities, with their more demanding sacramental obligations.[50] This would appear to pit them as rivals for popular support, but that is probably misleading. The Rosary and Holy Sacrament confraternities were held to be the most 'mutually' compatible confraternities within an average parish across France, and it is no accident that a demanding bishop like Vialart of Châlons-sur-Marne declared in 1661 that he would like to see one of each in every parish of his diocese 'in order to increase the devotion of the people'.[51] It may be that the massive influx of women into the Rosary confraternities itself initiated, or at least facilitated, a 'demand' for another kind of confraternity with different accents; it could also be an early phase of a gender dimorphism which by the mid-eighteenth century had produced confraternities that were, de facto, for men and for women.

Of all the confraternities scattered across seventeenth-century France, only one was wholly French in origin, as well as the only true newcomer, that of the Sacred Heart. It began in the Visitation convent of Paray-le-Monial near Mâcon, where Marie-Marguerite Alacocque experienced a series of visions between 1675 and 1688 during which the figure of Christ urged her to preach the need for devotion to the Sacred Heart of Christ: in that sense, the devotion resembled other Christocentric ones that we have already seen. The Visitation's historical closeness to the Jesuits enabled the devotion to spread outwards from Paray via both orders' houses and schools, initially in southern and south-eastern France and Savoy. Of the 427 confraternities recorded in

1733, 313 were still attached to the two orders' houses, and just over half of them (55 per cent) were located in France and Savoy. It was only gradually that they spread into the wider world of parishes.[52]

The successive emergence of various 'new' devotional confraternities should not imply that older concerns no longer mattered to contemporaries, or were somehow marginalised by the seventeenth-century church. New devotional confraternities remained in the minority. The numerous confraternities that focused on dying, death and burial are a prime example of this.[53] Conditions of life and high mortality rates, especially with the return of epidemics, did nothing to remove inherited fears of sudden death on a massive scale. The older confraternities of intercession, as we saw, strongly shaped the religious culture of the mass of the population and especially its sense of the solidarity between the dead and the living. Here, too, new confraternities with changing titles and patronages but with familiar preoccupations slipped into the shoes of older organisations. Innumerable confraternities of the 'Good Death' or of *Agonisants* – but not of Purgatory, it seems – flourished in our period, with the newer and more favoured ones – at least by the clergy – bearing titles such as the 'Agony of Jesus', 'Our Lady of the Agonisants' or the 'Agonisants of St Joseph'. The more traditional *Agonisants* prayed for their members at the moment of their death in an act of charity; mutual assistance in life and death was central to the history of occupational confraternities, especially artisans, whose social and festive activities continued to be such in a thorn in the side of the seventeenth-century church, even in such *dévot* cities as Dijon or Bordeaux. The new or reformed confraternities, especially those named after St Joseph or of the 'Good Death', also prayed for a good end and offered each other mutual assistance but, above all, their members sought to prepare for their own death through a lifetime of spiritual effort, the key elements of which – the sacraments, private prayer, daily examination of conscience – we have seen in other confraternites.[54] These confraternities were fewer in number and in members because they appealed mainly to a *dévot* elite.

As with the new religious orders and congregations of the seventeenth century, one could go on listing the names and 'families' of confraternities. Disentangling them from each other and defining their activities becomes almost impossible beyond a certain point. During the years 1676–84 and 1721–31, Roman briefs of indulgence were sought by no fewer than 700 different types of confraternity and devotional associations from across Europe, many of them French. This shows that the confraternal phenomenon remained just as 'plastic' and malleable as it had been for centuries. In countless places, as already observed, new ones appeared which took the places of older ones, with or without changing their names, so that labelling them is not always a sure guide to what they actually did.

It is also worth realising that there were forces at work within the French church that served to offset this balkanisation and to bring about a certain harmonisation of the confraternities. The role of the religious orders as creators, diffusers and hosts of confraternities is the most obvious of these mechanisms.[55] As already noted, especially in the case of the Sacred Heart confraternities, it took nearly a generation of work within the houses of the Ursulines, Visitation and Jesuits before it was ready for lay consumption, and for a long time the ensuing confraternities continued to be based in the orders' chapels. Thereafter, the geographical spread of the orders also ensured a certain coherence in confraternities' devotions, since they provided them within common statutes, commentaries and devotional books. To some degree, confraternities could themselves seek to escape the dangers of isolation and to consort with others. There is evidence from Lyon diocese, for example, of a search for affiliation among similar confraternities, with provision for three-yearly meetings for renewal and 'fraternity'. Even the adoption of certain devotional books and practices could achieve a minimum of standardisation among them.[56]

Perhaps the most unexpected – because only 'invented' during the sixteenth century – source of cohesion among early modern confraternities was that of affiliation to Roman arch-confraternities.[57] The phenomenon has only recently been studied for France, and it is easily assumed that such forms of contact would have been few and far between. But preliminary research indicates that French confraternities seeking indulgences from Rome were comparatively numerous during the period from the 1670s to the 1720s. The creation, in 1539, of the arch-confraternity of the Holy Sacrament in the Dominicans' Minerva church, in Rome, was an early strike in the struggle over the cult of the Eucharist, since it allowed affiliated confraternities to offer its indulgences to their members – an incentive which many found quite irresistible. As early as 1544, the Grasse Confraternity of the Holy Sacrament affiliated to the Roman one, to be followed by many others in due course.[58] The true extent of such affiliation throughout France by, say, 1600 or 1720–30 remains unknown, but it seems that it had fallen substantially over the years, owing to the simple fact that a confraternity of the Holy Sacrament founded with episcopal approval enjoyed exactly the same privileges and indulgences as those affiliated to Rome. The *Agonisants* and 'Good Death' had their Roman arch-confraternities, too. Affiliation was rendered all the easier by the fact that the major religious orders involved had their own entrées in Rome, which could simplify and reduce the cost of the whole process. Affiliated confraternities were required to adopt the statutes and, ideally, the practices of the Roman mother confraternity. Although its impact should not be overestimated, the wider the affiliation movement, the more harmonisation of practices ensued and the more devotions of a 'Roman' stamp took root.[59]

Penitents Revisited

This 'tour de France confraternel' during the Catholic Reformation would not be complete without considering the history of the Penitents *after* the wars of religion. As we saw, they were so compromised by their militant stance against Henri IV that they were abolished during the 1590s, and it seems that those of northern France withered away quickly. The local elites who had joined the Penitents there were anxious not to be compromised by their recent past, and they would soon find ample scope for their religious energies in the *dévot* movements that mushroomed in the following decades. But across southern France, the picture was markedly different: royal authority was more weak and distant, and the Protestant presence was more massive, both of which gave the Penitents a far better chance of survival. The ensuing geography of the Penitents is itself intriguing. Maurice Agulhon argued that they ultimately belonged within the cultural zone of the historic *langue d'oc*, but the correlation is not entirely perfect.[60] Around 1600, they were based predominantly in Provence, southern Dauphiné, the Rhone valley and Languedoc, the most densely urbanised areas of France. By then, they had disappeared from Dijon and Mâcon, and never really found a place in one of the south-west's most militant cities, Bordeaux – or in Guyenne generally. Quite surprising, in these circumstances, was their expansion northwards from Toulouse into the Limousin, which began as late as 1590 in Tulle, during the Catholic League. It continued into the following century, when a further fifty confraternities, scattered through the towns and *bourgs* of this 'outpost' province, were added. It was a notable record for a region that, unlike Provence or lower Languedoc, was heavily rural in character. By the mid-eighteenth century, it is possible that Limoges had up to 2,500 Penitents and Tulle between 600 and 800, both very substantial numbers for relatively medium-sized towns, and all the more so as the Penitents did not formally admit female members.[61]

Unlike the confraternity of the Rosary, which spread rapidly into rural areas, the Limousin Penitents remained urban and bourgeois in character. Interestingly, they quickly toned down the flagellant element of Penitent practice, and as early as 1613, the Aubusson confraternity made flagellation purely voluntary, to be conducted exclusively behind closed doors in their chapel, and at night.[62] For much of the century, these Penitents seem to have satisfied the church authorities, possibly because access was restricted via the entrance and membership fees they charged. Above all, they focused their attention on the confessional and Eucharistic exercises prescribed by their statutes, and engaged in charitable activities. But at some point before 1700, possibly in the 1680s, they seem to have begun making membership easier and cheaper, which would explain the very high numbers in the next century. Victims of their own success, perhaps, the Limousin penitents then followed the path taken by many confraternities elsewhere in the Midi. Their seventeenth-century clerical mentors and supporters gradually parted company with them, which led them to retreat more and more into their own chapels and rituals. That autonomy, in turn, made them more socially than religiously active, a pattern frequently encountered in confraternities with a large membership.[63]

The longer-established Penitent confraternities of Provence-Languedoc had reached that position earlier. They proved much more difficult to 'domesticate' after the religious wars, which had enabled them to assert considerable autonomy from church control, parochial or diocesan. Their popularity had already enabled them to build and decorate often impressive chapels; they were increasingly attached to their own separate religious services, inside and outside their chapels; they even regarded non-members as 'seculars', a hint at how strong their sense of being separate could be; most of all, they elected, and deferred to, their own officers rather than to the local *curé* or town council.[64] It is hardly necessary to suggest how little the idea of a group of lay confrères conducting their own Maundy Thursday ceremonies (with the washing of the feet and distribution of bread and wine) appealed to the post-Trent church. By the mid-century, serious worries about their behaviour arose, and when Bishop Antoine Godeau legislated in 1651 for the Penitents of Vence and Grasse, he was clearly attempting to disentangle the 'sacred' and 'profane' in their activities and to repress their profanity – with no great success, as it happened.[65] To counteract this, the seventeenth-century church encouraged the creation of Rosary and Holy Sacrament confraternities and, above all, the more recent 'reformed' Penitents. The record shows that large numbers of the latter took root in the heartlands of the Penitents, and that they were more confined from the outset in their activities and more carefully controlled by the local authorities, civil and clerical, to prevent them from developing non-religious roles in local society.[66]

It is typical of the history of confraternities that, judged by their names at least, hybrid formations also began to appear during the seventeenth century, notably the Penitents of the Holy Sacrament, which were more to the taste of the Catholic Reformation clergy. Clearly, there were many degrees of difference between the two ends of the spectrum which the Penitents of the Limousin and those of Provence represented. To the north of Provence, in the Lyonnais and the Dauphiné, the 'penitent' presence also seems to have been highly fluid and complex. Bishops or officials conducting parish visitations in Grenoble diocese referred indistinctly to confraternities as 'penitents', but it is impossible to be sure what they meant by such a generic term covering a range of activities. In Grenoble, the Penitents of the Holy Sacrament appeared during the 1620s and 1630s, with the intention of directing the Penitents towards a Christocentric, Eucharistic form of devotion, but a century later, they too seem to have drifted into the familiar southern penitent format. Old-style Penitents were also scattered throughout the sprawling Lyon diocese, but the parish clergy and their superiors were increasingly suspicious of them, and tried to encourage antidotes to them, especially the Rosary and Holy Sacrament confraternities.[67]

In Provence and its environs, a majority of the bishops were natives, and their dioceses were too small and too poor to provide seminaries to train a new-style clergy, which meant that pressure on the local confraternities to stay within a well-defined 'devotional' framework was probably weaker than elsewhere in France. This may also explain why northern prelates parachuted into southern dioceses and, unfamiliar with the Midi, from Antoine Godeau of Grasse and Vence (1638–72) and Le Camus of Grenoble (1672–1707) to Martin du Bellay of Fréjus (1739–66), were so shocked at the profanity and 'social' characteristics of southern confraternities. As Le Camus put it, 'down here, all they know of religion is confraternities, indulgences and congregations' – a damning verdict indeed, with confraternities heading the guilty list.[68] Judging by this comment, the wheel would seem to have come full circle, with the southern confraternities back in the firing line where they had been two centuries earlier during the age of Erasmus and Luther. Prelates like Le Camus could, when supported by their clergy, attempt to limit these developments, and Grenoble confraternities found themselves more tightly supervised under Le Camus, only for a a rash of new foundations, in which the Jesuits and the Capuchins took the lead, to be launched by his successors after his death. With their rigorist, and at times openly Jansenist predilections, clergy in the mould of Le Camus were virtually predestined to suspect, and enter into conflict with, such overtly 'social' and independently minded confraternities, and their disapproval of them inevitably appears as a form of killjoy puritanism.

Conclusion

If confraternities may be loosely – and poetically – characterised as 'associations which unite in charity the living and the dead of a particular place on earth in their search for a corner of heaven', then it is clear that seventeenth-century French society subscribed massively to such an aspiration.[69] Extrapolating from the data provided by a number of local studies, Jean de Viguerie suggested that by the early eighteenth century France had in the region of 15,000 confraternities with an average of 100 members each, giving a total confraternal population of 1.5 million – approximately 8 per cent of the population at the time.[70] Even if these projections proved accurate, they would only tell us a limited amount about our subject. It would be more useful to know something about the relevant densities and variety of confraternities – between particular provinces, towns, rural parishes – at a time when the biggest efforts to diffuse them had already occurred. But all attempts to produce such a map have so far failed, mainly because the archival base for the inter-diocesan comparisons that it would involve is simply too fragile.[71] Case-study substitutes have to be treated with caution, too. By 1760, only 30 per cent of parishes within the jurisdiction of the Paris *parlement* had a confraternity with fixed revenues, suggesting that the remaining 70 per cent of them, presumably mainly in rural areas, did not have one. A decade later, in 1774, the *grand archidiaconé* of Reims had such a confraternity in only one parish out of four. However, the dates in question, 1760 and 1774, may well be too late to reflect the situation a generation or so earlier, bearing in mind what is known about the often short-lived rural confraternities founded in the wake of missions. Above all, an unknown proportion of confraternities simply had no fixed revenues, but relied upon their members' regular donations to pay their expenses, so they, too, would have escaped the *parlement*'s 1760 enquiry.[72]

This way of looking at the phenomenon will always tend to underplay the scale of what was actually achieved during the long seventeenth century. A more illuminating measure of the changes in the confraternal landscape can be gleaned from a sample of local perspectives. Clearly, the big urban centres had a bazaar-like provision of confraternities. One author declared as early as 1621 that Paris alone had 337 confraternities, and a similar abundance was to be found in Lyon, Bordeaux, Angers, Rouen and a host of other towns. The great majority of the Paris confraternities of 1621 were old-style confraternities 'of intercession' rather than 'of devotion'.[73] At the other end of the scale, a remote place like Sennely-en-Sologne had up to five or six confraternities at various times from the 1620s to the early 1700s, with fluctuating fortunes and membership, in which fashion and perhaps indulgences may well have played a part at key moments. One of them was a Rosary confraternity founded there by the Dominicans in 1640, which grew strongly until 1660, not least because inhabitants of neighbouring parishes without a confraternity of their own joined it. Its membership, spread across several parishes, grew to around 400 at its height, yet by 1680 it had only half a dozen members left – a useful reminder of the short lifespan of some confraternities.[74]

A 'before' and 'after' comparison can be equally illuminating, as exemplified by the experience of the parishes of the north-eastern, and mainly rural, area of Lyon diocese. The archbishop's visitation of 1613–14 only recorded three confraternities – one of the Holy Sacrament, two of the Rosary – throughout the 108 parishes concerned. By the 1654–62 visitations that total had risen, steadily rather than spectacularly, to twenty-eight, equating to one confraternity on average for every four parishes. Twenty-two of those confraternities were either of the Holy Sacrament or the Rosary. By the period 1700–19, the total had risen to ninety, not far short of one per parish. But the underlying pattern had not changed much – seventy of the ninety confraternities were either of the Holy Sacrament (42) or the Rosary (28), leaving just 'scraps' for the Penitents, the Scapulary and the Christian Doctrine (which had only one). Because the Holy Sacrament and Rosary confraternities were so 'compatible', as we saw, they were often found in the same parishes, which explains why just under 40 per cent of the 108 parishes had *no* confraternity in 1710. At the same date, Marseille had 128 confraternities in all, of which 74 (58 per cent) were probably old-style ones 'of intercession' with traditional patron saints. If that is compared to Paris in 1620, the proportion of 'devotional' confraternities had risen substantially to about four in every ten.[75]

The *remue-ménage* that characterised seventeenth-century confraternities was driven by factors other than devotional fashion. The move to bring them inside the timetables and structures of parish Catholicism became increasingly strong as the century progressed. The history of the Penitents illustrates the kinds of problems that existed in places with a real history of autonomous lay sociability, of which the Penitents themselves were simultaneously both cause and effect. The occupational confraternities were an equally hard nut to crack, and in a city as firmly hitched to the Catholic Reformation as Dijon, the activities of the artisans were deplored for their excess and profanity by civic and church authorities alike up to at least mid-century.[76] Across many regions of France, older confraternities, such as those of the Holy Ghost, were often wound up altogether, and their properties or *rentes* assigned to the parish *fabrique*. A new confraternity, often of the Holy Sacrament, was installed in their place, one which, it was firmly hoped, would not waste its funds on banquets and other excesses when the real poor needed their charity.[77] In Normandy, which had seen a proliferation of 'charities' during the later Middle Ages, strenuous attempts were made both to ensure that every parish had one of its own, and to discourage as far as possible the existence of several such charities within a single parish.[78] With a 'one per parish' norm, each charity would be capable of discharging its duties towards the parish, duties which covered essentially funerals and services for the dead. The battle to control and discipline confraternities was not fought in isolation, since the 'social' confraternities of the kind the Catholic Reformation church disliked were hard to distinguish from other, mainly youth groups such as the *reinages*, the *royaumes* and the *abbayes*, whose licence and parodic-satirical practices were just as objectionable to *curés* and church authorities. The campaigns mounted against the apprentices and journeymen's *compagnonnages*, which were seen as inversions of confraternities, were another classic instance of official fears of the unauthorised and the subversive.[79]

It would be all too easy to see these efforts as a straightforward assertion of clerical power, but without the active participation of civic authorities and the lay *dévots*, the seventeenth-century church and clergy would never have been able to recover from the weakness they had experienced a century earlier. Membership of a confraternity was never a religious obligation, after all, and we have seen how quickly membership of new confraternities could collapse if they were unattractive. The manner in which confraternities like the Rosary or the Holy Sacrament developed took account of lay needs and capacities.[80] Local clergy, regular or secular, may have taken the leading role in creating them, but that should not disguise their sense of satisfying local lay expectations. Not every new confraternity of the period was 'high devotional', but the sheer range of devotions available ensured that most tastes were likely to be catered for. The policy of insisting that confraternities be open to all adults was a major departure from much past practice, and its most significant consequence was the massive entry of women, mainly but not exclusively into confraternities like the Rosary or the Holy Sacrament, where they increasingly became the majority of the membership by the later seventeenth and early eighteenth century. The problem with having up to 700 confraternities with 700 types of devotion was that small groups of individuals would separate themselves from the rest of their parishes and communities to pursue their own chosen paths. Some did just that, of course, gathering in their chapels, especially in the churches of religious orders. That was more likely to happen in towns with alternatives to the parish church, where the latter did not enjoy the same dominance as in village and rural society.

A major consideration for confraternities was whether a big membership was really compatible with anything other than a limited range of 'standard' religious practices; the smaller and more selective the membership was, the more likely confraternities were to engage in highly individualised devotion. The seventeenth-century French church would appear to have learned from the experiences of the previous century that, in certain situations or in certain forms, devotion itself could be difficult to keep under control. In this respect, the Penitents represented the most ambitious, and therefore most 'dangerous' search for an autonomous devotional society of their own, governed by their own rules and superiors. It could be said that the massive upsurge in new religious orders, both male and female, effectively guided the most demanding devotional aspirations of our period into acceptable channels, with many of these orders in turn diffusing and guiding the new devotions of the age within lay society. The vast majority of confraternities in small towns and rural areas were modest affairs with their own chapel or altar, increasingly in the parish church, and engaged in a limited number of devotional, funerary and charitable activities under clerical supervision. Yet the extent of their expansion during the generations after 1560 or 1600 and their readiness to adopt Marian or Eucharistic devotions, even on a limited scale, is among the best evidence we have that the Catholic Reformation did reach down into French village society.

CHAPTER 15

DÉVOTS: THE PIOUS AND THE MILITANT

The seventeenth century bequeathed many enduring terms to French culture, but few of them seem, even now, to belong so fully to the *grand siècle* as the word *dévot*. There is a subtle but important difference between its singular and plural forms. To translate the singular *dévot* as 'devout' would not be inadequate, as it would convey most of the meaning of the original. But to render *dévots* as 'the devout' or 'the devouts' would be far less satisfactory, because the plural form meant so much more in the original French than either 'devout' or 'devotion'. The term *dévots* always conveyed the idea of active groups of people who were imbued with the sense of a mission to influence and change the world in which they lived in accordance with their understanding of Christian religious and moral principles. The specific historical context suggests, therefore, that we would come closer to these *dévots* if we thought of them as 'the zealous' or 'the militant' – both of which take their spiritual 'devoutness' as a given.

Needless to say, historical labels undergo shifts in meaning over time, even within a relatively short span such as the seventeenth century. By the second half of the century, the criticism and mockery to which its *dévots* were subjected by libertines generally, but also by major figures like Molière and La Bruyère (who declared that 'a *dévot* is someone who would be an atheist in an atheistic society'), helped transform the term into one of ridicule and abuse. That reputation, too, is part of their history, but it should not be imagined that its appearance heralded the end of the *dévots*. Even a woman as decidedly 'of the world' as Mme de Sévigné could write in the 1680s, 'a *dévote*, that is what I would wish to be'. As if she had been eavesdropping on Mme de Sévigné, Mme de Maintenon claimed, in a decidedly firmer tone in the 1690s, 'a *dévote*, that is what I seek to become'. Having experienced the frankly anti-*dévot* atmosphere of Louis XIV's early court, she was certainly not alone in her convictions during his later years. In court politics alone, we find a long thread that extends from the *parti des dévots* of the 1610s and 1620s to the *parti dévot* of the eighteenth century. The world beyond the court moved in different ways and at different speeds, so that the scope and duration of the *dévot* phenomenon cannot be derived simply from trends at court. The *dévots* were the primary consumers of the devotional literature and new kinds of spirituality which, as we have just seen, were so abundant during our period. Many of their number were themselves writers, preachers and directors of conscience whose activities generated as well as satisfied such a demand. Quite simply, neither the major projects nor the accomplishments of seventeenth-century French Catholicism can be understood without the *dévots*, the great majority of whom still remain anonymous for historians. Even though Louis Châtellier has shown that the phenomenon was not a purely French one, and that it had analogues in other parts of Catholic Europe, it seems clear that it transcended its initial base in France to a degree not quite matched elsewhere.

The Early *Dévots*

Historians trace the origins of the *dévot* phenomenon to the wars of religion, and especially to its latter phases when the Catholic League mutated from a shadowy political conspiracy into a widespread movement of resistance, especially in urban areas, to Henri III and Henri IV. The processions, vigils, fasting and other penitential or ascetic activities of those involved were an essential element of that resistance. Some of this activity was organised by confraternities which would later continue to play a key role in channelling religious anxieties in both a devotional and an activist direction. The armed processions of Paris and other cities have remained one of the most powerful symbols of these years, but the failure to prevent the Bourbon succession and the political settlements which followed meant that those involved were anxious to bury the traces of their controversial political past. They were willing to engage in the *oubliance* that Henri IV was preaching during the 1590s as indispensable for peace, even though many remained wary of the king, especially over his dealings with the Huguenots.

It has, therefore, often been claimed that the *dévots* of the next century were either former Catholic Leaguers themselves or descendants of Leaguers.[1] Without denying the real importance of these groups in the emergence of the *dévots*, such a view is too limited. It would condemn the *dévots* to being no more than a lingering and ever-declining band of 'nostalgics' left over from the heady years of the League, which the evidence simply does not support. In fact, the hard political choices of the League period divided French Catholics as never before, and especially those belonging to the political elites, both nationally and locally. But the divisions generated by it were rarely absolute or long-lasting, and the challenges of restoring the French church and religious unity were more than sufficient to reunite the different groups thereafter: that project united those which the Bourbon succession had previously divided. Thus, considerable numbers of former *politiques* became *dévots* in due course demonstrating, as one recent historian has argued, that 'the processions of the League were not the only path to the cloisters of reformed Catholicism'.[2] So, too, did many of those who, having returned or converted to Catholicism from Calvinism, patronised and promoted some of the most emblematic elements of the Catholic Reformation. But the thesis that the *dévots* most committed to penitential and mystical forms of Catholicism were former Protestants with a prior history of financial activity again seems unnecessarily restrictive, and risks reducing the *dévot* phenomenon to an attempt at atonement by a minority for its past 'sins'. In any case, similar genealogies could be found for large numbers of Catholic *dévots*, whether they were former *politiques* or *ligueurs*, whose families had also held financial offices in royal service.

We shall return later to the question of the 'social' profile of the *dévots*, but it is worth noting here how important for the *longue durée* of the *dévots* – and for religious culture generally – were the different religious-spiritual affinities that did develop within individual families over several generations. They could take numerous forms, and concerned the 'small fry' as much as the great and the good – the latter, of course, being the best documented. The Séguiers, for example, were *politiques* in the 1580s and 1590s, but they were also overtly pro-Jesuit and would remain so during the following century, while also patronising the Carmelite nuns. Their cousins, the Bérulles, were no less heavily engaged politically and religiously, with Pierre de Bérulle becoming superior of the French Carmelites while also founding the French Oratory, which became the major counterweight to the Jesuits. The Arnauld family's religious commitments, centring on Port-Royal and the Jansenist cause, traversed the entire century, and are probably the best known of all.[3] Impressionistic evidence suggests that far less distinguished families, which we have previously observed patronising particular churches, confraternities or convents in provincial towns, also held steadfastly to their own distinctive traditions over several generations. Individual members might occasionally follow their own separate paths, but this rarely altered underlying family traditions.

If such traditions were vital, there were also 'institutions' (for want of a better term) which could lend a helping hand in perpetuating the *dévots* beyond the first generation. For many, especially in small towns, that might be the new confraternities that combined action with devotion, the frequentation of a newly established religious order, or (for women) membership of a third order. The early *dévots* were themselves active in creating many of these bodies in the first place, so the relationship between them was a highly reciprocal one. In Toulouse, for example, as many as twenty new confraternities were formed and four Penitent confraternities were reformed in the decades after the wars ended.[4] Probably the single most influential source, although only shaping a cross-section of France's *dévots*, was the Jesuit colleges and the Marian congregations that they organised for their students, alumni and local socio-professional groups seeking religious direction. These methods were first tried in Rome, Cologne and elsewhere before reaching their French colleges by the mid-1570s. Within what was already a disciplined and highly religious educational environment, the Jesuits singled out, as we have already seen, the best and most motivated of their senior students to become members of their Marian sodalities or congregations to engage in a range of additional religious exercises, under the guidance of a Jesuit director. Some of these students would go on to become Jesuits themselves, making the Marian congregations recruiting grounds for the society, but most members would follow careers within the secular world.

The Marian devotions were undisguisedly 'Catholic-confessional', having developed in the wake of the victory at Lepanto (1571), but insistence on frequent confession and communion was an even more central feature of these congregations. And, as we saw in another context, such sacramental practice required regular prayer, self-examination and other exercises of piety. Demands like these were meant to mark the members for life – to be a 'seminary of a life of holiness', as one author put it – so it is no surprise that the Jesuits developed corresponding congregations to accompany their alumni after their studies were completed. From there, other congregations emerged which brought together people from the same social groups or professions, only some of whom were former students of the Jesuits. By contrast, the indiscriminate mixing of different groups, even for spiritual exercises, was regarded as counterproductive: *messieurs* and artisans thus belonged to separate congregations. The gradual spread of Jesuit colleges across seventeenth-century France brought these congregations of both interns and externs in their wake, and it is hardly surprising that in many towns across France, the membership of these congregations numbered in their hundreds. What all had in common, beyond their devotions, was the Ignatian desire to act upon and improve the world beyond the chapels in which they met. Even while still college students, many of them were encouraged to engage in catechising in local parishes, visiting prisons and other 'good works'. Such an environment and activities paved the way for the proliferation of *dévots*.[5]

But, as already noted, the Jesuits did not have a monopoly on the 'making' of *dévots*. Their exclusion from northern and central France until 1603 and the gradual spread of their colleges thereafter are only two reasons why this remained so. An unknown number of towns opposed the presence of the Jesuits among them – such as in Clermont where there was stiff resistance to opening a Jesuit college in the early 1660s – but that did not prevent them from generating a strong *dévot* presence *without* the Jesuits. Above all, the Jesuits – and the other male orders or congregations – could not play a direct role in making female *dévots*, whose importance was never as crucial as during the early decades of the century.[6] It seems that the initial spur here was the experiences of the Catholic League, when women found themselves on different sides of the political divide, although in many cases that was not their personal choice to begin with. The absence or the death of husbands pitched many of them into roles where they assumed direct responsibility for their families, sometimes having to defend family property against confiscation by political adversaries. They carried over these experiences into the conditions of peace after the mid-1590s. It is also possible that there was more room than usual for female activism in the wake of the religious wars, if only because many of the men who had fought for the Catholic League were hampered by their recent past. Historians have frequently observed the role that women played in the diffusion of Calvinist ideas and piety in the sixteenth century, and it does not seem far-fetched to imagine early seventeenth-century *dévotes* having the same kind of influence within Catholicism. In this connection, Paris has always served as both model and shorthand for a wider phenomenon, but we should not forget the extent to which individual towns and cities differed from each other; the Parisian examples cited here should be regarded as indicators of the attitudes and approaches of the *dévots* of this early period.

The early phase of the post-war *dévot* movement seems to have been dominated by individuals and groups in search of penitential and sometimes mystical forms of piety. In Paris, the circle gathered around Mme Acarie attracted both clerics and laypeople, women and men. Some of the most influential 'gurus' of the early seventeenth-century church belonged to that group, which in turn exercised a 'ripple effect' influence on the next generation. The Acarie circle, and no doubt others like it elsewhere, acted as clearing houses for new religious ideas and practices, and they could call upon experienced preachers, spiritual directors and writers in their quest. On the one hand, mystics like the Capuchin, Benoît de Canfeld (originally an English émigré, William Fitch) or the Benedictine, dom Beaucousin, offered the prospect of access to mystical union with God to those seeking withdrawal from the world. On the other hand, the personal influence, letters and early works of François de Sales offered them a powerful legitimation for what they were already doing – living a Christian life in the world at large. The search for atonement led them in more than one direction, so that a simple binary opposition between withdrawal from the world and activity in the world does not accurately represent their behaviour. As important as such impulses articulated by individual clerics were, the role of lay *dévots* remained paramount, and in early seventeenth-century Paris, Mme Acarie herself emerged as a spiritual adviser in her own right, even to clerics like Bérulle who would themselves become famous in such roles. Her circle were the real founders of the contemplative Carmelite nuns in France, having attracted an initial group of nuns from Spain in 1605. Two years later, as we saw in an earlier chapter, they sponsored the very different Order of Visitation nuns to settle in Paris. Similar efforts were replicated numerous times in Paris itself, but above all in provincial towns.

The efflorescence of new religious orders, especially but not exclusively for women, that was so prominent a feature of the early Catholic Reformation in France, would be quite unthinkable without these *dévots*, whose efforts and methods would be copied and adapted by later generations. The efforts that they deployed, to clear legal obstacles, acquire or construct new buildings, obtain financial support and so on for the new orders or congregations, were without historical precedent, and in numerous cases could last for decades rather than years. No doubt, the slowness of the old orders, both male and female, to engage in self-reform made the search for new forms of religious life seem an obvious challenge for these *dévots*. Likewise, the highly uneven quality of the official church leadership at this juncture encouraged self-reliance and initiative on their part, even though it is equally clear how eagerly they gravitated towards those bishops who showed a real determination to reform their dioceses. But at the same time, many of these early *dévots* experienced the tug of the cloister and the urge to withdraw from a world of sin and corruption, and that was to prove a perennial motif throughout their history, for men as much as for women. They were not immune to the argument that the 'consecrated' life remained the most truly Christian one and, indeed, that strict cloister might be best of all. So it is no surprise that Mme Acarie herself, three of her daughters and large numbers of her fellow *dévotes* ended up joining the convents that they had helped to found.

The scale of the *dévot* phenomenon during the early seventeenth century is such that dividing it into two generations seems arbitrary, except insofar as it conveys a sense of its growing dynamism and widening activities. It was helped, as we shall see, by the fact that the political situation changed to their advantage from the 1610s onwards. As far as the Parisian female *dévots* are concerned, Diefendorf has argued that this second generation was more geared towards charitable activities than towards asceticism and contemplation. This interpretation can certainly be accepted if the term 'charitable' is understood in its widest possible connotation. Nothing illustrates better the extent of this shift than the well-known collaboration between Vincent de Paul, protégé of the powerful Gondi-Retz family and especially of its most prominent *dévot* members, and Louise de Marillac, herself the daughter of an equally well-connected *dévot* family. The experiences and projects of de Paul and Marillac, which we saw from another angle in an earlier chapter, would have had little impact were it not for the networks of *dévots* that supported and financed them. De Paul's own brief spell as a parish *curé* brought him into immediate contact with popular poverty, and led him to launch a parish confraternity of charity, an idea which was not hugely different from similar associations springing up within other parishes across France at the time, and whose objective was to organise the better-off, especially women, in order to feed and nurse the poor.

This was the origin of the Ladies of Charity, whose indispensability, but also limitations, became gradually evident by the late 1620s, when de Paul employed Marillac to survey their operations: by then, some of the ladies were employing their own servants to perform the charitable works on their behalf rather than engaging directly in them themselves. The next step, the creation of the Daughters of Charity recruited among lower-status women, was an attempt to restore the primacy of the charitable dimension to the operation, by replacing servants acting under obligation with women who saw it as a religious vocation. The double-pronged congregation that subsequently emerged was unprecedented because it involved retaining rather than superseding the Ladies of Charity, whose financial and social resources seemed so indispensable, in tandem with the daughters. Indeed, the survival of such a hybrid, which was Marillac's rather than de Paul's idea, is the best indicator of the ramifications of the wider *dévot* world, which included the highest circles at court. Without such powerful support, this pioneering *dévot* project, which opened the door for so many others in later decades, would probably not have survived at all.[7]

The *Parti des Dévots*: Politics and Religion

It will be clear from the example of the Daughters of Charity that the *dévots*, whatever their background and even when they were not politically attuned, were not averse to seeking the support of the monarchy for their projects. Throughout the seventeenth century, their history is one of periods of closeness to, and influence over, the crown on the one hand, and periods of distance and mutual suspicion on the other. The scale of their activities and the high-status support that they regularly enjoyed meant that the political dimension was never entirely absent. Under Henri IV, as might be expected, the signals were limited and mixed, and the strongest signal of all, namely the king's embrace of the Jesuits post 1603 and his subsequent decision to have a Jesuit as his confessor, did not please everyone.[8] But it did open the way, as we have just seen, for the proliferation of Jesuit colleges and their devotional congregations. By contrast, both personal inclination and the political circumstances of the post-Henri IV regency (and beyond) induced Marie de' Medici to rely quite heavily, from the early to mid-1610s onwards, on church leaders, and to admit *dévots*, lay and clerical, such as Michel de Marillac and Pierre de Bérulle respectively, into her confidence. After her return from disgrace (1617–20), a very loosely connected *parti des dévots* gathered around her rather than Louis XIII who, while by no means hostile to them, was more anxious to enforce royal authority than to pursue Catholic causes per se. This distinction, which Richelieu would emphasise in due course, only became fully clear at the end of the last Huguenot wars in 1629, with disastrous political results for the *parti des dévots*, which was blown apart during the political crisis of 1630. In the intervening years, thanks initially to Richelieu himself, the political *dévots* had brought elements of their activism with them into the realm of government. In particular, they elaborated plans for the reform of the realm that echoed those of Henri III's reign, and it is hardly an accident that their plans for church and religious reforms were better conceived than those for the improvement of governance, which have been characterised as unspecific and moralising.[9] And contrary to what is often imagined, the political defeat of the *dévots* in 1630 did not spell the end of their connections in government and at court. An emerging generation of major figures, such as de Paul, the Oratorian Charles de Condren, or Jean-Jacques Olier, the *curé* of Saint-Sulpice, was less openly political than Bérulle or Marillac, which enabled them in due course to secure high-level backing for their projects.

The Company of the Holy Sacrament

With so wide a panoply of congregations, sodalities, confraternities and devotional associations to choose from, it is hard to imagine why certain *dévots* should have thought it necessary to invent something more original, but the Company of the Holy Sacrament, a secret society founded in 1630, certainly fits the bill.[10] It remained totally forgotten until the late nineteenth century when a manuscript history (annals) of the Company, written in the mid-1690s by a surviving member who dreamed of reviving it, was exhumed and published. For a Catholic church used to denouncing secret societies (especially Freemasonry) as nefarious conspiracies, such a discovery was a serious embarrassment. It generated heated discussion at the height of the Third Republic's (anti-) clerical wars, so it is not surprising that early studies of the

Company were anything but dispassionate. Over a century later, well after the embers have cooled and despite the discovery of valuable additional sources, many questions remain unanswered and probably unanswerable; the contours of the Company are not easy to delineate and the exact nature of its influence hard to estimate, given the patchiness of the historical sources (due to both its own secrecy and the deliberate destruction of its principal archives). The analysis that follows, while not aiming at comprehensiveness, will attempt to show that the Company did 'capture' the *dévot* dynamic to such an extent that even when it was suppressed, there was no question of the *dévot* movement simply returning to the status quo ante of the late 1620s. The discussion here will confine itself to those issues which connect the Company to the major themes of this book.

The most difficult question for the historian is, quite simply, why such a creation at all and why in the late 1620s? The initial decision to found a society ('company') was formally made in 1627, but the idea itself may already have been a few years older by then, dating from around 1624–5, when a newly installed royal minister and relative of Richelieu, Jean Bochart de Champigny, was approached, but refused to take responsibility for launching it. It was, he responded, too 'dangerous' (*périlleux*) an undertaking, but it is hard to guess what exactly he may have meant by that. However, approaching him in the first place indicates a clear desire for highest-level approval – that of Louis XIII, Marie de' Medici and Richelieu included. The 1627 foundation hung fire because of the continuing Huguenot wars, hence the definitive refoundation in March 1630. The original idea is credited to a grandee of the realm, the duke of Ventadour, at the time lieutenant-governor of Languedoc, a province with a large Protestant population. His co-founders were a Capuchin friar, Philippe d'Angoumois, a preacher and spiritual writer, and a secular priest of old southern noble stock, François de Grignan, who would later become archbishop of Arles. Ventadour and his Capuchin confidant both emerge as emblematic 'crusading' figures of a decade that witnessed the reprise of the Huguenot wars in France. Ventadour, who would separate from his wife in 1631 so that both could pursue lives of renunciation and retreat in arch-*dévot* fashion, may be seen as prolonging, albeit in a very different register, contemporary aristocratic efforts to defend Catholicism in Europe as a whole, efforts which had generated projects like the *milice chrétienne* of the duke of Nevers and another, more famous Capuchin, Père Joseph, during the 1610s. Philippe d'Angoumois was an unsurprising ally for Ventadour to choose, given the Capuchins' involvement in anti-Protestant missions during these same years. It is known that the Huguenot wars of the 1620s generated almost messianic expectations among some French Catholics, and the choice of the Holy Sacrament as the new Company's motif immediately evokes the earlier militancy of the sixteenth-century leagues and confraternities. Yet these rapprochements do not really answer the question of how or why the idea of a secret society surfaced, for which there are no obvious precursors to which we can point. The Company itself, in 1660, underlined the ideal of secrecy as that which distinguished it most fundamentally from other bodies. This peculiarity, it may be argued, helps to explain why it took perhaps more time than is generally imagined to take on some of its most distinctive characteristics.

At any rate, by 1630 influential church and court figures knew of, and indicated their support for, the project, which still remained highly imprecise in its objectives. Via the king's confessor, the Jesuit Jean Suffren, they obtained royal support, as well as that of Richelieu. The secrecy which later became a trademark of the Company of the Holy Sacrament was perhaps not yet fully articulated, as the founders seem only progressively to have renounced the initial impulse to seek royal letters patent and a papal brief of approval, both of which would have rendered their existence public. The archbishops of both Paris and Lyon (the latter Richelieu's elder brother) quickly made it clear that they did not approve of the Company operating within their dioceses. Thus, actual experiences, rather than mere preconceived intentions, may have ensured that the kind of secrecy for which the Company was later notorious quickly became hard-headed and practical as well as mystical. The original idea of a 'hidden' society that corresponded to Christ's own early life and that wore 'the livery of a truly hidden God' (their term) was designed to facilitate 'the undertaking of good works with the greatest prudence, disinterestedness and the minimum of contradiction, since experience shows that display is the ruin of such works'. Secrecy thus became transmuted into a virtue, almost an end in itself, 'the soul of the Company' by the 1650s when, as we shall see, there was good reason to reiterate its mantra and to worry about the consequences of neglecting it.

The early surviving sources do not enable us to track the founders' thinking, and as already suggested we should perhaps not overestimate how fully formed their objectives were from the outset. It is perhaps best to regard them as knowing what they did *not* want, rather than what they actually wanted to be or do. They adopted statutes that were common among the Penitents and accompanied their regular Thursday meetings (in Paris at least) with prayers and spiritual readings, but they were clear that they did not wish to be a confraternity *comme les autres*.[11] The sanctification of its members was not the Company's primary objective, however much it encouraged them in that direction. Its disarmingly simple but Promethean motto of 'doing all good and preventing all evil' – or 'to build heaven on earth', as one historian of the *dévots* has put it – would have set them apart from confraternities of *every* stripe, but here, too, it is hard to grasp what the founders felt this to entail. Yet the initial grand design of doing all good and preventing all evil eventually acquired more tangible substance. A circular drafted after much discussion in 1660 and sent to local branches by the Paris chapter, when it was both at the height of its power and on the verge of suppression, spelt it out in impressive detail while simultaneously underlining its distinctiveness. It declared that, unlike other bodies or corporations, 'the Company has no frontiers, measures [limits?] or restrictions apart from those dictated by prudence and discernment. It engages *not only* in the habitual good works for the poor, the sick, prisoners and all other people in affliction, *but also* in missions, seminaries, the conversion of heretics, the propagation of the faith throughout the world, and the prevention of every kind of scandal, impiety, and blasphemy. In a word, it aims to prevent every kind of evil or to provide remedies for them; to achieve every kind of good, both general and individual; to engage in those works that are difficult and hard, neglected and abandoned; and to do so for the benefit of one's neighbour, in the full measure of charity.'[12]

Membership and Structure of the Company of the Holy Sacrament

There were many other respects in which the Company's make-up did not duplicate those of devotional or charitable associations that we have already discussed. It quite deliberately kept its membership limited, though the actual numbers did vary from place to place depending on the size of the towns and local *dévot* population, but probably also in relation to the scope of the local chapter's activities. Membership of the Paris mother-company was a minimum of 274 for the years 1630–60, while that of Vitré in Brittany for the years 1656–63 was only about fifteen, several of whom were inactive.[13] Secondly, admission was strictly by co-option, with individual members being delegated to approach potential recruits in a highly indirect manner, in order to sound out their 'dispositions', before either rejecting them or proposing them for membership. And that membership was far from representative of a cross-section of either the *dévots* or French society generally; such a 'balanced' objective had no place in the Company's thinking. For one thing, it was entirely male in composition. Yet the question of female membership did arise almost at the outset, for in late 1630 or early 1631, a proposal for a separate assembly of ladies with their own statutes was proposed, but it was voted down. It was proposed again in 1645, but by that point the opposition to it had hardened further, successfully arguing that such an idea was 'absolutely opposed to the spirit of the Company'.[14] This refusal of female membership of the Company may not have prevented one or two local companies from founding their own female counterpart society, but scarcely anything is known of them. It may also be, as was suggested in the 1645 debate, that potential female members were already being directed either towards the local *hôtel-Dieu*'s 'assembly of ladies' or towards the Company's own favoured affiliate, the Congregation for the propagation of the faith, in towns where they existed.

The Company of the Holy Sacrament is often depicted as an early precursor of lay 'Catholic action', but the absence of women is one glaring 'missing link' here. Furthermore, the membership of those branches for which we have information shows a clerical-lay equilibrium that cannot have been a series of local accidents. Alain Tallon's overall figures for known members shows a majority of laymen, but it was not an overwhelming one: at least 40 per cent of the known members were clerics of various rank and importance.[15] Well-intentioned bishops were routinely asked to join the company, and were given all the honour and deference due to their rank, but the business of the company was conducted by a regularly changing bureau of elected officers, clerical and lay. The precedent of Paris and Lyon, where the archbishop refused his blessing, was no doubt used in other dioceses to justify founding companies without episcopal permission or oversight. Thirty-nine bishops are known to have become members up to the early 1660s, but as some were missionaries outside France, this means that only a small minority of the episcopate was closely involved with the Company. Yet it did attract some of France's most distinguished bishops, such as Solminihac of Cahors, Godeau of Grasse, Pavillon of Alet and Zamet of Langres, while others such as Bossuet, Louis Abelly or Gabriel de Roquette were members before they became bishops. Some of them began as members of the Paris chapter and played a role in diffusing the Company in provincial France. 'Unclassifiable' figures like Vincent de Paul and Charles de Condren, Bérulle's successor at the Oratory, also joined its ranks from an early date. In numerical terms, though, it was the cream of the 'second order' secular clergy – diocesan officials, cathedral canons, *curés* of major urban parishes and so on – that filled the company's clerical ranks. Quite apart from the positions they held, these men were also local figures with good reputations and, frequently, family connections, whereas even a well-intentioned bishop might be just a temporary bonus.

Also worth noting in this connection is that, despite the role of a Capuchin in its foundation, the Company soon decided that it would no longer co-opt regulars or members of congregations; they were ultimately answerable to their own superiors, who might therefore have been in a position to ascertain what the Company's activities were. This ruling, of course, did not affect very early members like Philippe d'Angoumois, Suffren, de Paul or Condren. It is equally likely that the Company wished to steer clear of the habitual conflicts among the regulars and between regulars and secular clergy. The exclusion of Jesuits is particularly ironic – given the legends concerning their domination of the Company – since in many local branches, it was probably Jesuit alumni or Jesuit-directed confraternity members who dominated the

Company membership. As we shall see, the Company's philosophy of action, as well as its spirituality, owed much, but not all, to the Jesuits, something that appeared self-evident to the Jansenists, who contributed to the Company's demise in 1660.

As for its lay members, the Company was equally keen to select not just committed and devout Catholics, but to recruit men whose social and professional position would be particularly useful in promoting its objectives. A major consideration here was how effective they could be when seeming to act in a personal capacity, given the overriding need to protect the Company's secrecy and to offset its incapacity to act in its own name. Hence the selection of members of the old nobility, some with distinguished names like the prince of Conti or the duke of Liancourt. But most of its noble members were drawn from gentry families, such as the hyperactive Simiane de la Coste (Marseille and the Midi generally) or Gaston de Renty and Antoine de Fénelon (both key members of the Paris chapter). Throughout provincial France, the Company absolutely needed the support of royal magistrates from the local law courts and town halls, but it also welcomed, and needed, merchants, lawyers and a thin smattering of artisans, all of whom gave it a purchase on individual professions or social groups whose activities were of interest to it. Within these overall parameters, we should bear in mind that there were significant contrasts in the main functions of French towns – some were primarily political, economic or administrative-judicial centres – which probably meant that the internal balance of individual local chapters would vary somewhat. It is not superfluous to add here that although the Company insisted that all members be treated equally at meetings or when voting on projects, some members were nevertheless more equal than others. This is true not merely in respect of a Ventadour or a Conti, both grandees, but also of less socially elevated members whose connections were immensely valuable for the Company's projects – Renty, Vincent de Paul, Charles de Condren, Jean Eudes, Jean-Jacques Olier, to mention only a few. Weighing individual influence rather than counting heads is essential to understanding the *dévot* phenomenon generally.

Expansion of the Company of the Holy Sacrament

Whatever uncertainties the Company may have initially had about its aims, methods or membership, they clearly did not affect its desire to spread its wings across France. It was wholly in keeping with this attitude that a branch was founded in Lyon as early as 1630, just when the royal court was resident there, but what made the Company different from every other group we have seen in other contexts was the enduring desire, on the part of the founding Parisian chapter, to keep a firm grip on the whole process of expansion and subsequent communication between its member branches. The Company would not only be secret, it would also be centralised, though in several known instances that proved to be impractical.

The accompanying maps 5 and 6 (overleaf) give an initial idea of the chronology and the geographical scale of the Company's expansion, but what they depict is far from self-explanatory. The chronology of expansion shows that the decades either side of the Fronde (1648–53) were the most 'productive', which is not altogether surprising. It would have taken much of the 1630s to establish a method, make the necessary contacts and gauge the scope of support for a local chapter across French towns, while the final surge in new foundations after the Fronde may have been a question of 'catch-up' after the great revolt. By 1666, when Louis XIV renewed Mazarin's initial suppression order of 1660, there were chapters in at least sixty-four towns, with relatively few substantial towns lacking one by that point. On the other hand, the presence of chapters in several insignificant towns (Vitré, Beaucaire, Tarascon, Orange and Beaune) hints at how 'personal' rather than 'strategic' considerations could influence the company's expansion – as often happened with confraternities like the Penitents. It was frequently as a result of members of the Paris Company finding themselves on provincial missions – which is not surprising, given how many of them were royal officials of high rank – that local branches were founded. The personal relations that were thereby created, or reinforced, facilitated the process of transmitting statutes (which the Paris chapter absolutely refused to have printed for fear of their being divulged) and instructions thereafter; 'confidence' mattered as much as commitment. So the Angoulême chapter was founded in 1650 when the marquis d'Argenson returned to his native town for the marriage of his son, the Company's future historian. Brittany is another useful example. Both Rennes and Nantes had chapters from 1649 onwards, but nothing further happened until the 1655 session of the Breton provincial estates was held at Vitré, near Rennes. The royal commissioners in attendance were Lamoignon and Fouquet, the first a prominent *compagnon*, the second the finance minister with an impeccable *dévot* pedigree and a virtual *compagnon*. Lamoignon was commissioned to found a local company while on tour at Vitré. That two further chapters were added soon afterwards in north-western Brittany, at Morlaix (1656) and Saint-Brieuc (1657), is hardly a coincidence.

However, expansion was not always commanded or controlled from Paris. The Aix chapter (1638) founded the Marseille (1639) and, perhaps, the Arles (1640) and Toulon (1642) ones also. Yet it was the Marseille chapter which appears to have been the most energetic and independently minded in southern France, and it went on to found that of Toulouse (1641). How complete the Paris Company's control was, especially with the expansion of the post-Fronde years, is open to question. Sometimes it frankly accepted its

5. Expansion of the Company of the Holy Sacrament, 1629–49.

DÉVOTS: THE PIOUS AND THE MILITANT 381

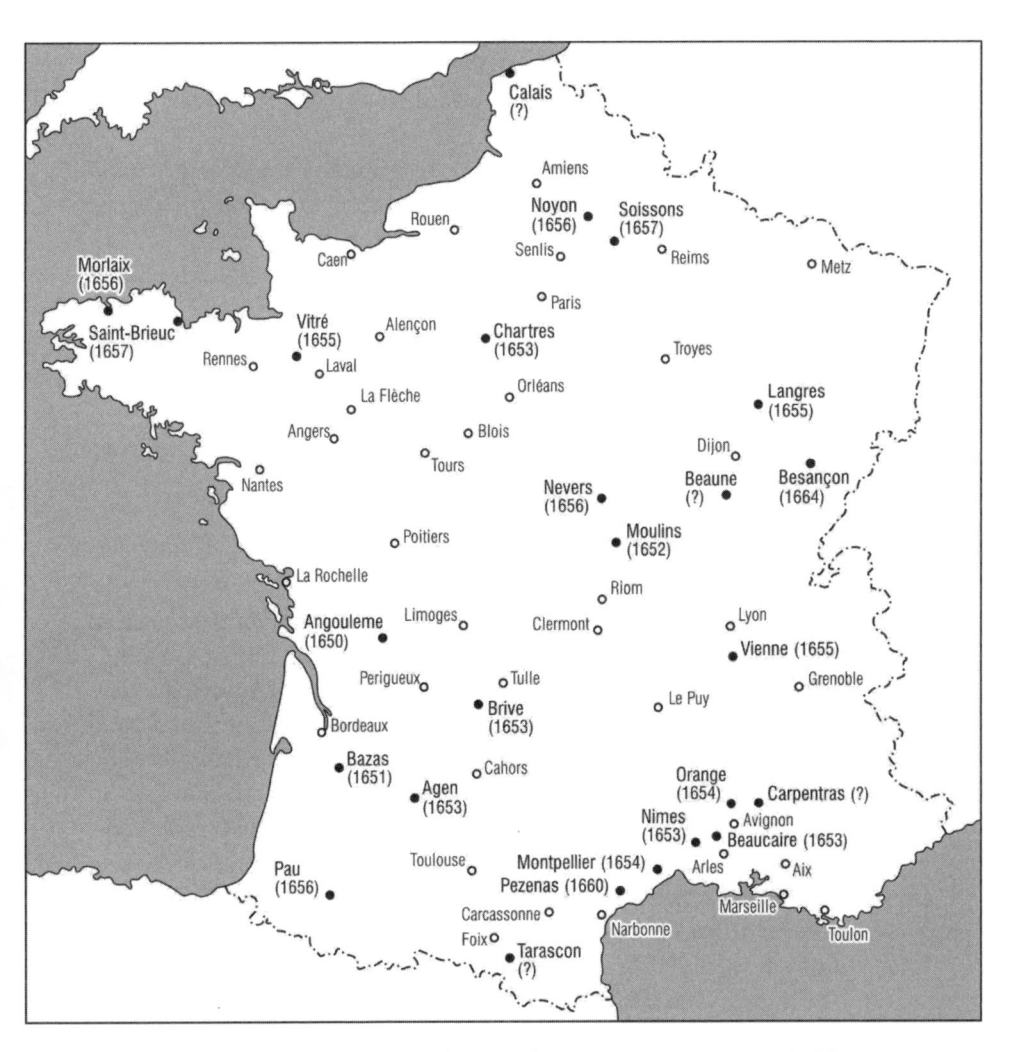

6. Expansion of the Company of the Holy Sacrament, 1653–67 (with post-1653 foundations marked in bold).

own limitations, as when it requested the new Vitré chapter in 1656 to take directions from its near neighbour at Rennes. The Limoges chapter appears to have been among the most energetic champions of 'downward' expansion from a provincial centre point, founding at least eight affiliated branches, 'little companies', some in quite small towns throughout the diocese.[16] In these towns, but also in places like Vitré or Beaucaire, the *compagnons* were, truly, worlds apart from those of Paris, Grenoble or Marseille, and their lay contingent would certainly have included churchwardens of relatively modest status, in other words, parish *dévots*!

Any attempt to measure the Company's impact must also keep firmly in mind the longevity – or lack of it – of local chapters, so as to avoid exaggeration or excessive generalisation. Being the first off the blocks did not make the Paris chapter the longest-lived! It lasted just over thirty years, declining quickly after its first suppression in 1660, whereas the Lyon, Grenoble and Marseille chapters lasted for several decades longer – that of Lyon until 1731. Nor were all chapters equally active throughout their period of existence. Lyon, the oldest after Paris, seems to have vegetated for the first dozen years or more of its existence. Some of the latecomers, like that of Vitré (1655), may have lasted fewer than ten years and had relatively little direct impact on their surroundings.

Activities of the Company of the Holy Sacrament

It would make little sense to propose a detailed analysis here of the manifold activities of the Company, either generally or locally; its own refusal to limit its fields of action should of itself be adequate deterrent against any such attempt. As we saw, when it did outline its multiple spheres of action in its 'mission statement' of 1660, it began with the classic 'works of mercy' ('the poor, the sick, prisoners, and all other people in affliction') that were recommended to all Christians, while placing greater emphasis on more difficult and troublesome, but also more unspecified, tasks. That distinction should not be misinterpreted, however, as meaning that the former were in any sense neglected. Indeed, it is particularly ironic that the Company's reputation remains closely wedded to its interventions in precisely the sphere of poverty and assistance to the poor, the sick and the imprisoned. Like the *dévots* among whom it recruited its members, the Company was soon faced with the problem of coping with unprecedentedly high levels of popular destitution, deracination and vagrancy resulting mainly from economic recession and warfare, civil and foreign – all of which reached a peak from the mid-1630s to the early 1660s. The surviving records of the Company's deliberations, whether in Paris or elsewhere, clearly show how constant a challenge this situation was, especially in relation to raising money, gathering food and clothes, despatching relief supplies and so on.

The problem of poverty, and its social, moral and religious consequences, had already forced governing authorities and social elites across Europe to search for new methods and institutions to deal with them. Neither the existing hospices nor the practice of conventional almsgiving to the 'poor of Christ' seemed capable of coping with the rising levels of indigence. The *dévots* of the generation of Louise de Marillac and Vincent de Paul were, as we saw, already seeking to alleviate poverty, using new confraternities and religious congregations, but they were also relying very heavily on the financial resources of the kind of wealthy *dévot* women, often widows, who became Ladies of Charity. Local confraternities of charity sprang up across the larger provincial cities which were most affected by such problems. The Company, because it tried to synthesise and co-ordinate these efforts, was more intrinsically likely than isolated individual groups of *dévots* to envisage new solutions. This positioned its approach to poor relief at the crossroads of the old and the new: its members still aspired to practise charity, working towards their own salvation by seeing Christ in the faces of the poor. But at the same time, they began to unravel the traditional image of the undifferentiated poor. The upshot was that they came to view some of the poor as more deserving than others: they were, for the most part, the familiar, settled and non-threatening poor of the parish, who managed to preserve their moral and religious dignity in severely straitened circumstances. But others fell far short of such an acceptance threshold, doubtless because so many of them were uprooted immigrants with no local family ties, which in turn made it easier to regard them as a danger to the existing social and religious order. Thus, they were perceived as ignorant, blasphemous, aggressive and, when thrown together in the same tenements or districts, often criminal.

In this kind of world, related problems of malnutrition, sickness, vagrancy, abandoned children and prostitution were never far away – so poor relief generated a series of interrelated activities. How far these shifting perceptions were based on the experiences and observations of 'ordinary' *dévots*, and how far they derived from the newer humanist and mercantilist thinking about poverty and its social causes, is hard to say. In any event, the Company's prime contribution was to insist that charity needed to be tied to the provision of religious instruction for the poor in question, something which existing municipal charity of the 'out of doors' kind was unable to provide. Only religious instruction would change their character and lead them to a life of virtue.

The Company's best-known, but by no means sole response, was to press for an improved institutional framework to deal with these social ravages. It took nearly twenty years, beginning as early as 1631, for the Paris chapter to develop and secure backing, particularly from the city's elites, for plans for a substantial *hôpital général*. It would be a place of confinement, a workhouse rather than a hospital in our sense of the word, whose inmates would be taught the basic tenets of religion, trained in some kind of skill or trade and, generally speaking, morally and socially disciplined. This ambitious scheme, designed to bring together a series of institutions under one roof, was first proposed for Paris shortly after the Fronde had ended (1653), and was driven from behind the scenes by the Company, which obtained the royal letters patent, but no less importantly, the funds to start building it. The Paris *hôpital général* began its operations in 1656, and for many years thereafter its governing body was dominated by members of the Company. Needless to say, it encouraged its provincial chapters to follow its lead, although it was only in 1662 that a royal edict called for an *hôpital général* to be founded in every city and town throughout France. Despite little real support from the crown, almost one hundred analogous institutions had been started across France by around 1700, thanks largely to Jesuit missionaries and *dévot* commitment.

Summarised in such bald terms, it is hard to imagine that the *hôpital général* could be considered as the epitome of a vast repressive project, the 'great enclosure of the poor', to quote its most famous exponent, Michel Foucault.[17] But the great enclosure of the poor never happened. Existing practices of domiciliary assistance to the poor and needy, in which the *dévots* still engaged in large numbers, continued to target far more people than the seventeenth-century *hôpital général* ever did; around 1700, fewer than 10 per cent of the latter's inmates in Paris were confined there against their will; towns were keener to expel immigrant paupers than to lock them up because of the expense of supporting them. As we saw, the monarchy gave the *hôpital général* project its blessing, but the refusal to put its money where its mouth was meant the crown had relatively little control over the project until conditions changed under Louis XV; above all, it would continue to be financed by various forms of charity, not by taxes. And of course, each *hôpital* continued to be staffed by (mainly) women congregationists such as the Daughters of Charity. There was not the philosophy, will or means to impose a state-driven *grand renfermement* under Louis XIV. It was not the distant monarchy, but rather local urban elites who were primarily interested in shaping the changes in poor relief, and that certainly enabled the *dévots* to make the running. Long after the Company had vanished, it was the *dévots* and the church more broadly, especially its bishops, who remained the principal supporters of the new institution. It is no great surprise, therefore, that after the Company's demise it was a handful of highly resourceful Jesuit missionaries, and not royal officials, who spread the gospel of the *hôpital général* from the 1670s to the 1710s. What is less often noted is that they also campaigned strongly for smaller-scale bureaux of charity in towns and villages, where local *dévots* could play an important role as benefactors and administrators of charity.[18]

As a 'grand project', the building of an *hôpital général* was definitely one of the 'hard' works, to use the Company's own language, even if it was an extension of a classic kind of 'good' work. So, too, were several others, such as their efforts to improve conditions for prisoners and those condemned to galley-service, both of whom were treated abysmally by royal officials: the dynamism of the Marseille chapter derived in large part from such campaigns. The Company's commitment to the 'propagation of the faith' was another 'hard' work and a logical outcome of the conditions of its foundation. A key element of it was not new, namely the drive to eradicate French Protestantism altogether, to which we will return later. More novel, by comparison, was its support for missions outside of Europe, an unfamiliar phenomenon in France until the 1610s. As the Paris chapter was preparing its prospectus of 1660, its leading members were preparing to found the first missionary society of secular clergy anywhere in Europe, the celebrated *Missions Étrangères de Paris*, a creation that its historian, Argenson, regarded as the most fitting monument to the Company's work. The Company had already singled out diocesan seminaries for attention at a time when the second, enduring wave of post-Trent seminaries was taking shape in France. As we noted in an earlier chapter, many of them were 'officially' founded in the decades from 1630 to 1680, but for a very long time, they remained mere 'paper' creations, for want of funds and buildings. It was here that the middle-ranking clergy and local magistrates, municipal officials, merchants and so on, who composed the Company's local chapters, could make a real difference. Obstructionism, legal problems over property and sites and, above all, lack of money – these were the kind of obstacles that a local company could deal with by mobilising its networks of influence.

Even this limited overview shows that the multitude and ambition of the Company's projects required considerable resources. One former *compagnon*, Jean du Ferrier, recorded attending chapter meetings in Paris at which 150,000 *livres* were donated by – or via – those present. Such a round figure may be an exaggeration, but Argenson, who had archives rather than personal memories on which to draw, wrote that by the late 1650s the funds available to the Paris chapter seemed limitless, regardless of the constantly growing number of projects that needed financing.[19] This was, of course, in addition to the funds that de Paul and others regularly solicited from high-status *dévots*, especially during the hardship of Fronde and the 1650s. Clearly, the Company had ready access to 'serious' money throughout its lifespan. The pinnacle of its success in this connection coincided with the years (1653–61) when Nicholas Fouquet was royal finance minister. If he was not actually a *compagnon* himself, he was the next best thing: a man whose parents, siblings and wider clientele were steeped in active devotion. He probably ensured that certain 'good works' received financial support from the crown, but this was not the full extent of his commitment.[20] But even before Fouquet took up office, the Company seems to have had little problem financing its enterprises. Several of the kingdom's most influential financial officials and tax-farmers, especially those originating from Tours, which still produced a disproportionate number of financiers, belonged to ultra-*dévot* circles. Leading financial families like the Bonneau, the Pallu and others, for example, were heavily involved with French Canada, the new religious orders (especially of women), and the missionary efforts that would culminate in the *Missions Étrangères de Paris*.[21] But funds were also forthcoming from members of the aristocracy, many of them familiar as Ladies of Charity. It was Richelieu's *dévot* niece, the ubiquitous duchess of Aiguillon who, advised by Vincent de Paul, did most to finance the Marseille hospital for the galley-prisoners. More generally, Argenson's history frequently acknowledges the Company's indebtedness to *dévot* women for the funds they provided for its projects. For once, the term *la finance catholique* is not an empty phrase, provided we realise that it included titled aristocrats as well as professional financiers.

Demise of the Company of the Holy Sacrament

In May 1631, Louis XIII wrote to Archbishop Gondi of Paris declaring that, having commissioned an assessment of the Company and its plans, he judged that it could 'only be beneficial for my realm'.[22] Almost exactly thirty years later, in December 1660, Louis XIV permitted his chief minister, Mazarin, radically to reverse that judgement, despite repeated entreaties from Anne of Austria and other influential political figures. Mazarin concluded that unauthorised assemblies and 'companies' were inherently dangerous to any state and could not be tolerated. Quite how much he knew about them (there were over sixty chapters by then) is impossible to tell, but it was not hard to exploit his well-known fear of conspiracy. By then, there was no shortage of circumstantial evidence against the Company for its excessive zeal in pursuit of moral reform. In particular, the unlawful locking up of prostitutes and other undesirables by members of local chapters such as Bordeaux, Caen or Rouen in the later 1650s contributed to the rumours and denunciations that brought it unwelcome attention. It was the extension of its zeal into spheres like the theatre – specifically, a campaign against comedy – which gained the *dévots* of the mid-seventeenth century their enduring reputation of snoopers and killjoys. It is important to note that some of the accusations launched against the Company came from clerics, led by the ambitious Archbishop Harlay of Rouen. If there was *raison d'état* at work in the suppression of the Company, there was a sprinkling of *raison d'église* too. The latter reflected, firstly, the fear of autonomous groups with a high level of lay leadership operating seemingly at will and, secondly, the higher clergy's growing determination to govern their dioceses without let or hindrance. The holding of a general assembly of Company representatives in Paris in 1660, not to mention the issuing of general instructions by the Paris chapter, could not but conjure up unacceptable images of a 'church within a church' as much as a state within a state. The first suppression order of December 1660 was actually issued by the Paris *parlement*, and was therefore not valid for the entire realm, nor did it make any explicit mention of the Company. Mazarin's death a few months later gave the Company hope that a new regime would ignore a dying man's obsessions, but the *dévots* soon found themselves on the wrong side of Colbert, Mazarin's closest political disciple, during the bitter political struggle that followed the fall of Fouquet in 1661, who was supported by so many of the *dévots*. Thus the Paris chapter's hopes of weathering the storm and of continuing to direct the Company nationwide foundered on an ongoing power struggle well before the definitive suppression by Louis XIV in 1666, even though their last meeting dates from April 1666. As an expression of the *dévot* phenomenon, the Company had come full circle: in 1630, the founding members had renounced any explicit political designs for it, but a generation later politics caught up with the Company, because its activities and membership seemed to make it a threat equivalent to the *parti des dévots* of the late 1620s.

After the Company of the Holy Sacrament

As a nationwide movement, run on what seem remarkably modern lines by the equivalent of a central committee, the Company of the Holy Sacrament was extraordinary by any standards. It was not, however, the equivalent of a central committee of the *dévot* movement in general. The vast majority of France's *dévots* knew even less about it than did the non-*dévots* like Molière who fell foul of it! It attempted to harness the multitude of groups of *dévots* throughout France and enrol them in ever-widening campaigns of religious and social reform which their own mostly single-activity confraternities and associations were incapable of conceiving, let alone pursuing. Its demise removed both the grand vision, as a practical programme rather than as a conception in itself, and the co-ordinating force behind it, but not the local *dévot* groups and their ability to continue acting according to their own lights.

In the short term, there was little place for *dévots* in the politics of the decidedly libertine court of the young Louis XIV. As already mentioned, the fall and subsequent scapegoating of Fouquet hit the *dévots* among the political elite hard, and the anti-*dévot* Colbert was perennially wary of them, whether in

Paris, Dijon or Toulouse. Raoul Allier argued that several of the Company's members attempted to revive it under various guises in the 1660s or 1670s. One such effort was, in Allier's view, the 'company of the hard [*fortes*] works', located in Dijon, whose doings in a highly *dévot* city nevertheless worried the local authorities enough that they issued a decree against it, rejecting anything that constituted an inquisition into people's behaviour.[23] Only further research could demonstrate whether the Saint-Sulpice parish's charitable confraternity acted as cover for a residual Paris chapter, given how many of those attending its meetings until the mid-1660s were former members of the Company. Yet despite the inauspicious political climate, the *dévots* did begin to resurface during the 1680s and 1690s, first in court circles around Mme de Maintenon, and then the duke of Burgundy (the king's eldest grandson and thus his eventual successor), around whom an entire programme for the reform of the realm, with strong *dévot* accents, was developed by Fénelon and others during the years before Burgundy's premature death in 1712. Some of the foundations of their critique of royal absolutism and its harmful moral and social effects had already been developed during the 1670s and 1680s by the so-called 'petit concile', which included Bossuet, a former secretary of the Parish chapter.[24]

Since the Company of the Holy Sacrament had not sought to absorb smaller *dévot* groups into its maw, but rather to orientate their activities from behind the scenes, it was actually in favour of more rather than fewer groups at work, and that, too, was one of its most important legacies. Regardless of whether the efforts at revival just discussed should be considered national rather than local, it is clear that local chapters of the Holy Sacrament continued to exist in several major cities like Marseille, Lyon, Grenoble and elsewhere. Despite the need to keep a low profile after 1660, they retained the earlier habits of the Company within their areas. In many ways, it seems that they achieved more of their objectives during the following decades than previously, as for example the founding of 'primary' schools, 'refuges' for repentant prostitutes and so on.[25] To that extent, there was no return to the status quo ante 1630; the Company was instrumental in adding to the existing stock of *dévot* groups, many of which survived it. Only a few of them can be considered here, essentially with a view to grasping the range of *dévot* activities under Louis XIV.

The Confraternity of the Passion is one of the most elusive of these groups, for the simple reason that it was, unusually, a secret offshoot of the Company; its other offshoots, as we saw, were public, although the links between them were well hidden. The Passion Confraternity was primarily dedicated to the eradication of duelling among the nobility, an early fixation of the Company, and it seems to have come into being during the Fronde.[26] Its Paris group, led by Antoine de Fénelon (uncle of the future archbishop of Cambrai), came together in Saint-Sulpice parish at Pentecost 1651, with the blessing of its *curé*, Olier, another key Company member, where its founders vowed to renounce duelling.[27] They quickly obtained the support of the Paris theology faculty, the 1651 Assembly of Clergy, and even the young Louis XIV for their stance, which demonstrates the effectiveness of their connections. But that was relatively easy compared to the task of persuading highly sceptical French nobles that refusing a duel was not proof of cowardice and a lack of honour. Indeed, it was the duke of Ventadour himself, the originator of the Company of the Holy Sacrament, who published, in 1653, a hard-hitting defence of their campaign, 'Christian and moral reasons against duelling'. In fact, their programme, which bears the hallmark of the Company, was far broader than the mere elimination of duelling. Essentially, it entailed inculcating typically *dévot* forms of religious practice (already manifest in the choice of the 'passion' in their title) and self-discipline among the military nobility, with a view to ending its culture of violence, blasphemy and profanity. Armed with this, the founders extended their efforts during the 1650s to places as far apart as Normandy, Dauphiné, Quercy, Périgord, Brittany and Languedoc, where they began by persuading the nobles attending the provincial estates to sign renunciations of duelling. Confraternities of the Passion were small (anywhere from two or three to fifteen members) and secret but, unlike the Company, they were probably unaware of each other's existence.[28] However, their methods and activities were precisely what worried Mazarin most: they targeted and banded together members of the nobility, some of them ranking military figures, at a time when associations of nobles, disgruntled or otherwise, were deeply suspect. It is quite possible that, in the period leading up to the suppression of the Company of the Holy Sacrament in late 1660, Mazarin actually feared the doings and members of the Passion Confraternity even more. Thereafter, it seems that their activities became more discreet, all the more so as Louis XIV himself offered no real support for anti-duelling campaigns.[29]

A similar logic was at work in another enduring *dévot* enterprise. It began, not untypically, with a seemingly limited issue, only to expand to cover several related concerns in due course. The starting point was the idea of an 'advocate of the poor' per law court, which the crown had proposed under Henri IV, but failed to implement after his murder in 1610. The Company of the Holy Sacrament took it up in the early 1650s. Its concern with the mediation of disputes and the avoidance of litigation, especially among poorer social groups which could ill afford it, also led it to push for the creation of 'parochial companies' or 'charitable confraternities', with a view to cost-free arbitration. It is not known if they were modelled on the parish confraternities that Vincent de Paul had founded in the 1610s, but it would be hard to discount his influence. The highly active Marseille chapter of the Holy Sacrament was probably responsible for founding such a confraternity in the 1640s. An important move was the establishment of one during 1650 in the Parisian parish of Saint-Sulpice which, thanks to the influence of its *curé*, Olier, a key member of the Paris chapter, served as a kind of laboratory for several *dévot* campaigns. By 1656, a city-wide 'central committee' met to draft a set of common statutes for charitable confraternities throughout Paris.[30]

Such a co-ordinated project may have been stillborn, but that did not prevent the idea from spreading more informally in subsequent years. It was still being adapted in places as widely separated as Tréguier in northern Brittany, Aix, Lyon and Grenoble in the 1670s and 1680s – with former or existing members of the Company involved in each case. Further evidence that these 'companies' tended to expand into replicas of the Company at parish level seeking, like it, 'to do all good and prevent all evil', comes in other guises. In Lyon, a charitable council was established specifically to administer a 'bureau of charitable loans' established there in 1679, which was itself the realisation of a long-standing *dévot* campaign to protect lower social groups from debt and usury.[31] Twenty years later, in 1699, Bishop Le Camus and a group of lay *dévots* founded a similar kind of pawnshop in Grenoble, followed some years later by a bureau of free legal aid.[32] But these seem relatively isolated successes, and with the exception of Provence, the *dévots* failed thereafter to diffuse across France their version of the *monti di pietà* so common in Italy and the Netherlands. As well connected as they were, this was a sphere in which vested interests were too strong to be easily overturned.

Perhaps the most active of the Company's offshoots after 1660 was the Congregation for the Propagation of the Faith (originally known as the Exaltation of the Holy Cross), founded in Paris in 1632 by yet another Capuchin friar, Hyacinthe Kerver, private secretary to Richelieu's confidant, Père Joseph. In this case, however, there was no question of it being a secret organisation, even though it shared several of the Company's other organisational innovations. Interestingly, Rome refused to recognise the new creation as a 'congregation', given that it included laypeople (who might include women), while its own members disdained the label of a confraternity, precisely because 'mere' devotion was no more their purpose than it was of the Company of the Holy Sacrament! From the outset, the two bodies had a number of members in common, and it is clear that the Company sought to use the congregation as its public face when it could not itself act effectively in secret. This was particularly the case in its dealings with the Huguenots, which was the congregation's principal *raison d'être*. However, the Paris chapter of the Propagation, the only one in existence until that of Grenoble was founded in 1647, was never as dominant as its counterpart within the Company. From the 1650s onwards, the Grenoble chapter in which, as it happened, female influence was particularly strong, was acknowledged as the leading chapter to which the others normally deferred. The 'Propagation', as it was known, spawned only five provincial branches in its first fifty years, all in cities close to Protestant strongholds (Lyon, Grenoble, Aix, Avignon and Montpellier), while plans for others in Nîmes and Toulouse failed to materialise.[33]

Offsetting this limited scope were the significant efforts to develop both female chapters and, more significantly, one or two of those congregations of nuns which, as we saw previously, were typical creations of the period. The convents and members of the ensuing *Institution chrétienne* and the *Filles des Nouvelles Catholiques* were designed to deal specifically with female converts from Protestantism, old and young; they were charged with both educating and preventing them from relapsing, if necessary by the 'sharpest' methods to hand. Because it was public, some of the Propagation's early ambitions, in particular that of training laypeople to engage in controversy with the Protestants, generated criticism, not least because it entailed access for them to banned books and the Scriptures. The church hierarchy, in both France and Rome, bridled at such dangerous innovation. Tellingly, it was not until the individual 'chapters' of the Propagation were brought under episcopal control that anxieties about these *dévot* busybodies died down, so it is arguable as to whether it truly remained a single organisation at all. Even the crown, which suspected it more than once of being the long arm of the Company of the Holy Sacrament, ultimately accepted the guarantee of episcopal surveillance, and channelled money to it for use in converting and subsiding Protestants. By then, the Propagation had done more than anyone else to pioneer the restrictive interpretation of the Edict of Nantes, and it intervened actively in the localities to ensure there would be no leniency in applying what was intermittently, but from the 1660s increasingly, a policy of harassment, chicanery and isolation of France's Protestants. If there was a genuine 'locking up' of any group within seventeenth-century France, it was of Huguenot children separated from their families in the institutions of the Propagation in order to ensure there would be no way back to their religion of birth.[34]

An even more peculiar *dévot* creation of this period was the 'Aa', a society that was so secret and so determined to protect itself that historians remain uncertain even as to what the term 'Aa' refers to! The best guess is that it meant, simply, *assemblée d'amis*, an 'association of friends'.[35] Its originators were all members of the Jesuits' Marian sodalities from which the Company of the Holy Sacrament and similar bodies drew many of their members. This, needless to say, has led to speculation that the 'Aa', too, was an offshoot of the Company of the Holy Sacrament, but the case remains unproven, although it teamed up with the Company in 1664 to found the *Missions Étrangères de Paris*, whose first superior, Vincent de Meur, was active in both organisations. Unlike the Company of the Holy Sacrament, however, Aa groups were totally independent and frequently ignorant of each other, even though they were typically established by 'itinerant' members from older foundations. Appearing first in France in 1632 at La Flèche and then in Paris, they seem initially to have been self-selecting groups operating secretly within existing confraternities or associations directed by the Jesuits; only later did they split away and acquire full autonomy. What set them apart from other *dévot* groups observed so far is that their membership was exclusively drawn from theology students and ordained clergy, originally regulars like the Jesuits. But in due course they attracted groups of secular clergy working mainly inside seminaries. The purpose of these explicit 'perfectionists' was to raise the calibre of future clergy, by disseminating the Berullian ideal of priesthood, with charitable and catechetical activities as their principal 'good works'. Their ultra-secrecy means it is impossible to say how much of an impact they had on future clergy, but it was probably minimal until well into Louis XIV's reign and later. As early as the 1660s, Aas existed in most of the major cities. Toulouse was a key centre of their activity and dissemination in the southern provinces, but the Aa of Rennes also appears to have been highly vigorous. Bordeaux had its Aa from 1658, and a number of the city's parishes were significantly marked thereafter by *curés* who belonged to the association, while higher-placed clergy, such as vicars-general, ensured that its influence extended to other parts of the diocese.[36] The most enduring of all seventeenth-century *dévot* groups, the Aas were still expanding across southern France, where they were especially well established, during the 1720s and later.

Conclusion

It will be evident by now that measuring the full impact of the *dévots* on French society is an impossible task, since we are dealing with something that mobilised people as diverse as churchwardens and titled aristocrats within a very broad spectrum of 'works'. In some ways, the various 'companies' discussed in this chapter, such as the Holy Sacrament or the Propagation of the Faith, could justifiably be seen as extensions of the equally wide-ranging confraternal phenomenon examined earlier, even though they categorically refused to see themselves as mere devotional groups. That refusal was, in turn, intended primarily to underline the broader scale of their ambitions. It is paradoxical that the history of the seventeenth-century *dévots* should be dominated by a relatively short-lived organisation that was almost pathologically obsessed with operating secretively and with using what can be termed 'front' organisations to achieve its ambitions. It is tempting to regard the generation from 1630 to the mid-1660s as an aberration but, as we saw, the desire to work from behind the scenes did not disappear completely with the Company of the Holy Sacrament. The Company was made possible by a combination of serious doubts about the reliability of the crown as a defender of religious causes, and a real impatience with the inadequacy of the church leadership as well as of the secular clergy generally in the face of the enormous task of the religious and moral reform of French society. For a crucial generation, it exerted itself to provide such leadership. It even wished that France's bishops place themselves at the service of its agenda, but by the 1660s, it was they who were determined, as the experience of the Congregation of the Propagation of the Faith shows, to direct religious activities within their dioceses. Indeed, those bishops most likely to support the Company's agenda were increasingly those least likely to tolerate independent operations within their jurisdictions. From then on, many of the Company's 'works' were continued and adapted by local networks of *dévots*. So many of the activities seen in previous chapters, such as catechisation, elementary schooling and so on depended crucially upon the commitment of those local, parish *dévots*. Finally, we should not forget how much religious activity the various companies actually required of their members, and how much those members helped to diffuse new devotions across the wider *dévot* spectrum. The titles that the different groups chose for themselves – Holy Sacrament, Passion, Exaltation of the Cross and so on – are telltale indicators of the new-style, frequently anti-Protestant devotions that they practised. Engaging in such devotions was a further spur to action in a mutually reinforcing cycle. The *dévot* phenomenon may be more about action than devotion, but ultimately it was the latter which made it possible.

CHAPTER 16

JANSENISTS: DISSIDENTS BUT ALSO MILITANTS

Introduction

It would be easy to conclude from the evidence of the previous chapters that, given the extent of the efforts and the mobilisation that France's Catholic Reformation produced, success was merely a matter of time. But it is rarely the case that reform movements born under the sign of strife and division escape altogether from their clutches thereafter. In France, older divisions continued to exist – Gallicans versus ultramontanes, regulars versus seculars, for example. The brand new division between Protestants and Catholics was the most intractable of all, and will be examined in a separate study. There is one development within seventeenth-century Catholicism, particularly in France, which combines old and new features, and which deserves scrutiny as much for its implications for religious practices and attitudes as for its intellectual and political repercussions.

In one respect, Jansenism represents unfinished business from the conflicts of the previous century, so that its appearance during the early 1640s triggered conflicts that were in some sense unavoidable in the long term. Yet there was nothing inevitable about either the scale or the significance of the Jansenist problem when it did arise in France: its early history there is marked by contingency, which in turn suggests that what we mean by the term 'Jansenism' is far from fixed or easy to define. As we shall see, it took root in France for complex reasons that have less to do with abstract theological debates than with practical religious challenges. It connected with elements of France's religious culture as it was developing by the 1630s and 1640s, thanks to the efforts of the religious reformers, spiritual writers and directors, religious orders and *dévots* with whom we are already familiar. Put at its simplest, what historians call Jansenism has to be viewed, not in isolation nor as a purely intellectual development, but in a wider framework – that of a gradual shift within French Catholicism towards greater rigour in the practice of religion, especially where the sacraments of penance and the Eucharist were concerned. Robin Briggs has provocatively and usefully labelled those involved in pushing Catholicism in that direction as 'Catholic puritans', but to imagine all rigorists as 'Jansenists' would be seriously mistaken, and to fall into the trap set at the time by France's own anti-Jansensists.[1] We shall return more than once to this problem.

French Jansenism, leaving aside for the moment the genuinely problematic nature of the '-ism' in question, has attracted a long line of historians of impressive originality and often polemically sharp standpoints. This is partly because the Jansenist disputes influenced French culture well beyond the narrow spheres of theology or religious activity. Thinkers and writers as diverse as Pascal, Racine, La Bruyère and La Rochefoucauld, even when they were not especially interested in religious questions, were all influenced by the legacy of St Augustine in its widest ramifications for human psychology, morality and behaviour; French intellectual history generally before the Enlightenment seems inseparable from that legacy. Above all, Jansenism divided opinion from the outset, and as early as the opening decades of Louis XIV's reign, rival historians like Racine (then a historiographer royal) and the Jesuit, René Rapin, produced detailed and circumstantial accounts of its beginnings. Rapin was even given access to the archives of the Holy Office in Rome, as well as documents seized earlier in France, something that no historian would be able to do again for centuries!

The first 'modern' historian of French Jansenism was in fact nineteenth-century France's greatest literary critic, Sainte-Beuve, whose classic *Port-Royal* (first published in 1840–48) already shows how contrasting approaches to the subject were possible long after the embers of the original conflicts had cooled. Following Racine, Sainte-Beuve deliberately focused on the heroic spirituality of the reformed Cistercian convent of Port-Royal and its nuns in their resistance to the tyranny of both church and state, an emphasis which enabled him to avoid what he took to be the 'debased' Jansenism of (mainly) the eighteenth century, with its political partisanship, chicanery and perceived lack of spiritual substance. Since then, major scholars like Henri Bremond, Jean Orcibal, René Taveneaux, Lucien Goldmann, Lucien Ceyssens, Bruno Neveu, Dale Van Kley and Catherine Maire have revealed just how wide and unexpected both the sources and the impact of 'Jansenism' (and of its related impulses) really were in the spheres of ideas, religious practices, culture and politics.[2] The marginal, crypto-Calvinist and sectarian aberration that its early opponents depicted Jansenism as being, is belied by its uncanny ability to connect with other forces, religious and political, that were anything but marginal and became essential to its survival. Lastly, despite the enormous pressures to which it was subjected, French Jansenism stayed inside the Catholic church rather than becoming the sect that its opponents in France often labelled it, and that, too, was crucial to its ability to influence the development of Catholicism there.

Post-Trent Theology

It is now generally accepted that the Council of Trent, so often berated for dogmatically closing debates on key theological issues, actually feared the dangers of making definitive pronouncements on questions that had remained undecided for centuries. Its decrees on fundamental issues of original sin, freedom of the human will and predestination to salvation or damnation, which were at the core of the legacy of Saint Augustine to medieval Christianity, and which Luther and Calvin had brought to the forefront during the Reformation, were compromises that left the door open to further discussion and, therefore, disagreement.[3] The idea that Augustinian theology might have to be jettisoned because some of its key positions had been captured and given a new lease of life by the Protestant reformers was simply not accepted by most of the universities or religious orders of Catholic Europe, before or after Trent. On the contrary, there was a widespread desire to reclaim a long tradition, which the Protestants were regarded as having hijacked and, most of all, traduced. Indeed, that stance was, if anything, fortified by an aggressive counter-pressure already emerging within Catholicism which would remain crucial throughout the history of Jansenism – namely the theological principles known as Molinism which were in many ways diametrically opposed to the Augustinian theses that remained, nominally at least, the common if not the 'official' doctrines of the Catholic church. The title of the 1588 treatise by Luis de Molina, *The Concord of Free Will and the Gifts of Grace*, was itself a manifesto: Molinist teachings minimised the enduring impact of original sin on the capacity of Christians to contribute to their own salvation, insisted that God's grace was freely given and readily available to all, and rendered the idea of predestination insignificant.

Such an approach appealed to humanists of post-Renaissance Europe, but what really made the Molinist approach powerful and influential was that it was championed by the Jesuits, of whom Molina himself was one. Thus, conventional institutional rivalries, especially between the Jesuits and the Dominicans (and, in France, the Oratorians), overlay these theological differences from the outset, and would harden into fixed positions well before what we call Jansenism emerged. Academic skirmishing in places like Salamanca and Louvain, but not Paris, kept those rivalries alive without rendering them particularly troublesome in the early post-Trent decades. When the papacy convened a prolonged debate in Rome (1598–1607) to deal with the appeals against Molina's work, it was unable to find a solution, so evenly balanced were the forces involved, and it ended up, despite its own dislike of Molinist ideas, by imposing a ban on further discussion and publication on the disputed questions. The appearance, a generation later (in 1640), of Cornelius Jansen's massive tome with the telling and simple title of *Augustinus*, revived these disputes with more serious and unexpected consequences, though not because there was by then a much greater interest in such debates. On its own, the *Augustinus* would certainly have raised some academic hackles, but nothing like what by the 1650s would become a major affair of church and state with, at least in France, a growing impact on educated public opinion. This is not to deny the continuing pervasiveness of a general Augustinian theological culture at the time, which is indispensable to understanding how the Jansenist question took shape in due course. The sixteenth century may have been the 'Augustinian' century because of Protestant reformations, but for much of Catholic Europe this description fits the seventeenth century at least as well.[4]

What may be called the 'theological' pre-history of Jansenism is one in which France had virtually no part. French theologians, especially those of the universities, were far less concerned than their Spanish or 'Belgian' counterparts with questions of grace and free will; on the contrary, it was questions of political and ecclesiastical power, a legacy of the wars of religion, which mobilised and divided them most. Until the mid-1620s, they were often reacting to defences of regicide or of papal power emanating from other parts of Europe, in which the most prominent figures were Jesuits like Bellarmine, Suarez, Becan and Santarelli. Moreover, French theology faculties, especially that of Paris, had been highly unwelcoming of the Jesuits from the beginning, and strenuously attempted to deny them academic space and influence. It is not altogether surprising that the biggest argument in France during the 1620s and 1630s was that between the seculars and the regulars, in which the Jesuits played a prominent role: it, too, turned on questions of power, jurisdiction and privilege within the church, and therefore on major themes within classic Gallican thinking.[5] It is only a slight anticipation to say at this point that if Jansenism in France escaped from the academy more completely than elsewhere in Catholic Europe, it was because it did not quite start there in the first place. Other reasons have to be sought for this outcome, and no single one can be identified as decisive.

From Saint-Cyran to Pascal

The early affinities which led to the emergence of Jansenism in France were more personal than intellectual, which is not to minimise or trivialise them: it would be as simplistic to attribute French Jansenism to Jansen's only known French acquaintance of any stature, Jean Duvergier de Hauranne (1581–1643), better known as the abbé de Saint-Cyran, as to Jansen himself. They had studied, simultaneously but unknown to each other, at Louvain in the early 1600s, and then intensively together in the privacy of Saint-Cyran's family estate near Bayonne between 1611 and 1616. During that spell, they both acquired a mastery of the early Church Fathers, whose influence on them, as on the French church generally, would be considerable, even though each man used that mastery for different causes and in different ways thereafter. Jansen became a strongly anti-Jesuit university professor determined to produce a definitive and unglossed 'true' account of Saint Augustine's teaching, both to rescue it from the Protestants and to restore it to its notionally dominant position in the church.[6] On the other hand, Saint-Cyran, as a conventional *abbé de cour*, gravitated from the mid-1610s onwards towards the highest *dévot* circles of church and court. It is his successive changes of orientation that are of central interest in the present context, since they vividly illuminate underlying tendencies and sources of conflict within the *dévot* milieux of his time. He only became what he represented for later generations during the 1620s, when he experienced a form of 'conversion' thanks to his prolonged encounters with Bérulle – as always a pivotal figure within the *dévot* world of this period. After Bérulle's death in 1628, Saint-Cyran assumed his legacy and leadership within the *dévot* movement, albeit in his own fashion, one in which the political was scarcely visible at all. He initially proved himself a redoubtable defender and invaluable evangelist of both Bérulle's spirituality and of the Oratory itself, combining vast learning and polemical skills that skewered opponents and their arguments. In the early 1630s, his defence, under the pseudonym of Petrus Aurelius, of the seculars – and specifically of episcopal authority – against the regulars, had the same effect, winning him the public thanks of an assembly of clergy and the enduring admiration of leading figures in the French church, despite the controversies to come. In the course of this particular controversy, Saint-Cyran developed and diffused Bérulle's ideas on the priesthood far more widely and successfully than Bérulle himself, whose writings were not readily available or easy to grasp. Throughout the controversies of the 1620s and 1630s, Saint-Cyran also found himself crossing swords with the Jesuits, his former teachers, though in ways that were different to Jansen in the Spanish Netherlands.[7]

But more than his learning, it was Saint-Cyran's conversion, leading ultimately to his refusal of high political or church office, which gradually set him apart within the evolving *dévot* movement. Having once frequented the same circles as Bérulle and Richelieu in the entourage of Marie de' Medici, he distanced himself from the Cardinal's policies and priorities during the 1630s, and was known to disapprove of war against fellow-Catholic powers like Spain. But for a figure like Saint-Cyran to engage in such a 'retreat' was problematic in the age of the ever-wary Richelieu: was it not in some sense a political gesture, especially if it influenced others and created the kind of discipleship that might 'contaminate' wider social groups? Even Saint-Cyran's assumption, during 1634–5, of the role of spiritual director to the reformed Cistercian monastery of Port-Royal soon began to generate curiosity and suspicion, because it was in this capacity that he began putting into practice a set of ideas that he had been developing in previous years, and which would be a key trigger for the kind of Jansenism that evolved later in France.[8]

Saint-Cyran was not the first spiritual director to work with, and then apply to his *dirigés* his understanding of, the practical implications of the spiritual ideas of his time; doing so within the enclosed environment of a celebrated reformed convent like Port-Royal was nothing new either. But that did not give a spiritual director (or a convent's confessor) an entirely free hand, and it was not unusual for nuns, particularly articulate women from elite social groups such as those of Port-Royal, to complain that their directors were insisting too much on particular practices or devotions. The quietist controversy of the 1690s is a reminder of how quickly a storm could brew up when dubious practices were feared to have gained too much influence. At Port-Royal, Saint-Cyran's direction provoked no such turmoil. His methods were new to the nuns, but it was not they who objected to them; criticism and disapproval came from outside, beginning with his predecessor who had suggested Saint-Cyran as his replacement! During the last five years of his life after his arrest in 1638, Saint-Cyran's opportunities to pursue his techniques were more limited and were largely conducted through the medium of letters of direction, but he continued to attract prominent figures, lay as well as clerical, who sought him out as their spiritual mentor. From his prison at Vincennes, where the inflexible Richelieu kept him from 1638 to 1643, despite being unable to convict him of anything, he was able to communicate his ideas to a more diverse audience than before.

At Port-Royal, Saint-Cyran was dealing with women who had turned their backs on the world and had already experienced some kind of conversion.[9] His efforts to sustain a high level of spiritual commitment among them led him to move away from the techniques of previous directors, who included François de Sales, and to insist on delaying the absolution of the sins they confessed, with the consequence of deferring the taking of communion for relatively long intervals. This was primarily a psycho-pastoral technique designed to provoke 'renewals' of religious fervour among those subjected to it, and also to improve the nuns' own spiritual life by obliging them to 'purify' their sorrow (contrition) for the sins that they confessed, rather than the application of theological first principles. Saint-Cyran was not the first director-confessor to insist on such delay and deferment – Bourdoise had already tried it elsewhere – but in doing so, he was nevertheless entering a theological minefield over which loomed the ever-problematic figure of Saint Augustine. Yet his profound knowledge of the Fathers and religious practices of the early church enabled Saint-Cyran to defend his approach as a necessary return to the purity of past practice in the present age of corruption. Rather than follow his former companion Jansen's lead and attempt to produce a systematic restatement of Augustinian theology – something that would have been impossible for him after his imprisonment in 1638 anyway – Saint-Cyran confided to a young disciple, Antoine Arnauld (1612–94), the task of defending the truth, as he saw it, as well as his penitential-sacramental practices at Port-Royal, where female members of the Arnauld family were the dominant presence for several decades. The outcome was, as might be expected, a very different kind of book to the *Augustinus*.

Arnauld's French-language best-seller, *On Frequent Communion*, was written under Saint-Cyran's supervision by 1641, but was published only weeks before Saint-Cyran's death in 1643.[10] Twenty-four French theologians and twenty-seven bishops vied with each other to give it their formal approbation. The book's full title explained its provenance and purpose: 'On frequent communion, in which the opinions of the Church Fathers, popes and councils regarding the sacraments of penance and the Eucharist are faithfully exposed for use by those persons who are seriously considering conversion to God, and for pastors and confessors who are zealous for the good of souls'. By contrast, the publication of Jansen's *Augustinus* in Paris in early 1641 in Paris had a far more limited impact, though it did elicit several noisy attacks in print and from the pulpit.

Saint-Cyran devised, and Arnauld defended, an approach to the sacraments and, beyond them, to living a Christian life generally that clashed sharply with recent practices. Firstly, as we have already seen, their approach reopened the discussion about the nature of sorrow for sin and the sacrament of penance. In their pessimistic, Augustinian view of human nature, the vast majority of people were driven by self-love, which made them fear eternal damnation for their sins. This self-centred sorrow for sin (attrition) contrasted sharply with the sorrow for sin that was generated by a purified love of God undiluted by self-regard (contrition). The aim of Saint-Cyran and those imitating him was to convince individuals that only the second was genuine and, therefore, capable of bringing them to salvation. Despite the ideas of predestination attributed to Jansenist thinking, there was nothing 'resigned' or inactive about this contritionist position: it positively demanded a very high degree of commitment, penitence and rejection of worldliness; it expected Christians to do everything as if salvation depended purely on their efforts. This, of course, was the basis of their indignant reaction to being labelled crypto-Calvinists, for their version of Augustinianism, which was still widespread across Catholic Europe, was one in which the idea of predestination did *not* exclude human co-operation with divine grace in the the pursuit of salvation.

The accusation of being 'really' Calvinists was not their only headache, because the notion that contrition was necessary for absolution of sin was also highly contested. Richelieu himself made no secret of his disapproval of it, not least because one of Louis XIII's confessors, the Jesuit Caussin, had tried to apply it during 1637, causing the king major scruples about his policies and behaviour. As both a theologian, who had expressed himself on the subject in his earlier writings, and a minister wary of potentially destabilising political influences, Richelieu could not approve of the alternative, contritionist approach, and it was that which led him to arrest Saint-Cyran in the first place. His objection, one shared by many, was that contritionism made a normal life within lay society incompatible with Christian living, and that it would drive those subjected to it either to outright despair or withdrawal from the world.[11] This particular perception, on Richelieu's part at least, was suddenly confirmed in 1637 when a brilliant young lawyer with a bright future, Antoine Le Maitre, abruptly quit public life altogether. He, too, was one of Saint-Cyran's disciples. What was, arguably, far worse, was that Le Maitre openly declared that he quit not with a view to a conventional career in the church, which Richelieu could have readily accepted, but to live as a simple layman and a 'solitary' in the shadows of Port-Royal. The likes of Le Maitre were made for the world of law, government or business, and should seek their salvation by achieving the kind of religious 'perfection' that corresponded to their 'estate', rather than by rejecting it for contemplation. Such gestures, the cardinal feared, were bound to have a social impact and, if widely imitated, would do serious damage to both church and monarchy.[12] Richelieu thus initiated a stance that Mazarin and Louis XIV would continue and which regarded internal 'exile', or alienation from the dominant political values for religious reasons, as dangerous.

In fact, the clash of penitential standpoints and their implications was part of a much wider transformation occurring during the early decades of the century. The greater frequency of confession and the proliferation of confessors and directors of conscience gave a real boost, as we saw in an earlier chapter, to what Briggs has called the 'science of sin', more familiar as casuistry and which Pierre Bayle later characterised as 'the art of haggling with God'.[13] Casuistry was not new to the seventeenth century, but the demand for it exploded as religious practices changed. It hints at moral laxity, but once again that is not necessarily so, and this is nowhere more clearly evident than in French Catholicism of this period, even though we should realise that much of the casuistry in circulation was not French in origin, emanating initially from Spain or Italy. Because confessors and directors of conscience – most of whom were regulars – sought to encourage and reassure their penitents, they were increasingly ready to allow them to adopt courses of action that represented sometimes considerable mitigations of Christian precepts. 'Probabilism' was the dominant school of thought in the early decades of the century, and it typically dispensed an individual from the obligation to obey the law if there existed a 'probable' opinion, expressed by a theologian or canonist, against the requirement to do so, however weak that opinion might actually be. One French casuist, the Jesuit Jean Ferrier, who would later become Louis XIV's own confessor, even argued that individuals with a clear conscience could not commit sin at all, which entirely removed the law and Commandments from the picture! Variations of these positions, most of them seeking to accommodate church precepts and social mores for members of the social elites, emerged during these decades of rapid change in religious practices.

As an example of such approaches, we can return briefly to a topic that we have seen in a previous chapter – duelling. It was a classic problem for the doctors and canonists who engaged in deciding 'cases of conscience' submitted to them for an authoritative opinion. Was the practice sinful, was killing someone in a duel murder, in accordance with the fifth commandment? Or were there instances where exceptions could, or should, be made to the general principle? In seventeenth-century France, the casuistry concerning duelling centred on the nobility, its main practitioners, and specifically on their need to preserve their honour, without which, it was argued, their status and identity as nobles would become meaningless. Behind that question lay others – for example, should one engage in a duel only to avenge a wrong or a slight already endured, or was it licit to kill someone in order to prevent an insult to one's honour? Depending on the answers to these initial questions, many sub-questions cascaded behind them, thereby creating a typical 'science of sin'. Duelling was one of the more egregious domains for casuistic activity, because of the social status of those involved, but casuistry was by no means confined to such questions. It also covered far wider areas of conduct that concerned commoners as well as nobles, women as well as men, from sexuality to economic affairs, and in even more inexhaustible detail. Collections of opinions by major casuists were published, and as the century progressed they became more widespread and more encyclopaedic. One such tome, published in 1728, claimed to provide opinions on 28,000 questions.[14] Paradoxically for French Jansenism, which instinctively disapproved of casuistry, its history was nevertheless closely bound up at particular moments with controversial cases of conscience. The most critical of these came in 1701, when forty doctors of the Paris theology faculty, who could not be classified as Jansenists, opined in response to a question to the effect that a priest could absolve a dying penitent who refused to accept that the five propositions condemned in 1653 were to be found in Jansen's *Augustinus*. Two years later, the papacy condemned the doctors for their opinion, and that proved to be the first of a series of moves which led to the second condemnation of Jansenist theses in 1713.

This excursus suggests that the ideas of Saint-Cyran and Arnauld generated controversy in the age of Richelieu and Mazarin because they addressed some fundamental religious developments. By comparison, the Jansenist-Augustinian theses on grace and human liberty were of far narrower interest, the overt discussion and teaching of which became highly marginalised after the expulsion of Arnauld from the Sorbonne and the purge of the theology faculties during the 1650s. But this did not of itself herald the triumph of Molinist theological views in France's theological centres. Major figures like Bossuet under Louis XIV were strongly Augustinian, as we shall see later in this chapter. His younger contemporary, the controversial biblical scholar Richard Simon, who, despite being an Oratorian, detested the Jansenists, strongly argued that the mixing of the two currents of thought – those of Jansen and Saint-Cyran – after 1640 was a mistake; it would have been far better, in his view, to have concentrated on moral-theological issues rather than on doctrinal ones.[15] Despite Simon's comments, it would be misleading to think that the Jansenist-Augustinian 'doctrinal' strand dominated French Jansenism thereafter, especially when compared to its history in Jansen's own Spanish Netherlands. The result was that French Jansenism retained its own original rigorist characteristics which would in subsequent generations make it highly attractive in Italy and other parts of Europe.

During the years following the publication of *Augustinus* and the *Frequent Communion*, everything was much more fluid, with far fewer certitudes than in later decades. In the heat of battle, the two strands of thought – Jansen's on questions of grace and Saint-Cyran's on sacramental-penitential practice – gradually became more closely conflated than they were at the outset. In defending Saint-Cyran from his critics, the combative and often imprudent Arnauld gave too many hostages to fortune, crucially enabling his opponents, particularly the Jesuits, to present Jansen and the abbé as just two sides of the same coin. Accusations of being crypto-Calvinists and of serving up 'reheated Calvinism' were rejected by Arnauld and his supporters, who claimed that they were no more than disciples of St Augustine, and that Jansenism was a pure fiction invented by the Jesuits the more easily to discredit their sacramental discipline. As early as 1643, Arnauld responded by attacking them in his *Moral Theology of the Jesuits*, a more promising terrain that would witness many subsequent clashes. Over the ten years after 1643, blast and counterblast succeeded each other, theological disputations on questions of grace multiplied and, finally, petitions and letters for and against papal intervention in the dispute were signed and despatched to Rome in 1650–51. After two years of hard lobbying by both sides in the Curia, a papal bull, *Cum Occasione*, rather cautiously condemned five propositions that were vaguely linked to the *Augustinus* in 1653, but it was in France that its public impact was the most far-reaching (see the 'brief chronology' for the successive events).

Table 16.1 *Brief chronology of French Jansenism, 1640–1713*

1640	Publication of Jansen's *Augustinus* (September).
1642	Papal bull *In Eminenti* condemns *Augustinus* in general terms (March).
1643	Antoine Arnauld, *Moral Theology of the Jesuits* and *Frequent Communion* (August). Death of Saint-Cyran (October).
1644	Arnauld publishes *Defence of Jansenius and the Doctrine of St Augustine* and *Apologia for Monsieur de Saint-Cyran*.
1645	Saint-Cyran's *Christian and Spiritual Letters*. Arnauld, *Second Defence of Jansenius*.
1649	Paris theology faculty examines seven (later reduced to five) propositions allegedly taken from Jansen's *Augustinus* (July).
1650	Assembly of Clergy petitioned to condemn five propositions, signatures collected from 85 bishops to petition pope to intervene.
1651–3	Debates in Rome, where Jansenists and anti-Jansenists lobby for papal support.
1653	Bull *Cum Occasione* condemns five propositions from Jansen (June). Crown demands acceptance of papal decision, reiterated by an Assembly of Bishops (July).
1654	Ad hoc Assembly of Clergy accepts papal bull and petitions for further clarification of its meaning (March).
1655	First proposal of a formulary subscribing to condemnation of Jansenism (January). Arnauld's two 'Letters to a Duke and Peer' distinguishing right (*droit*) and fact (*fait*). Assembly of Clergy (May until March 1657).
1656	Arnauld condemned and expelled (followed by supporters) from Sorbonne (February–March). Pascal begins publishing eighteen best-selling *Provincial Letters* anonymously (January – last one published March 1657). Pope Alexander VII issues new bull, *Ad Sacram*, reaffirming condemnation of five propositions as being taken from Jansen (October). *Ad Sacram* registered by Paris *parlement* (November).

JANSENISTS: DISSIDENTS BUT ALSO MILITANTS 405

1657   Assembly of Clergy imposes on clergy the signature of formulary accepting the condemnation of the five propositions; publication of Borromeo's *Instructions to Confessors*.

1661   Assembly of Clergy and crown reimpose anti-Jansenist formulary and extend it to nuns and schoolteachers (January). First resistance to formulary from Port-Royal (June).

1665   Papal bull to enforce signature of formulary (February).

1668   'Peace of the Church', accepted by Clement IX, allowing signature of the formulary by those maintaining a 'respectful silence' as to whether the five propositions were Jansen's work (October–January 1669).

1671   First edition of Quesnel's *Moral Reflections on the New Testament*.

1679   (and subsequent years) French Jansenists suspected of opposing crown on *régale* and other issues. Port-Royal banned from receiving new recruits by Archbishop Harlay of Paris. Arnauld in exile in Netherlands (1680), followed by Pasquier Quesnel (1684) and others.

1695   Death of Arnauld. Quesnel succeeds as major figure within Jansenist movement. Cardinal Noailles, suspected of Jansenist views, succeeds Harlay as archbishop of Paris.

1701   (and subsequent years) Renewed controversy over the 'respectful silence' provision of 1668 peace.

1705   Bull *Vineam Domini* outlaws the right to 'respectful silence' in signing formulary.

1709   Eviction of nuns of Port-Royal-des-Champs on Louis XIV's orders (October), destruction of buildings (1711).

1713   Bull *Unigenitus* condemns 101 propositions from Quesnel's *Moral Reflections on the New Testament* (September).

The process of making the papal condemnation 'stick' in the years immediately after 1653 showed that French Jansenists were by no means reducible to misguided theologians. The reception, clarification and subsequent confirmation of the original papal condemnation, orchestrated by Mazarin and his advisers, was itself a complex political and diplomatic affair that was not completed until 1657.[16] Along the way, it generated polemics more intense than anything up to then, ones that embraced theological, moral and ecclesiological themes. It led, among other things, to Arnauld and dozens of his supporters being expelled in uproar from the Paris theology faculty (1656), after debates supervised by the chancellor of France, Pierre Séguier, in person. That, in turn, was quickly followed by the preparation of a new statement of theological orthodoxy, the 'Formulary', initially drawn up by an assembly of clergy that was then in session, and which effectively superseded the declaration of faith of the Council of Trent – though without replacing it – as the key test of orthodoxy for members of the clergy. This move, designed to winkle out opponents of the condemnation of the five propositions, was a seriously risky one, but its makers appear not to have been unduly concerned about the possibility that it might create more dissent and defiance – more 'Jansenists' – than already existed. It did, and ten years later, in 1668–9, it had to be shelved.[17]

Of course, once the five propositions had been condemned and 'Jansenism' was 'magisterially' defined as a set of theological errors, there was no going back to the status quo ante – regardless of whether the condemnation corresponded to the reality of French Jansenism at this juncture. Arnauld and his friends initially declared themselves ready to accept the condemnation of the propositions taken as they stood, but by 1655 they refused to accept that they were actually in the text of the *Augustinus*. The distinction that Arnauld made at this point between *fact* (are they or are they not in Jansen's book?) and *right* (the pope's rightful authority to pronounce on religious questions) amounted to saying that what the pope had condemned was unexceptionable in itself, but had nothing to do with Jansen. Although Arnauld did not invent the distinction, his formulation of it openly questioned the whole basis of the condemnation of Jansen's work. The 1656 Formulary was designed to make such a distinction untenable, but Arnauld's argument was to trigger acrimonious dispute and opposition over the next fifty years.

However, what is most significant about the many clashes of the 1650s is the degree to which the focus was on moral-pastoral rather than doctrinal questions. Given how heavily involved the Assembly of Clergy of 1655–7 was in closing the loopholes and escape routes for Arnauld and his supporters, many of whom were in no sense Jansenists, it is surprising to find it deciding to publish, and commend for use throughout France, the *Instructions for Confessors* of Charles Borromeo.[18] That Borromeo was the model bishop and reformer in the eyes of seventeenth-century French clergy was undisputed, so broadcasting his works seems uncontroversial. In fact, the assembly's gesture was a calculated one, because until that point, the *Instructions* had been essentially the preserve of the pre- or non-Jansenist rigorists in their campaign against the casuists and laxists. The *Instructions* were scarcely known in France before Arnauld, who inherited Saint-Cyran's veneration of Borromeo, had included extracts from them in his *Frequent Communion* and, especially, in his 1644 work on 'the tradition of the church with regard to penitence and communion'. No less crucially, as the title of this last work indicates, Arnauld defined Borromeo as an authority in moral-sacramental questions precisely because of his fidelity to early church practices and the rigour with which he interpreted them. He was not alone in the 1640s in propagating this message, and he was supported by eminent episcopal figures like Jean-Pierre Camus and especially Antoine Godeau, who attacked laxist confessors and casuists. A full translation of Borromeo's *Instructions* was commissioned by the Jansenist-leaning Archbishop Montchal of Toulouse in 1648, but its circulation remained largely confined to his diocese. A decade later, the impact of the anti-laxist arguments, to which we will return presently, was such that when, in 1657, the Assembly of Clergy ordered the diffusion of the *Instructions*, its recommendation was prefaced by a vehement lament over the corruption of the age in which they lived, a corruption exemplified by a 'loosening of morality' (*morale relâchée*) that was visible everywhere. The assembly's gesture was a neatly calculated decoupling of the drive for tougher moral standards from the Jansenist theological positions of which it disapproved. Borromeo's greatest advantage here was that he was unassailably orthodox, unlike the confessed, but now increasingly 'untouchable', admirers of his like Saint-Cyran or Arnauld, so that his moral-sacramental principles could be safely recommended to the French church. But the act of rescuing Borromeo from the 'Jansenists' was itself a recognition of the success they had been having in changing attitudes on religious-moral questions.

If the publication of the *Instructions* did not receive much attention at the time, it was for a very good reason: they were completely overshadowed by a spectacularly public polemic over closely related issues, one with which the name of Pascal is inseparably linked.[19] His intervention owed something to his family's and to his own, as yet limited, connections to Port-Royal, where his sister was a nun, but up to the mid-1650s he was mostly known for his scientific work. It was when the heat was turned up on Arnauld and his friends in 1655–6 that they sought Pascal's help and provided him with the materials and ideas that he needed to defend their cause; his intervention was, therefore, in some sense 'commissioned' and it occurred well into a prior confrontation. As a result, it was only from the fourth of the celebrated *Provincial Letters* onwards, when Arnauld's cause in the theology faculty had been lost, that Pascal turned his fire on the Jesuits and their *morale relâchée*, building upon Arnauld's own earlier attack, *The Moral Theology of the Jesuits* (1643). Writing in clandestinity and in a great hurry, he ridiculed and lampooned their Molinist casuistry, picking out with an unerring eye the weakest features of their probabilist approach to questions of conscience and morality – not a particularly difficult task for a polemicist with Pascal's gifts. Unfair and grossly one-sided, the *Provincial Letters* were an instant success with the educated public, who for the first time were invited – and by a layman – to peek behind the normally closed doors of academic moral theology and to enjoy the skewering of a particular school of thought. After eighteen 'letters' written over a period of a year from January 1656 to February 1657, Pascal abruptly broke off. Some of his acquaintances feared, and rightly so, that for all their stunning success, the *Letters* would only strengthen their opponents' determination to crush what they viewed as a hydra that seemed to have tentacles everywhere within French Catholicism. Inevitably, the *Letters* also drew responses, mostly from Jesuits led by the royal confessor, François Annat, but they fell far short of the mark. The best known and most inept of their responses was the *Apologia of the Casuists* of 1657, which was so feeble that it provided a readymade target for defenders of the *morale sévère*. The so-called *Écrits des curés de Paris* of 1658–9 – whose real authors were friends of Arnauld and Port-Royal – widened the dispute further by taking up the defence of the rights of the secular clergy against the regulars, a reminder that clerical and institutional rivalries were never far away in such conflicts.

Thus by the late 1650s, as the political and doctrinal noose was tightened about doctrinal Jansenism, its more widely diffused 'moral' counterpart was on the offensive, and enjoying unprecedented support. The assembly of clergy's publication of Borromeo's *Instructions* was, as we saw, a perfect example of this paradox, since not a single one of its members had defended the five condemned propositions or Arnauld. This 'rigorist turn' within France would continue to gain ground in subsequent decades, almost regardless of whether church and crown were openly persecuting Jansenists and Port-Royalists or not. The spread of such rigorist views provided cover for those who were authentic Jansenists, but the great difficulty remains that of distinguishing between them. Pascal himself, as has been shown, traduced the actual teaching and practices of France's Jesuits by inflating out of all proportion those utterances that were an easy target. Interestingly, most of his incriminating evidence was taken from treatises written by foreign Jesuits, such as the Spaniard Escobar, while his main French source, Etienne Bauny, had already been condemned in both France and Rome for his tendentious ideas in the early 1640s.

The Age of Louis XIV

Louis XIV inherited his godfather Mazarin's instinctive hostility to the Jansenists and Port-Royal as rebels and fomentors of dissent, which in turn made him vulnerable to insinuations about their 'real' intentions. His experiences of the Fronde, of the continuing defiance of the exiled archbishop of Paris, Cardinal de Retz, and of the Jansenist controversies of the 1650s – all made him wary, as we saw, of *dévots* generally. Their support of Retz and the closeness of so many of them – including leading figures from the aristocracy – to Port-Royal, reinforced his suspicion that religious dissent was always at least incipiently political in character. The centrality of the tentacular Arnauld clan to so many of these flashpoints, and especially to Port-Royal, meant that he had no qualms when, in 1664, Retz's successor in Paris, Archbishop Péréfixe, began the process which would lead to the dispersal of Port-Royal's nuns and the ultimate physical destruction of the abbey in the Chevreuse valley (Port-Royal-des-Champs) in 1709. The nuns' refusal to sign the anti-Jansenist Formulary, on the grounds that theology was no business of women, did not save them; the lay *solitaires* who lived in the abbey's grounds and the 'little schools' that it had developed had already been dispersed or suppressed.[20]

Despite all this, the Formulary evoked increasing unease during the 1660s, especially among several of France's bishops, who were meant to be its chief enforcers. This mounting reticence made negotiations with Rome both possible and necessary, and the outcome, known as the 'peace of the church' of 1669, enabled those who hitherto would not sign the Formulary to do so while retaining a 'respectful silence' as to whether the condemned propositions were actually in Jansen's *Augustinus*. But there was no reversal of the condemnations of the 1650s in this at least partial vindication of Arnauld's 'right-versus-fact' argument. However, so long as it remained in operation – as it did in some respects for over thirty years – the 'peace of the church' eased the conflicts over the Jansenist question within the French clergy, the only group directly concerned by the Formulary. Indeed, the political climate changed sufficiently after 1668 for Antoine Arnauld himself to be presented at court, and for his nephew, Simon Arnauld de Pomponne, to become foreign minister in 1672.

In many respects, the following decades were the golden age of French Jansenism, provided we use that term in its broadest sense. Exiles and prisoners of the previous decade of defiance returned to France, or were released from confinement. The *solitaires* returned to Port-Royal, which regained its right to function normally again, taking in new members and boarders. The peace of the church ring-fenced the condemnation of Jansen's work and, provided this latter question was not reopened, it allowed unprecedented scope for action by former dissenters. The reaction against laxist moral propositions also went full steam ahead and, tellingly, it now became virtually 'official' church policy. Pope Alexander VII, who had approved the anti-Jansenist Formulary, initiated a series of papal condemnations of such propositions as early as 1665. A further condemnation occurred in 1679 under Innocent XI (1676–89), with whom Louis XIV frequently crossed swords on other matters.

Innocent took things much further than that, since he was the closest Rome got to having a Jansenist pope in this period. Many of his closest and most influential advisers were Jansenists or philo-Jansenist Augustinians, with close links to their counterparts in France. But even without this Innocentian interlude, it is clear that the climate in Rome was increasingly rigorist, which put the Jesuits in particular on the defensive, not just in relation to moral and sacramental issues, but also to their missionary strategy, especially in China.[21]

Within France itself, there was a corresponding rigorist turn. The Borromean 'signal' of 1657 was followed in 1675 by the condemnation of a whole set of 'probabilist' propositions about penance by Bishop Sève of Arras, a gesture publicly supported by at least twenty-seven French bishops. Rome did not appreciate any bishop seeming to 'usurp' the pope's role as doctrinal censor, but since the Roman Inquisition's decrees were not valid in France, its condemnations of 1665 and 1679 were, for practical purposes, non-events there. And Sève's attack on laxism was raised to a much more official level in 1700, when the Assembly of Clergy, dominated by Augustinian-rigorist bishops like Bossuet, Le Tellier of Reims and Noailles of Paris, condemned no fewer than 125 propositions, and recommended that confessors and directors of conscience follow henceforth the 'most probable', or safest, course of action in future. Here, too, there was no doubt that the main target of the censors was the Jesuits.[22]

In both France and Rome, these pronouncements were the consequence rather than the cause of changing attitudes. We find a clear echo of them in the casuistry of the age of Louis XIV, a period which not only witnessed the expansion of casuist activity generally – the best-known casuists began to publish summas of their wisdom – but, above all, was dominated by a rigorist approach. Its success was such that those religious orders, especially the Jesuits, which had been known for their probabilist standpoint, had to adjust to the new climate. One Parisian wit claimed around 1700 that the Jesuits were no longer really Jesuits any more, since their confessors gave their penitents and *dirigés* a hard time in the confessional! It is still unclear, however, whether the Jesuits changed to that extent, and it is perhaps worth distinguishing between the society in general and within France, where it was more dangerously exposed than elsewhere in Europe. There is reason to suppose that in France, at least, Jesuit moral teaching discreetly adjusted, well before 1700, to the prevailing wind, especially when it proved to be more than a passing gust. The victory of the rigorists was perhaps more rhetorically than practically conclusive, since it remains unclear how far it prevented directors and confessors from taking a more or less 'indulgent' view of the sins of their penitents.[23]

This broad shift in attitudes expanded the space for Augustinian-Jansenist activities opened up by the 1668 peace of the church.[24] One of the striking characteristics of the period was a continuing fascination with the early church which was already apparent in Saint-Cyran and his generation, but by no means confined to those of Jansenist leanings. This was no idle historical curiosity, but involved defining – 'inventing'? – a distinct, self-contained historical epoch, and to differentiate it from the long – and still unfinished – era of 'decay' and 'relaxation' that had set in thereafter. A major task was to uncover the actual practices of the early church and to strip away the accretions of subsequent ages as unwarranted deviations from true religion. Once this 'prelapsarian' church, if one can put it thus, and its practices had been recovered, it would be a question of applying them in the seventeenth-century present. Apart from Augustine himself, individual Church Fathers, such as Cyprian of Alexandria, were singled out for special attention, largely because of their strictures and writings on penitential and related issues. Much of this kind of work was unspectacular because scholarly, and it was only possible at all because a number of religious orders and congregations – the Benedictines, the Oratory and later the Augustinian canons-regular – had the resources, scholars and, above all, the Augustinian sympathies to pursue it. But even scholarly activities could create controversy, as the Maurists discovered when they began to publish a new edition of the works of St Augustine: the quality of the scholarship here was not irrelevant in the wars of words over Jansen's work and his followers. It was, of course, easier to identify later practices not accredited by the early church than it was to restore supposedly authentic ones, as is clear from the actual attempts made during this period to restore public penitence and the deferral of absolution to hardened sinners. But it is not difficult to see how the actual attempts of uncompromising Jansenist bishops like Pavillon of Alet or Vialart of Châlons-sur-Marne to impose early church practices upon their dioceses achieved the equivalent of cult status among their admirers.

However disconnected from the 'real' world much of this patristic scholarship might seem to be, its practitioners did not confine themselves to their research and editions. They turned out translations, anthologies, lives and hagiographies designed to nourish the spiritual lives of the educated *dévots* of their day, works which conveyed the gap between a corrupt present and a perfect past far better, because more subtly, than learned treatises ever could. They even provided abundant material for preachers to draw upon, although their ideal of simple 'apostolic' preaching was less likely to win converts in Louis XIV's France than any other part of Europe.

If there is one work to be singled out here for its contemporary impact, and not merely for its later destiny, it is the *Moral Reflections* of the Oratorian Pasquier Quesnel (1634–1719), first published in 1668 under the title *Words* of the Word Incarnate. It went through numerous reworkings, amalgamations and renamings in the following twenty-five years, becoming substantially longer from one edition to the next. Quesnel's book resembled Arnauld's *Frequent Communion* more than it did Jansen's *Augustinus*, but its full title, 'The New Testament in French, with moral reflections on each verse, in order to make it easier to read and to meditate upon', shows its difference in format and intention from both predecessors. Quesnel combined a mainstream Augustinianism with themes drawn from Gallican and more recent 'presbyterial' thinking associated with Edmond Richer (d.1630), which emphasised the nature of the church as a community rather than as a hierarchical institution, and the central importance of the parish clergy within it. New editions of the *Moral Reflections* were not merely longer, but Quesnel added stronger emphases and new themes over the years, although these did not immediately arouse undue comment or controversy; that would only come later, after 1700. Indeed, the book's popularity was enormous, as is evident enough from the rapidity of its consecutive editions. It was widely read by laypeople as well as clerics, and became the favourite spiritual reading of the likes of Bossuet (the king's confessor) Père La Chaize, and Cardinal Albani who, as Pope Clement XI, would nevertheless condemn 101 of its propositions as Jansenist and heretical in 1713!

Towards *Unigenitus*

It was apparent well before 1713 that the 'peace of the church' of 1668 was dead. Indeed, it had been fragile from the outset, and there were serious reservations about it on both sides of the divide. The Jesuits, led by the royal confessor, were convinced it was a public-relations victory for the Jansenists, who had conceded nothing and had behaved dishonestly in the negotiations that preceded it. Among their Jansenist opponents, there were influential voices claiming that signing a declaration while maintaining mental reservations as to its meaning was a shabby compromise that undermined their fight for the truth. As with the Huguenots around this time, royal policy vacillated depending on extraneous factors, such as whether France was at war or peace with other states. But from 1679 onwards, there was a significant initial shift towards persecution, especially of Port-Royal and the Oratory, one that quickly led Arnauld and Pierre Nicole to flee to safety in the Spanish Netherlands, followed in due course by Quesnel (1683) and others, who became a kind of Jansenist counterpart to the Huguenot 'refuge' in the Dutch Republic.

The peace of 1668 remained ostensibly unbroken until the decade after 1700, even if increasingly the atmosphere was such that individual incidents could trigger both renewed conflict and punitive action. Thus, when it became known that forty doctors had signed a *cas de conscience* of 1701 allowing, as we saw above, a confessor to accept a penitent's 'respectful silence' about the five propositions, they were quickly forced to disown their judgement. The papacy then weighed in, condemning their action in 1703 and more solemnly again, at Louis XIV's request, in 1705. No doubt, Louis XIV's gradual reconciliation with Rome after the Gallican disputes of the 1680s under Innocent XI made it easier to envisage a counter-attack against the Jansenists. The much harder-line Jansenist writings now emanating from the exiles around Quesnel in the Low Countries probably reinforced that temptation. The final destruction of Port-Royal-des-Champs in 1709 and 1711was conducted *manu militari*, and was redolent of the deliberate brutality hitherto reserved for the Huguenots or the Palatinate. It was a preface to the ultimate objective, to secure a new condemnation of Jansenism that would be more comprehensive and definitive than that of 1653 – and, ideally, without a messy aftermath. Clement XI duly gave in to French pressure and issued the bull *Unigenitus* in 1713, which was directed entirely against Quesnel's *Moral Reflections*, condemning en bloc and with no distinction between them, a whole series of themes central to the 'second' Jansenism, such as free access to the Bible, the idea of the church as a community, the central role of the parish clergy in church affairs, and so on.[25]

That proved the easiest part. This time, at least, there was no problem with the provenance of the condemned propositions: Quesnel was unmistakably their author. But thereafter, the entire project backfired spectacularly. Leaving aside the response of 'public opinion', however we define it, to the condemnation of so many 'heretical' propositions taken from one of the most widely read devotional books of the age, the crown failed even to persuade a hand-picked assembly of bishops to accept the papal bull without conditions. And the reign of Louis XIV ended with the unprecedented spectacle of a monarch whose two principal ecclesiastical advisers were openly at loggerheads – his confessor, Père Tellier, and Cardinal Noailles, the archbishop of Paris. In fact, it was Noailles who was the real target of *Unigenitus* for France's anti-Jansenists, so the confessor and his allies planned to hold an unprecedented 'national council' of the Gallican church which would depose Noailles and his episcopal supporters. The king's death, in September 1715, scuppered these audacious plans to decapitate the Janenist hydra – but not the uproar caused by *Unigenitus*, which would cause increasingly bitter conflict for several decades more.[26] The future chancellor, d'Aguesseau, correctly predicted that '*Unigenitus* will be the cross not merely of the theologians but of the highest magistrates of the kingdom'.[27] By this date French Jansenism had absorbed numerous influences – Gallican, richerist, conciliarist – that were to make it such a formidable and slippery problem during the following decades.

Pastoral and Liturgical Innovations

Because it is so often argued that the Jansenist version of Augustinian Christianity was for a tiny elite, ideally one withdrawn from the world, it has been all too easy to assume that it could have had very little impact on the wider French society of the day. Measuring that impact is indeed difficult, but it should not be foreclosed by denying the possibility of an impact or, more importantly, of considering the kinds of efforts its defenders made to evangelise their society according to their lights. As Louis Pérouas put it, the Augustinian movement's 'pastoral philosophy was probably the richest of the seventeenth century'.[28] Their 'archaic' instincts – to return to, and restore the early church's practices – were actually the source of attitudes which were often quite subversive of contemporary orthodoxies.

The status and use of the Bible was a particularly sensitive issue during and after the sixteenth-century Reformations. The full title of Quesnel's *Moral Reflections* is itself an excellent illustration of the desire of the Jansenist-Augustinians to put the Bible in the vernacular at the disposal of laypeople, and to encourage its use for meditative purposes. In fact, Quesnel's position was perhaps the most 'extreme' of its day within European Catholicism, since he insisted that the reading of the Bible was an obligation for everyone, women as well as men. He pushed to the limits an impulse inherited from the Augustinian-Jansenist generation before him, arguing, as they had, that such use of the Bible was in accord with the teaching and practice of the early Church Fathers. But the Jansenist-Augustininian stance would not have had the same impact were it not for France's confessional past and present, in which the argument for ready access to the Bible for Catholics was based on the constant need to respond to the Huguenots, who based their religious superiority on their fidelity to the Scriptures, which they read in the vernacular. In addition – and this was no less crucial – France did not formally recognise the instruments (the Inquisitions, the Roman Congregation of the Index) which so efficiently enforced the twin Tridentine limitations on the translation and the reading of the Bible in Italy and Spain that there was no vernacular Bible in either country. René Benoist's translation into French, made in the 1560s and known generally as the 'Louvain' Bible, was an unfortunate but not fatal start, despite being condemned by Rome for its excessive reliance on the Genevan Bible. *Faute de mieux*, it continued to be reprinted and to circulate in France into the seventeenth century, until alternatives to it gradually appeared. In the meantime, especially from the 1620s onwards, paraphrases rather than new translations were easier to provide and encountered fewer problems with church censors.[29]

The most famous and controversial translations were the 'New Testament of Mons' (1666) and the Old Testament (1672–95), both the work of Isaac

Lemaitre de Sacy, the *solitaire* of Port-Royal. Both contained French and Latin texts, with explanations based on Augustine's advice on how to read the Bible. A vast improvement on Benoist and expressed in elegant classical French, this monumental labour enjoyed support wider than that of France's Augustinians. At the point when Port-Royal and its Jansenist-Augustinian supporters began their work, the only point of difficulty in France seems to have been that of how easy, or under which conditions, access to a vernacular Bible for laypeople should be; that translations should be made at all seems to have worried relatively few people outside of the Sorbonne and sections of the episcopate. Port-Royal and its friends took what was a broad consensus to the next, but more controversial stage: instead of recommending Bible-reading as useful and meritorious, they presented it as obligatory for all people, regardless of gender, age or status. This drift, which Quesnel adopted and increasingly insisted upon at various places in his *Reflections*, split the wider consensus about the use of the Bible among French Catholics and lost the support of much of the episcopate, which played a decisive role in approving and protecting translations. By arguing, as they increasingly did, that reading the Bible was an obligation for laypeople, Quesnel and his generation of Jansenists were declaring, in effect, that access to it could no longer really be subject to church control. The French bishops' instinct was to resist such Bible democracy, even though they were usually content to allow ordinary parish priests the right to authorise individual lay reading of the Bible – a concession quite unthinkable in the rest of Catholic Europe.[30] The desire among France's wider *dévot* circles to read the Bible, especially the New Testament, *in extenso*, rather than be drip-fed with excerpts and paraphrases by preachers or spiritual authors, was essential to this development. When the Jesuit Bouhours produced his translation of the New Testament in 1697, it was, he claimed, because 'the faithful have never had such a wish to read the word of God as today'.[31]

Interestingly, it was not translating the Bible but rather the liturgical offices of the church that first put Port-Royal into the pastoral firing line. Compared with translating the Bible, this may seem innocuous, but it arguably raised more clerical hackles because it was a more telling indicator of the Jansenist-Augustinians' desire to reduce the gap separating laity from clergy.[32] The first such translation came as early as 1650: the 'Hours of Port Royal', as it was called, rendered the various offices of the liturgical year in both Latin and French. The presence of a French version alongside the clerical Latin was a provocation that was quickly denounced in both France and Rome. But the Port-Royalists were not discouraged, for an even more controversial effort, Joseph de Voisin's five-volume translation of the Roman missal appeared in 1660 with several episcopal and other 'approbations'. Mazarin secured its condemnation by the 1660 Assembly of Clergy and then by Rome just before his death in early 1661. Although the censure was apparently ignored in France (the book was never withdrawn from sale or use there), the stance of the assembly was perhaps more indicative of the reluctance of the French church authorities to encourage this particular path. However politically contrived the condemnations may have been, sections of the clergy clearly feared a drift towards a French vernacular liturgy. To give laypeople their own vernacular version of the prayers said by the priest, especially of the mass, which they could recite simultaneously during services, represented a serious 'invasion' of the sanctuary.[33] Against such reservations, several influential spiritual writers had been arguing since the 1630s that laypeople be encouraged to 'unite and associate themselves with the priest's prayers during the mass' rather than simply recite their own private prayers. The question was – what form should such 'association' take, and how far should it go?

In their efforts to promote a more vernacular liturgy that would achieve their ideal of a liturgical 'union' of priest and laity, the Jansenist-Augustinians were both drawing upon existing impulses and stretching them still further; their initiatives fitted naturally into the search for what has been called a 'neo-Gallican' liturgy, which self-evidently presumed the existence of vernacular texts. Under Louis XIV, they even benefited from quite unforeseen circumstances. In 1685–7, for example, in an effort to induce thousands of former Huguenots to embrace Catholic religious practices, up to a million volumes were distributed to them, including vernacular Bibles and other books. This huge effort, which simply ignored the 'normal' arguments about how far to go with vernacular texts generally, included the mass diffusion of works like Archbishop Harlay's *Manner of Hearing the Mass* (1651) and Nicolas Le Tourneux's more controversial *Best Manner of Hearing the Mass* (1680). Yet however much they encouraged active 'participation' in the mass, these works were not actual 'mass books'.[34] The first complete translation of the missal for the Paris diocese was only published in 1701, by which point the Quesnellian Jansenists had moved the goalposts further again, and were ready to embrace a liturgy of the mass conducted by a priest either wholly or partially in the vernacular. By the 1720s and 1730s, a handful of Jansenist priests were doing just that, reciting the canon of the mass in French, and allowing laypeople to join them in certain prayers of the mass or to read the Bible aloud in church.[35] These experiments were derived from an understanding of the historical evolution of the liturgy that was typical of certain Jansenist-Augustinian circles, which in turn drew on the wider pastoral philosophy at work within the French church.

It will be evident that the above activities had serious implications for pastoral and religious practices, and that only a thin filament of the population was capable of responding to them. From the middle decades of the seventeenth century, the Jansenist-Augustinians and the supporters of Port-Royal were aware of the problem, and some of their most despondent comments about the prospects of human salvation came from a realisation of how enormous the educational task was. The fact that they had numerous lay supporters, beginning with the committed *solitaires* of Port-Royal, meant they could hardly avoid doing something about it. The 'little schools' of Port-Royal (1637–60) did not last long and only involved a small number of children, but the experience produced a pedagogical philosophy unique for its time in being pragmatic and adaptable to individual temperaments. It was taken up and adjusted to local circumstances by a small number of Jansenist bishops from the 1660s onwards in dioceses as far apart as Alet and Châlons-sur-Marne. Wherever Jansenist *curés* managed to gain the goodwill of their parishioners – something virtually always confined to urban parishes – there was normally a joint push to promote schools there. The Jansenist parochial confraternities of charity did far more than relieve popular misery: they tried to educate as well as to catechise children, choosing their educators with care. Certain Paris parishes like Saint-Jacques-du-Haut-Pas were well known for this, while several Jansenist-run schools also flourished in the Faubourg Saint-Antoine. Nor were the Jansenist-leaning clergy afraid to draw on the services of laypeople of both sexes as catechists and assistants.[36]

Who Were France's Jansenists?

Throughout its history, the dominant tendency has been to think of Jansenism as an 'essence' that can be defined by one means or another. In more recent times, historians have variously insisted upon its bourgeois characteristic (Groethuysen) or its 'real' function as an ideology that 'sublimated' the dissatisfaction and incipient revolt of a class of royal officials who were in the process of losing their power and influence within the French monarchy (Goldmann).[37] Such approaches also tend to perpetuate the 'essentialist' approach, and thus to impose their own categorisations. It would be more helpful, in the wider context of the present study, to ask a different type of question: who were the Jansenists? This is not without its pitfalls. The simplest response to it would be: those who refused to sign the 1657 Formulary or who appealed to a future general council against *Unigenitus* in 1717 and later. But both the refusal and the appeal respectively were motivated by a complex mixture of reasons, so that it is ultimately impossible to know how far those involved were Jansenists. And, theoretically, both involved only members of the clergy. It is necessary to consider other approaches, while pointing out that any analysis of who the Jansenists were is unlikely to be a model of (statistical) rigour.

Given its origins, it is no surprise that the clergy are the most visible and most numerous category within the Jansenist world. Among the higher clergy, the number of overt Jansenists was always tiny – only three or four bishops could be described as Jansenists in the 1650s and 1660s, but they were surrounded by a more numerous nebulous outer ring of philo-Jansenist colleagues whose Augustinian credentials are indisputable. However, even such a reduced number could have disproportionate influence within the church, both generally and locally. It was their refusal to enforce the Formulary in the 1660s which gathered the support of nearly twenty bishops in all and led to the peace of the church of 1668. This pattern remained largely unchanged throughout Louis XIV's reign. The French monarchy never quite managed to exclude Jansenists or Jansenist-leaning Augustinians from the episcopate, for the simple reason that some of them only evolved towards such a position *after* their elevation.[38] And once they showed their colours there was really no way of getting rid of them! Despite their limited numbers, they were essential for the survival of Jansenist tendencies among the lower secular clergy. By the later seventeenth and early eighteeenth century, such bishops could shape the next generation of parish clergy by confiding their seminaries to Jansenist-Augustinian directors drawn from particular religious orders or congregations; they could also approve new works written by Jansenist authors and even distribute or recommend them to their clergy. Obviously, the principal threat to the perpetuation of an entrenched Jansenist clergy was royal patronage itself: once a Jansenist bishop died, it was certain that an anti-Jansenist would replace him, usually with instructions from the king's confessor to purge the local clergy. When Cardinal Coislin was succeeded as bishop of Orléans in 1706 by a known anti-Jansenist bishop intent on doing just that, many of them found refuge with Coislin's nephew, a known Jansenist bishop based in the distant diocese of Metz! 'Refuges' like Metz, but also Auxerre, Beauvais or Nantes, enabled Jansenist clergy to survive and, to an extent, regroup. Cardinal Coislin was one of a number of Augustinians who permitted rather than actively promoted a Jansenist secular clergy in his diocese, and he was probably not alone. Cardinal Noailles of Paris was another moderate Augustinian-cum-Gallican, during whose long reign (1695–1729), several of the capital's most prominent parishes became enduringly Jansenist, to the extent that when his successor, Vintimille du Luc, and Cardinal Fleury tried to purge them and install orthodox *curés* during the 1730s, there was a highly effective and protracted boycott of the intruded *curés*.[39]

Just as important to the Jansenist movement were the *regular* clergy, as we already noted in relation to patristic scholarship. Perhaps the most surprising aspect of this is the extent to which members and houses of older monastic orders, like the Benedictines or Cistercians, were centres of Jansenist activity.

René Taveneaux has shown how vital the Champagne-Lorraine abbeys were in maintaining contacts with the Low Countries, and how, aided in some dioceses by Jansenist *curés*, they acted as conduits for books, correspondence and the in- or exfiltration of Jansenists on the run.[40] The widely strewn Maurist Congregation of Benedictines developed a combination of scholarship and piety which echoed the reputation of Port-Royal. A major abbey in a particular area, especially if it belonged to a post-Trent reformed congregation like Saint-Maur, could resist pressure to conform far better than members of the secular clergy. The reformed canons-regular of the Congregation of France (or Sainte-Geneviève), naturally, defended the legacy of their 'founder', Augustine. Newer orders or congregations like Oratory or the Doctrinaires had no such historical affinities, but were drawn into the orbit of the Jansenist movement because of early Augustinian associations, which among the Oratory owed so much to their 'Augustinian' founder, Bérulle. The Oratory's loose structures enabled individual members to assert their personal positions more readily than in other orders, which led to many of them, like Quesnel, either going into exile, being expelled, or leaving it altogether. Archbishop Harlay of Paris tried to bring it to heel, but his authoritarian methods were not especially successful, while his successor Noailles positively approved of the Oratory. Thus it remained in charge of Paris's most intellectually prominent seminary, Saint-Magloire, and it was there that a succession of Oratorians studied and refined Augustinian thinking in ways that would continue to be highly influential into the next century.

Notwithstanding the caveat entered above about the variety of motives for individual appeals against *Unigenitus* from 1717 onwards, a more general impression of the make-up and geographical spread of clerical Jansenism at the end of Louis XIV's reign can be derived from a brief look at the phenomenon (see Map 7).[41] The appeal to a general council was initiated by four bishops from widely scattered dioceses (Boulogne, Senez, Montpellier and Mirepoix), and in each case the diocesan clergy followed their lead quite significantly. Thirteen bishops, including Noailles of Paris, followed suit soon afterwards, while a smaller group of known Jansenist bishops kept their heads down for various reasons, or changed tack later. The bishop of Metz was one of these, but his neighbour, the bishop of Verdun, who did join the appeal, absolutely refused to allow his clergy to become involved at all! In both dioceses, there were almost certainly many Jansenist clergy, yet they do not register on the map. The geography of French clerical Jansenism represented on the map is, therefore, somewhat approximate, but it does show that, with the exception of a number of dioceses with Jansenist bishops in Provence (plus Grenoble), southern France was almost a complete desert as far as adherence to the Jansenist cause was concerned. The biggest presence was in

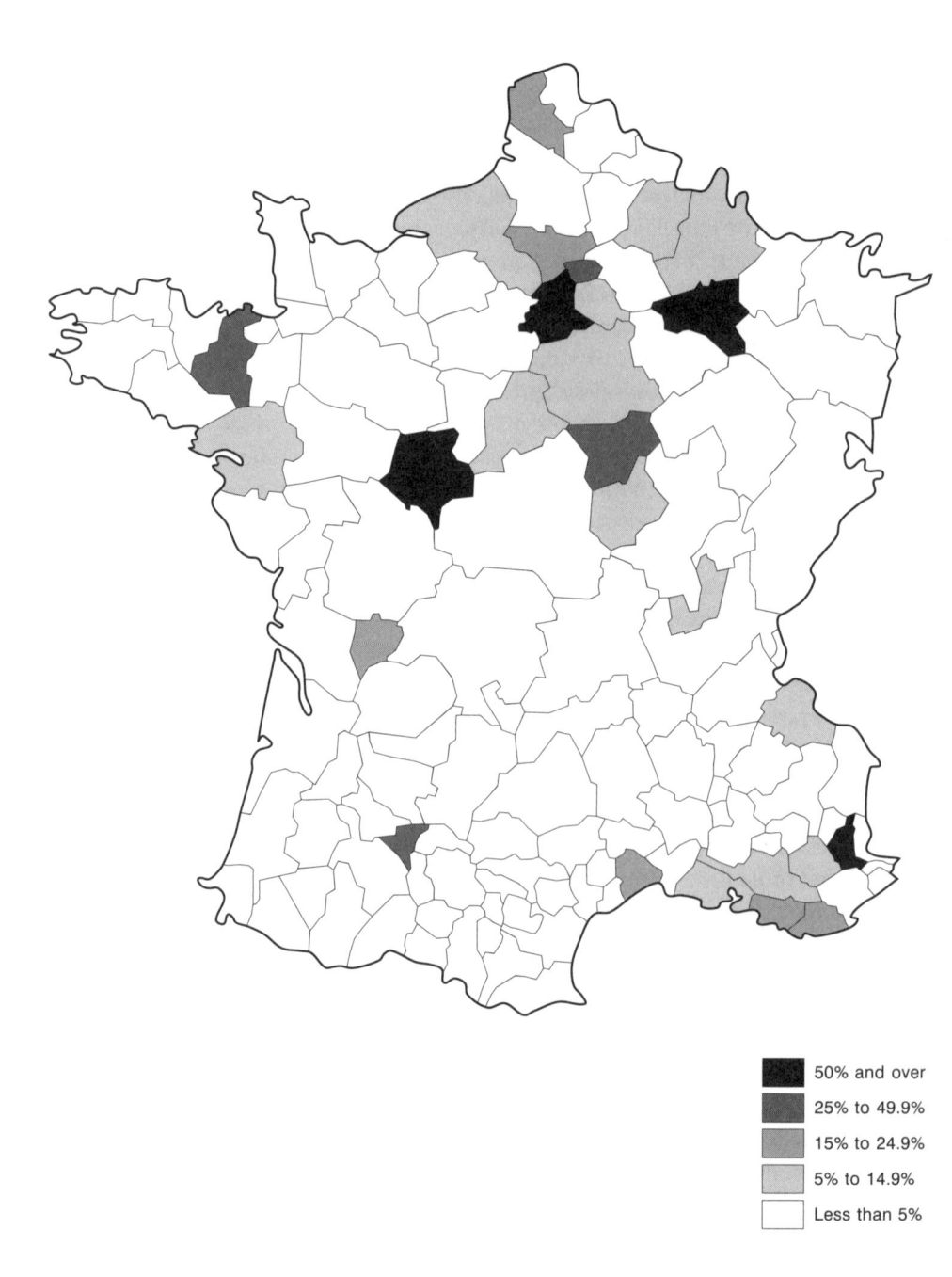

7. Geography and scale of clerical appeals against *Unigenitus*, 1717–28.

the greater Paris region, especially on its eastern and northern side, from Auxerre and Mâcon to Reims and Boulogne, along with a western fringe embracing Tours, Nantes and Saint-Malo (all three with Jansenist bishops). It is clear that dioceses once governed by Jansenist bishops (Angers, Alet, Pamiers) had been purged of their Jansenist clergy by 1717.

In terms of numbers, a maximum of 7,000 clerics, representing around 5 per cent of the French clergy, joined the appeals after 1717. Over 2,000 signatures came from Paris alone, and another 3,000 from the dioceses from the wider region around it, indicating just how disproportionate its influence within the Jansenist fold was. By contrast, only around 700 clerics from the Midi did so. What is much harder to gauge is how many sympathisers did not formally appeal because of fear of reprisals or simple opportunism. But more than the raw numbers involved, it is the categories of appellant which are significant. Graduates from the biggest and most active theology faculties (Paris, Reims, Nantes) were disproportionately prominent, not least because many of them held important urban parishes which served as their pastoral platforms. The appeal made by the Paris faculty was signed by 260 doctors. Cathedral chapters also appealed, sometimes with their bishop, but just as often against him, as was ever their wont. And over one-third of the 7,000 appellants belonged to the religious orders discussed above, evidence of how Augustinian they had remained; their appeals sometimes drew secular clergy in their wake in places like Nantes or Marseille. The big battalions of the regulars, the Jesuits, Capuchins and Récollets, were entirely absent.

By contrast, evaluating the lay element of French Jansenism is genuinely problematic. Nor can it have recourse to usable statistics. Yet it is remarkable that a movement which began among apostles of the priesthood like Saint-Cyran should have subsequently become so permeable to lay involvement. The *solitaires* of Port-Royal, who began in 1636, were the 'flagship' of such an association, and their participation in a whole range of 'Jansenist' activities, such as the 'little schools', the translations of the Bible and so on, consolidated that association by showing how indispensable they were. Their members' origins among, and continuing contacts with, the social circles of the court, law and government generally, gave them a 'voice' out of all proportion to their tiny numbers.[42] Without this dimension, it is hard to see Jansenism evolving towards its Quesnellian themes. But a handful of *solitaires* and their connections are not the full story. It seems highly unlikely that Jansenist-inclined parish clergy would have had much success in their efforts at reforming their parishes had they not encountered the goodwill and backing of the lay elites, epitomised by the churchwardens. Marie-José Michel demonstrated how different Paris parishes could 'feel', depending on whether they were Jansenist-run or not. Jansenist parishes were well ordered commonwealths, and not just in their religious practices. 'Temporal' matters were not irrelevant to the pursuit of parochial godliness, and the way churchwardens kept their archives and accounts was an integral part of an anti-baroque religiosity that prized a simplicity of worship and an atmosphere of recollection within churches. But here, too, there was a time factor at work, as in a Parisian parish it would take an active *curé*, supported by willing *habitué* clergy and churchwardens, up to twenty years to make a real impact on its religious practices.[43]

It will be obvious that there was much less scope for formal female roles within the Jansenist milieux. Yet, in the war of words to which Jansenism gave rise, accusations were regularly made against it for allowing women too many liberties, accusations which overlapped with wider social prejudices against women.[44] In the case of Jansenism, however, the role of women was in some ways *sui generis*. Nowhere was this more visible than in the history of the convent of Port-Royal, which was consubstantial with the movement during its crucial early decades, whether it be in Saint-Cyran's career, the Arnauld family's role inside and outside the abbey and the convent's emblematic resistance to the anti-Jansenist Formulary in the 1660s. Like the leading *dévot* women of the early seventeenth century, some of its nuns acted as advisers and mentors to men and women outside its walls. Angélique Arnauld, its reforming abbess, did not hesitate to write in 1635 to a *curé* in Boulogne whom she directed, 'I would like to know if you have worked as hard to make good Christians of your parishioners as you have to make good nuns of the sisters [of the Annunciation] ... These good people are your first and principal obligation, and it is a task that is never finished.' Port-Royal's travails from the 1660s gradually transformed it into a symbol of heroic suffering for the truth within wider Augustinian circles. Without the support of high-status women, it would have succumbed much earlier than it did, and Louis XIV's government only attacked it after 1679 because its principal protectress, the duchess of Longueville, died that year.[45] Individual women like Mme de Fontpertuis and Mlle de Joncoux have recently been shown to have been indispensable to Arnauld and Quesnel, especially after they went into exile.[46] Much further down the scale, it seems clear that Jansenist churchwardens in Paris in the 1730s 'were strongly seconded by their womenfolk', whose support 'was indispensable to the campaign' against Fleury's repression.[47]

Conclusion

Clearly, what we, for the sake of convenience, call Jansenism went through numerous stages of development and accretion, making it extremely difficult to use a single term to describe it at any one point in its history. Its capacity to attract and combine with other strands of thought is an essential feature of its history – and is doubtless the main reason why historians have defined and approached it in such different ways. In 1688, a Roman cardinal wittily divided the Jansenists into three types: those who believed in the five propositions, who were virtually non-existent since nobody had up to then been convicted of such an offence; those who supported strict morality and severe disciplinary rules, of whom there were many; and finally, those who for a multitude of reasons were opposed to the Jesuits, and their numbers were infinite! Precisely because its history involved unprecedented recourse to papal assistance by the French church and crown at critical moments, the Jansenists and their supporters were able to rally sympathy, if not always overt support, from a much wider 'Gallican' constituency. The magistrates who supported them during the crisis of the 1650s were more Gallican than Jansenist in their concerns, so the two could unite on the common ground of the defence of Gallican traditions. The conflicts of the 1650s also witnessed the more unprecedented intervention of the Parisian parish clergy, with their claims to their rightful place, as successors of Christ's seventy-two disciples, within the church. This kind of 'presbyterianism' would not percolate through the French secular clergy until at least a century later, but it is no accident that such themes were later developed by Quesnel and his followers, who were already steeped in the Berullian idea of the priesthood. Even during moments of the greatest danger, France's Jansenists were rarely without allies fighting their own, compatible causes.[48] Along the way, they developed a culture of resistance which was transferable to other domains, as both church and crown would discover to their cost.[49] So much emphasis has been placed on Jansenism as an 'ideology of withdrawal' – as if ample reasons for withdrawing did not already exist – that it remains difficult to appreciate the extent of its adherents' active engagement with changing the world in which they lived. They probably had their widest impact, pastoral and spiritual, during the decades after the 1668 peace of the church, only for much of it to be undone by the repression under Cardinal Fleury in the wake of *Unigenitus*. How the religious history of France would have evolved without Jansenism and especially its condemnation is impossible to say, as there is no doubt that it became a major force for division and polarisation within the wider *dévot*-reformist movement. But it is no less true that it was part and parcel of the French Catholic Reformation at its height. What François Lebrun noted for the diocese of Angers could be extended to many other areas of France – that in the domain of religious practice and morality rather than that of theology and politics the Jansenist problem was a 'false problem' since the anti-Jansenists had become just as demanding as their adversaries.[50]

Conclusion

French historians of the seventeenth century have conventionally labelled this period of their history the *grand siècle*, although the 'greatness' in question – essentially political and cultural – has mostly been associated with the rule of Louis XIV. Historians concerned with France's religious history, on the other hand, have no less frequently used another label, the *siècle des saints*, in order to emphasise the significance of the religious changes occurring then, but their 'century' has usually been shorter and earlier, stretching from the 1590s to the 1640s. That brevity is to some extent disguised by using the term 'saints' to characterise the period, as if to suggest that normal measures of time do not apply to such exceptional cases. The term 'century of saints' is not without its paradoxes, since surprisingly few individuals from the period were acclaimed as saints, either by the institutional church or by an increasingly disqualified vox populi. The purpose of this book has not been to dispute or demonstrate either the greatness or the saintliness of the seventeenth century, but to explore both the range and the continuity of religious change for well over a century after the wars of religion. If it has succeeded in showing the reality of a substantial *longue durée* of efforts to refashion, revive and reform French Catholicism, in the face of the inherited geographical, economic and institutional structures considered in the early chapters – structures which remained massively resistant to change – then it will have vindicated the approach taken in these pages.

In recent years, historians of Europe's sixteenth-century Protestant Reformations have proposed a 'success and failure' approach in order to measure the scale of contemporary religious change.[1] It has not always proved convincing, since the end results of any movement inevitably fall short – and often sharply so – of the initial expectations. And, as often as not, the successes that were recorded tended to expand earlier ambitions rather than evince satisfaction with a job well done. Furthermore, no period of change would be complete without at least some unexpected outcomes which were not on anyone's agenda at the outset. The scale of what was attempted and, to some extent, achieved in France during the 'long' seventeenth century should not be seen merely in terms of a relatively short-lived 'big bang' that occurred in the later sixteenth century and that energised a generation or two down to the late 1630s, only to fade away thereafter and allow a Weberian bureaucratic routine to dominate after the 1640s. That there was a high level of reformist activity during the early decades of the seventeenth century and that it derived from sixteenth-century conflicts is clearly beyond doubt, but the myth-making that it spawned has made the generations immediately after it seem insipid by comparison. The Catholic Reformation may have begun later in France than elsewhere in Europe, but it was more sustained and long-lasting than any other. Jean Delumeau observed years ago that the decades from the 1730s to the 1750s which are usually seen as belonging to the Enlightenment were also the high-water mark of France's Catholic Reformation.

The terms 'Reform' or 'Reformation' are too limited to cover the full range of religious changes occurring during our period, as if they were confined to existing dysfunctions that needed putting to rights. Several historians have in recent years criticised the once-liberating distinction between 'Counter-Reformation' and 'Catholic Reformation' on the grounds that, even taken together, the two terms do not fully account for the shifts and new dimensions of what they prefer to call 'early modern Catholicism'.[2] This term includes the substance of the other two, and is an extension of, rather than a substitute for them. France's religious landscape of, say, 1730 did not differ from that of 1580 or 1600 merely because particular reforms had been successfully pursued, but because substantial new elements had been added to that landscape. As we have seen in individual chapters, the French church could be highly inventive in seeking ways to improve the means that it needed to attain its objectives, and such efforts were spread out well into the eighteenth century. It also took a more 'creative' approach to several elements of the Tridentine reform agenda, not because it was sceptical towards it, but because it was free of the constraints imposed on the other parts of Europe which had formally 'received' Trent's decrees.

Because of the chronology and scale of the religious changes we are dealing with, it would be inadequate to assume that it derived exclusively from one initial 'moment' of mobilisation (the conflicts of the wars of religion). It makes more sense to think of it in terms of successive 'boosts' emerging from within seventeenth-century Catholicism itself. The history of the *dévots* shows not just how widespread and usable (by an organisation like the Company of the

Holy Sacrament, for example) was the desire to see extensive reforms within the French church, but that it was still gathering steam and self-confidence from the 1630s to the early 1660s when the company was suppressed. The fact that that particular organisation disappeared or fragmented thereafter did not signify that the impetus disappeared with it, as studies of local chapters such as Grenoble or Toulouse, have made quite clear.

Likewise, enduring hostility to France's Huguenots provided another major source of religious energy. The 'scandalous' toleration of 'heresy' after 1600 was a standing challenge to reinvigorate French Catholicism, while the monarchy's refusal between 1629 and 1685 to destroy Protestantism on French soil ensured that that challenge would be prolonged throughout most of the century. This had wider ramifications than we might imagine. The often sharp differences between the religious 'cultures' of the two churches acted as spurs to mutual competition which, on the Catholic side at least, prevented any early foreclosure of attempts at reform. This was more than a question of rival institutions rubbing up against each other. Polemic and controversy between Catholics and Huguenots turned not merely on big questions of 'high' theology or ecclesiology, but also on religious practices that were rejected as superstitions by the Huguenots, who continued until the later seventeenth century fiercely to accuse Catholicism of mixing ancient pagan practices with other forms of superstition. Although such attacks did not prevent the Catholic church from defending its practices, the criticisms could not simply be dismissed out of hand because of where they came from. If France's Huguenots were to be successfully converted, as churchmen from Richelieu to Bossuet hoped they would, then their objections had to be heeded in some way; the prospect of reconciliation between the churches always implied the possibility of shedding particular religious usages that the Huguenots could not accept. Moreover, the Huguenots had partly inherited their critique of superstition from pre-Reformation humanists like Erasmus, whose views were independently perpetuated during subsequent generations by erudite Gallicans and non-confessional Catholics like Pierre de l'Estoile. The 'learned libertines' of the seventeenth century would similarly take aim at numerous religious practices that they regarded as groundless, forcing the French church to continue examining the validity of many of those practices.

A more unexpected source of pressure for further change, and especially the cleansing of religious practices, emerged within Catholicism itself from the 1640s onwards, namely the rigorist neo-Augustinian 'movement' which included the Jansenists. Because the emphasis in the historiography of this subject has usually been on the conflicts that Jansenism created, the wider movement's contribution towards the 'further reformation' of Catholicism is often badly underestimated. Its approach to the sacraments of penance and the

Eucharist guaranteed it a reputation for taking a hard-line stance in pastoral matters when, paradoxically, its adherents were among the most forward-looking in other regards (especially the Bible, the liturgy in the vernacular, lay participation). It reproduced within Catholicism some of the elements of the Catholic–Protestant debates on religious practices, but its contribution to maintaining the momentum of French Catholicism is too often buried under the divisions that it produced, especially during the eighteenth century.

The theme of superstition in its multiple forms and the need to confront it was an important leitmotif throughout the successive phases of this drive for religious change. It is highly significant that, if anything, it took on greater importance during the later seventeenth and early eighteenth century, when both influential religious authors like Jean-Baptiste Thiers (1636–1703, a country *curé*) and Pierre Lebrun (1661–1729, an Oratorian) as well as church authorities like Cardinal Le Camus of Grenoble went to great lengths to itemise and denounce the varieties of magic and superstition which they still saw flourishing, especially but not exclusively among the peasantry. The continuing sharpness of Huguenot denunciations of 'concrete and spectacular features of baroque worship' in the decades immediately before 1685 also contributed significantly to these reassessments.[3] The increasingly elaborate questionnaires for pastoral visitations, which included numerous questions about popular religious practices, are evidence that such concerns were of practical rather than merely academic concern. Critics and reformers found some of their strongest intellectual support in the efforts of the Gallicans and neo-Augustinians to restore what they regarded as the 'purer' practices of the early church, and to purge not merely magical and related practices, but also adventitious devotions and saints with no demonstrable basis. It was symptomatic of their approach they they were no less critical of some recent devotions – elements of the cult of the Virgin, the Sacred Heart, 'excessive' exposition of the Holy Sacrament and so on – which seemed equally unfounded to them. They did not always agree among themselves on how far this work of 'epuration' should go, and figures like Thiers and Mabillon clashed sharply on how far scholarly evidence (or the lack of it) should be viewed as the sovereign arbiter of whether particular devotions should live or die.[4] The concept of 'cumulative radicalisation', used to describe the development of a particular twentieth-century regime, may not be an apt one in connection with the seventeenth-century French church, but the efforts made to pursue and expand the agenda of reform had become stronger and more entrenched by the early eighteenth century than during any previous generation, precisely because the 'scholarly' and the 'pastoral' campaigns had fused together. It is important to note that the 'scholarly' work in question was not disconnected from pastoral concerns, especially by the latter decades of the century, so there was nothing contrived about its connection with efforts to curb what seemed to be untenable religious practices. As far as superstitious beliefs or practices are concerned, there is no reason to believe that they were any more numerous than a century earlier, but the renewed assault launched against them around either side of 1700 came at a time when a generation of better-prepared clergy were capable of responding to the perceived challenge.[5]

Of course, 'on the ground' efforts to purge what were considered the grosser elements of popular Catholicism could meet stiff resistance. In 1707, the bishop of Châlons-sur-Marne was strongly opposed by an alliance of uncomprehending parishioners, including magistrates, lawyers and merchants, when he removed the relic of the 'holy umbilical cord' from a local church. What he regarded as utterly indefensible, they saw as a venerable local tradition with a history of devotion and miracles that were its warrant. Such incidents, especially when picked up by critics of a 'libertine' or 'enlightened' persuasion, provided ready ammunition to denounce not the well-intentioned 'reformers', but the idolatrous or the superstitious at the core of popular religion. In specific instances like this, a determined local bishop got his way and the dubious relics were put away, but the evidence suggests that the local clergy, even those of the more recent seminary-trained variety, were considerably more amenable to 'negotiating' changes in local practices.[6] Christophe Sauvageon, the *curé* of Sennely-en-Sologne, denounced the Rosary as a superstition, but does not appear to have acted upon his views.[7] As we saw, within their local environments, the clergy had, literally, to find a modus vivendi with their congregations, which inevitably blunted the thrust of many a 'reformist' initiative, but the efforts to effect religious change, sustained and revived across more than a century, did gradually produce results in France's religious culture that were far from negligible. It was usually only in areas where the local clergy were themselves as demanding as the bishop of Châlons that bitter conflicts with parishioners would arise. All too often, this is as far as the analysis can be taken, so that viewing religious practices through the eyes of the 'average' lay parishioner for the seventeenth century is exceptionally difficult.

By the later seventeenth century, the imitation of things French by other parts of Europe was not confined to the political or artistic spheres. Italy, the model that Europe had tended to follow in the arts and culture generally since the Renaissance, was the first to acknowledge that it was being culturally overtaken by France at this point. Spain would only begin seriously to look to France once the Bourbon succession had become permanent after 1713, and the German-speaking world later still. Initially, the Italian acknowledgement of France's new superiority occurred in the world of scholarship, in which the contribution of ecclesiastical history from the pens of figures like Mabillon and the Maurists was singled out early for attention. But this was far from being 'mere' history: its exemplarity lay for its admirers in its close alliance with an 'enlightened piety' which disdained 'laxist' casuistry and, above all, 'exterior' devotions. Such a verdict identified a particular vein of French religious experience, namely the Gallican and the Augustinian-rigorist, which was increasingly adopted thereafter by the religious elites of Italy as the core of the 'regulated devotion' (Ludovico Muratori) that they would seek to introduce within the peninsula in the name of the Catholic Enlightenment.[8] Yet in view of the latter's frequent anti-papal postures, it is worth recalling that such a penchant for French religious models actually began in Rome with Innocent XI (1676–89), as he sought to kick-start what is sometimes called the second Catholic Reformation in Italy.[9] The Bourbon succession opened up eighteenth-century Spain to French religious influences, with the local 'Jansenists' making much of the running in efforts to make Spanish religious culture less 'baroque'.[10] It is only fair to add that the limitations that France's Gallican principles and long-standing practice imposed on papal jurisdiction greatly strengthened the French model's attractiveness to the rest of eighteenth-century Catholic Europe.[11]

On this evidence, seventeenth-century France had built a religious culture that increasingly appealed to the Catholic elites of Europe. Of course, the reception of French influences by those elites was selective, depending as it did on their previous 'local' history and their current preoccupations; they knew far more about the programme of religious change, but much less about the actual synthesis worked out in practice on the ground in France. Among the features most visible to them by the early eighteenth century was the calibre of the French secular clergy, connected as it was to a serious reduction in the numbers of surplus clergy and a far higher proportion of ordained priests among the clergy than anywhere else in Europe, both of which enabled them seriously to challenge the dominance of the religious orders. It also helped that France had a well-defined parish system, the lack of which perpetuated dependence on the religious orders in certain parts of Europe, especially in Poland, parts of Germany and the Habsburg lands, where the funds provided by the suppression of monasteries later in the eighteenth century would be widely used to create a parochial system. It was no less significant that seventeenth-century France moved away from the classic format of regular orders towards congregations of secular priests, like the Oratorians or the Lazarists, whose influence in shaping French Catholicism was out of proportion to their size. When the Italian search for the 'good parish-priest' (*buon parocco*) took off in the early 1700s, it was naturally to the French model that its promoters turned.[12].

An equally important reason for the attractiveness of French Catholicism was that it was credited with diffusing a more refined, elevated kind of religion, not merely among the elites, but beyond them to the mass of the population. Such efforts had faltered in much of Italy by the 1620s and 1630s. Catholic Germany, it has been argued, also experienced a relatively brief 'Tridentine moment' which also ended about the same time (with the Thirty Years War), after which a different and more 'popular' form of Catholicism took shape there. The latter was embodied by the Capuchins rather than the Jesuits, with popular religious enthusiasms and needs forming the bedrock of a 'baroque' Catholicism which blossomed fully in the eighteenth century. When a reaction against this kind of Catholicism emerged after 1750, it drew for its inspiration on French models, albeit indirectly, via Muratori's synthesis on 'regulated devotion' that we saw above.[13]

Of course, to foreign observers or imitators alike, the actual extent of religious change across France as a whole was of far less concern; the model that they invoked did not have any geographical or other 'density' to it. Yet for historians, geographical variations in the chronology and scale of religious change of the kind explored in this book are of major importance, and taking France as a homogeneous entity is misleading. As we saw, provinces acquired during the seventeenth century, such as Roussillon, Franche-Comté and Artois-Hainaut, were perceived by French political and clerical elites at the time as unduly influenced by 'baroque' and 'popular' forms of Catholicism which stood in need of 'Gallican' correction. But Provence and much of Languedoc as far west as Toulouse continued, as in the past, to be open to Italian religious influences, which contributed an 'exotic' dimension to their religious practices that could surprise observers from northern France. Brittany, too, continued to have a distinctive religious culture of its own, and seventeenth-century preachers and missionaries reinforced rather than suppressed some of its more unusual features, notably the cult of the dead. But unexpected shifts occurred elsewhere, too. The papal enclave of Avignon, which had been home to some of the earliest Borromean impulses on French soil, found itself imitating forms of religious change emanating from northern France by 1700.[14] At the more local level, significant differences in clerical recruitment and popular religious 'fervour' have been detected by studies of dioceses as distant as Reims, La Rochelle or Tarbes. Pierre Chaunu argued many years ago, in a discussion of French Jansenism, that it took on more vigorous pastoral emphases in those areas, such as Lorraine, where it came into contact with Protestant populations. Chaunu speculated that Normandy might have had a similar experience to Lorraine, and for similar reasons. He also contrasted both provinces to those parts of Burgundy (Auxerre diocese) or Champagne (Châlons, Troyes) where the absence of exposure to Protestantism bred a more sterile form of Jansenism which would lead in due course to a precocious movement of de-Christianisation.[15] It is far from clear whether these and other 'frontiers of Catholicity' in other parts of France, especially in the south and west, actually had the effects of their religious behaviour that Chaunu anticipated; they may well have produced more defensive and mutually antagonistic relations between the confessions.[16]

Of course, variations of this and other kinds would have been undetectable inside or outside of France around 1680 or 1730. To contemporaries, it seemed that by expanding the Tridentine agenda of change much further than anywhere else, the French church had assumed the kind of religious leadership that had once belonged to Carlo Borromeo or Juan de Ribera. In the lengthy process of doing so, it forged, as these pages have tried to demonstrate, an impressive, if unevenly successful, arsenal of instruments of religious change, many of which spread across Europe and continued to be widely used during subsequent centuries.

NOTES

Preface

1. J. Michael Hayden and Malcolm R. Greenshields, *600 Years of Reform. Bishops and the French Church, 1190–1789* (Montreal, 2005).
2. John McManners, *Church and Society in Eighteenth-Century France*, 2 vols (Oxford, 1988).

Prologue: The Fire and the Ashes

1. Denis Crouzet, *Les Guerriers de Dieu. La Violence au temps des troubles de religion (vers 1525–vers 1610)*, 2 vols (Seyssel, 1990) remains the most ambitious account of the nature of conflicts in this period.
2. Their reports, as well as the instructions issued to them, can be found in the incomplete *Acta Nuntiaturae Gallicae* series (Rome, 1961–), the most recent volume of which is the *Correspondance du nonce en France Gasparo Silingardi évêque de Modène (1599–1601)*, ed. Bertrand Haan (Rome, 2002).
3. Alain Tallon, *Conscience nationale et sentiment religieux en France au xvie siècle* (Paris, 2002), esp. Ch. 1.
4. Alain Tallon, *La France et le concile de Trent (1518–1563)* (Rome, 1997) an exhaustive and illuminating study.
5. In addition to Tallon, *La France et le concile de Trent*, see Hayden and Greenshields, *600 Years of Reform*, Ch. 3.
6. Alain Tallon, 'Inquisition romaine et monarchie française au xvie siècle' in Gabriel Audisio, ed., *Inquisition et pouvoir* (Aix-en-Provence, 2004), 311–12.
7. Among the most useful narratives are R. J. Knecht, *The Rise and Fall of Renaissance France 1483–1610*, 2nd edn (Oxford, 2001); id., *The French Civil Wars* (London, 2000); Mack P. Holt, *The French Wars of Religion 1562–1629* (Cambridge, 1992); Arlette Jouanna et al., *Histoire et dictionnaire des guerres de religion* (Paris, 1998).
8. On this see, in addition to Tallon, *France et concile de Trente*, Jotham Parsons, *The Church in the Republic. Gallicanism and Political Ideology in Renaissance France* (Washington, DC, 2004), Ch. 6.
9. Mark Greengrass, *Governing Passions. Peace and Reform in the French Kingdom, 1576–1585* (Oxford, 2007), esp. 94–101, 286–303 and *passim*, for the most highly documented study of these efforts which supersedes earlier accounts.

10. Hayden and Greenshields, *600 Years of Reform*, 67–8, 87; Marc Venard, 'Un concile provincial oublié: le concile d'Embrun en 1583', *Provence Historique*, 42 (1992), 625–44.
11. Robin Briggs, 'Richelieu and reform: rhetoric and political reality' in Joseph Bergin and Laurence Brockliss, eds, *Richelieu and His Age* (Oxford, 1992), 71–97.
12. Victor Carrière, 'Les Épreuves de l'église de France au xvie siècle' in Carrière, ed., *Introduction aux études d'histoire ecclésiastique locale*, 3 vols (Paris, 1934–40), iii, 247–509, for the most extensive statement of this position.
13. Olivier Christin, *Une Révolution symbolique: l'iconoclasme huguenot et la reconstruction catholique* (Paris, 1991), pt i.
14. See Greengrass, *Governing Passions*, esp. 32ff., for local evidence.
15. See Ch. 9.
16. Carrière, 'Épreuves', 393–434; Claude Michaud, *L'Église et l'argent sous l'ancien régime* (Paris, 1991), esp. Chs 3, 5; Marc Venard, 'La Situation financière du clergé dans la France des guerres de religion' in Marcel Pacaut and Olivier Fatio, eds, *L'Hostie et le denier* (Geneva, 1991), 121–30, for a useful synthesis of research by Michaud, Ivan Cloulas and other historians.
17. Michaud, *Église et argent*, views the financial question primarily from the perspective of the receiver-general of the French clergy. For the evolution of the assemblies, see Parsons, *Church in the Republic*, Ch. 6.
18. The following pages owe much to Serge Brunet, 'Anatomie des réseaux ligueurs dans le sud-ouest de la France (vers 1562–vers 1610)' in Nicole Lemaitre, ed., *Religion et politique dans les sociétés du Midi* (Paris, 2002), 153–91; id., ' "Confréries ligueuses, confréries dangereuses". Fraternités de combat dans le sud-ouest de la France durant les guerres de religion' in Marc Venard and Dominique Julia, eds, *Sacralités, culture et dévotion* (Marseille, 2005), 129–70; id., 'Jeanne d'Albret, Pierre d'Albret évêque de Comminges, et la "trahison" de Blaise de Monluc. Aux origines de la Ligue dans le sud-ouest de la France' in Evelyne Berriot-Salvador et al., eds, *Jeanne d'Albret et sa cour* (Paris, 2004), 129–68; Kevin Gould, *Catholic Activism in South-West France 1540–70* (Aldershot, 2006); Robert R. Harding, 'The Mobilization of confraternities against the Reformation in France', *Sixteenth-Century Journal*, 11 (1980), 85–107.
19. See n. 18, for Serge Brunet's essays on this point.
20. Gould, *Catholic Activism*, for a detailed analysis of Bordeaux, Agen and Toulouse.
21. Jean Boutier et al., *Un Tour de France royal. Le voyage de Charles IX (1564–1566)* (Paris, 1984), 254–6; see also Greengrass, *Governing Passions*, 188–92, for a subsequent 'voyage' to Guyenne by Catherine de Médicis.
22. Harding, 'Mobilization', 86ff.; Brunet, 'Anatomie', esp. 146–7, 150–1.
23. Philip Benedict, 'The Catholic response to protestantism. Church activity and popular piety in Rouen 1560–1600' in James Obelkevich, ed., *Religion and the People 800–1700* (Chapel Hill, NC, 1979), 168–90. For Toulouse, see Robert A. Schneider, *Public Life in Toulouse 1463–1789* (Ithaca, NY, 1989), Ch. 3.
24. Greengrass, *Governing Passions*, 306–11.
25. Harding, 'Mobilization', 92–9; on Marseille, Brunet, 'Confréries ligueuses, confréries dangereuses', 165–8.
26. Denis Pallier, *Recherches sur l'imprimerie à Paris pendant la Ligue (1585–1594)* (Geneva, 1975), 173.
27. See Ann W. Ramsey, *Liturgy, Politics and Salvation. The Catholic League in Paris and the Nature of Catholic Reform 1540–1630* (Rochester, NY, 1999), for an analysis of these themes in a major city.
28. See Judith Pollmann, 'Countering the Reformation in France and the Netherlands: clerical leadership and Catholic violence 1560–1585', *Past and Present*, 190 (2006) 83–120.
29. Serge Brunet, *'De l'Espagnol dans le ventre'. Les catholiques du sud-ouest de la France face à la Réforme, vers 1540–1589* (Paris, 2007), extends his earlier research on the Spanish connection, but the *ligueurs* were not alone in playing that card: see Joan Davies,

'Neither politique nor patriot? Henri I, duc de Montmorency and Philip II, 1582–1589', *Historical Journal*, 34 (1991), 539–66.
30. See n. 1, above.
31. For an analysis of the 'no surrender' elements of the Catholic League, see Robert Descimon and José Javier Ruiz Ibàñez, *Les Ligueurs de l'exil* (Seyssel, 2005), Introduction.
32. Michel Cassan, 'Laïcs, ligue et réforme catholique à Limoges', *Histoire, Économie, Société*, 10 (1991), 159–75.
33. André Latreille et al., *Histoire du catholicisme en France*, 3 vols (Paris, 1957–62), ii, 269–70.
34. Marc Venard, 'Les Rapports de visites *ad limina* des évêques de France sous l'ancien régime' in Philippe Boutry and Bernard Vincent, eds, *Les Chemins de Rome* (Rome, 2002), 109; Joseph Bergin, *French Bishops: The Making of the French Episcopate 1589–1661* (New Haven and London, 1996), 385–9, for Medici's mission.

Chapter 1: From Dioceses to Parishes: the Geography of the French Church

1. The following pages are based mainly on Joseph Bergin, *The Making of the French Episcopate*, Ch. 1; id., *Crown, Church and Episcopate under Louis XIV* (New Haven and London, 2004), Ch. 1; McManners, *Church and Society*, i, Ch. 6.
2. Nicole Lemaitre, 'Le Culte épiscopal et la résistance au protestantisme au xvie siècle' in Gérald Chaix, ed., *Le Diocèse* (Paris, 2002), 307–26.
3. Marc Venard, 'Les Rapports de visites *ad limina*', 101–21.
4. Philippe Martin, 'Definir le diocèse. Débats en Lorraine à propos d'une définition (vers 1690–vers 1730)' in Chaix, ed., *Le Diocèse*, 344–5.
5. McManners, *Church and Society*, i, 178.
6. Bergin, *Crown, Church and Episcopate*, 20ff.
7. Ibid.
8. This trend is evident from the multi-volume history of the assemblies of clergy from 1615 to 1715 by Pierre Blet: *Le Clergé de France et la monarchie 1615–1666*, 2 vols, (Rome, 1959).
9. McManners, *Church and Society*, i, Ch. 10.
10. Jean-Pierre Gutton, *La Sociabilité villageoise dans l'ancienne France* (Paris, 1979), Ch. 1.
11. Anne Bonzon, *L'Esprit de clocher. Prêtres et paroisses dans le diocèse de Beauvais 1535–1650* (Paris, 1999), 219.
12. Michel Vernus, *Le Presbytère et la chaumière. Curés et villageois dans l'ancienne France (xiiie–xiiie siècles)* (Rioz, 1986), 20.
13. Numbers derived from *Répértoire des visites pastorales*, ed. Marc Venard, 4 vols (Paris, 1977–85), i, 41, 97.
14. Claire Dolan, *Entre Tours et clochers. Les gens d'église à Aix-en-Provence au xvie siècle* (Sherbrooke, 1981).
15. René Pillorget, *Paris sous les premiers Bourbons* (Paris 1988), 86–88; Ségolène de Dainville-Barbiche, *Devenir curé à Paris. Institutions et carrières ecclésiastiques (1695–1789)* (Paris, 2005), 30–50, shows that five parishes were suppressed and three suburban ones created during the period 1695–1789.
16. Philippe Loupès, *L'Apogée du catholicisme bordelaise 1600–1789* (Bordeaux, 2001), 101ff.
17. Louis Pérouas, *Le Diocèse de La Rochelle 1648–1724. Sociologie et pastorale* (Paris, 1964), 146–7.
18. What follows draws on Gutton, *La Sociabilité villageoise*, Ch. 6; Vernus, *Presbytère et chaumière*, 136ff.; McManners, *Church and Society*, i, 307ff.
19. David Garrioch, *The Formation of the Parisian Bourgeoisie 1690–1830* (Cambridge, MA, 1996), Chs 1–3; id., *The Making of Revolutionary Paris* (Los Angeles, 2002), 153–60.
20. Georges Couton, *La Vieillesse de Corneille 1658–1684* (Paris, 1949), 300.

436 NOTES to pp. 34–53

21. Nicole Lemaitre, 'Finances des consulats et finances des paroisses dans la France du sud-ouest xive–xviiie siècles' in Pacaut and Fatio, L'Hostie et le denier (Geneva, 1991), 101–15.
22. Nicole Lemaitre, ed., Histoire des curés (Paris, 2002), 186.

Chapter 2: Wealth into Benefices

1. See McManners, Church and Society, i, Ch. 3; Claude Michaud, Église et argent; Atlas de la Révolution française, ix, ed. Claude Langlois et al. (Paris, 1996), 50, for maps and analysis of the 1789 data.
2. See Jean Meuvret, 'La situation matérielle des membres du clergé séculier dans la France du xviie siècle' in Meuvret, Études d'histoire économique (Paris, 1971), 251–68.
3. For some details about episcopal holdings, see Bergin, Making of the French Episcopate, Ch. 3; on the monastic orders, Dominique Dinet, 'Les Grands domaines des reguliers en France (1560–1790): une relative stabilité?', Revue Mabillon, new series, 10 (1999), 257–69.
4. Gérard Sabatier, 'Le Géographie seigneuriale du Languedoc des montagnes: Velay, Gévaudan, Vivarais en 1734' in La France d'ancien régime. Études réunies en l'honneur de Pierre Goubert, 2 vols (Toulouse, 1984), 649–63.
5. See the map of the tithes in 1790 in Atlas de la Révolution française, ix, 50; McManners, Church and Society, i, 122ff.
6. Jacques Bottin, Seigneurs et paysans dans l'ouest du Pays de Caux, 1540–1650 (Paris, 1983), 228ff.
7. See René Favier, Les Villes du Dauphiné aux xviie et xviiie siècles (Grenoble, 1993), 84, 'seventeenth-century people identified towns primarily in terms of episcopal cities'.
8. John McManners, French Ecclesiastical Society Under the Ancien Régime. A Study of Angers in the Eighteenth Eentury (Manchester, 1960), 3–8; Pierre Deyon, Amiens capitale provinciale au xviie siècle (Paris, 1967), 363ff.
9. Pierre Goubert, Beauvais et le Beauvaisis au xviie siècle (Paris, 1958), 237–41.
10. Michaud, Église argent, pt i, Ch. 3.
11. Philip Hoffman, 'Taxes and agrarian life in early modern France: land sales 1530–1730', Journal of Economic History, 46 (1986), 37–55, discusses these issues with references to non-taxpaying elites generally.
12. For a brief summary of the enormous volume of research on early modern economic trends, see Françoise Bayard and Philippe Guignet, L'Économie française aux xvie–xviiie siècles (Paris, 1991), Chs 3–4 and dossier no. 1.
13. Emmanuel Le Roy Ladurie, Paysans du Languedoc, 2 vols (Paris, 1966), i, 373ff., 474ff.; Victor Carrière, Introduction aux études d'histoire ecclésiastique locale, 3 vols (Paris, 1934-40), iii, 287–352, 'Le Refus des dîmes'.
14. Le Roy Ladurie, Paysans du Languedoc, 474ff.
15. Marcel Lachiver, Les Années de misère 1680–1720 (Paris, 1991).
16. Le Roy Ladurie, Paysans du Languedoc, i, pt iv.
17. Bergin, Making of the French Episcopate, 105ff.; id., Cardinal Richelieu. Power and the Pursuit of Wealth (New Haven, 1985), 214ff.
18. Philippe Loupès, Chapitres et chanoines de Guyenne (Paris, 1985), pt ii, Chs 1–2; Dinet, 'Les Grands domaines des réguliers', 257–69.
19. Maarten Ultee, The Abbey of St Germain des Prés in the Seventeenth Century (New Haven, 1981), Ch. 9, 'The Monk as Steward'.
20. Philip Hoffmann, Church and Community in the Diocese of Lyon 1500–1789 (New Haven, 1984), 48ff.; Vernus, Presbytère et chaumière, pt i, Ch. 6.
21. Vernus, Presbytère et chaumière, 61–4.

NOTES to pp. 54–79   437

22. Serge Brunet, 'Les Prêtres des campagnes de la France du xviie siècle: la grande mutation', *XVII Siècle*, 59 (2007), 49–82, at 59ff.
23. Joseph Bergin, 'Cardinal Mazarin and his Benefices', *French History*, 1 (1987), 3–26.
24. See the discussions of these practices in McManners, *Church and Society*, i, esp. 630ff.
25. Ibid, i, Ch. 20, describes 'The Art of Obtaining a Benefice'.

Chapter 3: Clerics and Clergy: the World of the Seculars

1. Joseph Bergin, 'Between Estate and Profession: the Catholic Parish Clergy of Early Modern Western Europe' in M. L. Bush, ed., *Social Orders and Social Classes in Europe Since 1500* (London, 1992), 68–9.
2. Dominique Julia, 'The Priest' in Michel Vovelle, ed., *Enlightenment Portraits* (Chicago, 1997), 361.
3. See Brunet, 'Les Prêtres des campagnes', 56–9.
4. Bergin, 'Between Estate and Profession', 71.
5. Mario Rosa, *Clero cattolico e società nell'età moderna* (Rome, 2006), Ch. 2, for an up-to-date comparative analysis.
6. The best study of this question focuses on the eighteenth century, but contains both data and reflections that are relevant for the seventeenth: Timothy Tackett, *Religion, Revolution and Religious Culture in Eighteenth-Century France* (Princeton, 1986).
7. Bergin, 'Between Estate and Profession', 71–3. Pérouas, *La Rochelle*, 199–200, 205ff.; Dominique Julia and Denis McKee, 'Le Clergé paroissial dans le diocèse de Reims sous l'épiscopat de Charles-Maurice le Tellier: origines et carrières', *Revue d'Histoire Moderne et Contemporaine*, 29 (1982), 529–82, at 532ff.
8. Bergin, 'Between Estate and Profession', 73.
9. Lemaitre, *Histoire des curés*, 104.
10. Georges Viard, 'Chapitre et réforme catholique au xviie siècle: le chapitre cathédral de Langres' (unpublished doctoral thesis, University of Nancy-II, 1974), 409.
11. These passages are based mainly on Serge Brunet and Nicole Lemaitre, eds, *Clergés, communautés et familles des montagnes d'Europe* (Paris, 2005); Serge Brunet, *Les Prêtres des montagnes* (Aspet, 2001), esp. v; id., 'Les Prêtres des campagnes', 49–82; Yves Durand, 'Les Prêtres habitués en France aux xviie et xviiie siècles' in André Corvisier et al., eds, *Combattre, gouverner, écrire* (Paris, 2003), 369–84; Nicole Lemaitre, 'Les Communautés de "prêtres filleuls" dans le Rouergue d'ancien régime', *Ricerche di Storia Sociale e Religiosa*, 17 (1988), 33–58; Louise Welter, 'Les Communautés de prêtres dans le diocèse de Clermont du xiiie au xviiie siècle, *Revue d'Histoire de l'Église de France* 35 (1949), 5–35.
12. Durand, 'Prêtres habitués', 369–71.
13. Loupès, *Chapitres et chanoines*, is the most comprehensive study, despite its focus on the chapters of Guyenne province. There is useful comparative material in McManners, *Church and Society*, Chs 14–15; Viard, 'Chapitre et réforme', is an excellent case study.
14. Stéphane Gomis, *Les 'Enfants prêtres' des paroisses d'Auvergne, xvie–xviiie siècles* (Clermont-Ferrand, 2006).
15. Louise Welter, 'Le Chapitre cathédral de Clermont: sa constitution, ses privilèges', *Revue d'Histoire de l'Église de France*, 41 (1955), 5–42.
16. Loupès, *Chapitres et chanoines*, pt iii, Chs 2, 6.
17. Georges Viard, 'Les Chanoines de Langres au xviie siècle: recrutement, origines, fortunes', *Annales de l'Est*, 28 (1976), 94.
18. Georges Minois, *La Bretagne des prêtres en Trégor d'ancien régime* (n.p., 1987), 17, 208–9.
19. Loupès, *Chapitres et chanoines*, 260.
20. Viard, 'Chapitre et réforme catholique', 409ff.

21. See Ch. 7.
22. R. J. Knecht, *The French Renaissance Court* (New Haven and London, 2008); Jeroen Duindam, *Vienna and Versailles* (Cambridge, 2003), Ch. 3.
23. Bergin, *Crown, Church and Episcopate*, 127–32.
24. Dominique Dinet, 'Une Institution méconnue: la commende' in Jean-Pierre Bardet et al. eds, *État et société en France aux xviie et xviii siècles* (Paris, 2000), 195–208.
25. See Ch. 7.

Chapter 4: The Monastic Orders: Adjustment and Survival

1. Derek Beales, *Prosperity and Plunder. European Catholic Monasteries in the Age of Revolution 1650–1815* (Cambridge, 2003), Chs 1, 4, provides the best survey of *all* the orders and congregations for our period, despite the dates in its title; Mario Rosa, *Clero cattolico e società*, Ch. 3, also places France in a European context.
2. For a brief historical analysis of the constitutional-organisational dimension of this problem, see David Knowles, *From Pachomius to Ignatius* (Oxford, 1966).
3. The following pages owe much to Jean-Marie Le Gall, *Les Moines au temps des réformes* (Seyssel, 2001); Dominique Dinet, 'Une Institution méconnue: la commende', 195–208; id., 'L'Évolution de l'institution de la commende dans l'espace religieux des xviie et xviiie siècles' in Giles Constable and Michel Rouche, eds, *Auctoritas* (Paris, 2006), 727–39; Nicole Lemaitre, 'Abbés et abbesses de l'époque moderne, approches nouvelles de la prosopographie' in Marc Venard and Dominique Julia, eds, *Sacralités, culture et dévotion* (Marseille, 2005), 25–47.
4. Jules Gallerand, 'L'Erection de l'évêché de Blois (1697), *Revue d'Histoire de l'Église de France*, 42 (1956), 175–228; Robert Sauzet, 'La Création du diocèse d'Alès (1694), prototype de l'erection de celui de Blois' in Chaix, ed., *Le Diocèse*, 33–46; Dominique Dinet, *Religion et société: réguliers et vie régionale dans les diocèses d'Auxerre, Langres et Dijon (fin xvie–fin xviiie siècles)*, 2 vols (Paris, 1999), ii, 472–9.
5. *L'Intendance de Berry à la fin du xviie siècle*, ed. Claude Michaud (Paris, 2001), 90, n. 108.
6. Lemaitre, 'Abbés et abbesses', 40ff.; Bernard Chédozeau, 'La Congrégation de Saint-Maur et le renouveau architectural du monachisme dans les abbayes du Bas-Languedoc', *Revue Mabillon*, n.s., 13 (2002), 67–87, esp. 77.
7. For a single example of reform by contract, see Joseph Bergin, 'Ways and Means of Monastic Reform in Seventeenth-Century France: the Example of St Denis de Reims 1630–3', *Catholic Historical Review*, 72 (1986), 14–32.
8. See René Pillorget, 'Réforme monastique et conflits de rupture dans quelques localités de la France méridionale au xviie siècle', *Revue Historique*, 253 (1975), 77–106.
9. A brief survey is Gérard Michaux, 'Les Nouveaux réseaux monastiques à l'époque moderne' in *Naissance et fonctionnement des réseaux monastiques et canoniaux* (Saint-Étienne, 1991), 603–23, esp. 615ff.; Daniel-Odon Hurel, ed., *Guide pour l'histoire des ordres et des congrégations religieuses, France xvie–xxe siècles* (Turnhout, 2001) contains useful data on individual orders; Joseph Bergin, *Cardinal de la Rochefoucauld. Leadership and Reform in the French Church* (New Haven, 1987), 136–46.
10. Hurel, ed., *Guide*, 53–4, for these figures.
11. Bergin, *La Rochefoucauld*, Ch. 6, for the context and thinking behind such an approach to monastic reform.
12. Bergin, *La Rochefoucauld*, Ch. 9; Paul Denis, *Richelieu et la réforme des monastères bénédictins* (Paris, 1912); Guy Charvin, 'L'Abbaye et l'ordre de Cluny de la mort de Richelieu à l'élection de Mazarin 1642–1654', *Revue Mabillon*, 33 (1943), 85–114; id., 'L'Abbaye et l'ordre de Cluny sous l'abbatiat de Mazarin 1654–1661', ibid., 34–35 (1944–5), 20–81.
13. See Bergin, *La Rochefoucauld*, Ch. 9; Polycarpe Zakar, *Histoire de la stricte observance de l'ordre cistercien depuis ses débuts jusqu'au généralat du cardinal de Richelieu*

(1606–1635) (Rome, 1966); Louis J. Lekai, *The Rise of the Cistercian Strict Observance in Seventeenth-Century France* (Washington, DC, 1968).

14. See Bergin, *La Rochefoucauld*, Chs 7–8, for a detailed account of the congregation to 1645. Isabelle Brian, *Messieurs de Sainte-Geneviève* (Paris, 2001), deals mostly with its subsequent history.
15. See Hurel, *Guide*, 94ff.
16. Benoist Pierre, *La Bure et le sceptre. La congrégation des Feuillants dans l'affirmation des états et des pouvoirs princiers (vers 1560–vers 1660)* (Paris, 2006), a study that ranges more widely than its title might suggest.
17. A. J. Krailsheimer, *Armand-Jean de Rancé, Abbot of La Trappe* (Oxford, 1974), the best of many studies of Rancé.
18. *L'Intendance de Berry*, 91, n. 112.
19. Chédozeau, 'La Congrégation de Saint-Maur', 67–87.
20. Ultee, *St Germain des Prés*, 18–19.
21. Krailsheimer, *Rancé*, 45–7, 52–3.
22. Jean-Louis Quantin, *Le Catholicisme classique et les pères de l'église. Un retour aux sources (1669–1713)* (Paris, 1999), pt i, Ch. 5.
23. Lekai, *Rise of Strict Observance*, ch 13.
24. Dominique Julia, 'Les Bénédictins et l'enseignement aux xviie et xviiie siècles' in *Sous la Règle de Saint-Benoît* (Paris, 1982), 345–500.
25. Brian, *Messieurs de Sainte-Geneviève*, 241ff., 329ff.
26. *L'Intendance de Berry*, 87, n. 96.
27. Brian, *Messieurs de Sainte-Geneviève*, 270ff.

Chapter 5: From Mendicants to Congregations.

1. Marcel Bernos, 'Un Ordre italien en France à l'époque moderne: les Servites de Marie' in *Échanges religieux entre la France et l'Italie du moyen age à l'époque moderne* (Geneva, 1987), 173–91; Hurel, *Guide*, 170–76.
2. Bernard Montagnes, *Les Dominicains en France et leurs réformes* (Paris, 2001); id., *Sébastien Michaelis et la réforme d'Occitanie (1594–1647)* (Rome, 1984); Hurel, *Guide*, 136–9.
3. P. J. S. Whitmore, *The Order of Minims in Seventeenth-Century France* (The Hague, 1967).
4. Hurel, *Guide*, 145–51, for the essential statistics.
5. Fréderic Meyer, *Pauvreté et assistance spirituelle. Les Franciscains récollets de la province de Lyon aux xviie et xviiie siècles* (Saint-Étienne, 1997) is the only substantial modern study of a particular region; Hurel, *Guide*, 152–4.
6. The two major studies are those of Bernard Dompnier, *Enquête au pays des frères des anges. Les Capucins de la province de Lyon* (Saint-Étienne, 1993); Jean Mauzaize, *Le Rôle et l'action des capucins de la province de Paris au xviie siècle*, 3 vols (Paris, 1978). Relevant material can also be found in Dinet, *Religion et société,* and other studies of the orders generally within a provincial or local context. For European comparisons, see Marc Venard, ed., *Histoire du christianisme* (Paris, 1992, 1997), ix, 282–3.
7. Hurel, *Guide*, 154–7.
8. Meyer, *Pauvreté et assistance*, 277ff.
9. Hurel, *Guide*, 200. See also Ch. 6.
10. Jean de Viguerie, *Une Oeuvre d'éducation sous l'ancien régime* (Paris, 1976), for an exhaustive study. Hurel, *Guide*, 196–8, for some valuable statistics.
11. Studies of the Jesuits are highly uneven in quality, and with scarcely a single major synthesis. McManners, *Church and Society*, ii, Ch. 42, 'The Jesuits of France', has useful material for our period.
12. John W. O'Malley, *The First Jesuits* (Cambridge, MA, 1993).

13. Eric Nelson, *The Jesuits and the Monarchy. Catholic Reform and Political Authority in France (1590–1615)* (Aldershot, 2005), covers many of these themes; Robert Bireley, *The Jesuits and the Thirty Years War* (Cambridge, 2002), places France's Jesuit confessors in their European context.
14. See Dominique Julia, 'Entre Universel et Local: le Collège jésuite à l'époque moderne', *Paedagogica Historica*, 40 (2004), 15–31; id., 'Églises, société, éducation à l'époque moderne. La transformation des collèges aux xvie et xviie siècles', *Pédagogie chrétienne, pédagogues chrétiens* (Paris, 1996), 61–83; Michel Péronnet, 'Les Établissements des jésuites dans le royaume de France à l'époque moderne' in *Les Jésuites parmi les hommes aux xvie et xviie siècles* (Clermont, 1985), 463–79 (with maps).
15. Péronnet, 'Établissements des jésuites', 471.
16. Jean Dagens, *Bérulle et les origines de la restauration catholique 1575–1611* (Paris, 1952); Charles E. Williams, *The French Oratorians and Absolutism 1611–41* (New York, 1989).
17. Dominique Julia and Willem Frijhoff, 'Les Oratoriens de France sous l'ancien régime. Premiers résultats d'une enquête', *Revue d'Histoire de l'Église de France*, 65 (1979), 225–65; id., 'Le Recrutement d'une congrégation enseignante et ses mutations à l'époque moderne: l'Oratoire de France' in D. N. Baker and P. Harrigan, eds, *The Making of Frenchmen* (Waterloo, Canada, 1980), 443–58; id., 'Les Oratoriens et l'espace éducatif français du règne de Louis XIV à la Révolution française' in Jean Ehrard, ed., *Le Collège de Riom et l'enseignement oratorien au xviiie siècle* (Paris and Oxford, 1993), 12–27.
18. Yves Krumenacker, *L'École française de spiritualité* (Paris, 1998), 242–3.
19. Dominique Julia, 'L'Expansion de la congrégation de la Mission de la mort de Vincent de Paul à la Révolution française' in *Vincent de Paul* (Rome, 1983), 362–419.
20. Charles Berthelot du Chesnay, *Les Missions de Saint Jean Eudes* (Paris, 1967).
21. Yves Poutet, *Le xviie Siècle et les origines lasalliennes*, 2 vols (Rennes, 1970), for a broad account; Hurel, *Guide*, 219–21.
22. Julia, 'Expansion', 384.
23. Pillorget, *Paris sous les premiers Bourbons*, 496ff.
24. Yann Lignereux, *Lyon et le roi, de la 'bonne ville' à l'absolutisme municipal (1594–1654)* (Seyssel, 2004), 720–37; Schneider, *Public Life in Toulouse*, 35–6; Loupès, *Apogée du catholicisme bordelais*, 89.
25. This paragraph is based on Dinet, *Religion et société*, i, Chs 1–5.
26. Bernard Dompnier, 'Les Affiliations des laïcs aux communautés: tiers ordres et réseaux dévotionnels' in *Les Mouvances laïques des ordres religieux* (Saint-Étienne, 1996), 379–402.
27. See Ch. 14 below.
28. Bernard Dompnier, 'Ordres, diffusion des dévotions et sensibilités religieuses. L'exemple des Capucins en France (xviie–xviiie siècles)', *Dimensioni e Problemi della Ricerca Storica*, 10 (1994), 21–59.
29. Louis Châtellier, *Europe of the Devout* (Cambridge, 1989), is the standard account.
30. Hurel, *Guide*, 157–9.
31. Meyer, *Pauvreté et assistance*, 287ff.; id., 'Les Tertiaires chez les franciscains récollets aux xviie et xviiie siècles' in *Les Mouvances laïques des ordres religieux*, 415–27.
32. Dompnier, 'Les Affiliations des laïcs aux communautés', 397.
33. Louis Châtellier, *The Religion of the Poor* (Cambridge, 1997), Ch. 3; Bernard Dompnier, 'Les Missions des Capucins et leur empreinte sur la réforme catholique en France', *Revue d'Histoire de l'Église de France*, 70 (1984), 127–47; id., 'Les Jésuites et la mission de l'intérieur' in Luce Giard and Louis de Vaucelles, eds, *Les Jésuites à l'age baroque* (Grenoble, 1996), 155–79; D-O Hurel, 'Monachisme et missions intérieures en France au xviie siècle', *Revue Mabillon*, n. s., 10 (1999), 271–96.
34. Jean de Viguerie, 'Y a-t-il une crise d'observance régulière entre 1660 et 1715?' in *Sous la Règle de Saint Benoît* (Paris, 1982), 135–47.
35. Vladimir Malov, 'Le Projet colbertiste de la réforme monastique' in *Un Nouveau Colbert* (Paris, 1983), 167–76.

36. Frédéric Meyer, 'L'Évêque contre les Récollets', *Études Héraultaises* 30–32 (1999–2001), 75–85, for one of the most notorious conflicts.
37. H. G. Judge, 'The Congregation of the Oratory in France in the Late Seventeenth Century', *Journal of Ecclesiastical History*, 11 (1961), 46–55; Julia and Frijhoff, 'Le Recrutement d'une congrégation enseignante', 443–58; Hurel, *Guide*, 203.
38. Meyer, *Pauvreté et assistance*, 424ff.

Chapter 6: A Silent Revolution: Women as Regulars

1. Elizabeth Rapley, *A Social History of the Cloister. Daily Life in the Teaching Monasteries of the Old Regime* (Montreal, 2001), Ch. 5 and Appendix, 346–7.
2. Beales, *Prosperity and Plunder*, 85–6; McManners, *Church and Society*, i, 534–5.
3. *The Canons and Decrees of the Council of Trent*, ed. H. J. Schroder (St Louis, 1941), 220–21, *sessio* XXV, *de reformatione*, cap. 5.
4. For a case study, see Joan Davies, 'The Montmorencys and the Abbey of Sainte Trinité, Caen: Politics, Profit and Reform', *Journal of Ecclesiastical History*, 53 (2002), 665–85.
5. Manuscrits français 20969, Paris, Bibliothèque Nationale, fos 17v–19r, 16 Nov 1676; Hurel, *Guide*, 164.
6. Le Gall, *Les Moines au temps des réformes*, 32–3; Bernard Hours, *Madame Louise, princesse au Carmel, 1737–1787* (Paris, 1987).
7. Hurel, *Guide*, 144–5. Like their male counterparts, the Dominican nuns have largely escaped the attention of historians.
8. Ibid., 159–68.
9. Alexander Sedgwick, *The Travails of Conscience. The Arnaud Family and the Ancien Régime* (Cambridge, MA, 1998), Ch. 3; Louis Cognet, *La Réforme de Port-Royal 1591–1618* (Paris, 1950).
10. Pillorget, 'Réforme monastique et conflits de rupture', 78ff., documents such incidents involving female orders.
11. Benoist Pierre, *Le Père Joseph* (Paris, 2007), 111ff.
12. Barbara Diefendorf, *From Penitence to Charity. Pious Women and the Catholic Reformation in Paris* (Oxford, 2004), Chs 3–4 is the best account.
13. Elizabeth Rapley, *The Dévotes. Women and Church in Seventeenth-Century France* (Montreal, 1990), 48–61; Diefendorf, *Penitence to Charity*, 124ff.
14. Claude-Alain Sarre, *Vivre Sa Soumission. L'exemple des Ursulines provençales et comtadines* (Paris, 1997), for the slowness of full cloister to dominate south-eastern France.
15. Laurence Lux-Steritt, *Redefining Female Religious Life. French Ursulines and English Ladies in Seventeenth-Century Catholicism* (Aldershot, 2005), for a close analysis of how French Ursulines committed to teaching negotiated the obstacles to action while preserving their contemplative impulse.
16. Rapley, *Dévotes*, 43–8; Loupès, *Apogée du catholicisme bordelais*, 40–44.
17. Rapley, *Dévotes*, 34–41.
18. In addition to Rapley, *Dévotes*, this section owes much to Dominique Julia, 'L'Expansion de l'ordre de la Visitation aux xviie et xviiie siècles' in *Visitation et visitandines aux xviie et xviiie siècles* (Saint-Étienne, 2001), 115–76.
19. Julia, 'Expansion', 117.
20. Diefendorf, *Penitence to charity*, 242–3.
21. In addition to Diefendorf, *Penitence to Charity*, 203–16, and Rapley, *Dévotes*, Ch. 4, this account draws on Susan E. Dinan, *Women and Poor Relief in Seventeenth-Century France: The Early History of the Daughters of Charity* (Aldershot, 2006).
22. Vincent de Paul, *Correspondance, entretiens et documents*, ed. Pierre Coste, 14 vols (Paris 1920–23), x, 661.
23. Table assembled from material in Hurel, *Guide*.

24. These paragraphs owe much to the research of Marie-Claude Dinet-Lecomte, recently summarised in her book, *Les Sœurs hospitalières en France aux xviie et xviiie siècles: la charité en action* (Paris, 2005).
25. Dinet-Lecomte, 'La "cléricalisation" du personnel hospitalier en France aux xviie et xviiie siècles' in *Religion et enfermements (xviie–xxe siècles)* (Rennes, 2005), 115–29.
26. Colin Jones, *The Charitable Imperative. Hospitals and Nursing in Ancien Régime and Revolutionary France* (London, 1989), sections i–ii, esp. Ch. 1, 'Hospitals in Seventeenth-Century France'.
27. Case studies and plentiful evidence in Daniel Hickey, *Local Hospitals in Ancien Régime France* (Montreal, 1997), Ch. 5, 'Religious Congregations and Local Hospitals: Women Working in the World'; Dinet-Lecomte, *Sœurs hospitalières en France*, Ch. 2, 'From Local Association to Congregation'.
28. Dinet-Lecomte, 'Implantation et rayonnement des congrégations Hospitalières dans le sud de la France aux xviie et xviiie siècles', *Annales du Midi* (1992), 19–42, at 39; Rapley, *Dévotes*, 86–7. Abundant evidence of episcopal intervention in Hurel, *Guide*, 230–77.
29. Dinet-Lecomte, 'L'Hôpital, un lieu d'édification et de conversion dans la France moderne' in Christian Sorrel and Frédéric Meyer, eds, *Les Missions intérieures en France et en Italie du xvie au xxe siècle* (Chambéry, 2001), 215–32.
30. For one example of this, see Odile Robert, 'De la dentelle et des âmes. Les "Demoiselles de l'Instruction" du Puy (xviie–xviiie siècle)' in Jean Delumeau, ed., *La Religion dema mère* (Paris, 1992), 245–67.
31. Quoted in Roger Chartier, Dominique Julia and Marie-Madeleine Compère, *L'Éducation en France, xvie–xviiie siècles* (Paris, 1976), 238.
32. Diefendorf, *Penitence to Charity*, 136–7 (table of new Paris houses 1604–50); René Lehoreau, *Cérémonial de l'église d'Angers 1692–1721*, ed. François Lebrun (Paris, 1967), 47; Gilles Deregnaucourt and Didier Poton, *La Vie religieuse en France aux xvie, xviie, xviiie siècles* (Paris, 1994).
33. Cassan, *Le Temps des guerres de religion*, 395, table 27.
34. McManners, *Church and Society*, i, 545.
35. Lehoreau, *Cérémonial*, 47.
36. Dominique Dinet, 'Les Dots de religion en France aux xviie et xviiie siècles' in *Les Églises et l'argent* (Paris, 1989), 37–65, at 40–41.
37. Rapley, *Social History*, 20–21.
38. Dinet, 'Dots de religion', an informative synthesis to which the following reflections are indebted.
39. This is not to suggest a fixed sum, but merely the differences between what different orders and convents could expect – which in turn triggered negotiation of individual dowries.
40. Dinet, 'Dots de religion', 42–3.
41. Ibid., 58.
42. Loupès, *Apogée du catholicisme bordelais*, 96.
43. Rapley, *Social History*, 21–4.
44. Lux-Steritt, *Redefining Female Religious Life*, esp. Ch. 6, for these tensions among the Ursulines.
45. François Lebrun, *Les Hommes et la mort en Anjou aux xviie et xviiie siècles* (Paris, 1971), 246; Marie-Claude Dinet-Lecomte, 'Administrateurs d'hôpitaux et religieuses hospitalières' in Jean-Pierre Gutton, ed., *Les Administrateurs d'hôpitaux dans la France de l'ancien régime* (Lyon, 1999), 147–69.
46. Dominique Dinet, 'Les Religieuses des diocèses d'Auxerre, Langres, et Dijon: vie contemplative et action séculière (aux xviie et xviiie siècles)' in *Les Religieuses dans le cloître et dans le monde* (Saint-Étienne, 1994), 851–69, at 861.
47. Rapley, *Dévotes* and *Social History*, both study the organisation and daily routines of the major teaching orders; Odile Robert, 'De La Dentelle et des âmes',

245–67, studies those at the very opposite end of the scale, in both social and religious terms.

Chapter 7: The Bishops: Adaptation and Action

1. *Canons and Decrees of Trent*, ed. Schroeder, 153–4, sessio XXII, de reformatione, cap. 2.
2. The sections that follow are based upon material from Bergin, *The Making of the French Episcopate* and *Crown, Church and Episcopate*.
3. Tallon, *La France et le concile de Trente*, 770ff.
4. Louis Pérouas, 'L'Emploi du temps des évêques du xviie siècle dans les diocèses de Luçon et de La Rochelle', *Revue d'Histoire de l'Église de France*, 49 (1962), 89–95, one of the few documented attempts to deal with this question.
5. Pierre Blet, *Le Clergé de France et la monarchie 1615–1666*, 2 vols (Rome, 1959), ii, *livre iv*, Ch. 2.
6. The best guide here is Alison Forrestal, *Fathers, Pastors and Kings. Visions of Episcopacy in Seventeenth-Century France* (Manchester, 2004), esp. Chs 1–2.
7. Forrestal, *Fathers*, 83–4, 175–6.
8. Paul Broutin, *La Réforme pastorale en France au xviie siècle*, 2 vols (Tournai, 1956), i, 221.
9. Philippe Goujard, *Un Catholicisme bien tempéré. La Vie religieuse dans les paroisses rurales de Normandie 1680–1789* (Paris, 1996), 24–5; Bergin, *Crown, Church and Episcopate*, 140–41.
10. Peyrous, Bernard, *La Réforme catholique à Bordeaux (1600–1719)*, 2 vols (Bordeaux, 1995), i, 229–46.
11. Nicole Lemaitre, 'De l'évêque au curé: la communication des réformes vers les paroisses et ses mutations (xve–xviiie siècles)', in Ilana Zanguer and Myriam Yardeni, eds, *Les Deux Réformes chrétiennes* (Leiden, 2004), 331–53, for a suggestive analytical framework.
12. Bruno Restif, 'Les Synodes du diocèse de Saint-Malo aux xvie–xviie siècles', *Revue d'Histoire de l'Église de France*, 89 (2003), 345–61.
13. Jean-Marie Gouesse, 'Assemblées et associations cléricales, synodes et conférences ecclésiastiques dans le diocèse de Coutances aux xviie et xviiie siècles', *Annales de Normandie*, (1974), 37–71.
14. Ibid., 64.
15. Hayden and Greenshields, *600 Years of Reform*, for the most systematic study of synodal statutes, on which the following passages draw.
16. Lemaitre, 'De l'évêque au curé', 336–7.
17. The bibliography on the subject is vast. Visitation records constitute, alongside synodal legislation, the core sources for Hayden and Greenshields's study, *600 Years of Reform*. For valuable perspectives on visitations and the problems posed by the sources they generated, see Dominique Julia, 'La Réforme post-tridentine en France d'après les proces-verbaux de visites pastorales: ordre et résistances' in *La Società religiosa nell'età moderna* (Naples, 1973), 311–415; Marc Venard, 'Les Visites pastorales du xvie au xviie siècle' in Marc Venard, *Le Catholicisme à l'épreuve dans la France du xvie siècle* (Paris, 2000), 27–63; Georges Viard, 'Les Visites pastorales dans l'ancien diocèse de Langres, la réglementation épiscopale et sa mise en oeuvre', *Revue d'Histoire de l'Église de France*, 63 (1977), 235–72, offers a useful synopsis on visitations within a single diocese. All the major local/diocesan studies (e.g. Goujard, Hoffmann, Pérouas, Peyrous) have extensively used these records.
18. Lemaitre, 'De l'évêque au curé', 342–3.
19. Pérouas, 'L'Emploi du temps', 91.
20. See below, 'One Bishop's Agenda', 180ff.
21. Lehoreau, *Céremonial*, 41–2; Isabelle Bonnot, *Hérétique ou saint? Henry Arnauld, évêque janséniste d'Angers au xviie siècle* (Paris, 1984), 124.

444 NOTES to pp. 177–91

22. Loupès, *Chapitres et chanoines*, esp. 355–66.
23. Robert Sauzet, *Les Visites pastorales dans le diocèse de Chartres pendant la première moitié du xviie siècle. Essai de sociologie religieuse* (Rome, 1975), 101ff.
24. The most interesting and unabridged set of visitation records in print is the unfinished *Recueil des visites pastorales du diocese de Lyon aux xvie–xviie siècles* (Lyon, 1926). In fact, this volume contains only the visitations conducted by Archbishop Marquemont in 1613–14; no further volumes appeared subsequently.
25. See n. 17, above.
26. See Sandrine Messines, 'Contre-Réforme et Réforme catholique en Agenais, à travers les visites pastorales de Nicolas de Villars' in Nicole Lemaitre, ed., *Religion et politique dans les sociétés du Midi* (Paris, 2002), 193–201, esp. 194–7, 'la désolation matérielle du diocèse'; Nicole Lemaitre, 'Les Visites pastorales témoins de la christianisation? L'exemple du diocèse de Rodez (début xive–mi-xviiie siècles)' in *La Christianisation des campagnes*, 2 vols (Brussels, 1996), i, 206–7.
27. For a systematic visitor of the late seventeenth century, Cardinal Le Camus of Grenoble, see Jean Godel, 'Les Visites pastorales de Le Camus: objectifs et méthode' in Jean Godel, ed., *Le Cardinal des montagnes* (Grenoble, 1974), 213–39.
28. Gabriel Audisio, *Les Français d'hier. Des Croyants, xve–xixe siècles* (Paris, 1996), 387–8.
29. Venard, *Catholicisme à l'épreuve*, 42.
30. Goujard, *Un Catholicisme bien tempéré*, 27.
31. Paris, Archives Nationales, Archives privées, 259 AP 272, dossier 9, pièce no. 1.
32. Lehoreau, *Cérémonial*, 51–2.
33. Rosa, *Clero cattolico e società*, Ch. 1, esp. 11–16.

Chapter 8: Remaking the Secular Clergy

1. Sauzet, *Chartres*, 101ff.
2. Hayden and Greenshields, *600 Years of Reform*, 128.
3. This discussion is based partly on Bergin, 'Between Estate and Profession', 79–80.
4. Jean-François Soulet, *Traditions et réformes religieuses dans les Pyrénées centrales au xviie siècle (le diocèse de Tarbes de 1602 à 1716)* (Pau, 1975), 126–7.
5. Julia and McKee, 'Le Clergé paroissial dans le diocèse de Reims', 581–2.
6. Bergin, 'Between Estate and Profession', 80; Brunet, 'Les Prêtres des campagnes', esp. 73ff.
7. The discussion here draws mainly on Owen Chadwick, *The Popes and the European Revolution* (Oxford, 1981), 124–33, useful for European comparisons; Gilles Deregnaucourt, 'Le concours pour l'accès aux curés dans les anciens diocèses du Nord de la France (16–18 siècles)' in *Croire dans le passé. Études sur la vie religieuse dans les temps modernes offertes au professeur Michel Cloët* (Louvain, 1996), 111–29; Marc Venard, 'Examen ou concours? Réflexions sur la procédure de recrutement des curés dans la France d'ancien régime', in Gilles Deregnaucourt, ed., *Société et religion en France et aux Pays-Bas xve–xixe siècle* (Arras, 2000), 373–88.
8. Marc Venard, 'Les Rapports de visites *ad limina*', 113, 115.
9. Berthelot du Chesnay, *Prêtres séculiers en Haute-Bretagne*, 222ff.
10. Julia and McKee, 'Clergé paroissial', 563ff.
11. Venard, 'Examen ou concours?', 386–7.
12. Peyrous, *Réforme catholique à Bordeaux*, ii, 537–43; Brunet, 'Les Prêtres des campagnes', 71–2.
13. Anne Bonzon, 'Faire corps face aux pouvoirs: les communautés de curés dans les cités épiscopales de la province ecclésiastique de Reims', *Revue du Nord*, 81 (1999), 691ff.
14. Goujard, *Un Catholicisme bien tempéré*, 57–8.
15. Gouesse, 'Assemblées et associations', 56.

16. Goujard, *Un Catholicisme bien tempéré*, 59–60; Gouesse, 'Assemblées et associations', 65.
17. Bernard Dompnier, 'Les Hommes d'église et la superstition entre xviie et xviiie siècles' in Dompnier, ed., *La Superstition à l'âge des Lumières* (Paris, 1998), 13–47, at 14–17.
18. Goujard, *Un Catholicisme bien tempéré*, 58.
19. Dominique Julia, 'Reading and the Counter-Reformation' in G. Cavallo and R. Chartier, eds, *A History of Reading in the West* (Cambridge, 1999), 251–6, for a comparative overview.
20. Pierre Hurtubise, 'Le prêtre tridentin: idéal et réalité' in *Homo religiosus. Autour de Jean Delumeau* (Paris, 1997), 212–13.
21. Pérouas, *La Rochelle*, 253–4; Alain de Solminihac, *Lettres et documents*, ed. Eugène Sol (Cahors, 1930), 160–61. For some later instances of such demands, see Jacques Le Goff and René Rémond, eds, *Histoire de la France religieuse*, 4 vols (Paris, 1988–92), ii, 519 Julia, 'Reading and the Counter-Reformation', 252.
22. Jean Quéniart, *Les Hommes, l'église et Dieu dans la France du xviiie siècle*, (Paris, 1978), 69ff.; id., 'La Culture des prêtres de campagne bretons au xviiie siècle', in Marc Venard and Dominique Julia, eds, *Sacralités, culture et dévotion* (Marseille, 2005), 257–66; McManners, *Church and Society*, i, 346–7.
23. J. A. O'Donohue, *Tridentine Seminary Legislation: Its Sources and its Formation* (Louvain, 1957); Antoine Degert, *Histoire des séminaires français*, 2 vols (Paris, 1912), i, pt i, Ch. 1.
24. The standard account is Degert, *Séminaires français*.
25. Marc Venard, 'Les séminaires en France avant Saint Vincent de Paul' in *Vincent de Paul. Actes du colloque international d'études vincentiennes* (Rome, 1983), 1–16.
26. Degert, *Séminaires français*, pt i, Ch. 4.
27. Dominique Julia, 'La constitution du réseau des collèges en France du xvie au xviiie siècle' in *Objet et Méthodes de l'histoire de la culture* (Budapest and Paris, 1982), 73–94; George Huppert, *Public Schools in Renaissance France* (Urbana and Chicago, 1984).
28. Venard, 'Les séminaires en France', 6.
29. Joseph Bergin, *The Rise of Richelieu* (New Haven and London 1991), 94–6.
30. Vincent de Paul, *Correspondance*, ii, 458–61, letter of 13 May 1644.
31. Solminihac, *Lettres et documents*, 456, letter to Vincent de Paul, 16 April 1651.
32. For Lyon, see Hoffman, *Church and Community*, 76–77.
33. See discussion of congregations in Ch. 5 above.
34. Degert, *Séminaires français*, i, 121–8.
35. See Bergin, *La Rochefoucauld*, 108, for the context.
36. Dominique Julia, 'L'Éducation des ecclésiastiques en France aux xviie et xviiie siècles' in *Problèmes d'Histoire de l'Éducation* (Collection de l'École Française de Rome, 104) (Rome, 1988), 157.
37. McManners, *Church and Society*, i, 197; Goujard, *Un Catholicisme bien tempéré*, 53, for Rouen diocese; Hoffman, *Church and Community*, 79, for Lyon.
38. Pierre Delattre, 'La Compagnie de Jésus et les séminaires en France', *Revue d'Ascétique et de Mystique*, 20 (1953), 20–44, 160–76; Louis Châtellier, *Tradition chrétienne et renouveau catholique dans l'ancien diocèse de Strasbourg* (Strasbourg and Paris, 1981), 231ff.
39. Goujard, *Un Catholicisme bien tempéré*, 52.
40. See Dominique Julia, 'Système bénéficial et carrières ecclésiastiques dans la France d'ancien régime' in *Historiens et Sociologues d'aujourd'hui* (Paris, 1986), 79–107, esp. 99ff.
41. On the eve of the French Revolution, no fewer than 42 of the approximately 140 seminaries were still run by diocesan secular clergy. See Tackett, *Religion, Revolution and Regional Culture*, 100.
42. Degert, *Séminaires français*, pt ii, Ch. 8.
43. Julia, 'L'Éducation des ecclésiastiques', 146–9.

446   NOTES to pp. 204–15

44. Dominique Julia, 'La Formation du clergé dans l'espace catholique occidental (xvie–xviiie siècles)' in Maurizio Sangalli, ed., *Pastori, pope, preti, rabbini. La Formazione del ministro di culto in Europe (secoli xvi–xviii)* (Rome, 2005), 23–65, at 44–5.
45. Jean Orcibal, *Jean Duvergier de Hauranne, abbé de Saint-Cyran*, (Paris, 1948), 62.
46. In addition to n. 18 above, see Krumenacker, *L'École française de spiritualité*, 76–80, 350ff., and the essays in Danielle Pister, ed., *L'Image du prêtre dans la littérature classique (xviie–xviiie siècles)* (Frankfurt, 2001).

Chapter 9: The Triumph of the Parish?

1. Marc Venard, 'La Construction des églises paroissiales, du xve au xviiie siècle', *Revue d'Histoire de l'Église de France*, 73 (1987), 7–24, for a synthesis that draws on numerous local studies.
2. See Ch. 7, above, on visitations.
3. Nicole Périn, 'Le Diocèse de Reims après la Fronde', *Revue d'Histoire Ardennaise*, 8 (1973), 91–124; Lemaitre, 'Les Visites pastorales témoins de la christianisation?', 212; Jeanne Ferté, *La Vie religieuse dans les campagnes parisiennes (1622–1695)* (Paris, 1962), 80ff., esp. 88–94.
4. See the discussion in Hayden and Greenshields, *600 Years of Reform*, 134ff.
5. Michèle Ménard, *Une Histoire des mentalités religieuses aux xviie et xviiie siècles. Mille retables de l'ancien diocèse du Mans* (Paris, 1980), shows the scale of the change by including parish churches in her study; see also Bruno Restif, *La Révolution des paroisses. Culture paroissiale et Réforme catholique en Haute-Bretagne aux xvie et xviie siècles* (Rennes, 2006), 193ff.
6. Bernard Chédozeau, *Choeur clos, choeur ouvert. De l'église médiévale à l'église tridentine (France, xviie–xviiie siècle)* (Paris, 1998), esp. 95–7 for list of churches modified before 1789; Restif, *Révolution des paroisses*, 201–2.
7. See Ch. 7, n. 24, evidence from the visitation records from Lyon diocese for 1613–14.
8. Keith P. Luria, *Territories of Grace: Cultural Change in the Seventeenth-Century Diocese of Grenoble* (Los Angeles, 1991), 139–47, for an interesting case study of these changes.
9. Audisio, *Croyants*, 156.
10. See Restif, *Révolution des paroisses*, Ch. 6.
11. Audisio, *Croyants*, 156–8; Restif, *Révolution des paroisses*, 203ff.
12. For the Protestant attacks and the Catholic defence of images 'on the ground', see Christin, *Une Révolution symbolique* (Paris, 1991)
13. Julia, 'La Réforme post-tridentine', 334–5. Marie-Hélène Froeschlé-Chopard, *Espace et sacré en Provence (xvie–xxe siècle). Cultes, images, confréries* (Paris, 1994), 226ff., for the most exhaustive regional study of the shifting iconography.
14. As noted by Vernus, *Presbytère et chaumière*, 159.
15. Audisio, *Croyants*, 286–7.
16. Malcolm R. Greenshields, 'What happened in Quibou? The Catholic reformation in the village', *Proceedings of the Annual Meeting of the Western Society for French History*, 18 (1991), 80–88, at 86.
17. Jean Nicolas, *La Rébellion française. Mouvements populaires et conscience sociale 1661–1789* (Paris, 2002), 496–500, for riots in Brittany and elsewhere over questions of burial; Alain Croix, *L'Age d'or de la Bretagne 1532–1675* (Rennes, 1993), Ch. 19 (iii), which summarises his earlier monumental study of these themes, *La Bretagne aux xvie et xviie siècles. La Vie, la mort, la foi*, 2 vols (Paris, 1983), esp. ii, 1001–36.
18. Hayden and Greenshields, *600 Years of Reform*, 94, 'cemeteries and their fencing were of great interest to visitors of the Second Catholic Reformation'; Lebrun, *Les Hommes et la mort en Anjou*, 477–80.

19. Vanessa Harding, *The Dead and the Living in Paris and London, 1500–1670* (Cambridge, 2002), ranges wider than the two cities in its title, and discusses the eighteenth-century campaigns for removing cemeteries to peripheral locations.
20. Keith P. Luria, *Sacred Boundaries. Religious Coexistence and Conflict in Early Modern France* (Washington, DC, 2005), for a study based on Poitou.
21. Audisio, *Croyants*, 153–4; Gutton, *Sociabilité villageoise*, 194–6. Gutton notes that the presbytery may also have widened the gap between *curés* and parishioners, but this could be an eighteenth-century phenomenon.
22. Vernus, *Presbytère et chaumière*, 154–7; Lemaitre, *Histoire des curés*, 189; Nicole El Hajje-Kervévan, 'L'État moral du clergé forézien, 1650–1789', *Cahiers d'Histoire*, 30 (1985), 289–308, at 301.
23. See the extraordinary description written around 1700 by the prior of Sennely-en-Sologne about his dwelling and his memorandum ('devis') for its improvement: Christophe Sauvageon, 'Le Manuscrit original du prieur Sauvageon', *Mémoires de la Société Archéologique et Historique de l'Orléanais*, 32 (1908), lxxv–lxxxix – cited henceforth as Sauvageon, *Mémoires*, Ch. 15, cxxvi–cxxx.
24. Gutton, *Sociabilité villageoise*, 190–91.
25. Summary in Bergin, 'Between Estate and Profession', 77–81. See Minois, *La Bretagne des prêtres*, 15–21; Julia and McKee, 'Clergé paroissial', 530–56; Nicole El Hajje-Kervévan, 'Sociologie du clergé forézien, 1650–1789', *Histoire, Économie, Société*, 4 (1985), 497–517, at 500–6.
26. Minois, *La Bretagne des prêtres*, 202; Julia and McKee, 'Clergé paroissial', 563.
27. Timothy Tackett, *Priest and Parish*, 111.
28. Lemaitre, *Histoire des curés*, 187, 189; Gérard Bouchard, *Le Village immobile. Sennely-en-Sologne au xviie siècle* (Paris, 1972), which is based essentially on Sauvageon's memoirs and other writings.
29. Audisio, *Croyants*, 294.
30. Julia and McKee, 'Clergé paroissial', 570–76.
31. Ibid., 582.
32. El Hajje-Kervévan, 'Sociologie du clergé forézien', 514–15.
33. Brunet, 'Les Prêtres des campagnes', 59, n. 36. See also Rosa, *Clero cattolico e società*, Ch. 2, for interesting comparisons.
34. McManners, *Church and Society*, i, 393–8, for observations that fit the seventeenth century.
35. See the items listed by Gutton, *Sociabilité villageoise*, 199–200; Vernus, *Presbytère et chaumière*, 68–70.
36. Gutton, *Sociabilité villageoise*, 201.
37. Restif, *Révolution des paroisses*, 146ff.
38. David Garrioch, *The Formation of the Parisian Bourgeoisie 1690–1830* (Cambridge, MA, 1996), Ch. 2.
39. David Garrioch's suggestive studies of these questions deal with eighteenth-century Paris: *Neighbourhood and Community in Paris 1740–1790* (Cambridge, 1986) and *The Formation of the Parisian Bourgeoisie*.
40. Richard M. Golden, *The Godly Rebellion* (Chapel Hill, NC, 1981), Chs 2–4.
41. See Ch. 16 below.
42. Marie-José Michel, *Jansénisme et Paris 1640–1730* (Paris, 2000), esp. Ch. 6.

Chapter 10: Saints and Shrines

1. This section draws on François Lebrun, 'Le Calendrier agro-liturgique dans la société traditionnelle de la France de l'Ouest (xviie–xixe siècles)' in Lebrun, *Croyances et cultures dans la France d'ancien régime* (Paris, 2001), 97–104; Alain Cabantous, *Entre Fêtes et clochers. Profane et sacré dans l'Europe moderne, xviie–xviiie siècle* (Paris, 2002), Ch. 4; Peter

Hersche, 'Fest und Alltag. Das agro-liturgische Jahr in der frühen Neuzeit' in Eva Kreissl, ed, *Feste feiern* (Linz, 2002), 112–20; Bernard Dompnier and Françoise Hernandez, 'Fêtes des confréries, calendrier liturgique et dévotions (xviie et xviiie siècles)' in *Sacralités, culture et dévotions*, 171–91; McManners, *Church and Society*, ii, 202–8; Michael Maurer, 'Sonntag in der frühen Neuzeit', *Archiv für Kulturgeschichte*, 88 (2006), 75–100.
2. See the extensive and at times caustic commentary on feast days and activities which they generated in Sauvageon, 'Mémoires'.
3. Restif, *Révolution des paroisses*, 301ff.
4. Lehoreau, *Cérémonial*, 131.
5. Luria, *Territories of Grace*, 147.
6. Restif, *Révolution des paroisses*, 303.
7. Lebrun, 'Calendrier agro-liturgique', 101.
8. *Canons and Decrees of Trent*, 215–17; Miguel Gotor, *Chiesa e santità nell'Italia moderna* (Rome, 2004), Chs 1–2; Venard, ed., *Histoire du christianisme*, viii, 272–3.
9. Christin, *Une révolution symbolique*, pt ii, 'la riposte (catholique)'.
10. See Carlos Eire, *War Against the Idols: the Reformation of Worship from Erasmus to Calvin* (Cambridge, 1986); Dominique Julia, 'Pour Une Géographie européenne du pèlerinage à l'époque moderne et contemporaine' in Philippe Boutry and Dominique Julia, eds, *Pèlerins et pèlerinages dans l'Europe moderne* (Rome, 2000), 6–18; Dompnier, 'Les Hommes d'église', 13–47; Luria, *Territories of Grace*, 117–21.
11. Luria, *Territories of Grace*, Ch. 4, for a synoptic view of the shifting fortunes of the saints within one diocese.
12. François Lebrun, 'La place du pèlerinage thérapeutique dans la piété des Bretons aux xviie et xviiie siècles' in Lebrun, *Croyances et cultures*, 149–52.
13. Luria, *Territories of Grace*, 108, 127–8.
14. Simon Ditchfield, *Liturgy, Sanctity and History in Tridentine Italy* (Cambridge, 1995), 214ff.; Gotor, *Chiesa e santità nell'Italia moderna*, 79–93; Eric Suire, *La Sainteté française de la réforme catholique (xvie–xviiie siècles) d'après les textes hagiographiques et les procès de canonisation* (Bordeaux, 2001), 351ff.
15. Gotor, *Chiesa e santità*, 93–120; Peter Burke, 'How to be a Counter-Reformation Saint' in Burke, *Historical Anthropology of Early Modern Italy* (Cambridge, 1987), 48–62.
16. Luria, *Territories of Grace*, 110, for de Sales; Bernard Dompnier, 'La Dévotion à Charles Borromée dans la France du xviie siècle. Représentations d'un saint et histoire de son culte', *Studia Borromaica*, 20 (2006), 253–92.
17. Lebrun, 'La Place du pèlerinage thérapeutique', 155.
18. Soulet, *Traditions et réformes religieuses*, 280–81; Restif, *Révolution des paroisses*, 329.
19. Luria, *Territories of Grace*, 113–17.
20. See Ch. 14.
21. Luria, *Territories of Grace*, 161–3.
22. Dompnier and Hernandez, 'Fêtes de confréries', 180; Luria, *Territories of Grace*, 126–7, 150–60.
23. Luria, *Territories of Grace*, 160.
24. Sauvageon, *Mémoires*, xxxix, italics mine. See also Bouchard, *Village immobile*, 299–300.
25. In addition to Luria, see Froeschlé-Chopard, *Espace et sacré en Provence*, esp. pt ii, Chs 1–2.
26. Luria, *Territories of Grace*, 165.
27. See n. 24 above. Sauvageon recounts the episcopal visit of 1682 ordering the destruction and burial of 'unworthy' statues of St Anthony.
28. Marie-Hélène Froeschlé-Chopard, 'De L'Image protectrice à l'image enseignante. Une mutation du sentiment religieux au xviie siècle' in Olivier Christin, ed., *Crises de l'image religieuse*, (Paris, 2000), 156; ead., *Espace et sacré en Provence*, esp. pt ii, Chs 1–2.
29. Restif, *Révolution des paroisses*, 326–7; Dominique Julia, 'Sanctuaires et lieux sacrés à l'époque moderne' in André Vauchez, ed., *Lieux sacrés, lieux de culte, sanctuaires*, (Rome, 2000), 258ff.

30. Denis Crouzet, 'Recherches sur les processions blanches, 1583–4', *Histoire, Économie, Société*, 4 (1982), 511–63; Audisio, *Croyants*, 297; Deyon, *Amiens capitale provinciale*, 381–2 (Deyon considers further processions in the 1630s around Amiens).
31. Soulet, *Traditions et réformes religieuses*, 269.
32. Lebrun, 'La Place du pèlerinage thérapeutique', 155.
33. Alain Croix, ed., *Les Bretons et Dieu. Atlas d'histoire religieuse 1300–1800* (Rennes, n.d.), fiche no. 27.
34. Deyon, *Amiens capitale provinciale*, 382–3.
35. Soulet, *Traditions et réformes religieuses*, 270.
36. Alphonse Dupront, *Du Sacré. Croisades et pèlerinages. Images et langages* (Paris, 1987), contains Dupront's main contributions to the subject.
37. The following pages owe much to Jean Chélini and Henry Branthomme, eds, *Les Chemins de Dieu. Histoire des pèlerinages chrétiens des origines à nos jours* (Paris, 1982); Dominique Julia, 'Le Pèlerinage aux temps modernes (xvie–xviiie siècles)' in Gabriel Audisio, ed., *Religion et exclusion xiie–xviiie siècle*, (Aix-en-Provence, 2001), 183–95; id., 'Sanctuaires et lieux sacrés', 241–95; id., 'Pour Une Géographie européenne du pèlerinage à l'époque moderne', 2–126; id., *Gilles Caillotin, pèlerin. Le retour de Rome d'un sergier remois, 1724* (Rome, 2006); id. and Philippe Boutry, 'Les Pèlerins français à Rome au xviiie siècle d'après les registres de Saint-Louis-des-Français', in Boutry and Julia, eds, *Pèlerins et pèlerinages*, 403–54; Philippe Boutry and Françoise Le Hénard, 'Pèlerins parisiens à l'age de la monarchie administrative' in Philippe Boutry, Pierre-Antoine Fabre and Dominique Julia, eds, *Rendre Ses Vœux: les identités pèlerines dans l'Europe moderne (xvie–xviiie siècle)* (Paris, 2000), 401–37; Georges Provost, 'Identité paysanne et «pèlerinage de long cours» dans la France des xviie–xixe siècles' in ibid., 379–99; id., *La Fête et le sacré. Pardons et pèlerinages en Bretagne aux xviie et xviiie siècles* (Paris, 1998); McManners, *Church and Society*, ii, 140–55; Philippe Martin, *Les Chemins du sacré. Paroisses, processions et pèlerinages en Lorraine du xvie au xixe siècle* (Metz, 1995).
38. Nicole Lemaitre, 'La Vie religieuse des paysans dans la France centrale, xvie–xviie siècles' in *Le Paysan* (Paris, 1989), 319.
39. René Moulinas, 'Le Pèlerinage, victime des Lumieres' in Chélini and Branthomme, eds, *Les Chemins de Dieu*, 259–92. Julia, 'Pour Une Géographie européenne', 26–37.
40. Julia, 'Pèlerinage aux temps modernes', 293.
41. Bruno Maës, *Le Roi, la Vierge et la nation: pèlerinages et identité nationale entre guerre de Cent Ans et Révolution* (Paris, 2003); Isabelle Brian, 'Le Roi pèlerin. Pèlerinages royaux dans la France moderne' in Boutry and Julia, eds, *Rendre ses voeux*, 363–78.
42. Maës, *Le Roi, la Vierge et la nation*, 36–7.
43. Lebrun, 'La Place du pèlerinage thérapeutique', 156–7; Provost, 'Identité paysanne', 382.
44. Julia, 'Pour Une Géographie européenne', 106ff.
45. See Julia, *Gilles Caillotin, pèlerin*, for an extended study and edition (pp. 37–267) of Caillotin's account of his return journey from Rome; the rest of the original document is lost.
46. Provost, 'Identité paysanne', 397–9.
47. Lebrun, 'La Place du pèlerinage thérapeutique', 156.
48. Marie-Hélène Froeschlé-Chopard, 'Les Ordres religieux, témoins et acteurs dans les lieux de pèlerinage' in *Homo religiosus*, 52–60.

Chapter 11: Sacraments and Sinners

1. Restif, *Révolution des paroisses*, 354.
2. Jean Bernhard et al., *L'Époque de la Réforme et du concile de Trente* (Paris, 1990), 135–309, is valuable for its analysis of Trent's treatment of each sacrament.
3. For what follows, see McManners, *Church and Society*, ii, 3–6; Venard, ed., *Histoire du christianisme*, ix, 896–7.

4. Venard, ed., *Histoire du christianisme*, ix, 897.
5. The most extended account of this practice is Jacques Gélis, *L'Arbre et le fruit: la naissance dans l'Occident moderne, xvie–xixe siècle* (Paris, 1984), esp. pt i, Ch. 6, and pt iii, Chs 1–2.
6. Wendy Gibson, *Women in Seventeenth-Century France* (London, 1989), 118–19; Hayden and Greenshields, *600 Years of Reform*, 133.
7. Jean de Viguerie, *L'Institution des enfants. L'Éducation en France, xvie–xviiie siècles* (Paris, 1978), 56–7.
8. Jean de Viguerie, *Le Catholicisme des Français dans l'ancienne France* (Paris, 1988), 17–18.
9. McManners, *Church and Society*, ii, 6–8; Venard, ed., *Histoire du christianisme*, ix, 898.
10. The anonymous account of Bishop Le Peletier of Angers's visitations pays considerable attention to the confirmations he conducted: Paris, Archives nationales, 259 AP 272, dossier 9, pièce no. 3.
11. See the substantial essays on its early history in Jean Delumeau, ed., *La Première Communion* (Paris, 1987): Nicole Lemaitre, 'Avant La Communion solennelle' (15–32); Robert Sauzet, 'Aux Origines' (33–50); Maryvonne Goubet-Mahé, 'Le Premier Rituel de la première communion, xvie–xviie siècle' (51–76).
12. Sauvageon, *Mémoires*, lxxvii, lxxxxvi, discusses this problem in his parish.
13. The passages that follow owe much to Thomas N. Tentler, *Sin and Confession on the Eve of the Reformation* (Princeton, 1977); John Bossy, *Christianity in the West* (Oxford, 1984), Ch. 3; Jean Delumeau, *L'Aveu et le pardon. Les difficultés de la confession, xiiie–xviiie siècle* (Paris, 1990); W. David Myers, '*Poor Sinning Folk*'. *Confession and Conscience in Counter-Reformation Germany* (Ithaca, NY, 1996); Stephen Haliczer, *Sexuality in the Confessional* (Oxford, 1996), Ch. 3; McManners, *Church and Society*, ii, Ch. 31; Wietse de Boer, *The Conquest of the Soul. Confession, Discipline and Public Order in Counter-Reformation Milan* (Leiden, 2001).
14. On this point, see L. G. Duggan, 'Fear and Confession on the Eve of the Reformation', *Archiv für Reformationsgeschichte*, 75 (1984), 153–75, followed by Myers, '*Poor Sinning Folk*', Ch. 1.
15. Hubert Jedin, 'La Necéssité de la confession privée selon le concile de Trente', *Maison-Dieu*, 104 (1970), 88–115; Bernhard et al., *Époque de la Réforme et du concile de Trente*, 157–83.
16. See Ch. 16 below.
17. Nicole Lemaitre, 'Pratique et signification de la confession communautaire dans les paroisses au xvie siècle' in *Pratiques de la confession* (Paris, 1983), 139–64; id., 'Confession privée et confession publique dans les paroisses du xvie siècle', *Revue d'Histoire de l'Église de France*, 69 (1983), 189–208.
18. De Boer, *Conquest of the Soul*, esp. Ch. 3.
19. John Bossy, *Peace in the Post-Reformation* (Cambridge, 1998), 42–3. See the reproductions of three confession scenes in *A History of Private Life*, iii, ed. Roger Chartier (Engl. trans., Cambridge, MA, 1989), 68, 77–8.
20. Sauvageon, *Mémoires*, lxxxxiii–vi.
21. For the Jesuits and their approach, see Châtellier, *Europe of the Devout*.
22. See Ch. 16 for an analysis of Arnauld's work.
23. See the extensive discussions by Marcel Bernos, *Les Sacrements dans la France des xviie–xviiie siècles. Pastorale et vécu des fidèles* (Aix-en-Provence, 2007), Ch. 1, 'Des Sources maltraitées pour l'époque moderne. Manuels de confessions de recueils de cas de conscience' (first published in *Revue d'Histoire de l'Église de France*, 86 (2000), 479–92). This volume reprints eight other essays by this author on the literature and practice of the sacrament of penance. See also Robin Briggs, 'The Science of Sin: Jacques de Sainte-Beuve and His *Cas de Conscience*' in Nigel Aston, ed., *Religious Change in Europe 1650–1914* (Oxford, 1997), 23–40, for shrewd comments on this literature.
24. See Haliczer, *Sexuality in the Confessional*, Chs 2–3, and Sarah T. Nalle, 'Inquisitors, Priests and People During the Catholic Reformation in Spain', *Sixteenth-Century Journal*, 18 (1987), 557–87.

25. As quoted by Gregory Goudot, 'Capucins et Récollets à Montaigut-en-Combraille (vers 1620–vers 1660). Fondations franciscaines et enjeux socio-politiques', *Revue Mabillon*, new series, 17 (2006), 185–208, at 192.
26. See Ch. 13.
27. Sauvageon, *Mémoires*, xii, lxxxxv.
28. On missions and their impact, see the next chapter.
29. Delumeau, *L'Aveu et le pardon*, 27–8, quoting Eudes.
30. Bossy, *Peace in the Post-Reformation*, for European comparisons, starting with Italy.
31. Studies of liturgical history for this period are scattered and patchy. Restif, *La Révolution des paroisses*, Ch. 6, has valuable material. In general, see McManners, *Church and Society*, ii, Ch. 23, 'Liturgical Worship', which has forays back into the seventeenth century; Bernard Chédozeau, *La Bible et la liturgie en français: L'Église tridentine et les traductions bibliques et liturgiques, 1600–1789* (Paris, 1990), discusses the mass from the perspective of biblical translations and the use of the vernacular; Venard, ed., *Histoire du christianisme*, viii, 949–50; ix, 905–6. A key analysis is John Bossy's wide-ranging, 'The Mass as a Social Institution 1200–1700', *Past and Present*, 100 (1983), 29–61.
32. See Virginia Reinburg, 'Liturgy and the Laity in Late Medieval and Reformation France', *Sixteenth-Century Journal*, 23 (1992), 526–47, for sixteenth-century reformers' efforts at rejecting earlier practices; Audisio, *Croyants*, 204.
33. For one example see Sauvageon, *Mémoires*, xli–ii, who roundly condemns his parishioners and churchwardens for spending money on building a gallery, which only produced 'tumult' and distraction during religious services, rather than on buying sacred objects for those services.
34. Bossy, 'Mass as a Social Institution', 59.
35. Audisio, *Croyants*, 204–5.
36. Bernhard et al., *Époque de la Réforme*, 212–302. For the medieval heritage and context, Jean Gaudemet, *Le Mariage en Occident. Les mœurs et le droit* (Paris, 1987) and James A. Brundage, *Law, Sex and Christian Society in Medieval Europe* (Chicago, 1987), whose account includes the Council of Trent.
37. Gaudemet, *Mariage en Occident*, Ch. 12, *passim*. Pontchartrain quoted at 325–6.
38. See the sparkling essay by Robin Briggs, 'The Church and the Family in Seventeeth-Century France' in Briggs, *Communities of Belief* (Oxford, 1989), 235–76.
39. François Lebrun, *La Vie conjugale sous l'ancien régime* (Paris, 1975), 20–21; Audisio, *Croyants*, 53.
40. Audisio, *Croyants*, 222–3.
41. See Alain Lottin, *Lille, citadelle de la Contre-Réforme? (1598–1668)* (Westhoek, 1984), 218–19, for the bishop of Tournai's efforts to introduce these French ways after Louis XIV's conquest of Flanders.
42. Briggs, 'Church and Family', 258.
43. André Burguière, 'Le Rituel du mariage en France: pratiques ecclésiastiques et pratiques populaires (xvie–xviiie siècle)', *Annales ESC*, 33 (1978), 637–49, which is not confined to a discussion of 'superstitions'; Briggs, 'Church and Family', 244–5.
44. Marcel Bernos, 'L'Extrême Onction à l'époque moderne: Onction des malades ou démarche pénitentielle pour les mourants?' in Bernos, *Les Sacrements*, 267–76, for a concise analysis of the major questions about the sacrament.
45. Viguerie, *Catholicisme des Français*, 318–19.
46. Pierre Chaunu, *La Mort à Paris, xvie, xviie, xviiie siècles* (Paris, 1978), 231. In Ch. 1, Chaunu also summarised much of the existing historiography of death and dying.
47. Michel Vovelle, *Piété baroque et déchristianisation en Provence au xviiie siècle* (Paris, 1973) pioneered the study of wills in France, albeit for a later period. Among more recent studies that cover earlier periods, see Marc Bouyssou, *Réforme catholique et déchristianisation dans le sud du diocèse de Chartres xvie–xviiie siècle*, 2 vols (Chartres, 1998).

452 NOTES to pp. 273-83

48. Chaunu, *Mort à Paris*, pt iii, summarises this tradition. See also Philippe Ariès, *L'Homme devant la mort* (Paris, 1977) and Michel Vovelle, *La Mort et l'Occident de 1300 à nos jours* (Paris, 1983). John McManners, *Death and the Enlightenment* (Oxford, 1985), esp. Chs 7–8, surveys changing practices and beliefs during a period closer to this book.
49. Henri-Jean Martin, *Livre, pouvoirs et société à Paris au xviie siècle*, 2 vols (Paris, 1969), ii, 787.
50. Marie-Hélène Froeschlé-Chopard, *Dieu pour tous et Dieu pour soi. Histoire des confréries et de leurs images à l'époque moderne* (Paris, 2006), for the confraternities and death; see also the discussion of confraternies below, Ch. 14.
51. See McManners, *Death and the Enlightenment*, Chs 9–10; id., *Church and Society*, ii, 35–8.
52. Serge Brunet, 'Les Prêtres des campagnes', 59ff.
53. Croix, *Age d'or de la Bretagne*, 387–91, 502–3.

Chapter 12: Religion Taught and Learned

1. See the influential work of Gerald Strauss, *Luther's House of Learning: Indoctrination of the Young in the German Reformation* (Baltimore, MD, 1978), which generated a long-running debate about 'success and failure' in the Reformation.
2. *Canons and Decrees of Trent*, ed. Schroeder, 26, *sessio* V, Ch. 2 *de reformatione*.
3. Louis Le Gendre, *Mémoires*, ed. M. Roux (Paris, 1863), 8–22. See the work by A. Hurel, *Les Orateurs sacrés à la cour de Louis XIV* (Paris, 1872), which studies several episcopal preachers of the period.
4. For the longer history of preaching see Hervé Martin, Le *Métier de prédicateur en France septentrionale à la fin du Moyen-âge (1350–1520)* (Paris, 1988). The most valuable studies of sixteenth-century preaching are by Larissa J. Taylor, *Soldiers of Christ: Preaching in Late Medieval and Reformation France* (Oxford, 1992) and *Heresy and Orthodoxy in Sixteenth-Century Paris: François Le Picart and the Beginnings of the Catholic Reformation* (Leiden, 1999). See also her essay, 'Dangerous Vocations: Preaching in France in the Late Middle Ages and the Reformations' in Taylor, ed., *Preachers and People in the Reformations and Early Modern Period* (Leiden, 2001), 91–124 (with bibliography).
5. Marc Venard, 'Le Prédicateur de carême, semeur d'idées réformées' in Ilya Zinguer and Myriam Yardeni, eds, *Les Deux Réformes chrétiennes: propagation et diffusion* (Leiden, 2004), 60–73, ranges more widely than its title suggests; id., 'Du Carême à la mission' in Christian Sorrel and Frédéric Meyer, eds, *Les Missions intérieures en France et en Italie, du xive siècle au xxe siècle* (Chambéry, 2001), 9–18.
6. Venard, 'Du Carême à la mission', 9–13.
7. Isabelle Brian,'Prêcher à Paris de la Fronde aux Lumières' in *Être parisien* (Paris, 2004), 333–49.
8. Dominique Dinet, 'Quelle Place pour les missions en Bourgogne et en Champagne aux xviie et xviiie siècles?', in Sorrel and Meyer, eds, *Les Missions intérieures en France et en Italie*, 126.
9. Audisio, *Croyants*, 144.
10. Sauvageon, *Mémoires*, lxxxvi.
11. Thomas Worcester, 'Bishop Jean-Pierre Camus and the Christianisation of Rural France' in *La Christianisation des campagnes*, 2 vols (Brussels, 1996), i, 350–1.
12. J-B. Séguy, 'Langue, religion et société: Alain de Solminihac et l'application de la réforme tridentine dans le diocese de Cahors (1636–1659)', *Annales de l'Institut d'Estudis Occitans*, 5e sér. 1 (1977), 79–110.
13. Venard, 'Du Carême à la mission', 15–18.

14. Louis Châtellier, 'De L'Instruction à la conversion. La Prédication en question après le concile de Trente' in Matthieu Arnold, ed., *Annoncer l'Évangile* (Paris, 2006), 182–92.
15. The literature on missions is extensive, and the subject has received renewed attention from historians eager to advance beyond the stereotypes of 'heroic' missionaries. Châtellier, *Religion of the Poor*, is the most wide-ranging and original synthesis. Dominique Deslandres, *Croire et faire croire. Les Missions françaises au xviie siècle 1600–1650* (Paris, 2003), with a copious bibliography, emphasises the interaction of France's foreign and domestic missions. Venard, ed., *Histoire du christianisme*, ix, 310–35, for a Europe-wide synthesis by Bernard Dompnier. McManners, *Church and Society*, ii, 25, includes earlier material in his account of eighteenth-century missions. Recent essays include Sorrel and Meyer, eds, *Les Missions intérieures en France et en Italie, du xvie siècle au xxe siècle*; 'Les Frontières de la mission' in *Mélanges de l'École Française de Rome: Italie et Méditerranée*, 109 (1997), 485–792.
16. Berthelot du Chesnay, *Les Missions de saint Jean Eudes*, an important early contribution to the historiographical renewal of the subject.
17. Deslandres, *Croire et Faire Croire*, 32; Bernard Dompnier, 'La Compagnie de Jésus et la mission de l'intérieur', in Luce Girard and Louis de Vaucelles, eds, *Les Jésuites à l'age baroque 1540–1640* (Grenoble, 1996), 155–79, at 164ff.
18. Châtellier, *Europe of the Devout*, 25ff.; Dompnier, 'La Compagnie de Jésus et la mission de l'intérieur', 155–79; id., 'La France du premier xviie siècle et les frontières de la mission', in *Mélanges de l'École Française* 109 (1997), 621–52, esp. 633ff; id., 'Le Premier Apostolat des Capucins de la province de Lyon', *Revue d'Histoire de l'Église de France*, 75 (1989), 125–36; id., 'Les Missions des Capucins et leur empreinte sur la réforme catholique en France', 127–47.
19. Ferté, *Vie religieuse des campagnes parisiennes*, 199; Bernard Dompnier, 'Le Diable et les missionaires des xviie et xviiie siècles' in Sorrel and Meyer, eds, *Missions intérieures en France et en Italie*, 233–46.
20. See Ch. 5 above.
21. Ferté, *Vie religieuse des campagnes parisiennes*, 207, n. 68.
22. Nicole Lemaitre, 'Un Prédicateur et son public. Les Sermons du père Lejeune et le Limousin 1653–1672', *Revue d'Histoire Moderne et Contemporaine*, 30 (1982), 33–65.
23. Yves Krumenacker, 'La Mission dans l'Oratoire de France au xviie siècle' in Sorrel and Meyer, eds, *Missions intérieures en France et en Italie*, 73–86.
24. See the successive maps of missionary activity throughout France from 1600 to 1650 in Deslandres, *Croire et faire croire*, 34–40 and the commentary on them, 32–3. For the impact of the new orders/congregations from the perspective of one diocese, Paris, see Ferté, *Vie religieuse des campagnes parisiennes*, 202–23.
25. Ferté, *Vie religieuse des campagnes parisiennes*, 206.
26. See the extensive letter-report published by François Lebrun, 'Une Mission à Brissac en 1707' in Lebrun, *Croyances et cultures*, 23–42, at pp. 36–42.
27. Report quoted by Deregnaucourt and Poton, *Vie religieuse en France*, 104.
28. Bernard Dompnier, 'Les Missionaires, les pénitents et la vie religieuse aux xviie et xviiie siècles (à partir des exemples des diocèses de Grenoble, Valence et Die)' in *Les Confréries de pénitents (Dauphiné-Provence)* (Valence, 1988), 139–59, at 140ff.
29. Châtellier, *Religion of the Poor*, 24–5; Berthelot du Chesnay, *Missions de Saint Jean Eudes*, 3–7.
30. Berthelot du Chesnay, *Missions de Saint Jean Eudes*, 8.
31. Châtellier, *Religion of the Poor*, 52–9; Pérouas, *La Rochelle*, 309–37, for Fénelon in context.
32. Krumenacker, 'La Mission dans l'Oratoire', 82–4.
33. Dinet, 'Quelle place pour les missions?', 118–19.
34. Ferté, *Vie religieuse des campagnes parisiennes*, 202; Bernard Dompnier, 'Missions et confession au xviie siècle' in *Pratiques de la confession*, 206–7; id., 'La France du premier

xviie siècle et les frontières de la mission', 645; Dinet, 'Quelle place pour les missions?', 118.
35. Deslandres, *Croire et faire croire*, 32ff.; Dompnier, 'La France du premier xviie siècle', 642ff.
36. Dompnier, 'La Compagnie de Jésus et la mission de l'intérieur', 178–9.
37. Luria, *Territories of Grace*, 46.
38. Ferté, *Vie religieuse des campagnes parisiennes*, 223–6; Krumenacker, 'La Mission dans l'Oratoire', 82.
39. Ferté, *Vie religieuse*, 198.
40. Châtellier, *Religion of the Poor*, 37–40.
41. Dinet, 'Quelle place pour les missions?', 122–3.
42. François Lebrun, 'Les Missions des lazaristes en Haute-Bretagne au xviie siècle' in Lebrun, *Croyances et cultures*, 43–73.
43. Lebrun, 'Une Mission à Brissac en 1707', in ibid., 23–42.
44. Deslandres, *Croire et faire croire*, Ch. 10.
45. Quoted by Dompnier, 'Missions et confession', 216.
46. Dompnier, 'Les Missionaires, les pénitents et la vie religieuse', 154.
47. Dinet, 'Quelle Place pour les missions?', 119ff., raises some of these questions.
48. As suggested by Dompnier, 'La France du premier xviie siècle', 632.
49. Quoted in Venard, ed., *Histoire du christianisme*, ix, 313.
50. On what follows, see Nicole Lemaitre, 'Le Catéchisme, avant les catéchismes, dans les rituels' and Marc Venard, 'La fonction catéchétique des statuts synodaux', both in Pierre Colin et al., eds, *Aux Origines du catéchisme en France* (Tournai, 1989), 28–44, 45–54 respectively.
51. The most extensive account is that of Jean-Claude Dhotel, *Les Origines du catéchisme moderne d'après les premiers manuels imprimés en France* (Paris, 1967). See also Venard, ed., *Histoire du christianisme*, viii, 957–63.
52. Jean de Viguerie, 'Les Catéchismes enseignés en France au xviiie siècle, première approche', *Revue d'Histoire de l'Église de France*, 82 (1996), 85–108, at 86, n. 5; Guy Bedouelle, 'L'Influence des catéchismes de Canisius en France' in Colin et al., *Aux Origines du catéchisme*, 67–82.
53. Robert Sauzet, 'Les Résistances au catéchisme au xviie siècle' in Colin et al., *Aux Origines du catéchisme*, 208–13, at 208.
54. Jean Joncheray, 'L'Instruction du chrétien de Richelieu: prône ou catéchisme?' in Colin et al., *Aux Origines du catéchisme*, 229–45.
55. An informative diocesan case study of this in Pérouas, *La Rochelle*, 272–9.
56. *Catéchismes diocésains de la France d'ancien régime conservés dans les bibliothèques françaises*, ed. Antoine Monaque (Paris, 2002), 15; Venard, ed., *Histoire du christianisme*, ix, 340–41.
57. Dhotel, *Origines du catéchisme moderne*, 279–84; Ferté, *Vie religieuse*, 237–9; Dominique Julia, 'La Leçon de catéchisme dans *l'Escolle Paroissiale* (1654)' in Colin et al., *Aux Origines du catéchisme*, 161–83, on the catechetical experiments at St Nicholas.
58. *Catéchismes diocésains*, 66–71(Bourges), 143–50 (Paris).
59. Venard, 'Avant-propos' in *Catéchismes diocésains*, 13.
60. Marie-Hélène Froeschlé-Chopard and Michel Froeschlé, *Atlas de la réforme Pastorale en France de 1550 à 1790* (Paris 1986), 200–1; Hayden and Greenshields, *600 Years of reform*, 91, 132, 134–5, 142.
61. McManners, *Church and Society*, ii, 12. *Catéchismes diocésains*, 40 (Angers), 145 (Paris). Harlay's catechism had nineteen chapters on religious controversies.
62. *Catéchismes diocésains*, 170–78 (Sens), 111–31 (Montpellier).
63. Marcel Bernos, 'Le Catéchèse des filles par les femmes aux xviie et xviiie siècles' in Jean Delumeau, ed., *La Religion de ma mère* (Paris 1992), 277, notes that the eighteenth-

century Ursulines produced their own catechism in response to the changes of catechism occasioned by the Jansenist conflict in dioceses where they had convents.
64. Sauzet, 'Résistances au catéchisme' in Colin et al., *Aux Origines du catéchisme*, 208–13, for a brief survey.
65. Quoted by Jean-Marie Gouesse, 'Ad Utilitatem populi: catéchisme et remaniement des églises: deux "augmentations du culte divin" dans le diocèse de Coutances au xviie siècle', *Revue du Département de la Manche*, 24 (1982), 67–8 (italics mine). Gouesse notes similar foundations in Coutances around this time.
66. Gouesse, 'Ad Utilitatem populi', 68; Ferté, *Vie religieuse*, 232–6; Venard, ed., *Histoire du christianisme*, ix, 336–7.
67. *Catéchismes diocésains*, 103.
68. Ferté, *Vie religieuse*, 234.
69. Pérouas, *La Rochelle*, 426–7.
70. McManners, *Church and Society*, ii, 10.
71. Chartier, Compère and Julia, *Éducation en France*, Ch. 1, 'L'École au village'.
72. Viguerie, *Institution des enfants*, 64–6; Venard, ed., *Histoire du christianisme*, ix, 343–4.
73. Chartier et al., *Éducation en France*, 13–16.
74. Ferté, *Vie religieuse*, 242–3.
75. See above, p. 118; Venard, ed., *Histoire du christianisme*, ix, 346.
76. The following passages draw on Chartier et al., *Éducation en France*, Ch. 8, 'L'Éducation des filles' 233–47; Viguerie, *Institution des enfants*, Ch. 2; Delumeau, ed., *Religion de ma mere* (esp. essays by Bernos, 'Catéchèse des filles par les femmes aux xviie et xviiie siècles' 269–85, and Louis Châtellier, 'Le Premiers Catéchistes des temps modernes, confrères et consoeurs de la Doctrine chrétienne, 287–99); Venard, ed., *Histoire du christianisme*, ix, 345–7.
77. Venard, ed., *Histoire du christianisme*, ix, 337–8.
78. Bernos, 'Catéchèse des filles par les femmes', 270–71.
79. See Ch. 6.
80. Robert, 'De La Dentelle et des âmes', 245–67.
81. Quoted by Chartier et al., *Éducation en France*, 238.
82. For the overall scale of schooling for girls in one diocese, see Ferté, *Vie religieuse*, 252–64.

Chapter 13: The Forms and Uses of Spirituality

1. Jacques Le Brun, *La Spiritualité de Bossuet* (Paris, 1972), 666.
2. Lucien Febvre, 'Aspects méconnus d'un renouveau religieux en France entre 1590 et 1620', *Annales ESC* (1958), 639–50.
3. Works which provide the historical context for this chapter include: Venard, ed., *Histoire du christianisme*, viii, pt 3, Ch. 3 (Venard); ix, pt 4, Ch. 1 (R. Bertrand); *Dictionnaire de spiritualité*, v (Paris, 1963) (article 'France', by Jacques Le Brun), cols 917–53; Louis Cognet, *La Spiritualité moderne. L'Essor 1500–1650* (Paris, 1966); Martin, *Livre, pouvoirs et société*; Michel de Certeau, *Le Lieu de l'autre: histoire religieuse et mystique* (selected essays) (Paris, 2005).
4. Gigliola Fragnito, *La Bibbia al rogo. La censura ecclesiastica e i volgarizzamenti della Scrittura (1471–1605)* (Bologna, 1997), is not just concerned with Italy. Its last chapter is entitled, 'The Destruction of the Holy Book'. See Julia, 'Reading and the Counter-Reformation', 243–5.
5. Denis Pallier, 'Les Réponses catholiques' in Henri-Jean Martin and Roger Chartier, eds, *Histoire de l'édition française*, i (Paris, 1982), 327–47.
6. Ibid., 334; Dagens, *Bérulle et les origines de la restauration catholique*, 103–9.
7. Martin, *Livre, pouvoirs et société*, i, 135–8; Charles Chesneau, *Le Père Yves de Paris et son temps*, 2 vols (Paris, 1946); Pierre, *Le Père Joseph*.
8. Châtellier, *Europe of the Devout*, pts 1–2.

9. Certeau, *Le Lieu de l'autre*, 155–65 ('La Réforme de l'intérieur au temps d'Aquaviva'); Dominique Salin, 'La Spiritualité de la compagnie de Jésus en France au début du xviie siècle' in *Henri IV et les Jésuites* (La Flèche, 2006), 41–7.
10. The subject has attracted numerous historians since Brémond. Among the most influential and prolific have been Jean Orcibal, Michel de Certeau, Jacques Le Brun and Daniel Vidal (see bibliography under their names).
11. Dominique Salin, 'L'Invasion mystique en France au xviie siècle' in Henri Laux and Dominique Salin, eds, *Dieu au xviie siècle, crises et renouvellements* (Paris, 2003), 244–7.
12. The literature on Bérulle is voluminous. Apart from Henri Brémond, *Histoire littéraire du sentiment religieux en France depuis la fin des guerres de religion jusqu'à nos jours*, 11 vols (Paris, 1916–36), this account is derived largely from Cognet, *Essor*; Dagens, *Bérulle et les origines de la restauration catholique*; Krumenacker, *École française de spiritualité*; Venard, ed., *Histoire du christianisme*, ix, 839–43.
13. Krumenacker, *École française de spiritualité*, Chs 4, 6–8, devotes considerable space to this evolution.
14. The bibliography on de Sales is enormous, but notably uneven in quality. Cognet, *Essor* is the best modern survey. See also Michael J. Buckley, 'Seventeenth-Century French Spirituality: Three Figures' in Louis Dupré and Don E. Saliers, eds, *Christian Spirituality, Post-Reformation and Modern* (London, 1990), 32–41; Venard, ed., *Histoire du christianisme*, viii, 1011–14.
15. Quoted by Cognet, *Essor*, 284.
16. Ibid., 412ff.; Certeau, *Le Lieu de l'autre*, 170–71.
17. The literature on this subject is scattered rather than voluminous. See Charles Berthelot du Chesnay, 'La Spiritualité des laïcs', *XVIIe Siècle*, 62–3 (1964), 30–46; M-C. Guedré, 'La Femme et la vie spirituelle', ibid., 47–77.
18. Nicolas Le Roux, 'La Religion des courtisans dans la France de la Renaissance' in Klaus Malettke and Chantal Grell, eds, *Hofgesellschaft und Höflinge an europäischen Fürstenhöfen in der frühen Neuzeit*, (Münster, 2001), 507–24; Marcel Bernos, 'Les Nobles d'ancien régime face à leur conscience' in Chantal Grell and Arnaud Ramière de Fortanier, eds, *Le Second Ordre* (Versailles, 1999), 141–50.
19. Elfrieda Dubois, 'Le Père Le Moyne et la dévotion aisée' in *Les Jésuites parmi les hommes aux xvie et xviie siècles* (Clermont-Ferrand, 1988), 153–62.
20. Volker Kapp, 'La Théologie des réalités terrestres dans la *Cour Sainte* de N. Caussin', ibid., 142–51; Cognet, *Essor*, 440–2.
21. René Taveneaux, *Le Catholicisme dans la France classique*, 2 vols (Paris, 2nd edn, 1994), ii, 424–6.
22. Cognet, *Essor*, 442–5.
23. McManners, *Death and the Enlightenment*, 221.
24. Martin, *Livre, pouvoirs et société*, ii, 787, n. 55.
25. This discussion is based mainly on Agnès Walch, *La Spiritualité conjugale dans le catholicisme français, xvie–xxe siècles* (Paris, 2002) and her *Histoire du couple en France* (Rennes, 2003); Bernos, *Les Sacrements dans la France des xviie–xviiie siècles*, Chs 13–15.
26. Cognet, *Essor*, 495.
27. Ibid., 445–52; Certeau, *Le Lieu de l'autre*, 175.
28. Buckley, 'Seventeenth-Century French Spirituality: Three Figures', 53–63. Buckley rebuts the charge that Lallemant was banned outright from teaching by his nervous superiors.
29. Certeau, *Le Lieu de l'autre*, 183–4.
30. René de Voyer d'Argenson, *Annales de la compagnie du saint-sacrement*, ed. H. Beauchet-Filleau (Paris, 1900), 36–7.
31. Certeau, *Le Lieu de l'autre*, 268ff.
32. This account relies mainly on Louis Cognet, *Le Crépuscule des mystiques* (Paris, 1958); Jean-Robert Armogathe, *Le Quiétisme* (Paris, 1973); Fénelon, *Œuvres* (La Pléiade), ed. Jacques Le Brun, 2 vols (Paris 1983–92), i, 1001–1199, 1530–49.

33. Denis Richet, 'Fénelon contre Bossuet: la querelle du quiétisme' in Richet, *De la Réforme à la Révolution* (Paris, 1991), 136.
34. Julia, 'Reading and the Counter-Reformation', 248–9.
35. For example, the two parts of Cognet's *Essor* are entitled 'Spanish Preponderance' and 'French Preponderance'.
36. Henri-Jean Martin, ed., *Histoire de l'édition française*, i, 379–403.
37. *Livre, pouvoirs et société à Paris au xviie siècle*, 2 vols.
38. Martin, *Histoire de l'édition française*, ii, 177ff.
39. Julia, 'Reading and the Counter-Reformation', 268.
40. Giovanni Dotoli, 'La Religion dans la bibliothèque bleue au xviie siècle' in *La Pensée religieuse dans la littérature et la civilisation du xviie siècle en France*, ed. Manfred Tietz and Volker Kapp (Tübingen, 1984), 271–97, at 272–5.
41. Suire, *La Sainteté française de la Réforme catholique*, Ch. 1.
42. Marc Venard, 'Les Martyrs catholiques des affontements religieux du xvie siècle, d'après l'*Histoire Catholique* du père Hilarion de Coste (1625)', in Jürgen Beyer et al., eds, *Confessional Sanctity (c.1500–1800)*, (Mainz, 2003), 85.
43. Jacques Le Brun, 'La Sainteté à l'époque classique et le problème de l'autorisation' in Beyer et al., eds, *Confessional Sanctity*, 152.

Chapter 14: The Many Faces of the Confraternities

1. Gabriel Le Bras, 'Les Confréries chrétiennes: problèmes et méthodes', *Revue Historique du Droit Français et Étranger*, 4e sér., 19–20 (1940–41), 310–63 (reprinted in Le Bras, *Études de sociologie religieuse*, 2 vols (Paris 1956), ii, 423–62); Maurice Agulhon, *Pénitents et franc-maçons de l'ancienne Provence* (Paris, 1968).
2. The historiography of medieval confraternities is enormous. The most valuable synthesis is Catherine Vincent, *Les Confréries médiévales dans le royaume de France* (Paris, 1994); see also Froeschlé-Chopard, *Dieu pour tous*, Ch. 1.
3. R. N. Swanson, *Religion and Devotion in Europe, c.1215–c.1515* (Cambridge, 1995), 116ff., discusses these definitional problems; also helpful is Christopher Black, *Italian Confraternities in the Sixteenth Century* (Cambridge, 1989), Ch. 2, 'Confraternities: What, Where, For Whom?'
4. Marc Venard, 'Si On Parlait Des Confréries de métiers' in Venard and Julia, eds, *Sacralités, culture et dévotion*, 211–38, for an extensive discussion which brings out the extent to which the northern *métiers* acquired more religious dimensions in the fifteenth and early sixteenth centuries. See also Lottin, *Lille, citadelle de la Contre-Réforme?*, 271–3; McManners, *Church and Society*, ii, 159–64.
5. Catherine Vincent, *Des Charités bien ordonnées. Les Confréries normandes de la fin du xiiie siècle au début du xviie siècle* (Paris, 1988); Froeschlé-Chopard, *Dieu pour tous*, 35–40; Goujard, *Un Catholicisme bien tempéré*, Ch. 5.
6. Bonzon, 'Faire Corps face aux pouvoirs', 689–703; Croix, ed., *Les Bretons et dieu*, fiche 26 (G. Minois); McManners, *Church and Society*, ii, 181–8; Jean-Claude Meyer, 'La Réforme spirituelle du clergé. L'Aa de Toulouse', *Bulletin de Littérature Ecclésiastique*, 101 (2000), 149–80.
7. Luria, *Territories of Grace*, 32–3; Antoine Follain, 'Charités et communautés rurales en Normandie' in Claude Langlois and Philippe Goujard, eds, *Les Confréries du Moyen Âge à nos jours* (Rouen, 1995), 83–91; Marie-Hélène Froeschlé-Chopard and Roger Devos, 'Confréries et communautés d'habitants en Savoie et en Provence' in *Sociabilité, pouvoirs et société* (Rouen, 1987), 457–72.
8. The best discussion of this is by Marc Venard, 'Qu'est-ce Qu'une Confrérie de dévotion?' in Venard, *Catholicisme à l'épreuve au xvie siècle*, 237–48.
9. Philippe Goujard, *La Normandie aux xvie et xviie siècles* (Rennes, 2002), 103.

10. Froeschlé-Chopard, *Dieu pour tous*, Ch. 1 (vi); André Vauchez, *The Laity in the Middle Ages* (Notre Dame, IN, 1993), Ch. 10, 'Medieval Penitents'; Venard, ed., *Histoire du christianisme*, viii, 977–8; McManners, *Church and Society*, ii, 171ff.
11. François-Xavier Emmanuelli et al., *La Provence moderne 1481–1800* (Rennes, 1991), 230.
12. Andrew E. Barnes, *The Social Dimension of Piety* (New York, 1994), 12–18 and 248–64.
13. For what follows, Marc Venard, 'La Crise des confréries au xvie siècle' in id., *Catholicisme à l'épreuve*, 249–68; id., ed., *Histoire du christianisme*, viii, 976–9; Stefano Simiz, *Confréries urbaines et dévotion en Champagne (1450–1830)* (Lille, 2001), 118–20; Goujard, *Un Catholicisme bien tempéré*, 119–20.
14. Venard, 'Crise des confréries', 259.
15. Ibid., 264–5.
16. See Prologue, pp. 10–12.
17. Benedict, 'Catholic Response to Protestantism', 168–90.
18. See above, p.10.
19. Harding, 'Mobilization', 92.
20. Froeschlé-Chopard, *Dieu pour tous*, 104–11.
21. See the essays on confraternities during the Catholic League by Andrew E. Barnes, Ann W. Ramsey and Christopher W. Stocker in John P. Donnelly and Michael W. Maher, eds, *Confraternities and Catholic reform in Italy, France and Spain* (Sixteenth-Century Essays and Studies, xliv) (n. p., 1999), 123–89; Andrew E. Barnes, 'The Wars of Religion and the Origins of Reformed Confraternities of Penitents: A Theoretical Approach', *Archives de Sciences Sociales des Religions*, 64 (1987), 117–36; id., 'Religious Anxiety and Devotional Change in Sixteenth-Century French Penitential Confraternities', *Sixteenth-Century Journal*, 19 (1988), 389–405; Venard, ed., *Histoire du christianisme*, viii, 980–81.
22. Venard, 'Crise des confréries', 264–5.
23. Barnes, 'Religious Anxiety and Devotional Change', 391, 393–6.
24. Venard, 'Crise des confréries', 265–6; Goujard, *Un Catholicisme bien tempéré*, 134.
25. Froeschlé-Chopard, *Atlas de la réforme catholique*, 66–7, 196–7.
26. Venard, 'Crise des confréries', 250.
27. See the comments of Dinet, *Réguliers et société*, ii, 745; in one part of Normandy, Goujard found that the approval of statutes was already a feature of the years 1640–89: *Un Catholicisme bien tempéré*, 121–2.
28. Froeschlé-Chopard, *Dieu pour tous*, 155–60.
29. Hoffman, *Church and Community*, 107.
30. See Simiz, *Confréries urbaines*, 168ff., 'Le Triomphe de la paroisse après 1660'.
31. Barnes, 'Wars of Religion and Reformed Penitents', 123–4 and n. 3.
32. Both quotations taken from Michel Bée, 'Les Confréries de Vimoutiers aux xviie et xviiie siècles' in *Revue du Département de la Manche*, 24 (1982), 126 and 125 respectively; Goujard, *Un Catholicisme bien tempéré*, 134.
33. Goujard, *Un Catholicisme bien tempéré*, 119, 134.
34. Venard, 'Qu'est-ce Qu'une Confrérie de dévotion?', 241ff.
35. Froeschlé-Chopard, *Dieu pour tous*, 130–31; Barnes, 'Religious Anxiety and Devotional Change', 393–4, 405.
36. Simiz, *Confréries urbaines*, 166–8; Michel Cassan, 'Confréries et ordres religieux dans les combats confessionnels des xvie–xviie siècles', in *Les Mouvances laïques des ordres religieux* (Saint-Étienne, 1996), 320–21.
37. Cassan, 'Confréries et ordres religieux', 322–3.
38. Froeschlé-Chopard, *Dieu pour tous*, 168–9.
39. The standard account is Châtellier, *Europe of the Devout*, Chs 1–2.
40. In addition to Châtellier, see Michael W. Maher, 'How the Jesuits Used Their Congregations to Promote Frequent Communion' in Donnelly and Maher, eds, *Confraternities and Catholic Reform*, 75–95.

41. Dinet, *Réguliers et vie Régionale*, ii, 750.
42. Goujard, *La Normandie aux xvie et xviie siècles*, 238; Deregnaucourt and Poton, *Vie religieuse en France*, 98.
43. Dinet, *Réguliers et société*, ii, 739, 749–50.
44. The following passages owe much to Froeschlé-Chopard, *Dieu pour tous*, Ch. 2 (i), 3 (ii), 6(i), the most comprehensive account of its development.
45. A. D. Wright, 'Bérulle and Olier: Christ and the Blessed Virgin Mary', in R. N. Swanson, ed., *The Church and Mary (Studies in Church History*, 39) (Woodbridge, Suffolk, 2006), 271–9.
46. In addition to Froeschlé-Chopard, *Dieu pour tous*, Louis Pérouas, 'La Diffusion de la confrérie du Rosaire au xviie siècle dans les pays creusois' in Pérouas, *Culte des saints et anticléricalisme: entre statistique et culture populaire* (Ussel, 2002), 77–92; Restif, *Révolution des paroisses*, 180ff.
47. Pérouas, 'La Diffusion', 90.
48. Froeschlé-Chopard, *Dieu pour tous*, Ch. 2 (ii) and esp. 5 for the most extensive account.
49. Bernard Dompnier, 'Un Aspect de la dévotion eucharistique dans la France du xviie siècle: les prières des Quarante-Heures', *Revue d'Histoire de l'Église de France*, 67 (1981), 5–31.
50. Pérouas, 'La Diffusion', 91.
51. Quoted by Stefano Simiz, 'Les Confréries de Champagne du Nord, entre héritage et modernité, xviie–xviiie siècles' in Langlois and Goujard, eds, *Les Confréries du Moyen Âge à nos jours* (Rouen, 1995), 70.
52. Froeschlé-Chopard, *Dieu pour tous*, Chs 8–9; ead., 'La Dévotion au Sacré-Coeur: confréries et livres de piété', *Revue de l'Histoire des Religions*, 217 (2000), 531–46.
53. McManners, *Church and Society*, ii, 168–71.
54. Françoise Hernandez, 'Les Confréries de l'agonie de Jésus et des Agonisants à la lumière de leurs livrets et manuels', *Siècles*, 12 (2000), 29–56; Froeschlé-Chopard, *Dieu pour tous*, esp. Ch. 6 (ii–iv); Simiz, *Confréries urbaines*, 235–7; Lebrun, *Les Hommes et la mort en Anjou*, 457–8.
55. Marie-Hélène Froeschlé-Chopard and Françoise Hernandez, 'Les Dévotions des confréries, reflet de l'influence des ordres religieux?', *Dimensioni e Problemi della Ricerca Storica*, 10 (1994), 104–25, for a discussion based on Roman archival sources; Dompnier, 'Ordres, diffusion des dévotions et sensibilités religieuses', 21–59, for a rich, wide-ranging survey.
56. Bernard Dompnier, 'Réseaux de confréries et réseaux de dévotions' in *Siècles*, 12 (2000), 9–29.
57. Froeschlé-Chopard, *Dieu pour tous*, Chs 2 (ii), 4 (iv).
58. Emmanuelli et al., *Provence moderne*, 235–6.
59. Froeschlé-Chopard, *Dieu pour tous*, 162ff.
60. Agulhon, *Pénitents et francs-maçons*, Ch. 13, 'Géographie de la sociabilité méridionale', esp. 338–42.
61. Froeschlé-Chopard, *Dieu pour tous*, 127.
62. Cassan, 'Confréries et ordres religieux', 317.
63. Louis Pérouas, 'Les Confréries de pénitents au xviie siècle dans les petites agglomérations de la Marche et du Limousin' in id., *Culte des saints et anticléricalisme*, 225–49.
64. Cassan, 'Confréries et orders religieux', 321.
65. Emmanuelli et al., *Provence moderne*, 232–3.
66. See Barnes, *The Social Dimension of Piety*, for a study of the reformed Penitents of Marseille.
67. Bernard Dompnier, 'Les Confréries du diocèse de Grenoble d'après les visites pastorales (1665–1757) in *Les Confrèries, l'église et la cité*, 39–54; Hoffman, *Church and Community*, 111–12; Emmanuelli et al., *Provence moderne*, 239.

460 NOTES to pp. 361–73

68. Luria, *Territories of Grace*, 32ff., for Le Camus; for the other reactions, Agulhon, *Pénitents et francs-maçons*, 124–8; McManners, *Church and Society*, ii, 179.
69. Michel Bée, 'Religion, culture et société: les confréries en Normandie, xviie–xxe siècles', *Histoire, Économie, Société*, 11 (1992), 277–93, at 278.
70. Viguerie, *Catholicisme des français*, 162.
71. Michel Vovelle, 'Géographie des confréries des pénitents à l'époque moderne' in *Les Confréries de penitents (Dauphiné-Provence)* (Valence, 1988), 17–33, for an attempt at such mapping.
72. Simiz, *Confréries urbaines*, 251ff.
73. Froeschlé-Chopard, *Dieu pour tous*, 149–55.
74. Sauvageon, *Mémoires*, xiv, xli (where he denounces the Rosary as a superstition!); Bouchard, *Village immobile*, 306–9.
75. Hoffman, *Church and Community*, 109–10; Froeschlé-Chopard, *Dieu pour tous*, Ch. 4 (i, v).
76. James R. Farr, *Hands of Honor. Artisans and Their World in Dijon, 1550–1650* (Ithaca, NY, 1988), 250–1.
77. Dompnier, 'Les Confréries de Grenoble', 42–3.
78. Follain, 'Charités et communautés rurales en Normandie', 88.
79. Natalie Zemon Davis, 'The Reasons of misrule' in Davis, *Society and Culture in Early Modern France* (Stanford, 1975), 97–123; Jean-Pierre Gutton, 'Reinages, abbayes de jeunesse et confréries dans les villages de l'ancienne France', *Cahiers d'Histoire*, 4 (1975), 443–53; id., *Sociabilité villageoise*, 231–4; Hoffman, *Church and Community*, 111–12; Cynthia M. Truant, *The Rites of Labor. Brotherhoods of Compagnonnage in Old and New Régime France* (Ithaca, NY, 1994), Ch. 2, for the hostility to the *compagnonnages*.
80. Goujard, *Un Catholicisme bien tempéré*, 136–7.

Chapter 15: *Dévots*: the Pious and the Militant

1. Marguerite Pecquet, 'Des Compagnies de pénitents à la compagnie du Saint-Sacrement', *XVIIe Siècle*, 69 (1965), 3–36.
2. Barbara Diefendorf, 'An Age of gold? Parisian women, the Holy League and the roots of Catholic renewal' in Michael Wolfe, ed., *Changing Identities in Early Modern France* (Chapel Hill, NC, 1996), 171.
3. Sedgwick, *Travails of Conscience*.
4. Schneider, *Public Life in Toulouse*, 225.
5. Châtellier, *Europe of the Devout*.
6. The major study here is Diefendorf, *Penitence to Charity*.
7. In addition to Diefendorf, see Dinan, *Women and Poor Relief in Seventeenth-Century France*.
8. Nelson, *The Jesuits and the Monarchy*, esp. Chs 2–3.
9. Briggs, 'Richelieu and Reform: Rhetoric and Political Reality', 97.
10. The following sections rely mainly on Argenson, *Annales*; Raoul Allier, *La Cabale des dévots* (Paris, 1904); Alfred Rebelliau, 'La Compagnie du Saint-Sacrement' (six articles), *Revue des Deux Mondes*, 5 séries, 16 (1903), 49–82, 540–63; 17 (1903), 103–35; 46 (1908), 834–68; 53 (1909) 892–923; 54 (1909), 200–8; Emmanuel Chill, 'The Company of the Holy Sacrament 1630–1666' (PhD dissertation, Columbia University, 1960); Orest Ranum, *Paris in the Age of Absolutism*, 2nd edn (University Park, PA, 2002); Pillorget, *Paris sous les premiers Bourbons*; Alain Tallon, *La Compagnie du saint-sacrement, spiritualité et société* (Paris 1991); Jacques Depauw, *Spiritualité et pauvreté à Paris au xviie siècle* (Paris, 1999); Jean-Pierre Gutton, *Dévots et société* (Paris, 2004). Numerous local studies (e.g., Norberg, schneider, Restif, Hoffman) have also been utilised.

11. Argenson, *Annales*, 25.
12. Ibid., 196 (italics mine).
13. Restif, *Révolution des paroisses*, 159–67.
14. Argenson, *Annales*, 20.
15. Tallon, *Compagnie du saint-sacrement*, 168–71.
16. Argenson, *Annales*, 112.
17. Michel Foucault, *Folie et déraison à l'âge classique* (Paris, 1961).
18. See Gutton, *Dévots et société*, 65ff.
19. Argenson, *Annales*, 143.
20. Daniel Dessert, *Fouquet* (Paris, 1987), 47ff.
21. Jean-Claude Dubé, *Les Intendants de la Nouvelle France* (Montreal, 1984) for their social history; Deslandres, *Croire et faire croire*, for the missionary *elan* of the first half of the century.
22. Argenson, *Annales*, 22.
23. Allier, *Cabale des dévots*, 431–5.
24. François-Xavier Cuche, *Une Pensée sociale catholique. Fleury, La Bruyère, Fénelon* (Paris, 1991).
25. Gutton, *Dévots et société*, Ch. 4.
26. Ibid., 43ff.
27. *Correspondance de Fénelon*, ed. Jean Orcibal et al., i (Jean Orcibal, 'Fénelon et Sa Famille'), 65–7.
28. E. Albe, 'La Confrérie de la passion (contribution à l'étude de la compagnie du Saint-Sacrement)', *Revue d'Histoire de l'Église de France*, 3 (1912), 644–70.
29. Stuart Carroll, *Blood and Violence in Early Modern France* (Oxford, 2006), 315–16, 318; François Billacois, *Le Duel dans la société française des xvie et xviie siècles* (Paris, 1986), 290–92.
30. Gutton, *Dévots et société*, 47ff.
31. Ibid., 171–2.
32. Kathryn Norberg, *Rich and Poor in Grenoble 1600–1820* (Los Angeles, 1985), 83.
33. Catherine Martin, *Les Compagnies de la propagation de la foi (1632–1685)* (Geneva, 2000), for an exhaustive study.
34. Jean-Pierre Gutton, 'Enfermement et charité au xviie siècle', *Histoire, Économie, Société*, 10 (1991), 356.
35. See Châtellier, *Europe of the Devout*, 71ff.; McManners, *Church and Society*, 181–4; Meyer, 'La Réforme spirituelle du clergé: l'Aa de Toulouse', 149–80.
36. Loupès, *Apogée du catholicisme bordelais*, 153–6.

Chapter 16: Jansenists: Dissidents but Also Militants

1. Robin Briggs, 'Catholic Puritans', in Briggs, *Communities of Belief*, Ch. 8.
2. The literature on the subject is immense. For a brief 'Critical Bibliography of Studies of French Jansenism' (to c.1990), see Catherine Maire, 'Port-Royal' in Pierre Nora, ed., *Realms of Memory*, i (New York, 1996), 344–8. Also useful is the bibliography (with comments) in William Doyle, *Jansenism* (Houndmills, 2000), 96–104.
3. A. D. Wright, *The Counter-Reformation* (London, 1982), 15ff.; Alexander Sedgwick, *Jansenism in Seventeenth-Century France* (Charlottesville, VA, 1977), Ch. 1.
4. Wright, *The Counter-Reformation*, esp. Chs 1, 2, 6; Bruno Neveu, *Érudition et religion au xviie siècle* (Paris, 1994), includes four essays discussing the place of Augustinianism in seventeenth-century Catholicism; Jean-Louis Quantin, *Le Catholicisme classique et les pères de l'église. Un retour aux sources (1669–1713)* (Paris 1999).
5. L. W. B. Brockliss, *French Higher Education in the Seventeenth and Eighteenth Centuries* (Oxford, 1987), Ch. 5; Nelson, *The Jesuits and the French Monarchy*, passim.

6. The most complete studies are those of Orcibal, *Saint-Cyran*; id., *Jansénius d'Ypres (1585–1638)* (Paris 1989).
7. Orcibal, *Saint-Cyran*, pt ii.
8. In addition to Orcibal, see Sedgwick, *Travails of Conscience*, Chs 4–5.
9. Cognet, *Essor*, Ch. 12, 'Le Premier Port-Royal'.
10. Sedgwick, *Travails of Conscience*, Ch. 7, 'Le *Grand Arnauld* and the origins of Jansenism'.
11. Françoise Hildesheimer, 'Richelieu et le jansénisme, ou ce que l'attrition veut dire' in Hartmut Lehmann et al., eds, *Jansenismus, Quietismus, Pietismus* (Göttingen, 2002), 11–39.
12. Sedgwick, *Travails of Conscience*, Ch. 5; René Taveneaux, *La Vie quotidienne des jansénistes* (Paris, 1973), Ch. 3.
13. Briggs, 'The Science of Sin', 23–40. Jean-Louis Quantin, *Le Rigorisme chrétien* (Paris, 2001).
14. Quantin, *Rigorisme chrétien*, 54.
15. Quoted by Jean-Louis Quantin, 'Le Rigorisme: sur le basculement de la théologie morale catholique au xviie siècle', *Revue d'Histoire de l'Église de France*, 89 (2003), 26–7.
16. See Blet, *Le Clergé de France et la monarchie*, ii, 175–220; Jacques Grès-Gayer, *Le Jansénisme en Sorbonne 1643–1656* (Paris, 1996), esp. Ch. 3.
17. Pierre Blet, 'Louis XIV et les papes aux prises avec le jansénisme', *Archivum Historiae Pontificiae*, 31 (1993), 109–92; 32 (1994), 65–148; P. Dieudonné, *La Paix clémentine 1667–9* (Leuven, 2003).
18. Jean-Louis Quantin, 'De la Rigueur au rigorisme: les *Avvertenze ai confessori* de Charles Borromée dans la France du xviie siècle', *Studia Borromaica*, 20 (2006), 195–251, the most thorough study of the subject. See also Briggs, 'Catholic Puritans', 349–50.
19. What follows is based mainly on Marvin R. O'Connell, *Pascal* (Grand Rapids, MI, 1997), Ch. 7; Golden, *The Godly Rebellion*, esp. Ch. 4.
20. Sedgwick, *Travails of Conscience*, Chs 8–9.
21. Quantin, *Rigorisme chrétien*, Ch. 3, for an extensive discussion of this period.
22. Pierre Blet, *Le Clergé de France, Louis XIV et le Saint-Siège de 1695 à 1715* (Vatican City, 1989), 134–8; J. Grès-Gayer, *D'Un Jansénisme à l'autre. Chroniques de Sorbonne 1696–1713* (Paris, 2007), Ch. 2.
23. Jean-Pascal Gay, 'Laxisme et rigorisme: théologies ou cultures?', *Revue des Sciences Philosophiques et Théologiques*, 87 (2003), 525–48, esp. 545ff.
24. For what follows, see Quantin, *Catholicisme classique, passim*.
25. Venard, ed., *Histoire du christianisme*, ix, pt ii, Ch. 2 (iv) (Monique Cottret); Blet, '*Clergé de France, Louis XIV et le Saint-Siège*', pts ii–iii.
26. See also Dale K. Van Kley, *The Religious Origins of the French Revolution* (New Haven and London, 1996), Chs 1–2.
27. Quoted by Monique Cottret, *Culture et politique dans la France des Lumières* (Paris, 2002), 29.
28. Pérouas, *Culte des saints et anticléricalisme*, 70.
29. Julia, 'Reading and the Counter-Reformation', 243–9.
30. These passages are based on Julia, 'Reading' 243ff., Chedozeau, *La Bible et la liturgie*, Ch. 3; McManners, *Church and Society*, ii, 43–4; Linda Timmermans, *L'Accès des femmes à la culture sous l'ancien régime* (Paris, 2005), 702ff.
31. Quoted by Timmermans, *L'Accès des femmes à la culture*, 703.
32. Chedozeau, *La Bible et la liturgie*, 117–37; Grès-Gayer, *Le Gallicanisme de Sorbonne*, 53–65; McManners, *Church and Society*, ii, 44–5.
33. Blet, *Le Clergé de France et la monarchie*, ii, 292–300.
34. Ferté, *Vie religieuse*, 278–80. Parts of the 'ordinary' of the mass had been translated prior to 1701.
35. McManners, *Church and Society*, ii, 429–31.

36. McManners, *Church and Society*, ii, 429; Michel, *Jansénisme et Paris*, 285ff.; Monique Cottret, *Jansénismes et lumières* (Paris, 1998), 244ff.
37. Bernard Groethuysen, *The Bourgeois: Catholicism Versus Capitalism in Eighteenth-Century France* (Engl. trans., London, 1968); Lucien Goldman, *Le Dieu caché* (Paris, 1964).
38. See Bergin, *Crown, Church and Episcopate*, 218–23.
39. Pierre Chaunu et al., eds, *Le Basculement religieux de Paris au xviiie siècle* (Paris, 1998), 153–240, 'Au Temps de Noailles et de Vintimille'.
40. René Taveneaux, *Le Jansénisme en Lorraine (1640–1789)* (Paris, 1960), several chapters of which deal with the Benedictines and other orders.
41. This discussion is based on Dominique Dinet and Marie-Claude Dinet-Lecomte, 'Les Appelants contre la bulle *Unigenitus* d'après Gabriel-Nicolas Nivelle', *Histoire, Économie, Société*, 9 (1990), 365–89, maps at 386–9. See also McManners, *Church and Society*, ii, Ch. 37, p. 388ff., Dominique Julia, 'Le Catholicisme, religion du royaume' in *Histoire de la France religieuse*, iii, 19–21; Deregnaucourt and Poton, *Vie religieuse*, 175–7.
42. Sedgwick, *Travails of Conscience*, Ch. 5; Taveneaux, *Vie quotidienne des jansénistes*, Ch. 3.
43. Michel, *Jansénisme et Paris*, esp. pt 2.
44. The most extensive discussion of the question, seen in a wider context of women and religion generally, is in Timmermans, *L'Accès des femmes à la culture*, pt ii, section c, Chs 6–7.
45. Sedgwick, *Travails of Conscience*, Chs 9, 11.
46. F. Ellen Weaver, *Madame de Fontpertuis: une dévote janséniste, amie et gérante d'Antoine Arnauld et de Port-Royal* (Paris, 1998); ead., *Mademoiselle de Joncoux: polémique janséniste à la veille de la bulle* Unigenitus (Paris, 2002).
47. David Garrioch, *The Formation of Parisian Bourgeoisie 1670–1830* (Cambridge, MA, 1996), 46.
48. Albert N. Hamscher, 'The Parlement of Paris and the Social Interpretation of Early Jansenism', *Catholic Historical Review*, 63 (1977), 392–410; Golden, *Godly Rebellion*, Ch. 4.
49. Venard, ed., *Histoire du christianisme*, ix, 404 (Monique Cottret).
50. Lebrun, *Les Hommes et la mort en Anjou*, 414, n. 108.

Conclusion

1. The origin of this discussion was the essay by Gerald Strauss, 'Success and Failure in the German Reformation', *Past and Present*, 67 (1975), 30–63, and continued by Geoffrey Parker, 'Success and Failure in the First Hundred Years of the European Reformation', ibid., 136 (1992), 43–82.
2. The most influential contributor has been John W. O'Malley, *Trent and All That. Renaming Catholicism in the Early Modern Era* (Cambridge, MA, 2000).
3. Jacques Solé, *Les Origines intellectuelles de la révocation de l'édit de Nantes* (Saint-Étienne, 1997), 100.
4. Quantin, *Catholicisme classique*, 489–92.
5. Dompnier, 'Les Hommes d'église et la superstition', 13–47.
6. Quoted in Briggs, *Communities of Belief*, 377.
7. Sauvageon, *Mémoires*, xiv, xli.
8. Françoise Waquet, *Le Modèle français et l'Italie savante (1660–1750)* (Rome, 1989), Ch. 3, esp. 178ff.; see the similar verdict of Beales, *Prosperity and Plunder*, 89–90.
9. Neveu, *Érudition et religion*, Ch. 4.
10. C. C. Noel, 'Clerics and crown in Bourbon Spain' in John Bradley and Dale van Kley, eds, *Religion and Politics in Enlightenment Europe*, (Notre Dame, IN 2001), 119–153.

11. See the comparisons by Nigel Aston, 'Continental Catholic Europe' in Stewart J. Brown and Timothy Tackett, eds, *Enlightenment, Reawakening and Revolution 1660–1815* (*The Cambridge History of Christianity*, vii) (Cambridge, 2006), Ch. 1.
12. Rosa, *Clero cattolico e società*, for an excellent comparative survey.
13. Marc Forster, *Catholic Germany from the Reformation to the Enlightenment* (Houndmills, 2007), which summarises his earlier interpretations of the nature of German Catholicism.
14. Marc Venard, *Réforme protestante, réforme catholique dans la province d'Avignon au xvie siècle* (Paris, 1993), 1127.
15. Pierre Chaunu, 'Jansénisme et frontière de catholicité', *Revue Historique*, 227 (1962), 115–38, esp. at 122–3.
16. See Timothy Tackett, *Religion, Revolution and Religious Culture in Eighteenth-Century France*, 205–25, esp. 224–5.

BIBLIOGRAPHY

Adam, Antoine, *Du Mysticisme à la révolte. Les Jansénistes du xviie siècle*, Paris, 1968
Agulhon, Maurice, *Pénitents et franc-maçons de l'ancienne Provence*, Paris 1968
Albe, E., 'La Confrérie de la passion (contribution à l'étude de la compagnie du Saint-Sacrement)', *Revue d'Histoire de l'Église de France*, 3 (1912), 644–70
Allier, Raoul, *La Cabale des dévots*, Paris, 1904
Anatole, Charles, 'La Réforme tridentine et l'emploi de l'occitan dans la pastorale', *Revue des Langues Romanes*, 77 (1967), 1–29
Argenson, René de Voyer d', *Annales de la compagnie du saint-sacrement*, ed. H Beauchet-Filleau, Paris 1900
Ariès, Philippe, *L'Homme devant la mort*, Paris, 1977
——, and Duby, Georges, eds, *History of Private Life*, 5 vols, Cambridge, MA, 1987–91
Armogathe, Jean-Robert, *Le Quiétisme*, Paris, 1973
Aston, Nigel, 'Continental Catholic Europe' in Stewart J. Brown and Timothy Tackett, eds, *Enlightenment, Reawakening and Revolution 1660–1815* (*The Cambridge History of Christianity*, vii) (Cambridge, 2006), 15–32
Atlas de la Révolution française, ix, *La Religion*, ed. Claude Langlois et al., Paris, 1996
Audisio, Gabriel, *Les Français d'hier. Des Croyants, xve–xixe siècles*, Paris 1996
Baccrabère, Georges, 'La Pratique religieuse dans le diocèse de Toulouse aux xvie–xviie siècles', *Annales du Midi* (1962), 287–314
Barnes, Andrew E., 'The Wars of Religion and the Origins of Reformed Confraternities of Penitents: A Theoretical Approach', *Archives de Sciences Sociales des Religions*, 64 (1987), 117–36
——, 'Religious Anxiety and Devotional Change in Sixteenth-Century French Penitential Confraternities', *Sixteenth-Century Journal*, 19 (1988), 389–405
——, 'The Social Transformation of the French Parish Clergy 1500–1800' in Barbara Diefendorf and Carla Hesse, eds, *Culture and Identity in Early Modern Europe* (Ann Arbor, 1993) 139–58
——, *The Social Dimension of Piety*, New York, 1994
Bayard, Françoise and Guignet, Philippe, *L'Économie française aux xvie–xviiie siècles*, Paris, 1991
Beales, Derek, *Prosperity and Plunder. European Catholic Monasteries in the Age of Revolution 1650–1815*, Cambridge, 2003
Bedouelle, Guy, 'L'Influence des catéchismes de Canisius en France' in Pierre Colin et al., eds, *Aux Origines du catéchisme*, 67–82

466 BIBLIOGRAPHY

Bée, Michel, 'Les Confréries de Vimoutiers aux xviie et xviiie siècles', *Revue du Département de la Manche*, 24 (1982), 119–40
——, 'Religion, culture et société: les confréries en Normandie, xviie–xxe siècles', *Histoire, Économie, Société*, 11 (1992), 277–93
Benedict, Philip, 'The Catholic Response to Protestantism. Church Activity and Popular Piety in Rouen 1560–1600', in James Obelkevich, ed., *Religion and the People 800–1700* (Chapel Hill, NC, 1979), 168–90
——, *Rouen During the Wars of Religion*, Cambridge, 1981
Bergin, Joseph, *Cardinal Richelieu. Power and the Pursuit of Wealth*, New Haven, 1985
——, 'Ways and Means of Monastic Reform in Seventeenth-Century France: The Example of St Denis de Reims 1630–3', *Catholic Historical Review*, 72 (1986), 14–32
——, 'Cardinal Mazarin and His Benefices', *French History*, 1 (1987), 3–26
——, *Cardinal de la Rochefoucauld. Leadership and Reform in the French Church*, New Haven, 1987
——, *The Rise of Richelieu*, New Haven and London, 1991
——, 'Between Estate and Profession: The Catholic Parish Clergy of Early Modern Western Europe' in M. L. Bush, ed., *Social Orders and Social Classes in Europe Since 1500* (London, 1992), 66–85
——, *French Bishops: The Making of the French Episcopate 1589–1661*, New Haven and London, 1996
——, 'The Counter-Reformation Church and its Bishops', *Past and Present*, no. 165 (1999), 30–73
——, 'The Place of Seminaries and Colleges in Clerical Education in 17th-Century France', *Zeitschrift fur Historische Forschung* (*Beiheft*, vol. 28, Im Spannungsfeld von Staat und Kirche [2003]), 297–311
——, *Crown, Church and Episcopate Under Louis XIV*, New Haven and London, 2004
——, 'The King's Confessor and his Rivals in Seventeenth-Century France', *French History*, 21 (2007), 187–204
—— and Laurence Brockliss, eds, *Richelieu and His Age*, Oxford, 1992
Bernhard, Jean et al., *L'Époque de la Réforme et du concile de Trente*, Paris, 1990
Bernos, Marcel, 'Un Ordre italien en France à l'époque moderne: les Servites de Marie' in *Échanges religieux entre la France et l'Italie du moyen age à l'époque moderne* (Geneva, 1987), 173–91
——, 'Le Catéchèse des filles par les femmes aux xviie et xviiie siècles', in Jean Delumeau, ed., *La Religion de ma mère* (Paris 1992), 269–85
——, 'Les Nobles d'ancien régime face à leur conscience' in Chantal Grell and Arnaud Ramière de Fortanier, eds, *Le Second Ordre* (Versailles, 1999), 141–50
——, 'Des Sources maltraitées pour l'époque moderne. Manuels de confessions et recueils de cas de conscience', *Revue d'Histoire de l'Église de France*, 86 (2000), 479–92
——, *Femmes et gens d'église dans la France classique*, Paris, 2003
——, 'L'Extrême Onction à l'époque moderne: onction des malades ou démarche pénitentielle pour les mourants?' in Bernos, *Les Sacrements*, 267–76
——, *Les Sacrements dans la France des xviie–xviiie siècles. Pastorale et vécu des fidèles*, Aix-en-Provence, 2007
Berthelot du Chesnay, Charles, 'La Spiritualité des laïcs', *XVIIe Siècle*, 62–3 (1964), 30–46
——, *Les Missions de Saint Jean Eudes*, Paris, 1967
——, *Les Prêtres séculiers en Haute-Bretagne au xviiie siècle*, Rennes 1984
Beyer, Jürgen et al., eds, *Confessional Sanctity (c.1500–c.1800)*, Mainz, 2003
Billacois, François, *Le Duel dans la société française des xvie et xviie siècles*, Paris, 1986
Bireley, Robert, *The Jesuits and the Thirty Years War*, Cambridge, 2002
Black, Christopher, *Italian Confraternities in the Sixteenth Century*, Cambridge, 1989
Blet, Pierre, *Le Clergé de France et la monarchie 1615–1666*, 2 vols, Rome, 1959

——, *Les Assemblées du clergé et Louis XIV de 1670 à 1693*, Rome 1972
——, *Le Clergé de France, Louis XIV et le Saint-Siège de 1695 à 1715*, Vatican City, 1989
——, 'Louis XIV et les papes aux prises avec le jansénisme', *Archivum Historiae Pontificiae*, 31 (1993), 109–92; 32 (1994), 65–148
Boer, Wietse de, *The Conquest of the Soul. Confession, Discipline and Public Order in Counter-Reformation Milan*, Leiden, 2001.
Bonnot, Isabelle, *Hérétique ou saint? Henry Arnauld, évêque janséniste d'Angers au xviie siècle*, Paris, 1984.
Bonzon, Anne, *L'Esprit de clocher. Prêtres et paroisses dans le diocèse de Beauvais 1535–1650*, Paris, 1999
——, 'Faire Corps face aux pouvoirs: les communautés de curés dans les cités épiscopales de la province ecclésiastique de Reims', *Revue du Nord*, 81 (1999), 689–703
——, 'Paroissse rêvée, paroisse vécue: le point de vue de curés citadins au temps de la Réforme catholique. L'exemple de Beauvais', *Revue du Nord*, 83 (2001), 319–39
Bossy, John, 'The Counter-Reformation and the People of Catholic Europe', *Past and Present*, 47 (1970), 51–70
——, 'The Mass as a Social Institution 1200–1700', *Past and Present*, 100 (1983), 29–61
——, *Christianity in the West*, Oxford, 1984
——, 'Godparenthood: The Fortunes of a Social Institution in Early Modern Christianity' in Kaspar von Greyerz, ed., *Religion and Society in Early Modern Europe 1500–1800* (London, 1984), 194–201
——, *Peace in the Post-Reformation*, Cambridge, 1998
Bottin, Jacques, *Seigneurs et paysans dans l'ouest du Pays de Caux, 1540–1650*, Paris, 1983
Bouchard, Gérard, *Le Village immobile. Sennely-en-Sologne au xviie siècle*, Paris, 1972
Boutier, Jean et al., *Un Tour de France royal. Le voyage de Charles IX (1564–1566)*, Paris, 1984
Boutry, Philippe and Le Hénard, Françoise, 'Pèlerins parisiens à l'age de la monarchie administrative' in Philippe Boutry, Pierre-Antoine Fabre and Dominique Julia, eds, *Rendre Ses Vœux: les identités pèlerines dans l'Europe moderne (xvie–xviiie siècle)*, (Paris, 2000), 401–37
Bouyssou, Marc, *Réforme catholique et déchristianisation dans le sud du diocèse de Chartres xvie–xviiie siècles*, 2 vols, Chartres, 1998
Bradley, John, and Van Kley, Dale K., eds, *Religion and Politics in Enlightenment Europe*, Notre Dame, IN, 2001
Brémond, Henri, *Histoire littéraire du sentiment religieux en France depuis la fin des guerres de religion jusqu'à nos jours*, 11 vols (Paris, 1916–36), (Engl. trans., *A Literary History of Religious Thought in France*, 3 vols only, London 1928–36)
Brian, Isabelle, *Messieurs de Sainte-Geneviève*, Paris, 2001
——, 'Le Roi pèlerin. Pèlerinages royaux dans la France moderne' in *Rendre ses vœux*, 363–78
——, 'Prêcher à Paris de la Fronde aux Lumières' in *Être parisien* (Fédération des Sociétés Historiques et Archéologiques de Paris et de l'Île-de-France, Mémoires, lv) (Paris, 2004), 333–49
Briggs, Robin, *Communities of Belief*, Oxford, 1989
——, 'Catholic Puritans' in Briggs, *Communities of Belief*, 339–63
——, 'The Church and the Family in Seventeeth-Century France' in Briggs, *Communities of Belief*, 235–76
——, 'Richelieu and Reform: Rhetoric and Political Reality', in Joseph Bergin and Laurence Brockliss, eds, *Richelieu and His Age* (Oxford, 1992), 71–97
——, 'The Science of Sin: Jacques de Sainte-Beuve and His *Cas de Conscience*' in Nigel Aston, ed., *Religious Change in Europe 1650–1914* (Oxford, 1997), 23–40
Brockliss, L. W. B., *French Higher Education in the Seventeenth and Eighteenth Centuries*, Oxford, 1987
Broutin, Paul, *La Réforme pastorale en France au xviie siècle*, 2 vols, Tournai, 1956

Brundage, James A., *Law, Sex and Christian Society in Medieval Europe*, Chicago, 1987
Brunet, Serge, *Les Prêtres des montagnes*, Aspet, 2001
——, 'Anatomie des réseaux ligueurs dans le sud-ouest de la France (vers 1562–vers 1610)' in Nicole Lemaitre, ed., *Religion et politique dans les sociétés du Midi* (Paris, 2002), 153–91
——, 'Jeanne d'Albret, Pierre d'Albret évêque de Comminges, et la "trahison" de Blaise de Monluc. Aux origines de la Ligue dans le sud-ouest de la France' in Evelyne Berriot-Salvador et al., eds, *Jeanne d'Albret et sa cour* (Paris, 2004), 129–68
——, ' "Confréries ligueuses, confréries dangereuses". Fraternités de combat dans le sud-ouest de la France durant les guerres de religion' in Marc Venard and Dominique Julia, eds, *Sacralités, culture et dévotion* (Marseille, 2005), 129–70
——, 'Les Prêtres des campagnes de la France du xviie siècle: la grande mutation', *XVII Siècle*, 59 (2007), 49–82
——, '*De l'Espagnol dans le ventre*. Les catholiques du sud-ouest de la France face à la Réforme, vers 1540–1589*, Paris, 2007
——, and Lemaitre, Nicole, eds, *Clergés, communautés et familles des montagnes d'Europe*, Paris, 2005
Buckley, Michael J., 'Seventeenth-Century French Spirituality: Three Figures' in Louis Dupré and Don E. Saliers, eds, *Christian Spirituality, Post-Reformation and Modern* (London, 1990), 28–68
Burguière, André, 'Le Rituel du mariage en France: pratiques ecclésiastiques et pratiques populaires (xvie–xviiie siècle)', *Annales ESC*, 33 (1978), 637–49
Burke, Peter, 'How to be a Counter-Reformation Saint' in Burke, *Historical Anthropology of Early Modern Italy* (Cambridge, 1987), 48–62
Cabantous, Alain, *Entre Fêtes et clochers. Profane et sacré dans l'Europe moderne, xviie–xviiie siècle*, Paris, 2002
Canons and Decrees of the Council of Trent, ed. H. J. Schroder, St Louis, 1941
Carrière, Victor, ed., *Introduction aux études d'histoire ecclésiastique locale*, 3 vols, Paris, 1934–40
——, 'Les Épreuves de l'église de France au xvie siècle' in Carrière, ed., *Introduction aux études d'histoire ecclésiastique locale*, 3 vols, (Paris, 1934–40), iii, 247–509
Carroll, Stuart, *Blood and Violence in Early Modern France*, Oxford, 2006
Cassan, Michel, 'Laïcs, ligue et réforme catholique à Limoges', *Histoire, Économie, Société*, 10 (1991), 159–75
——, *Le Temps des guerres de religion. Le Cas du Limousin (vers 1530–vers 1630)*, Paris, 1996
——, 'Confréries et ordres religieux dans les combats confessionnels des xvie–xviie siècles' in *Les Mouvances laïques des ordres religieux* (Saint-Étienne, 1996), 301–23
Catéchismes diocésains de la France d'ancien régime conservés dans les bibliothèques françaises, ed. Antoine Monaque (Paris, 2002)
Certeau, Michel de, *Le Lieu de l'autre: histoire religieuse et mystique* (selected essays), Paris, 2005
Chadwick, Owen, *The Popes and the European Revolution*, Oxford, 1981
Chaix, Gérald, ed., *Le Diocèse: espaces, représentations, pouvoirs. France xve–xxe siècles*, Paris, 2002
Chartier, Roger, Julia, Dominique and Compère, Marie-Madeleine, *L'Éducation en France, xvie–xviiie siècles*, Paris, 1976
Charvin, Guy, 'L'Abbaye et l'ordre de Cluny de la mort de Richelieu à l'élection de Mazarin, 1642–1654', *Revue Mabillon*, 33 (1943), 85–114
——, 'L'Abbaye et l'ordre de Cluny sous l'abbatiat de Mazarin, 1654–1661', *Revue Mabillon*, 34–35 (1944–5), 20–81
Châtellier, Louis, 'Societé et bénéfices ecclésiastiques. Le cas alsacien', *Revue Historique* 224 (1970), 75–98
——, *Tradition chrétienne et renouveau catholique dans l'ancien diocèse de Strasbourg*, Strasbourg–Paris, 1981

——, *Europe of the Devout*, Cambridge, 1989
——, 'Le Premiers Catéchistes des temps modernes, confrères et consoeurs de la Doctrine chrétienne' in Delumeau, Jean, ed., *La Religion de ma mère*, 287–99
——, *Le Catholicisme en France 1500–1650*, 2 vols, Paris, 1995
——, *The Religion of the Poor*, Cambridge, 1997
——, 'De L'Instruction à la conversion. La Prédication en question après le concile de Trente' in Matthieu Arnold, ed., *Annoncer l'Évangile* (Paris, 2006), 182–92
Chaunu, Pierre, 'Jansénisme et frontières de catholicité', *Revue Historique*, 127 (1962), 115–38
——, *La Mort à Paris, xvie, xviie, xviiie siècles*, Paris, 1978
——, Foisil, Madeleine and Noirfontaine, Françoise de, *Le Basculement religieux de Paris au xviiie siècle*, Paris, 1998
Chédozeau, Bernard, *La Bible et la liturgie en français: l'Église tridentine et les traductions bibliques et liturgiques, 1600–1789*, Paris, 1990
——, *Choeur clos, choeur ouvert. De l'église médiévale à l'église tridentine (France, xviie–xviiie siècle)*, Paris, 1998
——, 'La Congrégation de Saint-Maur et le renouveau architectural du monachisme dans les abbayes du Bas-Languedoc', *Revue Mabillon*, new series, 13 (2002), 67–87
Chélini, Jean and Branthomme, Henry eds, *Les Chemins de Dieu. Histoire des pèlerinages chrétiens des origines à nos jours*, Paris, 1982
Chesneau, Charles, *Le Père Yves de Paris et son temps*, 2 vols, Paris, 1946
Chill, Emmanuel, 'The Company of the Holy Sacrament 1630–1666', PhD dissertation, Columbia University, 1960
Christin, Olivier, *Une Révolution symbolique: l'iconoclasme huguenot et la reconstruction catholique*, Paris, 1991
——, *La Paix de religion. L'autonomisation de la raison politique au xvie siècle*, Paris, 1997
Cognet, Louis, *La Réforme de Port-Royal 1591–1618*, Paris, 1950
——, *Le Crépuscule des mystiques*, Paris, 1958
——, *Le Jansénisme*, Paris, 1961
——, *La Spiritualité moderne: I. L'essor: 1500–1650*, Paris, 1966
Colin, Pierre, ed., *Aux Origines du catéchisme*, Paris, 1989
Cornette, Joël, 'Les Nobles et la foi du siècle des réformes au siècle de l'absolutisme', in *Société, culture et vie religieuse aux xvie et xviie siècles* (Paris, 1995), 139–96
Correspondance de Fénelon, ed. Jean Orcibal, Jacques Le Brun and Irénée Noye, 18 vols, Paris, 1972–2007
Correspondance du nonce en France Gasparo Silingardi évêque de Modène (1599–1601), ed. Bertrand Haan, Rome, 2002
Cottret, Monique, *Jansénismes et lumières*, Paris, 1998
——, *Culture et politique dans la France des Lumières*, Paris, 2002
Couton, Georges, *La Vieillesse de Corneille 1658–1684*, Paris, 1949
Croix, Alain, *La Bretagne aux xvie et xviie siècles. La vie, la mort, la foi*, 2 vols, Paris, 1983
——, *L'Age d'or de la Bretagne 1532–1675*, Rennes, 1993
——, ed., *Les Bretons et Dieu. Atlas d'histoire religieuse 1300–1800*, Rennes, n.d.
Crouzet, Denis, 'Recherches sur les processions blanches, 1583–4', *Histoire, Économie, Société*, 4 (1982), 511–63
——, *Les Guerriers de Dieu. La Violence au temps des troubles de religion (vers 1525–vers 1610)*, 2 vols, Seyssel, 1990
Cuche, François-Xavier, *Une Pensée sociale catholique. Fleury, La Bruyère, Fénelon*, Paris, 1991
Dagens, Jean, *Bérulle et les origines de la restauration catholique 1575–1611*, Paris, 1952
Dainville-Barbiche, Ségolène de, *Devenir curé à Paris. Institutions et carrières ecclésiastiques (1695–1789)*, Paris, 2005
Davies, Joan, 'Neither Politique Nor Patriot? Henri I, Duc de Montmorency and Philip II, 1582–1589', *Historical Journal*, 34 (1991), 539–66

Davies, Joan, 'The Montmorencys and the Abbey of Sainte Trinité, Caen: Politics, Profit and Reform', *Journal of Ecclesiastical History*, 53 (2002), 665–85
Davis, Natalie Zemon, 'The Reasons of Misrule' in Davis, *Society and Culture in Early Modern France* (Stanford, 1975), 97–123
Degert, Antoine, *Histoire des séminaires français*, 2 vols, Paris, 1912
Delattre, Pierre, 'La Compagnie de Jésus et les séminaires en France', *Revue d'Ascétique et de Mystique*, 20 (1953), 20–44, 160–76
Delumeau, Jean, *Catholicism between Luther and Voltaire*, Engl. trans., London, 1977
——, ed., *La Première Communion*, Paris, 1987
——, *L'Aveu et le pardon. Les difficultés de la confession, xiiie–xviiie siècle*, Paris, 1990
——, ed., *La Religion de ma mère: les femmes et la transmission de la foi*, Paris, 1992
Denis, Paul, *Richelieu et la réforme des monastères bénédictins*, Paris, 1912
De Paul, Vincent, *Correspondance, entretiens et documents*, ed. Pierre Coste, 14 vols, Paris 1920–23
Depauw, Jacques, *Spiritualité et pauvreté à Paris au xviie siècle*, Paris, 1999
Deregnaucourt, Gilles, 'Le Concours pour l'accès aux cures dans les anciens diocèses du Nord de la France (16–18 siècles)' in *Croire dans le passé. Études sur la vie religieuse dans les temps modernes offertes au professeur Michel Cloët* (Louvain, 1996), 111–29
—— and Poton, Didier, *La Vie religieuse en France aux xvie, xviie, xviiie siècles*, Paris, 1994
Descimon, Robert and Ruiz Ibàñez, José Javier, *Les Ligueurs de l'exil*, Seyssel, 2005
Deslandres, Dominique, *Croire et faire croire. Les Missions françaises au xviie siècle 1600–1650*, Paris, 2003
Dessert, Daniel, *Fouquet*, Paris, 1987
Deyon, Pierre, *Amiens capitale provinciale au xviie siècle*, Paris, 1967
Dhotel, Jean-Claude, *Les Origines du catéchisme moderne d'après les premiers manuels imprimés en France*, Paris, 1967
Diefendorf, Barbara, 'An Age of Gold? Parisian Women, the Holy League and the Roots of Catholic Renewal' in Michael Wolfe, ed., *Changing Identities in Early Modern France* (Chapel Hill, NC, 1996), 169–90
——, 'Give Us Back Our Children: Patriarchal Authority and Parental Consent to Religious Vocations in Early Counter-Reformation France', *Journal of Modern History*, 68 (1996), 265–307
——, 'Contradictions of the Century of Saints: Aristocratic Patronage and the Convents of Counter-Reformation Paris', *French Historical Studies*, 24 (2001), 471–500
——, *From Penitence to Charity. Pious Women and the Catholic Reformation in Paris*, Oxford, 2004
Dieudonné, P., *La Paix clémentine 1667–9*, Leuven, 2003
Dinan, Susan E., *Women and Poor Relief in Seventeenth-Century France: The Early History of the Daughters of Charity*, Aldershot, 2006
Dinet, Dominique, *Vocation et fidélité. Le Recrutement des réguliers dans les diocèses d'Auxerre, Langres et Dijon (xviie–xviiie siècle)*, Paris, 1988
——, 'Les Dots de religion en France aux xviie et xviiie siècles' in *Les Églises et l'argent* (Paris, 1989), 37–65
——, 'Les Religieuses des diocèses d'Auxerre, Langres, et Dijon: vie contemplative et action séculière (aux xviie et xviiie siècles)' in *Les Religieuses dans le cloître et dans le monde* (Saint-Étienne, 1994), 851–69
——, *Religion et société: réguliers et vie régionale dans les diocèses d'Auxerre, Langres et Dijon (fin xvie–fin xviiie siècles)*, 2 vols, Paris, 1999
——, 'Les Grands Domaines des réguliers en France (1560–1790): une relative stabilité?', *Revue Mabillon*, new series, 10 (1999), 257–69
——, 'Une Institution méconnue: la commende' in Jean-Pierre Bardet et al., eds, *État et société en France aux xviie et xviiie siècles* (Paris, 2000), 195–208

——, 'Quelle Place pour les missions en Bourgogne et en Champagne aux xviie et xviiie siècles?' in Christian Sorrel and Frédéric Meyer, eds, *Les Missions intérieures en France et en Italie du xvie au xxe siècle* (Chambéry, 2001), 117–31

——, 'L'Évolution de l'institution de la commende dans l'espace religieux des xviie et xviiie siècles' in Giles Constable and Michel Rouche, eds, *Auctoritas* (Paris, 2006), 727–39

Dinet, Dominique and Dinet-Lecomte, Marie-Claude, 'Les Appelants contre la bulle *Unigenitus* d'après Gabriel-Nicolas Nivelle', *Histoire, Économie, Société*, 9 (1990), 365–89

Dinet-Lecomte, Marie-Claude, 'Implantation et rayonnement des congrégations hospitalières dans le sud de la France aux xviie et xviiie siècles', *Annales du Midi* (1992), 19–42

——, 'Administrateurs d'hôpitaux et religieuses hospitalières' in Jean-Pierre Gutton, ed, *Les Administrateurs d'hôpitaux dans la France de l'ancien régime* (Lyon, 1999), 147–69

——, 'L'Hôpital, un lieu d'édification et de conversion dans la France moderne' in Christian Sorrel and Frédéric Meyer, eds, *Les Missions intérieures en France et en Italie du xvie au xxe siècle* (Chambéry, 2001), 215–32

——, 'La "Cléricalisation" du personnel hospitalier en France aux xviie et xviiie siècles' in *Religion et enfermements (xviie–xxe siècles)* (Rennes, 2005), 115–29

——, *Les Sœurs hospitalières en France aux xviie et xviiie siècles: la charité en action*, Paris, 2005

Ditchfield, Simon, *Liturgy, Sanctity and History in Tridentine Italy*, Cambridge, 1995

Dolan, Claire, *Entre Tours et clochers. Les gens d'église à Aix-en-Provence au xvie siècle*, Sherbrooke, 1981

Dompnier, Bernard, 'Un Aspect de la dévotion eucharistique dans la France du xviie siècle: les prières des Quarante-Heures', *Revue d'Histoire de l'Église de France*, 67 (1981), 5–31

——, 'Missions et confession au xviie siècle' in *Pratiques de la confession* (Paris, 1983), 202–22

——, 'Les Missions des Capucins et leur empreinte sur la réforme catholique en France', *Revue d'Histoire de l'Église de France*, 70 (1984), 127–47

——, 'Les Confréries de penitents au xviie siècle: essai de définition', *Cahiers d'Histoire* 30 (1986), 263–88

——, 'Les Confréries du diocèse de Grenoble, d'après les visites pastorales (1665–1757)' in *Les Confréries, l'église et la cité* (Grenoble, 1988), 39–54

——, 'Les Missionaires, les pénitents et la vie religieuse aux xviie et xviiie siècles (à partir des exemples des diocèses de Grenoble, Valence et Die)', in *Les Confréries de pénitents (Dauphiné-Provence)* (Valence, 1988), 139–59

——, 'Le Premier Apostolat des Capucins de la province de Lyon', *Revue d'Histoire de l'Église de France*, 75 (1989), 125–36

——, *Enquête au pays des frères des anges. Les Capucins de la province de Lyon*, Saint-Étienne, 1993

——, 'Ordres, diffusion des dévotions et sensibilités religieuses. L'exemple des Capucins en France (xviie–xviiie siècles)', *Dimensioni e Problemi della Ricerca Storica*, 10 (1994), 21–59

——, 'Les Affiliations des laïcs aux communautés: tiers ordres et réseaux dévotionnels' in *Les Mouvances laïques des ordres religieux* (Saint-Étienne, 1996), 379–402

——, 'Les Jésuites et la mission de l'intérieur' in Luce Girard and Louis de Vaucelles, eds, *Les Jésuites à l'age baroque* (Grenoble, 1996), 154–79

——, 'La France du premier xviie siècle et les frontières de la mission', *Mélanges de l'École Française de Rome: Italie et Méditerranée*, 109 (1997), 621–52

——, 'Les Hommes d'église et la superstition entre xviie et xviiie siècles' in Dompnier, ed., *La Superstition à l'âge des Lumières* (Paris, 1998), 13–47

——, 'Réseaux de confréries et réseaux de dévotions', *Siècles*, 12 (2000), 9–29

——, 'Le Diable et les missionaires des xviie et xviiie siècles' in *Les Missions intérieures en France et en Italie*, 233–46

——, 'La Dévotion à Charles Borromée dans la France du xviie siècle. Représentations d'un saint et histoire de son culte', *Studia Borromaica*, 20 (2006), 253–92

Dompnier, Bernard, and Hernandez, Françoise, 'Fêtes des confréries, calendrier liturgique et dévotions (xviie et xviiie siècles)', in Venard, Marc and Julia, Dominique, eds, *Sacralités, culture et devotions* (Marseille, 2005), 171–91

Donnelly, John P., and Maher, Michael W., eds, *Confraternities and Catholic Reform in Italy, France and Spain* (*Sixteenth-Century Essays and Studies*, xliv), n.p., 1999

Dotoli, Giovanni, 'La Religion dans la bibliothèque bleue au xviie siècle' in Manfred Tietz and Volker Kapp, eds, *La Pensée religieuse dans la littérature et la civilisation du xviie siècle en France* (Tübingen, 1984), 271–97

Doyle, William, *Jansenism*, Houndmills, 2000

Dubé, Jean-Claude, *Les Intendants de la Nouvelle France*, Montreal, 1984

Dubois, Elfrieda, 'Le Père Le Moyne et la dévotion aisée' in *Les Jésuites parmi les hommes aux xvie et xviie siècles* (Clermont-Ferrand, 1988), 153–62

Duggan, L. G., 'Fear and confession on the eve of the Reformation', *Archiv für Reformationsgeschichte*, 75 (1984), 153–75

Duindam, Jeroen, *Vienna and Versailles*, Cambridge, 2003

Dupront, Alphonse, *Du Sacré. Croisades et pèlerinages. Images et langages*, Paris, 1987

Durand, Yves, 'Les Prêtres habitués en France aux xviie et xviiie siècles' in André Corvisier et al., eds, *Combattre, Gouverner, Écrire*, (Paris, 2003), 369–84

Eire, Carlos, *War Against the Idols: the Reformation of Worship from Erasmus to Calvin*, Cambridge, 1986

El Hajje-Kervévan, Nicole, 'L'État moral du clergé forézien, 1650–1789', *Cahiers d'Histoire*, 30 (1985), 289–308

——, 'Sociologie du clergé forézien, 1650–1789', *Histoire, Économie, Société*, 4 (1985), 497–517

Emmanuelli, François-Xavier et al., *La Provence moderne 1481–1800*, Rennes, 1991

Farr, James R., *Hands of Honor. Artisans and Their World in Dijon, 1550–1650*, Ithaca, NY, 1988

Favier, René, *Les Villes du Dauphiné aux xviie et xviiie siècles*, Grenoble, 1993

Febvre, Lucien, 'Aspects méconnus d'un renouveau religieux en France entre 1590 et 1620', *Annales ESC* (1958), 639–50

Fénelon, François de Salignac de La Mothe, *Œuvres* (La Pléiade), ed. Jacques Le Brun, 2 vols, Paris 1983–92

Ferté, Jeanne, *La Vie religieuse dans les campagnes parisiennes (1622–1695)*, Paris, 1962

Follain, Antoine, 'Charités et communautés rurales en Normandie' in Claude Langlois and Philippe Goujard, eds, *Les Confréries du Moyen Âge à nos jours* (Rouen, 1995), 83–91

Forrestal, Alison, ' "Fathers, Leaders, Kings". Episcopacy and episcopal reform in the 17th C. French School', *The Seventeenth Century*, 17 (2002), 24–47

——, 'Making Bishops in Tridentine France: the episcopal ideal of Jean-Pierre Camus', *Journal of Ecclesiastical History*, 54 (2003), 254–77

——, *Fathers, Pastors and Kings. Visions of Episcopacy in Seventeenth-Century France*, Manchester, 2004

Forster, Marc, *Catholic Germany from the Reformation to the Enlightenment*, Houndmills, 2007

Foucault, Michel, *Folie et déraison à l'âge classique*, Paris, 1961

Fragnito, Gigliola, *La Bibbia al rogo. La censura ecclesiastica e i volgarizzamenti della Scrittura (1471–1605)*, Bologna, 1997

Froeschlé-Chopard, Marie-Hélène, *Espace et sacré en Provence (xvie–xxe siècle). Cultes, images, confréries*, Paris, 1994

——, 'Les Ordres religieux, témoins et acteurs dans les lieux de pèlerinage' in *Homo religious. Autour de Jean Delumeau* (Paris, 1996), 52–60

——, 'De L'Image protectrice à l'image enseignante. Une mutation du sentiment religieux au xviie siècle' in Olivier Christin, ed., *Crises de l'image religieuse*, (Paris, 2000), 133–56

——, 'La Dévotion au Sacré-Coeur: confréries et livres de piété', *Revue de l'Histoire des Religions*, 217 (2000), 531–46

——, *Dieu pour tous et Dieu pour soi. Histoire des confréries et de leurs images à l'époque moderne*, Paris, 2006
—— and Froeschlé, Michel, *Atlas de la réforme pastorale en France de 1550 à 1790*, Paris, 1986
—— and Devos, Roger, 'Confréries et communautés d'habitants en Savoie et en Provence' in *Sociabilité, pouvoirs et société* (Rouen, 1987), 457–72
—— and Hernandez, Françoise, 'Les Dévotions des confréries, reflet de l'influence des ordres religieux?', *Dimensioni e Problemi della Ricerca Storica*, 10 (1994), 104–25
'Frontières de la mission' in *Mélanges de l'École Française de Rome: Italie et Méditerranée*, 109 (1997), 485–792
Gallerand, Jules, 'L'Erection de l'évêché de Blois (1697)', *Revue d'Histoire de l'Église de France*, 42 (1956), 175–228
Garrioch, David, *Neighbourhood and Community in Paris 1740–1790*, Cambridge, 1986
——, *The Formation of the Parisian Bourgeoisie 1690–1830*, Cambridge, MA, 1996
——, *The Making of Revolutionary Paris*, Los Angeles, 2002
Gaudemet, Jean, *Le Mariage en Occident. Les mœurs et le droit*, Paris, 1987
Gay, Jean-Pascal, 'Laxisme et rigorisme: théologies ou cultures?', *Revue des sciences philosophiques et théologiques*, 87 (2003), 525–48
Gélis, Jacques, *L'Arbre et le fruit: la naissance dans l'Occident moderne, xvie–xixe siècle*, Paris, 1984
Gibson, Wendy, *Women in Seventeenth-Century France*, London, 1989
Godel, Jean, 'Les Visites pastorales de Le Camus: objectifs et méthode' in Jean Godel, ed., *Le Cardinal des montagnes* (Grenoble, 1974), 213–39
Golden, Richard M., *The Godly Rebellion*, Chapel Hill, NC, 1981
Goldman, Lucien, *Le Dieu caché*, Paris, 1964
Gomis, Stéphane, *Les 'Enfants prêtres' des paroisses d'Auvergne, xvie–xviiie siècles*, Clermont-Ferrand, 2006
Gotor, Miguel, *Chiesa e santità nell'Italia moderna*, Rome, 2004
Goubert, Pierre, *Beauvais et le Beauvaisis au xviie siècle*, Paris, 1958
Goubet-Mahé, Maryvonne, 'Le Premier rituel de la première communion, xvie–xviie siècle' in Jean Delumeau, *La Première Communion* (Paris, 1987), 51–76
Goudot, Gregory, 'Capucins et Récollets à Montaigut-en-Combraille (vers 1620–vers 1660). Fondations franciscaines et enjeux socio-politiques', *Revue Mabillon*, new series, 17 (2006), 185–208
Gouesse, Jean-Marie, 'Assemblées et associations cléricales, synodes et conférences ecclésiastiques dans le diocèse de Coutances aux xviie et xviiie siècles', *Annales de Normandie*, (1974), 37–71
——, 'Ad Utilitatem populi: catéchisme et remaniement des églises: deux "augmentations du culte divin" dans le diocèse de Coutances au xviie siècle', *Revue du Département de la Manche*, 24 (1982), 63–91
Goujard, Philippe, *Un Catholicisme bien tempéré. La Vie religieuse dans les paroisses rurales de Normandie 1680–1789*, Paris, 1996
——, *La Normandie aux xvie et xviie siècles*, Rennes, 2002
Gould, Kevin, *Catholic Activism in South-West France 1540–70*, Aldershot, 2006
Green, Ian M., 'Reformed Pastors and *Bons Curés*: The Changing Role of the Parish Clergy in Early Modern Europe' in W. J. Shiels and Diana Wood, eds, *Studies in Church History*, vol. 26, 249–86
Greengrass, Mark, *Governing Passions. Peace and Reform in the French Kingdom, 1576–1585*, Oxford, 2007
Greenshields, Malcolm R., 'What Happened in Quibou? The Catholic Reformation in the Village', *Proceedings of the Annual Meeting of the Western Society for French History*, 18 (1991), 80–88
Grès-Gayer, Jacques, 'The *Unigenitus* of Clement XI, A Fresh Look at the Issues', *Catholic Historical Review*, 49 (1988), 259–82

Grès-Gayer, Jacques, 'The Magisterium of the Faculty of Theology of Paris in the Seventeenth Century', *Theological Studies*, 53 (1992), 424–50
——, *Le Jansénisme en Sorbonne 1643–1656*, Paris, 1996
——, *D'un Jansénisme à l'autre. Chroniques de Sorbonne 1696–1713*, Paris, 2007
Groethuysen, Bernard, *The Bourgeois: Catholicism Versus Capitalism in Eighteenth-Century France*, Engl. trans., London, 1968
Guedré, M-C., 'La Femme et la vie spirituelle', *XVIIe Siècle*, 62–3 (1964), 47–77
Gutton, Jean-Pierre, 'Reinages, abbayes de jeunesse et confréries dans les villages de l'ancienne France', *Cahiers d'Histoire*, 4 (1975), 443–53
——, *La Sociabilité villageoise dans l'ancienne France*, Paris, 1979
——, 'Enfermement et charité au xviie siècle', *Histoire, Économie, Société*, 10 (1991), 353–7
——, *Dévots et société*, Paris, 2004
Halizcer, Stephen, *Sexuality in the confessional*, Oxford, 1996
Hamscher, Albert N., 'The Parlement of Paris and the Social Interpretation of Early Jansenism', *Catholic Historical Review*, 63 (1977), 392–410
Harding, Robert R., 'The Mobilization of Confraternities Against the Reformation in France', *Sixteenth-Century Journal*, 11 (1980), 85–107
Harding, Vanessa, *The Dead and the Living in Paris and London, 1500–1670*, Cambridge, 2002
Hayden, J. Michael, 'Social Origins of the French Episcopate in the Early 17th century', *French Historical Studies* (1977), 27–40
—— and Greenshields, Malcolm R., 'The Clergy of Early Seventeenth-Century France: Self perception and society's perception', *French Historical Studies* 18 (1993), 145–72
—— and Greenshields, Malcolm R., *600 Years of Reform. Bishops, and the French Church*, Montreal, 2005
Hernandez, Françoise, 'Les Confréries de l'agonie de Jésus et des Agonisants à la lumière de leurs livrets et manuels', *Siècles*, 12 (2000), 29–56
Hersche, Peter, 'Fest und Alltag. Das Agro-Liturgische Jahr in der Frühen Neuzeit' in Eva Kreissl, ed., *Feste Feiern* (Linz, 2002), 112–20
Hickey, Daniel, *Local Hospitals in Ancien Régime France*, Montreal, 1997
Hildesheimer, Françoise, 'Richelieu et le jansénisme, ou ce que l'attrition veut dire' in Hartmut Lehmann et al., eds, *Jansenismus, Quietismus, Pietismus* (Göttingen, 2002), 11–39
Hoffmann, Philip, *Church and Community in the Diocese of Lyon 1500–1789*, New Haven and London, 1984
——, 'Taxes and Agrarian Life in Early Modern France: Land Sales 1530–1730', *Journal of Economic History*, 46 (1986), 37–55
Holt, Mack P., *The French Wars of Religion 1562–1629*, Cambridge, 1992
Hours, Bernard, *Madame Louise, princesse au Carmel, 1737–1787*, Paris, 1987
——, *L'Église et la vie religieuse dans la France moderne, xvie–xviiie siècle*, Paris, 2000
Huppert, George, *Public Schools in Renaissance France*, Urbana and Chicago, 1984
Hurel, A., *Les Orateurs sacrés à la cour de Louis XIV*, Paris, 1872
Hurel, Daniel-Odon, 'Monachisme et missions intérieures en France au xviie siècle', *Revue Mabillon*, new series 10 (1999), 271–96
——, ed., *Guide pour l'histoire des ordres et des congrégations religieuses, France xvie–xxe siècles*, Turnhout, 2001
Hurtubise, Pierre, 'Le Prêtre tridentin: idéal et réalité' in *Homo religiosus. Autour de Jean Delumeau* (Paris, 1997), 208–17
L'Intendance de Berry à la fin du xviie siècle, ed. Claude Michaud, Paris, 2001
Jedin, Hubert, 'La Nécéssité de la confession privée selon le concile de Trente', *Maison-Dieu*, 104 (1970), 88–115
Joncheray, Jean, 'L'Instruction du chrétien de Richelieu: prône ou catéchisme?' in Pierre Colin et al., *Aux Origines du catéchisme*, 229–45
Jones, Colin, *The Charitable Imperative. Hospitals and Nursing in Ancien Régime and Revolutionary France*, London, 1989

Jouanna, Arlette et al., *Histoire et dictionnaire des guerres de religion*, Paris, 1998

Judge, H. G., 'The Congregation of the Oratory in France in the Late Seventeenth Century', *Journal of Ecclesiastical History*, 11 (1961), 46–55

Julia, Dominique, 'La Réforme post-tridentine en France d'après les procès-verbaux de visites pastorales: ordre et résistances' in *La Società religiosa nell'età moderna* (Naples, 1973), 311–415

——, 'La Constitution du réseau des collèges en France du xvie au xviiie siècle' in *Objet et Méthodes de l'histoire de la culture* (Budapest and Paris, 1982), 73–94

——, 'Les Bénédictins et l'enseignement aux xviie et xviiie siècles' in *Sous la Règle de Saint-Benoît* (Paris, 1982), 345–500

——, 'L'Expansion de la congrégation de la Mission de la mort de Vincent de Paul à la Révolution française' in *Vincent de Paul* (Rome, 1983), 362–419

——, 'Système bénéficial et carrières ecclésiastiques dans la France d'ancien régime' in *Historiens et Sociologues d'aujourd'hui* (Paris, 1986), 79–107

——, 'L'Éducation des ecclésiastiques en France aux xviie et xviiie siècles' in *Problèmes d'Histoire de l'Éducation* (Collection de l'École Française de Rome, 104) (Rome, 1988), 141–205

——, 'Le Catholicisme, religion du royaume', in *Histoire de la France religieuse*, 4 vols (Paris, 1988–92), iii, 11–50

——, 'La leçon de catéchisme dans *l'Escolle Paroissiale* (1654)' in Pierre Colin, et al., *Aux Origines du catéchisme*, 161–83

——, 'Églises, société, éducation à l'époque moderne. La transformation des collèges aux xvie et xviie siècles', *Pédagogie chrétienne, pédagogues chrétiens* (Paris, 1996), 61–83

——, 'The Priest' in Michel Vovelle, ed., *Enlightenment Portraits* (Chicago, 1997), 356–92

——, 'Reading and the Counter-Reformation' in G. Cavallo and R. Chartier, eds, *A History of Reading in the West* (Cambridge, 1999), 238–68

——, 'Sanctuaires et lieux sacrés à l'époque moderne' in André Vauchez, ed., *Lieux sacrés, lieux de culte, sanctuaires* (Rome, 2000), 241–95

——, 'Pour Une Géographie européenne du pèlerinage à l'époque moderne et contemporaine' in Philippe Boutry and Dominique Julia, eds, *Pèlerins et pèlerinages dans l'Europe moderne* (Rome, 2000), 3–126

——, 'Le Pèlerinage aux temps modernes (xvie–xviiie siècles)', in Gabriel Audisio, ed., *Religion et exclusion xiie–xviiie siècle* (Aix-en-Provence, 2001), 183–95

——, 'L'Expansion de l'ordre de la Visitation aux xviie et xviiie siècles' in *Visitation et visitandines aux xviie et xviiie siècles* (Saint-Étienne, 2001), 115–76

——, 'Entre Universel et local: le collège jésuite à l'époque moderne', *Paedagogica Historica*, 40 (2004), 15–31

——, 'La Formation du clergé dans l'espace catholique occidental (xvie–xviiie siècles)' in Maurizio Sangalli, ed., *Pastori, pope, preti, rabbini. La Formazione del ministro di culto in Europe (secoli xvi–xviii)* (Rome, 2005), 23–65

——, *Gilles Caillotin, pelerin. Le retour de Rome d'un sergier remois, 1724*, Rome, 2006

—— and Boutry, Philippe, 'Les Pèlerins français à Rome au xviiie siècle d'après les registres de Saint-Louis-des-Français' in Philippe Boutry and Dominique Julia, eds, *Pèlerins et pèlerinages dans l'Europe moderne* (Rome, 2000), 403–54

—— and Frijhoff, Willem, 'Les Oratoriens de France sous l'ancien régime. Premiers résultats d'une enquête', *Revue d'Histoire de l'Église de France*, 65 (1979), 225–65

—— and Frijhoff, Willem, 'Le Recrutement d'une congrégation enseignante et ses mutations à l'époque moderne: l'Oratoire de France' in D. N. Baker and P. Harrigan, eds, *The Making of Frenchmen* (Waterloo, Canada, 1980), 443–58

—— and Frijhoff, Willem, 'Les Oratoriens et l'espace éducatif français du règne de Louis XIV à la Révolution française' in Jean Ehrard, ed., *Le Collège de Riom et l'enseignement oratorien au xviiie siècle* (Paris and Oxford, 1993), 12–27

Julia, Dominique and McKee, Dennis, 'Le Clergé paroissial dans le diocèse de Reims sous l'épiscopat de Charles-Maurice le Tellier: origines et carrières', *Revue d'Histoire Moderne et Contemporaine*, 29 (1982), 529–83

Kapp, Volker, 'La Théologie des réalités terrestres dans la *Cour Sainte* de N. Caussin', *Les Jésuites parmi les hommes aux xvie et xviie siècles* (Clermont-Ferrand, 1988), 142–51

Knecht, R. J., *The French Civil Wars*, London, 2000

——, *The Rise and Fall of Renaissance France 1483–1610*, 2nd edn, Oxford, 2001

——, *The French Renaissance Court*, New Haven and London, 2008

Knowles, David, *From Pachomius to Ignatius*, Oxford, 1966

Krailsheimer, A. J., *Armand-Jean de Rancé, Abbot of La Trappe*, Oxford, 1974

Krumenacker, Yves, *L'École française de spiritualité*, Paris, 1998

——, 'La Mission dans l'Oratoire de France au xviie siècle' in Sorrel and Meyer, eds, *Les missions intérieures en France et en Italie*, 73–86

Lachiver, Marcel, *Les Années de misère 1680–1720*, Paris, 1991

Latreille, André et al., *Histoire du catholicisme en France*, 3 vols, Paris 1957–62

Le Bras, Gabriel, 'Les Confréries chrétiennes: problèmes et méthodes', *Revue Historique du Droit Français et Étranger*, 4e sér., 19–20 (1940–41), 310–63 (reprinted in Le Bras, *Études de sociologie religieuse*, 2 vols (Paris, 1956), ii, 423–62)

Le Brun, Jacques, *La Spiritualité de Bossuet*, Paris, 1972

——, 'France', in *Dictionnaire de spiritualité*, v (Paris, 1963), cols 917–53

——, 'La Sainteté à l'époque classique et le problème de l'autorisation' in Jürgen Beyer et al., eds, *Confessional Sanctity (c.1500–c.1800)* (Mainz, 2003), 149–62

Le Gall, Jean-Marie, *Les Moines au temps des réformes*, Seyssel, 2001

Le Gendre, Louis, *Mémoires*, ed. M. Roux, Paris, 1863

Le Goff, Jacques, and Rémond, René, eds, *Histoire de La France religieuse*, 4 vols, Paris, 1988–92

Le Roux, Nicolas, 'La Religion des courtisans dans la France de la Renaissance' in Klaus Malettke and Chantal Grell, eds, *Hofgesellschaft und Höflinge an europäischen Fürstenhöfen in der frühen Neuzeit* (Münster, 2001), 507–24

Le Roy Ladurie, Emmanuel, *Paysans du Languedoc*, 2 vols, Paris, 1966

Lebrun, François, *Les Hommes et la mort en Anjou aux xviie et xviiie siècles*, Paris, 1971

——, *La Vie conjugale sous l'ancien régime*, Paris, 1975

——, ed., *Histoire des catholiques en France*, Paris, 1980

——, 'La Place du pèlerinage thérapeutique dans la piété des Bretons aux xviie et xviiie siècles' in Lebrun, *Croyances et cultures*, 149–52

——, *Croyances et cultures dans la France d'ancien régime*, Paris, 2001

——, 'Le Calendrier agro-liturgique dans la société traditionnelle de la France de l'Ouest (xviie–xixe siècles)' in Lebrun, *Croyances et cultures*, 97–104

——, 'Les Missions des lazaristes en Haute-Bretagne au xviie siècle' in Lebrun, *Croyances et cultures*, 43–73

——, 'Une Mission à Brissac en 1707' in Lebrun, *Croyances et cultures*, 23–42

Lehmann, Hartmut, et al., eds, *Jansenismus, Quietismus, Pietismus*, Göttingen, 2002

Lehoreau, René, *Cérémonial de l'église d'Angers 1692–1721*, ed. François Lebrun, Paris, 1967

Lekai, Louis J., *The Rise of the Cistercian Strict Observance in Seventeenth-Century France*, Washington, DC, 1968

Lemaitre, Nicole, 'Un Prédicateur et son public. Les Sermons du père Lejeune et le Limousin 1653–1672', *Revue d'Histoire Moderne et Contemporaine*, 30 (1982), 33–65

——, 'Confession privée et confession publique dans les paroisses du xvie siècle', *Revue d'Histoire de l'Église de France* 69 (1983), 189–208

——, 'Pratique et signification de la confession communautaire dans les paroisses au xvie siècle', in *Pratiques de la confession* (Paris, 1983), 139–64

——, 'Avant la communion solennelle' in Jean Delumeau, ed., *La Première Communion* (Paris, 1987), 15–32

——, 'Les Communautés de "prêtres filleuls" dans le Rouergue d'ancien régime', *Ricerche di Storia Sociale e Religiosa*, 17 (1988), 33–58
——, 'La Vie religieuse des paysans dans la France centrale, xvie–xviie siècles' in *Le Paysan* (Paris, 1989), 315–32
——, 'Le Catéchisme, avant les catéchismes, dans les rituels' in Pierre Colin et al., eds, *Aux Origines du catéchisme en France* (Tournai, 1989), 28–44
——, 'Finances des consulats et finances des paroisses dans la France du sud-ouest, xive–xviiie siècles' in *L'Hostie et le denier* (Geneva, 1991), 101–15
——, 'Les Visites pastorales témoins de la christianisation? L'exemple du diocèse de Rodez (début xive–mi-xviiie siècles)' in *La Christianisation des campagnes*, 2 vols (Brussels, 1996), i, 199–220
——, ed., *Histoire des curés*, Paris, 2002
——, 'Le Culte épiscopal et la résistance au protestantisme au xvie siècle' in G. Chaix, ed., *Le Diocèse* (Paris, 2002), 307–27
——, 'De L'Évêque au curé: la communication des réformes vers les paroisses et ses mutations (xve–xviiie siècles)' in Ilana Zanguer and Myriam Yardeni, eds, *Les Deux Réformes chrétiennes* (Leiden, 2004), 331–53
——, 'Abbés et abbesses de l'époque moderne, approches nouvelles de la prosopographie' in Marc Venard and Dominique Julia, eds, *Sacralités, culture et dévotion*, (Marseille, 2005), 25–47
Lignereux, Yann, *Lyon et le roi, de la 'bonne ville' à l'absolutisme municipal (1594–1654)*, Seyssel, 2004
Lottin, Alain, *Lille, citadelle de la Contre-Réforme? (1598–1668)*, Westhoek, 1984
Loupès, Philippe, *Chapitres et chanoines de Guyenne*, Paris, 1985
——, *L'Apogée du catholicisme bordelais 1600–1789*, Bordeaux, 2001
—— and Suire, Eric, 'Noblesse française et réforme catholique: idéal religieux ou conformisme social?', in J. Pontet, M. Figeac and M. Boisson, eds, *La Noblesse de la fin du xve au début du xxe siècle*, 2 vols (Bordeaux, 2002), i, 347–67
Luria, Keith P., *Territories of Grace: Cultural Change in the Seventeenth-Century Diocese of Grenoble*, Los Angeles, 1991
——, ' "Popular Catholicism" and the Catholic Reformation' in Kathleen M. Comerford and Hilmar Pabel, eds, *Early Modern Catholicism* (Toronto, 2001), 114–30
——, *Sacred Boundaries. Religious Coexistence and Conflict in Early Modern France*, Washington, DC, 2005
Lux-Steritt, Laurence, *Redefining Female Religious Life. French Ursulines and English Ladies in Seventeenth-Century Catholicism*, Aldershot, 2005
McManners, John, *French Ecclesiastical Society Under the Ancien Régime. A Study of Angers in the Eighteenth Century*, Manchester, 1960
——, *Church and Society in Eighteenth-Century France*, 2 vols, Oxford, 1998
——, *Death and the Enlightenment*, Oxford, 1985
Maës, Bruno, *Le Roi, la Vierge et la nation: pèlerinages et identité nationale entre guerre de Cent Ans et Révolution*, Paris, 2003
Maher, Michael W., 'How the Jesuits Used their Congregations to Promote Frequent Communion', in John P. Donnelly and Michael W. Maher, eds, *Confraternities and Catholic Reform in Italy, France and Spain (Sixteenth-Century Essays and Studies*, xliv) (n.p., 1999), 75–95
Maire, Catherine, 'Port-Royal' in Pierre Nora, ed., *Realms of Memory*, i (New York, 1996), 301–51
——, *De La Cause de dieu à la cause de la nation: le jansénisme au xviiie siècle*, Paris, 1998
Malov, Vladimir, 'Le Projet colbertiste de la réforme monastique' in *Un Nouveau Colbert* (Paris, 1983), 167–76
Martimort, Aimé-Georges, *Le Gallicanisme*, Paris, 1973
Martin, Catherine, *Les Compagnies de la propagation de la foi (1632–1685)*, Geneva, 2000

Martin, Henri-Jean, *Livre, pouvoirs et société à Paris au xviie siècle*, 2 vols, Paris, 1969 (Engl. trans., *Print, Power and People in Seventeenth-Century France*, Metuchen, NJ, 1993)
——, 'Renouvellements et concurrences' in Martin and Chartier, Roger, eds, *Histoire de l'édition française*, i (Paris, 1983), 379–403
——, 'La Tradition perpetuée', in Martin and Chartier, eds, *Histoire de l'édition française*, ii (Paris, 1984), 175–85
——, *The French Book*, Baltimore, 1996
——, and Chartier, Roger, eds, *Histoire de l'édition française*, 4 vols, Paris 1983–6
Martin, Hervé, *Le Métier de prédicateur en France septentrionale à la fin du Moyen-âge (1350–1520)*, Paris, 1988
Martin, Philippe, *Les Chemins du sacré. Paroisses, processions et pèlerinages en Lorraine du xvie au xixe siècle*, Metz, 1995
——, 'Definir le diocèse. Débats en Lorraine à propos d'une définition (vers 1690–vers 1730)', in G. Chaix, ed., *Le Diocèse* (Paris, 2002), 329–54
Maurer, Michael, 'Sonntag in Der Frühen Neuzeit', *Archiv für Kulturgeschichte*, 88 (2006), 75–100
Mauzaize, Jean, *Le Rôle et l'action des capucins de la province de Paris au xviie siècle*, 3 vols, Paris, 1978
Mayer, Jean-Maire et al. eds, *Histoire du christianisme*, 13 vols, Paris, 1990–2001
Ménard, Michèle, *Une Histoire des mentalités religieuses aux xviie et xviiie siècles. Mille retables de l'ancien diocèse du Mans*, Paris, 1980
Messines, Sandrine, 'Contre-Réforme et Réforme catholique en Agenais, à travers les visites pastorales de Nicolas de Villars' in Nicole Lemaitre eds., *Religion et politique dans les sociétés du Midi* (Paris, 2002), 193–201
Meuvret, Jean, 'La Situation matérielle des membres du clergé séculier dans la France du xviie siècle' in Meuvret, *Études d'histoire économique* (Paris, 1971), 251–68
Meyer, Fréderic, 'Les Tertiaires chez les franciscains récollets aux xviie et xviiie siècles' in *Les Mouvances laïques des ordres religieux* (Saint-Étienne, 1996), 415–27
——, *Pauvreté et assistance spirituelle. Les Franciscains récollets de la province de Lyon aux xviie et xviiie siècles*, Saint-Étienne, 1997
——, 'L'Évêque contre les Récollets', *Études Héraultaises*, 30–32 (1999–2001), 75–85
Meyer, Jean-Claude, 'La Réforme spirituelle du clergé. L'Aa de Toulouse', *Bulletin de Littérature Ecclésiastique*, 101 (2000), 149–80
Michaud, Claude, *L'Église et l'argent sous l'ancien régime*, Paris, 1991
Michaux, Gérard, 'Les Nouveaux réseaux monastiques à l'époque moderne' in *Naissance et fonctionnement des réseaux monastiques et canoniaux* (Saint-Étienne, 1991), 603–23
Michel, Marie-José, *Jansénisme et Paris 1640–1730*, Paris, 2000
Minois, Georges, *La Bretagne des prêtres en Trégor d'ancien régime*, n.p., 1987
Montagnes, Bernard, *Sébastien Michaelis et la réforme d'Occitanie (1594–1647)*, Rome, 1984
——, *Les Dominicains en France et leurs réformes*, Paris, 2001
Morgain, Stéphane-Marie, *La Théologie politique de Pierre de Bérulle*, Paris, 2001
Moulinas, René, 'Le Pèlerinage, victime des Lumières', in Jean Chélini and Henry Branthomme, eds, *Les Chemins de Dieu. Histoire des pèlerinages chrétiens des origines a nos jours* (Paris, 1982), 259–92
Myers, W. David, *'Poor Sinning Folk'. Confession and Conscience in Counter-Reformation Germany*, Ithaca, NY, 1996
Nalle, Sarah T., 'Inquisitors, Priests and People During the Catholic Reformation in Spain', *Sixteenth-Century Journal*, 18 (1987), 557–87
Nelson, Eric, *The Jesuits and the Monarchy. Catholic Reform and Political Authority in France (1590–1615)*, Aldershot, 2005
Neveu, Bruno, *Érudition et religion au xviie siècle*, Paris, 1994

Nicolas, Jean, *La Rébellion française. Mouvements populaires et conscience sociale 1661–1789*, Paris, 2002
Norberg, Kathryn, *Rich and Poor in Grenoble 1600–1820*, Los Angeles, 1985
Noel, C. C., 'Clerics and Crown in Bourbon Spain', in John Bradley and Dale van Kley, eds, *Religion and Politics in Enlightenment Europe*, (Notre Dame, IN, 2001), 119–53.
O'Connell, Marvin R., *Pascal*, Grand Rapids, MI, 1997
O'Donohue, J. A., *Tridentine Seminary Legislation: Its Sources and its Formation*, Louvain, 1957
O'Malley, John W., *The First Jesuits*, Cambridge, MA, 1993
O'Malley, John W., *Trent and All That. Renaming Catholicism in the Early Modern Era*, Cambridge, Mass., 2000
Orcibal, Jean, *Jean Duvergier de Hauranne, abbé de Saint-Cyran*, Paris, 1948
——, 'Fénelon et sa famille' in *Correspondance de Fénelon*, vol. 1, Paris, 1972
——, *Jansénius d'Ypres (1585–1638)*, Paris, 1989
——, *Études d'histoire et de littérature religieuses xvie–xviiie siècles*, ed. Jacques Le Brun and Jean Lesaulnier, Paris, 1997
Pacaut, Marcel, and Fatio, Olivier, eds, *L'Hostie et le denier*, Geneva, 1991.
Palanque, J. R., Delaruelle, E. and Latreille, A., *Histoire du catholicisme en France*, 3 vols, Paris, 1957–62
Pallier, Denis, 'Les Réponses catholiques' in Henri-Jean Martin and Roger Chartier, eds, *Histoire de l'édition française*, i (Paris, 1982), 327–47
Parker, Geoffrey, 'Success and Failure in the First Hundred Years of the European Reformation', *Past and Present*, 136 (1992), 43–82
Parsons, Jotham, *The Church in the Republic. Gallicanism and Political Ideology in Renaissance France*, Washington, DC, 2004
Pecquet, Marguerite, 'Des Compagnies de pénitents à la compagnie du Saint-Sacrement', *XVIIe Siècle*, 69 (1965), 3–36
Périn, Nicole, 'Le Diocèse de Reims après la Fronde', *Revue d'Histoire Ardennaise*, 8 (1973), 91–124
Péronnet, Michel, *Les Évêques de l'ancienne France*, Lille-III, 1977
——, 'Les Établissements des jésuites dans le royaume de France à l'époque moderne' in *Les Jésuites parmi les hommes au xvie et xviie siècles* (Clermont, 1985), 463–79
——, 'La Crosse, le sceptre, l'épée: réflexions sur les évêques de France (début xvie–milieu xviie siècle), in *Sociétés et idéologies des temps modernes. Hommage à Arlette Jouanna* (Montpellier, 1996), 229–46
Pérouas, Louis, 'L'Emploi du temps des évêques du xviie siècle dans les diocèses de Luçon et de La Rochelle', *Revue d'Histoire de l'Église de France*, 49 (1962), 89–95
——, *Le Diocèse de La Rochelle 1648–1724. Sociologie et pastorale*, Paris, 1964
——, 'La Diffusion de la confrérie du Rosaire au xviie siècle dans les pays creusois' in Pérouas, *Culte des saints et anticléricalisme*, 77–92
——, 'Les Confréries de pénitents au xviie siècle dans les petites agglomérations de la Marche et du Limousin' in Pérouas, *Culte des saints et anticléricalisme*, 225–49
——, *Culte des saints et anticléricalisme: entre statistique et culture populaire*, Ussel, 2002
Peyrous, Bernard, *La Réforme catholique à Bordeaux (1600–1719)*, 2 vols, Bordeaux, 1995
Phillips, Henry, *Church and Culture in Seventeenth-Century France*, Cambridge, 1997
Pierre, Benoist, *La Bure et le sceptre. La congrégation des Feuillants dans l'affirmation des états et des pouvoirs princiers (vers 1560–vers 1660)*, Paris, 2006
——, *Le Père Joseph*, Paris, 2007
Pillorget, René, 'Réforme monastique et conflits de rupture dans quelques localités de la France méridionale au xviie siècle', *Revue Historique*, 253 (1975), 77–106
——, *Paris sous les premiers Bourbons*, Paris, 1988
—— and Pillorget, Suzanne, *France baroque, France classique*, 2 vols, Paris, 1995

Pister, Danielle, ed., *L'Image du prêtre dans la littérature classique (xvii*^{e}*–xviii*^{e} *siècles)*, Frankfurt, 2001

Pollmann, Judith, 'Countering the Reformation in France and the Netherlands: Clerical Leadership and Catholic Violence 1560–1585', *Past and Present*, 190 (2006) 83–120

Poutet, Yves, *Le xvii*^{e} *siècle et les origines lasalliennes*, 2 vols, Rennes, 1970

Provost, Georges, *La Fête et le sacré. Pardons et pèlerinages en Bretagne aux xvii*^{e} *et xviii*^{e} *siècles*, Paris, 1998

——, 'Identité paysanne et «pèlerinage de long cours» dans la France des xviie–xixe siècles' in Philippe Boutry, Pierre-Antoine Fabre and Dominique Julia, eds, *Rendre ses vœux: Les Identités pèlerines dans l'Europe moderne (xvi*^{e}*–xviii*^{e} *siècle)* (Paris, 2000), 379–99

Quantin, Jean-Louis, *Le Catholicisme classique et les pères de l'église. Un retour aux sources (1669–1713)*, Paris, 1999

——, *Le Rigorisme chrétien*, Paris, 2001

——, 'Le Rigorisme: sur le basculement de la théologie morale catholique au xviie siècle', *Revue d'Histoire de l'Église de France*, 89 (2003), 26–7

——, 'De La Rigueur au rigorisme: les *Avvertenze ai confessori* de Charles Borromée dans la France du xviie siècle', *Studia Borromaica*, 20 (2006), 195–251

Quéniart, Jean, *Les Hommes, l'église et Dieu dans la France du xviii*^{e} *siècle*, Paris, 1978

——, 'La Culture des prêtres de campagne bretons au xviiie siècle', in Marc Venard and Dominique Julia, eds, *Sacralités, culture et dévotion* (Marseille, 2005), 257–66

Ramsey, Ann W., *Liturgy, Politics and Salvation. The Catholic League in Paris and the Nature of Catholic Reform 1540–1630*, Rochester, NY, 1999

Ranum, Orest, *Paris in the Age of Absolutism*, 2nd edn, University Park, PA, 2002

Rapley, Elizabeth, *The Dévotes. Women and Church in Seventeenth-Century France*, Montreal, 1990

——, 'Women and the Religious Vocation in Seventeenth-Century France', *French Historical Studies*, 18 (1994), 613–31

——, *A Social History of the Cloister. Daily Life in the Teaching Monasteries of the Old Regime*, Montreal, 2001

Rebelliau, Alfred, 'La Compagnie du Saint-Sacrement', *Revue des Deux Mondes*, 5e sér., 16 (1903), 49–82, 540–63; 17 (1903), 103–35; 46 (1908), 834–68; 53 (1909) 892–923; 54 (1909), 200–28

Recueil des visites pastorales du diocese de Lyon aux xvie*–xvii*^{e} *siècles*, Lyon, 1926

Reinburg, Virginia, 'Liturgy and the Laity in Late Medieval and Reformation France', *Sixteenth-Century Journal*, 23 (1992), 526–47

Répertoire des visites pastorales de la France. Première série: anciens diocèses (jusqu'en 1790), ed. Marc Venard, 4 vols, Paris, 1977–85

Restif, Bruno, 'Les Synodes du diocèse de Saint-Malo aux xvie–xviie siècles', *Revue d'Histoire de l'Église de France*, 89 (2003), 345–61

——, *La Révolution des paroisses. Culture paroissiale et Réforme catholique en Haute-Bretagne aux xvi*^{e} *et xvii*^{e} *siècles*, Rennes, 2006

Richet, Denis, 'Fénelon contre Bossuet: la querelle du quiétisme' in Richet, *De la Réforme à la Révolution* (Paris, 1991), 119–39

Robert, Odile, 'De la dentelle et des âmes. Les "Demoiseilles de l'Instruction" du Puy (xviie–xviiie siècle)' in Jean Delumeau, ed., *La Religion de ma mère* (Paris, 1992), 245–67

Rosa, Mario, *Clero cattolico e società nell'età moderna*, Rome, 2006

Sabatier, Gérard, 'La Géographie seigneuriale du Languedoc des montagnes: Velay, Gévaudan, Vivarais en 1734' in *La France d'ancien régime. Études réunies en l'honneur de Pierre Goubert*, 2 vols (Toulouse, 1984), 649–63

Sainte-Beuve, C. A., *Port-Royal*, ed. Maxime Le Roy (*Pléiade* edn), 3 vols, Paris 1953–5

Salin, Dominique, 'L'Invasion mystique en France au xviie siècle' in Henri Laux and Dominique Salin, eds, *Dieu au xvii*^{e} *siècle, crises et renouvellements* (Paris, 2003), 241–64

——, 'La Spiritualité de la compagnie de Jésus en France au début du xviie siècle' in *Henri IV et les Jésuites* (La Flèche, 2006), 41–7
Sangalli, Maurizio, ed., *Pastori, pope, preti, rabbini. La Formazione del ministro di culto in Europe (secoli xvi–xviii)*, Rome, 2005
Sarre, Claude-Alain, *Vivre sa soumission. L'exemple des Ursulines provençales et comtadines*, Paris, 1997
Sauvageon, Christophe, 'Le Manuscrit original du prieur Sauvageon', *Mémoires de la Société Archéologique et Historique de l'Orléanais*, 32 (1908), i–cxxxx
Sauzet, Robert, *Les Visites pastorales dans le diocèse de Chartres pendant la première moitié du xviie siècle. Essai de sociologie religieuse*, Rome, 1975
——, *Contre-Réforme et réforme catholique en Bas-Languedoc. Le Diocèse de Nîmes au xviie siècle*, Louvain, 1979
——, 'Contestation et renouveau du pèlerinage au début des temps modernes (xvie et debut du xviie siècle)', in Jean Chelini and Henry Branthomme, eds, *Les Chemins de Dieu. Histoire des pèlerinages chrétiens des origines à nos jours* (Paris, 1982), 235–58
——, 'Aux Origines' in Jean Delumeau, ed., *La Première Communion* (Paris, 1987), 33–50
——, 'La Création du diocèse d'Alès (1694), prototype de l'érection de celui de Blois' in G. Chaix, ed., *Le Diocèse* (Paris, 2000), 33–46
——, 'Les Résistances au catéchisme au xviie siècle' in Pierre Colin et al., *Aux Origines du catéchisme*, 208–13
Schmitt, Thérèse-Jean, *L'Organisation ecclésiastique et la pratique religieuse dans l'archidiaconé d'Autun de 1650 à 1750*, Autun, 1957
Schneider, Robert A., *Public Life in Toulouse 1463–1789*, Ithaca, NY, 1989
Sedgwick, Alexander, *Jansenism in Seventeenth-Century France*, Charlottesville, VA, 1977
——, *The Travails of Conscience. The Arnauld family and the Ancien Régime*, Cambridge, MA, 1998
Séguy, J-B., 'Langue, religion et société: Alain de Solminihac et l'application de la réforme tridentine dans le diocese de Cahors (1636–1659)', *Annales de l'Institut d'Estudis Occitans*, 5e sér., 1 (1977), 79–110
Simiz, Stefano, 'Les Confréries de Champagne du Nord, entre héritage et modernité, xviie–xviiie siècles', in Langlois and Goujard, eds, *Les confréries du Moyen Âge à nos jours* (Rouen, 1995), 67–82
——, *Confréries urbaines et dévotion en Champagne (1450–1830)*, Lille, 2001
Solé, Jacques, *Les Origines intellectuelles de la révocation de l'édit de Nantes*, Saint-Étienne, 1997
Solminihac, Alain de, *Lettres et documents*, ed. Eugène Sol, Cahors, 1930
Sorrel, Christian, and Meyer, Frédéric, eds, *Les Missions intérieures en France et en Italie, du xvie siècle au xxe siècle*, Chambéry, 2001
Soulet, Jean-François, *Traditions et réformes religieuses dans les Pyrenées centrals au xviie siècle (le diocèse de Tarbes de 1602 à 1716)*, Pau, 1975
Strauss, Gerald, 'Success and Failure in the German Reformation', *Past and Present*, 67 (1975), 30–63
——, *Luther's House of Learning: Indoctrination of the Young in the German Reformation*, Baltimore, 1978
Suire, Eric, *La Sainteté française de la réforme catholique (xvie–xviiie siècles) d'après les textes hagiographiques et les procès de canonisation*, Bordeaux, 2001
Swanson, R. N., *Religion and Devotion in Europe, c.1215–c.1515*, Cambridge, 1995
Tackett, Timothy, *Priest and Parish in Eighteenth-Century France*, Princeton, 1977
——, *Religion, Revolution and Religious Culture in Eighteenth-Century France*, Princeton, 1986
Tallon, Alain, *La Compagnie du saint-sacrement, spiritualité et société*, Paris, 1991
——, *La France et le concile de Trent (1518–1563)*, Rome, 1997
——, *Le Concile de Trente*, Paris, 2000

Tallon, Alain, *Conscience nationale et sentiment religieux en France au xvie siècle*, Paris, 2002
——, 'Inquisition romaine et monarchie française au xvie siècle' in Gabriel Audisio, ed., *Inquisition et pouvoir*, Aix-en-Provence, 2004, 311–24
Taveneaux, René, *Jansénisme en Lorraine (1640–1789)*, Paris, 1960
——, *La Vie quotidienne des jansénistes*, Paris, 1973
——, *Le Catholicisme dans la France classique*, 2 vols, Paris, 2nd edn, 1994
Taylor, Larissa J., *Soldiers of Christ: Preaching in Late Medieval and Reformation France*, Oxford, 1992
——, *Heresy and Orthodoxy in Sixteenth-Century Paris: François Le Picart and the Beginnings of the Catholic Reformation*, Leiden, 1999
——, 'Dangerous Vocations: Preaching in France in the Late Middle Ages and the Reformations' in Taylor, ed., *Preachers and People in the Reformations and Early Modern Period* (Leiden, 2001), 91–124
Tentler, Thomas N., *Sin and Confession on the Eve of the Reformation*, Princeton, 1977
The Canons and Decrees of the Council of Trent, ed. H. J. Schroder, St Louis, 1941
Timmermans, Linda, *L'Accès des femmes à la culture sous l'ancien régime*, Paris, 2005
Truant, Cynthia M., *The Rites of Labor. Brotherhoods of Compagnonnage in Old and New Régime France*, Ithaca, NY, 1994
Ultee, Maarten, 'The Suppression of Fêtes in France, 1666', *Catholic Historical Review* 62 (1976), 181–99
——, *The Abbey of St Germain des Prés in the Seventeenth Century*, New Haven and London, 1981
Van Kley, Dale K., *The Religious Origins of the French Revolution*, New Haven and London, 1996
Vauchez, André, *The Laity in the Middle Ages*, Notre Dame, IN, 1993
Venard, Marc, 'Les Séminaires en France avant Saint Vincent de Paul' in *Vincent de Paul. Actes du colloque international d'études vincentiennes* (Rome, 1983), 1–16
——, 'La Construction des églises paroissiales, du xve au xviiie siècle', *Revue d'Histoire de l'Église de France*, 73 (1987), 7–24
——, 'The Influence of Borromeo on the French Church' in John M. Headley and John B. Tomaro, eds, *San Carlo Borromeo. Catholic Reform and Ecclesiastical Politics in the Second Half of the Sixteenth-Century* (Washington, DC, 1988), 208–27
——, 'La Fonction catéchétique des statuts synodaux' in Pierre Colin et al., eds, *Aux Origines du catéchisme en France* (Tournai, 1989), 45–54
——, 'La Situation financière du clergé dans la France des guerres de religion' in Pacaut and Fatio, eds, *L'Hostie et le denier* (Geneva, 1991), 121–30
——, 'Ultramontane or Gallican? The French Episcopate at the End of the 16th Century', *The Jurist*, 52 (1992), 142–61
——, 'Un Concile provincial oublié: le concile d'Embrun en 1583', *Provence Historique*, 42 (1992), 625–44
——, ed., *Histoire du christianisme*, vols viii–ix (Paris, 1992, 1997)
——, *Réforme protestante, réforme catholique dans la province d'Avignon, au xvie siècle*, Paris, 1993
——, 'Examen ou concours? Réflexions sur la procédure de recrutement des curés dans la France d'ancien régime' in Gilles Deregnaucourt, ed., *Société et religion en France et aux Pays-Bas xve–xixe siècle* (Arras, 2000), 373–88
——, 'Les Visites pastorales du xvie au xviie siècle' in Venard, *Le Catholicisme à l'épreuve dans la France du xvie siècle* (Paris, 2000), 27–63
——, 'Du Carême à la mission' in Christian Sorrel and Fréderic Meyer, eds, *Les Missions intérieures en France et en Italie, du xive siècle au xxe siècle* (Chambéry, 2001), 9–18
——, 'La Crise des confréries au xvie siècle' in Venard, *Catholicisme à l'épreuve*, 249–68
——, 'Les Rapports de visites *ad limina* des évêques de France sous l'ancien régime' in Philippe Boutry and Bernard Vincent, eds, *Les Chemins de Rome* (Rome, 2002), 101–21

——, 'Les Martyrs catholiques des affontements religieux du xvie siècle, d'après l'*Histoire Catholique* du Père Hilarion de Coste (1625)' in Jürgen Beyer et al., eds, *Confessional Sanctity (c.1500–1800)*, (Mainz, 2003), 81–91
——, 'Le Prédicateur de carême, semeur d'idées réformées' in Ilya Zinguer and Myriam Yardeni, eds, *Les Deux Réformes chrétiennes: propagation et diffusion* (Leiden, 2004), 60–73
——, 'Qu'est-ce Qu'une Confrérie de dévotion?' in Venard, *Catholicisme à l'épreuve au xvie siècle*, 237–48
——, 'Si On Parlait des Confréries de métiers', in Venard and Julia, eds, *Sacralités, culture et dévotion*, 211–38
——, *Le Catholicisme à l'épreuve dans la France du xvie siècle*, Paris, 2000
—— and Julia, Dominique, eds, *Sacralités, culture et devotion*, Marseille, 2005
Vernus, Michel, *Le Presbytère et la chaumière. Curés et villageois dans l'ancienne France (xviie–xiiie siècles)*, Rioz, 1986
Viard, Georges, 'Chapitre et réforme catholique au xviie siècle: le chapitre cathédral de Langres', unpublished doctoral thesis, University of Nancy-II, 1974
——, 'Les Chanoines de Langres au xviie siècle: recrutement, origines, fortunes', *Annales de l'Est*, 28 (1976), 87–138
——, 'Les Visites pastorales dans l'ancien diocèse de Langres, la réglementation épiscopale et sa mise en oeuvre', *Revue d'Histoire de l'Église de France*, 63 (1977), 235–72
Vidal, Daniel, *Critique de la raison mystique. Benoît de Canfeld, possession et dépossession au xviie siècle*, Grenoble, 1990
Viguerie, Jean de, *Une Oeuvre d'éducation sous l'ancien régime*, Paris, 1976
——, *L'Institution des enfants. L'Éducation en France, xvie–xviiie siècles*, Paris, 1978
——, 'Y a-t-il Une Crise d'observance régulière entre 1660 et 1715?' in *Sous la Règle de Saint Benoît*, (Paris, 1982), 135–47
——, *Le Catholicisme des Français dans l'ancienne France*, Paris, 1988
——, 'Les Catéchismes enseignés en France au xviiie siècle: première approche', *Revue d'Histoire de l'Église de France*, 82 (1996), 85–108
Vincent, Catherine, *Des Charités bien ordonnées. Les Confréries normandes de la fin du xiiie siècle au début du xvie siècle*, Paris, 1988
——, *Les Confréries médievales dans le royaume de France*, Paris, 1994
Vovelle, Michel, *Piété baroque et déchristianisation en Provence au xviiie siècle*, Paris, 1973
——, *La Mort et l'Occident de 1300 à nos jours*, Paris, 1983
——, 'Géographie des confréries des pénitents à l'époque moderne' in *Les Confréries de penitents (Dauphiné-Provence)* (Valence, 1988), 17–33
Walch, Agnès, *La Spiritualité conjugale dans le catholicisme français, xvie–xxe siècles*, Paris, 2002
——, *Histoire du couple en France*, Rennes, 2003
Waquet, Françoise, *Le Modèle français et l'Italie savante (1660–1750)*, Rome, 1989
Weaver, F. Ellen, 'Erudition, spirituality and women: the Jansenist contribution' in Sherrin Marshall, ed., *Women in Reformation and Counter-Reformation Europe*, (Bloomington, 1989), 189–206
——, *Madame de Fontpertuis: une dévote janséniste, amie et gérante d'Antoine Arnauld et de Port-Royal*, Paris, 1998
——, *Mademoiselle de Joncoux: polémique janséniste à la veille de la bulle* Unigenitus, Paris, 2002
Welter, Louise, 'Les Communautés de prêtres dans le diocèse de Clermont du xiiie au xviiie siècle', *Revue d'Histoire de l'Église de France*, 35 (1949), 5–35
——, 'Le Chapitre cathédral de Clermont: sa constitution, ses privilèges', *Revue d'Histoire de l'Église de France* (1955), 5–42
——, *La Réforme ecclésiastique du diocèse de Clermont au xviie siècle*, Clermont-Ferrand, 1956
Whitmore, P. J. S., *The Order of Minims in Seventeenth-Century France*, The Hague, 1967

Williams, Charles E., *The French Oratorians and Absolutism 1611–41*, New York, 1989
Worcester, Thomas, 'Bishop Jean-Pierre Camus and the christianisation of rural France' in *La Christianisation des campagnes*, 2 vols (Brussels, 1996), i 345–54
Wright, A. D., *The Counter-Reformation*, London, 1982
——, 'Bérulle and Olier: Christ and the Blessed Virgin Mary', in R. N. Swanson, ed., *The Church and Mary* (*Studies in Church History*, 39) (Woodbridge, Suffolk, 2006), 271–9
Zakar, Polycarpe, *Histoire de la stricte observance de l'ordre cistercien depuis ses débuts jusqu'au généralat du cardinal de Richelieu (1606–1635)*, Rome, 1966

INDEX

Aa, secret clerical association 342, 391–2
abbés de cour 83, 398; *see also* almoners; clergy, upper
Abbeville 10, 346
abbeys 22, 419; damage to 6, 131, 157; female 131–2, 135, 158–9; held by *commendataires*, 49–50, 55–6, 57, 81–2, 91; jurisdiction of 177; patronage rights of 103, 187, 189; royal patronage over 158–9, 163; wealth of 7, 40, 54, 90–1, 307; *see also commende*; religious orders, male monastic
Abelly, Louis, bishop of Rodez 377
absolution 259, 260–1, 268, 294, 399–400, 401, 411; *see also* confession
Acarie, Barbe 136, 267, 317, 329, 335, 371; circle around 136, 317, 318, 320, 329, 370
Ad limina, visitation 23
Advent 230, 270, 351; preaching during 12, 101, 125, 280–1, 283, 285, 288, 293, 295; *see also* preaching
Agen 9, 10; seminary of 197
Agonisants *see* confraternities of
Aguesseau, Henri-François d', chancellor of France 413
Agulhon, Maurice, historian 339, 359; *see also* penitents
Aiguillon, Marie-Madeleine de Vignerot, duchess of 386
Aix-en-Provence 31–2, 79, 83, 379, 390, 391
Alacocque, Marie-Marguerite 356
Albani, Cardinal *see* Clement XI
Albi, diocese of 25
Albigensian crusade 108
Alès, diocese of 21, 90
Alet, Étienne Pavillon, bishop of 377, 411, 421; diocese of 417
Alexander VII, pope 404, 409
Alise-Sainte-Reine, pilgrimage to 248, 250
All Saints 176, 182, 230, 264
All Souls 230
Allier, Raoul, historian 388
almoners/almonerships 80–1, 82, 91, 159, 163, 164
Alsace 23, 94
altars: main 210–11, 212, 241, 266, 274, 356; of confraternities 238, 241, 341, 350; secondary/chapel 210–11, 216, 233
Amboise, Georges Cardinal 55
Amboise, edict of 9
Amiens 44, 244, 245; chapter of 50
Angers 43, 44, 72, 146, 147, 346, 362, 421, 423; bishop of 180–2; cathedral chapter of 177; diocese of 174, 181, 231; *see also* Arnauld (Henri); Le Peletier
Angoulême 379
Annat, François, Jesuit 408
Anne of Austria 80, 109, 112, 124, 158, 249, 386
Annecy 138, 140, 320, 322; *see also* de Sales
Annonciades, female Franciscans 130, 132, 133, 137
anticlericalism 37
appel comme d'abus 177

Apt, diocese of 18
Aquaviva, Claudio, Jesuit superior-general 284
Aquitaine, province of 18
archconfraternities 358; *see also* confraternities; confraternity of Holy Sacrament
archdeacons, and parish visitations 175, 176, 209; powers of 28, 74, 79, 171, 172, 240
Ardilliers, Notre-Dame des, pilgrimage to 248
Argenson, René de Voyer d' 329, 379, 385, 386
Arles 69, 379; diocese of 22, 31; province of 25
Arnauld family 368, 400, 422
Arnauld, Angélique 134, 422
Arnauld, Antoine 404–5, 408, 409, 412, 422; and *droit* versus *fait*, 406, 409; and François de Sales 321; as controversialist 403; attacks on Jesuits by 262, 268, 403–4, 407; critical of missionaries 294; disciple of St Cyran 400, 403, 406; expelled from Sorbonne 403, 406; goes into exile 412; use of Borromeo by 406–7
Arnauld, Henri, bishop of Angers 181, 300
Arnauld de Pomponne, Simon 409
Arras, diocese 24, 187
artisans 186, 213, 217, 238, 249, 320, 325, 341, 357, 363, 378; Jesuit congregations of 353, 369
Artois 39, 431
Assemblies of clergy 25, 26, 157, 166, 279, 389, 398; against the Jesuits 410; and episcopal elections 156, 158; role in Jansenist question 404–5, 406–7, 408, 410; influence of 4, 8, 78, 168–9, 200, 231, 415; and church finances 7, 45, 46
Assembly of Notables 4
Assumption, feast of 243
attrition 260, 400; *see also* confession; penance
Aubarède 246
Aubusson 359
Auger, Edmond, Jesuit 10, 313, 346; catechism of 298
Augustinian canons-regular 62, 124; reform of 85, 87, 95, 98, 100, 120, 419; congregations of 86, 87, 94; traditions of 102, 103, 411; Augustinianism among 419; *see also* Congregation of France; La Rochefoucauld; Sainte-Geneviève
Augustinian hermits 107, 112
Augustinians, Discalced 107, 130
Augustinian-Jansenists 102, 116, 403, 410–11, 414, 415, 416, 417, 418; and Bible 331, 414–15; and liturgical change 416–17; attitudes to marriage 328; critical of Jesuits 322; views of human nature 321, 323, 328, 417; *see also* Jansenists; neo-Augustinians; Port-Royal; rigorists
Augustinus 397, 400, 403, 404, 406, 409, 412; *see also* Jansen
Auray, site of pilgrimage 248, 249, 251
Autun, diocese of 217
Auvergne 43, 67, 72, 186, 263
Auxerre 121, 355, 421, 431; cathedral chapter of 74; diocese 121, 281, 292, 418
Avignon 10, 21, 24, 68, 88, 112, 133, 136, 165, 188, 333, 391, 431
Avila, Teresa of 135, 235, 311, 314, 330, 335

Bagnères 243
baptism: sacrament of 30, 210, 215, 253, **254**–7, 260, 272, 276; miracles around 256; of children 255–6; reworking of 256; role of midwives 256; social dimensions of 255; vows of 256–7
baptismal font 30, 179, 210, 255
Barcos, Martin de, abbot of Saint-Cyran 90
Barillon, Henri de, bishop of Luçon 168, 300
Barnabites, congregation of 111, 112, 113, 120; conduct missions 112, 290
Barré, Nicholas, Minim 151
Barry, Paul de, Jesuit 323, 334
Bar-sur-Aube 121
Basville, Nicolas Lamoignon de 120
Bauny, Étienne, Jesuit 408
Bayonne 139, 211, 398
Bazas, diocese of 218
Béarn 24, 112, 165, 283
Beaucaire 379, 382
Beaucousin, dom Richard, Carthusian 318, 370
Beaujolais 167
Beaune 379; Carmelite convent in 136
Beauvais 43, 44, 103, 191, 342; bishop of 44; diocese of 29, 31, 67, 191, 418
Bec, abbey of 50
Becan, Martin, Jesuit 397

Bellarmine, Robert, Jesuit 397; catechism of 298
Belley, diocese of 24, 322; *see also* Camus
Benedict, Philip, historian 10, 131
Benedictines (Order of Saint Benedict), male, 85, 94–6, 100, 101, 103, 131, 322; abbeys 43, 103; congregations among 86, 94, 95, 118; Jansenist networks among 418–19; reforms of 94, 95–7; traditions of 85–6, 100, 101–2, 411
Benedictines, female 130, 135
benefices, 7, 23, 24, **37–58**, 64, 65, 70, 71, 76, 89–90, 148, 164, 170, 172, 183, 185, 186, 187, 192, 199, 218, 219, 220; accumulation of 49, 55, 88; bishops and 170, 184; distinctions among 49, 55, 58, 67, 88; graduates and 68–9, 190, 214; importance of 58, 61, 66; law of 54–5; management of 48–52; nature of, 54–5, 56; patronage of 56–7, 58, 189, 190, 217; resignations of 57, 76, 77, 89, 160, 189, 218; royal patronage of 57–8, 81–2, 160, 163; search for by clergy 26, 66, 68, 83, 188, 201; trafficking in 57, 63; uses of 22, 90, 195; with cure of souls 55, 181, 217; without cure of souls 55, 56, 64, 173, 188; *see also* bishops; *concours*
Benoist, René 313, 414–15; *see also* Bible
Bernières, Jean de 329, 330
Berry 10
Bérulle, family 368
Bérulle, Pierre de 115–17, 196, 197, 198, 285, 320, 328, 371, 398, 419 (*see also* Oratory; priesthood; spirituality); and *dévot* party 373; and St Cyran 398; and Marian devotions 318, 354; Augustinianism of 321; disciples of 117, 197, 205–6, 312, 318–19, 354, 377; ideas on priesthood, 128, 169, 205–6, 271, 318–20, 321–2, 342, 349, 392, 398, 423; spirituality of 237–8, 312, 317, 318–19, 330, 354, 398
Besançon, diocese of 24, 31; province of 25
Béthune 132
Béziers 48; chapter of 50
Bible: Council of Trent and 278, 313; French clergy and 193, 194; Jansenists and reading of 332, 414–15, 416; translations into French of 313, 331, 414–15, 421; use of 331–2; status within French Catholicism 414, 428
bibliothèque bleue 335
Binet, Étienne, Jesuit 323, 334

bishops/episcopate 7, 18, 53, 58, 80, 99, 109, **155–80**, 182, 185, 186, 193, 207, 215, 247, 254, 361; age of 166; and Bible 415; and catechism 296, 299, 300–1, 303, 304, 305; and chapters 62, 75–6, 76–7, 78, 79; and Company of the Holy Sacrament 377, 393; and *concours* 187–90; and condition of churches 212–13; and confraternities 348, 360; and control of benefices 57, 58, 69, 104, 184, 187–8, 189–90, 199; and crown patronage 63, 78, 155–9; and ecclesiastical conferences 181–2, 193; and female religious orders/ congregations 133, 135, 139, 144–5, 149; and general hospitals 144, 384; and governance of dioceses 20, 23, 24, 28, 83, 167, 170–2, 180, 183, 186, 193, 387; and Jansenism 114, 404, 409, 410, 413, 418, 419; and missions 289, 291, 292, 293, 294; and parish clergy 69, 70, 189; and parish *vicaires* 219; and parishes 29, 30, 31–2, 35; and preaching, 278, 279, 280, 281, 282, 283; and Protestants 21, 22; and religious orders/congregations 100, 114, 115, 116, 117, 119, 127, 177; and residence 167–8; and sacraments 254, 257, 263, 268; and saints 230, 231, 239–40; and seminaries, 103, 195, 196, 199–200, 203–4, 418; and synods 172–5; and visitations 175–80, 209; at court 80, 81, 82; common features of 164–70; dislike of lowest clergy, 71, 186; education of 161–3; financial means of 40–1, 42, 44–5, 48, 49, 51–2, 54, 55, 170; Gallican sensitivies of 127, 167, 203; hierarchy among 26–7; Jansenists among 204, 411, 417, 418, 419, 421; models of 169–70, 235–6, 406; origins of 2–3, 159–61, 164–5; outsiders among 80, 82, 91; pre-episcopal careers of 163–4
Blet, Pierre, historian 168
Bloch, Marc, historian 17
Blois 146; diocese of 21, 90; ordinance of 5, 26, 195
Bochart de Champigny, Jean 374
Bologna, concordat of: papacy and 24–5; and crown's church patronage 57, 81; and religious orders 88; and French bishops, 156, 161, 163, 166
bon curé, idea of 62, 169, 205–6, 216–17
Bonal, Raymond 118–19

Bonne Nouvelle, Paris parish of 32
Bonneau, family 386
Bons Enfants, seminary of 200
bonus pastor, ideal of 156, 170
Bonzi, Jean, Cardinal 27, 167
Bordeaux 9, 11, 20, 25, 44, 72, 112, 198, 357, 359, 362, 386, 392; archbishop of 138, 172; catechism of 305, 306; diocese of 174; parishes of 31, 32; provincial council of 1624 26, 168, 193; religious orders in 120, 146, 150; seminary of 197
Borromeo, Carlo 26, 112; and confession box 212, 261; as heroic saint 236, 335; as model bishop 169, 172, 235–6; influence of 5, 22, 136, 191, 194, 205, 261, 314, 405, 406–8, 432
Bossuet, Jacques-Bénigne, bishop of Meaux 81, 170, 246, 279, 331, 377, 388, 403, 410, 412, 427; catechism of 304, 328
Bouhours, Dominique, Jesuit 415
Bouillon, Emmanuel d'Albret, Cardinal 27, 49
Boulogne 421, 422; bishop of 419; diocese of 187
Bourbon, Charles de, Cardinal 55
Bourbon succession 367–8
Bourdoise, Adrien 197, 199, 285, 294, 299, 306, 400
Bourges 82, 103, 132; catechism of 300; diocese of 20, 90, 100; province of 25
Bourgoing, François 63, 285
Bourras, confraternity of reformed Penitents 351
Bremond, Henri, historian 311–12, 316–17, 322, 395
Briggs, Robin, historian 271, 328, 395, 401
Brissac, mission in 294
Brittany/Breton 6, 23, 67, 94, 103, 118, 135, 234, 248, 261, 293, 294, 342, 355, 376, 379, 389, 390, 431; clergy of 68, 77, 137, 186, 188, 194, 217, 242; cult of dead in 214, 275; language of 165, 283, 286
Brothers of the Christian Schools 114, 118, 128, 308; *see also* La Salle
Brou, mission to 285
Brûlart de Sillery, Charles 111
Burgundy 10, 40, 72, 85, 113, 121, 131, 250, 431
Burgundy, Louis de Bourbon, duke of 388

Caen 132, 343, 386
Cahors 98, 145, 346, 377; bishop of 309; diocese of 171, 283; university of 162
Caillotin, Gilles 249–50
calendar *see* liturgical year
Calends 174, 180, 191, 206; *see also* ecclesiastical conferences; synods
Calvin, Jean 232, 278, 320, 345, 396; catechism of, 297–8
Calvinism/Calvinists 1, 3, 4, 6, 8–9, 10, 11, 12, 66, 112, 127, 131, 194, 215, 233, 345, 368, 370, 403 *see also* Huguenots/Protestants
Cambrai 389; diocese of 24, 31, 39, 187; province of 25
Camus, Jean-Pierre 169, 279, 282, 321, 327, 333, 407
Canfeld, Benoît de, Capuchin 315, 318, 330, 370
Canisius, Peter, Jesuit 297–8
canons *see* Augustinian canons-regular; chapters, cathedral
Capuchins 120, 263, 333, 431; activities of 12, 111, 113, 123, 224, 225, 239, 251; and confraternities 354, 361; and missions 125, 246, 284–5, 288, 290–1, 294, 295, 296, 374; and Rosary devotions 354; and spiritual direction 151, 315; anti-Jansenist 128, 421; attractiveness of 14, 123, 128; growth of 110
Capucines, female order of 137
Carcassonne 211
Caribbean 291
Carmelite nuns 107, 108, 130, 135, 137, 140, 318, 329, 368, 371; from Spain 14, 133, 135–6, 137, 318
Carmelites, male order of 107, 112, 120
Carmelites, discalced 107–8
Carre, Thomas 120
Carthusians 87, 88, 101
cases of conscience 192, 193, 259, 262, 401–2
casuistry/casuists 262–3, 327, 333, 401–2, 406–7, 410, 430; *see also* cases of conscience
catechism 181–2, **296–305,** 306–7, 326, 332, 339, 356; (anti-)Jansenist 301; classes/teaching of 30, 79, 277, 287–8, 298, 308; diocesan 299–301; during missions 286, 287, 294; extent of 305, 306–7; for children 288, 294, 303–4; format/content of 297–300, 303–4; of the Council of Trent/Roman, 193, 205, 213, 277–8; of 'three Henries' 300; oral 305; practice of 301, 305, 308–9; taught by clergy 181, 193, 251, 283, 302; taught

by women 308–9, 354; *see also* Auger; Bellarminer; Calvin; Canisius; Council of Trent; Luther
Catholic League, 8, 9–10, 11, 12, 13–14, 20–1, 47, 115, 119, 131, 135–6, 158, 243, 279, 280, 320, 346–7, 359, 367–8, 370
Catholic Reformation, 1, 13–14, 84, 107, 110, 114, 134, 138, 211, 233–4, 235, 237, 239, 241, 248–9, 251, 253, 267, 274, 283, 289, 311, 315, 327, 333, 335–6, 342–3, 350, 355, 359, 360, 363–4, 365, 368, 371, 394, 426, 430
Caussin, Nicholas, Jesuit 323, 325, 334, 401
Cazaulx, Charles 11
Celestines, religious order 86
celibacy, clerical 55, 57, 62, 124, 184, 271, 326
cemeteries 214–15
Certeau, Michel de, historian 329
Cévennes 290
Ceyssens, Lucien, historian 395
Châlons-sur-Marne, bishop of 429; diocese of 170, 217, 417
Champagne 10, 39, 40, 94, 121, 131, 250, 419, 431
Chancelade, Augustinian congregation of 86, 98
Chantal, Jeanne de 138, 139, 151, 317, 320; *see also* Visitation, order of
chapters, cathedral 6, 7, 21, 40, 42, 43, 44, 62, 163, 189, 195, 209, 387, 39; and bishops 78, 79, 171, 164, 177; and Jansenist crisis 421; and local families 76–7; and seminaries 195, 198; and visitations 175; canons of 74, 75–7, 78–9, 82–3; density of in France 68, 72, 74–5; local power/roles of 18, 21, 27, 31–2, 43, 75, 76, 78–9, 171, 177; loss of power 78; patronage rights of 57, 69–70, 187, 219; temporalities of 42, 48, 50, 51, 65, 75
chapters, collegiate 6, 7, 40, 44, 50, 51, 62, 69–70, 71, 72, 74–5, 77, 81, 164, 186, 187, 189, 209, 219
chapters, female 77
charities, Norman 274, 341, 363; *see also* confraternities
Charles IX, king of France 9
Charmoisy, Mme de 320
Chartres 11, 243, 249; cathedral chapter of 50, 74, 75; diocese of 20, 21, 25, 184, 285; site of pilgrimage 248
Châtellier, Louis, historian 367

Châtillon 121
Châtillon-les-Dombes, parish of 141
Chaumont 121
Chaunu, Pierre, historian 273, 431–2
Chelles, abbey of 132
Cherbourg 343
Chezal-Benoît, abbey and congregation of 86, 94
choir nuns 146, 151
choir schools 195; *see also* seminaries
Christian and charitable schools of the Infant Jesus, Rouen 142, 151
Christian Union of Fontenay 142
Christmas 230, 264
churchwardens/*fabriques*, 30, 177, 179, 214, 223, 240, 245, 342, 363, 382, 392, 421–2; activities of, 33–4, 53, 209, 212, 213, 214, 222, 245, 255, 261, 280; and parish priests, 35, 222–3; and parish schools, 307
Cistercians (Order of Cîteaux), 86, 87, 92, **95–9**, 105, 107, 134, 135, 418; Common Observance 87; female houses of 135, 138, 395; reform of 95–8; Strict Observance (Abstinents) 86, 87, 96, 97–8, 99, 100, 102; *see also* Feuillants; La Rochefoucauld; Port-Royal; Richelieu
Clamecy 121
Clarisses, female order of St Clare 130, 133
Clement VIII, pope 348
Clement XI, pope 412, 413
clergy, secular **61–83**, 84, 106, 113, 126, 131, 151, 158, 159, 161, 172, 178, 180, **183–207**, 217, 235, 236, 385, 429, 430; absenteeism of 68–9; access to 64–6; and benefices 54–8, 63–4; and church property 7, 37–8, 41, 42–54, 89; and churchwardens 34, 35, 222–3; and *commende* 89–92; and confraternities 123, 342, 348, 349–50, 355, 356, 360–1, 364; and cult of saints 232–3, 237, 239–40, 242; and Jansenism 412, 413, 415–16, 417, 418–19, 421–2, 423; and laypeople 42–3, 71, 177–8, 184–5, 186–7, 209, 212, 215, 216, 217, 222, 226, 245, 255, 263, 264, 265, 266, 348, 349, 415–16, 417, 421, 429; and missions 285–6, 287, 289–92, 294, 295; and popular religious practices 232, 243, 243–4, 245, 246, 247, 249, 265, 266, 429; and preaching 278, 279–82, 285; and processions 245–6; and sacraments 254–5, 256, 260, 262, 263–4, 265, 268,

269–70, 271, 275–6, 326, 328; and spirituality 314, 315, 319, 329, 334; and superstition 192, 214, 251, 278, 296, 428, 429; and synods 172–4; and taxation 7–8, 45, 58, 150; and tithes 41, 42, 47, 48; and visitations 175, 177–8, 180, 181, 182; and/in Company of the Holy Sacrament 377, 385, 392; as catechists 278, 296–7, 298–9, 301, 302, 305, 307, 309; as confessors 260–1, 265; behaviour of 68, 184–5, 275; books owned by 193–4; calibre of 252, 392; celibacy of 55, 57, 62–3, 124, 184, 271, 326; court-based 80–3; economic activities of 48–54; education/formation of 116, 117, 118, 161, 190, 191–3, **194–204**, 213; geographical origins of 67–8; in chapters 74–9, 162; in parishes 29, 30–1, 68–72, 208–26; in towns 6, 43; numbers of 8, 66–7; outsider 53, 209, 221; privileges of 45–6, 48, 64–5; problems of 6, 8; reform of 106, 115, 118, 155–6, 194, 196, 198–9, 289, 299, 319, 361; response to Protestantism 12–13; rivalry with regulars 29, 165, 168, 377, 408, 430; 'second-order' 72–9, 164, 377; social origins of 65, 66, 77–8, 186; subject to Formulary 406, 409; types of 54, 69; unbeneficed 32, 54, 70, 71, 117, 186, 225, 307; upper 10, 79–83, 387; *see also* assemblies of clergy; bishops; chapters, cathedral; chapters, collegiate; *curé*; parishes; regulars; religious orders, male monastic

clerical 'title' 65–6, 148, 185–6, 217

clerics 8, 22, 37, 45, 61, 63–4, 77, 88, 89, 90, 125, 148, 156, 157, 159, 165, 166, 167, 186, 191, 192, 194–5, 197, 199, 200, 204, 217, 219–20, 221, 272, 285, 294, 302, 307–8, 345, 370, 371, 377, 412, 421; and benefices, 26, 56, 57, 58, 64, 66; and *commende*, 88, 89; and confraternities, 342, 349; as schoolteachers, 307–8; at court 80–3; in chapters, 74, 75, 77; in parishes, 68–9, 219; orders of 64–6; *see also* clergy; clerical titles; orders

Clermont 370; cathedral chapter of 74; diocese 20, 146, 187, 191

Clichy 63

cloister 92, 103, 134, 136–7, 137–8, 138–9, 140, 141, 145, 312, 327, 352; adoption of 142; appeal of 371; problems with 143; spirituality outside of 320

Cloud of Unknowing 335

Cluny, abbey and order of 85–6, 99, 107; reform of 92–3, 95–7

Coëffetau, Nicolas, Dominican 279

Cognet, Louis, historian 328, 331

Coislin, Pierre du Cambout, Cardinal 418

Colbert, bishops 160

Colbert de Croissy, Joachim, bishop of Montpellier 301

Colbert, Jacques-Nicholas, archbishop of Rouen 166, 176, 179, 191, 203

Colbert, Jean-Baptiste 67, 231; and religious orders 126, 127, 147, 150; dislike of *dévots* 387

colleges/*collèges* 43, 90, 111, 113–14, 116, 125, 126, 156, 161, 184, 190, 195–6, 197, 199, 200, 201–2, 217, 284, 298, 306, 315, 324, 352, 353, 369–70, 373; *see also* Doctrinaires; Jesuits; Oratory; seminaries

collégiales see chapters, collegiate

Cologne 354, 369

commendataires 88, 89, 91, 92, 93

commende (*in commendam*) 49, 56, 81–3, **88–92**, 99, 100, 101, 131, 132; and reform of old orders 91, 92, 95; impact of 87, 88–91, 93

Commission des secours 130, 150

Commission of the Regulars 91, 129

Communion, Holy 250, 254, **265–8**, 276, 286, 288, 298, 302, 304, 352, 404, 406, 407; as last rite 272–3; at Easter 221, 223, 224, 259, 260, 264, 267; deferral of 399; first/solemn 258, 268, 271–2, 287, 294, 303; frequency of 258–9, 260, 261–2, 263–4, 267–8, 344, 351, 353, 354, 356, 369, 400, 403; hosts 212, 258; refusal of 265

Community of St Joseph (Josephists) 114, 292

compagnonnage 364

Company of the Holy Sacrament 273, **373–90**, 391, 392, 393; activities of 382–5; and Aa 391–2; and Congregation for the propagation of the faith 390–1; and seminaries 198; and general hospitals 383–5; and mysticism 329; and poor/poverty 128, 383; and reform of French church 426–7; creation of 373–6; expansion of 378–81; feared by clergy 387; finances of 385–6; impact of 382; legacy of 388–91, 393; membership of 376–8, 388; objectives of 375–6, 385;

INDEX 491

refuses female members 376; refuses regulars as members 377; secrecy of 375, 393; suppression of 386–7, 427
Company of Our Lady Mary, female congregation 137
Compostella, Santiago de 248, 250
Comtat Venaissin 112, 137
concours 187–8, 190, 199
Condé, Henri de Bourbon, prince of 250
Condren, Charles de, Oratorian 117, 205, 312, 319, 373, 377, 378
conférences ecclésiastiques see ecclesiastical conferences
confession 29, 133, 224, 251, **258–65**, 266, 272, 280, 287, 288, 298, 303, 304, 312, 344, 353, 354, 356, 359, 369, 401; during missions 287–8; frequency/regularity of 29, 262, 267–8, 353, 354, 356, 369, 401; 'general' 287; manuals of 260; denial of 265; practice of 212, 225, 265, 288; use of box 211–12, 261, 265, 280; *see also* Borromeo; cases of conscience; penance; rigorists
confirmation, sacrament of 176, 177, 181, 253–4, 257–8, 281, 304
confraternities, 23, 206, 211, 222, 224, 233, 234, 235, 237, 238, 239, 240, 242, 265, 273, 274, 275, 314, 320, 332, 333, 340–1, 344, **339–65**, 368, 369, 373, 375, 377, 379, 383, 392; affiliated to arch-confraternities 358; and 'good death' 274, 275; and catechism 301, 305; and church authorities 348, 350; and Jesuit colleges 353–4; and parish 33, 341, 349–50; and pilgrimages 250; and processions, 245; and religious orders 109, 123, 125, 126, 140, 152, 352; and rural missions, 352; and sacraments 264, 265, 267; and saints 234, 241, 244, 343; and schools 307; and spirituality 334; anti-clericalism of 342; anti-Protestantism of 375; arch-confraternity of Holy Sacrament 354, 358, 364; as 'schools of piety' 347, 352–8; banquets of, 343; characteristics of 340–3, 358; crisis of 344, 345; devotions of 240–1, 251, 306, 343, 351, 355, 356, 357, 361; evolution of 350–1 357, 363; historiography of 340; in rural areas 342; in urban areas 362; inversions of 364; lay features of 342; local densities of 362–3; membership of 355, 361, 364; mobilisation of 8, 10–11, 12–13, 233, 346, 347, 367; new types of 289, 346, 356, 364; of charity 141, 387, 388, 389–90, 417; of clergy 191, 349; officers of 349; statutes of 340–1, 343, 344, 346, 347–9, 350–1, 358, 375, 390; trades-based 341; within parishes 152, 211, 245, 265, 289, 372, 388; 'works' of 343; *see also* Dominicans; Franciscans; Jesuits; penitents
confraternity of St Joseph 275
confraternity of the *Agonisants* 238, 274, 357, 358
confraternity of the Agonisants of St Joseph 357
confraternity of the Cross 142, 356, 390
confraternity of the Five Wounds of Christ 356
confraternity of the Holy Ghost 10, 274, 341, 342, 343, 346, 348, 363
confraternity of the Holy Sacrament 124, 264, 267, 289, 343, 345–6, 351, 354, 355–6, 358, 360, 361, 362–3, 364
confraternity of the Name of Jesus 346
confraternity of the Passion of Christ 356, 388–9
confraternity of the Sacred Heart 289, 356, 358
Congregation for the propagation of the faith 377, 390–1, 392
Congregation of France *see* Augustinian canons-regular
Congregation of Our Lady of Charity, Caen 151
Congregation of St Thomas of Villanova 142
Congregation of the Daughters of the Holy Virgin of Vannes 142
Congregation of the Mission *see* Lazarists; de Paul
conseil de conscience 158, 161
Conti, Armand de Bourbon, prince of 378
contrition 260, 399–400, 401; *see also* penance
converses (lay sisters) 146
Cordeliers 109; *see also* Franciscans
Cordoux, *seigneurie* of 51
Coret, Jean-Jacques, Jesuit 334
Corneille, Pierre 33, 314
Corpus Christi, feast of 230, 243, 341
Corpus Domini, feast of 343
Coton, Claude, Benedictine monk 51
Coton, Pierre, Jesuit 323, 324, 325
Council of Trent 2–3, 5, 23, 26, 58, 67, 115, 171, 174, 175, 193, 238, 262, 263, 264, 333, 340, 385, 419, 426; and Bible 313;

492 INDEX

and catechism 193, 213, 278, 297–8, 301; and *concours* 187–8, 190; and confraternities 345, 348; and cult of saints 232, 234, 248; and defence of sacraments 253, 260, 263; and enclosure 136, 140, 143, 151; and godparenting 255; and marriage 268–9, 270, 326; and mass, 266; and pilgrimages 248; and preaching 278; and priesthood 205, 271; and private confession 258, 260, 265; and reform of clergy 75, 183, 187, 194, 199; and religious orders 94, 131, 133; and role of episcopate 23, 155–6, 161, 166–7, 168, 169; and role of parish 29, 30, 208; and seminaries 195, 197, 199; and theological disputes 396; French views of 2, 4; profession of faith of 406
Cour Sainte 325; *see also* Caussin
Coutances, diocese of 180, 185, 191, 192, 300, 302; synods of 173–4
Crasset, Jean, Jesuit 274
Crouzet, Denis, historian 13
crown *see* Henri IV; Louis XIII; Louis XIV; Mazarin; Richelieu
Cum Occasione, papal bull 404
curé/parish priest, 29, 40, 42, 47, 62, 63, 64, 72, 117, 181, 183, 187, 191, 198, 215, 216, 268, 349, 372, 373, 377, 389, 390, 392, 408, 428, 429; and Bible-reading, 415; and catechism 278, 279, 296, 300, 301–2, 305, 307; and churchwardens 35, 222–3; and *concours* 188; and confession 261, 263, 264; and confraternities 274, 360–1, 363; and cult of saints, 239–40; and devotions 241; and ecclesiastical conferences 192; and marriage, 269, 270; and midwives, 256; and missions, 295; and other clergy 72, 197, 219–20, 225, 422; and parishes 221–5; and preaching, 281–3; and sacraments 263, 268; and schools 306–7; and synods 173, 180; and visitations 180, 182; as locals/outsiders 239–40; books owned by 193–4; careers of 218–19; Jansenists among 417, 418–19, 421; origins of 217–18; parishioners and 216, 226, 265; primacy of 216–17, 220, 225, 270; residence of 184, 216; responsibilities of 220–1, 225; Richerist views among, 423; status of 69–70, 103–4, 218; use of curates by, 219; *see also* clergy; clerics; parish
curé primitif 32, 69, 70, 103, 169, 205, 216–17

curia, Roman 1, 2, 3, 404
Cyprian of Alexandria 411

Daughters of Charity 140–2, 143, 144, 145, 372, 384
Daughters of instruction of the Infant Jesus of Le Puy 142, 309
Daughters of the Cross 142
Daughters of the Good Saviour of Caen 142
Daughters of the Trinity, Valence 142
Daughters of Wisdom 142
Dauphiné 14, 41, 67, 70, 87, 107, 234, 236, 290, 295, 342, 359, 360, 389
Dax, bishop of 170
de Meur, Vincent 392
de Paul, Vincent 63, 151, 235, 278, 335, 389; and Company of Holy Sacrament 377, 378, 385; and Daughters of Charity 140–1; and *dévots* 372, 383, 386; and missions 285–6, 289, 295; and seminaries, 196–8, 199–200, 203; disciple of Bérulle 116, 205, 319, 373; founder of Lazarists 116–17, 198, 201, 205; *see also dévots*; Lazarists; Marillac, Louise de
de Sales, François 112, 194, 289; and marriage, 326–7; as model bishop, 169; as model saint 235–6, 279; co-founder of Visitation order 138–9; influence of, 370; spirituality of 311, 320–4, 325, 333–4, 370, 399; *see also* Chantal; Geneva/Annecy; *Introduction to the devout life*
décimes 7–8, 23, 46, 48
Delumeau, Jean, historian 426
Démia, Charles 151, 307
Déols, abbey of 103
Desmarest, family 160
dévotes 136, 145, 152, 370, 371, 383; as spiritual directors 422
devotions, christocentric 232, 237–8, 261–2, 266, 356, 361
dévots 161, 357, **366–92**, 393, 398, 426; activities of 368–9, 371–2, 375–6, 377, 382, 384–5, 386, 389–90; against duels 388–9; and Catholic League 367–8; and Company of Holy Sacrament 198, 373–92; and financial milieux 385–6; and new confraternities/sodalities 124, 352, 359, 364, 368–9, 389–90; and new religious orders 135–6, 141, 143–4, 145, 152, 371–2; and poverty 383–4; and

Protestants 390–1; and schools 307; beginnings of 367–72; devotions/ spirituality of 314, 317, 320, 324–5, 334, 335, 369–70, 393, 411, 415; divided by Jansenism, 423; impact on society 392–3; parish 241, 265, 289, 307; *parti des* 367, 372–3, 387, 388; *politiques* among, 368; social profile of 368, 372, 377–8; suspect under Louis XIV, 387–8, 409; women as 136, 143–4, 145, 300–1, 371, 376–7, 383, 386, 422
devout humanism 322
Die, diocese of 21
Diefendorf, Barbara, historian 371
Digne, chapter of 75
Dijon 20, 121, 136, 149, 329, 353, 357, 359, 363, 388; diocese of, 21
dioceses 14, **18–25**, 71, 77, 78, 82, 158, 171, 173, 186, 188, 198, 209, 230, 271; and clerical titles, 66, 185–6, 217; as 'fiscal' units 4, 7; attractiveness of 82, 157, 165; catechisms for 299–300; chapters in, 72, 74–5, 78–9; clerical densities in, 64, 67–8, 71; creation of new 18, 21, 90; endowment of 22, 40–1, 48; geography of 23–5, 72; governance of 4, 33, 49, 164, 170–2, 383, 389; identity of, 22–3; 'Jansenist' 188, 411, 417, 418, 421; numbers in France 80; organized into provinces, 25–7; parishes in 27, 28–9, 31–2, 36; religious orders in, 119, 121, 144, 146; size of, 20, 28, 172; subdivisions of 27–8, 172, 190–1, 192; visitations of 175–8, 180, 183; *see also décimes*; *don gratuit*
Discalced Augustinians 107
Discalced Carmelites 107, 108
Doctrinaires (*congrégation de la doctrine chrétienne*) 111, 112, 114, 115, 120, 136; and seminaries 198, 203; Augustinian leanings of, 419; colleges of 102, 113, 196, 306
Dol, diocese of 23
Dôle 308
Dominicans (Order of Preachers) 105, 107, 108, 109, 111, 113, 120, 124, 130, 132, 133, 280, 358; activities of, 108; and confraternities, 339, 362; and Marian devotions, 354; and missions, 290; as preachers, 281; history of, 108; rivalry with Jesuits, 396
don gratuit 23, 46, 48
Douai 146

dowries, for nuns 147–9, 50
du Bellay, Martin, bishop of Fréjus 361
Dubois, Guillaume, Cardinal 89
du Ferrier, Jean 385
duelling 263, 265, 388–9, 402
Dupront, Alphonse, historian 247

early church 400, 407, 411, 414, 428
Easter 174, 176, 181, 182, 350; confession and communion at (Easter 'duty') 221, 223–4, 259–60, 262, 264, 267
ecclesiastical conferences (*conferences ecclésiastiques*) 103, 173, 174, 191–3, 206, 221, 289, 301, 332
Einsiedeln, pilgrimage to 248
Embrun 25
enclosure, religious 86, 101, 102, 134; Council of Trent and 151; and female orders/congregations 133, 136–8, 140, 141, 144, 309
Enlightenment 231, 395, 426, 430
Erasmus of Rotterdam, Desiderius 2, 246, 278, 312, 322, 361, 427
Escobar, Antonio, Jesuit 408
Estaing, Joachim d', bishop of Clermont 263
Estates General 4, 38, 47, 113, 136
Estrées, César, Cardinal 27, 160
Eucharist, sacrament of *see* Communion; Easter
Eudes, Jean 116, 117–18, 151, 264, 284–5, 286, 292–3, 302, 330, 378; disciple of Bérulle 205, 312, 319–20
Eudists (Congregation of Jesus and Mary) 114, 116, 117–18, 125, 198, 199; *see also* seminaries
Exempts, Benedictine congregation of 86
Extreme unction, sacrament of 30, 253, 254, 272, 276

fabriques see churchwardens
Febvre, Lucien, historian 311
Féline, spiritual writer 327
Fénelon, Antoine de La Motte-Salignac, marquis de 378, 389
Fénelon, François de La Motte-Salignac 81, 117, 162, 290, 311, 317, 330–1, 388–9
Ferté, Jeanne, historian 307
Feuillants, congregation of 86, 99, 113, 127, 138
Flagellants/flagellation 11, 344, 351, 359; *see also* Penitents

Flanders 24, 94, 165, 188, 256, 341
Fleuriau d'Armenonville, Louis, bishop of Aire/Angers 182
Fleury, Hercule, Cardinal 418, 423
Fleury, Claude 296
Fontainebleau 250
Fontenay-le-Comte 32
Fontevraud, abbey of 130–1, 135
Fontgombault, abbey of 100
Fontpertuis, Mme de 422
Forbin-Janson, Toussaint, Cardinal 27
Forez 167, 216, 217
Formulary, anti-Jansenist 168, 404, 405, 406, 409, 417, 418, 422; *see also* Jansenism
Forty Hours 267; devotion of 126, 238, 267, 285, 289, 356
Foucault, Michel, historian 384
Fouquet, François, bishop of Bayonne 139
Fouquet, Nicholas 379, 385–6, 387
Fourier, Pierre 335
Fourth Lateran Council 223, 259
Franche-Comté 24, 94, 137, 188, 210, 220, 308, 342, 431
Francis of Assisi 105; cult of 239
Franciscans 107, 113, 124, 165, 239; and confraternities 339; and missions 290; and Rosary devotions 354; anti-Jansenism of 128; as preachers 280, 281; characteristics of 105, 108, 109; Conventuals 107, 109, 110; Observants 107, 109, 110, 111, 133; presence in France 12, 108, 109–11, 123
Franciscans, female 130, 132–3
François I, king of France 80, 345, 347
French Canada 291, 336, 386
French Revolution 17, 18, 21, 26, 39, 63, 67, 121, 142, 301, 334
Frequent Communion (Arnauld) 262, 321, 400, 403, 404, 406–7, 412; *see also* Arnauld, Antoine; Jansenism
Fronde 51, 139, 158, 160, 210, 379, 384, 385, 388, 408

Gallia Christiana 23
gallican, attitudes 4, 26, 112; church council 4, 413; traditions 94, 115, 127, 167–9, 170, 188, 203, 231, 247, 291, 394, 397, 412, 413, 418, 423, 427, 428, 430, 431
Gap 112, 198; diocese 300
Gascony 72, 182

Gassendi, Pierre 75
Gaultier, René 329
Geneva 138, 320
Genovéfains 98, 102, 103, 104; *see also* Augustinian canons-regular; Sainte-Geneviève
Germany/Holy Roman Empire 2, 17, 77, 89, 131, 248, 334, 430, 431
Gerson, Jean 278, 282, 297, 312
Gévaudan 40
Gien 121
Godeau, Antoine, bishop of Grasse and Vence 162, 169, 325, 333, 360, 361, 377, 407
godparents 255, 296
Goldmann, Lucien, historian 395, 417
Gondi, Jean-François, archbishop of Paris 386; *see also* Retz
good death: idea of 273–4; preparation for 235, 239, 272, 273–5, 326; *see also* confraternities
Goubert, Pierre, historian 36
graduates 75–6, 162, 171, 203, 221, 280, 421; and church benefices 68–9, 72, 75–6, 188, 190, 204
Granada, Luis de, 193, 194, 314
grand renfermement (enclosure of poor) 384
grand siècle 366, 425
Grande Chartreuse 88
Grandmont, order of 107
Grasse 358, 360, 361, 377; diocese of 20
Greenshields, Malcolm R., historian xi, 5
Gregory the Great, pope 193
Gregory XV, pope 95
Grenoble 20, 72, 88, 127, 231, 355, 382, 388, 390, 391, 427; diocese of 238, 239, 240, 292, 360, 419
Grignan, François de, archbishop of Arles 374
Grignion de Montfort, Louis-Marie 296
Groethuysen, Bernard, historian 417
gros décimateurs 35, 209
Guide for sinners 194, 314; *see also* Granada
Guise, Henri de Lorraine, duke of 3
Guise, Henri de Lorraine, archbishop of Reims 166
Guise, house of 13, 49, 89, 132, 160
Guyart, Marie 317
Guyenne 9, 10, 78, 359
Guyon, Jeanne-Marie de la Motte, Mme, mystic 318; ideas condemned 330; fate of 331

habitué clergy 71, 185, 186–7, 192; uses of in parishes 71–2, 220, 275, 422; *see also* clergy, secular; clerics
hagiography 169, 257, 335, 336
Harlay, Francois de, archbishop of Paris 27, 292, 293, 300, 386, 405, 416, 419
Harphius, Hendrik 317
Hayden, J. Michael, historian xi, 5
Henri II, king of France 2, 11
Henri III, king of France 3, 4, 9, 10, 11, 13, 119, 346, 313, 367, 373
Henri IV, king of France 5, 7, 11, 13, 14, 21, 24, 47, 51, 90, 94, 109, 112, 113, 157, 158, 159, 160, 165, 166, 324, 333, 347, 359, 367, 372, 373, 389
Henry VIII, king of England 2
heresy 2, 12, 283, 291, 306, 313, 347, 351, 427
Hilarion de Coste 336
Holy Ghost *see* confraternities
Holy Land, pilgrimage to 248
holy orders, sacrament of 253–4, 257, 271–2, 319
Holy Roman Empire *see* Germany
Holy Sacrament, devotions of, 124, 126, 428; *see also* confraternities; Company of the Holy Sacrament
Holy Sacrament, priests of 118
Holy Sacrament and Charity of Bourges, sisters of 142
Honoré de Cannes, Capuchin 292
Honoré de Paris (Bochart de Champigny), Capuchin 111
hôpital général 90, 143–4, 384–5; *see also* Company of the Holy Sacrament; hospitals; Paris
Hospitallers of Dieppe 142
Hospitallers of La Flèche 142, 144
Hospitallers of Le Havre 144
Hospitallers of Our Lady of Charity of Dijon 142
Hospitallers of St Augustine 130
hospitals 71, 90, 112, 143, 144–5, 151, 164, 384, 386
Huguenots/Protestants xiii, 9, 10, 13, 21, 131, 209, 215, 242, 289–90, 290–1, 297, 346, 367, 373, 374, 390–1, 398, 412, 413, 414, 416, 427, 428; *see also* Calvinism/Calvinists

Ile-de-France 28
Imitation of Christ 312, 313–24, 333, 335
Immaculate Conception 238, 354

in commendam see commende
Index of prohibited books 330, 331, 414
indulgences 246, 247, 264, 287, 354, 357, 358, 361, 362
Innocent X, pope 127
Innocent XI, pope 409–10, 413, 430
Inquisition 3, 328; Roman 3, 410, 414; Spanish 263
Instructions for confessors 194, 405, 406–7, 408; *see also* Borromeo
Introduction to the devout life 194, 320–1, 323, 326; *see also* de Sales
Italy 3, 11, 67, 89, 110, 120, 127, 162, 165, 196, 197, 265, 284, 294, 317, 330, 334, 390, 402, 403, 414, 429, 430, 431

Jacobins 108; *see also* Dominicans
Jansen, Cornelius 397, 398, 400, 403, 404–5, 406, 409, 411, 412; five propositions attributed to 403, 404, 405, 406, 413, 423
Jansenism/Jansenists 90, 181, 331, 332, **394–423**; among regulars 127–8, 418–19; and 'further' reform of Catholicism 427; and Company of the Holy Sacrament, 378; and frequent communion 268, 399–400, 403, 406–7; and penance 260; and social withdrawal 423; and use of Bible 415, 331–2; as crypto-Calvinism 395, 401, 403; as fiction 403; clandestine movements of 419; components of 403, 408; contours of 413, 417–23; formulary against 404–5, 406, 409, 417, 418, 422; geography of 419–20; 'golden age' of 409–12; hostility to casuistry, 402–3; influence in Bourbon Spain, 430; laypeople as 421–2; origins of 394–5, 396–7; pastoral dimensions of 414–17, 429, 431; persecution of 405–6, 408–9, 412–13; rigorism of in France 403, 406, 408, 410, 427; Saint-Cyran and development of 397–401, 403–4; *see also* Arnauld; Augustinians; *Augustinus*; Frequent Communion; Jansen; Port-Royal; Quesnel; Saint-Cyran
Jerusalem, pilgrimage to 246, 248
Jesuits 12, 14, 44, 90, 111, 115, 118, 120, 126, 138, 140, 224, 251, 320, 321, 333, 368, 398, 431; and Aa 391–2; and christocentric devotions 261–2; and Company of the Holy Sacrament 377–8; and confraternities 354, 358, 361; and

dévots 369–70, 384; and frequent communion 262, 263–4, 268; and good death 274; and marriage 327; and missions 125, 284–5, 288, 290, 292, 294; and Molinism 396–7; and mysticism 316, 328–9; and new devotions 251, 352, 353, 356; and seminaries 114, 128, 196, 201, 204; and spiritual direction 315–16, 328; and Visitation order 356; anti-Jansenists 109, 403–4, 412, 421, 423; attack Bérulle 318; catechisms of 298; controversial in France 112–13; clash with bishops 127, 292; colleges of 102, 112, 113–14, 116, 198, 199, 201, 204, 306; confessors to kings 127, 373; defend probabilism 410; influence of 44, 95, 113, 116, 139, 211, 378; Marian congregations of 124, 268, 306, 316, 324, 352–4, 369; politics of 14, 373, 397; spirituality of 315–16, 321, 322–3, 323–5, 327, 328, 358; under attack 225, 268, 403, 407–8, 410, 423
John of the Cross 314, 330
John the Baptist 232
John XII, pope 20
Joncoux, Mlle de 422
Joseph, père, Capuchin 111, 135, 289, 315, 374, 390
Josephists *see* Community of St Joseph
Joyeuse, Ange de, Capuchin 111
Joyeuse, François, Cardinal 14, 27, 50, 55, 111, 197, 203
jubilees 247, 264
Jura 31, 70

Kerver, Hyacinthe, Capuchin 390

L'Estoile, Pierre de 427
La Bruyère, Jean de 366, 395
La Chaise-Dieu, abbey of 43
La Chaize, François de, royal confessor 290, 412
La Cour, Didier de, Benedictine 101
La Flèche 332, 392; college of 90; *see also* Hospitallers of La Flèche; Jesuits
La Rochefoucauld, François, Cardinal 160; reformer of old orders 95–8, 100, 103, 106
La Rochefoucauld, François, duke of 395
La Rochelle 32, 289, 355, 431; bishop of 168; diocese 21, 32–3, 67, 176, 194, 305
La Salle, Jean-Baptiste de 118

La Trappe, abbey of 86, 91, 99, 101, 102, 135; *see also* Cistercians; Rancé
La Valette, Louis, Cardinal 50, 89
La Vallière, Louise de 133
Ladies of Charity 141, 372, 383, 386; *see also* Daughters of Charity; de Paul; Marillac, Louise de
Ladies of St Maur, congregation of 151
laity/parishioners 22, 177, 187, 192, 206, 221, 270, 281, 282, 283; and church property 6, 42, 52; and clergy 41, 42, 71, 177–8, 184–5, 206, 215, 216–17, 219, 226, 254, 265, 348, 349, 429; and confraternities 12, 356, 390–1; and missions 289, 302; and parish 213, 215, 216, 223, 224; and processions 246; and religious orders 44, 109; and sacraments 221, 253, 254, 255, 260, 261, 262, 263, 264, 266; and saints 236, 240; and the mass 266–7, 416; and visitations 177–8, 184; anticlericalism among 37; as catechists 301, 417; Bible for use by 415; devotions/spirituality of 271, 312, 314, 315, 319, 320, 324–7, 329, 356, 412; generosity of 233, 240; Jansenists among 417; vernacular liturgy for 416; *see also* churchwardens; *curé*/parish priest; parish
Lallemant, Louis, Jesuit 328
Lamoignon, Guillaume 379
Langres 21, 69, 79, 353, 377; cathedral chapter of 74, 77; diocese 20, 121
Languedoc 18, 20, 40, 72, 127, 167, 291, 295, 359, 360, 374, 389, 431
Languet de Gergy, Jean-Joseph, archbishop of Sens 300
Laon 10, 248, 249, 346; diocese 300
Lardière, Jean 218
Latreille, André, historian 14
Laval-Boisdauphin, Henri de, bishop of La Rochelle 168, 300
Lavaur, bishop of 167
Law, John 39, 150
Lazarists (Congregation of the Mission) 144, 430; and missions, 117, 125, 285–6, 289, 292, 293, 295; and seminaries, 117, 128, 198–200, 201, 203, 204; expansion of, 118–19; foundation of 116–17, 285; *see also* de Paul
Le Bras, Gabriel, historian 339–40
Le Camus, Étienne, Cardinal 127, 231, 292, 294, 361, 390, 428
Le Gendre, Louis 279

Le Gouverneur, Guillaume, bishop of Saint-Malo 212
Le Jay, Nicholas, bishop of Cahors 145
Le Maitre de Sacy, Louis-Isaac 314, 331, 415
Le Maitre, Antoine 401
Le Mans, diocese of 20
Le Moyne, Pierre, Jesuit 324–5, 334
Le Peletier, Michel, bishop of Angers 180–2, 231, 282, 300
Le Puy, diocese 40, 309; pilgrimage to, 248
Le Tellier, Charles-Maurice, archbishop of Reims 179, 186, 189, 410
Le Tourneux, Nicholas 416
Lebrun, François, historian 423
Lebrun, Pierre 233, 428
Lectoure, diocese of 18
Lefebvre d'Etaples, Jacques 2
Lejeune, Jean, Oratorian 285, 292
Lent, preaching during 12, 101, 125, 260, 280–1, 283, 284, 285, 288, 293, 295; penitential season of 230, 262, 270, 280, 351
Lepanto 354, 369
Lescar, diocese of 24
Lestonnac, Jeanne de 138
Liancourt, duke of 378
Liesse, Notre-Dame de, pilgrimage to 11, 243, 248, 249, 250
Lille 74, 146, 353
Limoges 14, 359; company of Holy Sacrament in 382; diocese of 103, 146, 178, 191
Limousin 10, 72, 293, 359, 360
Lisieux, dean of 349; diocese of 185
litugical/religious, books 193, 222, 313, 332, 333, 414; calendar 71, **229–32**, 243, 245, 252, 265, 276, 280, 286, 297, 325, 351, 415; innovations 414–16; services 30, 71, 78, 111, 151, 173, 178, 191, 199, 278, 311; vestments 178, 212, 222, 266
liturgy, neo-gallican 416; *see also* Jansenism
Lombez, diocese of 18
Longchamp, female abbey of 132
Longueville, duchesse de 422
Loretto, pilgrimage to 248, 250
Lorraine, Charles, Cardinal of 4, 27, 49, 55, 194
Lorraine, duchy of 23, 39, 77, 86, 94, 137, 165, 188, 419, 431
Loudun 328
Louis XI 132
Louis XII 132

Louis XIII 21, 51, 95, 124, 137, 157, 274, 323, 333, 354, 373, 401; and Company of Holy Sacrament, 374, 386; church patronage under 81, 90, 158; pilgrim king 249
Louis XIV 24, 25, 27, 31, 32, 34, 47, 67, 79, 83, 86, 93, 94, 99, 100, 101, 102, 110, 113, 114, 116, 117, 125, 126, 127, 133, 142, 143, 144, 147, 150, 162, 164, 167, 168, 170, 171, 174, 181, 191, 201, 214, 221, 225, 240, 252, 261, 270, 274, 282, 291, 293, 326, 330, 331, 336, 352, 384, 388, 389, 392, 395, 402, 403, 405, 410, 411, 416, 418, 419, 422, 425; against pilgrimages, 248, 249; and new saints 231; church patronage under 24, 26–7, 81, 82, 90, 132, 158–60, 165–6; court of 367, 387; dislike of Jansenists, 401, 408, 413; fiscality of 39, 44–5, 48, 149, 307; quarrels with papacy 24, 409; suppresses Company of the Holy Sacrament, 379, 386, 387
Louis XV 89, 95, 133, 250, 384
Louise de France 133
Loupès, Philippe, historian 72
Louvain 396, 398
Louviers 328
Loyola, Ignatius of 235, 284, 329, 335
Luçon, bishop of 168; diocese of 116, 166, 196; *see also* Oratorians; Richelieu
Luther, Martin 232, 259, 260, 278, 297, 345, 361, 396; catechism of 298
Luynes, Antoinette d'Albert de 137
Lyon 10, 11, 31, 32, 110, 111, 120, 121, 138–9, 140, 142, 151, 333, 355, 378, 382, 388, 390, 391; archbishops of 166, 375, 377; cathedral chapter of, 75; confraternities in diocese 345, 346, 347, 353, 358, 361, 362–3; diocese of 172, 185, 203, 216, 217, 307, 358, 361, 362, 377; religious orders in 120, 121, 142, 151, 292
Lyonnais 342, 360

Mabillon, Jean, Maurist and scholar 86, 89, 102, 428, 429
Mâcon 10, 77, 356, 359
Maillezais, bishop of 193; diocese of 21
Maintenon, Madame de 330, 366, 388
Maire, Catherine, historian 395
Malta, knights of 40
Marian congregations/sodalities 264, 315–16, 324, 352–4, 369, 391; devotions

238, 240–1, 251, 315, 332, 352–4, 369, 391; pilgrimages 249; *see also* confraternities; Jesuits; Rosary
Marie-Thérèse, queen of France 124
Marillac, Louise de 141, 144, 372, 383; *see also* Daughters of Charity; de Paul; Ladies of Charity
Marillac, Michel de 314, 373
Marmoutier, abbey of 94
Marquemont, Denis Simon de, archbishop of Lyon 138, 145
marriage, sacrament of 253, 254, 268–71
Marseille 11, 214, 249, 344, 346–7, 351, 363, 378, 379, 382, 385, 386, 388, 390
Martin, Claude, Benedictine 336
Martin, Henri-Jean, historian 333, 334
mass 34, 71, 75, 205, 210, 212, 215–16, 224, 232, 233, 250, 258, 260, 265–6, 267, 281, 302, 304, 344, 350, 351, 354, 416
Massif Central 70
Massillon, Jean-Baptiste, preacher 279
Mathurines of Paris 142
Maubeuge 288
Maubuisson, abbey of 132
Maunoir, Julien, Jesuit 286, 292
Maurists (congregation of Saint-Maur) 51, 86, 94–5, 96–7, 101–3, 118, 120, 125, 151, 322, 411, 419, 429
Mazarin, Jules, Cardinal 27, 109, 165, 403, 415; and Company of the Holy Sacrament 379, 386–7, 389; and crown church patronage 158; and reform of monastic orders 96, 97, 99; as benefice-holder 49, 56, 89; dislike of Jansenists 401, 405, 408
McManners, John xii
Meaux 103, 211; catechism of 304; diocese 25, 191, 192; *see also* Bossuet
Medici, Alessandro de', Cardinal (Pope Leo XI), 14
Medici, Marie de' 374, 398
Melun, edict of 195
Mende, diocese of 40
Mersenne, Marin, Minim 109
Messieurs, Jesuit congregations of 353, 369
Metz 94; bishop of 418, 419; diocese of 24
Michaelis, Sébastian, Dominican 108, 119
Michelet, Jules, historian 229
Midi 18, 20, 74, 108, 346, 360, 361, 421
midwives 256
Minims, order of 107, 109, 111, 113, 124

miracles 235, 237, 242, 246, 247, 248, 249, 251, 253, 256, 429; *see also* pilgrimage; saints
Miramionnes, female congregation of 142
Mirepoix, bishop of 197, 419
missions 79, 103, 114, 116, 125, 164, 171, 198, 212, 220, 239, 240, 246, 256–7, 264–5, 276, 277, 281, **283–96**, 332, 333, 339, 352, 354, 355, 356, 362, 376, 382, 385, 386; and reform of clergy 285, 286, 289, 296; and religious instruction 296, 301–2, 303, 307; conduct of 285–6, 289–90, 292; diffusing devotions 334; duration of 283, 287, 288, 292, 294, 295; evolution of 283–4, 284–5, 286, 287, 293, 294, 296; impact of 288, 295; in Protestant regions 289–90, 295; Jansenist criticisms of 295; patchiness of 291–2, 295; preaching during 286–7; religious orders and 125, 288, 290–1, 354; secular clergy and 117, 119, 285–6, 289, 290, 291–2, 294; *see also* Advent; Lent; preaching
Missions Étrangères de Paris 114, 291, 385, 386, 392
Molière 366, 387
Molina, Antonio de, Carthusian 193
Molina, Luis de, Jesuit theologian 396–7; theological system of 204, 396–7, 403, 407; *see also* Jansenism; Jesuits
Molinos, Miguel de, mystic 330
Monluc, Jean de 9, 10
Montaigne, Michel de 138
Montauban 289
Montchal, Charles de, archbishop of Toulouse 407
Montfaucon, Bernard de, Maurist and scholar 102
monti di pietà (pawn banks) 390
Montivilliers, abbey of 42
Montmartre 112; female abbey of 135
Montpellier 48, 289, 290, 391; bishop of 419; catechism of 301; chapter of 50
Mont-Saint-Michel, pilgrimage to 248
Mont-Valérien, pilgrimage to 249
Moral Reflections, 331–2, 405, 411–12, 413, 414; *see also* Quesnel; *Unigenitus*
morale relâchée, 407; *see also* Jesuits
morale sévère 408; *see also* rigorists
Morlaix 379
mortmain 38, 43, 45, 55, 149, 150
Moutiers-Sainte-Marie 256
Muratori, Ludovico 430, 431

mysticism/mystics, 115, 119, 135, 205, 237, 267, 310, 313–4, 315, 316–18, 321, 323, 327, 328–31, 335, 368, 370, 375; *see also* Bérulle; Guyon; quietism; spirituality

Nanterre 103
Nantes 379, 421; diocese of 103, 418; edict of 313; revocation of edict of 21, 145, 220, 290, 307, 391
Narbonne 48; cathedral chapter of 50, 75; diocese of 22, 167
Navarre 165
Navarre, Henri de (Henri IV) 13, 24
neo-Augustinians 329, 427–8; *see also* Augustinians-Jansenists
Neri, Filippo 115, 335
Netherlands, 1, 3, 20, 390, 403, 405
Nevers, diocese of 90
Nevers, Charles de Gonzague, duke of 374
Neveu, Bruno, historian 395
'new' Catholics 221, 290, 307; *see also* Calvinists; Huguenots; Protestants
Nicole, Pierre 329, 412
Nîmes 289, 391; diocese of 21
Noailles, Louis-Antoine, Cardinal, 27, 127, 405, 410, 413, 418, 419
Normandy 34, 50, 67, 71, 102, 113, 118, 131, 185, 206, 220, 293, 302, 342, 346, 363, 389, 431
Notre Sauveur, congregation of 86
Noyers 121
Nuncio, papal 2, 3, 4, 156; *see also* baptism

official 79, 171
Olier, Jean-Jacques 116, 117, 198, 199, 205, 286, 294, 306, 307, 312, 319, 320, 373, 378, 389, 390
Oloron, diocese of 24
ondoiement 254, 256; *see also* baptism
oraison 311
Orange 379; prince of 24
Oratory/Oratorians 63, 102, 117, 118, 119, 124, 126, 151, 198, 201, 251, 318, 319, 377, 412, 430; and missions 125, 285–6, 288, 290, 292; and reform of secular clergy 116, 197; Augustinian leanings of 114, 127–8, 204, 411, 419; colleges of 113, 116, 199, 306; evolution of 128; origins of 115–16; rivalry with Jesuits 368, 396; running seminaries 116, 196, 197, 199, 200, 204; *see also* Bérulle, Pierre de; Jansenism; Quesnel
Orcibal, Jean, historian 395

Orléanais 6
Orléans 25, 38, 132; diocese of 103, 182; Estates General of 38
Our Lady of Pity 238
Our Lady of Rosary 238
Our Lady of Charity, Caen, congregation of 142

pain bénit 222, 266, 267, 276
Pallier, Denis, historian 11
Pallu, *dévot* family 386
Pamiers 421
papacy 3, 4, 12, 14, 26, 112, 117, 163, 197; and Bible 414, 415–16, 431; and confraternities 348, 354, 358; and cult of saints 235; and ecclesiastical patronage/benefices 20, 24, 57, 78, 88–9, 95, 166, 188, 189; and French church, 26, 169; and French crown, 24, 35, 45, 78, 413; and new orders/congregations 109, 117, 137, 141, 390, 391; and reform of orders 95, 98, 99; and theological disputes 330–1, 332, 396–7, 403, 404, 408, 409, 410, 413; *see also* Jansenism; quietism
Paray-le-Monial, 356
Paris 27, 51, 82, 83, 88, 119, 125, 167, 168, 181, 210, 214, 248, 249, 267, 278, 285, 306, 320, 396, 400; and *dévots* 317, 370–1; and religious orders 98, 102, 108, 109, 110, 119–20, 131, 135–6, 139, 140, 146; and wars of religion 3, 13, 346, 367; archbishop of 44, 127, 117, 158, 159, 165–6, 200, 223, 292, 375, 377, 386, 405, 408–9, 410, 413, 418, 419 (*see also* Gondi; Harlay; Noailles; Retz, Paul de Gondi); catechism of 300; cathedral chapter of 74, 75; clergy of 67, 71–2, 278; Company of Holy Sacrament in 329, 375–6, 377, 378, 379, 382, 383–4, 385, 387–8, 388–9, 390; confraternities in 10, 346, 362, 363; diocese 25, 27, 67, 292, 301, 302, 304, 307, 377, 416; general hospital 384–5; Jansenist parishes in 225, 421–2; parishes of 31–2, 33, 117, 164, 222, 292, 299, 302, 306, 417; parlement 113, 149, 329, 362, 387, 404; *petites écoles* in 307; preaching in 279–80, 280–1; publishing trade in 333; seminaries in 196, 197, 199–200, 203, 419; theology faculty 83, 162, 203, 285, 389, 397, 402, 404, 406; *see also* Sorbonne

parish(es) 7, 9, **27–36**, 53, 56, 67, 68, 69, 70, 71, 79, 82, 114, 125, 141, 152, 164, 173, 182, 189, 199, 203, **208–26**, 233, 236, 256, 261, 265, 266, 280, 283, 286, 288, 289, 297, 299, 341, 356, 390, 413, 430; and communities 28–30; and confraternities 342, 343, 350, 355, 360, 363; and dioceses 17, 18, 20, 23; and new devotions 352; and testators 273; and tithes 53; as a benefice 55; baptismal font 254; basis of future seminaries 197; churches in/of 126, 212, 364; clergy resident in 69, 70, 71, 72; creation of 29–31; *dévots* of 393; in towns 31–2, 223–5; missions in 264, 288; number in France 28; patron saints of 243; primacy of 208–25, 252, 348, 349; processions 243, 244, 245, 247; property of 33, 34, 35, 52; reclothing of churches in 212–14; registers 221, 254; regulars serving in 56; resignations of 218; resources of 209; running of 33, 34; rural 32–3, 225–6; schools 306, 307; source of identity 223; state of 211; status of 208, 210; structures of 31; tithes, 52; triumph of 208, 225; *see also* curé
parlements 113, 149, 347
parti des dévots 367, 372–3, 387
Pascal, Blaise 395, 397, 404; attacks Jesuits 322, 324, 407–8
patois, preaching in 283
Paul V, pope 95, 157
Pavillon, Nicholas, bishop of Alet 377, 411
Peace of the church 405, 409, 410, 412, 418; *see also* Jansenism
peasantry 9, 28–9, 40, 49, 296; among clergy 186; and church property 46, 49, 53; and pilgrimages/processions 242, 243, 248, 252; and tithe 41–3, 48, 53
penance 101, 268; sacrament of 253, **258–65**, 268, 272, 400, 410, 427; *see also* confession
pénitencier 171
Penitents, confraternities of 123, 126, 344–7, 359–61, 363, 375, 379; after wars of religion 359; autonomy of 349, 360, 364; devotions of 344, 351; evolution of 346, 360, 363; geography of 10–11, 359, 361; membership of 350, 359; militancy of 347; of the Holy Sacrament, confraternity of 356, 360; of the Virgin, confraternity of 354; origins and growth of 344–6; spirituality of 345

Pentecost 230, 243, 264, 341, 389
Percin de Montgaillard, Jean-François, bishop of Saint-Pons 127
Péréfixe, Hardouin de, archbishop of Paris 409
Périgord 216, 389
Pérouas, Louis, historian 356, 414
Perpignan, diocese of 24
Perron, Jacques du, Cardinal 27, 162, 170, 279
Perseigne, abbey of 102
petites écoles 220, 306–8; *see also* Paris; Port-Royal; schools
petits séminaires 199
Philip II, king of Spain 13
Philippe d'Angoumois, Capuchin 374, 377
Picardy 39, 137, 256, 342; *illuminés* of 328
Picpus, fathers of 124
pilgrimage/pilgrims 71, 232, 236, 242, 243, **246–51**, 252, 335, 336; historiography of 247; during religious wars 11–12; result of vows 244; religious impact of 250–1; French sites of 248–9; criticism of in France 246, 248, 250
Poissy, colloquy of 3; contract of 7, 8
Poitiers 135; diocese of 20, 103, 172, 300
Poitou 6, 290, 291; Capuchin mission in 289, 295
Poland 11, 17, 51, 430
politiques 14, 368
Pontlevoy, abbey of 103
Pontoise, Estates General of 38, 136
Port-Royal, abbey of 101, 132, 331, 368, 405, 407, 408–9, 412, 415, 417, 419; and Jansenists 395, 399, 409, 412–13, 417, 422; Arnauld family and 134, 368, 409; little schools of 409, 417, 421; persecution of 409, 412, 413, 422; reform of 134, 135, 399; *solitaires* of 401, 409, 417, 421; *see also* Arnauld, Angélique; Jansenism; St Cyran
preaching 8, 79, 101, 103, 117, 123, 127, 170, 171, 173, 177, 191, 194, 198, 212, 257, 260, 263, 264, 267, 276, 277, 278, **279–83**, 320, 332, 333, 339, 354, 356, 367, 411; during missions **283–96**; regulars and 106, 108, 111, 114, 116, 125, 224, 239, 251, 263, 264, 354; *see also* Advent; Lent; missions; *prône*; sermons
Prémontré, congregation of 86, 99, 102, 103, 124; *see also* Augustinian canons-regular
presbyterianism 423

prêtres-filleuls 71, 186
priesthood 64, 199, 218, 271, 297, 326, 398, 421, 423; French rethinking of 62, 115, 169, 169, 205–6, 319, 326, 342, 349, 392, 398, 421, 423
priestly orders 8, 64, 68, 74, 76, 148, 189, 199, 206, 271, 305
printing trade 120, 332
probabilism/ist 402, 407, 410
processions 11, 34, 44, 71, 75, 223, 232, **242–6**, 247, 249, 252, 267, 285, 288, 354, 367; confraternities and 344, 346, 349; during religious wars 11–12, 243, 367–8
prône 266; and religious instruction 297, 281–2, 298–9, 301, 303; character/content of 216
Propaganda Fide, and missions 289, 291
Protestant Reformation(s) 37, 69, 84, 108, 123, 134, 155, 194, 248, 259, 261, 312, 322, 396
Protestants *see* Calvinists; Huguenots
Provence 10, 11, 18, 41, 68, 75, 107, 137, 165, 241, 242, 256, 340, 344, 345, 346, 359, 360, 390, 419, 431
Provincial Letters 404, 407–8
Psaume, Nicholas, bishop of Verdun 194
Puente, Luis de la 314
Pyrenees 54, 70, 72, 186

Quercy 389
Quesneger 29
Quesnel, Pasquier, 326, 331–2, 405, 411–14, 415, 416, 419, 421, 422, 423; *see also* Jansenism; *Moral Reflections*; Oratory
quietism 26, 330; *see also* Fénelon; Guyon; Molina, Luis de
Quintaine, Nicholas 302

Racine, Jean 395
Rancé, Armand-Jean Bouthillier, abbot 86, 89, 99, 102, 135
Rapin, René, Jesuit 395
Récollets 12, 107, 113, 120, 127, 133, 151, 225, 239, 263; and local society 123, 124, 126 and missions 290; and Rosary devotions 354; anti-Jansenist 128, 421; growth of 110–11; female branch of 130, 133
régale 168, 405
Régis, Jean-François, Jesuit 284
regulars, female, 84, 119, 123, 127, **129–52**; and nursing 143, 144–5, 147, 151, 152;
as educators 134, 136–8, 145, 148, 151, 152, 309; enclosure of 133, 134, 136–7, 137–8, 140–1, 144, 151–2, 215, 309; expansion of 134–47; financial problems of 147–50; governance of 151–2; mendicants among 105, 132–4; monastic houses among 130–2; new congregations of 140–7, 151; numbers of 130, 131; orders/congregations, 419
regulars/religious orders 12, 24, 56, 61–2, 66, 67, 71, 74, 80, 81, **84–104, 105–28, 129–52,** 161, 168, 177, 180, 208, 223, 225, 235, 262, 264, 269, 273, 319, 326, 364, 371, 377, 392, 394, 396, 402, 408, 410, 411, 421; members among episcopate 80, 81, 165; and Augustinian theology 396; and casuistry 410; and catechism 302; and colleges 196, 198–200; and confraternities 123, 289, 339, 340, 350, 352, 357, 358, 364; and cult of saints 235, 239, 241, 242, 251; and local society 123–5; and missions 264, 284–6, 287–8, 289, 290–1, 292–3, 295; and pilgrimage sites 242, 251; and preaching 125–6, 280, 284; and running of parishes 69, 101; and sacraments 262, 263–4, 267, 268; and spirituality 312, 314, 315, 329; as confessors/directors of conscience 402; attractiveness of 14, 126, 186; chapels/churches of 211, 214; growth of 43–4, 106–8, 114–21, 126–8, 134–47; Jansenists among 418–19, 421; pastoral activities of 30, 32, 106, 125, 224, 225; presence in France 84, 111, 119, 133, 152; relations with bishops 168, 177; quarrels with seculars 29, 115, 169, 205, 223–5, 291, 377, 394, 397, 398, 408; scholarly activities of 411
Reichskirche 12; *see also* Germany
Reims 11, 43, 67, 103, 118, 186, 249, 333, 421, 431; archbishop of 166, 187; diocese of 179, 185, 209, 217, 218, 362, 421; seminary of 197; pilgrimage to 248
reinages 244, 363
religious congregations, female **140–6**
religious congregations, male **114–19**
religious orders, female monastic **130–2**, 133, 135, 177
religious orders, female mendicant **132–4**
religious orders, male mendicant, **105–12**; *see also* Capuchins; Dominicans; Franciscans; Récollets

religious orders, male monastic 50, 52, 56, 66, 81, **84–104**, 105, 120, 131, 418; and *commende* 55–6, 81, 88–92; presence in France 105–6; similarities to mendicants 106, 107; reform of 93–100; *see also* Augustinian canons-regular; Benedictines; Cistercians; regulars

Remiremont, female chapter of 77

Rennes 379, 382, 392; bishop of 230; saints' days in 230–1, 232

Renty, Gaston de 136, 329, 378

retables 210

Retz family 372

Retz, Henri de Gondi, Cardinal 27

Retz, Paul de Gondi, Cardinal 200, 408

Ribera, Juan de 432

Richelieu, Armand-Jean du Plessis, Cardinal 5, 27, 49, 55, 116, 135, 196, 290, 328, 390, 403, 427; and Company of Holy Sacrament 373–4, 375, 386; and crown patronage 156, 157–8, 160, 161, 166; and *dévots* 373, 398–9; and religious orders 45, 93, 96–7, 99–100, 150; benefices held by 49, 55, 89; catechism of 299; imprisons Saint-Cyran 399, 401; theological views of 323, 401

Richelieu, town 31

Richeome, Louis, Jesuit 323

Richer, Edmond, ideas of 412, 423

rigorism/ists, 'turn' towards in France 263, 322, 328, 408, 410, 427–8; and Jansenism 395, 403; critical of popular religious practices 239, 246, 361; dislike cult of saints 239; pastoral dimensions of 265, 280, 292, 294; scope of 265; use of Borromeo by 406, 410; *see also* Augustinians

Rocamadour, pilgrimage to 248

Rodez, diocese of 209

Rogations 243

Roman Oratory 112, 115

Rome, city of 14, 27, 138, 188, 197, 247, 358, 274, 316, 369, 395, 397, 404, 410, 430; papal curia 1, 2, 3, 404; *see also* papacy

Roquette, Gabriel de, bishop of Autun 377

Rosary, confraternities of 240–1, 264, 289, 354–5, 356, 359, 360–1, 362, 363, 364; devotion of 124, 126, 238, 239, 242, 354, 355–6, 362–3

Rouen 10, 11, 33, 171, 333, 346, 353, 362, 386; diocese of 20, 180, 191, 192, 203, 282; seminaries in 196, 197; *see also* Colbert, Jacques-Nicholas

Roussillon 431

Ruysbroeck, Johannes, mystic 317

sacramentals, 253

sacraments, 30, 106, 111, 123, 125, 133, 134, 173, 175, 177, 180, 181, 182, 188, 190, 192, 200, 215, 220, 224, **252–76**, 280, 297, 298, 299, 302, 303, 357, 395, 400, 427–8; *see also* baptism; confirmation; Communion, Holy; extreme unction; marriage; holy orders; penance

Sacred Heart, devotion to 124, 238, 428; *see also* confraternities

Sainctes, Claude de 313

Saint-Antoine-de-Viennois 98

Saint-Brieuc 379

Saint-Cyr 330

Saint-Cyran, abbey of 90

Saint-Cyran, Jean Duvergier de Hauranne, abbé de 90, 116, 205, 206, 319, 324, 328, 397, 404, 406, 407, 422; and early church 411; and priesthood 421; and sacraments, 400, 403; as leading *dévot* 398–9; as spiritual director 399–400; disciple of Bérulle 398; imprisoned by Richelieu 401; influence of 401, 403

Saint-Denis, abbey of 86, 87, 90, 94, 249; congregation of 86, 90, 94, 249; pilgrimage to 248; town of 146

Saint-Dié, diocese of 23

Saint-Firmin 245

Saint-Germain-des-Prés, abbey of 51, 71, 102, 120; *see also* Maurists

Saint-Germer, abbey of 103

Saint-Jacques-du-Haut-Pas, Paris parish 32, 417

Saint-Jean of Lyon, chapter of 77

Saint-Jean-de-Losne 121

Saint-Julien of Brioude, chapter of 77

Saint-Jure, Jean-Baptiste, Jesuit mystic 328, 329

Saint-Lazare 162, 319; *see also* Lazarists

Saint-Leu, Paris parish of 32

Saint-Louis, feast of 230

Saint-Louis-en-l'Ile, Paris parish of 32

Saint-Magloire, seminary 162, 200, 419

Saint-Malo, diocese 174; Jansenists in 421; missions in 293; synods 173

Saint-Marcoul of Corbeny, pilgrimage to 249

Saint-Maur, congregation of 86, 94, 101, 102; growth of 95; *see also* Maurists; Saint-Germain-des-Prés
Saint-Maximin, pilgrimage to 248, 249
Saint-Médard, Paris parish 33, 222
Saint-Méen, pilgrimage to 249
Saint-Nicholas-du-Chardonnet: catechism of 299–300; parish of 72, 117, 197, 285; schools of 306; seminary of 117; *see also* Bourdoise
Saint-Pierre, Mâcon, chapter of 77
Saint-Pons, diocese of 18
Saint-Roch, Paris parish of 32
Saint-Ruf, congregation of 87, 98
Saint-Sulpice 114, 117, 198, 201, 203, 319; Company of 117, 198; *curé* of 300, 306, 373; parish of 32, 72, 117, 198, 388, 389, 390; seminary of 162, 181, 182, 197, 200; *see also* Olier; Sulpicians
Saint-Vanne, congregation of 86, 94, 101, 102
Saint-Victor, abbey and congregation of 86, 87, 98
Sainte-Beuve, Charles-Augustin, historian 395
Sainte-Foy-les-Lyon 348
Sainte-Geneviève, abbey of 98, 102, 103, 104, 114, 120, 218; *see also* Augustinian canons-regular; Congregation of France; Genovéfains; La Rochefoucauld, François, Cardinal
Sainte-Marguerite, Paris parish of 32
Saintes, diocese of 21
saints 11, 14, 23, 116, 125, 126, 194, 211, **229–42**, 243, 252, 273, 276, 302, 304, 355, 428; as friends of man 237, 238; as miracle workers 234, 236–7, 242, 251, 343; as intercessors 229, 232, 237, 241, 251, 275; as models 233, 235, 236, 248; Catholic Reformation and 233, 235–6, 237–9, 241; confraternities and 233, 343, 363; critiques of 233; cult of 234, 235, 236, 239, 240–1, 242, 244, 247, 248, 302; feast days of 230–2; lives of 194, 312, 335, 336; new additions to 230, 231, 240; pilgrimages and 247, 248, 251; processions and 242, 244; rejected by Protestants, 229, 232–3, 242–3; religious orders and 125, 126, 239; representations of 213, 241–2; universal 234–5
Salamanca 396
Sandret, Pierre 327

Santarelli, Antonio, Jesuit 113, 397
Sarpi, Paolo 107
Satan 274, 285, 287, 288, 296, 315
Saulx-Tavannes, Gaspard de 10
Saumur 332
Sauvageon, Christophe 103, 218, 282, 429
Savonarola, Girolamo 344
Savoy 24, 138, 236, 321, 356, 357
schools 79, 194, 199, 224, **305–9**, 276, 330, 345, 388, 393; and catechism, 301; choir 195; for girls 137, 142, 145, 151, 308–9, 356; 'little schools'/*petites écoles* 220, 306–8; pressure for 307; run by orders/congregations 102–3, 111, 112, 118, 128, 198, 268, 315, 333, 352–3; teachers in 34, 145, 179, 220, 405
Scupoli, Lorenzo 314
Séez, bishop of 206, 349
Séguier family 368
Séguier, Dominique, bishop of Meaux 191
Séguier, Pierre, chancellor 136, 406
Séguier, Jeanne, Carmelite 136
seminaries 52, 79, 102, 111, 116, 156, 162, 171, 173, 181, 182, 184, 186, 187, 190, 192, **194–204**, 206, 217, 221, 282, 283, 293, 307, 316, 361, 369, 376, 392, 429; and catechism 301, 302; as places of confinement 180; differences among 201–2, 203; failure of early 195, 196–7, 199; financial problems of 195, 198; for ordinands 72, 199, 202–3; Jansenism and 128, 204, 418, 419; Jesuits and 114, 196, 201, 204; limitations of 197, 198, 204; new views on 117, 197–8, 198, 199; relation to colleges 195–6, 199, 204; run by regulars/congregations 103, 112, 116, 117–18, 119, 126, 127–8, 199, 201, 293; second wave of 199–200, 385; Tridentine 162, 194–5
Senez, bishop of 419
Senlis 103
Sennely-en-Sologne 103, 218, 240, 261, 264, 282, 362, 429; *see also* Sauvageon
Sens, cathedral chapter of 74; catechism of 300; council of 2; diocese of 292; province of 25
sermons 101, 111, 168, 173, 181, 192, 223, 224, 266, 279, 281, 282–3, 286, 294, 302, 303, 305, 334–5; *see also* Advent; Lent; missions; preaching; *prône*
Servites, order of 107
Sève, Guy de, bishop of Arras 410
Sévigné, Mme de 125, 366

siècle des saints 425
Simiane de la Coste 378
Sisteron, diocese of 18
Sisters of Charity and Christian instruction of Nevers 142
Sisters of Charity of Our Lady of Evron 142
Sisters of Charity of Sainville 142
Sisters of Charity of St Charles, Nancy 142
Sisters of Saint Joseph of Le Puy, 144
Sisters of St Anne of Providence, Saumur 142
Sisters of St Charles of Lyon, congregation of 142
Sisters of St Paul of Chartres 142
Sisters of the Holy Sacrament of Autun 142
Sisters of the Sacred Heart of Ernemont 142
Société de Bretagne, Benedictine congregation of 86
Socrates 322
Soissons, cathedral chapter of 74; diocese of 300
solitaires see Port-Royal
Solminihac, Alain de, bishop of Cahors 98, 170, 172, 193, 198, 283, 377
Sorbonne 3, 200, 403, 404, 415; *see also* Paris, theology faculty
Sorèze 103
Sourdis, Cardinal François de 26, 172, 191
Spain 3, 13, 67, 89, 110, 136, 159, 165, 330, 371, 399, 402, 414, 429; Bourbon succession in 430
Spanish Netherlands 398, 403, 412
Spiritual Combat 314; *see also* Scupoli
Spiritual Exercises 315, 316
spirituality 126, 128, 135, 169, 271, **310–36**, 367, 395, 398; 'French school' of 312, 319, 322; and Bible 331–2; and mysticism 316–20, 328–31; christocentric 138, 237, 318; diffusion of 321, 332–4; evolution of 314–18; for lay people 271, 323–8; foreign sources of 313–14; forms of 310–12; hagiography and 335–6; impact of 334–5; Jesuits and 284, 306, 322–6, 378; of marriage, 271, 327, 328; printing and 312–13, 332–4; Salesian 138, 320–2; spiritual direction and 315–16; *see also* Bérulle; de Sales; Penitents; Saint-Cyran

St Anne 237; cult of 235, 238–9
St Anthony of Padua 235, 239, 240
St Augustine 102, 103, 130, 139, 404; disciples of 403; influence of 395, 396, 400; teaching of 326, 398; works published 411; Rule of 85; *see also* Jansenism; rigorism
St Benedict 131; rule of 85
St Bernard, college of 102
St Bernard of Clairvaux, works of 193
St Charles of Lyon, congregation of 151
St Clare 133
St Jerome 2
St Joachim 239
St John of God, congregation of 111, 112, 143
St John's Eve 230; targeted by reformers 232
St Joseph 142, 232, 237, 239; feast of 231; as model saint 238
St Joseph of Le Puy, sisters of 142
St Martin of Tours 213; chapter of 72
St Roch 234, 244, 343
St Sebastian 234, 244, 343
Strasbourg 114, 201
Suarez, Francisco, Jesuit 397
Suffren, Jean, Jesuit 323, 325, 375, 377
Sulpicians 116, 199; *see also* Saint-Sulpice
superstition, attacks on 1, 179, 192, 213, 214, 233, 251, 270, 271, 275, 278, 296, 427–8, 429
Surin, Jean-Jacques, Jesuit 317, 328, 330
synods 2, **172–5**, 177, 181, 183, 184, 191, 193, 206, 234, 240, 282; against confraternities 345, 350; and religious instruction 297, 301, 307; and *concours* 188; legislation/statutes of 163, 174–5, 180, 190, 193, 210, 215, 281, 297; limitations of 192; problems of 191; purposes of 180; revival and use of 172, 188

Tallon, Alain, historian 4, 377
Tarascon 379
Tarbes 214, 244; bishop of 186, 431
Tarisse, Grégoire, Maurist 322
Tauler, Johannes 317
Taveneaux, René, historian 395, 419
théologal 79, 171
Thiers, Jean-Baptiste 233, 428
third orders 107, 123, 124, 125, 133, 152, 264, 314, 369; *see also* Dominicans; Franciscans

Third Republic 373
Thiron, abbey of 103
Thomas Aquinas 193
tithes 6, 33, 35, 39, 41–3, 46–7, 48, 52–3, 54, 69, 75, 209, 281
Toledo, Francisco, Cardinal 193
Tonnerre 121
Toul 94; diocese 23, 24, 179
Toulouse 9, 10, 11, 20, 43, 44, 67, 83, 108, 112, 133, 138, 333, 346, 347, 359, 379, 388, 391, 392, 427, 431; confraternities in 369; diocese of 14, 203; religious orders in 120; seminaries of 196; university of 162, 197
Touraine 6
Tournai, diocese of 24
Tournon, François, Cardinal 27
Tours 211, 386, 421; diocese of 20, 29, 31, 103
Tréguier, 390; diocese of 217, 218
Trent *see* Council of Trent
Tronson, Louis 205, 319
Troyes 146, 335, 431
Tulle 359; diocese, 146, 191
Turgot, 221

ultramontane 394
Unigenitus 95, 168, 295, 405, 412, 413, 423; appeals against, 419; appellants against, 417
Urban VIII, pope 231, 235
Ursulines, order of 136, 137, 138, 139, 145, 147, 150, 309, 354, 358
Utrecht, peace of 24

Val d'Aran 54
Val des Ecoliers, congregation of 86
Valence, diocese of 21
Vallées, Marie des 330
Valois, Jeanne de 132
Van Kley, Dale, historian 395
Vannes 186, 248
Vassy, massacre of 1
Vauvert, monastery of 88
Velay 40, 41
Venard, Marc, historian 196
Vence 360, 361; diocese of 20
Ventadour, duke of 374, 378, 389
Verdun 94; bishop of 419; diocese of 24
vernacular, Bible in 313, 414–15, 331; liturgy in 313, 416, 428; preaching in 283; uses of 5, 297, 313, 332–3, 416
Versailles 167, 250

Vespers 220, 232
Vialart, Félix, bishop of Chalons-sur-Marne 170, 356, 411
vicaires forains 172, 174, 191, 193, 240
vicariats forains 172, 190
vicaires/curates, in parishes 56, 69–70, 103, 174, 219
vicars-general 78, 79, 91, 164, 171–2, 176, 177, 203, 240, 392
Vienne 25
Viguerie, Jean de, historian 361
Villeroy, Camille Neufville de, archbishop of Lyon 167, 219
Vincennes 11; château of 399
Vineam Domini, papal bull 405
Vintimille du Luc, Charles-Guillaume, archbishop of Paris 418
Virgin Mary 124, 230, 232, 340, 352; devotions to 124, 232, 320; France dedicated to 249; *see also* Marian, sodalities
Visitation, order of the 137, 138, 139, 140, 145, 151, 309, 320, 356, 358, 371
visitations 3, 6, 14, 125, **175–80**, 181, 182, 183, 184, 190, 193, 201, 209–10, 211, 212, 216, 219, 234, 239, 240, 254, 257, 281, 282, 301, 305, 342, 347, 362, 428; and catechism 300, 301; and confraternities 347–8, 360; and preaching 279, 283; and sacrament of confirmation 176, 257; and superstition 428; evolution of 178–9; objectives of 176, 177–8, 178–9; obstacles to conduct of 176–7, 178; records of 179–80, 194, 213, 241, 300
Vitré 376, 379, 382
Vivarais 40, 41
Viviers, diocese of 40
Voisin, Joseph de 415
Vosges 31
vows 62, 85, 92, 93, 112, 115, 117, 118, 124, 131, 134, 136, 138, 139, 141, 145, 149, 232, 236, 244, 245, 249; baptismal 255, 257, 288; of religion 144, 309; to go on pilgrimage 247

Walch, Agnès, historian 327
wars of religion 1, 3, 4, 5–6, 8–11, 12–13, 14, 20, 37, 39, 45, 46, 48, 49, 50, 66, 74, 77, 78, 89, 91, 93–4, 106, 110, 113, 119, 123, 126, 131, 134, 135, 140, 143, 156–7, 159, 170, 176, 179, 184, 195, 209, 210, 224, 233, 242–3, 248, 279, 283, 306, 307,

313, 315, 332, 345, 346–7, 349, 359, 360, 367, 369, 370, 397, 425, 426
widows 145, 146, 309, 383
women: abbeys of 131–2, 135, 158–9; and confraternities 342, 352, 355, 359, 376–7; and marriage 269; and third orders 124; as *dévots* 136, 143–4, 145, 152, 241, 300–1, 370–1, 372, 376–7, 383, 386, 422; as catechists 308–9, 354; as regulars 13–14, 56, 84, 106, 108, 112, 119–20, 123, 127, 127, 129–52, 281, 312, 364, 371, 400; chapters of 77; education of 309; Jansenists among 422; mystics among 330

Xavier, Francisco, 235

Ypres, diocese of 24
Yves de Paris, Capuchin 315, 333

Zamet, Sebastien, bishop of Langres 377